A New Nation

ADVENTURES IN TIME AND PLACE

James A. Banks

Barry K. Beyer

Gloria Contreras

Jean Craven

Gloria Ladson-Billings

Mary A. McFarland

Walter C. Parker

THE FIRST OFFICIAL FLAG OF THE UNITED STATES CONTAINED 13 FIVE-POINTED STARS, ONE FOR EACH OF THE FORMER 13 COLONIES. IT WAS ADOPTED BY CONGRESS ON JUNE 14, 1777. THE STARS WERE SOMETIMES PLACED IN A CIRCLE, AS ON THIS FLAG, AND SOMETIMES IN VERTICAL ROWS. AS THE COUNTRY GREW, STARS WERE ADDED TO REPRESENT THE ADDITIONAL STATES. IT WASN'T UNTIL 1912, WHEN THERE WERE 48 STARS FOR 48 STATES, THAT THE PLACEMENT OF THE STARS BECAME FIXED. TODAY THE 13 STRIPES REMAIN TO REPRESENT THE ORIGINAL COLONIES FROM WHICH THIS NATION GREW.

NATIONAL GEOGRAPHIC SOCIETY

THE PRINCETON REVIEW

McGraw-Hill School Division

New York   Farmington

PROGRAM AUTHORS

Dr. James A. Banks
Professor of Education and Director of
the Center for Multicultural Education
University of Washington
Seattle, Washington

Dr. Barry K. Beyer
Professor Emeritus, Graduate School of
Education
George Mason University
Fairfax, Virginia

Dr. Gloria Contreras
Professor of Education
University of North Texas
Denton, Texas

Jean Craven
District Coordinator of
Curriculum Development
Albuquerque Public Schools
Albuquerque, New Mexico

Dr. Gloria Ladson-Billings
Professor of Education
University of Wisconsin
Madison, Wisconsin

Dr. Mary A. McFarland
Instructional Coordinator of
Social Studies, K–12, and
Director of Staff Development
Parkway School District
Chesterfield, Missouri

Dr. Walter C. Parker
Professor and Program Chair for
Social Studies Education
University of Washington
Seattle, Washington

NATIONAL
GEOGRAPHIC
SOCIETY
Washington, D.C.

THE
PRINCETON
REVIEW
The Princeton Review is not affiliated
with Princeton University or ETS.

HISTORIANS/SCHOLARS

Dr. Carlos E. Cortés
Professor Emeritus of History
University of California
Riverside, California

Dr. John Bodnar
Professor of History
Indiana University
Bloomington, Indiana

Dr. Sheilah Clark-Ekong
Professor, Department of Anthropology
University of Missouri, St. Louis
St. Louis, Missouri

Dr. Darlene Clark Hine
John A. Hannah Professor of History
Michigan State University
East Lansing, Michigan

Council on Islamic Education
Fountain Valley, California

Dr. John L. Esposito
Professor of Religion and International
Affairs
Georgetown University
Washington, D.C.

Dr. Gary Mason
Department of Geography
Michigan State University
East Lansing, Michigan

Dr. Juan Mora-Torres
Professor of Latin American History
University of Texas at San Antonio
San Antonio, Texas

Dr. Valerie Ooka Pang
Professor, School of Teacher Education
San Diego State University
San Diego, California

Dr. Curtis C. Roseman
Professor of Geography
University of Southern California
Los Angeles, California

Dr. Joseph Rosenbloom
Professor, Classics Department
Washington University
St. Louis, Missouri

Dr. Robert Seltzer
Professor of Jewish History
Hunter College
City University of New York
New York, New York

Dr. Robert M. Senkewicz
Professor of History
Santa Clara University
Santa Clara, California

Dr. Peter Stearns
Dean, College of Humanities and Social
Studies
Carnegie Mellon University
Pittsburg, Pennsylvania

Dr. Clifford E. Trafzer
Department of Ethnic Studies
University of California
Riverside, California

CALIFORNIA PROGRAM CONSULTANTS

Diane Bowers
Former Assistant Director of Education
for the Yurok Tribe
Klamath, California

Dr. Karen Nakai
Lecturer of History-Social Science
Department of Education
University of California
Irvine, California

Shelly Osborne
Teacher-Literacy Mentor
Franklin School
Alameda, California

Lyn Reese
Director, Women in History Project
Berkeley, California

Evelyn Staton
Librarian
San Francisco School District
Member, Multiethnic Literature Forum
for San Francisco
San Francisco, California

CONSULTING AUTHORS

Dr. James Flood
Professor of Teacher Education,
Reading and Language Development
San Diego State University
San Diego, California

Dr. Diane Lapp
Professor of Teacher Education,
Reading and Language Development
San Diego State University
San Diego, California

GRADE-LEVEL CONSULTANTS

Karen Geathers
Fifth Grade Teacher
Grass Valley School
Oakland, California

Holly Nolan
Fifth Grade Teacher
Martin Luther King, Jr.,
Elementary School
Santa Ana, California

Dr. Karen Skalbeck
Fifth Grade Teacher
Bayside Elementary School
Imperial, California

CONTRIBUTING WRITERS

Kate Connell
Holliston, Massachusetts

Cheryl Edwards
Pennington, New Jersey

Gaynor Ellis
New York, New York

Deborah Golden
Pittsburgh, Pennsylvania

Linda Scher
Raleigh, North Carolina

Acknowledgments

From **They Have Yarns From the People, Yes** by Carl Sandburg. Copyright © 1936 by Harcourt Brace & Company and renewed 1964 by
Carl Sandburg, Reprinted by permission of the publisher.
From **Native Ways: California Indian Stories and Memories,** edited by Margolin & Montijo. Copyright © 1995 by Heydey Books.
From **Four Ancestors** told by Joseph Bruchac. Published by Bridgewater Books Copyright © 1996 by Joseph Bruchac.
From **Conquest: Montezuma, Cortes and the Fall of Old Mexico** by Hugh Thomas. Reprinted with the permission of Simon & Schuster.
Copyright © 1994 by Hugh Thomas.
From **The Aztecs** by Francis F. Berdan. Copyright 1989 by Chelsea House Publishers. Excerpt from the Indians of North America series.
From **The Log of Christopher Columbus** translated by Robert H. Fuson. Copyright 1987 by Robert H. Fuson. International Marine Publishing Company.

(continued on page R95)

McGraw-Hill School Division
A Division of The McGraw-Hill Companies

McGraw-Hill School Division
Two Penn Plaza
New York, New York 10121

Printed in the United States of America

ISBN 0-02-148825-8

8 9 027/046 03

CONTENTS

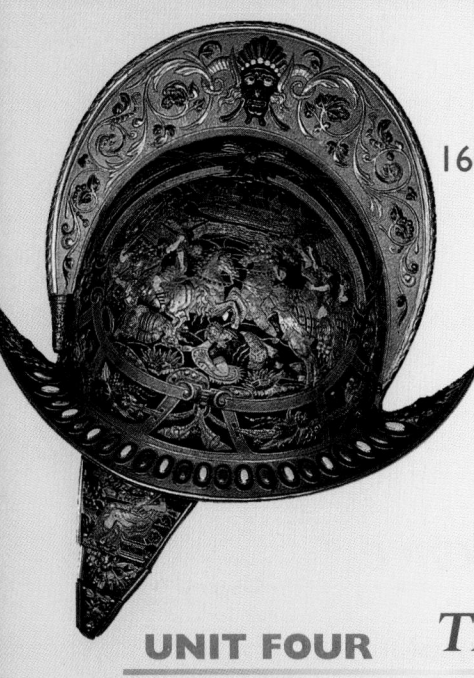

UNIT FOUR

The 13 English Colonies

186

UNIT FIVE   The Fight for Independence

292

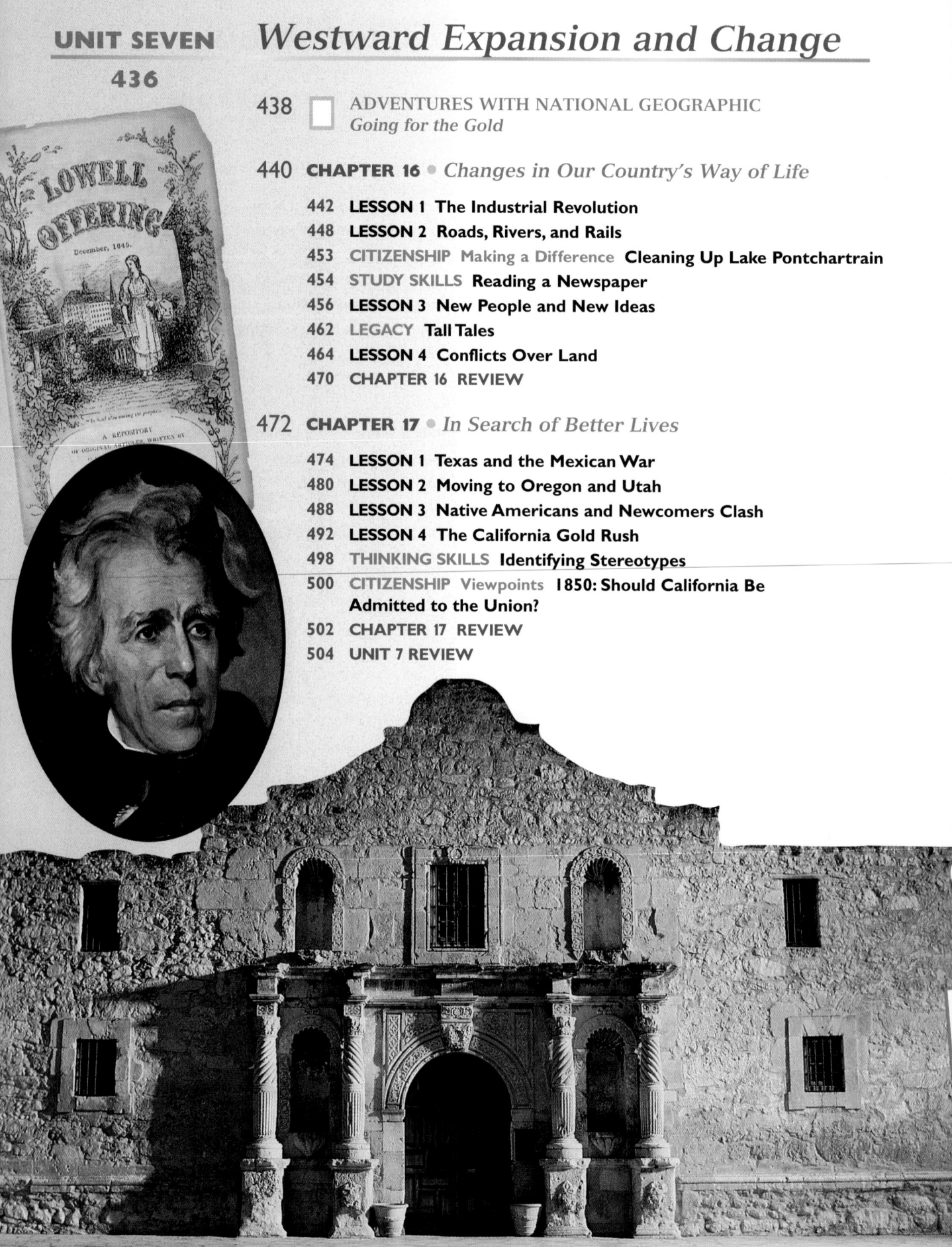

UNIT SEVEN Westward Expansion and Change
436

REFERENCE SECTION

STANDARDIZED TEST SUPPORT

THE PRINCETON REVIEW

FEATURES

MANY VOICES

CHARTS, GRAPHS, & DIAGRAMS

TIME LINES

MAPS

YOUR TEXTBOOK
at a glance

Your textbook is called *A New Nation: Adventures in Time and Place*. It has 20 chapters. Each chapter has three or more lessons. There are also many special features for you to study and enjoy.

NATIONAL GEOGRAPHIC

Five Themes of Geography

Region
What are some things that help make the West a special region!

Human/Environment Interactions
How have people changed this landscape in Alaska?

▲

Special pages right after these two pages and before each unit bring you ideas and Adventures in geography with National Geographic.

LESSON 3

1640   1670   1700   1775

COLONIAL CITIES GROW

Focus Activity

READ TO LEARN
How did colonial cities grow?

VOCABULARY
almanac
Great Awakening

PEOPLE
Benjamin Franklin

PLACES
Philadelphia
Boston

READ ALOUD

Andrew Burnaby, an Englishman traveling in North America in 1760, was surprised at the bustling cities he visited. He wrote: "Philadelphia, if we consider that not eighty years ago the place where it now stands was a wild . . . desert . . . must certainly be the object of everyone's wonder and admiration. . . . The city is in a very flourishing state, and inhabited by merchants, artists, tradesmen, and persons of all occupations."

THE BIG PICTURE

By the time Burnaby was traveling through the colonies, several cities were growing rapidly. There were no large inland cities, but those that were ports were actively trading with the West Indies, Europe, and each other. These cities grew according to the amount of goods they exported. Philadelphia grew fastest. Its population increased from 4,000 people in 1690 to 40,000 people in 1775. It was bigger than any English city except London. Boston, which mostly imported goods, did not grow much in the early 1700s. Charles Town and New York got bigger, but not as much as Philadelphia.

Benjamin Franklin, Philadelphia's most famous citizen, helped it become the largest city in the 13 colonies. He grew up at a time when the colonies were changing rapidly. Before 1700, eight out of ten colonists were English or had English parents. By 1750 colonists from Germany, Ireland, France, and other countries had begun to shape the 13 colonies.

282

WHY IT MATTERS

The arrival of the horse on the Great Plains changed the lives of the Native Americans of the Plains in many ways. It made buffalo hunting easier and helped the Lakota become a powerful people. It also made them much more dependent on the buffalo than they had ever been before.

The buffalo, in fact, became central to the Plains people's way of life. Their very existence now maintaining large Great Plains.

When Europear the Plains, problem still be enough lan graze? You will lea developments on t in this book.

DID YOU KNOW?

How did different Plains people communicate with each other?

Although Native Americans on the Great Plains often spoke at least 20 different languages, at times different groups did not have a language in common. In these

People such as the Huron, Chippewa, and Ottawa taught many French trappers to use lightweight birchbark canoes and to survive in the forests.

An adventurous life attracted many voyageurs and coureurs de bois. According to one voyageur:

There is no life so happy as a voyageur's life; none so independent; no place where a man enjoys so much variety and freedom.

WHY IT MATTERS

By building settlements throughout New France, the French surrounded English lands in North America. The 13 English colonies had no way to expand. By the mid-1700s, the French had won many Native American allies. The voyageurs and coureurs de bois helped to form strong partnerships with them.

Links to LANGUAGE ARTS

Parlez-vous français?

Parlez-vous français? (PAHR lay VOO frahn SAY) means "Do you speak French?" You may know more French words than you think. As you learned in Chapter 3, the Iroquois call themselves the Hodenosaunee. The French called them the Iroquois, and that name stuck. The Wyandot are also generally known by their French name—Huron. Until recently, most people called the Lakota by their French name—the Sioux.

Other French words are now part of the English language. Among them are glacier, plateau, lacrosse, and prairie.

Bonjour! I'm a prairie dog!

✓ Reviewing

MAIN IDEAS

- Before they learn horse, most Nati Great Plains wer in permanent vil
- With the horse, began moving t hunt the buffalo
- The Lakota bega buffalo about 17 animal for food pemmican, for c covering for the
- Th . i¿Fota kept fact, t/e s in th calendar called i rians use the wi stand the history

Reviewing Facts and Ideas

MAIN IDEAS

- Samuel Champlain built the first permanent French settlement in North America, called Quebec, in 1608.
- Explorations by Marquette and Jolliet in 1673, and by La Salle in 1682, led trol of the entire Missis-

THINK ABOUT IT

1. Who were some of the French explorers who came to North America? Why did they come?
2. How did Native Americans such as the Huron help the French?
3. **FOCUS** How did the fur trade shape the growth of New France?
   NG SKILL Compare and contrast English colonies

◀ **Some lessons have features called Links or Did You Know?— activities to try and interesting information to share.**

Look for a variety of lessons and features. **Infographics** bring you information with pictures, charts, graphs, and maps. You will build your **Skills**, learn about **Legacies** that connect us to the past, and meet people who show what **Citizenship** is. ▶

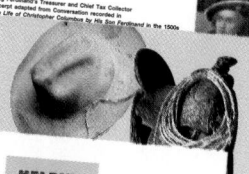

CITIZENSHIP VIEWPOINTS

Three DIFFERENT Viewpoints

Legacy
LINKING PAST AND PRESENT

VAQUEROS

STUDYSKILLS

Infographic

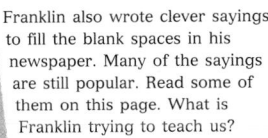

TECHNOLOGY DURING THE AGE OF EXPLORATION

Imagine explorers sailing the seas in the 1400s and coming upon lands and cultures unknown to them. Sailors could not determine their exact location at sea until the 1700s. During the 14

COMPASS
Earth is like a huge magnet. The magnetic force around Earth causes the magnetic needle in a compass to point always to the North Pole. In Europe the compass was first mentioned in 1187. By the 1400s Europeans

CROSS STAFF
Persians used the cross staff at least 300 years before Europeans did. Like the astrolabe, the cross staff measured the angle of the height of the sun or stars. It was the most popular navigating tool until the end of the 1500s.

TRIANGULAR SAILS
Europeans first saw triangular sails on Arab ships called caravos. Smaller than a single square sail, triangular sails were easier for sailors to handle. Triangular sails helped explorers stay on course more easily in strong winds and rough seas.

BENJAMIN FRANKLIN

Ben Franklin, the grandson of an indentured servant, grew up to become the most famous person in the colonies. Born in 1706 into a large Boston family, Franklin learned at a young age that reading was a key to success. He read everything he could get his hands on.

At age 16 he wrote funny stories for his brother's newspaper under the name Mrs. Silence Dogood. His brother published them, not knowing that Ben had written them. This was the beginning of Franklin's work as a writer.

Franklin the Writer

In 1729 Franklin founded Philadelphia's first newspaper, the *Pennsylvania Gazette*. As a writer, one of Franklin's greatest successes was *Poor Richard's Almanack*. Now spelled without a *k*, an almanac is a reference book that contains information about the stars and the weather. Franklin added jokes and sayings to his almanac. From 1732 to 1757, Franklin's almanac sold more copies than any other book in the colonies except for the Bible.

Poor Richard, 1733:
AN Almanack
For the Year of Chrift
1733,

Franklin also wrote clever sayings to fill the blank spaces in his newspaper. Many of the sayings are still popular. Read some of them on this page. What is Franklin trying to teach us?

MANY VOICES
PRIMARY SOURCE

Excerpts from *Poor Richard's Almanack* by Benjamin Franklin, published from 1732 to 1757.

Early to bed, early to rise, makes a man healthy, wealthy and wise.

Little strokes fell great oaks.

Glass, china, reputation, are easily cracked, and never well mended.

An open foe may prove a curse; but a pretended friend is worse.

One today is worth two tomorrows.

Haste makes waste.

Franklin the Scientist

As a scientist Franklin is best known for his experiments with electricity and his invention of the lightning rod. Among his other inventions that are still used today are bifocal eyeglasses and a wood-burning stove called the Franklin stove.

Franklin received many honors and prizes. His writings and experiments made him the best-known North American in Europe. When he visited Europe, people crowded in the streets to get a glimpse of him.

The Franklin stove heated rooms and tea kettles during the cold winters.

283

Use the **Reference Section** at the end of your book to look up words, people, and places. This section includes the **Constitution of the United States** and three **American History Time Lines**.
▼

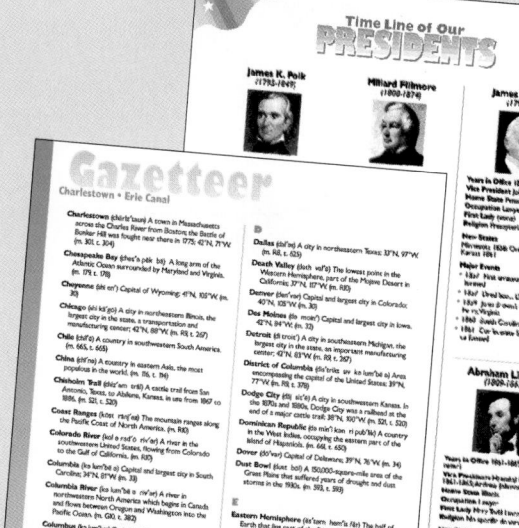

Time Line of Our PRESIDENTS

Gazetteer

▲
Lessons begin with a **Read Aloud** selection and **The Big Picture**. Study the **Read to Learn** question and the list of words, people, and places. Enjoy **Many Voices**—writings, songs, and art by people who actually witnessed the events being written about.

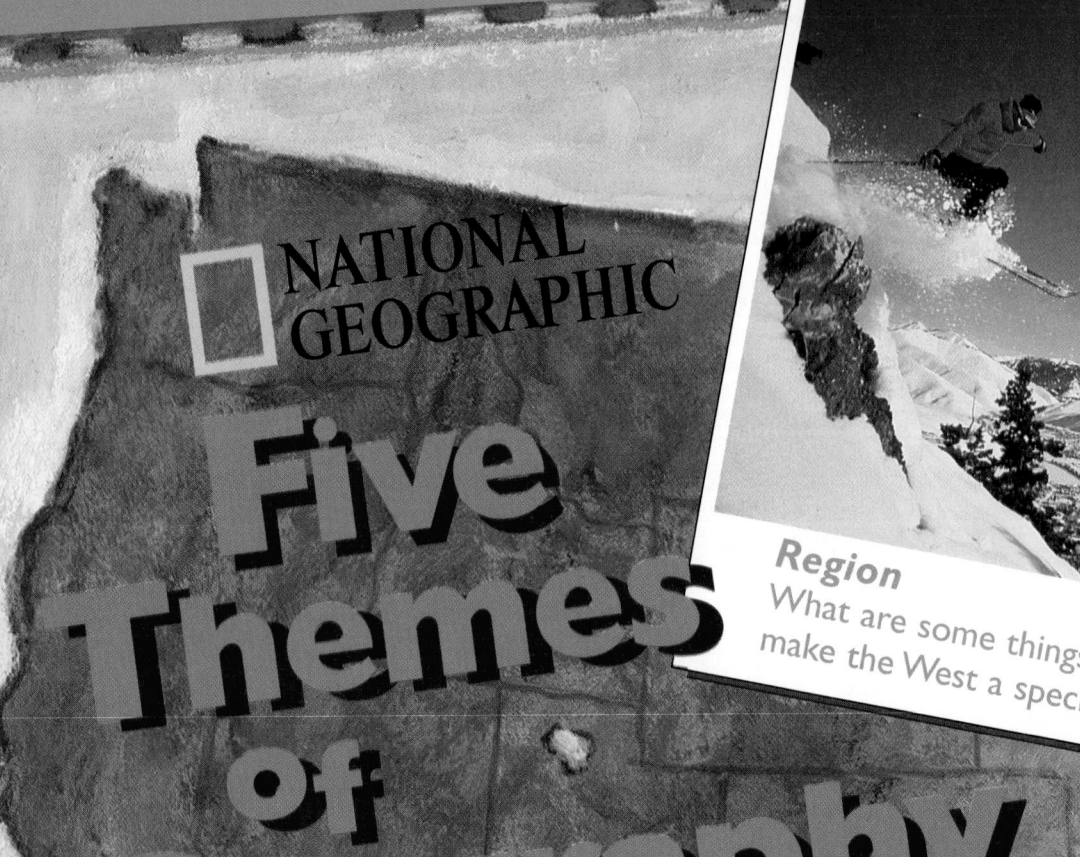

NATIONAL GEOGRAPHIC

Five Themes of Geography

Region
What are some things that help make the West a special region?

Human/Environment Interactions
How have people changed this landscape in Alaska?

Movement
How do people and goods travel from place to place?

Location
How do people know exactly where things are?

Place
What makes Niagara Falls different from other places?

GEOGRAPHY SKILLS

PART 1
Using Globes

VOCABULARY

continent	parallel
ocean	longitude
hemisphere	meridian
equator	prime meridian
latitude	

What is a globe? What does it show?

- A globe is a model of Earth. It is a useful tool for showing what Earth looks like.

- A globe shows Earth's seven continents, or large bodies of land. They are Africa, Antarctica, Asia, Australia, Europe, North America, and South America. What continents do you see on this globe?

- A globe also shows Earth's four oceans, or large bodies of salt water. They are the Atlantic, Arctic, Indian, and Pacific oceans. Look at the globe. On which continent do you live? What ocean is nearest to you?

What is a hemisphere?

- Like Earth, globes are spheres. A sphere is an object shaped like a ball. At any one time, you see only one half of a globe.

- Another word for half a sphere or globe is hemisphere. *Hemi* means half. Earth can be divided into four hemispheres.

- The equator is an imaginary line running halfway between the North Pole and South Pole. Into which two hemispheres does the equator divide Earth?

- Earth is also divided into the Eastern and Western hemispheres. Look at the maps at the top of the next page. Which two hemispheres show North America? Which hemispheres show South America?

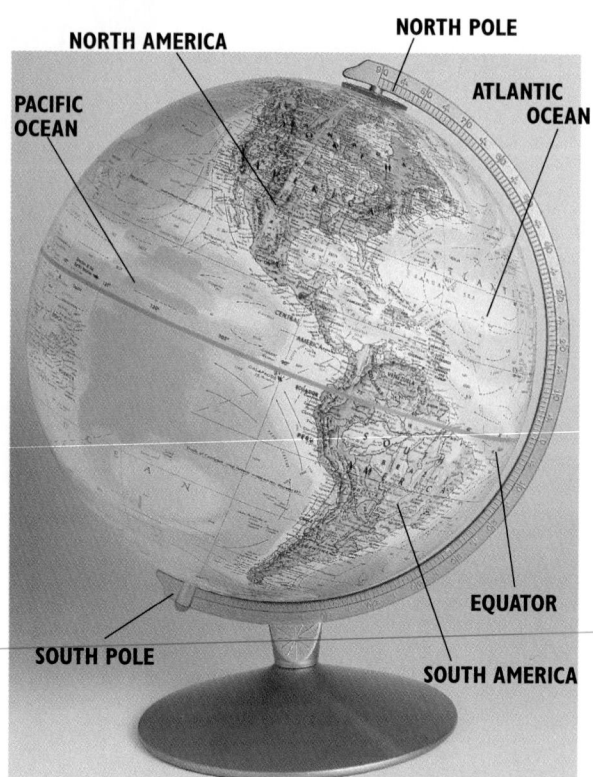

NORTH AMERICA · NORTH POLE · ATLANTIC OCEAN · PACIFIC OCEAN · EQUATOR · SOUTH POLE · SOUTH AMERICA

What are latitude and longitude?

- Maps and globes use a system of imaginary lines to help us locate places.

- Latitude lines run east and west. They measure the distance north or south of the equator. Latitude lines are also called parallels. Look at the lines of latitude at the bottom of the next page. What latitude line is shown just below the continent of South America?

- Longitude lines run north and south. Longitude lines are also called meridians. The starting line for measuring longitude is the prime meridian. Look at the lines of longitude. Where do they all meet?

More Practice

More maps in this book use lines of latitude and longitude. For examples, see pages 30, 33, and 37.

THE HEMISPHERES

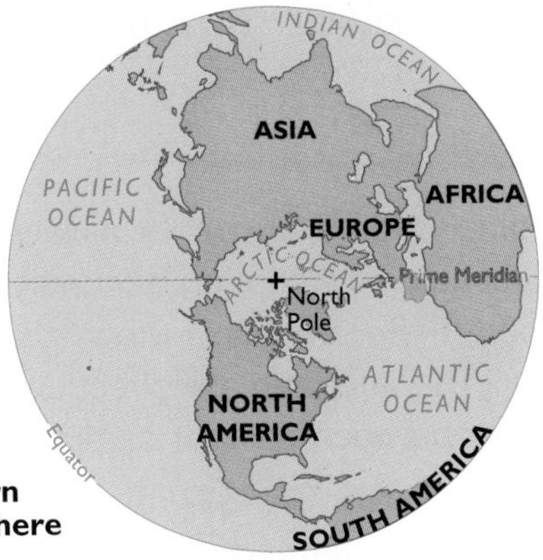

Northern Hemisphere

ASIA · AFRICA · EUROPE · NORTH AMERICA · SOUTH AMERICA · PACIFIC OCEAN · ATLANTIC OCEAN · ARCTIC OCEAN · INDIAN OCEAN · Prime Meridian · North Pole · Equator

Southern Hemisphere

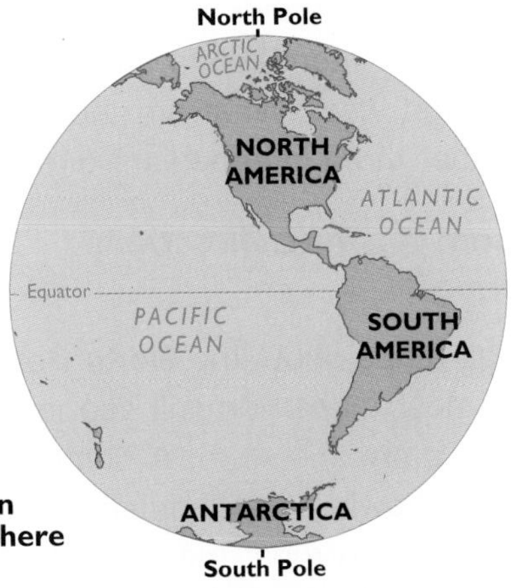

SOUTH AMERICA · ANTARCTICA · AFRICA · AUSTRALIA · ASIA · PACIFIC OCEAN · ATLANTIC OCEAN · INDIAN OCEAN · South Pole · Prime Meridian · Equator

Western Hemisphere

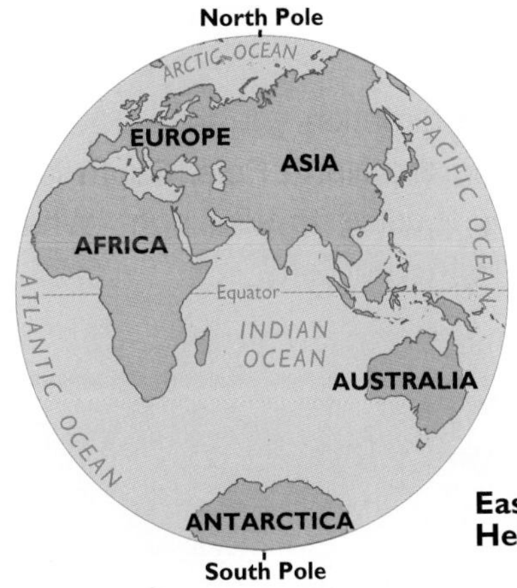

North Pole · NORTH AMERICA · SOUTH AMERICA · ANTARCTICA · ATLANTIC OCEAN · PACIFIC OCEAN · ARCTIC OCEAN · Equator · South Pole

Eastern Hemisphere

North Pole · EUROPE · ASIA · AFRICA · AUSTRALIA · ANTARCTICA · ARCTIC OCEAN · PACIFIC OCEAN · ATLANTIC OCEAN · INDIAN OCEAN · Equator · South Pole

LINES OF LATITUDE (PARALLELS)

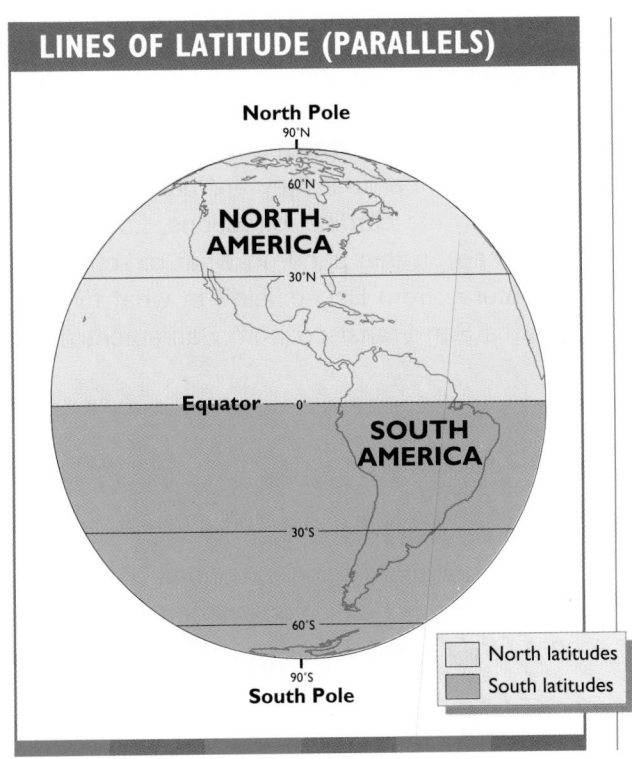

North Pole · 90°N · 60°N · 30°N · Equator 0° · 30°S · 60°S · 90°S · South Pole · NORTH AMERICA · SOUTH AMERICA

North latitudes
South latitudes

LINES OF LONGITUDE (MERIDIANS)

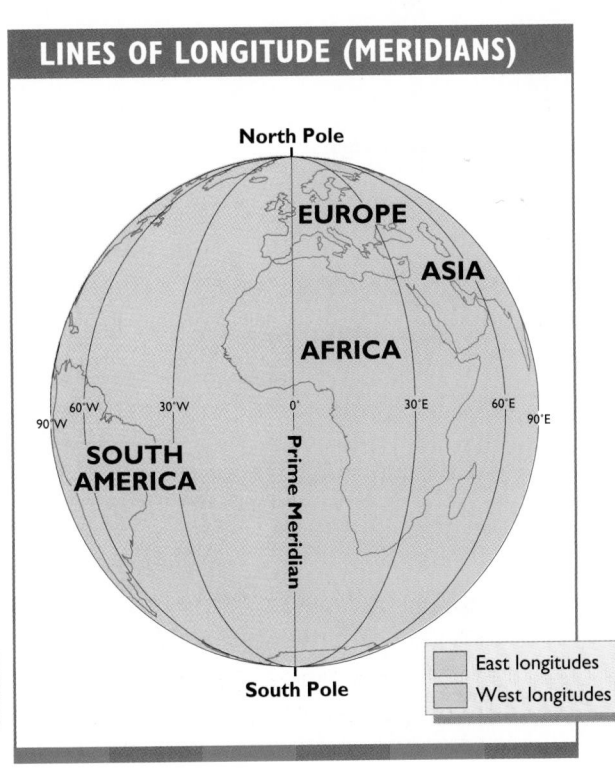

North Pole · EUROPE · ASIA · AFRICA · SOUTH AMERICA · 90°W · 60°W · 30°W · 0° · 30°E · 60°E · 90°E · Prime Meridian · South Pole

East longitudes
West longitudes

G5

PART 2
Using Maps

VOCABULARY
cardinal directions
intermediate directions
compass rose
scale
symbol
map key
locator

What are cardinal directions?

- There are four main or cardinal directions.

- North is the direction you face when you stand facing the North Pole. South is behind you. East is to your right. What direction is to your left?

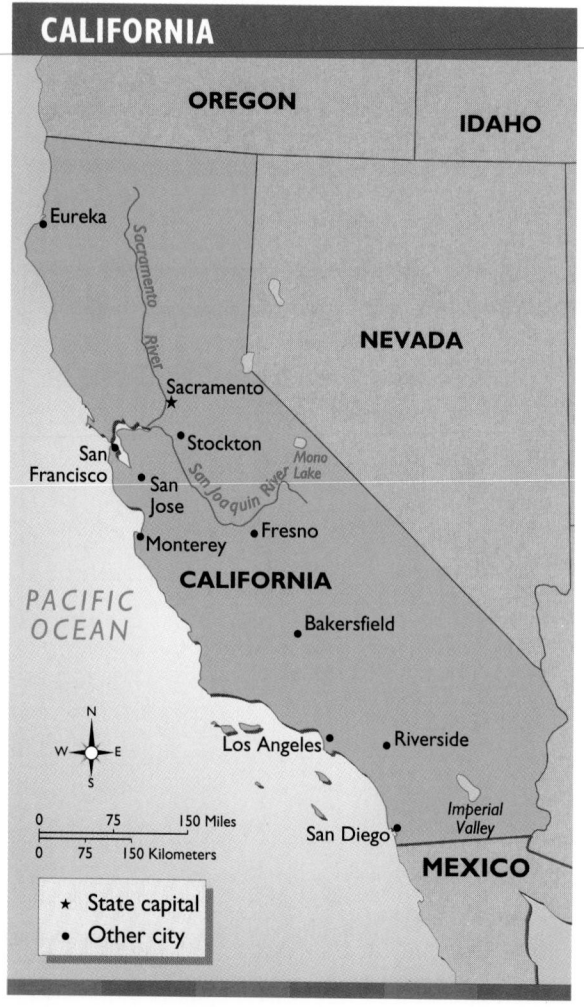

- The letters **N**, **S**, **E**, and **W** stand for these cardinal directions. What direction does **N** stand for? What direction does **E** stand for?

What are intermediate directions?

- Cardinal directions cannot always describe a direction with enough accuracy. For this reason, there are also intermediate directions. The intermediate directions are halfway between pairs of cardinal directions.

- The letters **NE**, **SE**, **SW**, and **NW** stand for the four intermediate directions. For example, **SW** stands for southwest. Southwest is the intermediate direction between south and west. What are the names of the other three intermediate directions?

How can you find directions on a map?

- Not all maps show the North Pole. However, most maps you will see in this book have a compass rose. A compass rose is a small drawing that indicates directions on a map. On most maps, north is the direction that is pointing toward the top of the map. Look at the compass rose for the map to the left. How are the cardinal directions marked?

- A compass rose sometimes includes both cardinal and intermediate directions. If it does not incude intermediate directions, just remember that they are halfway between the cardinal directions. Look at the map on this page. In what direction is Monterey from Bakersfield? In what direction is San Fransisco from Sacramento?

More Practice
You can practice finding directions on almost any map in this book. For examples, see pages 30, 33, and 37.

MAP A: HAWAII

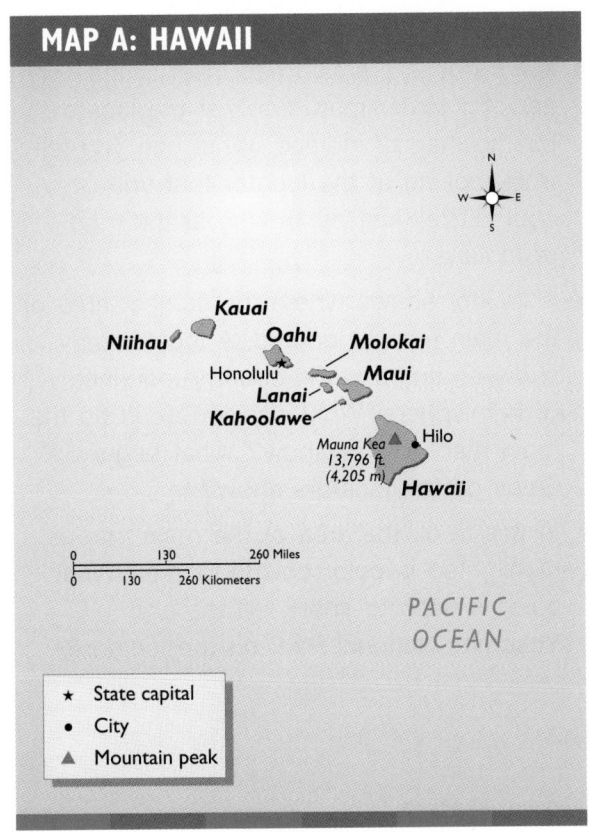

MAP B: HAWAII

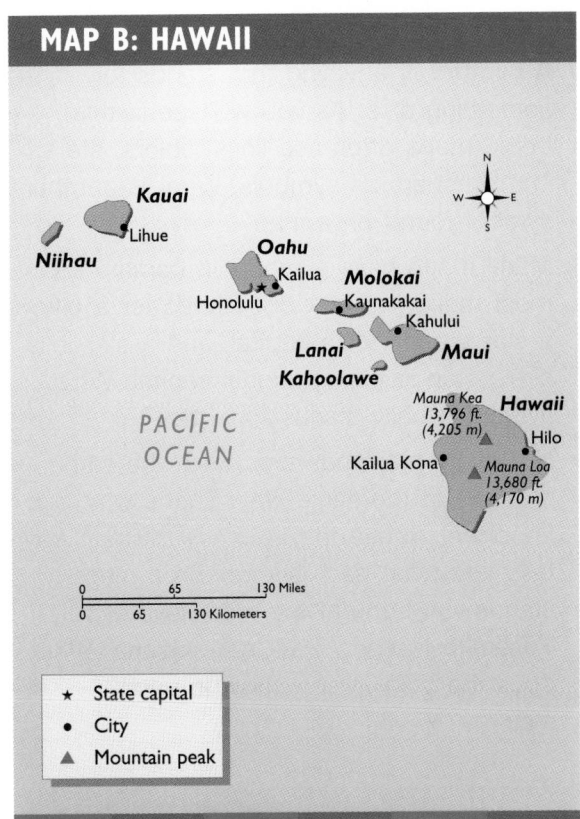

What is a scale?

- Maps are much smaller than the actual places they show. The **scale** tells how much smaller. Scale explains the relationship between real distances on Earth and distances on the map.

- For the maps in this book, scale is indicated by two lines. One line shows miles. What does the other line show?

How can you use a scale? How are map scales different?

- To measure distances on a map, you can use a ruler. You can also make a scale strip like the one at right.

- Find the distance between the island of Molokai and the peak of Mauna Kea on Map A. First make a scale strip using the Map A scale. Place the edge of the strip on a line between the two places. The zero should be on Molokai. What is the distance in miles between the two places?

- Maps are drawn at different scales. Maps A and B both show the Hawaiian Islands,

but the islands look larger on Map B. They look larger because Map B has a larger scale. This means that it shows more detail.

- Even though the scales are different, the distance between places on both maps are the same. Make a scale strip using the Map B scale. What is the distance in miles between Molokai and Mauna Kea on Map B?

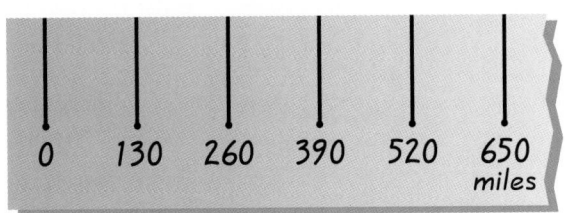

More Practice

You can practice using map scales on almost any map in this book. For examples, see pages 41, 148, and 419.

G7

How are symbols used on maps?

- A **symbol** is anything that stands for something else. As you will see in this book, maps often use lines, colors, stars, and numbers as symbols. What is another symbol found on a map?

- Many maps have symbols in common. On most maps, a black dot stands for a city, a star stands for a capital, and a star in a circle stands for a national capital. What symbol usually stands for water?

- Not every map, however, uses the same symbols in the same way. That's why it is important to use the **map key**. A map key tells you what each symbol on a map stands for. Look at the map keys of Yosemite National Park and Indiana. What does the color green show in each map?

What is a locator? What does it show?

- A **locator** is a small map inset in the corner of a larger map. Look at the locator for the map of Indiana. What can you tell from looking at the locator that you couldn't tell just by looking at the map of Indiana?

- A locator shows where the subject area of the main map is located. A locator may show an entire state, country, continent, or hemisphere. What subject areas do the main maps below show? What larger areas do the locators show?

- In this book the area of the main map is highlighted in color on the locator. What color is used to show Indiana and Yosemite National Park on the locators?

More Practice

Many maps in this book have keys and locators. For examples of map keys, see pages 32, 368, and 485. For examples of locators, see pages 61, 152, and 468.

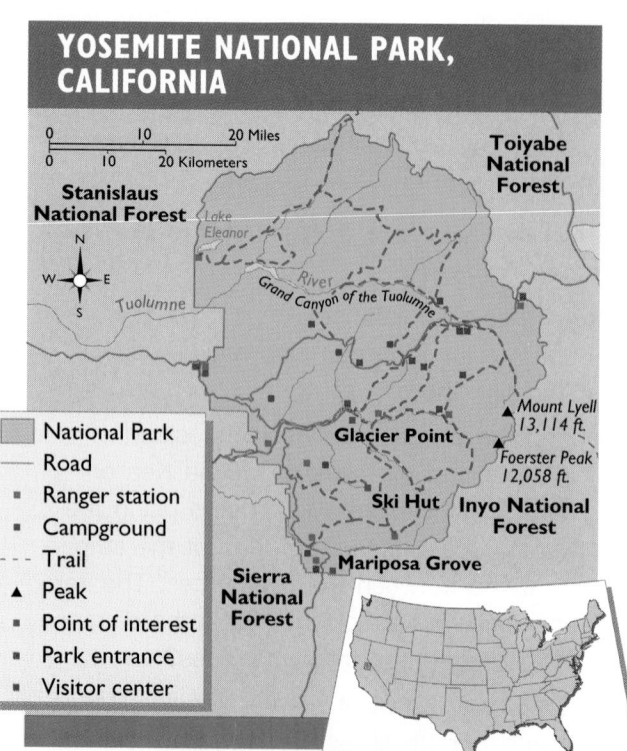

INDIANA: Corn and Dairy

Key
- ★ State capital
- • Other city
- Corn-growing area
- Dairy-farming area

ILLINOIS

Hammond, Michigan City, South Bend, Elkhart, Gary, La Crosse, Warsaw, Rensselaer, Fort Wayne, Monticello, Lafayette, Marion, Portland, **INDIANA**, Muncie, Crawfordsville, Indianapolis, Richmond, Connersville, Shelbyville, Terre Haute, Columbus, Lawrenceburg, Bedford, Madison, Vincennes, Washington, Scottsburg, Paoli, New Harmony, Evansville, Corydon, Cannellton

KENTUCKY

0 25 50 Miles
0 25 50 Kilometers

YOSEMITE NATIONAL PARK, CALIFORNIA

0 10 20 Miles
0 10 20 Kilometers

Stanislaus National Forest — Lake Eleanor — Toiyabe National Forest — Grand Canyon of the Tuolumne — Tuolumne River — Glacier Point — Mount Lyell 13,114 ft. — Foerster Peak 12,058 ft. — Ski Hut — Inyo National Forest — Mariposa Grove — Sierra National Forest

Key
- National Park
- — Road
- ▪ Ranger station
- ▪ Campground
- --- Trail
- ▲ Peak
- ▪ Point of interest
- ▪ Park entrance
- ▪ Visitor center

PART 3
Different Kinds of Maps

VOCABULARY

political map   elevation map
physical map   road map
relief map   historical map

Why read a map title?

- There are many kinds of maps. This section discusses four kinds of maps.

- It is important to read the map title first. It may tell you what information the map shows and what the map's subject area is. What is the title of the map below?

- Sometimes a map includes areas that are not part of its subject area. For example, the map of the Middle West region, below, also shows part of Canada. In this book nonsubject areas are usually shown in gray. What colors are used in the subject area of the map below?

What is a political map?

- Many maps show borders between states or countries. As you can see below, a political map often uses colors to show the boundaries between states or countries.

- A political map usually labels capital cities. Look at the map below. How many states are in the Middle West? What is the capital of Iowa?

More Practice

To study other political maps in this book, see pages R4–R5, R10–R11, and R12.

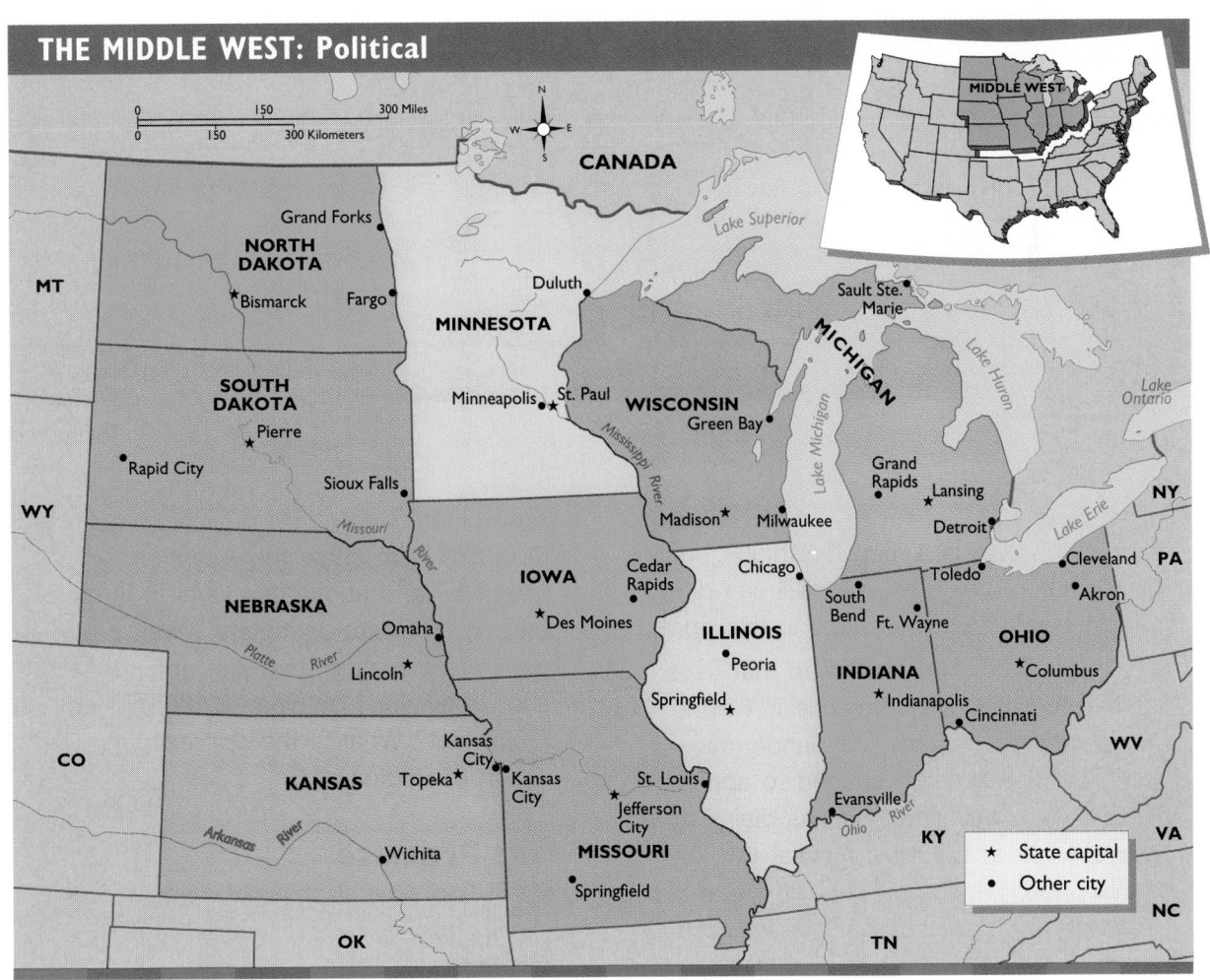

THE MIDDLE WEST: Political

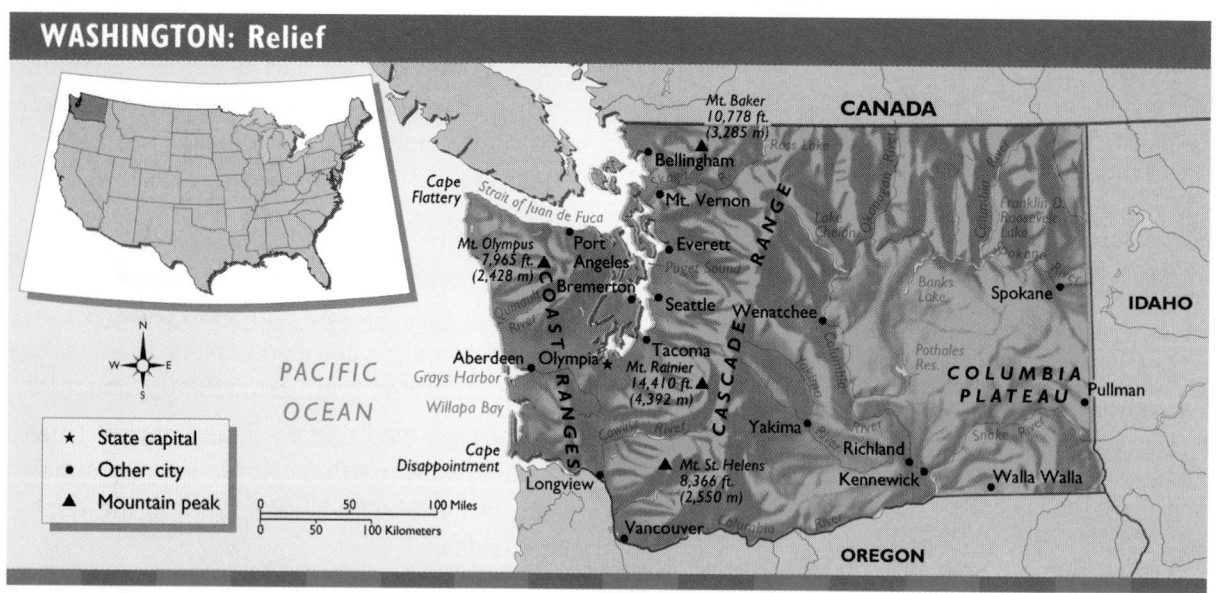

WASHINGTON: Relief

WASHINGTON: Elevation

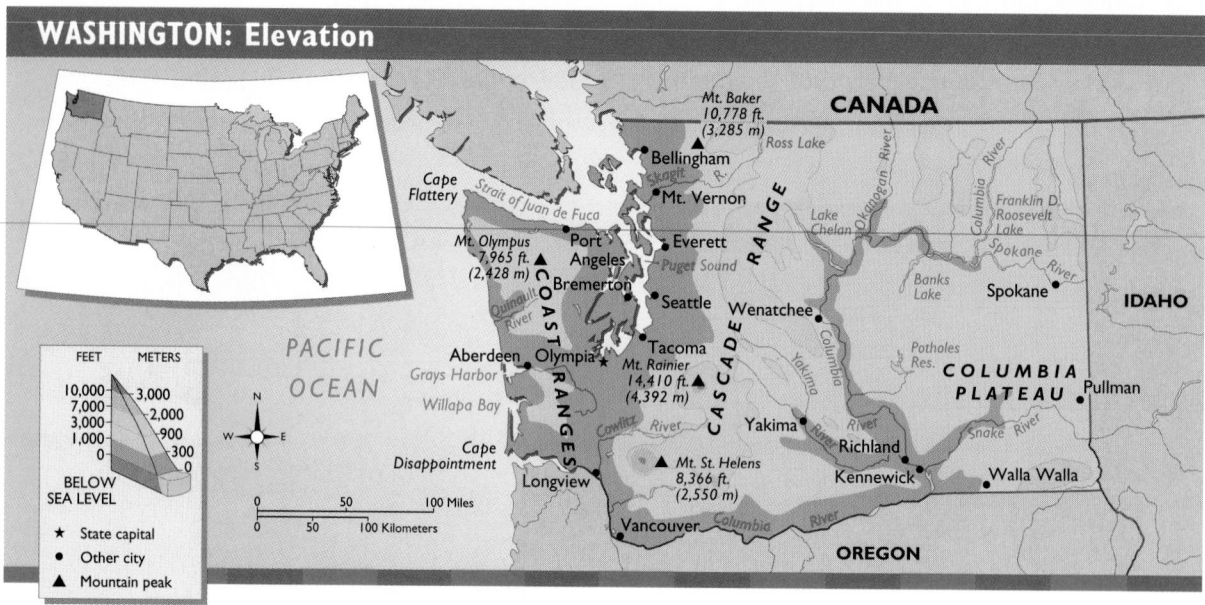

What is a physical map?

- A physical map is a map that highlights Earth's natural features. You will see different types of physical maps in this book.

- A relief map is a physical map that uses shading to show the difference in height between areas of land. High landforms such as mountains are shaded to appear higher than lower land, such as plains or valleys. Look at the relief map at the top of this page. Which part of Washington state has the greatest relief? Which area has the least?

- An elevation map is a physical map that uses colors to show the elevation, or height of land above sea level. It is usually measured in feet or meters. What color does the elevation map just above use to show elevations between 3,000 feet and 7,000 feet? What is the approximate elevation of Spokane?

More Practice

You will find several physical maps in this book. For examples, see pages 34, 230–231, and R6–R7.

G10

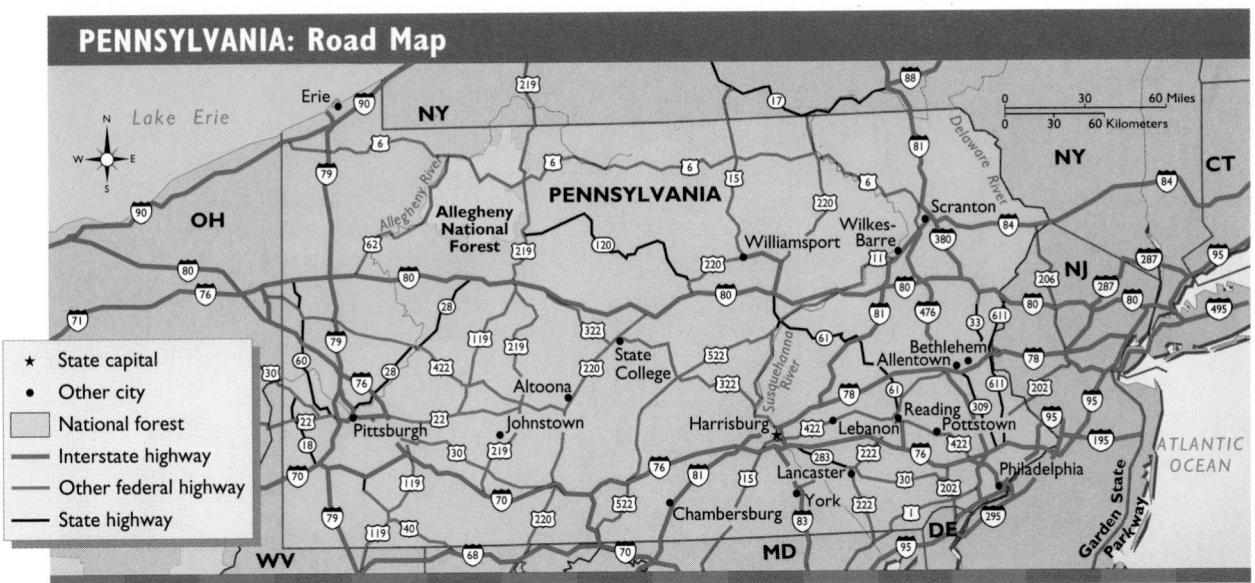

PENNSYLVANIA: Road Map

Legend:
- ★ State capital
- • Other city
- National forest
- — Interstate highway
- — Other federal highway
- — State highway

What is a road map?

- A **road map** shows you how to get from one place to another. Road maps usually show cities and highways. They may also show natural features, points of interest, rest stops for drivers, and even the number of miles between places.

- Look at the road map above. What is the number of the road you would take to get from Chambersburg to Scranton? What type of road is it? If you travel west on federal highway 422 from Reading, what city would you pass through first?

What is an historical map?

- An **historical map** is a map that shows information about the past or where past events took place.

- The title of a map will help you determine that it is historical. Look at the historical map shown at right. What time in history does it show? The map key can give you more information. In which group of colonies is Virginia shown? What color is used to show the New England colonies?

More Practice

You will study a variety of maps in this book. For more practice using different kinds of maps, see pages 149, 302, and 449.

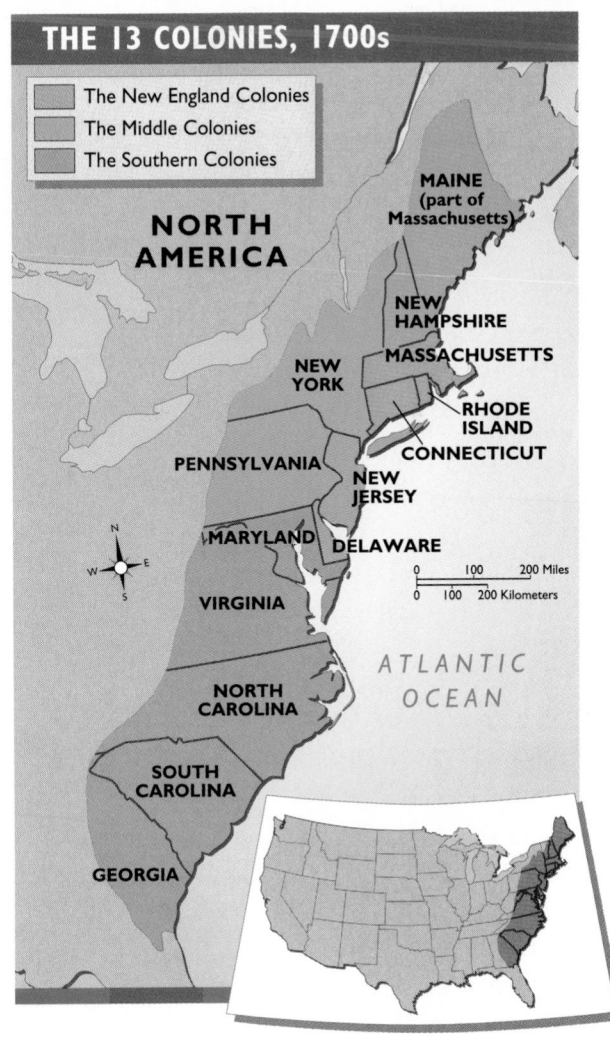

THE 13 COLONIES, 1700s

- The New England Colonies
- The Middle Colonies
- The Southern Colonies

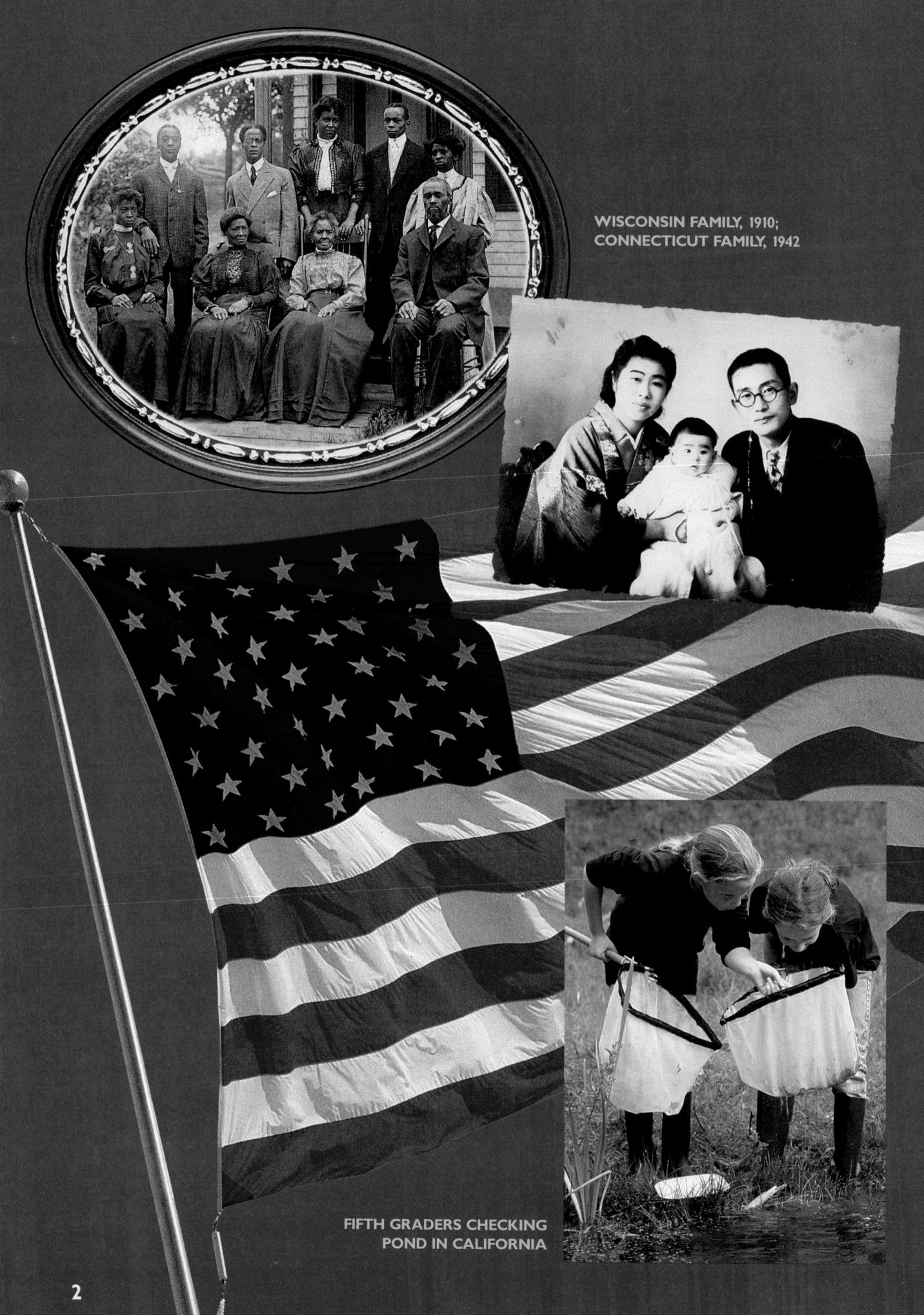

WISCONSIN FAMILY, 1910;
CONNECTICUT FAMILY, 1942

FIFTH GRADERS CHECKING
POND IN CALIFORNIA

Americans and Our Environment

"America! . . . From sea to shining sea."

from *America, the Beautiful* by Katharine Lee Bates
See page 47.

WHY DOES IT MATTER?

We live in a country of great natural beauty. Breathtaking views delight the eye in every region of the United States. In fact, the quote above, from the song *America, the Beautiful,* was inspired by the American land. Katharine Lee Bates wrote of our country's mountains and deserts, its rolling hills and plains, the bounty and richness of its environment.

As rich and varied as our land is, so too is the population of the United States. Yet while we come from different backgrounds, we share many things. We are, for example, united by our belief in freedom and justice for all.

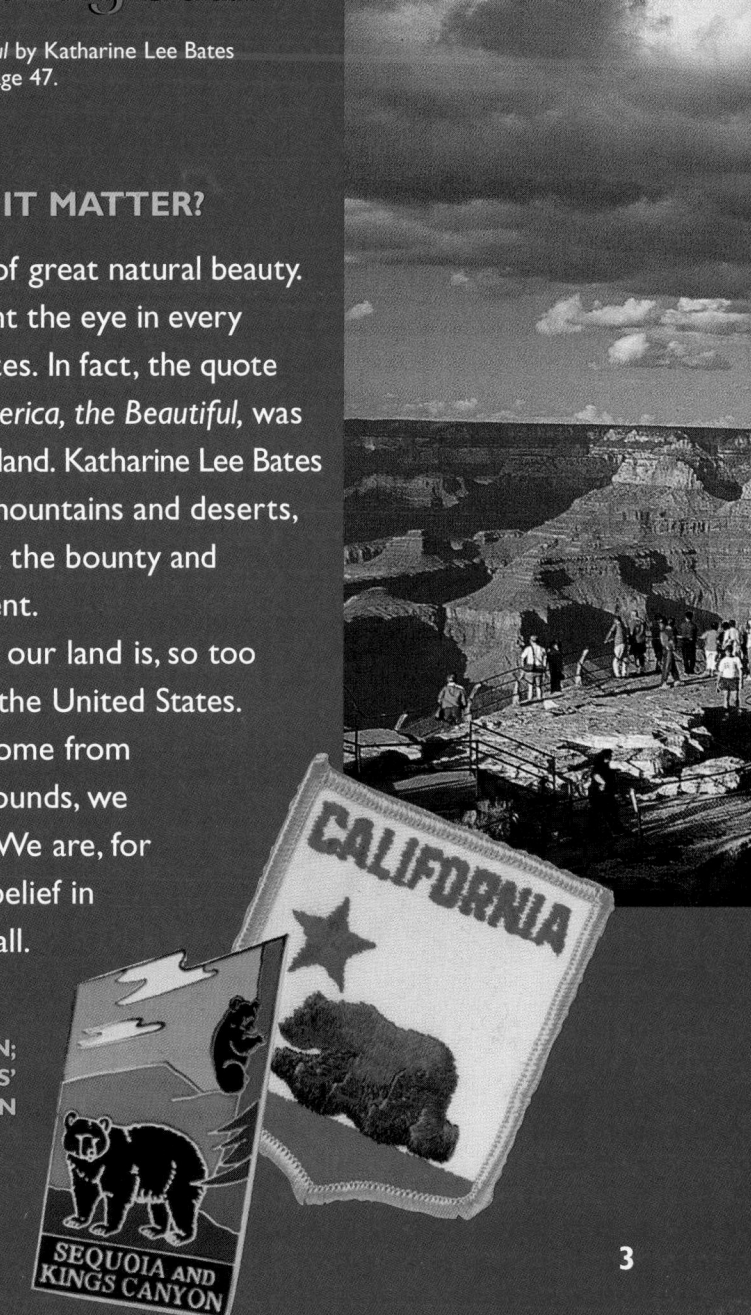

GRAND CANYON;
CALIFORNIA NATIONAL PARKS'
"BEAR STATE" PATCH AND PIN

Adventures with
NATIONAL GEOGRAPHIC

TALL TALES

They're even older than your teacher! The giant sequoias of California started growing centuries ago—before Columbus, before Washington, before most of the history in this book. Soaring 20 stories into the sky, their reddish trunks amaze visitors. Their roots make a natural jungle gym, and their stumps are a perfect place for a picnic. Between bites, you can digest a silent history lesson. Like Nature's diary, the tree rings chart the passing years. And, as you'll learn, a whole lot happened during those years.

GEO JOURNAL

Stretch your imagination and listen real hard. What stories might you hear from a 2,000-year-old tree?

CHAPTER 1

Life in the United States

THINKING ABOUT
PEOPLE AND HISTORY

The history of the United States is the story of its people. You will begin in Chapter 1 to meet the people whose words and deeds have contributed to our history. Our country's people come from all over the world, yet we are united in our belief in freedom and equality for all.

ALASKA

CANADA

New York Harbor

UNITED STATES

PACIFIC OCEAN

MEXICO

HAWAII

New York Harbor, **NEW YORK**

The Statue of Liberty, or Miss Liberty as it is known, was a gift from the people of France to celebrate our country's first 100 years.

AMERICANS TODAY

Focus Activity

READ TO LEARN
Who are the people of the United States?

VOCABULARY
culture
diversity
unity
values
immigrant
ancestor
ethnic group
census
population
prejudice

READ ALOUD

E pluribus unum (EE PLUR uh bus YOO num). You may have heard these words before. What do they mean? They are Latin for "Out of many, one," the motto, or saying, of the United States for more than 200 years. This motto has defined an important goal of our country—that the many different peoples in our 50 states live together as one people.

THE BIG PICTURE

Today as in the past, the United States is home to people from many cultures. A culture is the entire way of life of a people—their customs, beliefs, and language.

People came to this country, and continue to come, from all over the world. Each group has brought its different ideas and traditions to the United States. These differences in cultures bring a great deal of diversity (dih VUR sih tee) to our country. Diversity is variety.

Although Americans come from different backgrounds, we share many basic beliefs. We believe in the freedom to worship and to earn a living as we choose. Americans also believe in fairness and equal treatment of people. Such shared beliefs have helped to create a sense of unity among our country's people. *Unity* means "being as one or being in agreement."

As you read this book, notice how people from many diverse cultures, places, and backgrounds have helped to make the United States a great and special country.

AMERICAN PEOPLE

What do Americans have in common? Most speak English. Many have a similar style of dress and enjoy similar sports, books, and movies. Most important, people in the United States share similar values about the rights and freedoms they enjoy as Americans. Values are the beliefs or ideals that guide the way people live. Americans also respect the laws and the government that protect those rights.

Ancestors from Different Shores

Most people in the United States have someone in their family background who was an immigrant. An immigrant is a person who leaves one country to go and live in another land.

Many newcomers to the United States keep some of the traditional ways of their ancestors. Ancestors are the relatives who lived before you. We all have many ancestors. In the United States you can see the influence of different cultures everywhere. Recent immigrants might speak Spanish, Arabic, or Korean. They may celebrate the holidays of their ancestors, such as the Chinese New Year.

Ethnic Backgrounds

An example of our country's diversity is the variety of ethnic groups that live in the United States. An ethnic group includes people who share the same customs and language. Many also have a common history.

Some ethnic groups, such as Native Americans, have lived here for thousands of years. It was not until about 500 years ago that people from Europe and Africa began arriving here. Until after the Civil War, most African Americans were forced to come to the United States in chains.

In recent years the largest numbers of immigrants have come from Asia and Latin America. Latin America includes Mexico, the Caribbean islands, Central America, and South America. People whose ancestors are from Spanish-speaking countries in the Western Hemisphere are called Hispanics or Latinos. Asian Americans are descendants of people from China, Korea, Japan, Vietnam, India, and many other countries in Asia. You will read about many of our ethnic groups in this book.

Our country's diversity is seen in its many ethnic groups—from Native Americans to people from almost every country in the world.

Infographic

The People of the United States

How can we find out facts about our country's people? One way is to study the census that our government takes every ten years. A census is an official study of the people of a country. It provides information about the number of people in an area, where they live, and how they live. Such information helps the government plan for our future needs. Below are some facts about the American people today.

POPULATION

The population is the number of people living in a place. The population of the United States has grown from less than 4 million people in 1790 to 267 million in 1997.

Population in 1997: 267 million
Estimated population in 2000: 273 million
Estimated population in 2050: 381 million

MAJOR ETHNIC GROUPS, 1997

- European American
- African American
- Hispanic*
- Asian American
- Native American

32,158,000

28,910,000

194,365,000

9,387,000

1,969,000

Source: U.S. Bureau of the Census 1997
* of any race

AGE

In a few families, members' ages span an entire century from newborn to more than 100 years of age.

RELIGION
Americans follow many religious faiths. About 56 percent are Protestant, the largest Christian group in the country.

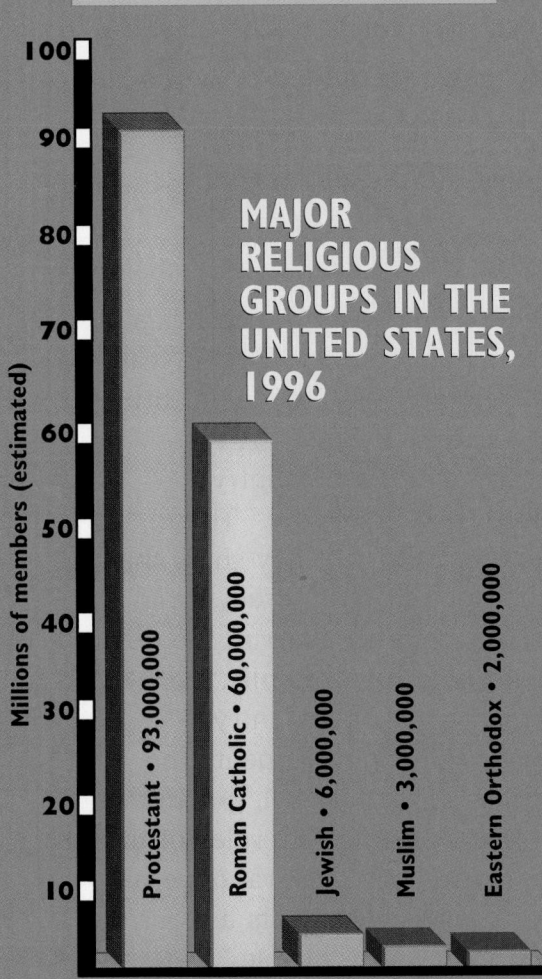

MAJOR RELIGIOUS GROUPS IN THE UNITED STATES, 1996

Millions of members (estimated)

100
90
80
70
60
50
40
30
20
10

Protestant • 93,000,000
Roman Catholic • 60,000,000
Jewish • 6,000,000
Muslim • 3,000,000
Eastern Orthodox • 2,000,000

Source: *The World Almanac, 1996*

WHY IT MATTERS

Most of the people in our country are proud of their heritage. The writer Ishmael Reed has described the United States as a place "where the cultures of the world crisscross."

However, the acceptance of differences has not always come easily. Many ethnic groups have faced prejudice because their backgrounds, skin color, or beliefs were different from those of other groups. Prejudice is a negative opinion formed without proof.

Despite their differences, Americans share a common culture and values such as "liberty and justice for all," freedom of speech, religious freedom, and the hope for a better life.

Reviewing Facts and Ideas

MAIN IDEAS

- The United States is a diverse country, but its people share a number of basic beliefs and values.
- Many ethnic groups have come together to form a rich variety of traditions and customs in our country.
- Many different religions are practiced in the United States.

THINK ABOUT IT

1. What is meant by the motto *E pluribus unum?*

2. What are some of the places in which our ancestors were born?

3. **FOCUS** Why is the United States home to many different peoples?

4. **THINKING SKILL** What kinds of information would you use to _classify_ the variety of Americans today?

5. **WRITE** Write a paragraph explaining what immigrants might enjoy about the United States.

11

OUR COUNTRY'S GOVERNMENT

Focus Activity

READ TO LEARN
What is the role of citizens in our country's democratic republic?

VOCABULARY
Constitution
democracy
republic
federal
citizen
civil rights

PLACE
Washington, D.C.

READ ALOUD

"I pledge allegiance (uh LEE juns) to the flag of the United States of America and to the Republic for which it stands, one Nation under God, indivisible, with liberty and justice for all." Most likely you already know these words to the Pledge of Allegiance. By reciting them, we promise our loyalty to our flag, our country's government, and the values they represent.

THE BIG PICTURE

In 1776 colonial leaders decided that the 13 British colonies should found their own country. Eleven years later many of the same leaders wrote the Constitution (kahn stih TOO shun) of the United States. A constitution is a plan of government for a country.

"We the People of the United States. . . ." These famous words begin our Constitution. They show that our country's founders believed in democracy. In a democracy the people make the laws and run the government. The United States is also a republic. Here the people elect representatives to run the country.

Our country has three levels of government. The Constitution set up the federal, or national, government in Washington, D.C. It also explained the roles of the state and local governments. Like the federal government, all of our state and local governments are run by representatives elected by "we the people."

PEOPLE AND GOVERNMENT

Our government serves the people in many ways. We expect it to protect our lives and property, to enforce laws, to build highways, and to provide schools.

"The Consent of the Governed"

The government gets its power "from the consent of the governed," says the Declaration of Independence. *Consent* means "approval." How do citizens give their consent? A citizen is a person who is born in a country or who chooses to become a member of that country by law. Citizens give their consent by voting. Americans vote in many kinds of elections. They vote for the President of the United States, for the governor of their state, and for the mayor of their city. They vote for local school-board members, as well.

Citizens often have different opinions about who should be elected or what the government should do. They get to voice their opinions in public meetings. Newspapers, radio, and television are also ways to speak out on issues. One big job that citizens have is staying informed about the issues.

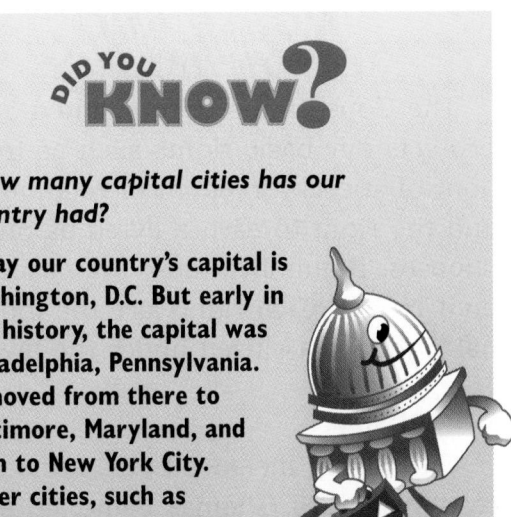

DID YOU KNOW?

How many capital cities has our country had?

Today our country's capital is Washington, D.C. But early in our history, the capital was Philadelphia, Pennsylvania. It moved from there to Baltimore, Maryland, and then to New York City. Other cities, such as Trenton and Princeton in New Jersey, also served briefly as the national capital.

Government Responds

The government responds to citizens in a number of ways. When disaster strikes, Americans receive help from the federal, state, and local governments. They use tax money and can draw upon resources of the entire country in times of major crisis. How has our government helped people in your area in normal times and in times of need?

Federal workers stack bales of hay to keep back flood waters; in the 1930s more than 250,000 young men maintained national forests (inset).

RIGHTS AND RESPONSIBILITIES

The Constitution of the United States protects our basic rights such as freedom of speech, freedom of religion, and the right to earn a living as one chooses. Rights like these are called civil rights. Civil rights are the individual rights of a citizen under the law.

Citizenship

Citizenship includes both rights and responsibilities. Thomas Paine, an early writer, put it this way:

Those who expect to reap [receive] the blessings of freedom must . . . undergo the fatigue [weariness] of supporting it.

As citizens we have important responsibilities, such as voting, obeying the law, taking part in government, and paying taxes to provide for the benefits that we receive. Respecting the rights of others is another responsibility that we all share.

Taking Part in Government

Citizens have many opportunities to take part in government. When you are 18 years old, you will be able to vote. Even now you could help in a political campaign. Eventually you will pay taxes, or money that pays for the costs of running the government. Some citizens defend our country in times of peace as well as war. Others take a direct role by running for government office.

Ben Nighthorse Campbell was elected to represent the citizens of Colorado in the United States Senate in 1992. Read the following excerpt in which Senator Campbell talks about his job in Congress. What do you think about the Senator's view that our government is run by the people?

MANY VOICES PRIMARY SOURCE

Excerpt from an interview with Senator Ben Nighthorse Campbell in 1994.

We are lucky to live in a country that grants us rights in the Constitution such as freedom to speak, write, read, work, worship, and live as we choose. These freedoms place a responsibility on each of us to become involved in our system of government. America is run by the people—that includes you.

There are many reasons why I ran for the Senate. . . . I wanted this job because I care about my state and its people, and I wanted to ensure that the people's interests were well represented in Congress.

More than 500 men and women meet regularly in the United States Capitol Building to make our country's laws.

The Levels of Government

Our country's government works on three separate levels—federal, state, and local. The federal government handles issues that affect the entire country. As you have read, Senator Campbell works in the federal government—in Congress. Only the federal government can declare war or make peace agreements with other countries.

Our country's state governments deal with issues that affect an entire state or parts of a state. Their responsibilities include managing public schools and holding elections.

Our country's people live in cities, counties, townships, and parishes. They have needs that are best met by local government. The people who work in local government are responsible for keeping law and order and building roads, among other duties.

Most important is how the levels of government work together. Such issues as energy and fuel use and highway and aircraft transportation involve the government at all levels—local, state, and federal.

WHY IT MATTERS

In our democratic republic the people are the government. We elect citizens like ourselves to speak for us at the local, state, and federal levels. If we do not approve of the views or actions of these representatives, we have the right to vote for others.

"The people's government, made for the people, made by the people, and answerable to the people." In those words Daniel Webster, an American statesman, described how the people and the government are the same. Since our country's beginning, people have proudly taken part in running it. You will read in the next lesson how the words and deeds of American people have created our country's history.

✔️ Reviewing Facts and Ideas

MAIN IDEAS

- The Constitution of the United States organizes our government into a democratic republic.

- Americans give consent to the government by voting and by taking part in the government themselves.

- Citizenship in a democratic republic involves rights and responsibilities.

THINK ABOUT IT

1. What kind of government does the United States have?

2. Describe the rights and responsibilities of American citizens.

3. **FOCUS** What are some jobs that citizens can do for our government?

4. **THINKING SKILL** Why would being elected influence the *decisions* of the people who hold government offices?

5. **WRITE** Write a paragraph explaining "consent of the governed."

THINKINGSKILLS

Problem Solving

VOCABULARY
problem
define
clarify
evaluate

WHY THE SKILL MATTERS

Every day you solve—or try to solve—dozens of problems. A problem is a question or issue that needs to be answered or solved. You use problem solving to find a lost book, to figure out how much time you need to do your homework, or to arrive at the answer to a question about something you have read. Problem solving is a process we use to overcome difficulties or find answers.

To begin the process of problem solving, you first define, or name, the problem. Sometimes you need to clarify, or make clear, the main difficulty or question by stating it clearly in your own words. You then identify and collect the information that you believe will help you to solve the problem. Next you evaluate, or judge the accuracy of, this information and then use the material to arrive at a solution or answer. The final result is sometimes called a conclusion.

USING THE SKILL

Here is an example of problem solving in action. Jason Stone is a fifth grader in a Los Angeles school. One day his teacher spoke

about the importance of taking part in school government. She said that students, like adults, need to be responsible members of their communities. Jason wanted to know whether his fellow students were responsible citizens. He knew that one way to be a responsible citizen was to vote. He defined his problem by asking this question: How many fifth graders actually vote in school elections? To solve the problem, he set out to find out how many fifth graders would vote in the next day's election for class president.

Jason asked each of the six fifth-grade teachers to count the number of votes cast on voting day. He evaluated the numbers they reported by checking them against the classroom attendance numbers for that day. Then he added the number of votes from each of the six classes. As a result, Jason discovered that 139 students had voted but 29 students had not. Jason came up with two answers. Most students in the six classes were responsible citizens as far as voting was concerned. However, 29 students were not.

TRYING THE SKILL

As you read this book, you will come across many people who used problem-solving skills. You will recognize the same steps that Jason followed. The Helping Yourself box on this page lists key steps in the process of problem solving. Suppose, for example, that you wanted to explore why

some students in your class vote while others do not. Where would you start? What steps would you follow?

REVIEWING THE SKILL

1. When did you use problem solving this week? How did you clarify the problem?

2. When solving a problem, why is it important to evaluate information before you state a conclusion?

3. Suppose you wanted to know what life was like in your hometown 100 years ago. What kinds of information might you gather?

4. How does problem solving help you in your daily life?

Percentage of Students Who Voted			
Class	Size	Votes	Percent
	30	30	100%
5-305	28	21	75%
5-306	30	24	80%
5-308	32		

OUR COUNTRY'S HISTORY

READ ALOUD

"All our stories are different," explained Tomo Shoji as she spoke to a group of Asian Americans in 1988. Shoji urged children to listen to their ancestors' stories. Through those tales they can learn about their families' pasts. Such stories form part of our country's history, which includes the experiences of the many people who have settled on these shores.

THE BIG PICTURE

History is the study or record of what happened in the past. The history of the United States is rich and varied. But when does that story begin? What and whom does that story include?

It begins far back in time. The first people to shape this land were the Native Americans. Our story continues with later arrivals from Europe, Africa, Asia, and Latin America. A book like this cannot tell every story. Instead it will look at how some people—some famous, some not—contributed to our country's development.

When Minnie Miller, an immigrant from Europe, wrote of her life, she included her ancestors. "My history is bound up in their history, and the generations that follow should know where they came from to know better who they are." History helps us to see how the lives of our ancestors affect the way we live today.

Focus Activity

READ TO LEARN
How do the stories of many different people help us to understand our country's history?

VOCABULARY
history
historian
primary source
oral history
secondary source
perspective

HISTORY AND ITS CLUES

Think about what you did yesterday or last week or even last year. Can you remember all of the details? Historians have an even harder task. Historians are people who study the past. They examine clues and records left behind by others. Then they try to figure out what happened and why.

Primary and Secondary Sources

Historians, like detectives, comb through much written and unwritten evidence. By studying homes, pottery, or other objects, they learn about the people who made and used them.

Historians depend upon primary sources. A primary source is information that comes from the time being studied. Many are written documents such as letters. A film or photograph from the time an event happened is also a primary source. So are eyewitness accounts. An eyewitness is a person who saw an event happen.

Another kind of primary source is oral history, or spoken records. Stories passed from one generation to the next tell of our ancestors' hopes and fears.

Historians also use secondary sources. A secondary source is an account of the past written by someone who was not an eyewitness to those events. A history textbook like this one is a secondary source. So are encyclopedia articles or recent films about an event that occurred in the past.

A Matter of Perspective

Historians cannot list all the facts about past events. Instead they sort the evidence and try to make sense of what happened and why. As they weave the information into a story, they include some facts and leave out others.

Historians must also be careful about interpreting the clues that they find. *Interpret* means "make understandable." Historians' own perspectives, or points of view, sometimes affect how they look at information. At other times historians may get two or more different accounts of the same event. The responsibility of the historian is to be as accurate as possible.

George Catlin's 1834 painting *Keokuk on Horseback* shows one perspective on Native Americans. This Navajo mural in Canyon del Muerto, Arizona, is one on Europeans.

Smithsonian Institution

PEOPLE AND HISTORY

People are the chief participants in history. They make and experience it. They also record and interpret it. A book like this one is about people whose thoughts and actions formed our past.

Speaking of History

The following accounts written by two historians describe the parts played by immigrants in our country's history.

Ronald Takaki wants to share stories of the people who helped make our country strong. In the first excerpt he gives his view of how different ethnic groups helped shape our country.

Arthur M. Schlesinger, Jr., has studied times in the past when our country was changing rapidly. In the second excerpt he discusses his perspective on American values. Read both excerpts. What similarities can you find in their views of America?

MANY VOICES PRIMARY SOURCE

Excerpt from
A Different Mirror:
A Multicultural History of America
by Ronald Takaki, 1993.

The signs of America's ethnic diversity can be discerned [seen] across the continent. . . . Much of what is familiar in America's cultural landscape actually has ethnic origins. The Bing cherry was developed by an early Chinese immigrant named Ah Bing. American Indians were **cultivating** *corn, tomatoes, and tobacco long before the arrival of Columbus. . . . Jazz and blues as well as rock and roll have African American origins. The "Forty-Niners" of the Gold Rush learned mining techniques from the Mexicans. . . . Popular songs like "God Bless America," "Easter Parade," and "White Christmas" were written by a Russian-Jewish immigrant named Israel Baline, better known as Irving Berlin.*

cultivating: growing

Excerpt from
The Disuniting of America
by Arthur M. Schlesinger, Jr., 1998.

The genius [greatness] of America lies in its capacity to forge a single nation from peoples of remarkably diverse racial, religious, and ethnic origins.

Our democratic principles **contemplate** *an open society founded on tolerance of differences and on mutual respect. In practice, America has been more open to some than to others. But it is more open to all today than it was yesterday and is likely to be even more open tomorrow than today. The persistent movement of American life has been from* **exclusion** *to inclusion.*

contemplate:
think about
exclusion:
not including

WHY IT MATTERS

The United States is a fascinating mixture of peoples and cultures. This is one of our country's greatest strengths.

History is not only about famous people. It is about ordinary people as well. It is the story of men, women, and children of many ethnic groups. It is the story of people who worked ten-hour days in the factories and children who helped clear land for farms or labored underground in coal mines. It is the story of cowhands who slept on the hard ground of the trail. All these stories, like small creeks, flow into the great river of American history.

The story of the American past is your story. Today you are a participant in our history. You are creating the stories that future students will learn.

✓ Reviewing Facts and Ideas

MAIN IDEAS

● Our country's history is the story of many different people with many experiences.

● History is recorded in different ways. Historians gather, sort, and interpret all kinds of evidence about the past.

● By studying the past, we learn how our ancestors acted and how their experiences affect who we are today.

THINK ABOUT IT

1. Describe the job of historians.

2. When might historians use a primary source? A secondary source?

3. **FOCUS** Why do we listen to the stories of different peoples in order to understand our country's history?

4. **THINKING SKILL** How does an historian *solve problems* in the same way that a detective does?

5. **WRITE** Write a paragraph about how your history is linked to that of your parents and grandparents.

Legacy

PRESERVING
HISTORIC PLACES

Is history a subject in a textbook? Or is it something we can see and touch? History is the study of the past, but its legacies are all around us. Legacies are traditions that are handed down from one generation to the next.

Almost everywhere in the United States, there are historic places that people have preserved. In preserving historic places we show future generations that the past is more than dates and names—it is, in fact, alive.

In 1963 First Lady Jacqueline Kennedy said that she wanted the White House to be a "museum of our country's heritage." The Diplomatic Reception Room (above) has changed little since she restored and redecorated it. This plate of china (right) was part of a set the Kennedys used during state dinners at the White House.

A nineteenth-century tenement building in New York City is now part of the Lower East Side Tenement Museum. In kitchens like the one above, immigrant families discussed their future in their new country.

Established in 1769, San Diego de Alcalá was the first Spanish mission in California. Today visitors admire the building's striking architecture and remember the Spanish influence on American history.

CHAPTER 1 REVIEW

THINKING ABOUT VOCABULARY

Number a paper from 1 to 15. Beside each number write the word or term from the list below that matches the description.

ancestor
census
citizen
civil rights
Constitution
culture
ethnic group
immigrant

perspective
prejudice
primary source
republic
secondary source
unity
values

1. a person who leaves one country to come and live in another

2. a country in which people elect representatives to serve in the government

3. a person who is born in a country or who chooses to become a member of that country by law

4. the rights of a citizen under the law

5. historical information from the time that is being studied

6. the entire way of life of a people, their customs, beliefs, and language

7. the beliefs or ideals that guide the way people live

8. a negative opinion formed without proof

9. an official study of the people of a country

10. the plan of government for the United States

11. being in agreement or being as one

12. the point of view a person brings to information and ideas

13. people who share, among other things, the same customs and language

14. an historical account written by someone who is not an eyewitness

15. a relative who lived before you

THINKING ABOUT FACTS

1. Why can the United States be considered a country of much diversity?

2. What was the population of the United States in 1997?

3. What are some of the basic beliefs or values that Americans share?

4. What are the three levels of government in the United States?

5. List two ways each level of government in the United States serves the people.

6. What famous words begin our Constitution? Why are these words important?

7. What is history? Is history only about famous people?

8. Why is it important to study history?

9. How does his or her perspective affect an historian's work?

10. How can the study of history help show our country's diversity?

THINK AND WRITE

WRITING A REPORT

Write a brief report in which you describe the government of the United States and the role a citizen plays in it.

WRITING AN ESSAY

Write an essay in which you discuss how the motto *E pluribus unum* applies to the United States.

WRITING FROM ORAL HISTORY

Write a paragraph that describes a true event from before you were born. Ask a relative, neighbor, or friend to tell you this piece of oral history.

APPLYING THINKING SKILLS

PROBLEM SOLVING

To apply the skill of problem solving, answer the questions below.

1. What is problem solving?

2. What are three problems you solve during a normal school day?

3. What is the first step when you are solving a problem? Why is it important?

4. When solving a problem, why should you evaluate the information you used before you state your conclusion or solution?

5. How could you use problem solving to find out why some students litter while others do not?

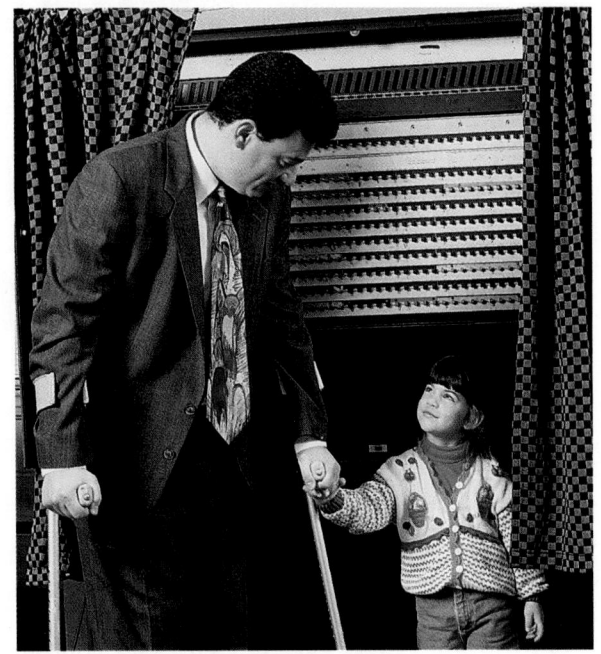

Summing Up the Chapter

Copy the main idea map on a separate piece of paper. Review the chapter to fill in the blank sections. After you have completed the map, use the information to write a short essay answering the question "How have historians helped us to learn about the people who made our country what it is today?"

Primary sources

The Study of History

MAIN IDEA

Historians use various sources to find out about the past of the United States—its people and government.

The People

Many different cultures

A federal system

Consent of the people

CHAPTER 2

Geography of the United States

THINKING ABOUT HISTORY AND GEOGRAPHY

Chapter 2 introduces you to the land and resources of the United States. From the Rocky Mountains of the West to the shores of the Atlantic Ocean in the East, our country is a mixture of many different physical features. As you read this chapter, you will see how magnificent this land of ours is.

ALASKA

CANADA

Wisconsin

New York

UNITED STATES

California

Texas

Florida

PACIFIC OCEAN

MEXICO

HAWAII

**Sierra Nevada
WEST**
California's Yosemite National Park contains some of our country's most spectacular scenery, including the peaks and valleys of the remarkable Sierra Nevada.

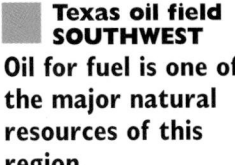

**Texas oil field
SOUTHWEST**
Oil for fuel is one of the major natural resources of this region.

**Wisconsin farmland
MIDDLE WEST**
This region is one of our country's largest producers of grain, hay, and livestock.

**Miami, Florida
SOUTHEAST**
Miami and its scenic coast is a popular place for tourists to visit.

**Niagara Falls
NORTHEAST**
The rushing waters of the New York falls create low-cost electric energy for many industries.

THE AMERICAN LAND

Focus Activity

READ TO LEARN
What are the five regions of the United States?

VOCABULARY
geography
region
landform
megalopolis
interdependent

PLACES
Rocky Mountains
Continental Divide
Grand Canyon
Corn Belt
Mississippi River
Boswash

READ ALOUD

Have you ever kept a scrapbook? A scrapbook holds photographs, ticket stubs, letters, postcards— things that remind us of special times or special places. It is also a way to hold on to memories of things we have done. You can visit a special place by taking a car trip, by gazing out the window of a plane, or by watching a movie. You can also visit a special place through the pages of a book. In the pages that follow, you will find a scrapbook of the United States.

THE BIG PICTURE

Every year millions of Americans take to the roads to see our land. They climb snowcapped mountains and explore deep canyons. They sail along rugged coasts or paddle in fish-filled lakes and rivers. They gaze in awe at waterfalls and deserts. They tour large cities and small towns. Although these vacationers might not realize it, they are studying our country's geography.

Geography is the study of Earth and the way people live on it and use it. Since earliest times the land has affected how people live. In turn, people have shaped the land to make houses for themselves or to earn a living. Geographers often divide the United States into smaller areas in order to study and compare these areas more closely. Read about these areas on the following pages. You may want to make a scrapbook of your own.

OUR COUNTRY'S REGIONS

The United States can be divided into several regions. A region is a large area that has common features that set it apart from other areas. Look at the map below. Into what five regions does it divide the United States?

Geographers, students, or teachers can divide a place into many kinds of regions. Suppose you want to learn about how people earn a living in the United States. You might divide our country into regions according to whether people work at large city jobs, in mines, or on farms. The regions shown on the map below have been created to help us study our country's culture, history, and geography. Find the region in which you live. Read on to find out what similarities the states in your region share.

Each region, such as the Middle West (top) and Northeast (above), is affected by how people use the land.

REGIONS OF THE UNITED STATES

WEST — WASHINGTON, MONTANA, OREGON, IDAHO, WYOMING, NEVADA, UTAH, COLORADO, CALIFORNIA

MIDDLE WEST — NORTH DAKOTA, MINNESOTA, SOUTH DAKOTA, WISCONSIN, MICHIGAN, NEBRASKA, IOWA, INDIANA, OHIO, ILLINOIS, KANSAS, MISSOURI

NORTHEAST — NEW HAMPSHIRE, VERMONT, MAINE, NEW YORK, MASSACHUSETTS, RHODE ISLAND, PENNSYLVANIA, CONNECTICUT, NEW JERSEY, DELAWARE, MARYLAND

ALASKA

HAWAII

SOUTHWEST — ARIZONA, NEW MEXICO, OKLAHOMA, TEXAS

SOUTHEAST — WEST VIRGINIA, VIRGINIA, KENTUCKY, TENNESSEE, NORTH CAROLINA, SOUTH CAROLINA, ARKANSAS, MISSISSIPPI, ALABAMA, GEORGIA, LOUISIANA, FLORIDA

MAP WORK

Each region in the United States has features that set it apart from the others. However, they work together to make our country strong.

1. How many states are part of the Southwest?

2. Which two regions have the most states?

3. Compare this map with the map on page 26. Which region contains the northernmost state?

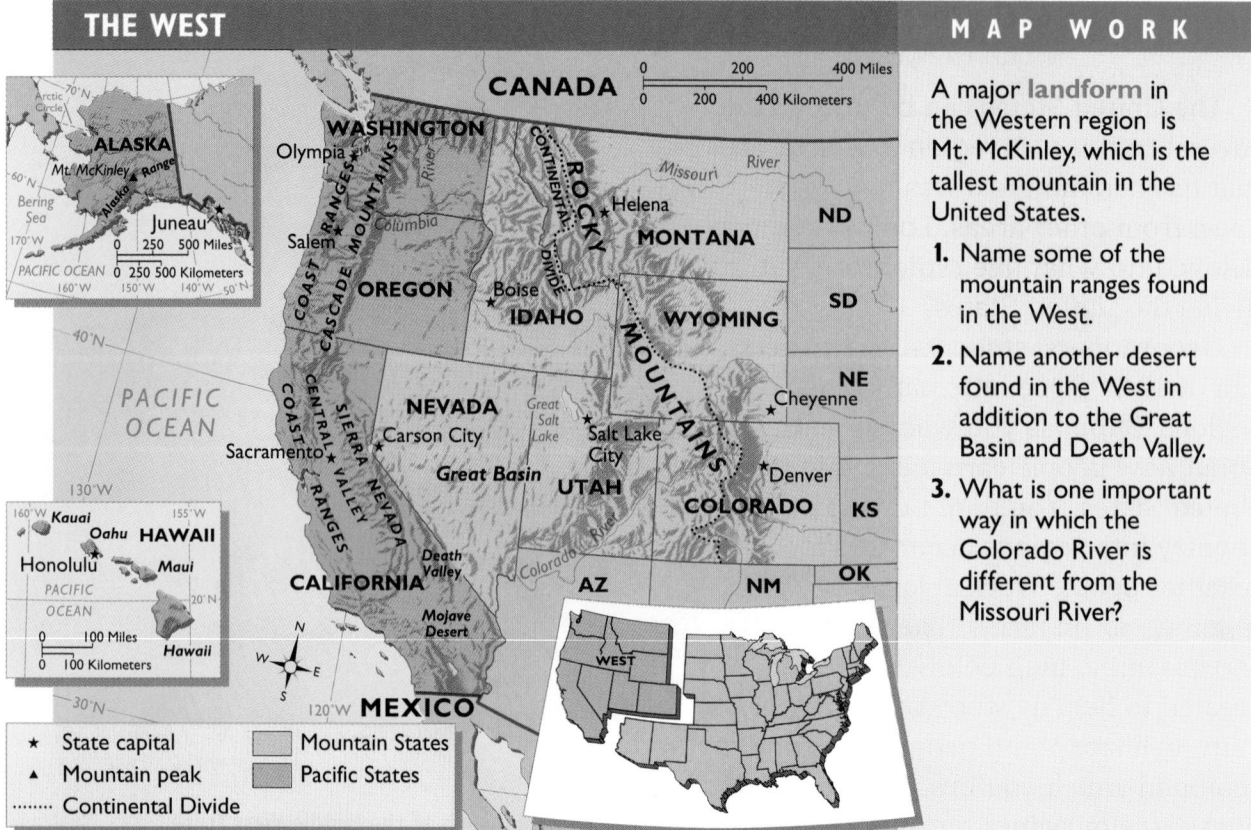

A major **landform** in the Western region is Mt. McKinley, which is the tallest mountain in the United States.

1. Name some of the mountain ranges found in the West.

2. Name another desert found in the West in addition to the Great Basin and Death Valley.

3. What is one important way in which the Colorado River is different from the Missouri River?

Map labels: CANADA, WASHINGTON, Olympia, ROCKY, Missouri River, ND, Helena, MONTANA, Columbia River, Salem, OREGON, Boise, IDAHO, WYOMING, SD, CASCADE MOUNTAINS, COAST RANGES, CONTINENTAL DIVIDE, MOUNTAINS, NE, Cheyenne, PACIFIC OCEAN, NEVADA, Great Salt Lake, Salt Lake City, Carson City, Sacramento, SIERRA NEVADA, CENTRAL VALLEY, COAST RANGES, Great Basin, UTAH, Denver, COLORADO, KS, Death Valley, CALIFORNIA, AZ, NM, OK, Mojave Desert, MEXICO, Colorado River

Alaska inset: Arctic Circle, ALASKA, Mt. McKinley, Alaska Range, Bering Sea, Juneau, PACIFIC OCEAN, 0 250 500 Miles, 0 250 500 Kilometers

Hawaii inset: Kauai, Oahu, HAWAII, Honolulu, Maui, PACIFIC OCEAN, Hawaii, 0 100 Miles, 0 100 Kilometers

Scale: 0 200 400 Miles, 0 200 400 Kilometers

Legend:
★ State capital
▲ Mountain peak
······· Continental Divide
Mountain States
Pacific States
WEST

People in the Western region enjoy gazing at beautiful views of the Pacific Coast. (left) and skiing in the snowy Rocky Mountains (below).

THE WEST

Look at the map of the West above. It is a vast region of thick green forests, rugged ocean coastlines, bustling big cities, and beautiful mountains. Mountains are a major **landform** of the West. A landform is a shape on Earth's surface. The **Rocky Mountains** are our longest mountain range. They attract millions of tourists each year.

There is an imaginary line in the Rockies that geographers call the **Continental Divide**. Rivers to the west of the divide drain into the Pacific Ocean. Rivers to the east flow into the Atlantic Ocean or Gulf of Mexico. Imagine standing on the Continental Divide. You have one foot to the west and one foot to the east and are looking down over the continent of North America.

THE SOUTHWEST

More people have moved to the Southwestern United States in recent years than to any other region of the country. As the map on this page shows, four very large states form this region. People from all over the United States and the world come to Arizona to gaze at the Grand Canyon. "It is the grandest of God's terrestrial [earthly] cities," said American geographer John Wesley Powell in 1869.

The fast-moving waters of the Colorado River carved out the Grand Canyon. You can look down at its blazing colors from the rim of the canyon. Or you can gaze up at the canyon walls from a raft in the Colorado River. You can even ride a mule down a narrow trail along the canyon.

Often-visited places of the Southwest include the Grand Canyon (top) and buildings made from sunbaked clay (right).

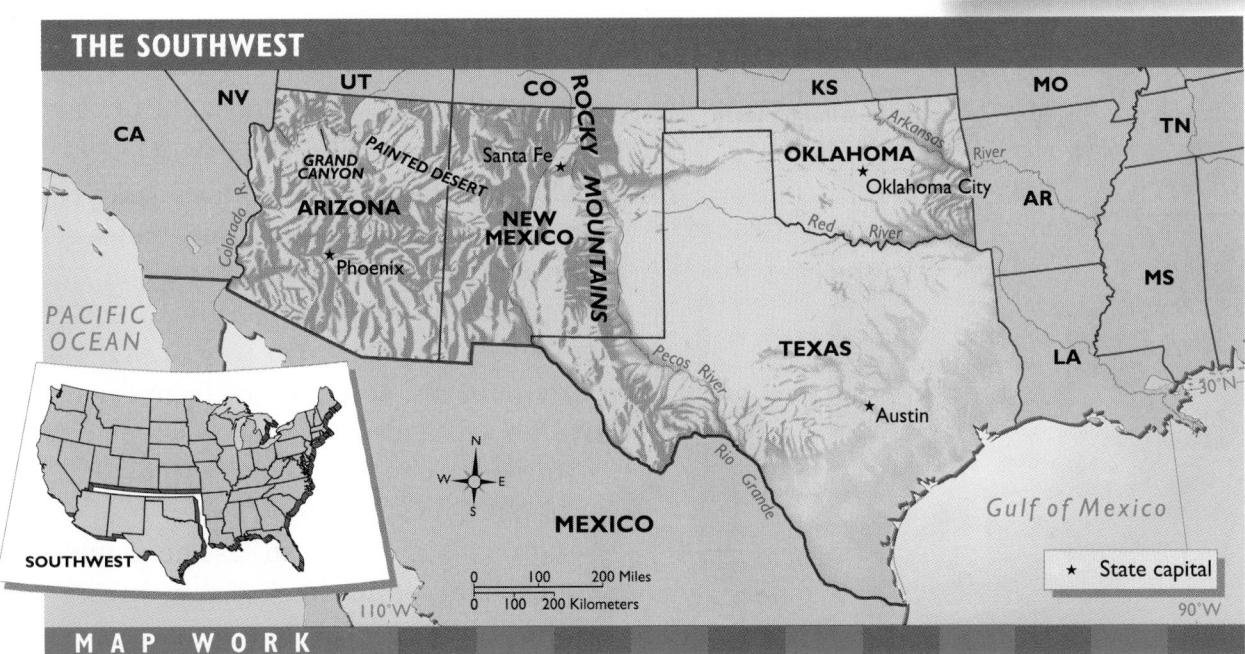

THE SOUTHWEST

SOUTHWEST

★ State capital

MAP WORK

Besides the Grand Canyon, another place of note is the Painted Desert. Its hills and plateaus are shades of blue, purple, red, and gold.

1. Which bodies of water border the Southwestern region?

2. Which states lie to the north of the Southwest region?

3. How does the Southwest change as you travel from west to east?

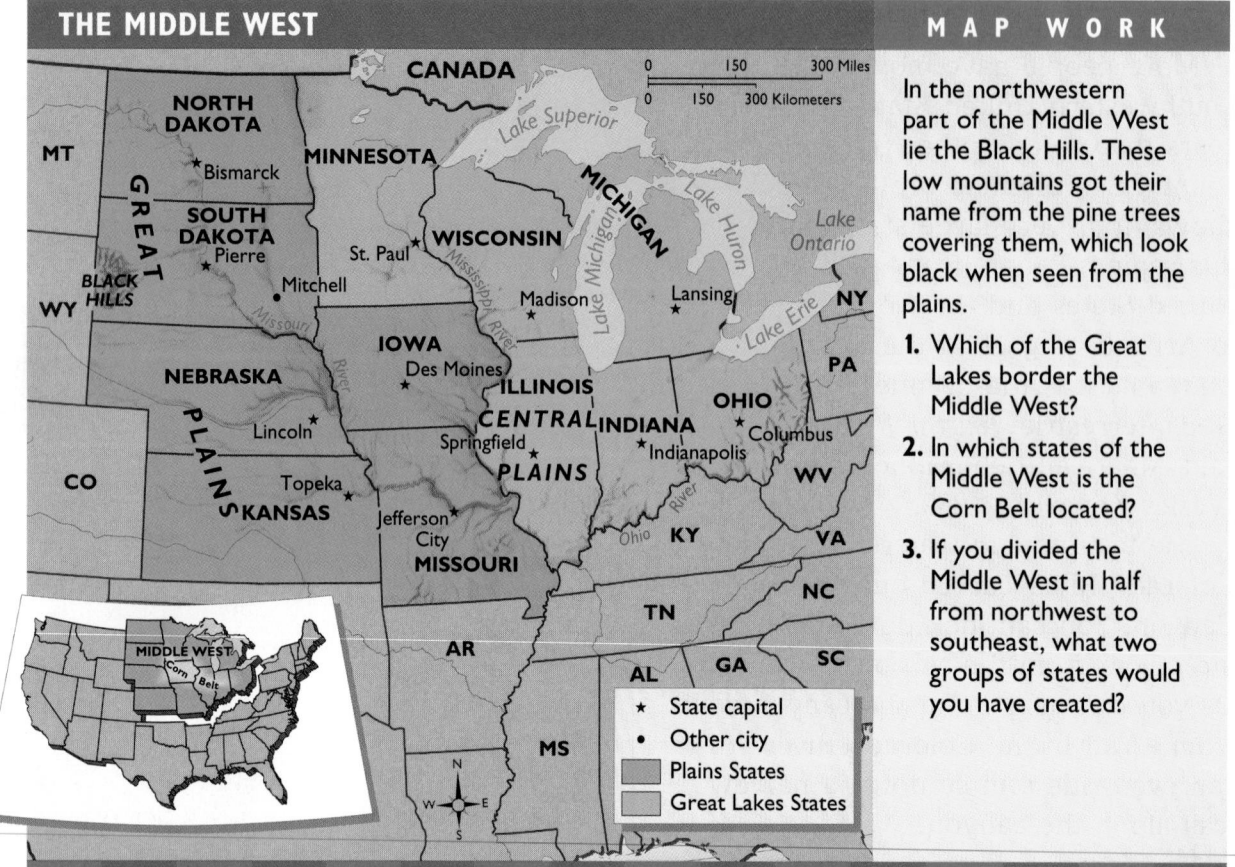

In the northwestern part of the Middle West lie the Black Hills. These low mountains got their name from the pine trees covering them, which look black when seen from the plains.

1. Which of the Great Lakes border the Middle West?

2. In which states of the Middle West is the Corn Belt located?

3. If you divided the Middle West in half from northwest to southeast, what two groups of states would you have created?

Chicago is the largest city in the Middle West, where many prize-winning farm animals are raised.

THE MIDDLE WEST

The Middle West has been called the breadbasket of the United States. Nowhere is that nickname more true than at the Corn Palace in Mitchell, South Dakota. Here people have put up a palace to honor a plant on which they have built their own way of life. People here are so proud of their corn that they tell and write stories about it.

The poet Carl Sandburg wrote about "the boy who climbed a cornstalk growing so fast he would have starved to death if they hadn't shot biscuits up to him."

Mitchell is in a part of the Middle West called the Corn Belt. Find the Corn Belt on the small locator map. Here, on the flat land of the Great Plains, growing corn is a way of life.

THE SOUTHEAST

Big things sometimes start out small. In northern Minnesota, a stream so narrow you can almost jump across it flows out of Lake Itasca. As the stream flows south, it gets bigger, much bigger. This is the mighty Mississippi River.

Native Americans who speak Algonkian (al GAHNG kee un) call it "big water" and "great river." It also is known as "the father of waters." Find the Mississippi River on the map on this page. People in the Southeast farm the rich lands along the Mississippi. Barges carry goods south to ports in New Orleans or north to cities such as Memphis and St. Louis. The Mississippi River is both beautiful and valuable.

The Mississippi River (above) forms the western border of the state of Mississippi, birthplace of Charley Pride (left) and other country music singers.

THE SOUTHEAST

★ State capital
• Other city

0   150   300 Miles
0   150   300 Kilometers

PA
OH
IL   IN
KS
MO
Ohio River
Charleston
Frankfort
KENTUCKY
Allegheny Mountains
WEST VIRGINIA   Richmond
VIRGINIA
NJ
MD
DE
Chesapeake Bay
OK
Nashville
TENNESSEE
ARKANSAS   Memphis
Tennessee River
APPALACHIAN MOUNTAINS
NORTH CAROLINA   Raleigh
Little Rock
Mississippi River
SOUTH CAROLINA
Columbia
Atlanta
Savannah River
Charleston
MISSISSIPPI
Jackson
ALABAMA   GEORGIA
Montgomery
ATLANTIC OCEAN
TX
LOUISIANA   Lake Pontchartrain
Baton Rouge
New Orleans
Tallahassee
30°N
90°W
FLORIDA
Gulf of Mexico
Lake Okeechobee
N   W   E   S
BAHAMAS
Florida Keys
80°W

SOUTHEAST

MAP WORK

New Orleans, near the delta of the Mississippi River, is the busiest port in the United States.

1. Identify the rivers that flow through the Southeastern region.

2. What landforms other than rivers does the map show?

3. What are three ways in which the Southeast is different from the Middle West?

33

THE NORTHEAST

What is Boswash? No, it is not a new video game or a new kind of laundry detergent. It is the name geographers have given to the Northeastern cities running south from Boston, Massachusetts, to Washington, D.C. These cities form a huge megalopolis (meg uh LAHP uh lihs). A megalopolis is a group of cities that have grown so close together they seem to form one city. Find Boswash on the map. At night pilots flying over the Northeast see an unbroken string of city lights.

From above, the nighttime view of Boswash may look like one big mass, but do not tell that to the people who live there! These cities have neighborhoods with their own foods and ways of life. You can almost travel to a different city by only going across town!

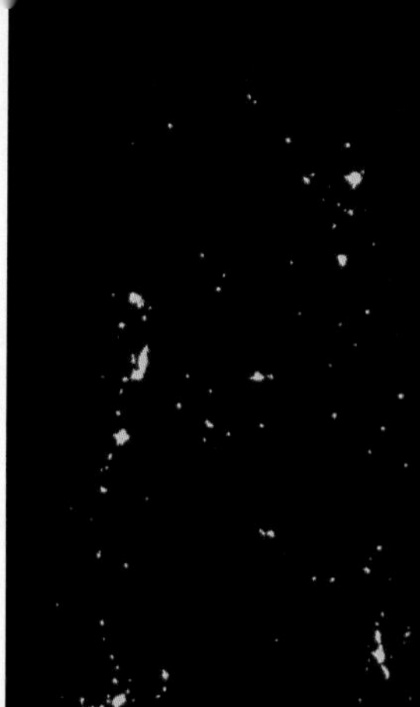

THE NORTHEAST

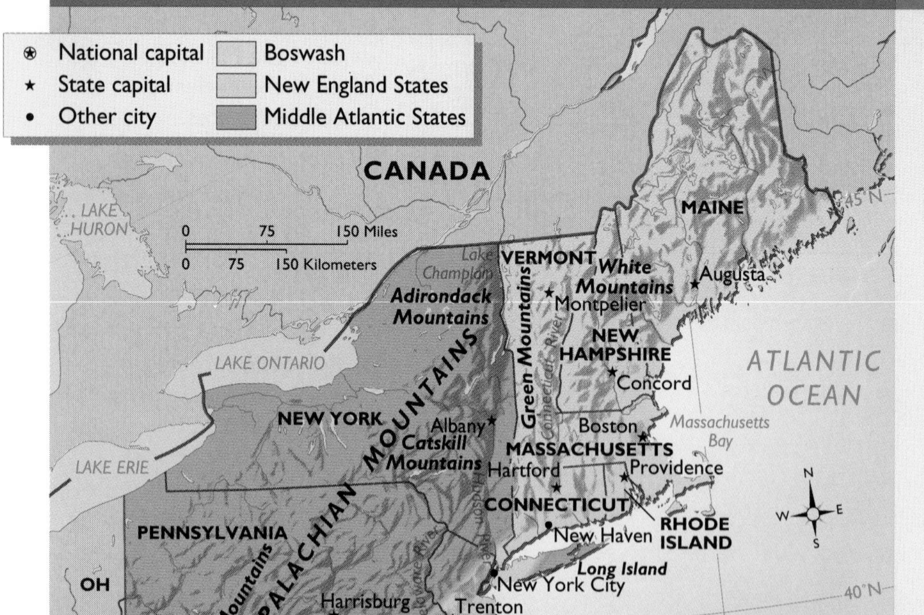

Legend:
- ⊕ National capital
- ★ State capital
- • Other city
- Boswash
- New England States
- Middle Atlantic States

CANADA

LAKE HURON

0   75   150 Miles
0   75   150 Kilometers

MAINE

Lake Champlain

VERMONT

White Mountains

Augusta ★

Adirondack Mountains

★ Montpelier

LAKE ONTARIO

NEW HAMPSHIRE

Green Mountains

ATLANTIC OCEAN

★ Concord

NEW YORK

Albany ★

Catskill Mountains

Boston •

Massachusetts Bay

LAKE ERIE

MASSACHUSETTS

Hartford ★

• Providence

APPALACHIAN MOUNTAINS

CONNECTICUT

RHODE ISLAND

N
W   E
S

PENNSYLVANIA

New Haven •

OH

Long Island

New York City

40°N

Allegheny Mountains

Harrisburg ★

Trenton ★

70°W

Philadelphia •

NEW JERSEY

MARYLAND

• Wilmington

Potomac River

• Baltimore

★ Dover

WV

Washington, D.C. ⊕

★ Annapolis

DELAWARE

VA

Chesapeake Bay

75°W

NORTHEAST

M A P   W O R K

In our country's smallest region, coastal plains and mountain ranges are the major landforms.

1. As shown on the map, which mountains are located in the Northeastern region?

2. Name the cities on the map that form the megalopolis Boswash.

3. Why do you think most of the people in the Northeast live near the Atlantic Coast?

The light that beams from this lighthouse (left) in the Northeast and the other lights from Boswash's large cities (above, rectangle) can be seen at night from outer space.

There are many other large cities in the Northeast. Some are hundreds of years old. There are also small towns and farms. A scrapbook of the Northeast would show that its people enjoy a variety of ways of life.

WHY IT MATTERS

This scrapbook has taken you all over the United States. It has also given you a look at some of the special places in each of our country's regions. As you read about the history of the United States in the pages ahead, you will revisit these regions.

Although each region of our country is special, all of our country's regions are becoming more interdependent. *Interdependent* means "depending on each other to meet needs and wants." Our country's regions depend on each other in many different ways. Metals

mined in the West are turned into tools and cars by Middle Western workers in factories. Fruits and vegetables grown in the Southeast feed city dwellers in other regions.

Often the weather will affect this interdependence. For example, a bad storm in Florida might cause a shortage of oranges in Boston markets. In the next lesson, you will read more about weather in the United States and how it affects people's lives.

Reviewing Facts and Ideas

MAIN IDEAS

- A region is a large area with common features that set it apart from other areas.
- Regions discussed in this lesson are the West, Southwest, Middle West, Southeast, and Northeast. However, there are other ways to divide our country into regions.
- Our country's regions depend on each other to meet needs and wants.

THINK ABOUT IT

1. What are some of the features geographers can use to define a region?

2. Describe a landform that is located in the region where you live. Explain how the landform affects the way of life there.

3. **FOCUS** What are the five regions of the United States, and what are some special features of each?

4. **THINKING SKILL** *Compare* the Northeast with the West. How are they similar? How are they different?

5. **WRITE** Suppose that you had visited the special places in this lesson. Prepare a scrapbook describing your visit to a friend.

OUR COUNTRY'S CLIMATE

READ ALOUD

"Everybody talks about the weather but nobody does anything about it," complained a witty writer named Mark Twain. How often have you said, "It's too hot!" or "It's too cold!" Perhaps you have also said, "I hope it doesn't rain on our game" or "I can hardly wait for the first snow day!"

THE BIG PICTURE

We talk a great deal about the weather because it affects our lives so much.

Weather in the United States differs a great deal from region to region. This means that each region also has a different climate. Climate is the weather an area has over a number of years. The climate of a place includes its general temperature, or the measurement of heat. Precipitation (prih sihp ih TAY shun) is another important part of climate. Precipitation is the moisture that falls to earth as rain or snow.

Climates vary for several reasons. One factor is a region's distance from the equator. Generally, the farther from the equator, the colder the climate. Near the equator, it is usually hot most of the year.

Death Valley, California

Focus Activity

READ TO LEARN
What kinds of climates do the arid and humid regions of America have?

VOCABULARY
climate
temperature
precipitation
arid
humid

ARID AMERICA

Geographers study the climate of the United States by dividing it into two different areas of precipitation. They use two key words. One is arid, which means "dry." The other is humid, which means "wet." On the map on this page, find the line that divides arid and humid America. Most of arid America receives less than 20 inches of precipitation a year. In humid America more than 20 inches of precipitation usually falls each year.

A Varied Climate

Much of the most arid part of the United States lies in the Great Basin of the West and the deserts of the Southwest. The driest place in the U.S. is Death Valley, California, with less than 2 inches of precipitation a year. But other kinds of places have a variety of temperatures. In the Rocky Mountains the peaks are capped with snow all year. In Washington State and Oregon, a wetter, warmer climate allows vast forests of pine and fir to grow.

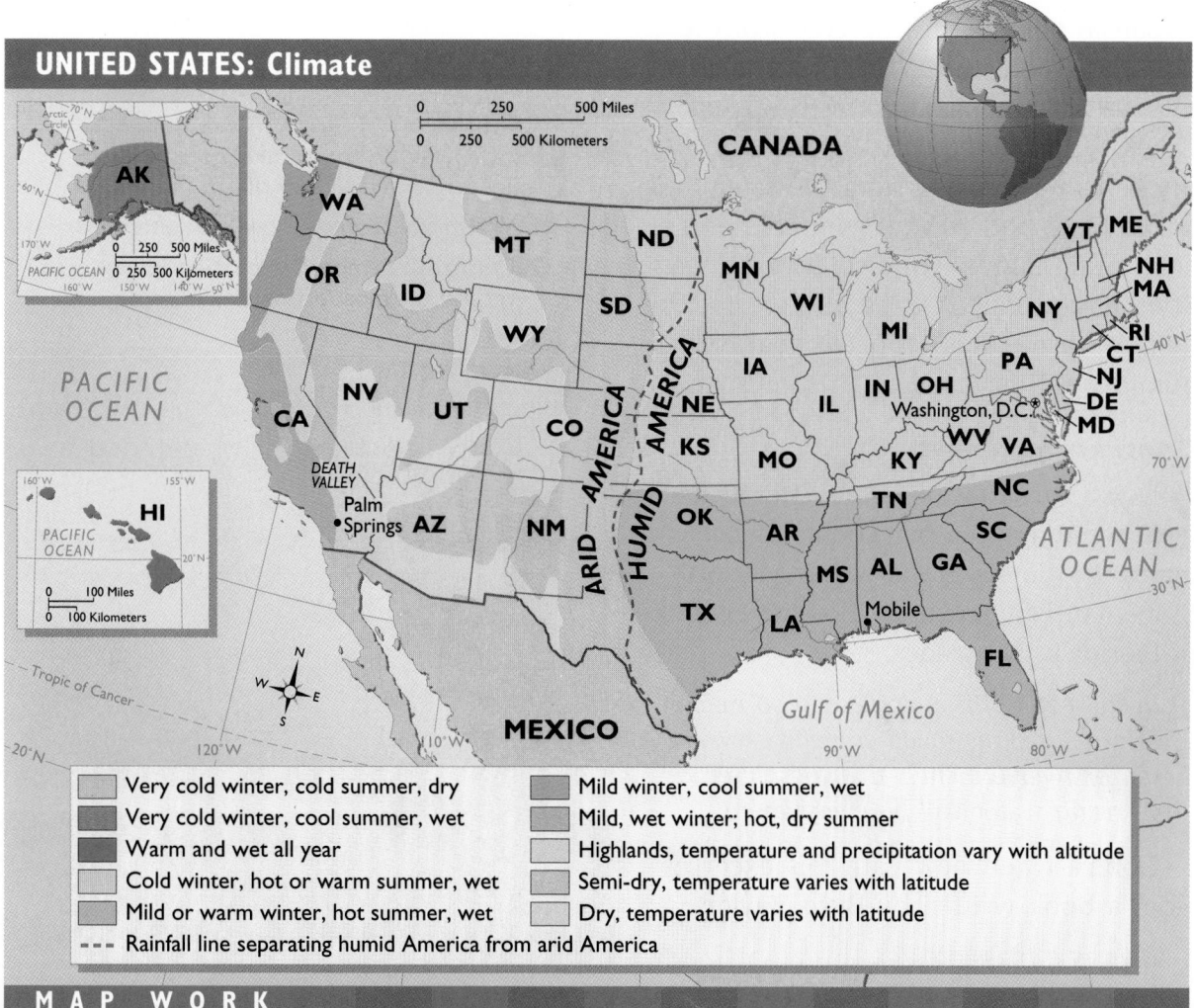

UNITED STATES: Climate

Legend:
- Very cold winter, cold summer, dry
- Very cold winter, cool summer, wet
- Warm and wet all year
- Cold winter, hot or warm summer, wet
- Mild or warm winter, hot summer, wet
- Mild winter, cool summer, wet
- Mild, wet winter; hot, dry summer
- Highlands, temperature and precipitation vary with altitude
- Semi-dry, temperature varies with latitude
- Dry, temperature varies with latitude
- - - Rainfall line separating humid America from arid America

MAP WORK

As the map shows, the United States has a variety of climates—from tropical heat to arctic cold.

1. Which states are found in both arid America and humid America?

2. Which states have a wet climate with mild winters and cool summers?

3. Which part of humid America has a warmer climate?

HUMID AMERICA

"It's not the heat. It's the humidity." You are more likely to have heard this in the humid sections of the country than in the arid parts.

The bar graph on this page shows precipitation in Mobile, Alabama, and Palm Springs, California. Use the map on page 37 to find whether they are located in arid or in humid areas.

A Moist Climate

The more humid sections of the United States stretch from the Atlantic Ocean in the East to the edges of the Great Plains in the West. From north to south, they extend from the Great Lakes to the Gulf of Mexico. People in the Northeast and around the Great Lakes have hot, steamy summers and cold, often snowy winters. In the Southeast frequent rains and warmer temperatures create a great deal of humid weather.

Contrasting Views

Down through the years Americans have written about our country's climates. In the 1940s the writer Marjory Stoneman Douglas described the climate of Florida's Everglades.

In the course of a single day so much rain will fall, as much sometimes as ten or twelve inches, that the glitter of rising water will be everywhere.

Contrast her view with this excerpt from a book written by Byrd Baylor.

*Rain is a blessing
counted
drop
by
drop.*

Did you recognize the two areas of precipitation?

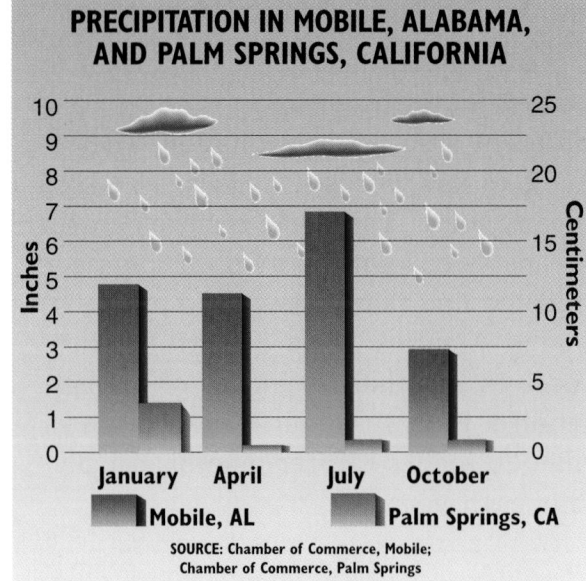

PRECIPITATION IN MOBILE, ALABAMA, AND PALM SPRINGS, CALIFORNIA

SOURCE: Chamber of Commerce, Mobile; Chamber of Commerce, Palm Springs

GRAPH WORK

For the people of Mobile, Alabama, and Palm Springs, California, **precipitation** is a major factor in their way of life.

1. Which city receives more precipitation?
2. During which month does Palm Springs receive the most precipitation?

WHY IT MATTERS

As you have read, the different regions of the United States have different climates. If someday you were to travel across the country, you would have to be sure to pack the right kinds of clothes for each of the different climates. During your trip you would see how the different climates have influenced the way people work and play. You would also see the creative ways in which people have improved their lives in difficult climates.

In the next lesson you will read about other ways people react to many different surroundings.

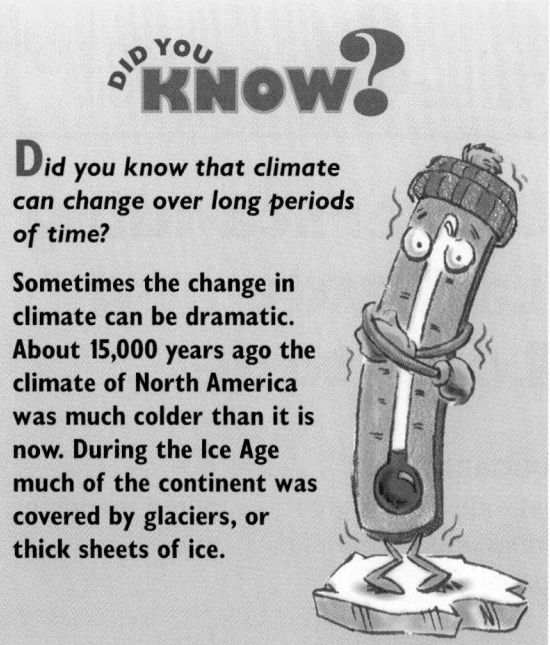

DID YOU KNOW?

Did you know that climate can change over long periods of time?

Sometimes the change in climate can be dramatic. About 15,000 years ago the climate of North America was much colder than it is now. During the Ice Age much of the continent was covered by glaciers, or thick sheets of ice.

✓ Reviewing Facts and Ideas

MAIN IDEAS

- Climate is the weather an area has over a long period of time. It includes temperature and precipitation.
- Climate affects people's daily lives, as well as activities such as farming.
- The West and Southwest regions are generally dry and receive less than 20 inches of precipitation a year.
- The Northwest, Midwest, and Southwest are generally wet, receiving over 20 inches of precipitation a year.

The saguaro cactus (far left) is a common plant in the arid climate of the desert. In humid areas (left), on the other hand, rainfall is plentiful.

THINK ABOUT IT

1. What is the difference between weather and climate?

2. A man named Philander Johnson wrote this jingle about weather:

   *Oh, what a blamed uncertain thing
   This pesky weather is;
   It blew and snew and then it thew,
   And now, by jing, it friz.*

   Did he live in the arid or the humid part of America? Explain your answer.

3. **FOCUS** What kinds of climates do the arid and humid regions of America have?

4. **THINKING SKILL** What <u>conclusions</u> would you make about how living in the arid or the humid sections of America would affect your way of life?

5. **GEOGRAPHY** Make a chart that describes each climate of the United States.

GEOGRAPHY SKILLS

Understanding Latitude and Longitude

VOCABULARY

latitude   degree   prime meridian
longitude   meridian   grid
parallel

WHY THE SKILL MATTERS

You have been reading about the climates of the United States. As you know, places near the equator are warmer than places far from the equator. To locate places on Earth, geographers have drawn two sets of imaginary lines on maps and globes called latitude and longitude. Lines of latitude run east and west. Lines of longitude run north and south.

USING LATITUDE AND LONGITUDE

Lines of latitude measure distance north and south of the equator. Lines of latitude are also called parallels. *Parallel* means "always the same distance apart." Parallels never meet. Find the equator on the map below. The equator is labeled 0° latitude. The symbol ° stands for a degree. A degree is a unit of measurement.

Lines of latitude north of the equator are labeled **N**. Those south of the equator are labeled **S**. On the latitude map below, the lines of latitude running through the United States are 45°N and 30°N.

Longitude lines are also called meridians. They measure distance east and west of the prime meridian. The prime meridian is the line of longitude labeled 0° longitude. Any place east of the prime meridian is labeled **E**. Any place west of the prime meridian is labeled **W**.

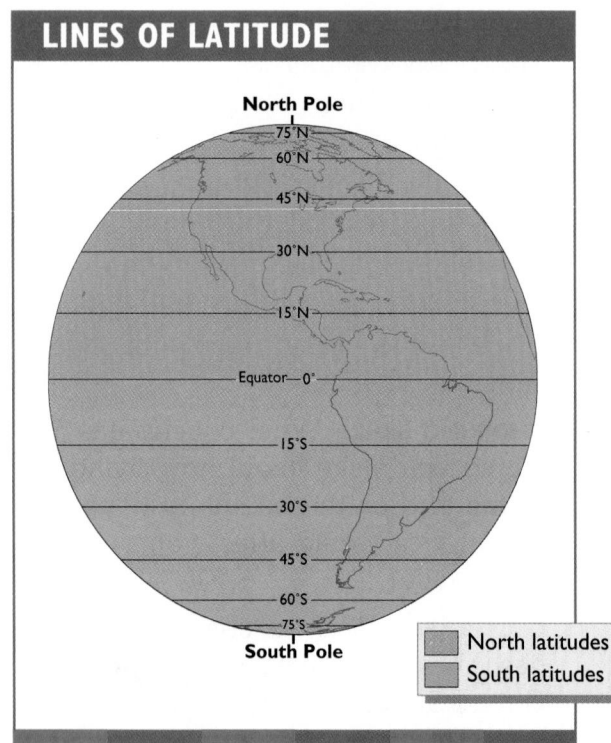

LINES OF LATITUDE

North Pole
75°N
60°N
45°N
30°N
15°N
Equator—0°
15°S
30°S
45°S
60°S
75°S
South Pole

North latitudes
South latitudes

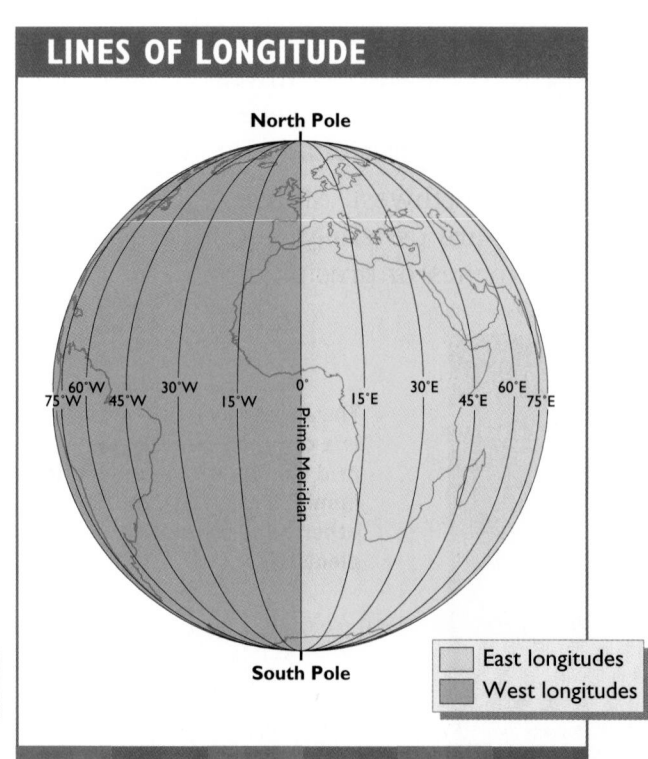

LINES OF LONGITUDE

North Pole
75°W 60°W 45°W 30°W 15°W 0° 15°E 30°E 45°E 60°E 75°E
Prime Meridian
South Pole

East longitudes
West longitudes

Because 180°E and 180°W are the same, most maps do not mark it as east or west.

USING THE GRID

A grid helps you use lines of latitude and lines of longitude to find places on a map. A grid is a set of crisscrossing lines. On the map below, each line of latitude crosses the same line of longitude in a different place. Memphis, Tennessee, for example, is located at 35°N latitude and 90°W longitude. Its grid location is 35°N, 90°W.

TRYING THE SKILL

Now use the grid on the map to find New Orleans, Louisiana. At what lines of latitude and longitude is it located? The Helping Yourself box on this page gives a summary of how to use these lines.

When cities are not shown exactly on a line of latitude or longitude on a particular map, use the lines that are closest. Find Springfield, Illinois. What are its closest lines of latitude and longitude?

REVIEWING THE SKILL

1. How do you find a place on a map using lines of latitude and longitude?

2. Between which lines of longitude is the state of Ohio located?

3. Give the grid location of Bakersfield, California.

4. In which states do the following lines of latitude and longitude intersect?
   • 35°N, 105°W   • 40°N, 80°W

5. When would it be helpful to be able to find latitude and longitude on a map?

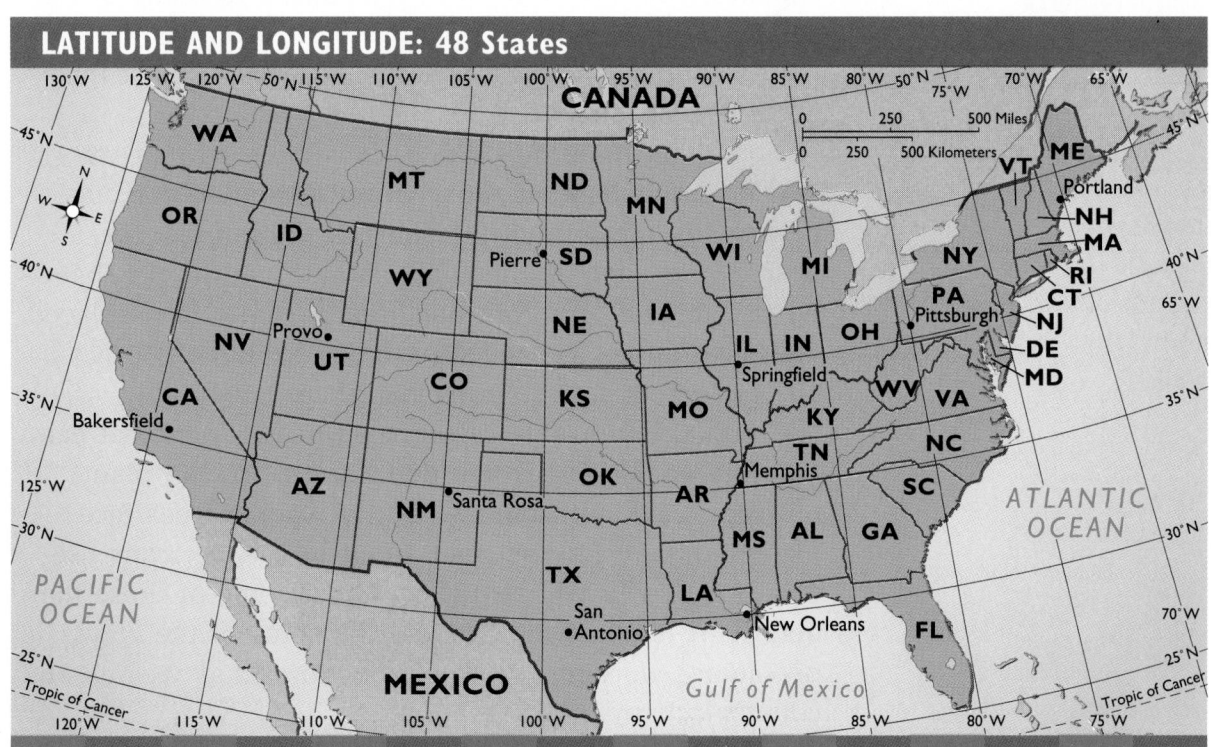

LATITUDE AND LONGITUDE: 48 States

OUR COUNTRY'S NATURAL RESOURCES

Focus Activity

READ TO LEARN
What is a natural resource?

VOCABULARY
natural resource
nonrenewable resource
renewable resource
mineral
fossil fuel
environment
economy
pollution
acid rain
conservation
recycle

READ ALOUD

"When the well's dry, we know the worth of water," wrote Benjamin Franklin in the 1750s. His words are still true today. In the United States we have a great many valuable resources, including water. But we do not always appreciate their value until they become scarce.

THE BIG PICTURE

As you have read about our country's regions and its climates, you have also been introduced to many of our country's natural resources. Natural resources are materials found in nature that people use to meet their needs and wants.

For a long time most Americans believed that we would always have enough natural resources for our needs. But our country's resources will not last forever. Some, such as the coal, oil, and natural gas that we use to heat and light our homes, cannot be replaced. These resources are called nonrenewable resources.

Our forests, on the other hand, are renewable resources. Renewable resources are resources that can be replaced. When we cut down trees, we can plant new ones. Yet both old and newly planted trees face many dangers. As you read about how Americans use our forests, you will also learn about some of these dangers. This lesson will also describe some of the ways people are working to protect our forests as well as our country's many other resources.

RICH IN RESOURCES

As the chart on this page shows, all the regions of the United States have important natural resources. People use these resources to make a variety of goods. Some goods are as simple as bottled water taken from fresh mountain springs. Others, such as computers, are made from many different natural resources. How many items in your classroom can you identify that came from natural resources?

Different Kinds of Resources

The United States has many, many natural resources. Where do they come from? How are they used? To identify and discuss resources, you can divide resources into groups, as shown on the chart on this page. You can see from the chart that some people in the Northeast earn their living by harvesting from the sea such animal resources as lobster. In all regions people use forests, a plant resource, to provide wood for building and paper.

The United States has vast mineral resources. A mineral is a substance found in the earth that is neither a plant nor an animal. Minerals include metals such as iron, copper, gold, silver, and zinc.

Among the most widely used mineral resources are fossil fuels. These fuels were formed over millions of years from fossils, which are the remains of ancient plants or animals. Fossil fuels include the nonrenewable resources oil, coal, and natural gas.

OUR COUNTRY'S NATURAL RESOURCES

REGION	MINERALS	FORESTS PLANTS	FISH WILDLIFE	FOSSIL FUELS
West	Zinc Lead	Cedar Birch	Salmon Tuna Deer	Oil
Southwest	Iron Copper	Oak Cactus	Shrimp Deer Rabbit	Natural Gas Oil
Middle West	Iron Copper	Maple Sunflower	Bass Deer	Oil Coal
Southeast	Iron	Pine Mangrove	Shrimp Bear	Coal Natural Gas
Northeast	Granite Copper	Fir Maple	Lobster Scallop Deer	Coal

CHART WORK

The United States government has long been working to preserve our natural resources.

1. What wildlife is included among each region's natural resources?

2. What natural resources are found in the Western region?

3. In which region are mangroves found? In which regions is copper found?

FORESTS

The resources that you have been reading about are all part of Earth's environment. The environment is made up of all the surroundings in which people, plants, and animals live. One of the most important parts of the environment, and one of our greatest natural resources, is forests.

Forests contribute in important ways to the health of the environment. As trees soak up sunlight, they keep the temperature of the air from getting too hot. A tree's roots hold together the soil in which they grow and prevent that soil from washing away. By producing oxygen and removing carbon dioxide from the air, the leaves of trees provide fresh air for us to breathe.

Using Forests

Most people do not think about oxygen and soil when they think about trees, however. You, for example, may think of the forest as a place to camp, to hike, to bird-watch, and to enjoy our country's natural beauty. Some of the most popular places in the United States are national and state parks. As you have read, many parks are covered with forests.

People use forests for many other purposes besides recreation. Forests are an important part of our economy. A country's economy is the way its people use natural resources, money, and knowledge to produce goods and services. Can you think of some ways that forests might play a role in our country's economy?

Chairs, houses, pencils, desks—we use the trees of our forests to make a variety of goods. You are looking at one of the most important forest products right now as you read this page: paper. The flow chart on this page shows the many steps involved in turning a tree into paper.

Dangers to Our Forests

People called foresters work to understand how forests grow and how to take care of them. They often decide how many trees can be cut down—and

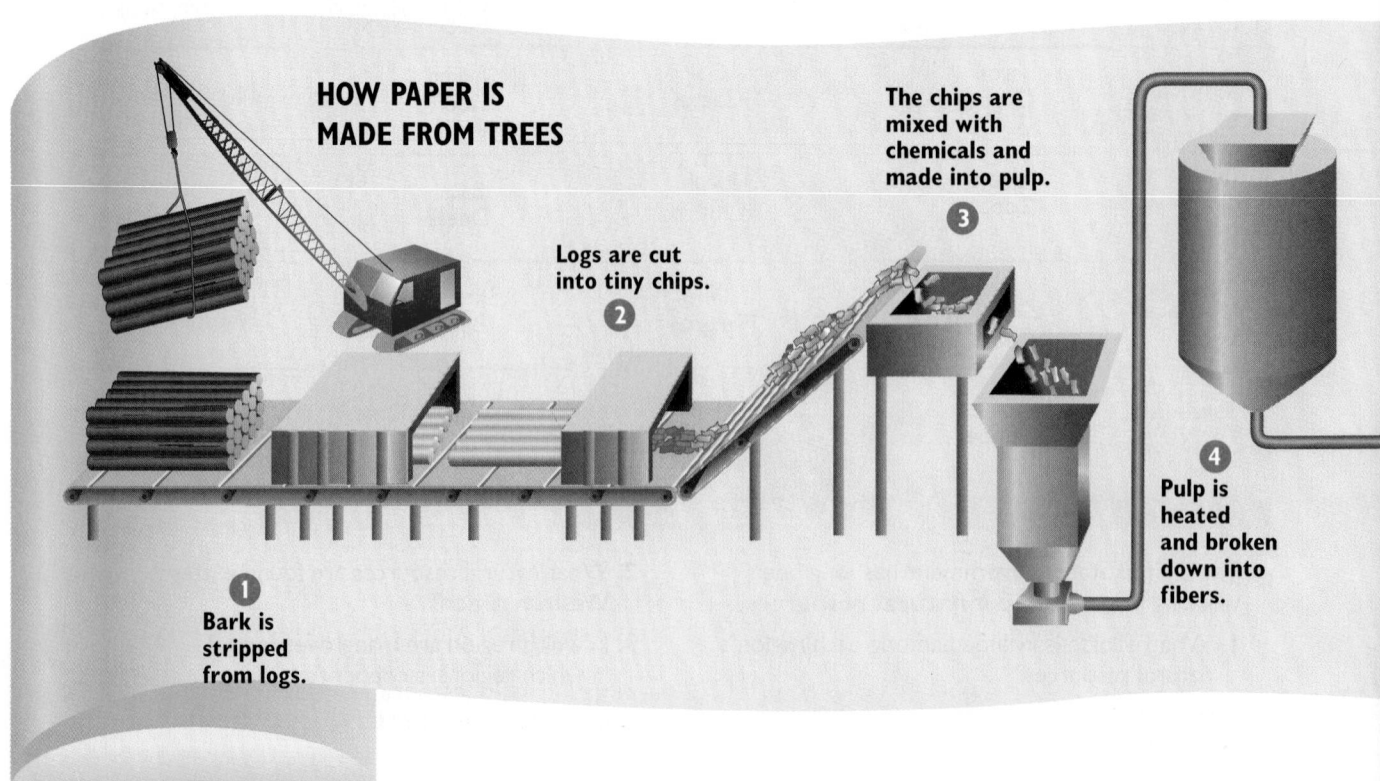

HOW PAPER IS MADE FROM TREES

1 Bark is stripped from logs.

2 Logs are cut into tiny chips.

3 The chips are mixed with chemicals and made into pulp.

4 Pulp is heated and broken down into fibers.

The lushness of this healthy green forest in North Carolina (left) seems remarkable when compared to the damage caused by acid rain (below).

when, where, and how many new trees to plant. They also work to protect forests from insects and diseases.

One of the most serious threats to our forests comes from pollution. Pollution is something—such as harmful chemicals—that makes our air, soil, and water dirty. Sometimes these chemicals mix with moisture in the air. When the polluted moisture falls to the ground, it is called acid rain. In spite of its name,

acid rain can take the form of snow, dew, or frost.

Acid rain can destroy trees and pollute the soil so it cannot support new growth. But the problem does not stop there. When forests die, animals must find new shelter. Acid rain can also pollute rivers and lakes and, therefore, kill fish as well.

How can we reduce the effects of acid rain? One thing that people can do is limit the amount of harmful chemicals that are released into the air. These chemicals often come from burning fossil fuels, such as gasoline in automobiles. Scientists and workers from business and government are studying cleaner ways to burn fossil fuels.

Chemicals and unwanted materials are removed from the fibers.
5

Dried sheets of paper are pressed smooth on rollers.
7

The paper is rolled onto reels and stored.
8

Fibers are poured onto a wire mesh, dried, and shaped into sheets.
6

The making of paper from trees involves a number of complex steps. In which step has the wood been turned into something else?

45

OTHER RESOURCES

You read on the chart on page 43 that the United States has many natural resources in addition to its forests. Such natural resources add to our country's beauty. Katharine Lee Bates wrote about this beauty as she traveled west to Colorado. Her poem "America, the Beautiful" was published in 1910 as the song many know today. You also read about the effects of acid rain and how our natural resources are related. There would be no forests without plentiful, clean water and rich, healthy soil.

Soil and Water

Soil, like forests, must be protected. Scientists are researching ways to use soil wisely. Using fewer harmful chemicals and growing different crops at different times help to restore the soil and to keep it healthy.

The water from our country's lakes, rivers, and streams is another valuable resource. Did you know that Americans use about 400 billion gallons of water each day? But only a small amount is used for washing and drinking. Most water is used to irrigate farmlands or to provide steam for power plants. People are working hard to find ways in which farms and factories can use water more wisely.

People Are a Resource

When people work to protect our environment and its natural resources, they are practicing conservation. Conservation is the protection and careful use of natural resources.

When people practice conservation they are using another important resource: themselves! Without people's creativity and skill, it would not be possible to make natural resources like forests into useful goods like paper.

Irrigation puts to use two valuable natural resources, water and soil (left). Scientists (below) looking for ways to help farmers are an important human resource.

America, the Beautiful

Words by Katharine Lee Bates, 1893;
music by Samuel Ward, 1882.

O beau - ti - ful for spa - cious skies, For am - ber waves of grain.

For pur - ple moun - tain maj - es - ties, A - bove the fruit - ed plain,

A - mer - i - ca! A - mer - i - ca! God shed His grace on thee,

And crown thy good with broth - er - hood, From sea to shin - ing sea.

RESOURCES FOR THE FUTURE

Americans work together to conserve our country's resources. One way that you can practice conservation is by recycling. Recycling means using something again. All over the country people are no longer only throwing things away. They are saving them so that they can be used again. We can cut down fewer trees if, instead of throwing paper away, we recycle it to make cardboard or other paper products. Only by protecting and using natural resources carefully can we be sure they will be available in the future. Have you used any items that have been recycled?

WHY IT MATTERS

Natural resources are an important part of our country's economy. Many factors affect the types of goods and services people can afford. A plentiful supply of resources is one. If a resource were to be all used up, people might not be able to buy a particular product or service at all. We can prevent such harm to our country's economy by conserving and recycling natural resources today.

✓✓ Reviewing Facts and Ideas

MAIN IDEAS

- The United States has many natural resources. Some are renewable, but others are nonrenewable.
- One of the most important natural resources is our forests. Forests serve the environment, provide recreation areas, and support our country's economy.
- People are also an important resource. They use their creativity and skill to practice conservation of natural resources.

THINK ABOUT IT

1. Name one natural resource for the headings *animal, plant,* and *mineral.*

2. Describe three products that people make out of trees.

3. **FOCUS** Why are forests one of our country's most important natural resources?

4. **THINKING SKILL** What are some ways you could _solve_ the _problem_ of too much waste in your community or your school?

5. **WRITE** Write a poem or song that celebrates the beauty of the United States or your region of the country.

Recycling **is one way that all Americans can help to conserve our country's natural resources.**

PLASTIC   GLASS

CITIZENSHIP
MAKING A DIFFERENCE

Making the Land Green Again

NORTH ARLINGTON, NEW JERSEY. Little by little, seventh graders at North Arlington Middle School are turning landfills—areas where garbage is buried—into wildlife garden parks where butterflies, birds, owls, and bats come to feed and nest. Since 1996, 118 student volunteers have planted 1,000 flowering plants and shrubs in an area that was once a landfill. So far their work has created three butterfly gardens on a half acre of land.

The land is located near the city of Newark, New Jersey, one of the most populated urban areas in the United States. "The former landfill," says teacher Loris Chen, "is one of the few remaining areas of open space around here. The students are helping to preserve it and make it into an area where people can enjoy bird-watching, bicycling, walking, and jogging."

Before volunteers planted the flowers and shrubs, they researched what plants to buy. They wanted plants that would attract butterflies, bluebirds, and songbirds. "We chose," says volunteer Kathy Lam, "flowering plants like butterfly bush and butterfly weed and brown-eyed Susan. They all make good food for caterpillars and for butterflies."

The town of North Arlington is on the flight path of birds that fly north to Canada from South America in the spring. Kathy says, "We wanted the birds to make our gardens a stopping place and nesting ground."

On Earth Day, April 22, 1996, the planting began. Four months later, students knew their gardens were a success. By August, volunteers had seen 12 different species of butterflies in the gardens and as many as 100 butterflies at a time.

The students' work is far from over. Many landfills remain. As each fills up, county workers will cover it with layers of new earth. Students will be adding a nature discovery center and planting trees. Kathy is looking forward to this new project. "Instead of just sitting around doing nothing for the environment, I feel good knowing that I am helping to make it green again."

"... I feel good knowing that I am helping ..."

Kathy Lam

CHAPTER 2 REVIEW

THINKING ABOUT VOCABULARY

Number a paper from 1 to 10. Beside each number write the word or term from the list below that correctly completes the sentence.

climate
conservation
economy
environment
geography

interdependent
megalopolis
nonrenewable resources
precipitation
regions

1. The study of the planet Earth and the way people live on it and use it is called _____.

2. _____ is the moisture that falls to earth as rain or snow.

3. Coal, oil, and natural gas are all examples of _____.

4. Earth's _____ is made up of all the surroundings in which people, plants, and animals live.

5. _____ is the weather that an area has over a number of years, including its general temperature.

6. The United States can be divided into _____, or large areas with common features.

7. A _____ is a group of cities so close together that they seem to form one large city.

8. The protection and careful use of our planet's natural resources is called _____.

9. The way a country uses its natural resources, money, and knowledge to produce goods and services is called its _____.

10. To be _____ is to depend on each other for needs and wants.

THINKING ABOUT FACTS

1. Why do geographers divide the United States into regions?

2. This chapter divides the United States into regions of West, Southwest, Middle West, Southeast, and Northeast. Name another way to divide the United States into regions. Why might you want to do it that way?

3. What is the name of the large river that starts as a small stream in northern Minnesota?

4. What is Boswash?

5. What is the nickname of the Middle West? Why is this a good nickname for the region?

6. How are the regions of the United States interdependent?

7. In what ways does the distance of a country or region from the equator affect its climate?

8. What areas of the United States are included in the humid parts of America? What areas are included in the arid regions of America?

9. How does climate affect our daily lives?

10. What are natural resources? Name two categories into which natural resources can be divided.

11. What are fossil fuels? Name two examples of fossil fuels.

12. Use the chart on page 43 to name one natural resource from each region in the United States.

13. In what ways are forests important to our economy?

14. What is acid rain? How does it affect the environment?

15. How can people be considered a resource?

THINK AND WRITE

WRITING A TRAVEL BROCHURE

Choose a location in the United States, such as the Corn Palace or some spot you have visited. Write a brochure that describes the attractions of the place for visitors.

WRITING DIARY ENTRIES

Suppose that you are on a trip across the United States. Write a series of diary entries that describe what you might see in each region you visit.

WRITING A PARAGRAPH OF CONTRAST

Write a paragraph that summarizes the differences between the arid regions of America and the humid regions of America.

APPLYING GEOGRAPHY SKILLS

UNDERSTANDING LATITUDE AND LONGITUDE

Answer the following questions, using the grid map of the 48 states on page 41 to practice the skill of understanding latitude and longitude.

1. How can you recognize maps showing latitude and longitude?
2. Which steps would you follow to find 90°N, 120°W?
3. Locate Springfield, Illinois, on the grid map. At what line of latitude is it found?
4. Is the state of New Mexico east or west of 110°W?
5. How are maps showing latitude and longitude useful?

Summing Up the Chapter

Copy this chart on a separate piece of paper. Review the chapter to fill in the blank sections of the matrix chart below. After you have finished, use the information in the chart to answer the question "How would you describe the geography of the United States?"

REGION	CLIMATE	RESOURCES	LANDFORMS
West	Arid, rainy in northwest, varied		
Southwest			Painted Desert, Grand Canyon
Middle West	Arid to west, humid to east		
Southeast		Minerals, forests, soil	
Northeast			

UNIT 1 REVIEW

THINKING ABOUT VOCABULARY

Number a paper from 1 to 15. Beside each number write the word or term from the list below that best matches the description.

ancestor

arid

democracy

economy

ethnic group

federal

landform

mineral

natural resource

oral history

pollution

problem

temperature

unity

values

1. a shape on Earth's surface
2. another word for *dry*
3. something that makes air, soil, or water dirty
4. beliefs or ideals that guide the way people live
5. another word for *national*
6. a country in which the people create laws and run the government
7. people whose backgrounds include the same customs and language
8. being as one
9. a question or issue that needs to be answered or solved
10. a relative who lived before you
11. a material found in nature that people use to meet needs and wants
12. spoken records
13. the way a country's people use their natural resources, money, and knowledge to produce goods and services
14. the measurement of heat and cold
15. a substance found in the earth that is neither plant nor animal

THINK AND WRITE

WRITING AN EDITORIAL

Think about the issues affecting natural resources, such as the dangers forests face from acid rain. Write a newspaper editorial in which you discuss the need to pay closer attention to conserving natural resources.

WRITING A REPORT

Choose a culture different from your own, and find out about one of its holidays. You may find your information in a book or by speaking to someone who celebrates the holiday you choose. Write a report about what the holiday means and when and how it is celebrated.

WRITING ABOUT PERSPECTIVES

Think of a place in the United States in which the climate is completely different from that in the area in which you live. Write a letter in which you describe a typical day from the point of view of a fifth grader who lives there.

BUILDING SKILLS

1. **Problem solving** What can you do to *solve* the *problem* of not getting good grades on your report card?
2. **Problem solving** How did the leaders who wrote our constitution *solve* the *problem* of how to organize the government of a representative democracy?
3. **Problem solving** How might you use *problem solving* to learn more about your ancestors?
4. **Latitude and longitude** What lines of latitude and longitude run through the state in which you live? Refer to the Atlas map on pages R4–R5.
5. **Latitude and longitude** How can a grid map help you locate a city or a specific area?

YESTERDAY, TODAY & TOMORROW

Historic places help us to keep history alive. Are there any historic places in your area that have been preserved for the future? Think of a place, like your school, that you use or visit every day. What would people from the future learn about daily life today if that place were preserved?

READING ON YOUR OWN

Here are some books you might find at the library to help you learn more.

. . . IF YOUR NAME WAS CHANGED AT ELLIS ISLAND
by Ellen Levine

This book explains the experience of coming to the United States for various immigrants.

OUR NATIONAL PARKS
by Donald Young

This guided tour of our nation's parks highlights their history and describes their main attractions.

WHO BELONGS HERE? AN AMERICAN STORY
by Margy Burns Knight

The author describes the story of a ten-year-old who comes to live in a new country.

UNIT REVIEW PROJECT

Make a Community Guide

1. Take a walk around your community. What are some of the things that you see? Notice the parks, statues, and schools.

2. Research historical and cultural places in your community, such as buildings and museums. One place to look for information is your local library.

3. Then draw pictures of what you find. Cut out your pictures and glue them onto separate sheets of colored construction paper.

4. Write a description under each picture.

5. Finally, create a cover, including the name of your community, and staple your guide together.

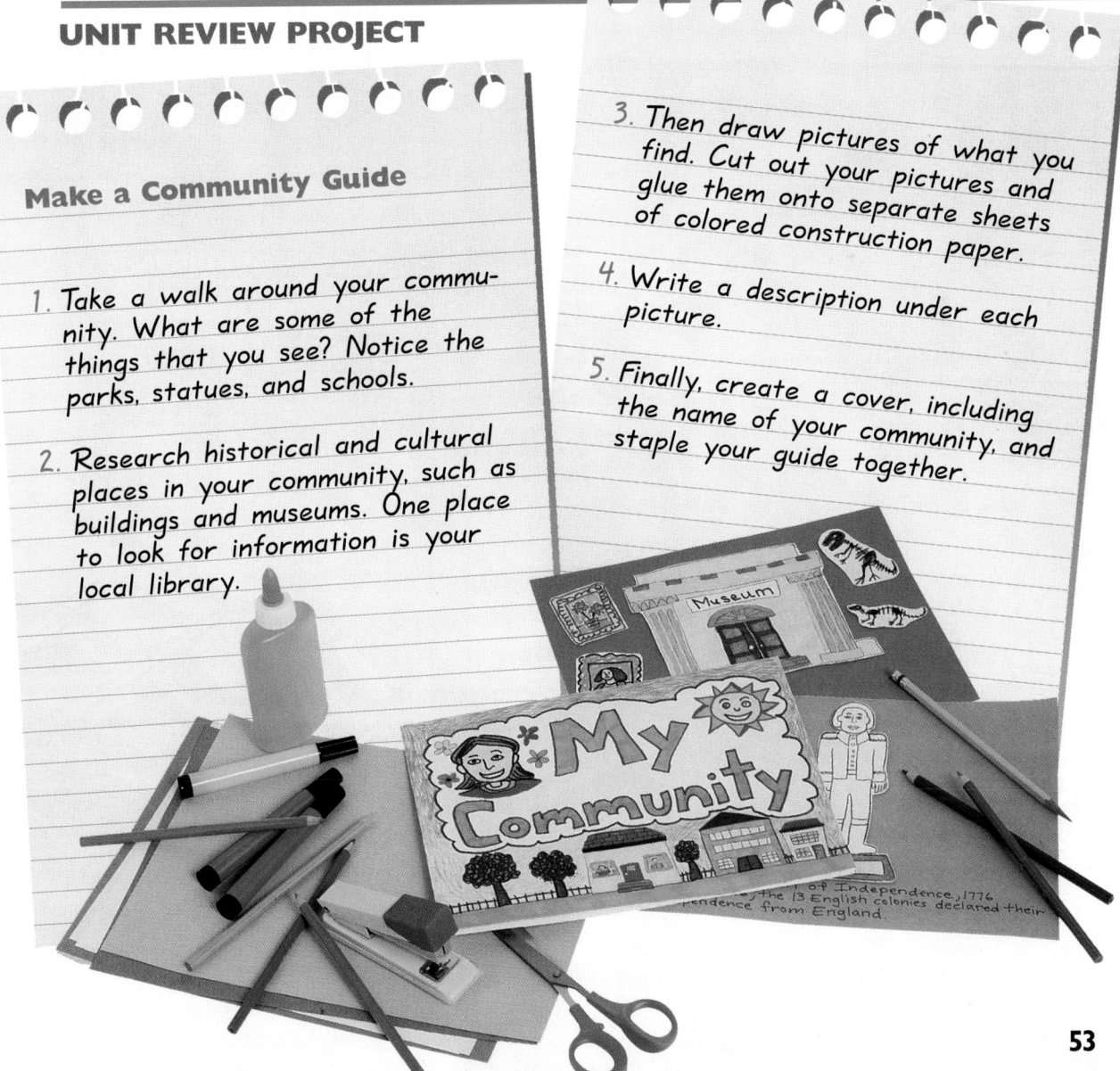

YUROK BASKET;
AZTEC KNIGHT CARVING (RIGHT);
MAYA MURAL (BELOW)

NORTHWEST COAST
TOTEM POLE (BELOW);
NIGERIAN BRONZE
SCULPTURE (RIGHT)

Culture West and East

"We must have but one voice."

from a speech by Hiawatha
See page 96.

WHY DOES IT MATTER?

Many thousands of years ago, a land bridge rose out of the cold northern sea, connecting the Western and Eastern hemispheres. People and animals probably crossed back and forth between the continents of North America and Asia.

Many centuries later, the people of the Western and Eastern hemispheres were building great cities, farming, trading, and developing unique cultures. The quote above from Hiawatha, an Iroquois leader, explains why different Iroquois groups united to form a representative government. This government is one example of the ways in which many cultures have shaped our country.

LEONARDO DA VINCI'S PAINTING
MONA LISA; CHINESE PORCELAIN VASE

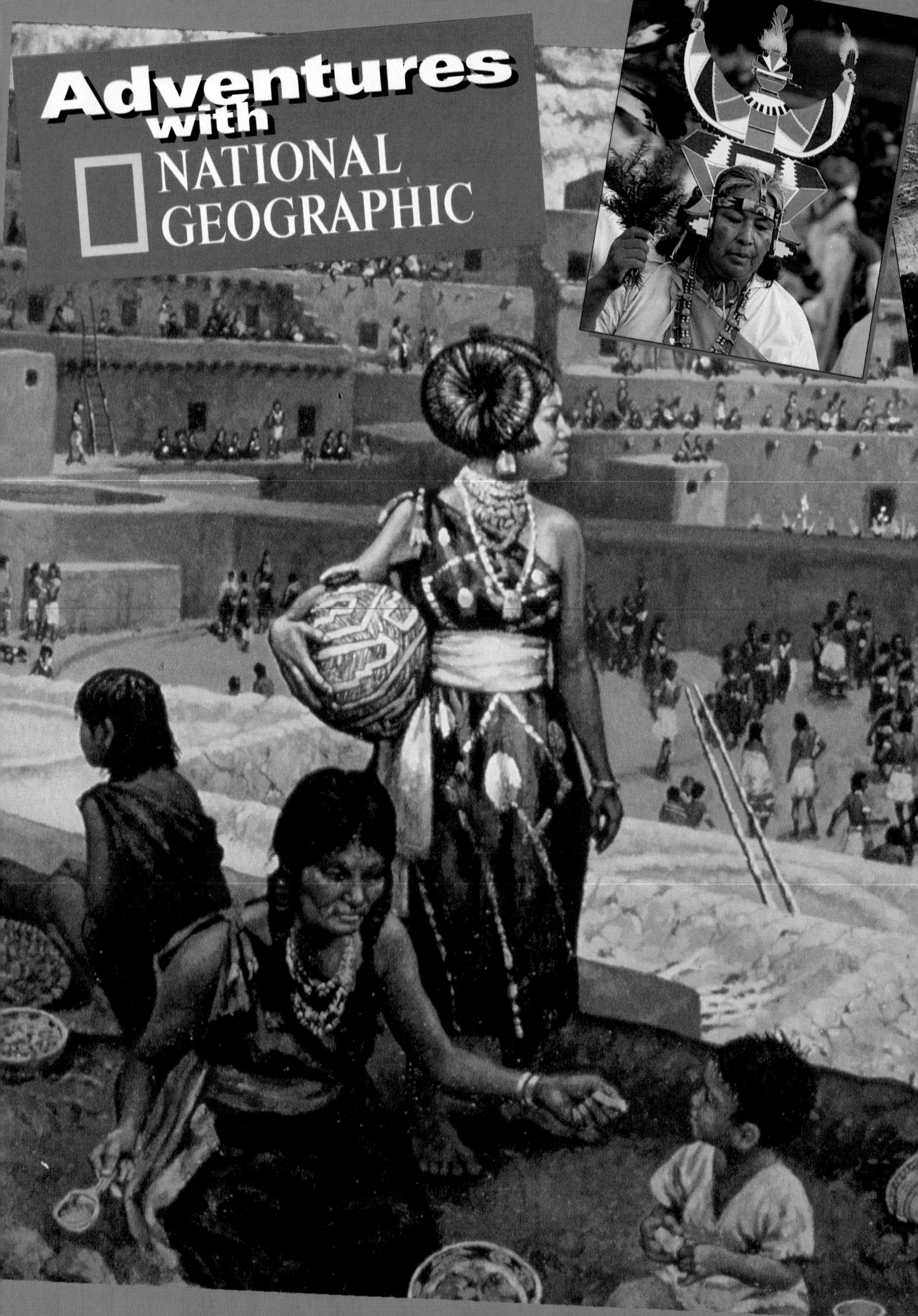

Adventures with NATIONAL GEOGRAPHIC

A World Without End

Pueblo Bonito is empty now. Or is it? It's true that no one lives in the New Mexico village that sheltered a thousand Anasazi in the 1100s. But if you walk among these ancient walls, you just might sense the presence of those who lived here long ago. Carefully constructed sandstone rooms and decorated clay pots suggest the creativity of the Anasazi. And, if your timing's right, you might catch a glimpse of a modern festival nearby. The descendants of the Anasazi live on to this day, and their traditions fill the pueblos with new life.

GEO JOURNAL

Suppose that the ancient women pictured here could meet the modern one. What might they say to each other?

CHAPTER 3

Native Peoples of North America

THINKING ABOUT
HISTORY AND GEOGRAPHY

The story of Chapter 3 begins nearly 2,000 years ago in Mexico and Central America, the home of the Maya. Read the time line below to follow the major events of the chapter. Notice that the background color of each event matches a square on the map. Each square marks the location of that event. As you read, you will learn more about different native peoples of North America.

195
TIKAL
The Maya build cities in Mexico and Central America

900s
PUEBLO BONITO
The Anasazi build large towns

1500s
HODENOSAUNEE TRAIL
The Iroquois trade and hunt in the Eastern Woodlands

Sitka

Black Hills

NORTH AMERICA

Hodenosaunee Trail

Pueblo Bonito

ATLANTIC OCEAN

Gulf of Mexico

PACIFIC OCEAN

Caribbean Sea

Tikal

CENTRAL AMERICA

SOUTH AMERICA

1600s

SITKA

The Tlingit of Alaska hold celebrations to honor leaders and family members

1700s

BLACK HILLS

The Lakota Sioux hunt on the Great Plains

EARLY AMERICANS

READ ALOUD

Imagine you are an early traveler in the Americas, searching for clues about the first people who lived here. What would you think if you stumbled upon a temple that towered 150 feet above the rain forest floor? What if you saw an entire village perched on a Colorado cliff side? Imagine finding a mound of earth, shaped like a snake, that stretched longer than a football field, or a clay figure that tells of life in ancient Mexico.

THE BIG PICTURE

The buildings and objects described above came from early American civilizations that you will learn about in this lesson. A civilization is a culture with complex systems of government, education, and religion. Lesson 1 begins about 1,800 years ago in what is today Mexico and Central America, the region between Mexico and South America. Here, a people known as the Maya began building some of their most important temples. Farther north, people had already been settling along the Ohio and Mississippi rivers for about 900 years. Hundreds of years later, between 1050 and 1250, one group built a city now called Cahokia (kuh HOH kee uh) in present-day Illinois. The group is known today as the Mound Builders. Miles away, in what is now the Southwest, the Anasazi (ah nuh SAH zee) were creating apartmentlike homes. Lesson 1 ends where it began, in Mexico, with the Aztec empire that rose to power in the 1440s.

Focus Activity

READ TO LEARN
What were early North American civilizations like?

VOCABULARY
civilization
archaeologist
land bridge
surplus
specialize
irrigation
empire
tribute
slavery

PLACES
Central America
Cahokia
Beringia
Bering Strait
Tikal
Four Corners
Mesa Verde
Tenochtitlán

60

EARLY PEOPLES

Not everyone agrees on who the first Americans were or when they came here. Native Americans believe that their people have always lived here. Some remains from the past support this belief. Many **archaeologists** (ahr kee AHL uh jihsts), however, think that people traveled to North America from Asia about 40,000 years ago. An archaeologist is a person who studies the remains of past cultures. A **land bridge**, or land connecting two large land areas, called **Beringia** (buh RIHN jee uh) once stretched across the **Bering Strait**, joining present-day Alaska with northeast Asia. Find the Bering Strait on the Atlas map on page R6. People may have crossed Beringia into the Americas in search of animals to hunt.

About 10,000 years ago, an important change took place in the way North Americans lived. They began to grow plants for food, in addition to hunting animals or gathering. Farming created a food **surplus**, an amount greater than what is needed. Farming allowed groups to settle in one place.

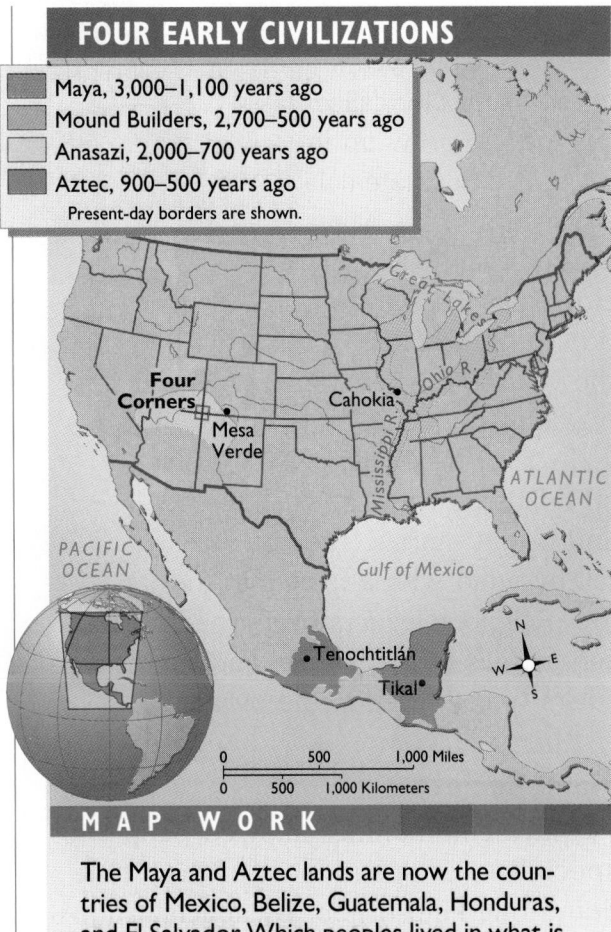

FOUR EARLY CIVILIZATIONS

Maya, 3,000–1,100 years ago
Mound Builders, 2,700–500 years ago
Anasazi, 2,000–700 years ago
Aztec, 900–500 years ago
Present-day borders are shown.

Four Corners
Cahokia
Mesa Verde
ATLANTIC OCEAN
PACIFIC OCEAN
Gulf of Mexico
Tenochtitlán
Tikal

Great Lakes
Ohio R.
Mississippi R.

0   500   1,000 Miles
0   500   1,000 Kilometers

M A P   W O R K

The Maya and Aztec lands are now the countries of Mexico, Belize, Guatemala, Honduras, and El Salvador. Which peoples lived in what is now the United States?

Over time, settled communities developed more complex ways of living. One such community was the Maya.

Many people of the Southwest have Anasazi ancestors (left). A Maya farmer collects honey (below).

THE MAYA

About 1,800 years ago, an amazing city called Tikal (tih KAHL) grew up in present-day Guatemala. Ancestors of the Maya lived in the area 3,000 years ago. However, the Maya civilization did not flourish until the year 195, when Tikal was built.

In Tikal the Maya decorated buildings with carved figures and bright murals. They built a tall pyramid with a temple at the top. Religious leaders performed ceremonies in the temple, and rulers were buried in the pyramid.

This statue of a Maya corn god was probably used by farmers during both planting and harvesting ceremonies.

Maya Farms and Food

Maya farmers grew enough food to feed people in the cities. The Maya got the most out of the land. In hilly areas the men grew crops on raised, level platforms of earth called terraces. Although the Maya grew many crops, their main crop was corn.

Maya Society

Maya communities allowed people to specialize, or spend most of their time doing one kind of job. By specializing, the Maya developed many skills. They used their knowledge of the stars, planets, and moon to create a calendar with 365 days, and also invented a symbol for zero long before other cultures. Why would it take a long time to learn how to write using their symbols, as shown below?

The Maya Today

After 909 the Maya cities were abandoned. What happened to the Maya? Some archaeologists believe that wars and food shortages may have helped bring the end of the great Maya communities. However, Maya people continued to live on in the surrounding countryside. Descendants of the Maya live today in Central America and Mexico. They still follow many ancient Maya customs and traditions.

MANY VOICES PRIMARY SOURCE

Maya writing symbols from a wall inside Temple 18 at Palenque, Mexico.

The Maya were the first people in the Americas to develop an advanced form of writing. Their writing system used symbols, such as these copies, that stood for both pictures and sounds.

BUNDLE

ENTERED THE ROAD

BUILDING

THE MOUND BUILDERS

North of Tikal other civilizations flourished in what is now the United States. Although these people were different from the Maya, they had two very important things in common—they farmed and they built civilizations.

Early People of the Woodlands

About 2,700 years ago, groups of people lived along the Mississippi River and the Ohio River in North America. No one knows what they called themselves. Today we know them as the Mound Builders. Can you guess why?

The Mound Builders lived in an area with plenty of natural resources. They grew squash and corn. They hunted wildlife and gathered nuts and berries. The many rivers that crossed through this land provided fish and also served as trade routes. By the year 700 the Mound Builders had a highly developed system of agriculture and trade. They traded with people as far away as the Rocky Mountains and present-day

The shape of the Great Serpent Mound can only be seen from the air. How do you think its makers were able to build it and view it from above?

Florida and Minnesota. We know this because in nearby grounds, archaeologists have found grizzly bear teeth from the Rockies, seashells from the Florida coast, and copper from mines in Minnesota.

The Mound Builders built earth structures to celebrate their religion and bury their dead. One of the largest mounds, Great Serpent Mound, is found near present-day Cincinnati, Ohio. It measures over 1,000 feet in length and rises up to 100 feet high.

After the year 1050 the Mound Builders often erected flat-topped mounds with buildings on top of them. These pyramid-shaped structures look similar to Maya temples. Such mounds appear in Cahokia. Between 1050 and 1250, Cahokia was the center of a city with as many as 15,000 inhabitants.

THE ANASAZI

In the Southwest region of the United States, in an area now called the Four Corners, lived the Anasazi. These people came to the Southwest about 2,000 years ago. Look at the map on page 61 to see which present-day states come together at the Four Corners. The Anasazi farmers faced many challenges caused by the geography. In order to farm in this desert environment, the Anasazi used irrigation to water their crops. Irrigation is a method by which water is brought into dry areas. The Anasazi built special ditches to bring rainwater to their crops.

Up to the year 700, the Anasazi lived in underground houses. After that time they began to build large villages that looked like apartment houses. Imagine creating villages beneath rock cliffs, tucked into the sides of canyons, and on the tops of tall, flat hills called mesas. Pueblo Bonito was a town of 800 rooms in what is now New Mexico. Cliff Palace, located on top of Mesa Verde, had 150 rooms built with sandstone blocks into the side of a cliff. It was built around 1100.

By 1300 the Anasazi towns were empty. Archaeologists are not sure what happened to the Anasazi. Some think that a long drought caused a food shortage that drove the Anasazi from their homes. A drought is a period with very little rainfall. Others think that quarrels among the Anasazi caused them to leave. However, many Native Americans and archaeologists believe that the Hopi and Pueblo peoples who live in this region today are descendants of the Anasazi.

The dry environment of Mesa Verde (right) helped to preserve its ruins and objects found there, such as Anasazi ceramics like the ones shown above.

THE AZTEC

After the Maya abandoned their cities in the 900s, a powerful new civilization grew up nearby. The Aztec came to the Valley of Mexico in the 1100s. Much of inland Mexico is dry, but the valley has several lakes. Around 1325 the Aztec settled on the shores of Lake Texcoco and on a small island in the lake.

Tenochtitlán

The Aztec named the place where they settled Tenochtitlán (te nawch tee TLAHN). This name meant "land of the prickly pear cactus." By 1440 Tenochtitlán had become the capital of a mighty empire. An empire is a large area with different groups of people controlled by one ruler or government. The Aztec ruled neighboring people such as the Tlaxcalan (tlah SKAH lahn) and Zapotec (zah puh TEK). Tenochtitlán's broad avenues, beautiful plazas, and great markets served a population of over 200,000, the largest of any city in the world at that time. The city even had a zoo with animals from all over the empire.

Religion was very important to Aztec life. The Aztec planned their city to honor their gods and the sun. Each building's location marked the position of the sun at an important time of the year, such as planting time. For the Aztec each day was special. Children were given names that honored their birth date.

Most Aztec children went to school, where they learned Aztec history and religion.

The quetzal (left) is an endangered species. The Aztec decorated objects with its feathers. The stone altar (below) was used to make human sacrifices.

Boys learned military skills. Girls learned to weave and to embroider feather cloaks. Children were taught to be honest and respectful. One Aztec book said: "Do not stare into another person's face" and "When you are called, do not be called twice or you will be thought lazy or rebellious."

The Aztec Market

The market in Tenochtitlán was one of the largest in the world at that time. Foods for sale included squash, corn, and cactus. The most prized items sold were those made from the feathers of the quetzal (ket SAHL) bird. This bird was very important to the Aztec. A poem in an Aztec language called Náhuatl (NAH wah tul) described it.

I am the blue-and-green bird
I make the [books] speak
I am the quetzal.

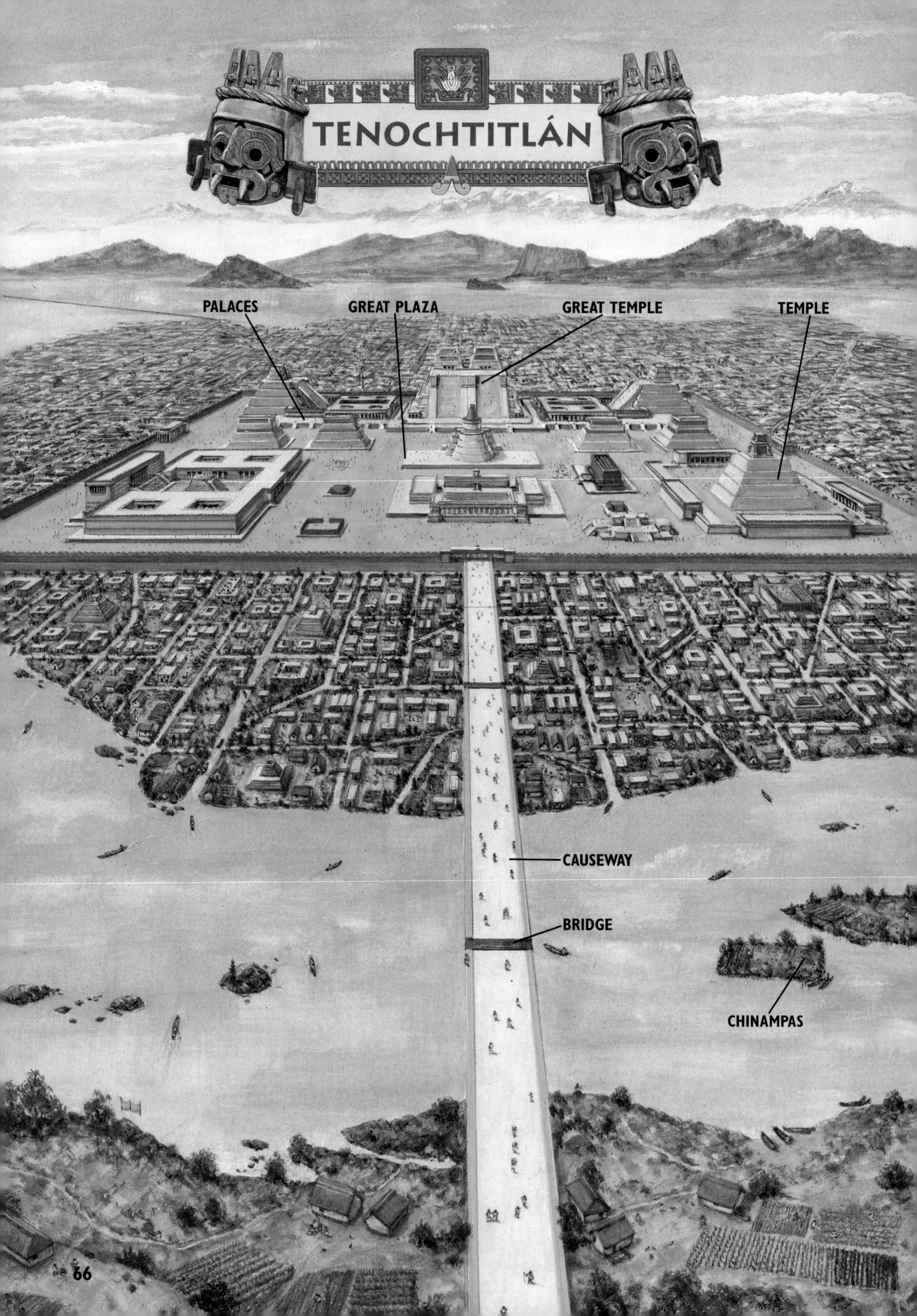

TENOCHTITLÁN

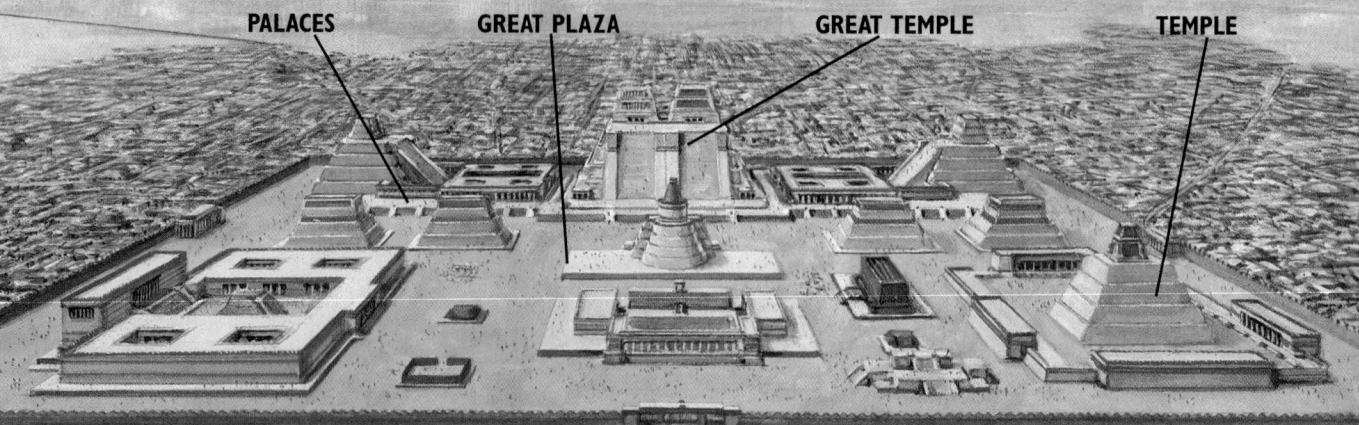

PALACES

GREAT PLAZA

GREAT TEMPLE

TEMPLE

CAUSEWAY

BRIDGE

CHINAMPAS

The Importance of War

The Aztec were constantly at war. They defeated many of their neighbors and demanded tribute, or payment, in the form of goods. From an early age Aztec boys were trained as soldiers.

Aztec soldiers often took enemies as prisoners. Prisoners are people whose freedom has been taken away. Some prisoners were forced into slavery, the practice of owning people and forcing them to work. Other prisoners were sacrificed to Aztec gods. *To sacrifice* means "to give up or destroy for the sake of something else." The Aztec believed that sacrifices were necessary to please their gods.

WHY IT MATTERS

These four major civilizations in North America and Central America before 1500 left many legacies. For example, some people in Central America and Mexico still speak Maya languages. The land farmed by the Mound Builders continues to give rich harvests today. The pottery and other crafts of the Anasazi inspire artists to this day. Many traditional Aztec foods, such as tacos and chocolate, are part of our daily lives.

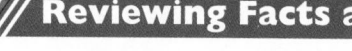

MAIN IDEAS

- Farming allowed early Americans, such as the Maya, to settle in one area and develop civilizations.
- The Mound Builders created great earth mounds along the Mississippi and Ohio rivers.
- The Anasazi lived and farmed in the desert region of the Four Corners.
- By 1440 the Aztec had developed a great empire in the Valley of Mexico.

THINK ABOUT IT

1. Why did the Mound Builders create earth mounds?

2. What method did the Anasazi use to farm the dry desert land?

3. **FOCUS** What did the early civilizations of the Americas have in common?

4. **THINKING SKILL** What things do archaeologists look for to *decide* how people in early civilizations lived?

5. **GEOGRAPHY** Look at the map on page 61. How do you think the location of Tenochtitlán helped the Aztec to maintain their empire?

This present-day descendant of the Maya weaves cloth on a loom in much the same way her ancestors did.

STUDYSKILLS

Reading Time Lines

VOCABULARY

time line   B.C.
century   A.D.
decade

WHY THE SKILL MATTERS

In Lesson 1 you read about four important early civilizations in North America and Central America. One way to understand the history of early civilizations is to use a time line. A time line is a diagram of a series of events in time. It shows events in the order in which they took place. Dates are marked to identify these events. Putting events in correct time order helps you to see relationships—like cause and effect—among and between events.

USING DECADES AND CENTURIES

Look at the general time line below. All time lines are divided into time periods. The time line on this page shows time in periods of 100 years, or centuries. The years 1 to 100 are considered to be the first century. The second century includes the years 101 to 200. The jagged line shows that a long period of time has been left out. A ten-year time period is called a decade. The years 1980 to 1989 make up the decade of the 1980s. In what decade were you born?

We use a system of dating events that divides time into two periods called B.C. and A.D. The letters B.C. stand for the time "before Christ," or before Jesus Christ was born. B.C. marks events that took place before the year 1. The letters A.D. stand for the Latin phrase *anno Domini*, or "in the year of the Lord." A.D. before a date means the years after the birth of Christ.

When reading B.C. dates, the numbers get smaller as you read from left to right. For example, the year 100 B.C. is followed by the year 99 B.C. Dates after the year 1 are much simpler to read because the numbers get higher. For example, A.D. 100 is followed by the year A.D. 101.

USING TIME LINES

The Early American History Time Line on page 69 shows when the four civilizations you read about began and ended. The yellow bar shows that the Maya civilization started around 2000 B.C. Look at the pink bar. Did the civilization of the Mound Builders begin before or after the Maya civilization?

Time lines are also useful for learning how things change over time. The Maya built Tikal in A.D. 195. This is the first event shown on the time line. How many years went by between the building of Tikal and the peak of the Maya civilization?

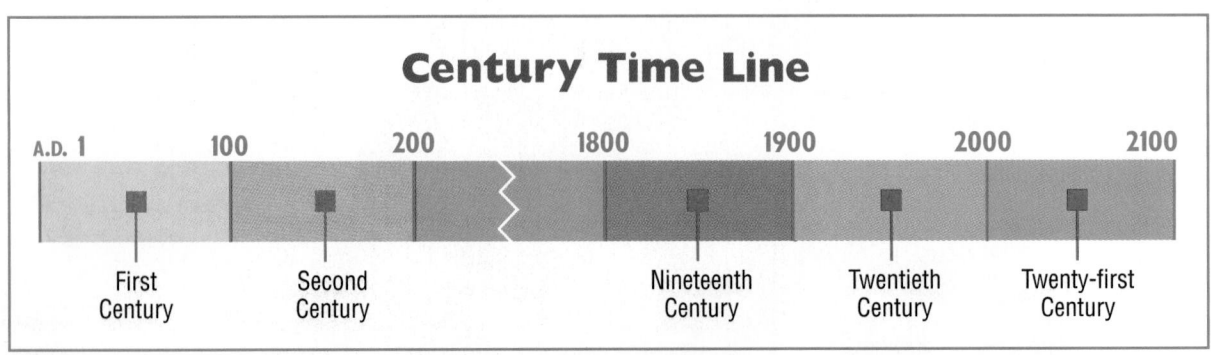

Century Time Line

A.D. 1	100	200	1800	1900	2000	2100

First Century   Second Century   Nineteenth Century   Twentieth Century   Twenty-first Century

You can also use a time line to compare events that occurred in different places during the same time period. At about the time the Maya civilization ended, what event was taking place in North America? This information is useful for historians, who study how different civilizations interact with one another. For example, the Mound Builders built mounds at Cahokia beginning around A.D. 1050. By looking at the time line, it is easy to see that this event happened many years after the Maya built their stone pyramids. Some historians believe that the Mound Builders picked up some of their customs from the Maya and other groups that lived in present-day Mexico.

TRYING THE SKILL

Now try reading the Early American History Time Line on your own. If you need help, use the Helping Yourself box on this page. What happened to the Maya civilization at the time the Anasazi started building?

REVIEWING THE SKILL

1. What is a time line? What types of information does it show?

2. Did the Aztec civilization begin before or after the Maya civilization ended?

3. How many years after the Anasazi built the many-roomed homes in Four Corners did the Mound Builders erect mounds at Cahokia?

4. What are some things that reading time lines can help you to do?

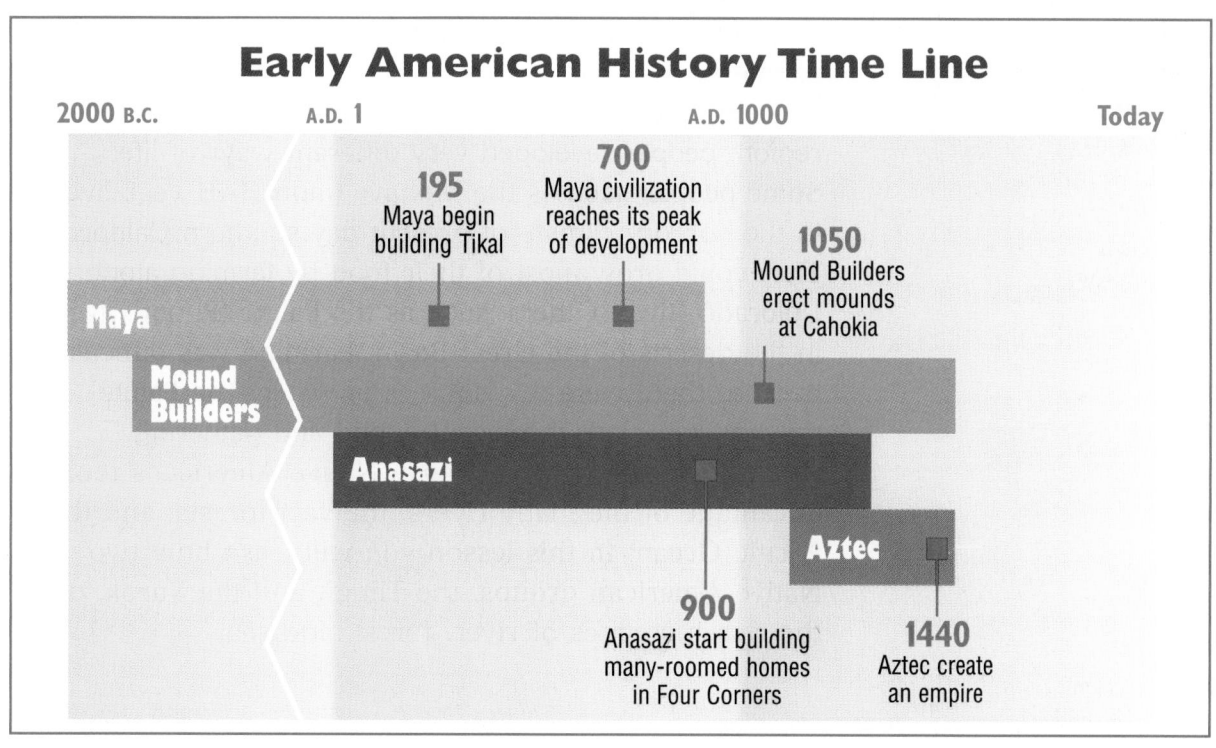

Early American History Time Line

| 2000 B.C. | A.D. 1 | A.D. 1000 | Today |

195 Maya begin building Tikal

700 Maya civilization reaches its peak of development

1050 Mound Builders erect mounds at Cahokia

Maya

Mound Builders

Anasazi

Aztec

900 Anasazi start building many-roomed homes in Four Corners

1440 Aztec create an empire

PEOPLE OF THE PACIFIC NORTHWEST

Focus Activity

READ TO LEARN
How did the environment of the Pacific Northwest affect the cultures of the people who lived there?

VOCABULARY
technology
totem pole
potlatch

PLACES
Sitka
Klamath River

READ ALOUD

"When I was growing up," says Marie Olson, whose Tlingit (KLIHNG iht) name is Kaayistaan (KĪ yih stan), "I was taught to treat the environment with respect. . . . A fisherman would talk to a fish before catching it. He would say thank you for coming to his net."

THE BIG PICTURE

As you read earlier, Native Americans have lived for thousands of years in North America. In each of the five regions of the United States, Native Americans created ways of life that were strongly influenced by their environment.

Even within a single region, such as the Western region, people developed very different ways of life. Some people, such as the Mohave (moh HAH vee), lived in the hot, dry climate of present-day southern California. They could grow most of their food by farming along the Colorado River. Others, such as the Paiute (PĪ oot), lived in the deserts of the Great Basin. Farming was difficult because there were few sources of water. The Paiute moved from place to place, hunting and gathering.

Along the Northwest Coast, Native Americans took advantage of the many rivers, the vast forests, and the Pacific Ocean. In this lesson you will learn how two Native American groups, the Tlingit and the Yurok, used the rich resources of river, forest, and sea.

GEOGRAPHY OF THE NORTHWEST COAST

The Northwest Coast is a narrow area of land along the Pacific Ocean. It begins around Anchorage, Alaska, and stretches south to northern California. There are forests, plateaus, basins, and rivers to the east of the area.

Riches from the Sea and Forest

The sea environment provided the people of the Northwest Coast with almost everything they needed for food, from whale meat to seabird eggs. Of all the resources the Native Americans took from the sea, salmon was the most important. Native Americans knew when and where large numbers of these fish could be caught.

Every year, from May to September, salmon swam from their homes in the Pacific Ocean to lay eggs in the freshwater rivers along the Northwest Coast. This yearly return of fish, called the salmon run, was an important event to the Northwest Coast peoples.

Native Americans developed many ways to catch salmon. One method was to build a weir (WEER) across a river. A weir is like a fence in the water, made from wood or brush. The salmon would get trapped against the weir, and people came and took what they needed. However, the Native Americans always left plenty for the people who lived upriver. They also made sure there would be enough fish left to produce young for the following year.

Lucy Thompson was a Yurok woman who lived in the early 1900s. She described some Yurok fishing rules.

Families come in the morning, and each one takes from the fish trap as many salmon as they need. They dip out fish with a special net, and they must not let a single one go to waste.

On the Columbia River, a present-day Native American fisher catches a salmon.

THE TLINGIT

Today if you visited Sitka, Alaska, you would find a busy American city. You might not guess that this city stands in the heart of the Tlingit homeland of long ago. As you can see on the Infographic on page 76, the Tlingit lived in the northernmost part of the Northwest Coast. Many descendants of the early Tlingit live here today. The Tlingit got most of their food from the sea. In addition to fish, they caught seals, porpoises, and even whales. During the winter they hunted animals from the forests and mountains of the region.

The Tlingit had direct water routes from the coast to other parts of the country. This enabled them to trade their surplus food for other goods. The Tlingit also helped other Native Americans to the north, south, and east trade with each other. This trade helped to make the Tlingit a wealthy people.

Technology and Art

The Tlingit specialized in making art and developing technology. Technology is the design and use of tools, ideas, and methods to solve problems. The Tlingit used their technology to build weirs and traps for catching salmon.

As highly skilled woodworkers, the Tlingit built large homes. In front of most houses stood a totem pole. Totem poles are tall logs carved with many designs. Most totem poles were 40 to 60 feet tall, but some were as high as 150 feet. Many totem poles were built to honor family members or new chiefs, or to mark special events.

Even everyday objects made by the Tlingit were often as beautiful as they were useful. Almost everything—from spoons to blankets to wooden storage boxes—was highly decorated.

A Tlingit teaches his daughter to carve a totem pole (far left). Someday her carvings may look like this totem pole (near left) in Haines, Alaska.

72

![A Northwest Coast potlatch ceremony with participants in traditional dress]

The Potlatch

To mark an important event, a family sometimes held a potlatch (PAHT lach). Potlatches are special feasts at which the guests, not the hosts, receive gifts. A potlatch, for example, might be held to honor a new chief or to celebrate a wedding.

Suppose that you could attend a potlatch of today. Everyone would be dressed in the finest clothing. The host would wear one of the family's best woven blankets.

A Northwest Coast potlatch (above) was an elaborate event. Handmade baskets, such as those shown below, were often given as gifts by the hosts of the feasts.

The ceremony, which could last for days, would include songs and dances. Excitement would mount as guests waited to see what each gift would be. An important guest might receive a canoe or fur robe.

To show their generosity, each host's family tried to give more gifts than the hosts of the last potlatch they attended. Sometimes the family gave away all of their valuables. But over time, wealth would return when the potlatch was held by another host. Potlatches were, and still are, a way of sharing wealth, determining social standing, and celebrating.

Shells, such as these from northwestern California, served as money. The purse is made of hollow elk horn.

National Museum of the American Indian

"How the Prairie Became Ocean" from Four Ancestors, 1996.

Long ago . . . the ocean was a treeless plain. . . . "How will the people be able to live?" Thunder turned to his companion, Earthquake. . . . "Should we place water here?"

Earthquake thought. "I believe we should do that," he said. "Far from here, at the end of the land, there is water. Salmon are swimming there."

So Earthquake and Water Panther went to the end of the land. . . . They picked up two abalone shells and filled the shells with salt water. Then they carried the shells back to Thunder.

Earthquake began to walk around. As he walked, the ground sank beneath him. Water Panther filled the sunken ground with the salt water. . . .

"Now this will be a good place for the people to live," Thunder said.

THE YUROK

The Yurok lived on the Pacific coast near the border of California and Oregon. Since people, goods, and ideas traveled up and down the coast, the Yurok had many things in common with the Tlingit. Both groups relied on the salmon run each spring, and both built large dugout canoes.

Resources from the Sea

In the early 1800s about 2,500 Yurok lived near the Klamath River in northwest California. The Klamath Mountains rose to the east, and the Pacific Ocean stretched to the west. The environment in which the Yurok lived had a strong influence on their lives. In fact, the word *Yurok* means "downriver," which describes the place along the Klamath River where they lived. The Yurok story on this page reveals how important the ocean was for the Yurok. Why did Thunder, Earthquake, and Water Panther create the ocean?

The Yurok used the sea as a resource for many of their needs. Yurok canoes carried people from one place to another. The sea also provided food. Even Yurok money came from the water. The Yurok used special shells the way we use coins and paper money today. Large shells had more value than small shells. The Yurok kept these shells on strings about two feet long. A person could buy a house for five strings, pay for medical help with two strings, or buy whale meat with one string of shells.

Resources from the Forest

People hunted deer and gathered nuts and berries in the forest. Each fall Yurok women collected acorns in large baskets they made themselves. The acorns were dried, cracked, and peeled and then ground into flour. Yurok women washed the flour many times with hot water to remove its bitter taste. The acorn flour was then baked into bread or used in soup.

The Yurok also made good use of the trees in the forest. They created canoes from redwood trees by splitting logs in half and burning out the centers. Then they hollowed them out with elk horns and smoothed them with clam shells. Other Native Americans prized these beautiful and strong boats, and they often traded with the Yurok.

Plank Houses

The Yurok also used redwood trees to build their houses. They split redwood planks with tools made from elk antlers. The Yurok used these planks to build rectangular houses with triangular roofs. A hole was carved into one wall to form a door. The houses were built half into the ground and half above the ground. The floor was dirt, and there was a fire pit in the center. The family slept on a wooden platform above the fire pit.

Yurok Ceremonies

The Yurok people did not practice the potlatch like the Tlingit. Yet they had many ceremonies of their own. Women played an important role in these events. One ceremony, called the Brush Dance, was led by a medicine woman. Her job was to cure sick people. Brush from the sugar pine tree was thrown on the fire, making a crackling sound. Then the sticks were waved over a sick child. As this three-day ceremony continued, the medicine woman used many other medicines, all made from local plants. Today the Yurok who live in California still perform the Brush Dance and other ceremonies.

Smithsonian Institution

Thaw Collection, Fenimore House Museum

A Yurok woman is shown pounding acorns above. This gracefully shaped Yurok spoon was carved from an elk antler.

Infographic

Native Americans, 1500s

In the 1500s, millions of Native Americans lived throughout North America. This map shows some of the largest groups that lived in this region at this time. Which Native Americans made their home near where you live today?

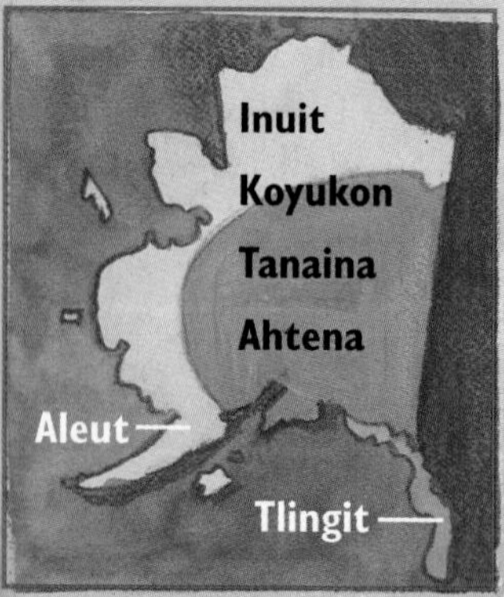

Alaska

Inuit
Koyukon
Tanaina
Ahtena
Aleut —
Tlingit —

Hawaii

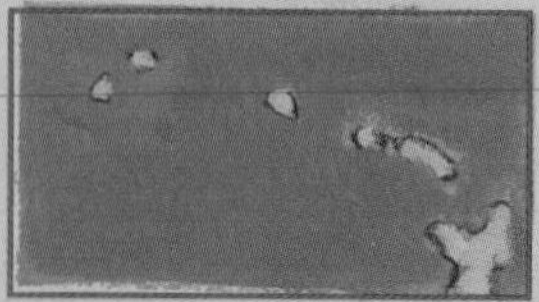

Hawaii was settled by people from Polynesia about 2,000 years ago.

Spokane
Yakima
Flathead
Lakota Sioux
Nez Percé
Crow
Klamath
Chinook
Modoc
Yurok
Pomo
Hupa
Yokuts
Paiute
Chumash
Mohave
Papago
Bannock
Shoshone
Ute
Arapaho
Pawnee
Hopi
Navajo
Pima
Zuni
Pueblo
Kiowa
Apache
Comanche
Cheyenne
Hidatsa
Mandan
Kickapoo
Winnebago
Iowa
Kansa
Osage
Quapaw
Wichita
Caddo
Coahuiltec
Sauk
Fox
Huron
Potawatomi
Miami
Illinois
Erie
Cherokee
Shawnee
Chickasaw
Muscogee
Natchez
Timucua
Calusa

YUROK PLANK HOUSE

Yurok houses were made with thick planks of wood and had small round doorways.

MANDAN LODGE

The Mandan built low, round houses made of wood covered with earth.

Native American Cultural Areas of the United States

Native Americans in what is now the United States lived in eight major cultural areas.

- [ ] Arctic
- [ ] Subarctic
- [ ] Northwest Coast
- [ ] California
- [ ] Basin and Plateau
- [ ] Southwest
- [ ] Plains
- [ ] Eastern Woodlands

Penobscot
Abenaki

Narragansett
Wampanoag
——— Iroquois
——— Lenape

Powhatan

——— Tuscarora

WATTLE-AND-DAUB HOUSE

The Muscogee used clay and a mixture of mud and moss to build houses with grass roofs.

WHY IT MATTERS

Many of the customs of the Tlingit and Yurok peoples are carried on today. Of the 15,000 Tlingit in our country, many work at logging or fishing. They also continue to hold potlatches and create beautiful artwork.

The modern-day Yurok make their homes in cities and towns. However, many Yurok still carry on traditions of their ancestors and keep close ties with their environment. Later in this book you will read about other Native Americans who have played important roles in our country's history.

✓ Reviewing Facts and Ideas

MAIN IDEAS

- Native Americans of the Northwest Coast developed a rich way of life that was based on resources of the sea.
- Because food was plentiful in their region, the Tlingit had time to develop technology and art.
- The Yurok depended on the resources of the sea and forest, such as salmon, acorns, and redwood trees.

THINK ABOUT IT

1. What is a potlatch?

2. What was one way that the Native Americans used resources carefully?

3. **FOCUS** How did the geography of the Pacific Northwest affect the lives of the Native Americans who lived there?

4. **THINKING SKILL** *Compare* the traditional lives of the Tlingit and the Yurok. What things did they have in common? How were their lives different?

5. **WRITE** Suppose that you were spending a day in a Yurok village during the 1800s. Write a journal entry describing what happened during that day.

NATIVE AMERICAN Games

What is your favorite game? Perhaps you like soccer or chess or even video games. All cultures have their own special games. Native Americans of North America had different games that reflected their beliefs as well as their environments. Many are still played by Native Americans today to keep their cultures alive.

Some games, such as hide-and-seek or cat's cradle, a string game, are probably familiar to you. One game called shinny is somewhat like field hockey. Others, like the hoop-and-pole game, may be like nothing you've ever seen before. Each of these games is a legacy of an earlier time, and they all join history, geography, and fun.

The Brooklyn Museum

In one game players toss rings strung on a cord (left) and try to catch them on this stick. The rings in this example from the Northwest Coast are made of salmon bones. A game of tag (above) is more fun in water than on land!

In this traditional southern California game, players try to correctly guess which small bones another player hides in his or her hand.

Shinny is played with long sticks and an object called a tossle. Players run up and down the field, trying to hit the tossle into the opponents' goal (below). Both males and females play this game, though not together. Talbert Alvarado, a Yurok from California (left), with his shinny stick.

NATIVE AMERICANS OF THE SOUTHWEST

Focus Activity

READ TO LEARN
What traditions have helped shape Hopi life?

VOCABULARY
pueblo
adobe
kachina

PEOPLE
Nampeyo

PLACE
Old Oraibi

READ ALOUD

"Before dancing, I get a little nervous," says Timmy Roybal, a ten-year-old from the San Ildefonso Pueblo in New Mexico. *"My legs start shaking, but they settle down once I am dancing. When I am dancing, I feel I am part of everything."* Timmy is talking about the Green Corn Dance, in which Pueblo peoples give thanks for all that nature has given them.

THE BIG PICTURE

In Lesson 1 you read about the Anasazi, who lived in what is today the southwestern United States. Many Native Americans and historians think that the Anasazi were the ancestors of today's Pueblo peoples, such as the Hopi and the Zuni (ZOO nee), who live in the Southwest.

Also living in the region are non-Pueblo Native Americans such as the Navajo (NAHV uh hoh) and Apache (uh PACH ee). Historians believe the Navajo and Apache may be newer arrivals to the Southwest.

Scholars often divide Native Americans in the Southwest into two groups. The first includes the Navajo and Apache, who were mainly hunters and herders. The second includes Pueblo peoples, who were mainly farmers. In this lesson you will read about the Hopi, a Pueblo people who became skilled farmers of the desert.

THE LAND OF THE HOPI

The Hopi call themselves *Hopiti,* which in their own language means "the gentle people." When the Spanish arrived in the 1500s, they called the Hopi apartment-style homes pueblos which means "villages" in Spanish. The Spanish used the word *pueblo* to describe both the people and the type of home in which they lived. Over time Native Americans living in pueblos have become known as the Pueblo people. The Hopi pueblo of Old Oraibi (oh rah EE bee) is one of the oldest settlements in the United States. The Hopi have lived there for about 800 years.

Farmers of the Desert

The land of the Hopi is mostly made up of deep canyons and wide mesas. This dry land is not a place where you would expect to find farming people. Yet the Hopi were among the most successful farmers in North America.

The Hopi have been growing crops in the Southwest for hundreds of years. Some of their farming methods were probably passed down to them by the Anasazi. To grow their crops, the Hopi use a method called *dry farming*. Dry farming is a way of growing crops in places where there is little water. The Hopi found clever ways to water their crops. They collected rainwater after storms and dug ditches to send the water to dry fields. They also grew special corn plants with long roots to reach the underground water.

Farming was sacred to the Hopi. Each plant had to be tended according to ancient religious practices. Every person in the community performed a task. Some planted, some weeded, some kept pests away. Success depended on everyone working together and carefully observing nature. As you can tell from the Hopi poem below, respect for nature is important to the Hopi and other Native Americans.

Power is very mysterious.
Power is all around us
in the wind
and the clouds
and the earth.

A Hopi uses dry farming to grow corn (above) in Old Oraibi, Arizona. Taos Pueblo (left) looks much the same today as it did long ago.

This piece of Zuni jewelry shows a kachina called Long Hair (below). In this painting (right) the kachina dancers perform in a Hopi village.

The Heard Museum

HOPI LIFE

The Hopi built homes made of adobe (uh DOH bee). Adobe is a type of clay found in the earth. It protected the house from the desert's blistering heat and extreme cold as well as floods and blizzards. In summer the roof of an adobe house could get as hot as 140°F. Even then, the temperature inside remained between 75°F and 85°F.

To keep invaders out, the Hopi built the first floor of most pueblos without doors or windows. To get in and out, people climbed ladders up to and down from doors in the roofs. Like Anasazi towns, most pueblo towns had underground rooms called kivas (KEE vuz) for religious ceremonies.

The Kachinas

Kachina ceremonies are an important part of Hopi religion. The Hopi kachinas are spirits who can visit Hopi villages for half of every year. The Hopi believe the kachinas bring the rains and help the crops to grow. They also show people how to live and behave, and bring peace and prosperity.

Kachina ceremonies are held throughout the six months the kachinas are said to dwell in the Hopi villages. Kachina dances are an important part of these ceremonies. Each kachina dancer represents one of the hundreds of different kachinas. For example, one dancer might become the kachina Crow Mother. Crow Mother is the mother of all kachinas. Other dancers represent clowns who follow the kachinas and cause mischief. One clown named Tcutckutu (koot KOO too) is known for his love of food. It takes years of training to become a kachina dancer, which is a position of honor among the Hopi.

During the kachina festivals, some kachina dancers give girls colorful wooden dolls that look like the kachinas they represent. Kachina dolls are used to teach Hopi children about the powers and abilities of each of the hundreds of different kachinas.

Generations of Artists

The skill of Hopi artists can also be seen in their pottery. A Hopi woman named **Nampeyo** (nahm PAY oh) was one of these artists. In 1895 Nampeyo's husband was working with an archaeologist digging up the ruins of an ancient Hopi pueblo. When Nampeyo saw the pottery that had been found there, she was struck by its beauty. She thought the ancient designs were more beautiful than the designs she and other artists of her time were creating. She began to visit the digging site to study the ancient pottery.

At first she tried to copy the designs she saw. Then she began to create her own designs in the ancient style. Over the next 20 years, Nampeyo made many beautiful pots. Her work soon gained wide recognition. Determined to spread interest in the traditional Hopi pottery, Nampeyo taught her skill to her daughters. Today many Hopi potters, including Nampeyo's grandchildren, carry on her work.

Southwest Museum

The Hopi artist Nampeyo (above) displays her pottery. The pottery shown at right includes many of the traditional designs that were brought back into use by Nampeyo.

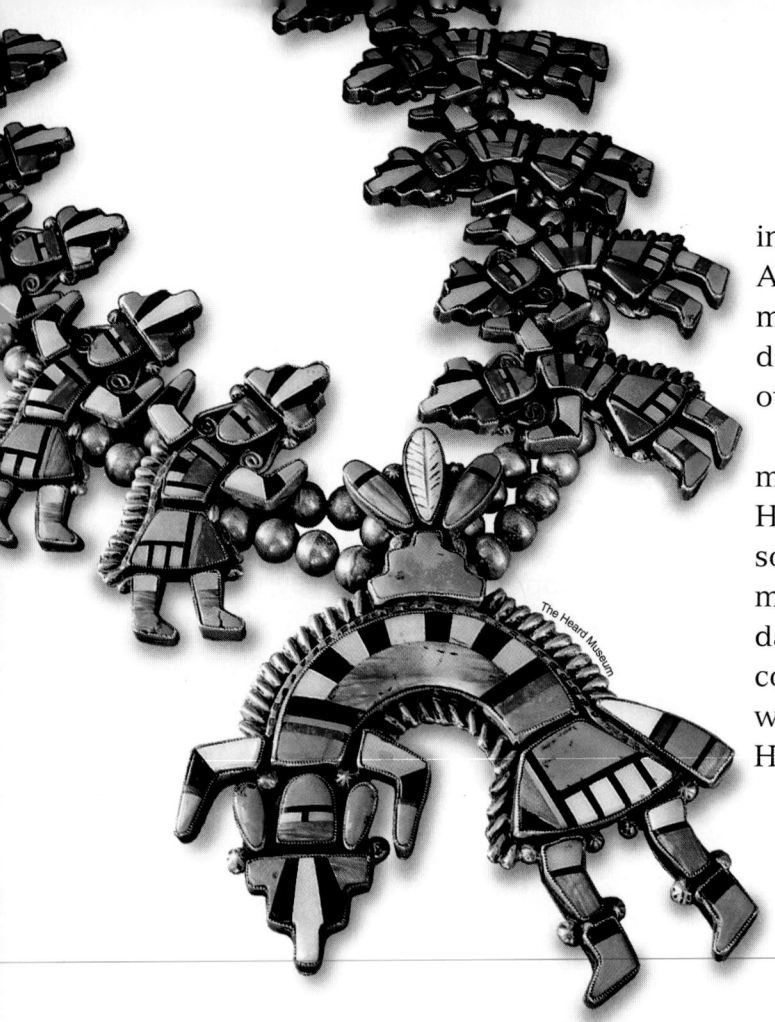

The Heard Museum

WHY IT MATTERS

Today the Pueblo peoples' way of life includes a mix of the old and the new. Adobe homes exist alongside buildings made of other materials. Many modern-day Hopi farm in traditional ways while others work in big cities.

The Hopi have worked hard to maintain their traditional way of life. Hopi ceremonies, government, and social organizations continue to exist much as they always have. Kachina dances are still being held. Visitors come from all over the world to watch these ceremonies and to buy Hopi artwork.

This Zuni necklace uses the traditional Pueblo materials of silver, turquoise, and other stones.

✓ Reviewing Facts and Ideas

MAIN IDEAS

- Native Americans in the Southwest include such Pueblo peoples as the Hopi and the Zuni, and such non-Pueblo peoples as the Apache and the Navajo.
- The Hopi were skilled dry farmers in a harsh, desert climate.
- Art and tradition have been and still are central to Hopi life.
- In 1895 a Hopi artist named Nampeyo revived the art of making traditional Hopi pottery.

THINK ABOUT IT

1. Name some of the Native American peoples who live in the Southwestern region. How and when did they come here?

2. How did the Hopi succeed at farming in their dry environment?

3. **FOCUS** Explain how art and tradition influence and enrich the life of the Hopi people.

4. **THINKING SKILL** What _problems_ did the Hopi have to consider when building their homes? What steps did they take to _solve_ these _problems_?

5. **GEOGRAPHY** What might the Hopi's belief in kachinas show about the effect of geography on their lives? Explain your answer.

Sharing the Old Ways

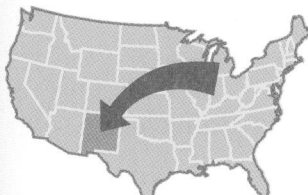

Laguna Pueblo, New Mexico, is one of 19 Pueblo communities in the state. At Laguna Elementary School, Ron Sarracino's students begin the day with the greeting "Guwatzi" (guh WAHT zee). In the Keres (KE rez) language, this word means "How are things here?"

Today English has replaced Keres as the main language spoken in many pueblos. Because of this, few young people have learned to speak Keres. To Mr. Sarracino, the Keres language plays an important part in the Laguna community. He explains:

All our ceremonies are based on our traditional language. The elders of our pueblo are telling us that if the young people do not learn the language, then our culture, ceremonies, and everything else that goes with it will be lost.

Mr. Sarracino learned Keres from his parents as he was growing up in Laguna. Today, in his classroom, the learning continues. The older people, or elders, in the community are helping Mr. Sarracino and his students. He says "the elders share the old ways with our children." They tell traditional stories of long ago and talk about events from their own childhoods. "The students are surprised," says Mr. Sarracino, "at how different life in Laguna was then.

Children herded sheep and went to the river for water for cooking and drinking."

Dancing is also important to the Keres. Students dance the arrow dance or the deer dance to songs Mr. Sarracino sings in Keres. One of the dancers is fifth grader Samantha Fernando. She has been learning Keres at home from her grandparents, as well as from Mr. Sarracino in school. "I'm glad we're learning our Laguna language," she says. "When we grow up, we don't want our traditions to be forgotten." Thanks to the efforts of the elders and people like Mr. Sarracino, they will be remembered.

"All our ceremonies are based on our traditional language."

Ron J. Sarracino

THE PLAINS PEOPLE

READ ALOUD

The Pawnee have a story that explains how their ancestors learned to live on the Great Plains. In the story four old men named Wind, Cloud, Lightning, and Thunder give instructions: "See how this lodge is made. See how we cover it with buffalo hide. This is the kind of lodge that you and the people to come should make. Those plants that grow outside our lodge will also be yours. Corn will help feed the people to come."

THE BIG PICTURE

For thousands of years Native Americans lived on the Great Plains of the Middle West, the land between the Missouri River and the Rocky Mountains. They settled mostly in villages located near rivers, where there was plenty of water for farming. The Plains people lived in lodges. Lodges are homes made of logs covered with grasses, sticks, and soil. Some lodges, such as those of the Pawnee, were covered with buffalo hide. During the summer, the men left their villages to hunt buffalo. They returned in the fall to harvest their crops.

In the 1500s the Spanish arrived in North America. They brought something that would change the Plains people's lives forever—the horse. In this lesson you will read about the Lakota Sioux (luh KOH tah SOO), one people of the Plains, from about 1500 to 1800. You will read about how their taming of the horse led to major changes in their way of life.

Focus Activity

READ TO LEARN
How did the Lakota adapt the horse to their culture?

VOCABULARY
lodge
prairie
teepee
travois
coup stick
jerky

PLACE
Black Hills

LIFE ON THE GREAT PLAINS

The Great Plains are made up of dry prairies that cover much of the Middle West. A prairie is flat or gently rolling land covered mostly with grasses and wildflowers. Summers can be extremely hot, and winters extremely cold. The lack of rain makes growing corn and other crops difficult except in river areas. Until the late 1800s, herds of buffalo roamed the Great Plains.

When they were hunting buffalo, the Plains people lived in teepees (TEE peez). Teepees are cone-shaped tents made of animal skins. Some Plains people still use teepees today. Jerry Flute says this about the teepee:

> We live in a very harsh climate. . . . It's not unusual to hear the [reporter] say it's going to be 85°F below zero with the wind chill. . . . [The teepee is] a dwelling that is cool in the summer, that is warm in the winter, and that is extremely mobile.

When it was time to move, the teepee was folded up and loaded onto the travois (truh VOY). A travois was a sledlike device used for carrying people and belongings. Plains people used the travois to carry buffalo meat home after a hunt. Before the arrival of the horse, the travois was often pulled by dogs.

Taming the Horse

By the 1600s runaway horses roamed freely across the Plains. By the 1700s the Lakota were taming these wild horses. The most important change the horse brought was in the economy of the Plains people. The buffalo replaced farming as the Lakota's main source of food. Many stopped living in permanent settlements. Instead, they moved from one campsite to another to hunt the buffalo.

This doll (right) was made from deerskin and horsehair. The Plains rider (below) is using a travois in the early 1900s.

Buffalo Bill Historical Center

THE LAKOTA

The Lakota Sioux live in the northern part of the Great Plains. The time is 1800. You are about to meet Standing Bear and Red Deer, young members of the Lakota people. They live near the Black Hills of South Dakota. This area was and still is sacred to the Lakota.

A Young Lakota Boy

Standing Bear, an 11-year-old boy, is at a buffalo hunt with his father and other men from their camp. First the hunters ride straight into the buffalo herd to create confusion. Then they go after a single buffalo, using a lance, bow and arrow, or rifle. Standing Bear admires the great courage and skill it takes to do this. He is only here to help, but someday he will kill his own buffalo. His father cuts out the liver of a buffalo that has just been killed. It is the most nutritious part, so he and Standing Bear eat some of it now. They save the rest for Standing Bear's mother and sister.

After the hunt Standing Bear practices riding. Someday he would like to

The Buffalo Hunt, a painting by Edgar S. Paxon, shows hunters using their skill and their knowledge of the horse and the buffalo.

become one of the leaders who govern his community. To be a leader, he must show courage in the face of danger—during the buffalo hunt and in battle. Standing Bear knows the bravest act that he can perform in battle is to touch an enemy without killing him. To do this, Standing Bear would have to use a special pole called a coup (KOO) stick. *Coup* is a French word that means "strike" or "hit."

Standing Bear can also bring honor to himself in other ways. Speaking well and generosity are other qualities that the Lakota admire.

A Young Lakota Girl

Red Deer, Standing Bear's older sister, works hard beside her mother. The hunt is over, but Red Deer's tasks have just begun. As you can see in the diagram on the next page, the buffalo serves many purposes. Thousands of pounds of buffalo meat lie in the field. If the meat is not cut and cured quickly, it will spoil.

Red Deer and her mother slice the buffalo meat in thin strips and leave it to dry in the sun. This dried meat is called jerky. Sometimes they make pemmican by adding berries and fat to jerky. Red Deer's family will eat this food all through the winter.

After the buffalo meat is prepared, Red Deer helps her mother make a teepee. The teepee will use about ten buffalo skins. First the skins must be cleaned and scraped. Then Red Deer and her mother will cut them and sew them together. Finally they will stretch the skins over several wooden poles.

Tomorrow Red Deer might go with her mother to search for herbs. Many Native Americans use herbs to cure common sicknesses. The major ingredient in aspirin today, for example, comes from an herb used by many Native Americans to treat illnesses.

HOW TO MAKE A TEEPEE, ABOUT 1800

What are the different steps the Plains women are using to make a teepee?

1. A buffalo hide is scraped clean to prepare it for making a teepee.

2. Several buffalo hides are sewn together to make the teepee cover.

3. Wooden poles are used to form the teepee frame.

4. The buffalo hides are stretched over the poles to cover the teepee.

THE WINTER COUNT

The Lakota kept track of time with calendars called winter counts. Each winter the Lakota met to choose an important event of the past year. An artist then recorded this event by drawing a symbol, or picture of it, on the hide of an animal.

Studying winter counts has helped historians understand the history of the Lakota. On this page is a winter count from the 1800s. What other means do people use to record important events from their past?

An 1801–1870 winter count by Lone Dog, published by the Smithsonian Institution.

Most of this winter count was recorded on a buffalo hide by a Lakota who lived in what is today Montana. The symbols are read in a counterclockwise spiral. The key tells the meaning of some of the symbols.

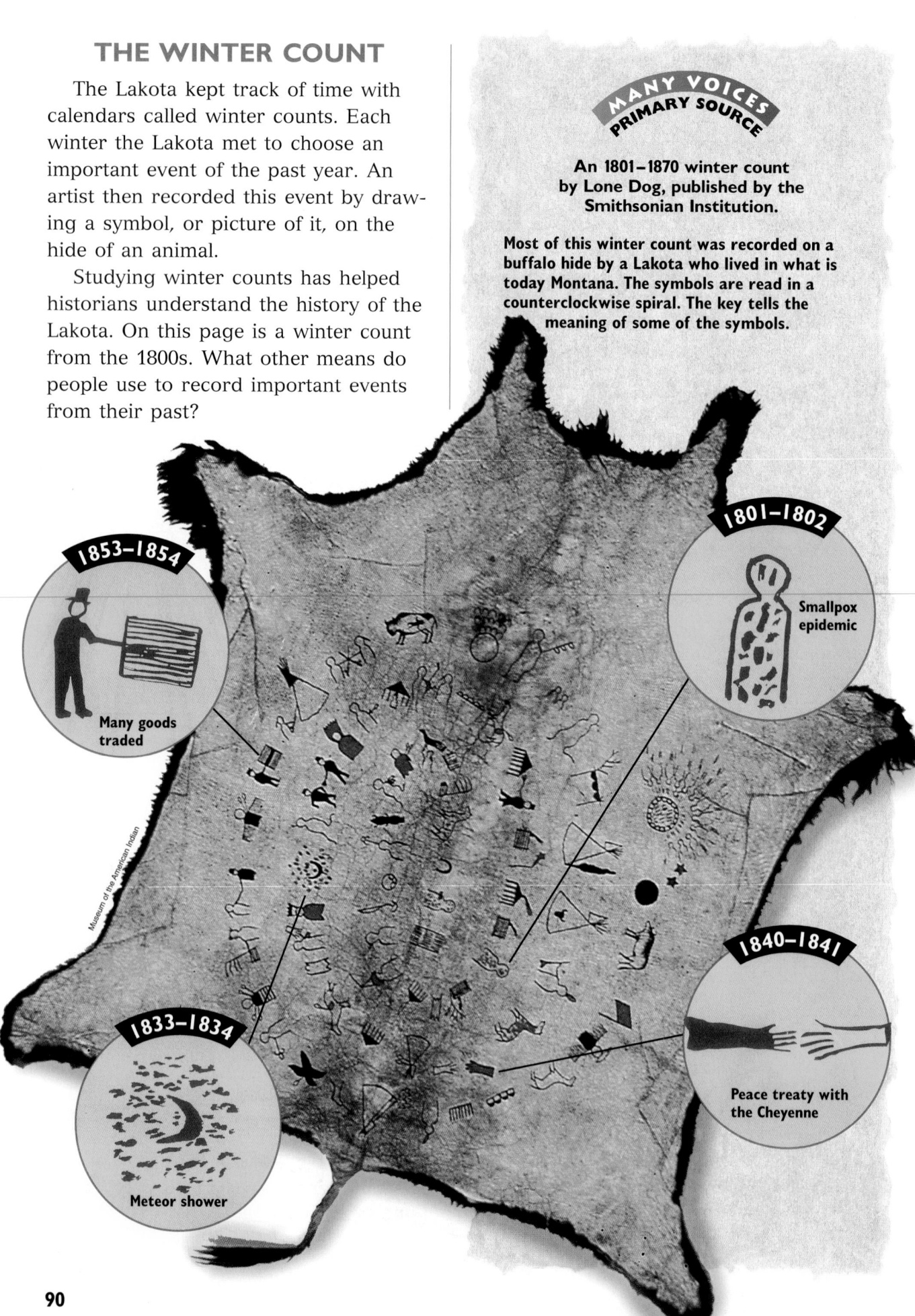

1853–1854
Many goods traded

Museum of the American Indian

1801–1802
Smallpox epidemic

1840–1841
Peace treaty with the Cheyenne

1833–1834
Meteor shower

WHY IT MATTERS

The arrival of the horse on the Great Plains changed the lives of the Native Americans of the Plains in many ways. It made buffalo hunting easier and helped the Lakota become a powerful people. It also made them much more dependent on the buffalo than they had ever been before.

The buffalo, in fact, became central to the Plains people's way of life. Their very existence now depended on their maintaining large buffalo herds on the Great Plains.

When Europeans started moving to the Plains, problems arose. Would there still be enough land for the buffalo to graze? You will learn more about these developments on the Great Plains later in this book.

How did different Plains people communicate with each other?

Although Native Americans on the Great Plains often spoke at least 20 different languages, at times different groups did not have a language in common. In these instances Plains people communicated through a special sign language they developed. Hand signals stood for important words. For example, to express the word *buffalo*, a person would raise an index finger to each side of his or her head to show horns.

✓ Reviewing Facts and Ideas

MAIN IDEAS

- Before they learned to tame the horse, most Native Americans on the Great Plains were farmers who lived in permanent villages.

- With the horse, many Plains people began moving from place to place to hunt the buffalo herds.

- The Lakota began to depend on the buffalo about 1700. They used the animal for food such as jerky and pemmican, for clothing, and as a covering for the teepee.

- The Lakota kept a record of important events in their history with a calendar called a winter count. Historians use the winter counts to understand the history of the Lakota.

THINK ABOUT IT

1. For what purposes did the Lakota people use the different parts of the buffalo?

2. What skills did Lakota boys learn? What skills did Lakota girls learn?

3. **FOCUS** How did the Lakota's taming of the horse lead to changes in their way of life?

4. **THINKING SKILL** *Predict* how the roles of the Lakota children Standing Bear and Red Deer, described in this lesson, might be different today.

5. **WRITE** Write your own version of a winter count. Pick one event from each year of your life and draw a symbol for it. Write down the meaning of each symbol.

Rochester Museum

NATIVE AMERICANS OF THE EASTERN WOODLANDS

READ ALOUD

"Into our bundle we have gathered the causes of war. We have cast this bundle away. . . . Our great-grandchildren shall not see them," spoke the Mohawk leader Hiawatha (hī uh WAH thuh). Hiawatha helped to bring peace to the Iroquois (IHR uh kwah).

THE BIG PICTURE

In Chapter 2 you read about arid and humid America. Because of its fertile soil and plentiful rainfall, hundreds of years ago humid America was almost completely covered by forest. This region was home to many Native Americans. Today these people are known as Native Americans of the Eastern Woodlands.

In the southern part of this region were the Cherokee and the Muscogee (mus KOH gee). In the northern part lived the Penobscot (puh NAHB skaht), the Lenape (lay NAH pay), and others. The Potawatomi (poh tuh WAH tuh mee) and the Winnebago (wihn uh BAY goh) lived near the Great Lakes.

Scholars usually divide the Native Americans in the Eastern Woodlands into two major language groups. The larger of the two groups spoke a language called Algonkian (al GAHNG kee un). In this lesson you will learn about the second group, the Iroquois, who spoke Iroquoian. By the 1700s the Iroquois had become a major power in the Eastern Woodlands.

Focus Activity

READ TO LEARN
How did the Iroquois bring peace among their people?

VOCABULARY
longhouse
wampum
clan
Iroquois Confederacy
compromise

PEOPLE
Hiawatha
The Peace Maker

PLACE
Hodenosaunee Trail

THE EASTERN WOODLANDS

The Eastern Woodlands is a vast area that extends roughly from the Atlantic Coast to west of the Mississippi River. In addition to forests, the area has many lakes and rivers.

Natural resources are plentiful. The Atlantic Ocean, the lakes, and the rivers are rich sources of fish. The forests provide animals for food and wood for building homes and canoes. Wild rice grows in the Great Lakes area. Along the coastal plains and river valleys, the soil is excellent for farming.

North and South

Different environments helped to bring about different ways of life among the peoples of the Eastern Woodlands. In what is now Maine, the Penobscot lived in mountainous areas where farming was difficult. They moved from place to place, hunting animals for food. The Penobscot also gathered fruits, nuts, and berries from the forests. They wore warm clothes made from deerskin.

The Natchez, who were descendants of the Mound Builders, lived in what is now the state of Mississippi. In the south the Natchez and other peoples depended mostly on farming. To keep cool in their warm climate, the Natchez wore light clothes woven from the fibers of plants.

These Native American peoples had much in common. Most were farming people who lived in permanent villages. They built homes out of wood and grew crops of corn, squash, and beans. They also hunted and fished. Using the area's many lakes, rivers, and streams Native Americans of the Eastern Woodlands traveled far in their canoes. Most importantly, they shared similar beliefs and traditions.

Rochester Museum

In Iroquois culture, women played an important role. They were mainly responsible for growing and harvesting crops, as shown in this painting by Iroquois artist Ernest Smith.

MAJOR IROQUOIS PEOPLES, 1500

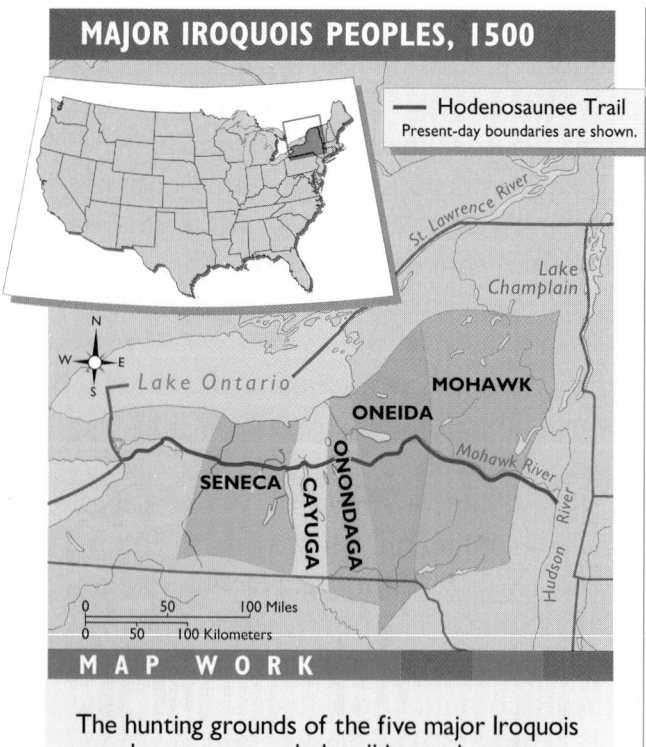

— Hodenosaunee Trail
Present-day boundaries are shown.

MAP WORK

The hunting grounds of the five major Iroquois peoples once extended well beyond present-day New York State to the Mississippi River. Which people lived near Lake Champlain?

THE IROQUOIS

In the 1500s most Iroquois lived in what is now New York State. The map above shows where the five Iroquois peoples were located. Historians have

named them after the Iroquoian language they spoke. The Iroquois, however, call themselves *Hodenosaunee* (hoh den oh SAH nee). In Iroquoian this means "people of the longhouse." Longhouses are long buildings built with poles covered with sheets of bark.

In the 1500s each longhouse—which could be 200 feet long—provided a home for several families. Each family had its own living space on either side of a central aisle, where they also cooked over fires. Goods were stored overhead.

The Iroquois Homeland

During the 1500s the homelands of the Iroquois were connected by well-used trails. One central route, the Hodenosaunee Trail, ran through the main villages of all five peoples. This winding path was 250 miles long.

The Iroquois were expert farmers. Women did most of the farming. They grew 15 types of corn and over 60 different kinds of beans. From the forest, the Iroquois obtained animals for meat, maple syrup, nuts, roots, vegetables, oils, fruits, all kinds of berries, herbs for medicines, and teas.

Wampum

Wampum (WAHM pum) was one thing the Iroquois could not get from the forest. Wampum—belts or necklaces made of small polished beads—was often given on special occasions. In the early 1600s the Iroquois began trading wampum to the Europeans for other goods. The beads used for wampum were made by hand, usually from seashells.

The Iroquois used wampum necklaces or belts like this one to commemorate special occasions.

Wampum was often used to celebrate important events. It was very valuable, because it took a lot of time and effort to make. Each bead had to be carefully carved from part of a shell. A hole was made with a small, slender drill, and the bead was polished with sand. Finished beads were woven into belts or strung into necklaces.

The Clan Mother

Women held a great deal of power—and still do—in the Iroquois world. They decided how the land would be used and who would use it. They were also the leaders of the clans. A clan is a group of families who share the same ancestor. Hopi and Navajo women held similar positions of power.

Almost all Iroquois property was controlled by clans. This meant that women were the owners of the land. They owned the longhouses and everything in them. When a man married, he moved into his wife's longhouse and lived with her family. The head of each clan was called a *clan mother*.

No important decision could be made without the consent of the clan mother. Although the leaders of each village were men, they were chosen by the clan mothers. If a leader failed in his duties, the clan women would decide who would replace him.

Conflicts Among the Iroquois

Around 1300, Iroquois numbers began to grow, and arguments and fighting broke out. The Iroquois also fought other Eastern Woodlands peoples, often over hunting grounds.

The Iroquois believed that if one person was wronged, it hurt the whole clan. For this reason, wrongs had to be punished. Warfare soon became a constant problem for the Iroquois.

ONE FAMILY'S LIVING SPACE   SMOKE HOLE

IROQUOIS LONGHOUSE, 1500s
What kinds of activities took place inside an Iroquois longhouse?

CENTRAL AISLE   STORAGE AREA   COOKING FIRE   SLEEPING PLATFORM   ANOTHER FAMILY'S LIVING SPACE

IROQUOIS CONFEDERACY

According to the Iroquois legend, two Iroquois leaders, Hiawatha and a man known as the Peace Maker, saw that fighting was destroying their people. Read Hiawatha's speech below. How does Hiawatha think uniting will help the Iroquois?

This Iroquois lacrosse team comes from a long tradition of great athletes.

MANY VOICES PRIMARY SOURCE

Excerpt from a speech by Hiawatha in about 1570, as told by Iroquois chief Elias Johnson, 1881.

Friends and Brothers: You being members of many tribes, you have come from a great distance; the voice of war has aroused you up; you are afraid . . . [for] your homes, your wives and your children; you tremble for your safety. Believe me, I am with you. My heart beats with your hearts. We are one. We have one common object. We come to promote our common interest, and to determine how this can be best done.

*To oppose those **hordes** of northern tribes, singly and alone, would prove certain destruction. We can make no progress in that way. We must unite ourselves into one common band of brothers. We must have but one voice. Many voices makes confusion. We must have one fire, one pipe [of peace] and one war club. This will give us strength.*

hordes: crowds

The Great Laws

In about 1570 five separate Iroquois peoples banded together to form the Iroquois Confederacy, also known as the Iroquois League. A confederacy is a union of people who join together for a common purpose. The five peoples that made up the Iroquois Confederacy were the Onondaga (ahn un DAW gah), the Mohawk, the Oneida (oh NĪ duh), the Seneca (SE nih kuh), and the Cayuga (kah YOO guh).

The Peace Maker and Hiawatha developed rules for the Iroquois to follow. These were called the Great Laws. The Great Laws were not only rules, though. They were also guidelines for living together in peace.

The Grand Council

The Peace Maker described the Iroquois Confederacy as a great longhouse that stretched the length of the Hodenosaunee Trail. To keep peace within the confederacy, the Peace Maker set up a Grand Council.

Representatives to the council were chosen by the clan mothers from each of the Iroquois peoples. The Grand Council made decisions through discussion and compromise. A compromise is the settling of a dispute by agreeing that each side will give up something.

WHY IT MATTERS

The Peace Maker's ideas brought peace to the Iroquois and helped make them powerful. By the 1700s they had influence over Native Americans from the St. Lawrence River in the north to present-day Tennessee in the south and all the way to Minnesota in the west. In the early 1700s the Tuscarora (tus kuh RAWR uh), an Iroquoian-speaking people from the woodlands of the South, moved to New York State. The Tuscarora joined the Iroquois Confederacy about 1722. Today the Grand Council governs the Iroquois, using discussion and compromise.

✓/// Reviewing Facts and Ideas

MAIN IDEAS

- Algonkian and Iroquoian were two major language groups in the Eastern Woodlands.
- Most Native Americans in the Eastern Woodlands, such as the Iroquois, were farming peoples living in permanent villages.
- Women had a great deal of power in Iroquois communities of the 1500s, and still do today.
- According to Iroquois legend, The Peace Maker and Hiawatha formed the Iroquois Confederacy in around 1570. The confederacy brought peace and unity to the Iroquois.

THINK ABOUT IT

1. How did Native Americans of the Eastern Woodlands use the natural resources in their environment?

2. What role do clan mothers play in Iroquois communities?

3. **FOCUS** How did the Iroquois Confederacy bring peace to its members?

4. **THINKING SKILL** How did members of the Iroquois Grand Council use compromise to _solve problems_ in their community?

5. **GEOGRAPHY** Look at the Infographic on page 76. Name four Native American groups that lived in the Eastern Woodlands region.

A present-day Iroquois couple (left) joins in a traditional community dance.

97

THINKINGSKILLS

Identifying Cause and Effect

This Iroquois council meeting took place in New York State in the early 1900s.

VOCABULARY

cause

effect

WHY THE SKILL MATTERS

History is the study of events that happened in the past. You can gain a better understanding of an event by also studying events that happened before and after it. These events are often connected. One of the most important connections between events is cause and effect.

A cause is an event or situation that makes something else happen. The thing that happens as a result of a cause is an effect. Here is an example. Suppose you close your window on a cold winter night.

Closing the window is a cause that produces an effect—the room stays warm.

Understanding cause and effect allows you to connect events in a meaningful way. It explains why things happen—in history, in movies, and in real life.

USING THE SKILL

Nearly every event causes an effect. The effect, in turn, causes yet another effect. In many cases an effect is caused by a series of events. Suppose you did not complete your homework this weekend. Why didn't you?

Here's one possible series of events. On Friday you came down with the flu. Because of this you didn't go to school. Because you missed school, you could not get your homework assignment. Catching the flu and missing school are both events that led to the effect of not completing your homework.

Rochester Museum

In the last lesson you read about how five Native American nations formed the Iroquois Confederacy. You can show how a series of events led to the confederacy by making a cause-and-effect chain. In the chain, events that link causes and effects are shown in the order in which they occurred.

Each event in the chain causes the next event in the chain. The effect of one event becomes the cause of another. A cause-and-effect chain makes it clear how one event is connected to another.

TRYING THE SKILL

Read the following paragraph. Make a cause-and-effect chain that shows the connections between the events. Use the Helping Yourself box to help you identify causes and effects.

Next Monday a traffic light will be put in outside the Maple Lane Social Center. Drivers on the busy road do not take the time

to stop when people are crossing. Over the last year there were three occasions when children narrowly escaped being hit by vehicles. Because of these near accidents, the director of the social center asked the town council to correct the situation last month. Therefore, the council responded quickly with a helpful solution.

On your cause-and-effect chain, what is the first cause? What two events link the first cause to the final effect? What is the final effect?

REVIEWING THE SKILL

1. What is a cause? What is an effect?

2. Pick an event in the middle of the chain about the traffic light. Explain why the event is a cause and why it is an effect.

3. Name an effect caused by putting in the traffic light.

4. How can finding cause-and-effect connections help you understand historical events?

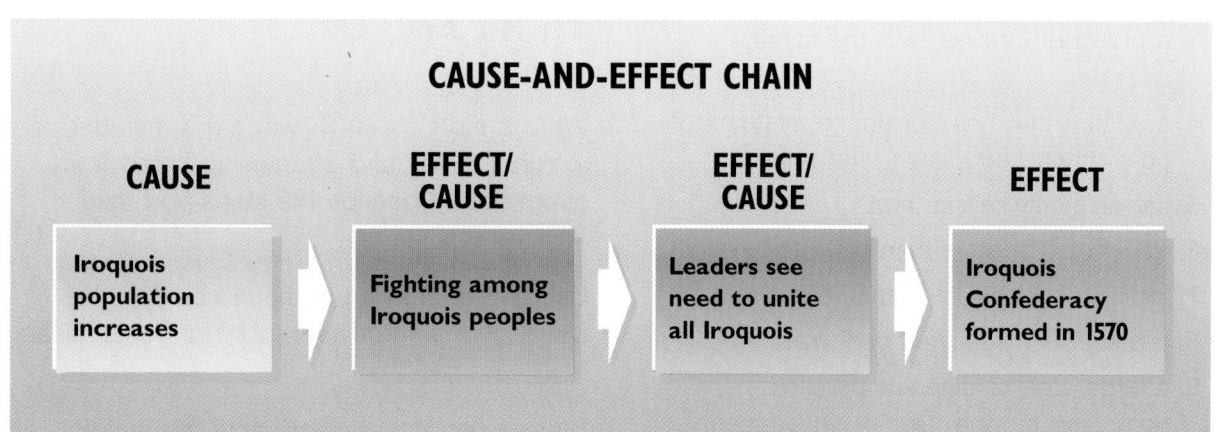

CAUSE-AND-EFFECT CHAIN

CAUSE	EFFECT/ CAUSE	EFFECT/ CAUSE	EFFECT
Iroquois population increases	Fighting among Iroquois peoples	Leaders see need to unite all Iroquois	Iroquois Confederacy formed in 1570

CHAPTER 3 REVIEW

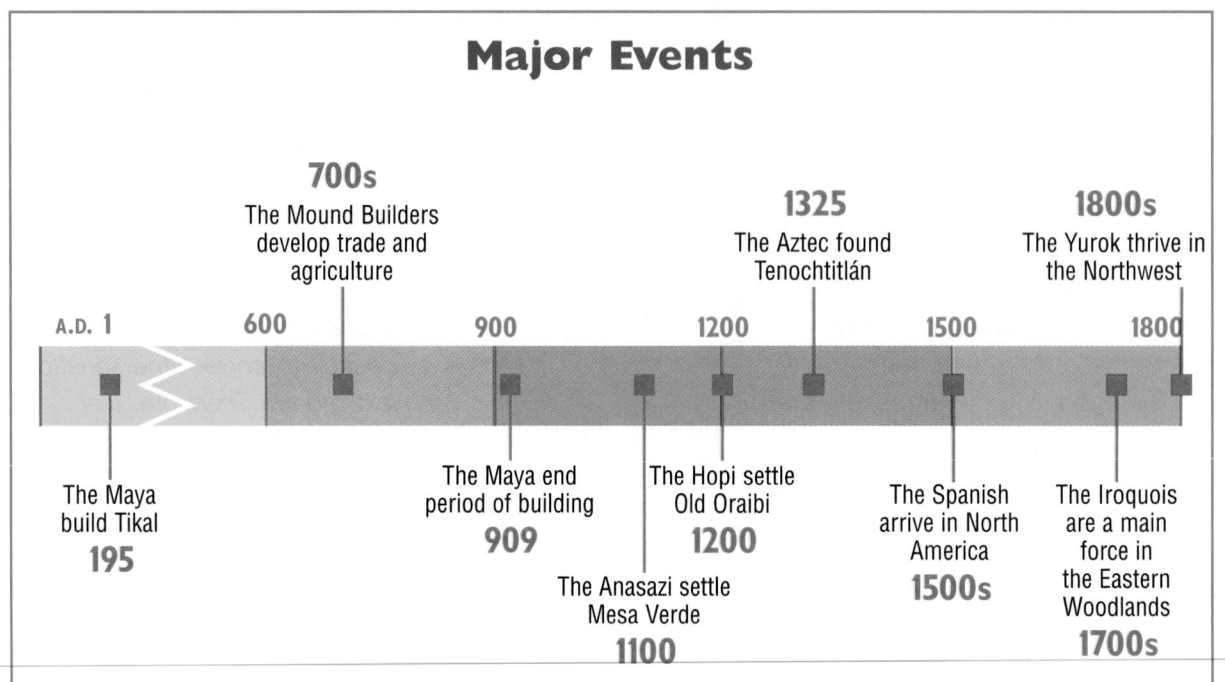

Major Events

700s
The Mound Builders develop trade and agriculture

1325
The Aztec found Tenochtitlán

1800s
The Yurok thrive in the Northwest

A.D. 1   600   900   1200   1500   1800

The Maya build Tikal
195

The Maya end period of building
909

The Hopi settle Old Oraibi
1200

The Spanish arrive in North America
1500s

The Iroquois are a main force in the Eastern Woodlands
1700s

The Anasazi settle Mesa Verde
1100

THINKING ABOUT VOCABULARY

Number a sheet of paper from 1 to 10. Beside each number write the word or term that best matches the description.

archaeologist	empire	pueblo
civilization	land bridge	surplus
clan	prairie	technology
compromise		

1. the design and use of tools, ideas, and methods to solve problems
2. a village with adobe dwellings
3. a group of families with the same ancestor
4. a culture that has developed systems of government, education, and religion
5. flat or gently rolling land
6. an amount greater than what is needed
7. a narrow connecting landmass
8. a person who studies past cultures
9. a large area of different peoples controlled by one ruler or government
10. the settlement of a dispute

THINKING ABOUT FACTS

1. Which Native Americans grew powerful in the Central Valley of Mexico after the 1200s?
2. What natural resources were available to the Tlingit and Yurok?
3. What role do kachinas play in Hopi culture?
4. Which culture occupied the Four Corners region about 2,000 years ago?
5. What evidence is there that the Mound Builders contacted other peoples?

THINK AND WRITE

WRITING A STORY

Write a story in which you are a member of a Yurok family and are making bread from acorn flour. Describe the steps you take.

WRITING A DESCRIPTION

Use the information in the lesson and the diagram to write a description of Tenochtitlán.

WRITING A REPORT

Write a report describing how the buffalo supported the Plains Indians' way of life.

APPLYING STUDY SKILLS

READING TIME LINES

Use the time line on page 100 to answer the questions below.

1. How much time is covered on the time line?

2. How many centuries come between the settling of Mesa Verde by the Anasazi and the arrival of the Spanish in North America?

3. By the year 1325, which cities had been built in Mexico and Central America?

4. If you arrived in Tenochtitlán a decade after it was founded, what year would it be?

5. How does a time line help you understand historical events?

APPLYING THINKING SKILLS

IDENTIFYING CAUSE AND EFFECT

Answer the questions below to apply the skill of identifying cause and effect.

1. What is a cause? What is an effect?

2. What does a cause-and-effect chain show?

3. Identify two causes for the Hopi's use of dry farming.

4. What was the most important effect of horses from Spain arriving on the Great Plains?

5. How is understanding cause and effect important in the study of history?

Summing Up the Chapter

Copy this matrix chart on a separate sheet of paper. Fill in the blank spaces to help you organize the information you have read about some of the early civilizations of North America. Then use the information in it to write a paragraph that answers the question, "Which civilization would you like to have lived in, and why?"

NATIVE PEOPLES OF NORTH AND CENTRAL AMERICA	LOCATION	SOURCE OF FOOD	TYPE OF BUILDINGS
Maya	Mexico, Central America		
Anasazi		farming with irrigation	
Hopi			pueblo, kiva
Lakota Sioux	Plains		
Iroquois			longhouse

CHAPTER 4

The World Gets Smaller

THINKING ABOUT
HISTORY AND GEOGRAPHY

The story of Chapter 4 stretches across Europe, Africa, and Asia before the peoples of the Eastern and Western Hemispheres met. Following the time line, you see that throughout the world people were exploring and trading. It would be only a few years before Europeans began making voyages to the Americas.

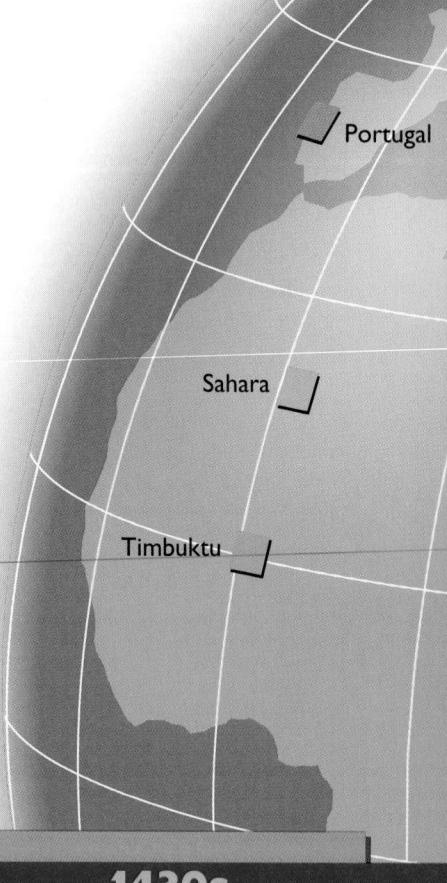

Portugal

Sahara

Timbuktu

1300s
SAHARA

Caravans crisscross the Sahara in West Africa

1400s
TIMBUKTU

Gold and valuable goods are sold at markets in West Africa

1430s
CHINA

Zheng He explores the coasts of Asia and Africa

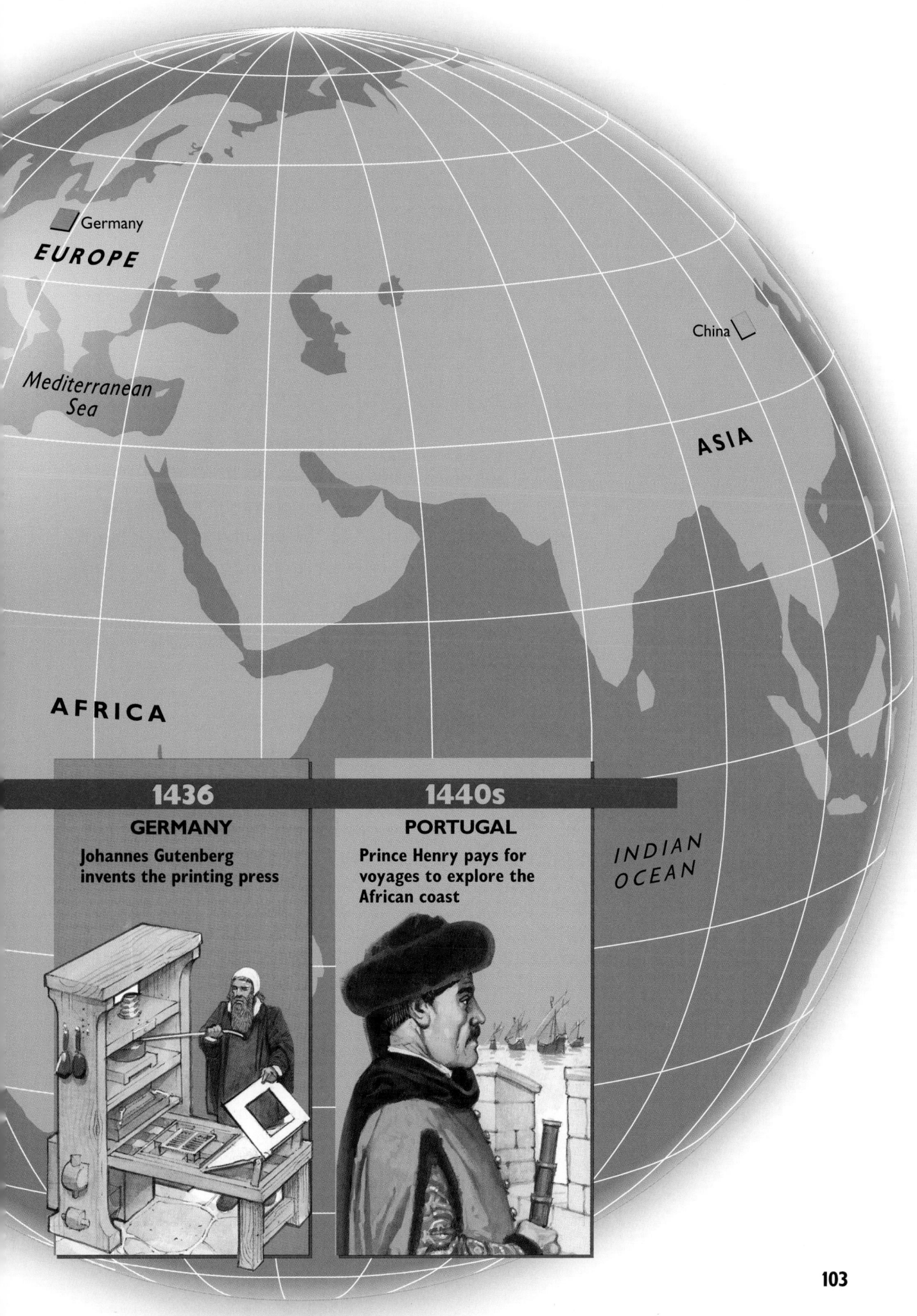

Germany

EUROPE

China

Mediterranean
Sea

ASIA

AFRICA

*INDIAN
OCEAN*

1436

GERMANY

**Johannes Gutenberg
invents the printing press**

1440s

PORTUGAL

**Prince Henry pays for
voyages to explore the
African coast**

ASIA'S VOYAGES OF DISCOVERY

READ ALOUD

"Let the dark water dragons go down into the sea and leave us free from calamity," prayed the Chinese sea captains.* *In the autumn of 1405, more than 300 Chinese ships were made ready to sail to the east coast of India. The captains' prayer asked their gods to protect them from danger. They were worried about what lay ahead.*

THE BIG PICTURE

You have read about early civilizations in the Western Hemisphere. Now you will read about great empires in the Eastern Hemisphere. In the 1300s and 1400s, contact between peoples within the Eastern Hemisphere increased. A desire to expand trade led to more contact between peoples of Asia, Africa, and Europe. Trade allows people to exchange goods that they have for goods or items that they do not have. As empires learned about lands and goods previously unknown to them, they began to search for trade routes to other continents.

You will begin this chapter by looking at one of the world's oldest civilizations. In eastern Asia, northeast of the Himalaya Mountains, is the country of China. While the Aztec were building their empire in the West, the Chinese were expanding their empire in the East.

Focus Activity

READ TO LEARN
How did the Chinese increase trade in the East?

VOCABULARY
magnetic compass

PEOPLE
Zhu Di
Zheng He

PLACES
China
Great Wall
Silk Road
Persia
India

*Mariner's prayer from *When China Ruled the Seas* (1994), translated by Chu Hung-lam and James Geiss.

THE CHINESE EMPIRE

The people of China viewed their land as a great empire at the middle of everything. As you will see from the map on page 106, this huge area was protected by the Himalayas to the west, the Gobi Desert to the north, and the Pacific Ocean to the east. Despite these barriers, invaders sometimes broke through. In the late 1200s, after years of fighting the Chinese, the Mongols from northern Asia gained control of the empire.

The Chinese pushed the Mongols out in 1368. In 1402 the new emperor, Zhu Di (ZHOO DEE), set out to re-build China. The Great Wall, which began as several older walls built around 200 B.C, was repaired. New bridges and roads were also built.

The Silk Road

Zhu Di also increased trade on the ancient Silk Road. The Silk Road was a network of overland trade routes that stretched from China to Persia, which is today the country of Iran. During the late 1200s, Europe's demand for Chinese silk was so high that the ancient trade route became known as the Silk Road. Find the Silk Road on the map on the next page.

Through a chain of Chinese, Indian, Arab, and Italian traders, the silk made its long journey over Asia's mountains and deserts to Europe. In exchange, gold was brought to China. Few traders traveled the entire Silk Road because it was such a long way to go. Most of them passed goods from one trading post to the next.

The Great Wall of China is the longest human-made feature ever built. It is 4,600 miles long and was built by hand. Construction went on for centuries.

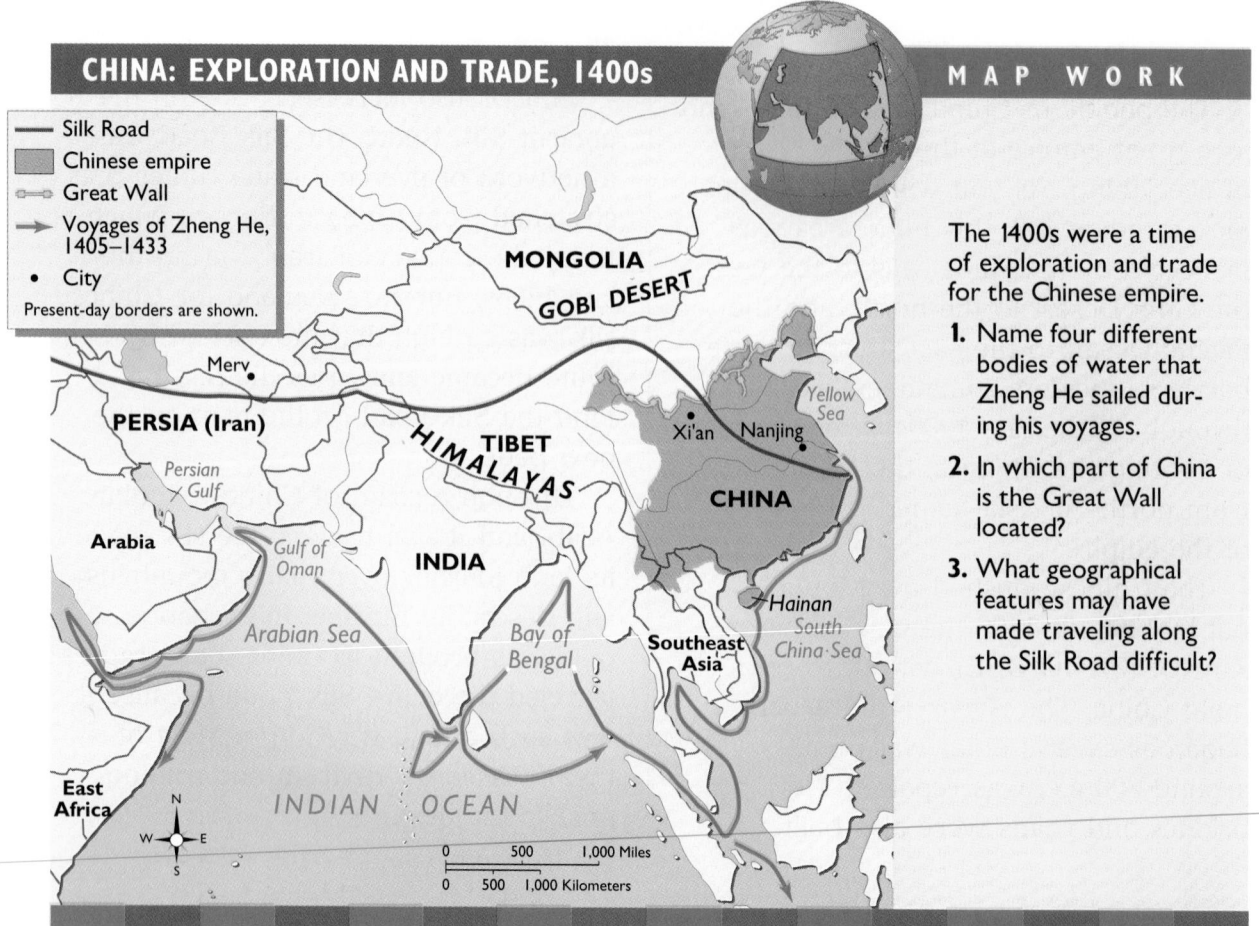

Legend:
- Silk Road
- Chinese empire
- Great Wall
- Voyages of Zheng He, 1405–1433
- City

Present-day borders are shown.

MONGOLIA

GOBI DESERT

Merv

PERSIA (Iran)

HIMALAYAS

TIBET

Xi'an   Nanjing

Yellow Sea

CHINA

Persian Gulf

Arabia

Gulf of Oman

INDIA

Arabian Sea

Bay of Bengal

Southeast Asia

Hainan

South China Sea

East Africa

INDIAN OCEAN

0   500   1,000 Miles

0   500   1,000 Kilometers

The 1400s were a time of exploration and trade for the Chinese empire.

1. Name four different bodies of water that Zheng He sailed during his voyages.

2. In which part of China is the Great Wall located?

3. What geographical features may have made traveling along the Silk Road difficult?

ZHENG HE'S VOYAGES

In 1403 Emperor Zhu Di ordered the building of thousands of ships. He put Zheng He (ZHAHNG HUH), a Chinese Muslim sea captain, in command of a fleet of more than 300 ships. Muslims are followers of the religion of Islam. From 1405 to 1433 the fleet made voyages to India, southeast Asia, Arabia, and the coast of East Africa.

The Ships of Zheng He

Several of Zheng He's ships were more then 400 feet long—the largest ever built at the time. To help them find their way on the open seas, the sailors used a magnetic compass,

invented by the Chinese about A.D. 100. Traders used the compass to guide them across the deserts along the Silk Road. Sailors used compasses with needles that floated in containers of water.

Scholars today do not agree on why Zheng He made these voyages. Perhaps the emperor wished to find new trading centers or to show outsiders the power of the Chinese empire. China's days of exploration ended in 1525 when a new emperor ordered the ships destroyed. Why did the emperor make this decision? He may have been concerned about protecting China's borders or may have wanted to save the cost of keeping the ships. Whatever the reasons were, China's chances for becoming a sea power were over.

Chinese explorers used the magnetic compass to find the direction of north.

A Chinese Tale

Zheng He's voyages helped peoples in the Eastern Hemisphere exchange tales. The Chinese may have been the first to write down a tale about a young woman who lost her shoe. Below is an excerpt from the Chinese tale of Yeh-hsien (YE SHEN). How is her story like a tale that you may know?

PRIMARY SOURCE

Excerpt from "Yeh-hsien" translated by Arthur Waley, in *The Chinese Cinderella Story*, adapted by Judy Sierra, 1992.

*The man who had picked up the gold shoe sold it in T'o-han (TOH HAHN), and it was brought to the king. He ordered all the women of the court to put it on, but it was too small even for the one among them that had the smallest foot. He then ordered all the women in his kingdom to try it on, but there was not one that it fitted. It was as light as **down**, and it made no noise even when **treading** on stone. His search finally took him to the place where Yeh-hsien lived with her stepmother, and the shoe fitted her perfectly.*

T'o-han: an imaginary kingdom
down: fine, soft feathers
treading: walking

WHY IT MATTERS

China is one of the world's oldest civilizations. Its roots go back more than 3,000 years. Today China has more people than any other nation. Until the 1400s, China had done little direct trading with Europe, but during the voyages of Zheng He, it began exploring countries in the Eastern Hemisphere. This was before Europe started exploring the Western Hemisphere. China's voyages soon ended, however, which prevented it from competing with Europe.

✓ Reviewing Facts and Ideas

MAIN IDEAS

- In the 1400s, while the Aztec empire was growing, the Chinese were strengthening their already powerful empire.
- Traders on the Silk Road carried silk and other goods from China to Europe, and gold back to China.
- From 1405 to 1433, Zheng He explored India, southeast Asia, Arabia, and the east coast of Africa.

THINK ABOUT IT

1. What natural and human-made features helped protect China from invasions? Which people successfully invaded China in the late 1200s?
2. How did the Silk Road get its name?
3. **FOCUS** What did Zheng He's voyages accomplish for the Chinese empire?
4. **THINKING SKILL** List the *cause* and *effect* connections between the Chinese invention of the magnetic compass and Zheng He's voyages.
5. **WRITE** Write an account describing how Zheng might have felt as he led his fleet to India for the first time.

STUDYSKILLS

Reading Line and Circle Graphs

VOCABULARY
circle graph
graph
line graph

WHY THE SKILL MATTERS

As you have read, the Chinese empire went through a great period of shipbuilding in the early 1400s. The Chinese built warships, passenger ships, and transport ships for the empire's fleet. A fleet is a group of ships under one command. Some of these ships took part in Zheng He's voyages.

One way to picture how large the Chinese fleet was is by using a graph. A graph is a diagram that presents information in a way that makes it easy to understand. Graphs are especially useful for showing such things as patterns, trends, amounts, or how things change over time.

USING LINE GRAPHS

Line graphs show changes over time. The graph below shows how the size of the Chinese fleet changed from 1410 to 1530.

To read a line graph, first look at its title. What is the title of the line graph on this page? Then read the years shown on the bottom of the graph. The numerals on the left side show the number of ships that made up the Chinese fleet.

For each year, a dot is placed on the graph to show the number of ships in the fleet during that year. The first dot shows that in 1410 China had about 3,500 ships. How many ships were there in 1470?

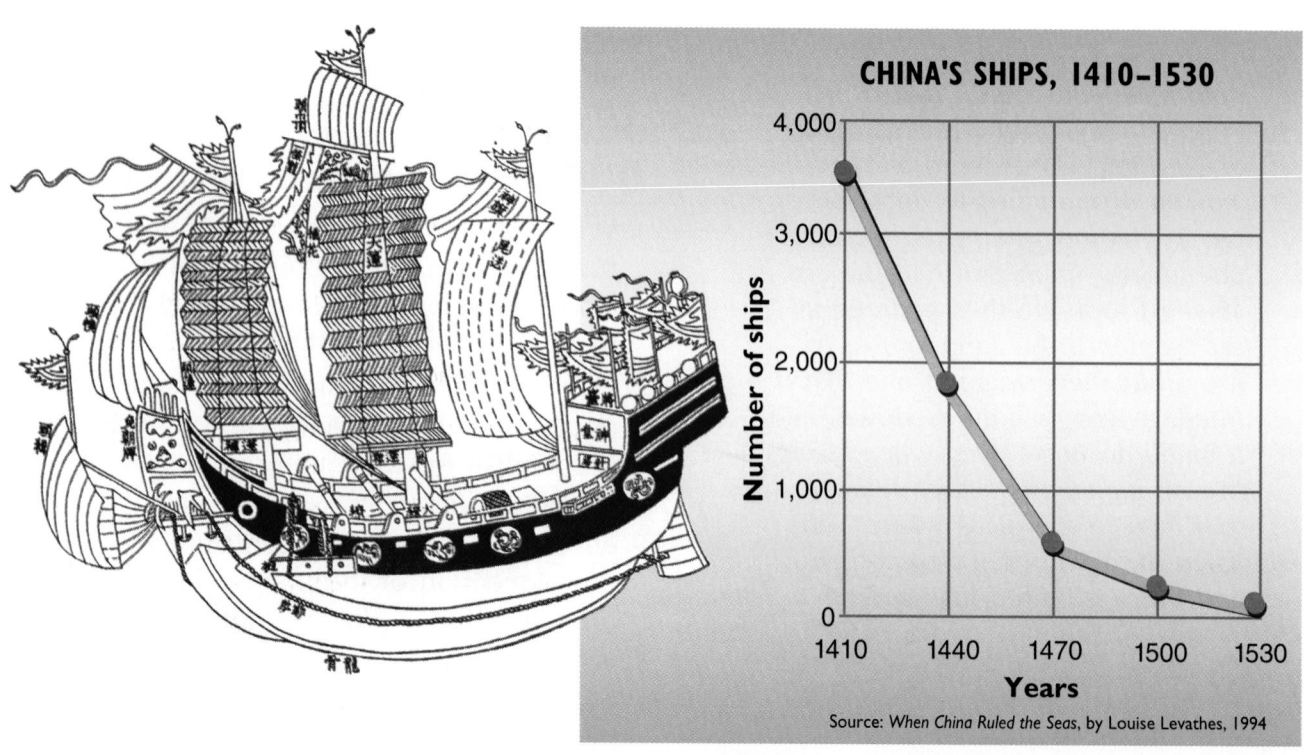

CHINA'S SHIPS, 1410–1530

Source: *When China Ruled the Seas*, by Louise Levathes, 1994

When you look at a line graph, pay special attention to patterns. For example, if you trace the line of dots in the graph on page 108, you can see that the number of ships decreased over time. When did the empire have the highest number of ships?

USING CIRCLE GRAPHS

A circle graph shows how something can be divided into parts that make up the whole. Circle graphs are also called pie graphs because the parts look like slices of a pie. The circle graph on this page shows what kinds of ships China had in the early 1400s.

Looking at the graph, you can see how many of each type of ship there were in the

HELPING Yourself

- **Line graphs** show how information changes over time. Trace the line of dots to see how the information changes.

- **Circle graphs** show how something can be divided into parts. Look at the sizes of the parts of the circle graph to see how they compare.

Chinese fleet. For example, you can see that there were 400 transport ships. Look at the sizes of the parts of the graph to see how they compare with each other. Of which ships did the Chinese have the largest number?

TRYING THE SKILL

Take another look at each of the graphs. Then answer the questions about the Chinese fleet. The Helping Yourself box on this page can give you hints about how to read circle graphs and line graphs.

Which graph or graphs would you use to find out the size of the fleet in 1410? In 1450? Which graph tells you how many warships were built? Which graph shows how many ships existed over time?

REVIEWING THE SKILL

1. How are line graphs different from circle graphs? How are they the same?

2. During which span of years did the greatest drop in the number of Chinese ships occur? How do you know?

3. Which kind of graph would be better for showing how the population of your school changed over several years?

4. Which kind of graph would be better for showing the number of boys and the number of girls in your school?

5. When might it be useful to know how to read line graphs and circle graphs?

THE CHINESE FLEET, EARLY 1400s

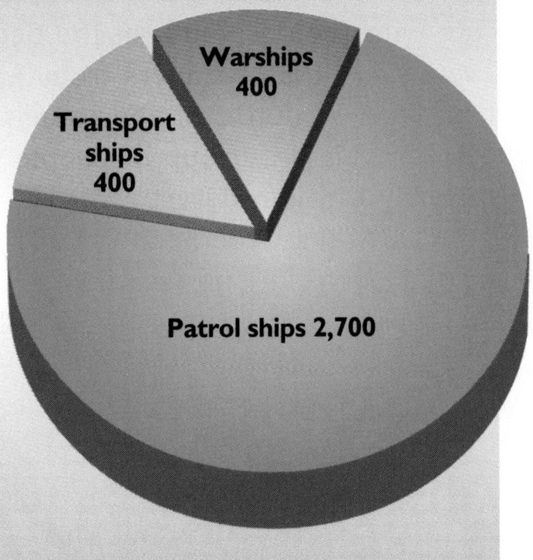

Warships 400

Transport ships 400

Patrol ships 2,700

Source: *When China Ruled the Seas,* by Louise Levathes, 1994

AFRICAN TRADE ROUTES

READ ALOUD

"Life is a perpetual coming and going," says a West African song. The endless comings and goings of trade have long been a part of life in Africa. Many great kingdoms that began as villages became powerful because of trade.

Focus Activity

READ TO LEARN
How did trade routes connect different parts of Africa?

VOCABULARY
caravan
malaria

PEOPLE
Sunni Ali
Leo Africanus

PLACES
Sahara Desert
Songhai
Timbuktu
Jenne
Gao

THE BIG PICTURE

One of the continents visited by Zheng He's fleet during the early 1400s was Africa. Africa is home to many peoples. It is the second largest continent in the world. Stretching across most of North Africa up to the Mediterranean Sea is the Sahara Desert. The Sahara is the largest desert in the world.

People called Berbers lived in the Sahara and along the Mediterranean coast. They had been in contact with Europe for centuries. Yet the Sahara made it difficult for them to communicate with regions south of the desert. In the 1200s, however, caravans of traders from Arabia began riding south on horses, donkeys, and camels across the Sahara. A caravan is a group of people traveling together, especially through desert areas. In the late 1400s most of the caravans were headed for Songhai (SAWNG hī), a powerful and wealthy kingdom whose king ruled a large part of West Africa.

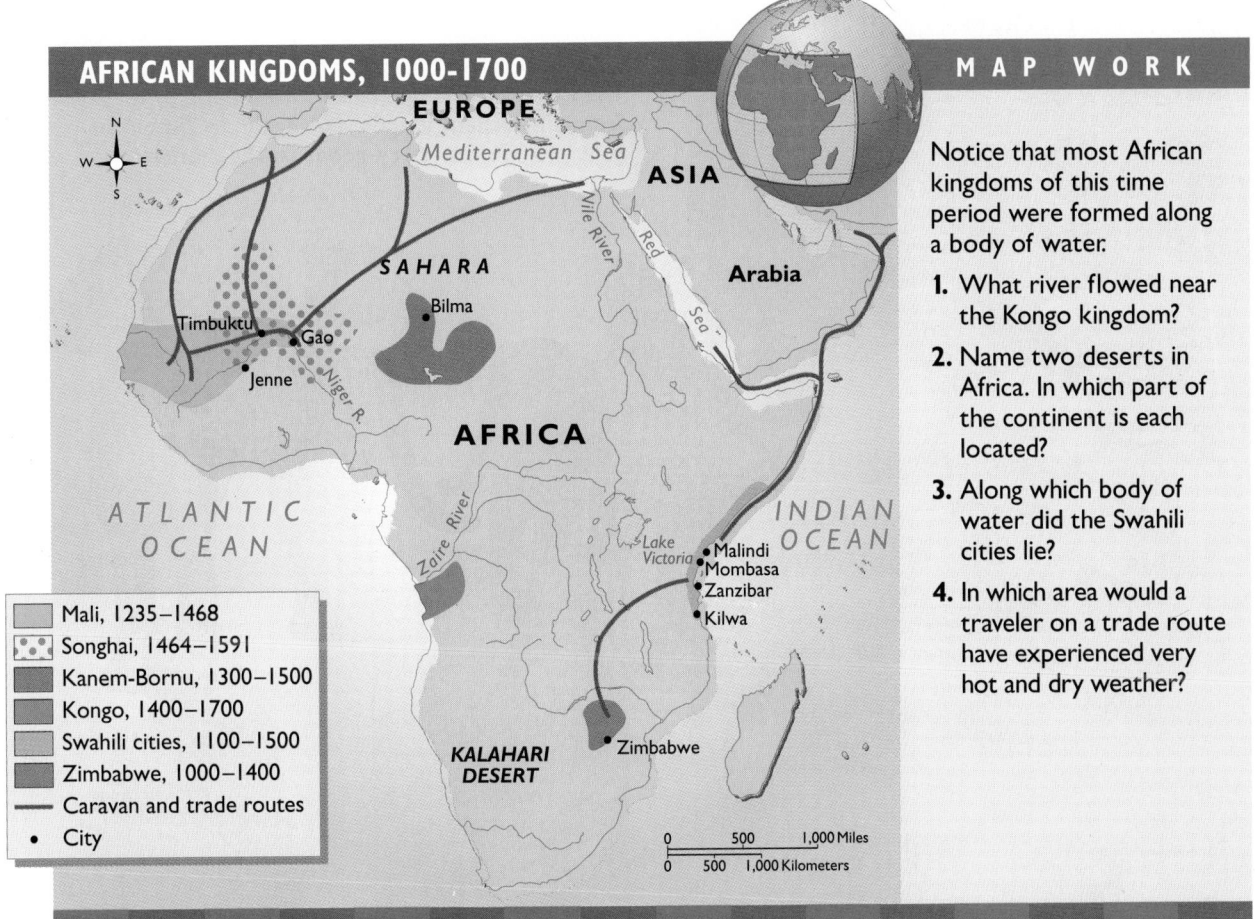

AFRICAN KINGDOMS, 1000-1700

EUROPE

Mediterranean Sea

ASIA

SAHARA

Bilma

Arabia

Timbuktu
Gao
Jenne

Niger R.

Nile River

Red Sea

AFRICA

ATLANTIC OCEAN

Zaire River

Lake Victoria

INDIAN OCEAN

Malindi
Mombasa
Zanzibar
Kilwa

KALAHARI DESERT

Zimbabwe

Mali, 1235–1468
Songhai, 1464–1591
Kanem-Bornu, 1300–1500
Kongo, 1400–1700
Swahili cities, 1100–1500
Zimbabwe, 1000–1400
— Caravan and trade routes
• City

0   500   1,000 Miles
0 500 1,000 Kilometers

MAP WORK

Notice that most African kingdoms of this time period were formed along a body of water.

1. What river flowed near the Kongo kingdom?

2. Name two deserts in Africa. In which part of the continent is each located?

3. Along which body of water did the Swahili cities lie?

4. In which area would a traveler on a trade route have experienced very hot and dry weather?

KING SUNNI ALI

In 1464 Sunni Ali became the ruler of Songhai. He captured Timbuktu from the Berbers in 1468 and Jenne (je NAY) about 1475. Find them on the map on this page. Both cities are located along the Niger River, which runs mostly through the present-day country of Mali.

Ruling Songhai

At its peak Songhai stretched over 1,000 miles across West Africa. To maintain power, Sunni Ali enslaved the people he conquered. Many African rulers did this. In Africa criminals and prisoners of war were often enslaved. African rulers traded slaves with Arab sailors in the 1400s. Although they could be sold, African slaves were often given food and shelter in difficult times and even treated as family members rather than as property.

Sunni Ali's tolerance of different religions encouraged traders of gold, ivory, cloth, and salt to come to Songhai. Diversity brought a great variety of goods to the kingdom.

A man and some children travel in a caravan through the Sahara in the northern part of Nigeria.

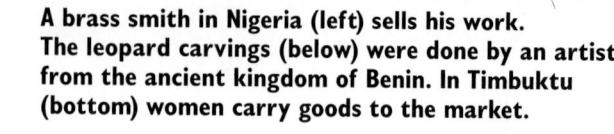

A brass smith in Nigeria (left) sells his work. The leopard carvings (below) were done by an artist from the ancient kingdom of Benin. In Timbuktu (bottom) women carry goods to the market.

THE SONGHAI KINGDOM

Sunni Ali ruled until his death in 1492. Songhai had become one of the largest kingdoms in West Africa during the 1400s. It controlled almost all trade coming south from the Sahara to the Niger River valley. It also controlled the valuable salt and gold mines of central Africa. The trading of salt and gold with people from North Africa helped make Songhai a wealthy kingdom.

Songhai's Cities

Gao, Timbuktu, and Jenne were the major centers of trade in Songhai. But each also had its own special character. Gao was a city full of skilled workers, craftworkers, and artists. The historian al-Kati called Gao an "artist's paradise." Leo Africanus, an Arab historian born in Spain, wrote that in Gao "it is a wonder to see . . . how costly and sumptuous [rich] all things be." Gold was so plentiful that miners sometimes had trouble finding a buyer.

Timbuktu, on the other hand, was a great cultural center. Scholars from far and wide studied astronomy, mathematics, music, and literature at Timbuktu's university. Arabic was the main language used by most people at the university. Leo Africanus was deeply impressed with the value the Songhai people placed on learning. Books, he reported, were "sold for more money than any other merchandise."

While Timbuktu was a place of learning, scholars at Jenne were known for their knowledge of medicine. Doctors there performed operations on the human eye. They also made the discovery that some mosquitoes carry malaria, a disease that causes fever and sweating. People can get malaria from the bite of these mosquitoes.

WHY IT MATTERS

In the 1400s Songhai, one of Africa's wealthy kingdoms, increased trade with other peoples in the Eastern Hemisphere. Over the centuries, traders and explorers from Europe came seeking Africa's gold, ivory, and other riches. Arab traders sailing off the east coast of Africa would bring the religion of Islam to the people there. Today people in many countries throughout Africa are Muslim.

DID YOU KNOW?

How did African gold miners trade without giving away the location of their secret gold mines?

A tenth-century Arab writer described how silent trading took place in Africa. Traders spread out goods such as salt and ivory near a stream. Then they left. Later gold miners crept in and put down bags filled with gold. Then they left also. The trading continued until both sides were satisfied with the amount the other group had left behind. Neither group of traders ever saw the other. In this way the gold miners did not fear that they would be kidnapped and forced to tell the location of their secret gold mines.

✓ Reviewing Facts and Ideas

MAIN IDEAS

- In the 1400s Arab traders coming from North Africa traveled in caravans to parts of Africa south of the Sahara Desert.

- Sunni Ali ruled the Songhai kingdom in West Africa from 1464 to 1492.

- Trade brought great wealth to Songhai. Artists and scholars in music, astronomy, mathematics, literature, and medicine flocked to its cities.

Traders measured amounts of gold with this brass warrior weight.

THINK ABOUT IT

1. Why might people have traveled in caravans when crossing the Sahara Desert?

2. What did Sunni Ali accomplish as king of Songhai?

3. **FOCUS** What were the main trade routes, and what parts of Africa did they connect?

4. **THINKING SKILL** *Compare* the features of Songhai's three major cities. How are they different?

5. **GEOGRAPHY** Look at the map on page 111. What geographic features might have made Songhai culture different from Berber culture in North Africa?

1292   1498 1500

Bodleian Library, Oxford University

EUROPE LOOKS OUTWARD

READ ALOUD

In 1292 Marco Polo started his trip back to Europe from Zaitun, a city in eastern China. After years of travel in Asia, he was still amazed by what he saw there. Later he wrote: "The noble and handsome city of Zaitun . . . has a port on the seacoast celebrated for . . . shipping, loaded with merchandise. . . . The quantity of pepper [available in the city] is so considerable [large], that what is carried . . . to supply the demand of the western parts of the world, is trifling [tiny] in comparison. . . . The country is delightful."

Focus Activity

READ TO LEARN
How did new technology affect European exploration of other parts of the world?

VOCABULARY
merchant
profit
Crusades
Renaissance
navigation
caravel

PEOPLE
Marco Polo
Johannes Gutenberg
Prince Henry
Bartholomeu Dias
Vasco da Gama

PLACES
Jerusalem
Portugal
Cape of Good Hope

THE BIG PICTURE

At the age of 17, Marco Polo began a great journey with his father and uncle, who were merchants in Italy. A merchant is a person who buys and sells goods to make money. The two elder Polos had traded in western Asia for years. In 1271, when they set off once again for Asia, they took Marco along. Marco Polo spent years in the court of China's powerful rulers. By the time he returned to Italy in 1295, Marco Polo knew more about Asia than anyone in Europe. Few believed his stories about a land rich in spices, silk, gold, and precious gems. Several years after his return, Marco Polo wrote a book describing his travels and China's vast wealth. Merchants and explorers began trading goods directly with Asia. Trade was one reason Europeans reached beyond their own borders in the 1400s.

114

TRADE AND RELIGION

Marco Polo also wrote about practical items such as cotton cloth, wool, and many types of grain. He found that people in Asia were already trading along river and sea routes. Europeans also wanted these goods.

Silks and Spices

In Europe people desired all kinds of goods, including luxury items. Luxuries are goods used for extra comfort. As you learned in Lesson 1, European demand for Asian silk was very high. Europeans also wanted spices such as pepper and cloves. These spices could be used to preserve food.

Europeans paid high prices for their goods. Every time pepper was traded along the long and difficult Silk Road, its price would rise. If a direct sea route to Asia could be found, the goods could be traded at a much lower cost. This would allow greater profits. *Profit* means the amount of money remaining after the costs of business have been paid.

The Crusades

Another reason that Europeans wanted to travel to Asia was to recapture the holy lands. This region,

sacred to many faiths, was now under Muslim control. In 1095 Pope Urban II, the leader of the Roman Catholic Church, called for Christians to conquer Jerusalem. The pope wanted to drive out the non-Christian people living there. Jerusalem was located in present-day Israel. Then and now it has been a holy city for the Jewish, Muslim, and Christian people. Pope Urban II's appeal began about 200 years of fighting called the Crusades. The Crusades were a series of wars fought by European Christians to gain back parts of Asia where Christianity had begun.

Europeans who fought in the Crusades brought back goods such as cotton and sugar. They also learned about advances in mathematics and science. Before the Crusades few Europeans had even left their own hometowns. Now they knew of exotic luxuries and new peoples with different ways.

El Escorial, Madrid

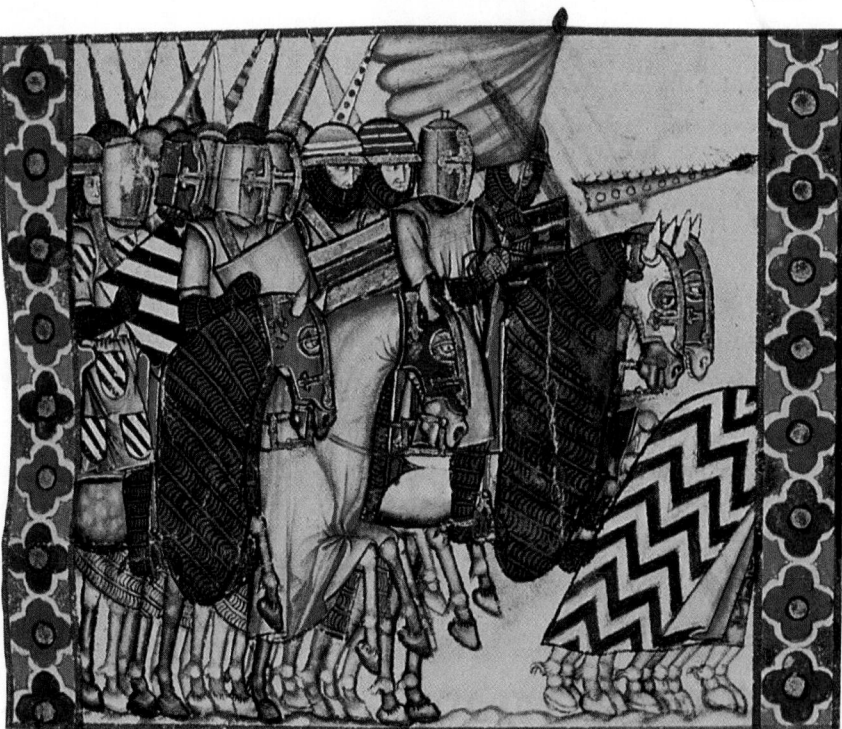

Europeans celebrated the Crusades with paintings such as these. Eastern spices such as those shown to the far left were prized by Europeans.

"REBIRTH" IN EUROPE

Inside its borders, Europe was changing a great deal. The Crusades had brought about a clash of cultures. Now that clash had led to a Renaissance (ren uh SAHNS). The Renaissance was a period when European culture and art flourished. The Renaissance began in Italy in the 1300s. This new way of thinking caught on throughout Europe in the 1400s and 1500s.

The Printing Press

Renaissance is a French word that means "rebirth." The Renaissance in Europe included a rebirth of learning from the past. Renaissance artists looked back to ancient Greek and Roman sculptures of the human figure. Using ideas from these artworks, they created masterpieces expressing the dignity of human experience.

In 1436 a world-changing event occurred. Johannes Gutenberg invented the printing press. This machine made copies of printed words and pictures. Before 1450 there were about 100,000 books in Europe—all hand copied. By 1500 there were close to 6 million printed books in Europe. The first book to be printed on the new printing press was the Bible, a version now called the Gutenberg Bible. Most of the early printed books were about religion, science, and law. Printed books helped to spread learning. They also made more people want to learn to read. As people learned more, they became more curious about the world around them.

The *Pietà* (left) was carved by the great Renaissance artist Michelangelo in 1498. The Gutenberg Bible (above) was one of the first books made using the new printing press.

NEW TECHNOLOGY

Europeans had many reasons for wanting to travel far across the seas. But they needed to improve their ships and their tools for navigation. Navigation is the science of determining a ship's sailing direction and location. Europeans were not the first people to study navigation. You have already read that the Chinese invented the magnetic compass. As contact with other cultures increased, Europeans learned from the Chinese, Greeks, and Arabs ways to help them travel farther. In the 1400s Europeans worked to improve what they knew about the compass and other navigational instruments.

New Ships for Stormy Seas

Explorers needed navigational tools in order to find their way, but how would they travel long distances in slow, heavy ships? In the 1440s the Europeans created a new kind of sailing ship called the caravel. The caravel was different from the earlier European ships. It used three small triangular sails instead of one large square sail. The caravel was lighter and easier to steer than earlier ships. It was built so that wooden planks fit together without overlapping. These new features allowed the caravel to sail more swiftly. The new ship also had storage space for carrying large amounts of goods. Only 12 to 25 sailors could work on the caravel at one time.

The pictures on this page show some of the improvements that led to faster, smoother sailing. By the 1600s large ships had square sails on all three masts and a triangular sail on the rear mast.

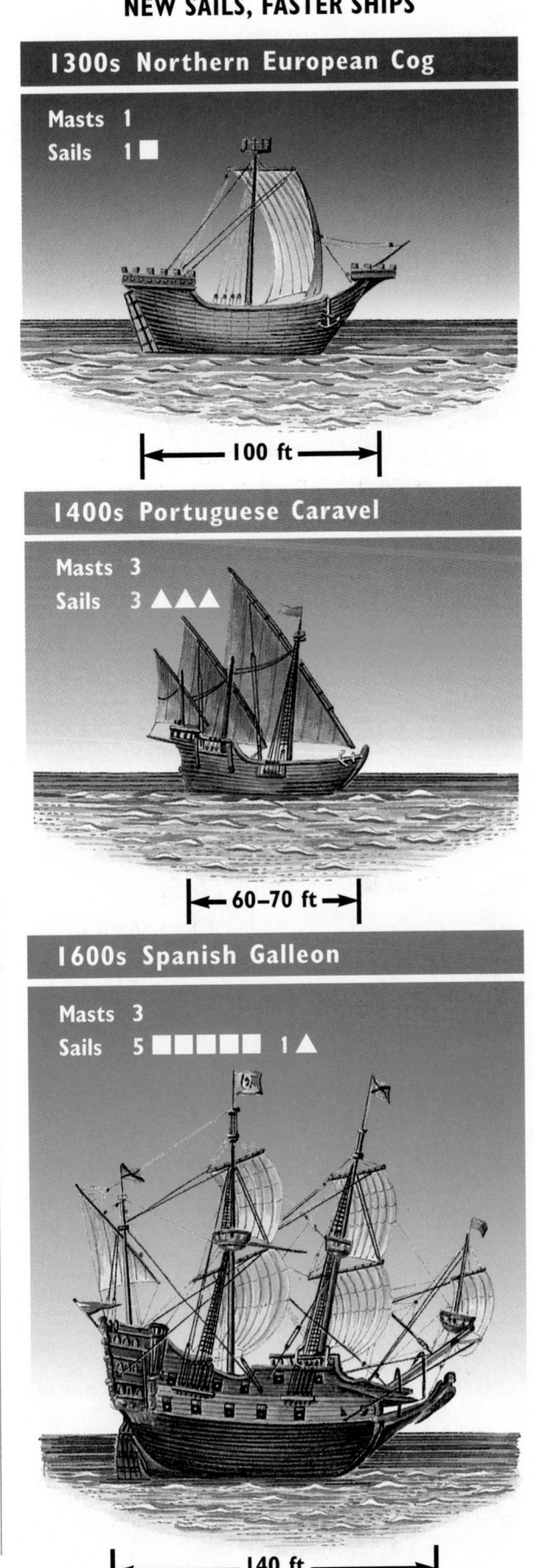

NEW SAILS, FASTER SHIPS

1300s Northern European Cog
Masts 1
Sails 1
⟵ 100 ft ⟶

1400s Portuguese Caravel
Masts 3
Sails 3
⟵ 60–70 ft ⟶

1600s Spanish Galleon
Masts 3
Sails 5   1
⟵ 140 ft ⟶

Infographic

Imagine explorers sailing the seas in the 1400s and coming upon lands and cultures unknown to them. Sailors could not determine their exact location at sea until the 1700s. During the 1400s, however, improvements in technology allowed sailors to navigate better from east to west. Study the Infographic to learn more about the kinds of technology explorers used to find their way.

COMPASS

Earth is like a huge magnet. The magnetic force around Earth causes the magnetic needle in a compass to point always to the North Pole. In Europe the compass was first mentioned in 1187. By the 1400s Europeans had improved the tool's accuracy and used it in every voyage.

ASTROLABE

The word *astrolabe* means "star finder." As early as the first century B.C., the Greeks used astrolabes to measure the angle of the sun and stars above the horizon. In the 1400s Europeans developed astrolabes that sailors used to estimate the time of day and the latitude where their ship was located.

Science Museum, London

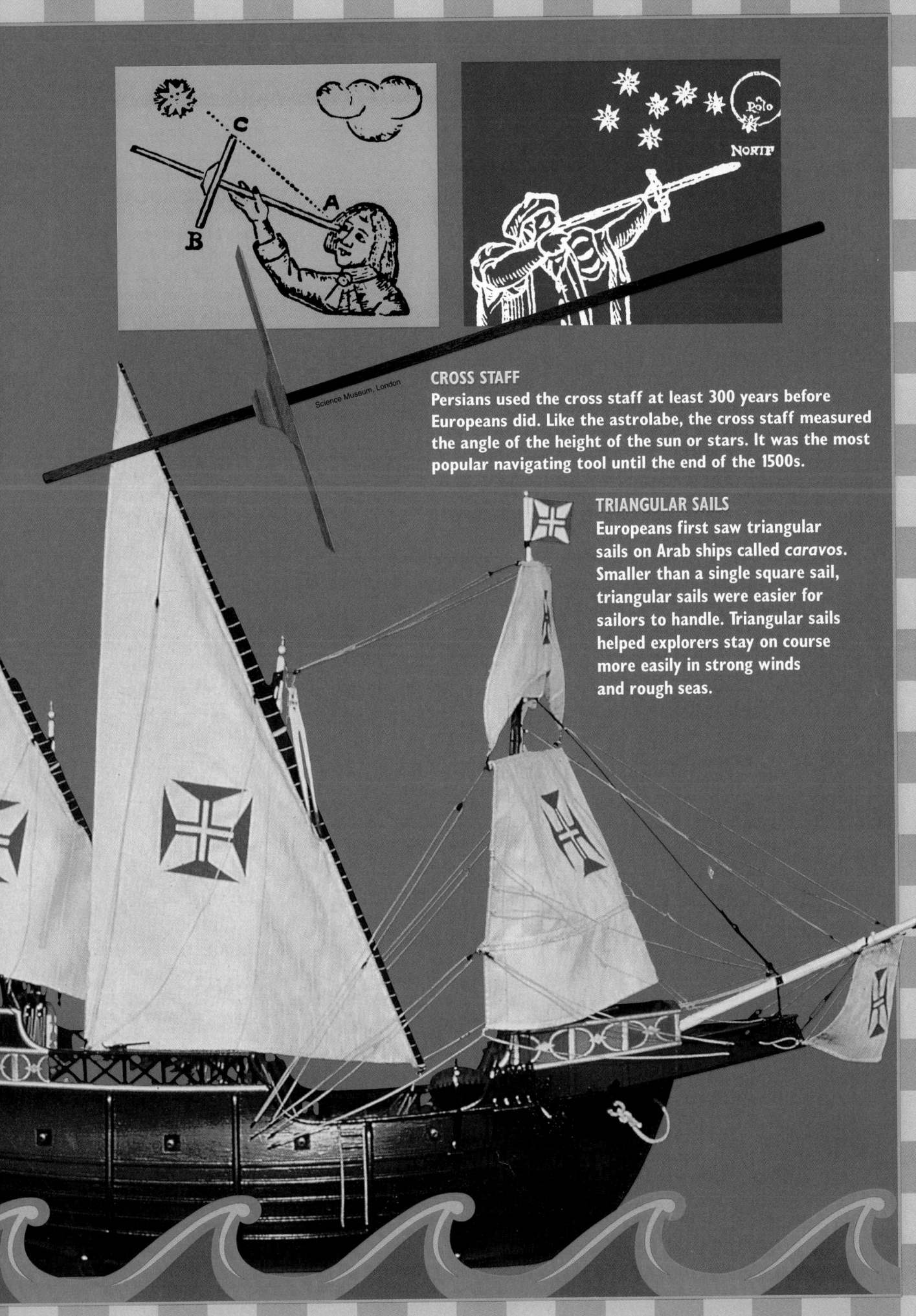

Science Museum, London

CROSS STAFF

Persians used the cross staff at least 300 years before Europeans did. Like the astrolabe, the cross staff measured the angle of the height of the sun or stars. It was the most popular navigating tool until the end of the 1500s.

TRIANGULAR SAILS

Europeans first saw triangular sails on Arab ships called *caravos*. Smaller than a single square sail, triangular sails were easier for sailors to handle. Triangular sails helped explorers stay on course more easily in strong winds and rough seas.

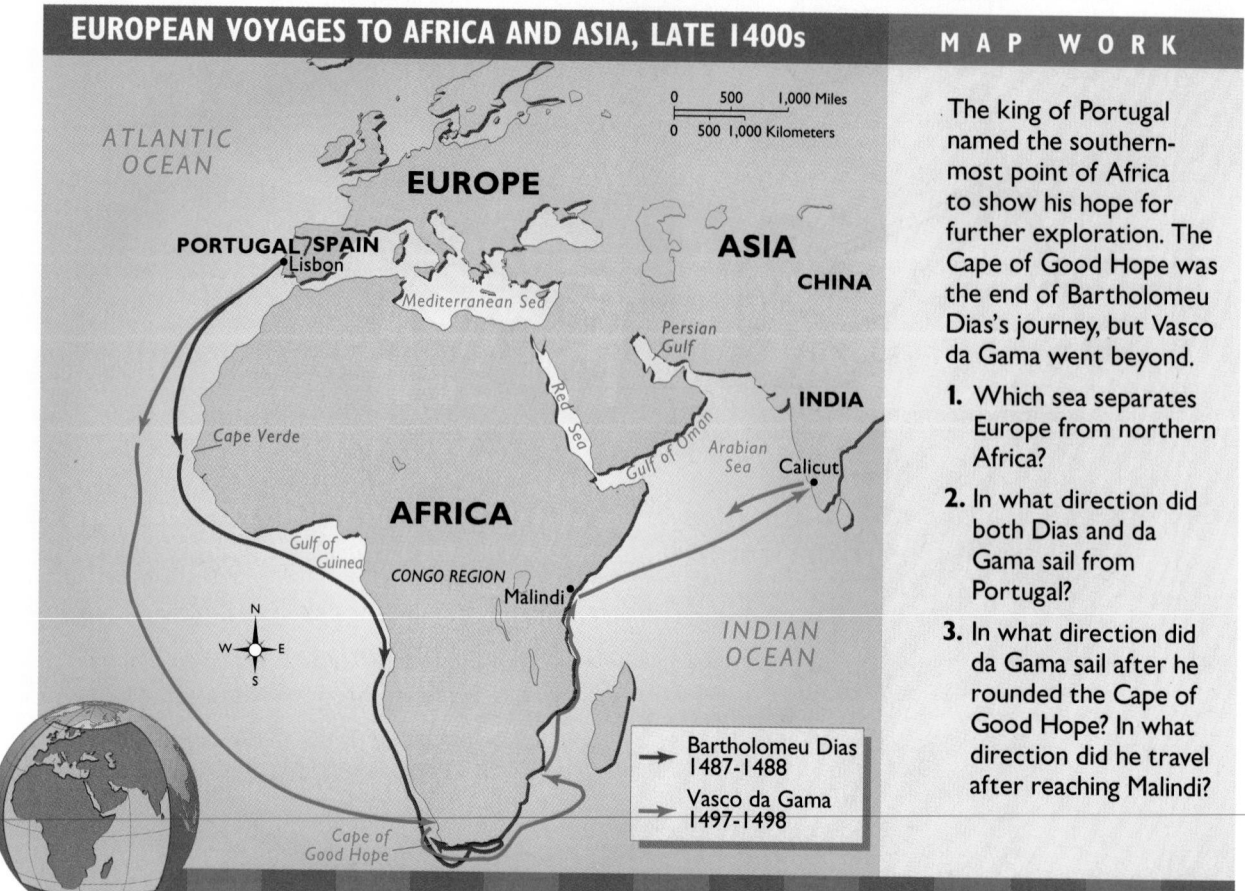

The king of Portugal named the southernmost point of Africa to show his hope for further exploration. The Cape of Good Hope was the end of Bartholomeu Dias's journey, but Vasco da Gama went beyond.

1. Which sea separates Europe from northern Africa?

2. In what direction did both Dias and da Gama sail from Portugal?

3. In what direction did da Gama sail after he rounded the Cape of Good Hope? In what direction did he travel after reaching Malindi?

PORTUGUESE EXPLORATION

It was dangerous and expensive for Europeans to travel directly on overland routes to Asia. The people who controlled most of these routes would not let Europeans pass. The Turks, for example, controlled Greece and the eastern Mediterranean. They wouldn't let Europeans travel through this area. To find a cheaper, safer route to Asia, Europeans looked to the sea. Study the map on this page. Was it possible to reach the shores of Asia by ship? As you just read in the Infographic, new technology in sailing was making exploration by sea possible.

Prince Henry

Prince Henry of Portugal, known as "Henry the Navigator," was very interested in new sailing technology.

He gathered the best mapmakers, astronomers, shipbuilders, and instrument makers around him. He also gave prizes to those people who invented better sailing instruments or who took risks at sea. The people Prince Henry surrounded himself with developed new sailing technology. Prince Henry insisted that all ocean pilots keep a "log," or detailed record, of everything that happened on their journeys. These logs helped mapmakers draw better and more accurate maps. He also ordered the first observatory in Europe to be built. An observatory is a place with tools for studying the moon, planets, and stars. The study of the stars and their locations would help guide sailors to their destinations. Prince Henry's aim was to discover a southern route to India to increase trade and spread Christianity.

Voyages to Far Away

Despite advances in navigation, sailors were afraid to sail into unknown seas. Many believed that the waters of the Atlantic boiled, with currents so strong that no ship could return.

In 1487 Bartholomeu Dias (bar TOH loh myoo DEE ush) set off from Portugal to explore the African coast and find an ocean route to India. In 1488 Dias sailed around the southern tip of Africa. This spot was later called the Cape of Good Hope.

In 1498 Vasco da Gama led four caravels past the Cape of Good Hope, across the Indian Ocean, and on to India. Da Gama's voyage opened up direct trade between Portugal and India. The map on page 120 shows the routes that Dias and da Gama sailed.

About thirty years after Prince Henry (below) died, the explorations he had hoped for began to take place. Henry himself may have used this map (right).

WHY IT MATTERS

As Europeans made contact with other cultures, they exchanged goods, ideas, and technologies with people they met. Advances in knowledge helped to increase exploration. In the next chapter you will read about Christopher Columbus, who sailed on two ships designed in 1440 by Prince Henry.

Reviewing Facts and Ideas

MAIN IDEAS

- Marco Polo's 1274 visit to China made Europeans interested in Asia.

- The desire to trade and to spread Christianity inspired Europeans to seek a direct sea route to Asia.

- Prince Henry of Portugal helped to improve ships and navigational tools. Portuguese explorers used new technology to reach Africa and Asia.

THINK ABOUT IT

1. Why were Europeans interested in finding a sea route to Asia?

2. What was the Renaissance?

3. **FOCUS** What kinds of new technology made European sea exploration successful?

4. **THINKING SKILL** Suppose you are a Portuguese sailor who has been blown off course on the way to eastern Africa. What steps could you take to solve the problem and reach your destination?

5. **GEOGRAPHY** Use the map on page 120 to find the land and sea routes from Europe to China. Which route, do you think, took longer to travel?

CHAPTER 4 REVIEW

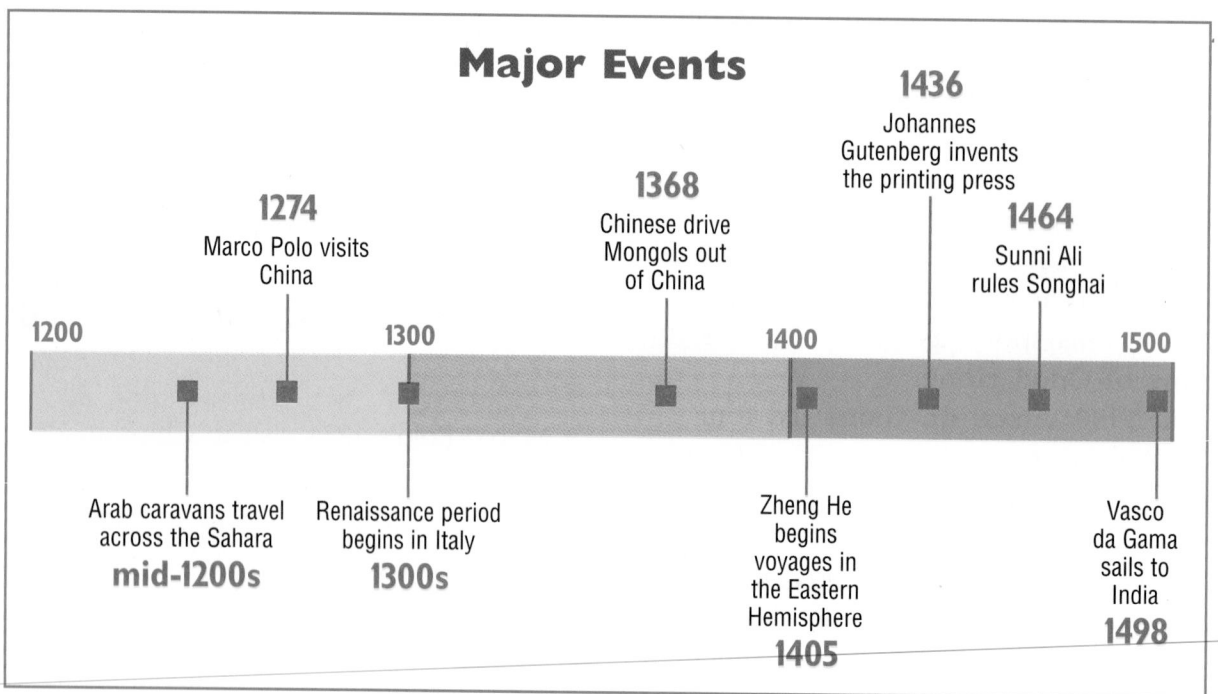

Major Events

1436
Johannes Gutenberg invents the printing press

1368
Chinese drive Mongols out of China

1274
Marco Polo visits China

1464
Sunni Ali rules Songhai

1200   1300   1400   1500

Arab caravans travel across the Sahara
mid-1200s

Renaissance period begins in Italy
1300s

Zheng He begins voyages in the Eastern Hemisphere
1405

Vasco da Gama sails to India
1498

THINKING ABOUT VOCABULARY

Number a sheet paper from 1 to 5. Beside each number write the word or term from the list below that best matches the description.

astrolabe   malaria
caravel   Renaissance
magnetic compass

1. a disease that causes fever and sweating and is transmitted by certain mosquitoes

2. a period of great cultural and artistic rebirth in Europe

3. an instrument used to find direction by measuring the angle of the sun and stars above the horizon

4. a kind of small, fast-sailing ship that can be steered easily

5. a navigational instrument with a needle whose end points to the North Pole

THINKING ABOUT FACTS

1. What was the main reason for increased contact between Asians, Africans, and Europeans during the 1400s?

2. What was the Silk Road?

3. To which places did Zheng He travel?

4. What navigational instrument was used by Zheng He?

5. What goods did Songhai trade to make it a wealthy kingdom?

6. Name the three great cities of Songhai, and tell what each was known for.

7. How did Johannes Gutenberg contribute to the Renaissance?

8. What was a caravel? Why was it important?

9. Who was "Henry the Navigator"? Why did people call him by that name?

10. In 1503 the price of pepper in Portugal was less than half of what it had been in the 1400s. What event on the time line led to this drop in price?

THINK AND WRITE

WRITING LOG ENTRIES

Suppose that you are on da Gama's trip to India in 1498. Write three log entries that describe 1) the beginning of your trip; 2) a day during the trip; 3) the day you reach India.

WRITING A PARAGRAPH OF COMPARISON AND CONTRAST

Reread the sections about the Silk Road and African trade routes. Write a paragraph in which you compare and contrast the lengths of different routes, the goods that were traded, and the people who traded them.

WRITING A REPORT

Research more information about the achievements of the kingdom of Songhai in art, education, and medicine. Write a brief report about these achievements.

APPLYING STUDY SKILLS

READING CIRCLE GRAPHS

To practice the skill of reading circle graphs, answer the questions below. Use the circle graph on page 109.

1. What do circle graphs show?
2. How many types of ships did China have in the early 1400s? What types were they?
3. What type of ship made up the greatest part of the Chinese fleet?
4. How many warships did the Chinese fleet have in the early 1400s?
5. How are circle graphs useful?

Summing Up the Chapter

Copy the main idea map on a separate sheet of paper. Review the chapter to find details that will complete the blank sections. After you have finished, use the map to write a few short paragraphs that answer the question "How would you describe each person in the chart?"

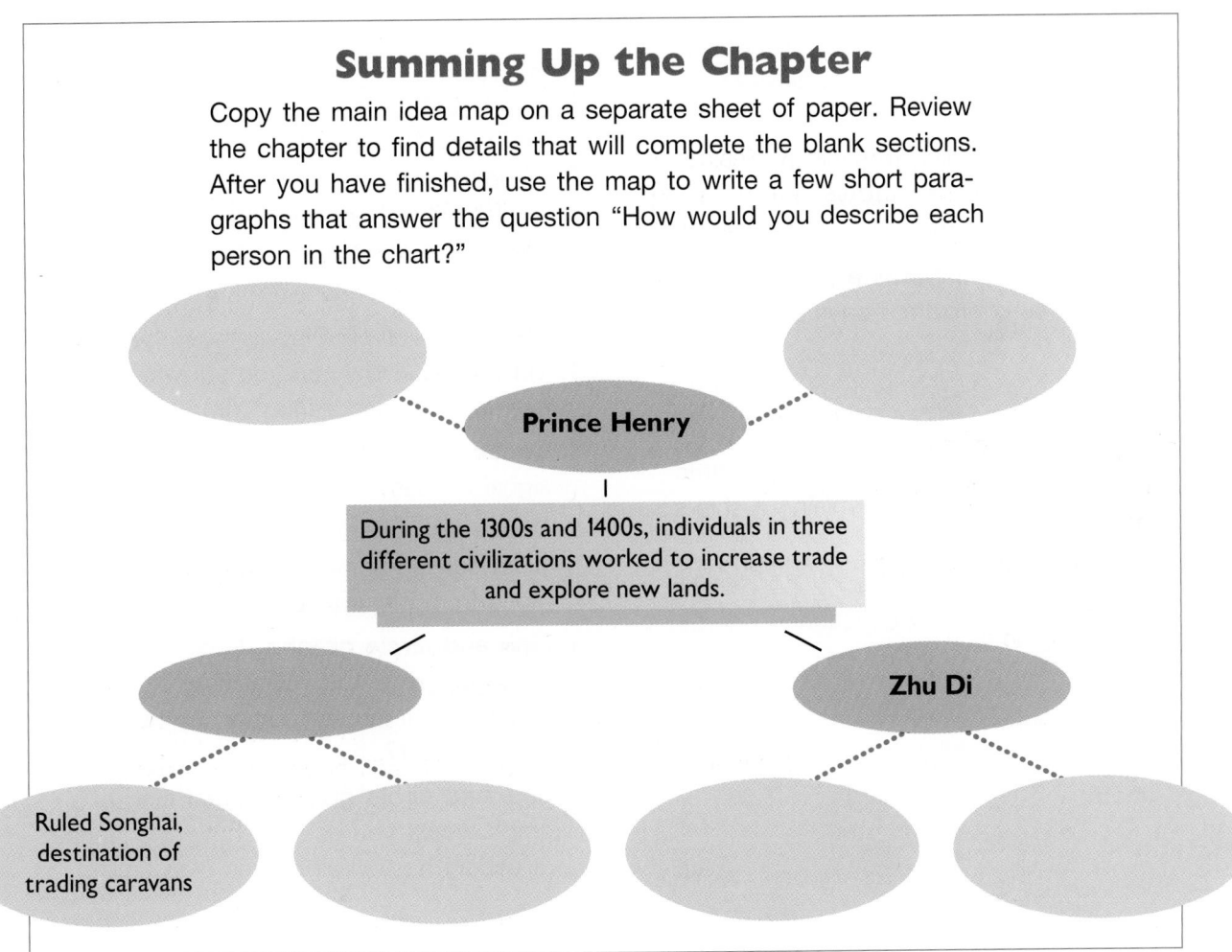

Prince Henry

During the 1300s and 1400s, individuals in three different civilizations worked to increase trade and explore new lands.

Zhu Di

Ruled Songhai, destination of trading caravans

UNIT 2 REVIEW

THINKING ABOUT VOCABULARY

A. On a separate sheet of paper, write sentences for the word pairs below.

1. caravan	malaria
2. Iroquois Confederacy	compromise
3. jerky	coup stick
4. magnetic compass	navigation
5. prairie	lodge
6. pueblo	kachina
7. specialize	archaeologist
8. technology	irrigation
9. teepee	travois
10. totem pole	wampum

B. Number a sheet of paper from 1 to 5. Beside each number write the term that best completes the sentence.

astrolabe   navigation
caravel   Renaissance
magnetic compass

1. If you were traveling through the desert and wanted to find your way by the stars, you might use a(n) _____.

2. The _____, which was a period of cultural and artistic growth, began in Italy in the 1300s.

3. In the 1400s a small, fast ship called the _____ was created.

4. Prince Henry had a nickname that came from the science of determining a ship's direction, or _____.

5. The Chinese invented the _____, which helps sailors find the directions of north and south.

THINK AND WRITE

WRITING A LETTER
Suppose that you are an archaeologist. What from this unit would you like to study? A Maya ruin? The remains of an Iroquois long-house? Write a letter to a fellow archaeologist in which you use facts to help describe your area of study.

WRITING A PARAGRAPH OF COMPARISON AND CONTRAST
In this unit you have read about many different people and their ways of life. Choose one group of people from Chapter 3 and another group from Chapter 4. Write a paragraph describing the similarities and differences in the way that they lived.

WRITING ABOUT PERSPECTIVES
What would Zheng He have thought about people traveling through outer space? How might Sunni Ali compare Gao to present-day Chicago? Write a description of an aspect of present-day life from the perspective of a person you read about in this unit.

BUILDING SKILLS

1. **Time lines** How can you tell which events happened earliest on a time line?

2. **Cause and effect** What clue words signal causes? Which signal effects?

3. **Cause and effect** Think about Chapter 3. What caused some native peoples to move from place to place to get food?

4. **Line and circle graphs** Look at the graph on page 109. What kind of ship made up the largest portion of the Chinese fleet?

5. **Line and circle graphs** What kind of graph would you use to show attendance at school basketball games over time?

YESTERDAY, TODAY & *TOMORROW*

Nampeyo, the woman who helped bring back the art of traditional Hopi pottery, at first tried to copy ancient designs. Then she created her own designs in the ancient style. What do you think of what Nampeyo did? Should she have continued copying designs? Why is remembering the past important for the future?

READING ON YOUR OWN

Here are some books you might find at the library to help you learn more.

MARCO POLO: HIS NOTEBOOK
by Susan L. Roth
This journal describes Marco Polo's journeys, as if in his own words.

CHILDREN OF THE LONGHOUSE
by Joseph Bruchac
A boy and his twin sister grow up in a Mohawk village in the 1400s.

PUEBLO BOY: GROWING UP IN TWO WORLDS
by Marcia Keegan
A young boy's life includes both ancient traditions and present-day activities.

UNIT REVIEW PROJECT

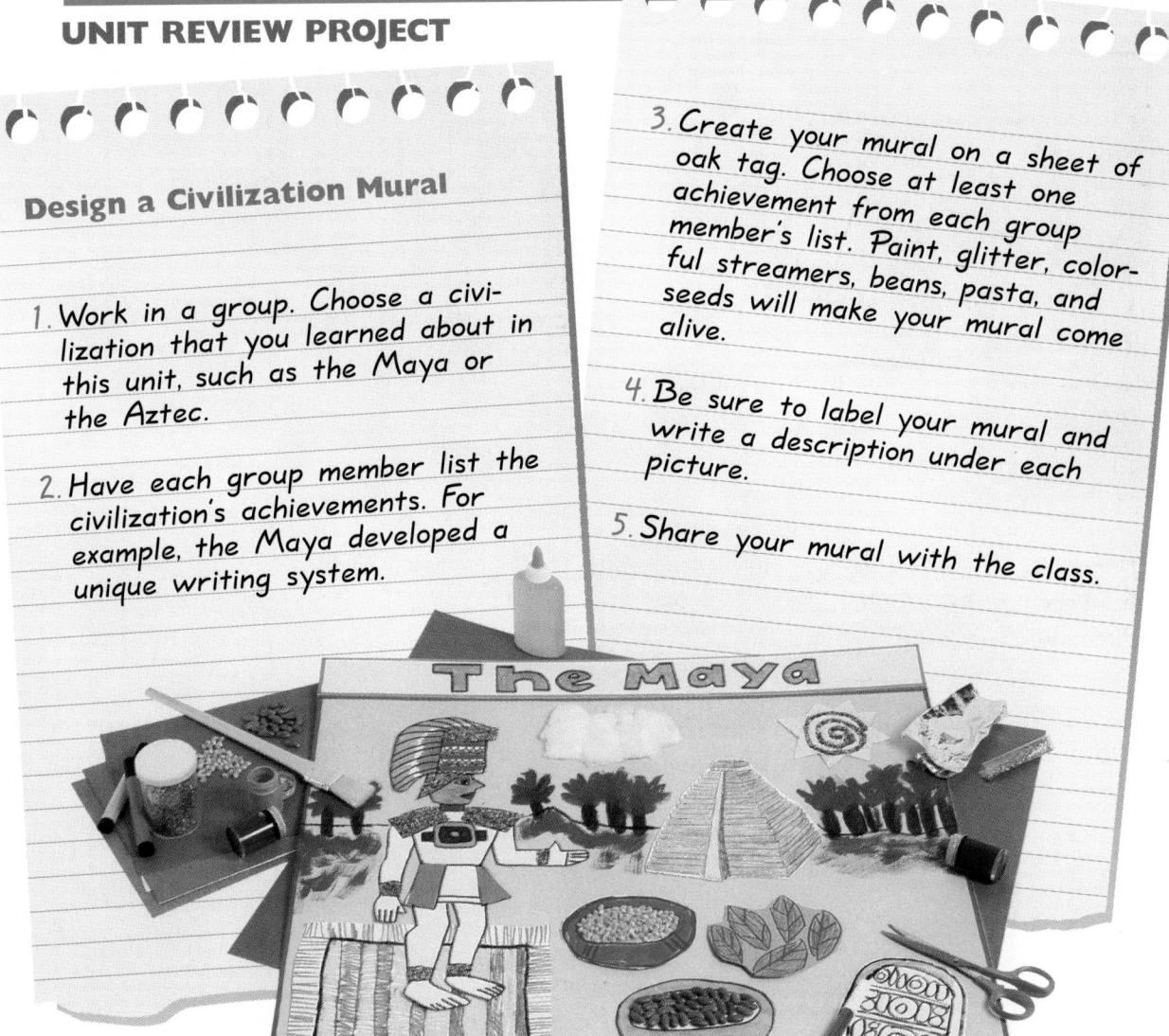

Design a Civilization Mural

1. Work in a group. Choose a civilization that you learned about in this unit, such as the Maya or the Aztec.

2. Have each group member list the civilization's achievements. For example, the Maya developed a unique writing system.

3. Create your mural on a sheet of oak tag. Choose at least one achievement from each group member's list. Paint, glitter, colorful streamers, beans, pasta, and seeds will make your mural come alive.

4. Be sure to label your mural and write a description under each picture.

5. Share your mural with the class.

The British Museum

AZTEC ATLATL;
TURQUOISE MASK;
COPY OF THE
HEADDRESS MOCTEZUMA
PROBABLY WORE

The British Museum

PILGRIM'S PEWTER
PLATTER; CHIEF
POWHATAN'S CLOAK

The Smithsonian Institution

The Ashmolean Museum

Contact and Exploration

"At dawn we saw people."

from the log of Christopher Columbus
See page 135.

National Museum, Mexico City

WHY DOES IT MATTER?

A European sea captain named Christopher Columbus wrote the words above about one of the most important meetings in history. On an October morning in 1492, Columbus arrived in the Americas and was greeted by the Taino people. The peoples of two hemispheres—east and west—were now in contact, and neither would ever again be the same.

This meeting started a chain of events that would reshape lives around the world. European ships raced westward across the Atlantic Ocean. Their captains claimed Native American lands and new riches for their countries. Many of the Native Americans lost their freedom and their lives. Before the end of the 1500s, a different America—not quite Indian, not quite European—was beginning to take shape.

CHRISTOPHER COLUMBUS;
SPANISH SOLDIER'S HELMET

Adventures
with
NATIONAL
GEOGRAPHIC

MAN OF MYSTERY

You sail across an uncharted sea and bump into a world unknown back home. You become one of the most famous men in history. Everyone remembers your face, right? Wrong. The only portraits we have of Columbus were painted after his death; the artists could only guess what he looked like. But we have a much better idea of what his ships looked like. Thanks to careful work by historians and shipbuilders, modern sailors now re-create Columbus's journey aboard reproductions of the *Niña*, the *Pinta*, and the *Santa María.*

GEOJOURNAL

Describe what you think it would be like to sail on one of the reconstructed ships.

Contact: East Meets West

THINKING ABOUT HISTORY AND GEOGRAPHY

The story of Chapter 5 begins in 1492, the year Christopher Columbus reached the Americas. Read the time line below. Notice the different ways in which Europeans interacted with the many peoples of the Americas. Europe brought many changes to the Western Hemisphere.

1492
BAHAMA ISLANDS

The Taino and Columbus meet

1519
TENOCHTITLÁN

Cortés is greeted by Moctezuma in Mexico

1542
SAN DIEGO

Cabrillo sails into the natural harbor of what is now San Diego

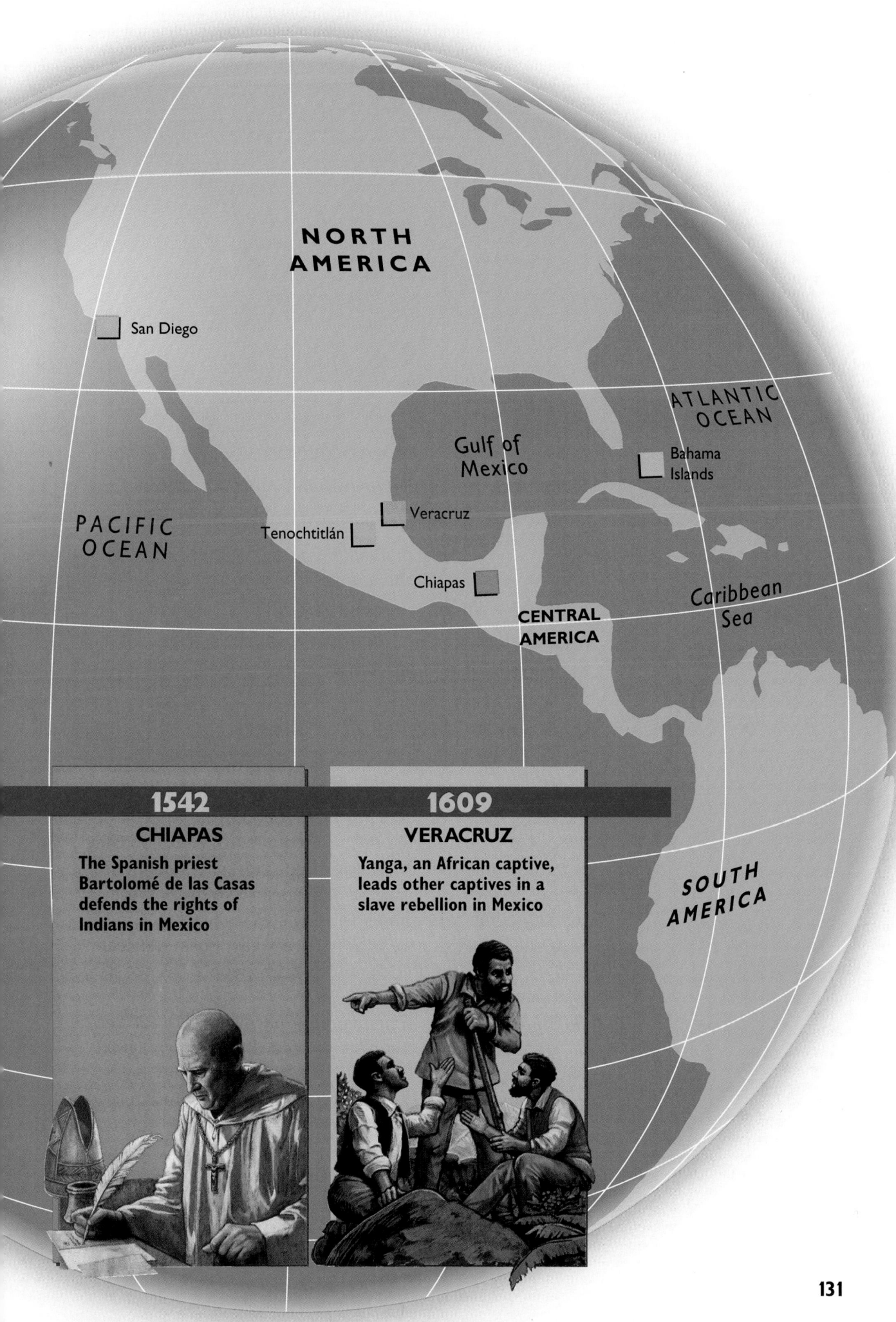

NORTH
AMERICA

San Diego

ATLANTIC
OCEAN

Gulf of
Mexico

Bahama
Islands

PACIFIC
OCEAN

Veracruz

Tenochtitlán

Chiapas

Caribbean
Sea

CENTRAL
AMERICA

SOUTH
AMERICA

1542

CHIAPAS

**The Spanish priest
Bartolomé de las Casas
defends the rights of
Indians in Mexico**

1609

VERACRUZ

**Yanga, an African captive,
leads other captives in a
slave rebellion in Mexico**

North Wind Picture Archives

COLUMBUS AND THE TAINO

Focus Activity

READ TO LEARN
How did the meeting of Columbus and the Taino people change the world?

VOCABULARY
expedition
colony
Columbian exchange

PEOPLE
Leif Ericson
Christopher Columbus
King Ferdinand
Queen Isabella

PLACES
Bahama Islands
San Salvador

READ ALOUD

October 12, 1492. On this fall morning, three ships landed near a small island in the Western Hemisphere. The island was home to the Taino (TĪ noh) people. A sea captain named Christopher Columbus, who was sailing under the flag of Spain, waded ashore. Neither the Taino nor Columbus knew that their meeting would change the world.

THE BIG PICTURE

As you have read, the 1400s was a time of human movement and exploration. In the Western Hemisphere the Aztec were conquering other peoples in what is today Central America and the country of Mexico. They were also building the magnificent city of Tenochtitlán. In the Eastern Hemisphere, European explorers were searching for new routes to Asia's rich markets. Chinese sailors were exploring Africa's east coast. African traders were exchanging goods with people from Asia and Europe.

The people of one hemisphere hardly knew that people of the other hemisphere existed. In about A.D. 1000 the Vikings, led by Leif Ericson, came from northern Europe and started a small settlement in northeastern Canada. They called it Vinland. Vinland did not survive long, and memory of it soon faded.

Nearly 500 years later the worlds of the West and the East came together again, this time forever.

THE TAINO

You read that in 1492 many peoples were living throughout the Americas. The Taino were one of the peoples living on islands in the Atlantic Ocean. Find the Taino's home islands on the map on this page.

On the morning of October 12, 1492, explorers from Spain arrived on one of the Taino's islands. We do not know what the Taino thought about their visitors. In fact, very little is known today about the Taino. Most of them died within a few decades. Some were killed by the Spanish, others by disease. What we do know about them comes from artifacts the Taino left behind.

The Taino Language

Some of the words from the Taino language, however, have survived. By studying these words and by examining artifacts from their lives, we can learn something about how the Taino lived.

One Taino word that we use in English is *canoe*. Like the Yurok and the Tlingit, the Taino made sturdy boats by hollowing out the centers of tree trunks with special tools. Since the Taino lived on islands, canoes were their lifelines. They used the boats to fish, to trade with their neighbors, and sometimes

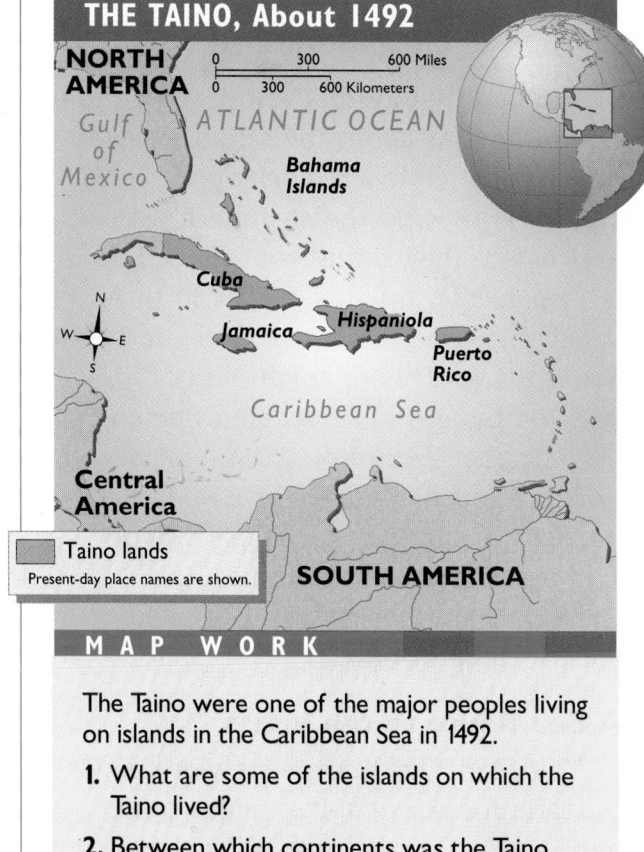

THE TAINO, About 1492

NORTH AMERICA
Gulf of Mexico
ATLANTIC OCEAN
Bahama Islands
Cuba
Jamaica
Hispaniola
Puerto Rico
Caribbean Sea
Central America
SOUTH AMERICA

0   300   600 Miles
0   300   600 Kilometers

Taino lands
Present-day place names are shown.

MAP WORK

The Taino were one of the major peoples living on islands in the Caribbean Sea in 1492.

1. What are some of the islands on which the Taino lived?

2. Between which continents was the Taino homeland located?

to make war. Some Taino canoes held over 30 people and could travel for hundreds of miles over the open sea.

Another word from the Taino language is *hamaca,* or *hammock.* This simple bed was perfect for the Taino's tropical climate. Made from woven cotton or other plant fibers, a hammock was easy to set up between two posts or trees. It did not take up much room in the Taino's small houses, and it was cool in the warm night air.

The Granger Collection

Taino hammocks might have looked like the one in this Spanish drawing (left). It is almost the same as hammocks used today.

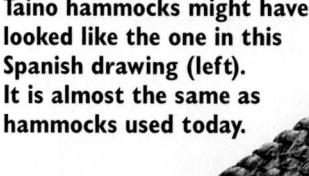

133

CHRISTOPHER COLUMBUS

Although we do not know what the Taino thought about the strangers who arrived that October morning in 1492, we do know who the strangers were and where they came from. They had left Spain two months earlier in three small ships: the *Niña,* the *Pinta,* and the *Santa María.* This Spanish expedition was led by an Italian seaman named Christopher Columbus. An expedition is a journey made for a special purpose. Columbus's purpose was to find a sea route to the Indies, the islands of Southeast Asia, by sailing west instead of east.

A Sea Route to the Indies

You read that Europeans were eager to trade for Asian spices, silks, gold, and jewels. But the cost of bringing Asian goods to Europe by land was very high. Columbus thought there might be a way to reach the Indies by sailing west across the Atlantic Ocean. Then the cost of trade with Asia would drop. In Europe the price of spices from Asia would become cheaper.

This painting of Christopher Columbus was done in the early 1500s. No one really knows what he looked like because none of his portraits were painted during his lifetime.

Museo Navale, Genoa

Links to MATHEMATICS

Columbus Miscalculates!

Why was Columbus confused about where he was in 1492?

One reason is that he thought Asia lay about 3,000 miles (4,827 km) west of Europe. Use the scale of miles on the world map in your Atlas to figure out how great this distance actually is.

How much farther would Columbus have had to sail to reach Asia if he had not run into the Americas first?

Money for Columbus's Expedition

For years Columbus tried to raise money for an expedition across the Atlantic. The king of Portugal listened to Columbus's plan and turned him down. The distance to Asia sailing west, the king said, was much greater than Columbus thought. Next, Columbus took his plan to King Ferdinand and Queen Isabella of Spain. He waited six years before the king and queen gave him money for his first expedition.

Reaching the Americas

On August 3, 1492, Columbus left Spain with three ships and sailed west into the unknown. Week after week dragged by with no sight of land. His men began to be afraid they would never see home again. To calm their fears, Columbus kept two records, or ship's logs. In the first he recorded the actual distance sailed each day. In the second he recorded a shorter distance. He showed his crew the second log so they would not know how far they really were from Spain.

Still the men worried, demanding that he turn back. Columbus asked them to wait two more days. If no land was sighted by then, he would return to Spain.

It was just enough time. Early on October 12, 1492, a lookout shouted, "¡Tierra! ¡Tierra!" (Land! Land!). Ahead a small island rose out of the blue sea.

Columbus was certain that he was near the coast of Asia. Instead, his ships had sailed to the Bahama Islands off the coast of North America.

Columbus Describes the Meeting

The next morning Columbus visited the island first seen the night before. In his log he wrote that he named the island San Salvador, or Holy Savior, and claimed it for Spain. Today many historians believe that Columbus may have landed at Watling Island. Read Columbus's description of his meeting with the Taino people. Believing he had reached the Indies, Columbus called these people "Indios," or Indians. What opinions did Columbus have about the Taino? How might the Taino have felt about Columbus?

One of the tools Christopher Columbus used to guide his ships across the Atlantic Ocean was an astrolabe (above). It helped him to find his latitude and to sail a straight course. The hawks' bells that Columbus wrote about in his log looked like these (right).

MANY VOICES
PRIMARY SOURCE

Excerpt from
The Log of Christopher Columbus,
presented to Queen Isabella in
1493.

At dawn we saw . . . people, and I went ashore in the ship's boat. . . .

*The people here call this island Guanahani (gwahn uh HAHN ee) in their language, and their speech is very **fluent**, although I do not understand any of it. They are friendly . . . people who [carry no weapons] except for small spears, and they have no iron. I showed one my sword, and through **ignorance** he grabbed it by the blade and cut himself. Their spears are made of wood, to which they attach a fish tooth at one end, or some other sharp thing.*

. . . They traded and gave everything they had with good will, but it seems to me that they have very little and are poor in everything. . . .

*This afternoon the people . . . came swimming to our ships and in boats made from one log. They brought us parrots, balls of cotton thread, spears, and many other things. . . . For these items we traded them little glass beads and **hawks' bells**.*

. . . They ought to make good and skilled servants, for they repeat very quickly whatever we say to them. . . . I will take six of them to Your Highnesses when I depart.

fluent: smooth and rapid
ignorance: not knowing
hawks' bells: small bells that are attached to the legs of a captive hawk

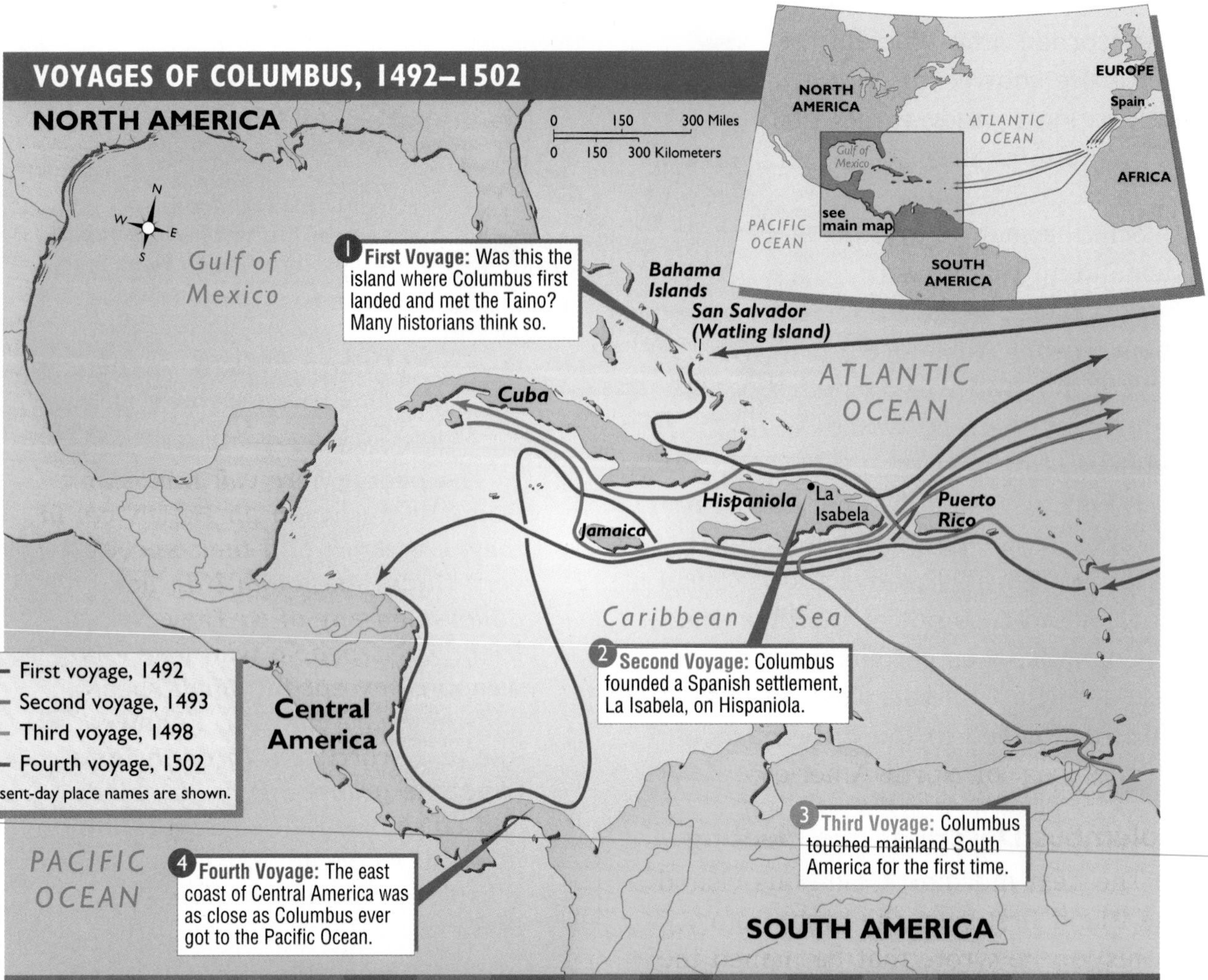

NORTH AMERICA

EUROPE
Spain

NORTH AMERICA

ATLANTIC OCEAN

Gulf of Mexico

PACIFIC OCEAN

see main map

AFRICA

SOUTH AMERICA

Gulf of Mexico

0   150   300 Miles
0   150   300 Kilometers

1 First Voyage: Was this the island where Columbus first landed and met the Taino? Many historians think so.

Bahama Islands

San Salvador (Watling Island)

ATLANTIC OCEAN

Cuba

Hispaniola • La Isabela

Puerto Rico

Jamaica

Caribbean Sea

2 Second Voyage: Columbus founded a Spanish settlement, La Isabela, on Hispaniola.

← First voyage, 1492
← Second voyage, 1493
← Third voyage, 1498
← Fourth voyage, 1502
Present-day place names are shown.

Central America

3 Third Voyage: Columbus touched mainland South America for the first time.

PACIFIC OCEAN

4 Fourth Voyage: The east coast of Central America was as close as Columbus ever got to the Pacific Ocean.

SOUTH AMERICA

MAP WORK

Many historians believe that Watling Island is where Columbus first landed in 1492. For this reason it was renamed San Salvador.

1. On which voyage did Columbus sail along the coast of Central America? South America?

2. Calculate the shortest distance between La Isabela and the coast of Central America.

3. What other parts of the Americas would you predict would be first colonized by the Spanish? Why?

THE COLUMBIAN EXCHANGE

From San Salvador, Columbus sailed south to islands in the Caribbean Sea. A few months later he returned to Spain with parrots and plants unknown in Europe. He had also kidnapped at least six Taino men and women and had taken them back to Spain. Columbus wrote in his journal that the Taino women would teach his people their language.

The Columbian exchange brought American plants to Europe, including chili peppers, tomatoes, and corn.

The Granger Collection

King Ferdinand and Queen Isabella asked Columbus to return to the Caribbean to found a colony. A colony is a settlement far away from the country that rules it.

Contact Brings Change

In 1493 Columbus set off on his second voyage. You can trace his route on the map on page 136. With him were 17 ships full of colonists. Most of the colonists were soldiers and nobles with little money who were seeking land and wealth. The colonists brought horses, cattle, and sheep as well as seeds and cuttings for growing wheat, onions, sugar, and other crops from the Eastern Hemisphere. The colonists also unknowingly carried germs that caused smallpox, measles, and other diseases.

Columbus also took more American plants and animals back to Spain. Colonists loaded ships with turkeys, corn, potatoes, tomatoes, chili peppers, pumpkins, beans, peanuts, avocados, tobacco, and pineapples and sent them back with him.

Historians call this movement of people, plants, animals, and germs across the Atlantic Ocean the Columbian exchange. Historians often use a form of Columbus's name to describe events that happened in the Americas before and after his arrival. Why do you think his name is used in this way?

The Columbian exchange affected the population of five continents. Some of these changes were welcome. American foods, for example, improved the diets of people in the Eastern Hemisphere. The new crops grew so well in the

The Columbian exchange brought wheat and horses to the Americas. However, as this drawing (above) by a Spanish priest shows, diseases such as smallpox brought a terrible death to many Indians.

Eastern Hemisphere that they increased food supplies in Europe, Africa, and Asia. As a result, the population of those continents increased rapidly.

For the peoples of the Americas, the Columbian exchange had both good and bad effects. The horse, as you have read, changed the lives of Native Americans on the Great Plains. But diseases that were brought unknowingly by Europeans killed millions of Caribbean Indians. The Indians had not built up any resistance to diseases from the Eastern Hemisphere.

137

THE SEEDS OF CHANGE

Among all of the items included in the Columbian exchange, five were especially important. Once planted on distant shores, they changed the lives of countless people. All five still have an effect on our lives today. For this reason they have been called the "seeds of change." Look at the chart on this page to find out what effect the seeds of change had on the peoples of the world.

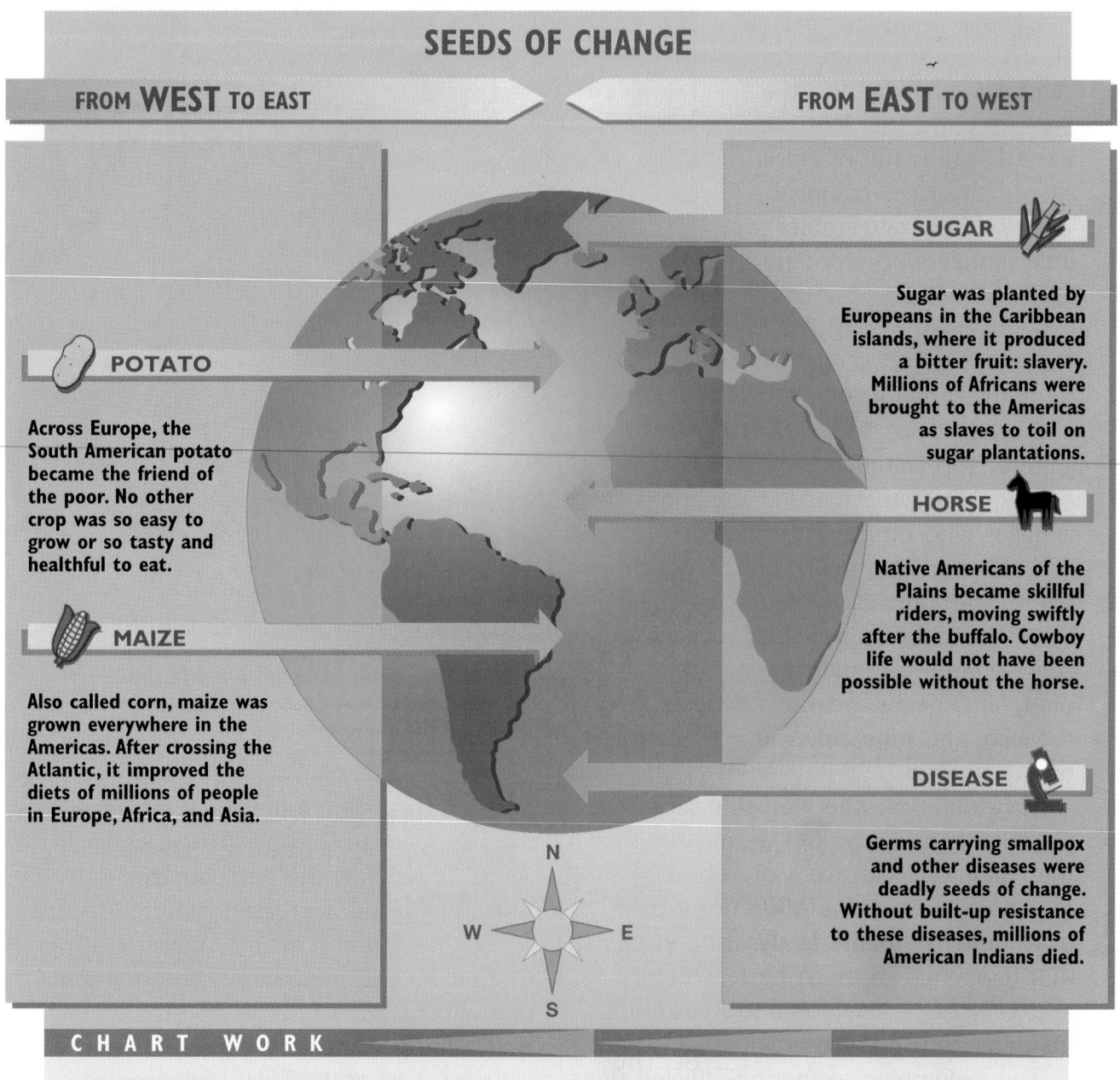

SEEDS OF CHANGE

FROM WEST TO EAST

FROM EAST TO WEST

SUGAR

Sugar was planted by Europeans in the Caribbean islands, where it produced a bitter fruit: slavery. Millions of Africans were brought to the Americas as slaves to toil on sugar plantations.

POTATO

Across Europe, the South American potato became the friend of the poor. No other crop was so easy to grow or so tasty and healthful to eat.

HORSE

Native Americans of the Plains became skillful riders, moving swiftly after the buffalo. Cowboy life would not have been possible without the horse.

MAIZE

Also called corn, maize was grown everywhere in the Americas. After crossing the Atlantic, it improved the diets of millions of people in Europe, Africa, and Asia.

DISEASE

Germs carrying smallpox and other diseases were deadly seeds of change. Without built-up resistance to these diseases, millions of American Indians died.

N
W · E
S

CHART WORK

The Columbian exchange was a major event in the worldwide movement of living things.

1. Which seeds of change moved from east to west? West to east?

2. Which seeds of change moved to the Caribbean? To Europe, Asia, and Africa?

3. How did the introduction of sugar affect the lives of Africans and Spanish colonists in the Americas?

4. Why did the Indians have no resistance to European diseases?

WHY IT MATTERS

When Christopher Columbus brought the Taino people back to Spain, Europeans thought that he had "discovered a new world." They began calling the Americas the "New World." But people had been living in both the Western Hemisphere and the Eastern Hemisphere for thousands of years. A new world did begin when Columbus and the Taino met. It was created by a joining of two old worlds, the Western and Eastern hemispheres.

Columbus was determined to cross the Atlantic Ocean despite great risks. He faced shipwreck, drowning, and storms. But he overcame them and showed Europe the way to the Americas. People from Spain and other European countries soon began sailing to the Americas. In the next lessons you will read about some of the people who followed Columbus. You will also find out what happened to the native peoples of the Americas.

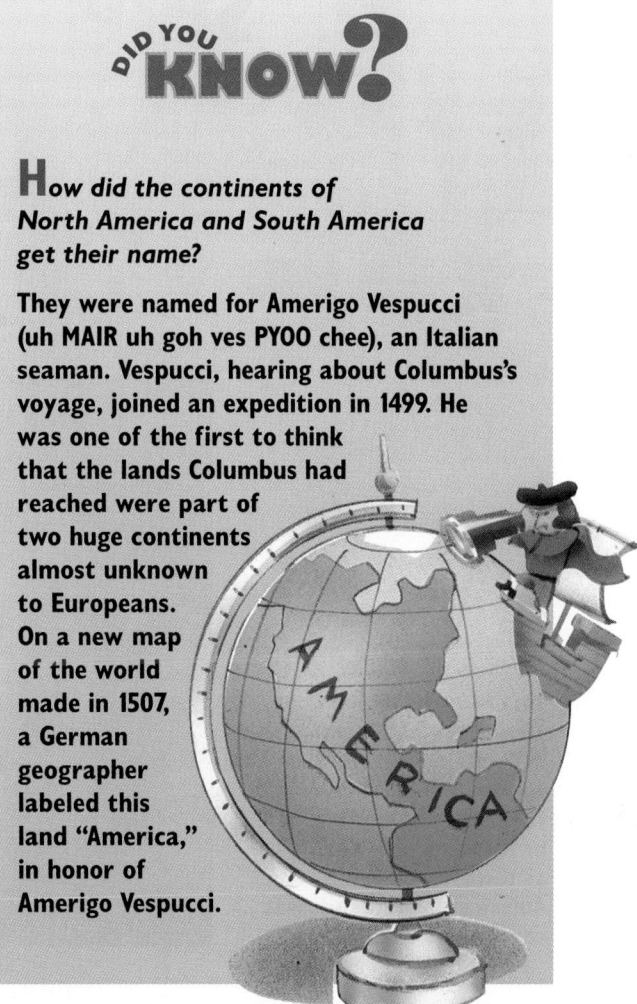

DID YOU KNOW?

How did the continents of North America and South America get their name?

They were named for Amerigo Vespucci (uh MAIR uh goh ves PYOO chee), an Italian seaman. Vespucci, hearing about Columbus's voyage, joined an expedition in 1499. He was one of the first to think that the lands Columbus had reached were part of two huge continents almost unknown to Europeans. On a new map of the world made in 1507, a German geographer labeled this land "America," in honor of Amerigo Vespucci.

Reviewing Facts and Ideas

MAIN IDEAS

- In both the Western and Eastern hemispheres people were moving into and exploring new lands.

- The Taino lived on many islands between the Caribbean Sea and the Atlantic Ocean. In 1492 Christopher Columbus left Spain to sail west across the Atlantic. After two months at sea his ships reached the Bahama Islands, one home of the Taino people.

- The Columbian exchange of people, plants, animals, and diseases changed life west and east of the Atlantic Ocean forever.

THINK ABOUT IT

1. What do we know about the Taino way of life, and how do we know it?

2. What was the Columbian exchange? Why is it called this?

3. **FOCUS** How did the meeting between the Taino and Christopher Columbus change the world?

4. **THINKING SKILL** Compare the effects of the Columbian exchange on the peoples of Europe, Africa, and the Americas.

5. **WRITE** Suppose you were there at the first meeting of Columbus and the Taino. Describe the meeting from the point of view of a Taino.

CITIZENSHIP VIEWPOINTS

This painting by John Vanderlyn, *The Landing of Columbus*, hangs in the Capitol Building in Washington, D.C. Painted in 1846, it shows Columbus as discoverer of the Americas, a view that was common at the time.

1492: WHAT DID THE SPANISH THINK ABOUT PAYING FOR COLUMBUS'S VOYAGE?

Christopher Columbus went to the royal court of Spain in 1486. He wanted to ask Queen Isabella and King Ferdinand to pay for a voyage of exploration. Columbus spread out his map of the world. He spoke of the riches and fame his voyage to Asia would bring to Spain. Knowing of Queen Isabella's deep Catholic faith, he also said his voyage would bring Christianity to distant parts of the world. The rulers listened carefully. When Columbus finished, they decided they needed to study seriously whether to support him.

Isabella and Ferdinand asked a committee of learned men to examine Columbus's proposal. The leader of this group was an official in the Catholic Church named Fernando de Talavera. The group became known as the Talavera Commission. As you will read in the third viewpoint, the commission advised the rulers to reject Columbus's project. Other advisers believed that Columbus offered the rulers an opportunity that should not be missed. Read and consider the three viewpoints. Then answer the questions that follow.

Three DIFFERENT Viewpoints

1 DON LUIS DE LA CERDA
Duke of Medina Celi
Excerpt from Letter to the Grand Cardinal of Spain, 1492

For some time I had staying in my house Christopher Columbus, who came here . . . to get the king's backing for a voyage in search of the Indies. Having three or four caravels available, I was minded to take a chance on this myself, . . . but it occurred to me that the Queen . . . might be interested, so I wrote to Her Highness about it. . . . She wrote back telling me to send Columbus to Her, so I did.

". . . take a chance on this myself . . ."

The Granger Collection

2 LUIS DE SANTANGEL
King Ferdinand's Treasurer and Chief Tax Collector
Excerpt adapted from Conversation recorded in
***The Life of Christopher Columbus by His Son Ferdinand* in the 1500s**

Queen Isabella has always shown bravery and firmness in matters of great importance. Why should she lack it now for a project of so little risk, yet which could be of such great service to God and the glory of Spain? Columbus's project is so important that if any other ruler agrees to do what Columbus offers the Queen, it will greatly hurt her Crown, disappoint her friends, and cause her enemies to criticize her.

". . . so little risk, yet which could be of such great service . . ."

The Granger Collection

3 FERNANDO DE TALAVERA
Excerpt from Report of the Talavera Commission,
made public about 1490

We can find no justification [*reason*] for their Highnesses' supporting a project that rests on extremely weak foundations and appears impossible to translate into reality to any person with any knowledge, however modest, of these questions.

". . . appears impossible . . ."

BUILDING CITIZENSHIP

1. What was the viewpoint of each person? How did each support his opinion?

2. In what ways did some of the viewpoints agree? In what cases did they disagree?

3. What other viewpoints might people have had on this issue? What are some cases in which the issue of paying for explorations might be discussed today?

SHARING VIEWPOINTS

Discuss why groups such as the Talavera Commission might have argued against supporting Columbus while others might have favored helping him. Write a letter to King Ferdinand and Queen Isabella describing the risks and possible rewards of paying for Columbus's voyage.

National Geographic Society

EXPLORERS AND CONQUERORS

READ ALOUD

On a bright November day in 1519, two men faced each other at the entrance to Tenochtitlán, one of the world's great cities. Moctezuma (mahk tuh ZOO muh) II, the ruler of Mexico's mighty Aztec empire, looked into the eyes of Hernán Cortés, the leader of a small Spanish army. Their meeting was the painful joining of two civilizations.

THE BIG PICTURE

In the 20 years after Christopher Columbus's meeting with the Taino, Spain claimed most of the islands in the Caribbean Sea. Its soldiers, who hoped to find gold and other riches, conquered new lands for Spain. They were known as conquistadors (kahn KEES tuh dohrz), from a Spanish word that means "to conquer."

During this time, Spanish and Portuguese explorers also began traveling to other parts of the Americas. The conquistadors claimed lands throughout present-day Mexico and explored what is now the southeastern United States. You can locate the areas of Spanish exploration on the Infographic on pages 146–147. A Portuguese explorer named Pedro Álvares Cabral (AHL vahr ez kuh BRAHL) reached South America and landed at present-day Brazil in 1500.

In the 1400s, as you have read, Spain and Portugal led the way for European exploration of Asia and Africa. Now, in the 1500s, Spain was beginning to take the lead in exploring the Americas.

Focus Activity

READ TO LEARN
How did the battle for Tenochtitlán change the Americas?

VOCABULARY
conquistador

PEOPLE
Pedro Álvares Cabral
Moctezuma II
Hernán Cortés
Doña Marina
Cuauhtémoc
Vasco Núñez de Balboa
Álvar Núñez
  Cabeza de Vaca
Francisco Pizarro
Hernando De Soto
Juan Ponce de León
Ferdinand Magellan

PLACES
Tenochtitlán
New Spain

MOCTEZUMA'S AZTEC EMPIRE

Tenochtitlán had been the capital of the Aztec empire since the early 1300s. Under Moctezuma I, who ruled from 1440 to 1468, the Aztec conquered their neighbors to the south and east. Under the following three rulers, the empire expanded to include most of present-day Mexico.

Ruling an Empire

In 1502 the great-grandson of Moctezuma I was chosen emperor. A strong leader in his own right, he was called Moctezuma II, or Moctezuma the Younger. In Aztec tradition the title of emperor was not passed on from father to son to grandson. Nobles chose from the royal families one male thought to be best suited for the job.

Early in his rule Moctezuma faced challenges to his power. People inside the empire were beginning to rebel against those in control. They no longer wanted to pay tribute or give up prisoners to the Aztec.

Moctezuma also had enemies outside his empire. The Aztec were bitterly hated by the Tlaxcalan people, who lived less than 100 miles east of Tenochtitlán. For years the Tlaxcalan had been fighting to keep from being conquered by their powerful neighbors. Despite these problems, however, Moctezuma was still firmly in control of his empire.

News of Strangers

Early in 1519 over 500 Spanish troops landed on the east coast of Mexico. Rumors of gold had brought them there. From the moment the Spaniards landed, Aztec messengers began reporting their movements to Moctezuma.

Moctezuma sent the Spaniards two disks of solid gold and silver. He did not know whether they were enemies to be feared or friends to be respected. In either case he hoped that his gifts would persuade the Spaniards to return home. This was a mistake. Moctezuma did not know the men were looking for gold. Nothing would keep the Spanish from trying to reach Tenochtitlán now.

Moctezuma probably wore a headdress like this one made from feathers of the quetzal bird. The Spanish melted down Aztec artworks like the gold mask and made them into coins.

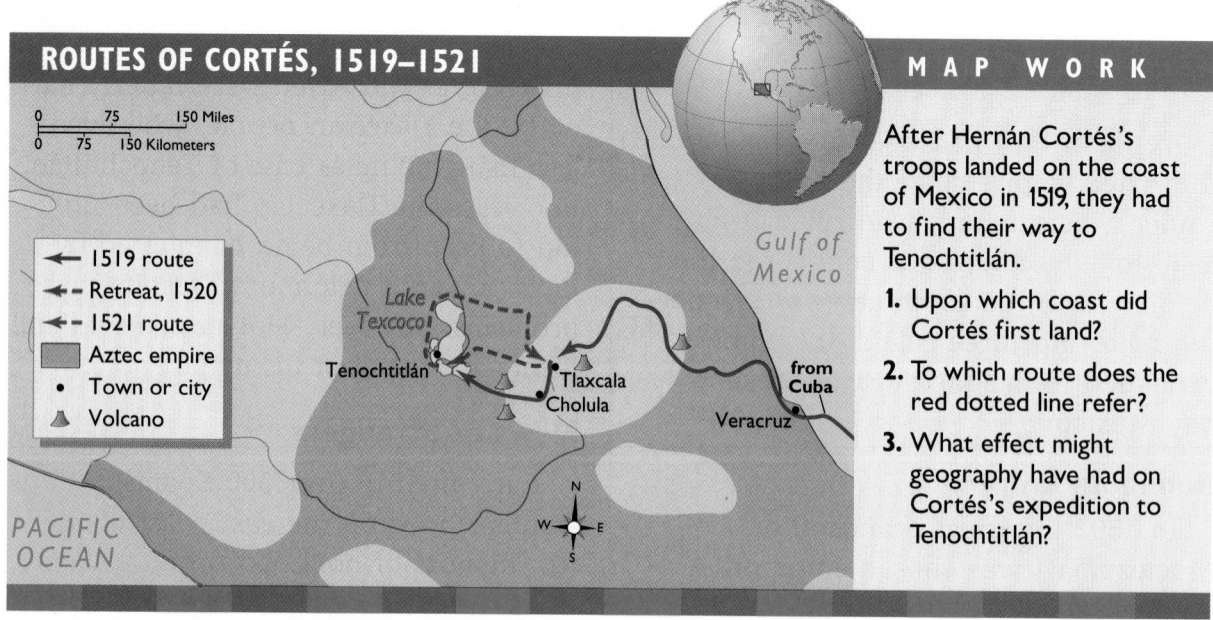

0 75 150 Miles
0 75 150 Kilometers

← 1519 route
←- Retreat, 1520
←-- 1521 route
▨ Aztec empire
• Town or city
▲ Volcano

Gulf of Mexico

Lake Texcoco
Tenochtitlán
Tlaxcala
Cholula
Veracruz
from Cuba

PACIFIC OCEAN

After Hernán Cortés's troops landed on the coast of Mexico in 1519, they had to find their way to Tenochtitlán.

1. Upon which coast did Cortés first land?

2. To which route does the red dotted line refer?

3. What effect might geography have had on Cortés's expedition to Tenochtitlán?

CORTÉS DEFEATS THE EMPIRE

At the age of 19, Hernán Cortés came from Spain to the Caribbean island of Cuba. Cortés was given land to farm. But he had other ideas. "I don't want land," he wrote. "I came for gold." When the governor of Cuba asked Cortés to lead an expedition to Mexico, he jumped at the chance.

Galleria degli Uffizi, Florence

Hernán Cortés (above) and his men probably wore armor similar to this one.

Heading for Tenochtitlán

Cortés came upon several Indian cities as he made his way inland to Tenochtitlán. You can trace his route on the map above. The people of these cities were bitter enemies of the Aztec. Before Cortés arrived in Veracruz, he met an Indian woman who was called Doña Marina (DOHN yah mah REE nah) by the Spanish and Malinche (mah LEEN che) by the Indians.

Doña Marina was the daughter of a chief but had been sold as a captive after her father died. She knew several languages, including those of the Aztec and Maya. Doña Marina helped Cortés convince many Indians to join him. Soon his small army grew into a force big enough to challenge the Aztec.

When the two leaders finally met in 1519, Moctezuma welcomed Cortés to Tenochtitlán. The Spaniards could hardly believe their eyes when they first saw the city. One of them wrote:

We were amazed because of the huge towers, temples, and buildings. . . . We were seeing things which had never been heard of or seen before, nor even dreamed about.

For reasons that are not understood today, Moctezuma did not resist the Spaniards. Cortés took Moctezuma prisoner and gained control of the city. Then the Aztec fought back. In a furious attack they drove the Spaniards out of the city. Moctezuma was killed during the fighting.

Tenochtitlán Falls

Cortés returned to Tenochtitlán in 1521 with more soldiers. His goal was to recapture the city. A young man named Cuauhtémoc (kwah TAY mahk) was now ruler of the Aztec. He led his warriors in the battle for Tenochtitlán. But again Cortés was helped by the Aztec's enemies. The Spaniards and their Indian allies blocked all the entrances to the city. No food or water could be taken inside. An Aztec who survived this battle later reported that

Many died of hunger. . . . The people ate anything—lizards, barn swallows, corn leaves, saltgrass. They gnawed . . . leather and buckskin, cooked or toasted; or . . . adobe bricks. Never had such suffering been seen.

After 75 days Tenochtitlán fell to Cortés. Cuauhtémoc was captured and later killed. Then the Spaniards and their Indian allies destroyed the Aztec temples and burned their sacred books. The Spaniards had conquered a great city. The fall of Tenochtitlán allowed the creation of the Spanish empire in the Americas. This colony would be called New Spain.

How the Spanish Won

How was a small group of Spaniards fighting in a strange land able to conquer an empire? One important reason was the thousands of Indian supporters who fought with the Spanish. A second reason was an outbreak of smallpox that killed many Aztec.

Yet another reason for the success of the Spaniards was their deadlier weapons. The Aztec fought with wooden spears and arrows tipped with stone points. They wore armor made of tightly woven cotton. Their weapons were no match for Spanish steel and gunpowder. Study the drawing below. What were some differences between Spanish and Aztec weapons?

Biblioteca Nacional, Madrid

Drawing by an unknown artist, created during the late 1500s.

As the drawing of the battle for Tenochtitlán shows, the Spanish musket, or rifle, was one of the main weapons used by the Spanish.

145

Infographic
Spanish Explorers and Conquistadors

After Columbus's voyage in 1492, Spanish explorers and conquistadors sailed across the Atlantic Ocean. Some came in search of routes to Asia. Others came to seek gold or to achieve glory for God. Study the Infographic to learn about the expeditions of the Spanish explorers and conquistadors in the Americas.

1528–1536

ÁLVAR NÚÑEZ CABEZA DE VACA

Shipwrecked during an expedition from Cuba, he reached what is now Texas in 1528. He became the first Spaniard to explore Texas.

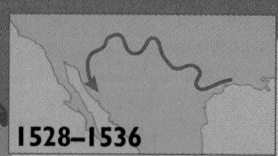

1540–1542

FRANCISCO CORONADO

With a small group, he began to explore the American Southwest in search of the rumored Seven Cities of Gold.

HERNÁN CORTÉS

He led an expedition from Cuba to Mexico that ended with the conquest of Moctezuma and the Aztec.

1519–1521

1513

VASCO NÚÑEZ DE BALBOA

He led an expedition across Central America to what later was named the Pacific Ocean.

FRANCISCO PIZARRO

His forces conquered the Inca empire ruled by Atahualpa.

1531–1533

146

HERNANDO DE SOTO

He led an expedition through the American Southeast in search of gold. He became the first European to see the Mississippi River.

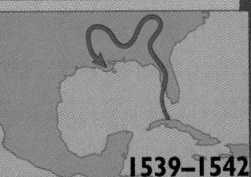

1539–1542

JUAN PONCE DE LEÓN

Stories of a fountain of youth led him to sail north from Puerto Rico. He reached a land he called Florida.

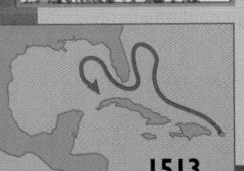

1513

CHRISTOPHER COLUMBUS

Sailing under the flag of Spain, he reached a group of islands in the Atlantic Ocean while seeking a route to Asia.

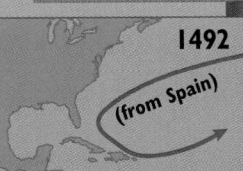

1492

(from Spain)

FERDINAND MAGELLAN

Sailing for the Spanish, he set out to find a route to the Indies by sailing around the southern tip of South America. Although he was killed, some of his crew returned to Spain, completing the first known voyage around the world.

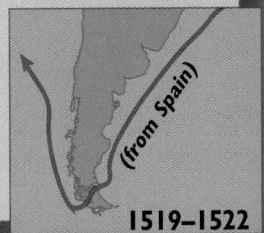

(from Spain)

1519–1522

WHY IT MATTERS

By the middle of the 1500s, the peoples of the Western and Eastern hemispheres were bonded together in many ways. Europeans explored and conquered much of the Americas. They forever changed the land and the peoples they met. But they, too, were changed. The king of Spain became the ruler of New Spain. And Tenochtitlán became known as Mexico City. As you will read, from all of these changes a very different culture was born.

✔️ Reviewing Facts and Ideas

MAIN IDEAS

- Other European explorers and conquerors soon followed Columbus to the Americas.

- By the 1500s the Aztec had built a large and powerful empire in Mexico.

- In 1521 the conquistador Hernán Cortés conquered the Aztec empire.

- After the Aztec's defeat, Mexico became part of what was called New Spain.

THINK ABOUT IT

1. In what way did Doña Marina help Hernán Cortés?

2. How did Moctezuma and Cortés treat each other when they met? What other options might Moctezuma have chosen?

3. **FOCUS** How did the fall of Tenochtitlán change the Americas?

4. **THINKING SKILL** _Predict_ how Mexico might be different today if Moctezuma had defeated Cortés.

5. **GEOGRAPHY** Use the map on page 144 to evaluate the advantages and disadvantages of other routes Cortés might have taken to Tenochtitlán.

GEOGRAPHYSKILLS

Reading Historical Maps

VOCABULARY
historical map

WHY THE SKILL MATTERS

Exploration in the 1500s allowed European countries to expand their empires. As you read earlier, the Portuguese explorer Pedro Álvares Cabral reached South America in 1500. His journey would help to change the history of the Western Hemisphere.

One way to study an historical event, such as Cabral's voyage, is to use an historical map. Historical maps show information about past events. For example, the map below traces a voyage that took place about 500 years ago. Use the Helping Yourself box on the next page as a guide for reading historical maps.

USING HISTORICAL MAPS

Study the map on this page. What is its title? What clues help you to know that it is an historical map?

On March 11, 1500, Cabral set sail. His main goal was to find a direct sea route to India. Cabral had received directions for his voyage from Vasco da Gama, whom you read about in Chapter 4.

Cabral's ships went much farther west than he had planned to go. Scholars disagree about exactly why this happened. One of the 13 ships soon became lost, and Cabral may have been trying to find it. Another possibility is that winds or a strong ocean current carried the ships off course.

On April 21, 1500, Cabral's men saw land. Two days later the crew anchored the ships and went ashore. Look at the map. On which continent did Cabral land?

Cabral named this land Santa Cruz, which means Holy Cross. Cabral then recrossed the Atlantic Ocean and continued his voyage to India. He returned to Portugal in July 1501.

The land that Cabral explored later became a colony of Portugal. This eventually became the country of Brazil, where Portuguese is still spoken today.

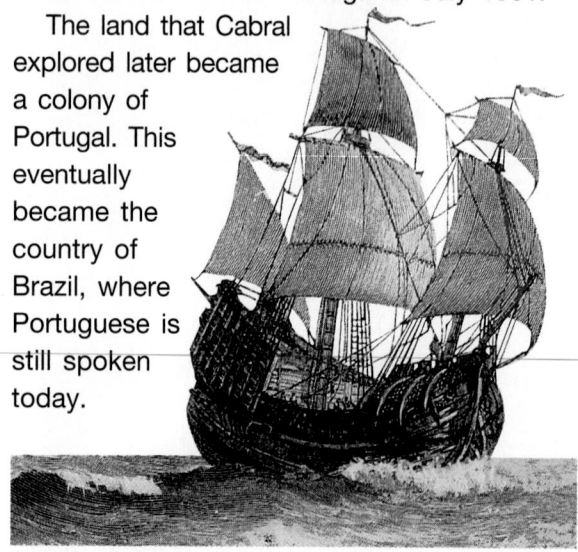

North Wind Picture Archives

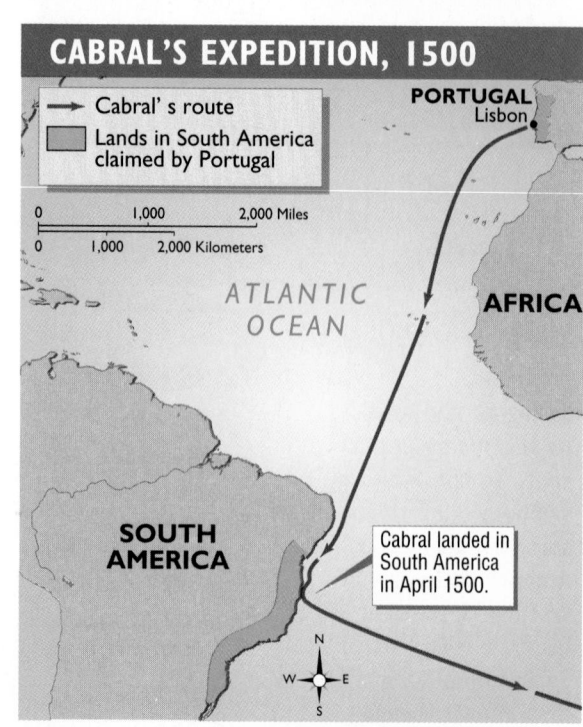

CABRAL'S EXPEDITION, 1500

→ Cabral's route

▢ Lands in South America claimed by Portugal

0   1,000   2,000 Miles
0   1,000   2,000 Kilometers

PORTUGAL
Lisbon

ATLANTIC OCEAN

AFRICA

SOUTH AMERICA

Cabral landed in South America in April 1500.

TRYING THE SKILL

You have practiced reading an historical map about Cabral's journey. Now try reading a map about an important voyage made by another Portuguese explorer Ferdinand Magellan who was sailing for Spain.

In September 1519, Magellan left Spain with five ships. He hoped to find a sea route from Europe to Asia that was shorter than the route around Africa.

At the southern tip of South America, Magellan reached a strait, or narrow water-way. Find this strait on the map. He sailed for four more months before he reached the Philippine Islands. Magellan thought his expedition had failed. He did not find a shorter route to Asia. However, he did prove

HELPING Yourself

● An **historical map shows places or events from the past.**

● **Study the title, date, and map key.**

● **Look for other information on the map.**

that a ship could circumnavigate (sur kum NAV ih gayt), or entirely circle, the world.

Where was Magellan killed? His death did not end the first known voyage around the world. One of his ships returned to Spain in 1522.

REVIEWING THE SKILL

1. What is an historical map?

2. What country claimed part of South America in 1500?

3. In which direction did Cabral travel after leaving South America?

4. What route did Magellan's crew take to sail home from the Philippines?

5. What are some ways in which reading historical maps can be useful to you?

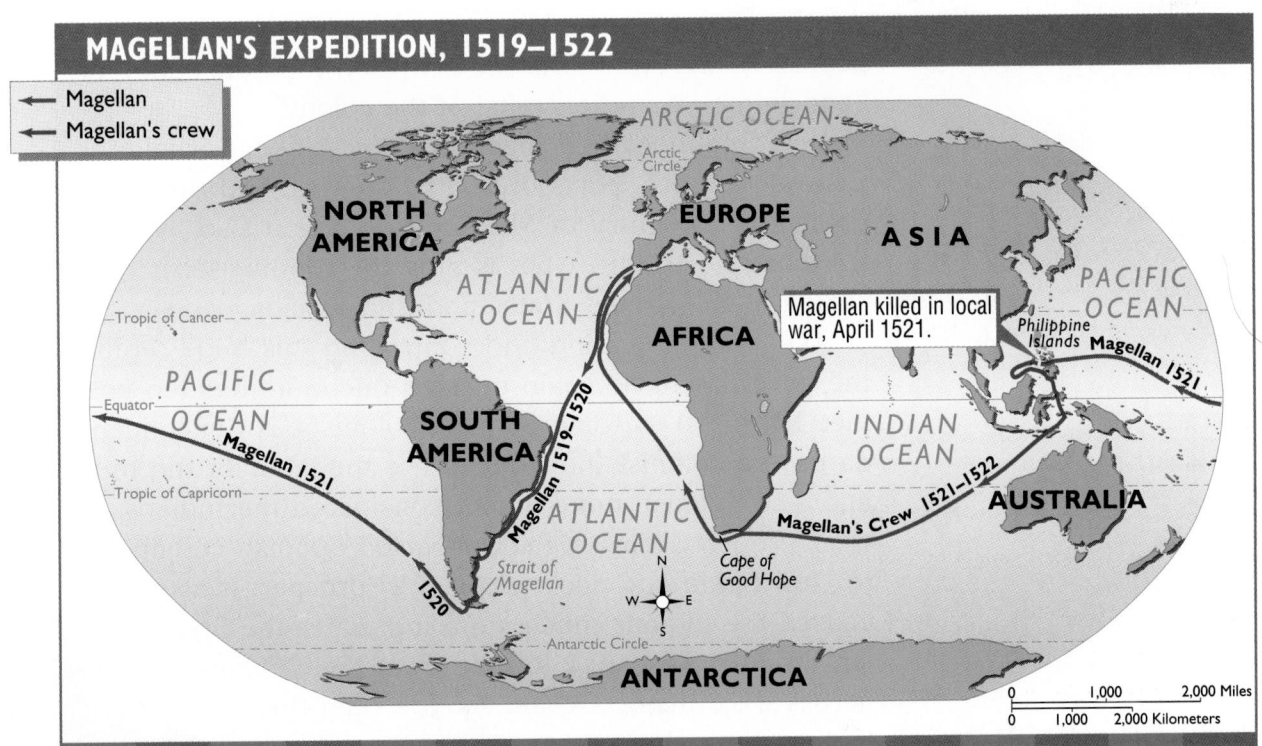

MAGELLAN'S EXPEDITION, 1519–1522

1450   1500   1521   1609   1650

THE SPANISH BUILD AN EMPIRE

Focus Activity

READ TO LEARN
What was life like in New Spain?

VOCABULARY
encomienda
missionary

PEOPLE
Francisco Coronado
Estevanico
Fray Marcos de Niza
Juan Rodríguez Cabrillo
Sebastian Vizcaíno
Bartolomé de las Casas
Yanga

PLACES
New Spain
Mexico City

READ ALOUD

"The strangers did not sleep. They ate silver and gold . . . they were all encased [by armor], and their faces completely covered in wool, so that all that could be seen was their eyes." This is how one Indian writer recorded the arrival of the Spanish in South America in the 1500s.

THE BIG PICTURE

In the 1500s the colony of New Spain grew to include the conquered lands of the Aztec, the Maya, and other peoples of the Americas. Mexico City, the new name for Tenochtitlán, was the capital of the colony.

New Spain covered much of the Caribbean islands, Central America, parts of South America, and the present-day country of Mexico. New Spain also stretched north into what is now the southwestern region of the United States and into Florida.

As a way of settling and controlling this huge region, the government of Spain granted encomiendas (en koh mee EN dahs) to some Spanish colonists. An encomienda gave a colonist the right to use the labor of the Indians. The Spanish government considered the Indians their property. This system attracted Spanish colonists to New Spain and allowed them to prosper. It also caused the Indians much suffering. Later the Spanish brought Africans by force from their homes across the Atlantic Ocean. As you read this lesson, think about what life was like in New Spain.

SPAIN CONQUERS THE AMERICAS

After the fall of Tenochtitlán, the Spanish began to move their conquest further south, towards the area that is now Peru. There, a people called the Inca had built a large civilization with road systems, irrigation, and cities throughout the Andes Mountains. They also had huge amounts of gold and silver. The Spanish conquered the Inca in 1532.

Spanish soldiers also headed southeast into the Yucatán peninsula to find Maya treasures. You read about the Maya in Chapter 3. Their descendants were still living in that area. By 1546 most of the Maya, like the Aztec and Inca, had fallen under Spanish rule. The Spanish burned the Maya's valuable collection of books. Only four Maya books written before the Spanish conquest are known to survive today. They are about astronomy, religion, and the Maya calendar.

Life in New Spain

As Spain's empire expanded, the lives of the people who lived in the colonies changed greatly. Some Spanish colonists received encomiendas, while others worked as soldiers, traders, farmers, or miners. Most Indians were forced to work for the colonists. They grew sugarcane, cotton, grain, and fruits. A part of all crops grown in the Americas was collected as a tax for Spanish rulers.

Gold and silver mining was also very important in the Americas. Indians did most of the mining, but the riches went to Spanish mine owners. Also, the king of Spain collected one-fifth of all the takings. Twice a year, ships loaded with gold, silver, and other goods sailed across the Atlantic Ocean to Spain.

The ruins of the Inca city of Machu Picchu lie hidden high in the mountains of Peru.

NEW SPAIN EXPANDS NORTH

Spain was not the only European country claiming land in the Americas. Spanish explorers competed with explorers from England, France, Portugal, and other countries. All of these countries were looking for gold.

Coronado Searches for Gold

In 1540 Francisco Coronado (koh roh NAH doh) led an expedition in what is now the southwestern United States. On an earlier expedition an African scout, Estevanico (e ste vah NEE koh), and a Spanish priest, Fray Marcos de Niza (FRÍ MAHR kohs DE NEE sah), had heard stories about "cities of gold." Before they could find the cities, Estevanico was killed. Fray Marcos returned with the stories and joined Coronado's expedition.

For two years Coronado searched for the rumored Seven Cities of Gold. These cities did not really exist. Coronado returned to Mexico with wonderful stories but no gold.

Journeys Along the Pacific Coast

Rumors of a continuous water route across North America, which the English called the Northwest Passage, were common in Europe in the early 1500s. If it existed, the Straits of Anián, as the Spanish called it, would take weeks off the journey from Europe to Asia.

In 1542 Juan Rodríguez Cabrillo (kah BREE yoh), a Portuguese explorer working for Spain, sailed north from the west coast of Mexico, searching for the Straits of Anián. Cabrillo's two ships took three months to reach what is now San Diego Harbor. Cabrillo then sailed north along the California coast. He claimed territory for Spain all along the way, but died during the voyage.

In 1602 a merchant named Sebastian Vizcaíno (vees kah EE noh) traveled along the same route that Cabrillo had sailed and then continued farther north. Vizcaíno gave names we still use today to many of the places that he saw, such as the bays of San Diego and Monterey. More than 150 years would pass before the Spanish settled this area.

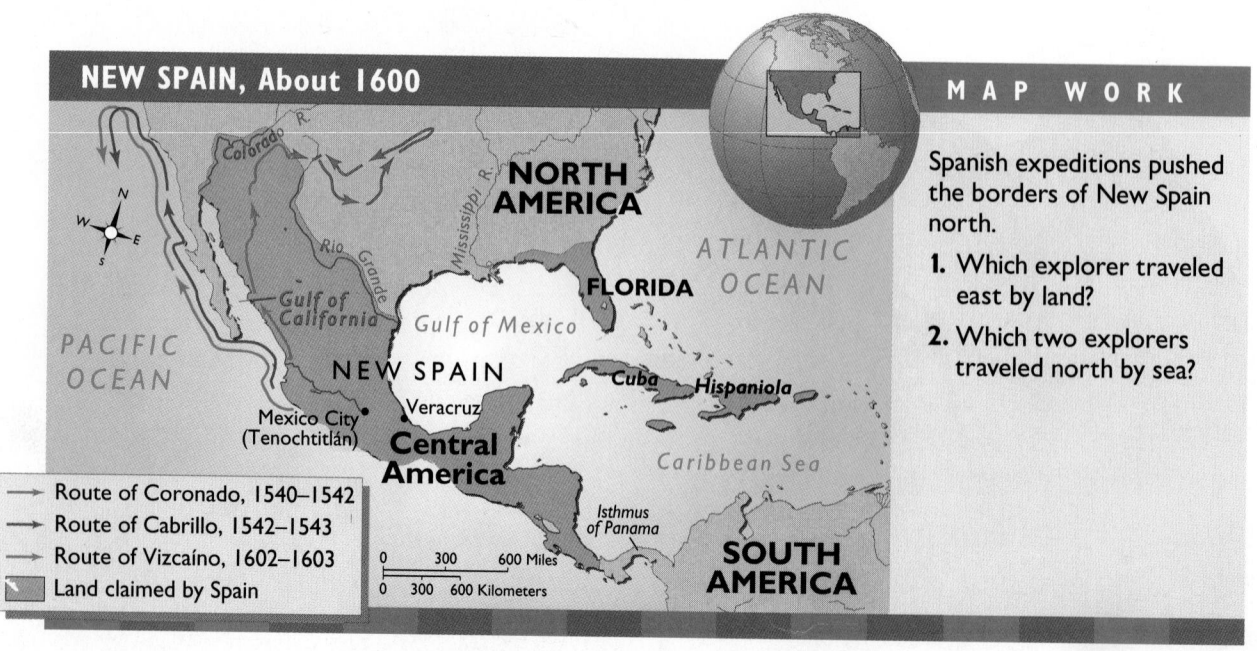

NEW SPAIN, About 1600

NORTH AMERICA

ATLANTIC OCEAN

FLORIDA

PACIFIC OCEAN

Gulf of California

Rio Grande

Gulf of Mexico

NEW SPAIN

Mexico City (Tenochtitlán)

Veracruz

Central America

Cuba

Hispaniola

Caribbean Sea

Isthmus of Panama

SOUTH AMERICA

→ Route of Coronado, 1540–1542
→ Route of Cabrillo, 1542–1543
→ Route of Vizcaíno, 1602–1603
▨ Land claimed by Spain

0   300   600 Miles
0   300   600 Kilometers

MAP WORK

Spanish expeditions pushed the borders of New Spain north.

1. Which explorer traveled east by land?

2. Which two explorers traveled north by sea?

BUILDING NEW SPAIN

Religion was another important reason that the Spanish wanted to build their empire in the Americas. Roman Catholic **missionaries** came to the Americas to spread their religion among the Indians. A missionary is a person who teaches his or her religion to people who have different beliefs.

Many missionaries worked on lands where Indians were forced to work growing corn, tending cattle, and building. In exchange for their labor, Indians received food, shelter, and teachings about Christianity. Often Indians were forced to work from dawn to dusk with very little to eat, and sometimes they were whipped and treated very cruelly.

"Protector of the Indians"

In the early 1500s a Catholic priest named Bartolomé de las Casas (bahr toh loh ME DE LAHS KAH sahs) came to New Spain to run an encomienda. A few years later he became a missionary.

Las Casas was given his own encomienda in 1513, but he gave it up a year later. Las Casas knew that thousands of Indians were dying from disease and overwork. For the next 50 years, he worked to end the encomienda system, and became known as the Protector of the Indians. Finally Las Casas's work caused the king to pass the New Laws of 1542, stating that Indians had to be paid for their work.

Las Casas's concern did not extend to enslaved Africans. They, too, labored under terrible conditions. Until late in his life, Las Casas saw no similarity between enslavement of Indians and Africans. In the excerpt at right, who is Las Casas speaking to in his writing?

Biblioteca Colombina, Seville

MANY VOICES
PRIMARY SOURCE

Excerpt quoted in
History of the Indies,
completed by
Bartolomé de las Casas in 1563.

Tell me, by what right or justice do you hold these Indians in such a cruel and horrible **servitude?** *On what authority have you [tried to destroy] these peoples, who dwelt quietly and peacefully on their own land? . . . Why do you keep them so* **oppressed** *and exhausted, without giving them enough to eat or curing them of the sicknesses they [get] from the excessive labor you give them, and they die, or rather, you kill them, in order to extract and acquire gold every day?*

And what care do you take that they should be instructed in religion, so that they may know their God and creator, may be baptized, may hear Mass, and may keep [observe] Sundays and feast days? Are these not men? . . . Are you not bound to love them as you love yourselves? Do you not understand this? Don't you feel this?

servitude: slavery
oppressed: cruelly, or unjustly, controlled

SLAVERY IN NEW SPAIN

The hard conditions under which the Indians worked and the diseases brought over from Europe caused many deaths. In 1519 between 8 and 30 million Indians lived in Mexico. By 1568 there were less than 3 million.

As the Indians in New Spain died, Spanish colonists sought other workers to bring to the colony.

The first enslaved Africans were brought to New Spain in 1502. By 1570 over 200,000 enslaved Africans had been brought to the Western Hemisphere. Most were brought to the Caribbean islands of Cuba and Hispaniola and forced to work growing sugarcane. Enslaved Africans also worked in the mines of Mexico. Others loaded silver and other products onto treasure ships bound for Spain.

Some Captives Break Free

By law, enslaved Africans in New Spain could work extra time to make money to buy their freedom. But it was very difficult for slaves to get enough time or make enough money to do this. Some African captives who could not buy their freedom escaped. In the 1560s and 1570s, many Africans and Indians rose up against the Spanish rulers.

In 1609 about 600 Spanish soldiers marched into the mountains around Veracruz to recapture an escaped African slave named Yanga. This elderly man had more than 80 followers. For 30 years the Spanish continued the hunt for Yanga's people. Finally, the government left them alone. The Africans later built a town called San Lorenzo de los Negros.

Diego Rivera, a Mexican artist, painted *Disembarkation of the Spanish at Vera Cruz* (right) in 1951. Many captive Indians and Africans were held in shackles such as those shown above.

The Detroit Institute of Art

The Spanish erected The National Palace, above, during colonial times. It is located on the Zócalo on the former site of Moctezuma's palace.

THE CAPITAL OF NEW SPAIN

The city that had once been Tenochtitlán was rebuilt by the forced labor of Indian slaves. Before long there was no trace of the Aztec capital. By 1554 Mexico City had many of the features of a European city.

Freshly arriving Spaniards marveled at the fine houses and wide streets of New Spain's capital. Mexico City had flowering parks, schools, a university, a theater, a post office, and a printing press. The Great Plaza, or the Zócalo, at the center of the city served as the main marketplace. One Spaniard wrote, "Everything that is best in Spain comes to this square."

WHY IT MATTERS

New Spain grew out of the ashes of the Aztec empire. European culture and customs took hold where Indian peoples had once ruled. As you will read in the Legacy on pages 156–157, the culture of New Spain still influences our lives today.

✓✓ Reviewing Facts and Ideas

MAIN IDEAS

- The Spanish colonies grew from the capital of Mexico City to include much of North America and parts of South America.

- Coronado, Cabrillo, and other explorers for Spain traveled north from Mexico City in search of gold and a water route across North America.

- The Spanish began the encomienda system in New Spain. Millions of Indians died from overwork and disease. Thousands of Africans were brought to New Spain as slaves.

- Colonial Mexico City was built over the ruins of Tenochtitlán as a European-style city.

THINK ABOUT IT

1. What goods from New Spain brought wealth to Spanish rulers?

2. What was Cabrillo looking for on his voyage?

3. **FOCUS** What was life like for Spanish colonists in New Spain? What was life like for Indians and for Africans?

4. **THINKING SKILL** What _effect_ did Las Casas have on life in New Spain? Explain your answer.

5. **WRITE** Suppose that you are on a voyage with Coronado, Cabrillo, or Vizcaíno. Write a journal entry describing your journey.

OUR HERITAGE IN
SPANISH NAMES

You read that Sebastian Vizcaíno gave names to many of the places that he visited during his explorations. For many years after Vizcaíno's journey, other Spanish explorers, settlers, and missionaries named the lands that were new to them. Many of the names have religious meanings or describe things that the Spaniards saw. We still use many of these Spanish names today. These names remind us of our country's long history and help us link the present with the past.

Did you know that *California* is a name from New Spain? Scholars believe that the name *California* was first used to describe an imaginary place in a Spanish novel in about 1500. In the story California was an island in the ocean, full of gold and riches. Can you think of any other states that have Spanish names?

Santa Fe, New Mexico
The words *Santa Fe* mean "Holy Faith." Houses made of adobe—sun-dried clay —were first built in New Mexico by Pueblo peoples.

San Francisco, California
This house from the late 1800s is typical of architecture in the city the Spanish named after Saint Francis of Assisi.

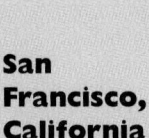

Monterey, California
When Vizcaíno reached California in 1602, he landed at Monterey. He named it for the Viceroy of Mexico, Count of Monte Rey.

Florida
The explorer Juan Ponce de León first used this name in 1513. *Florida* is a Spanish word meaning "full of flowers."

CHAPTER 5 REVIEW

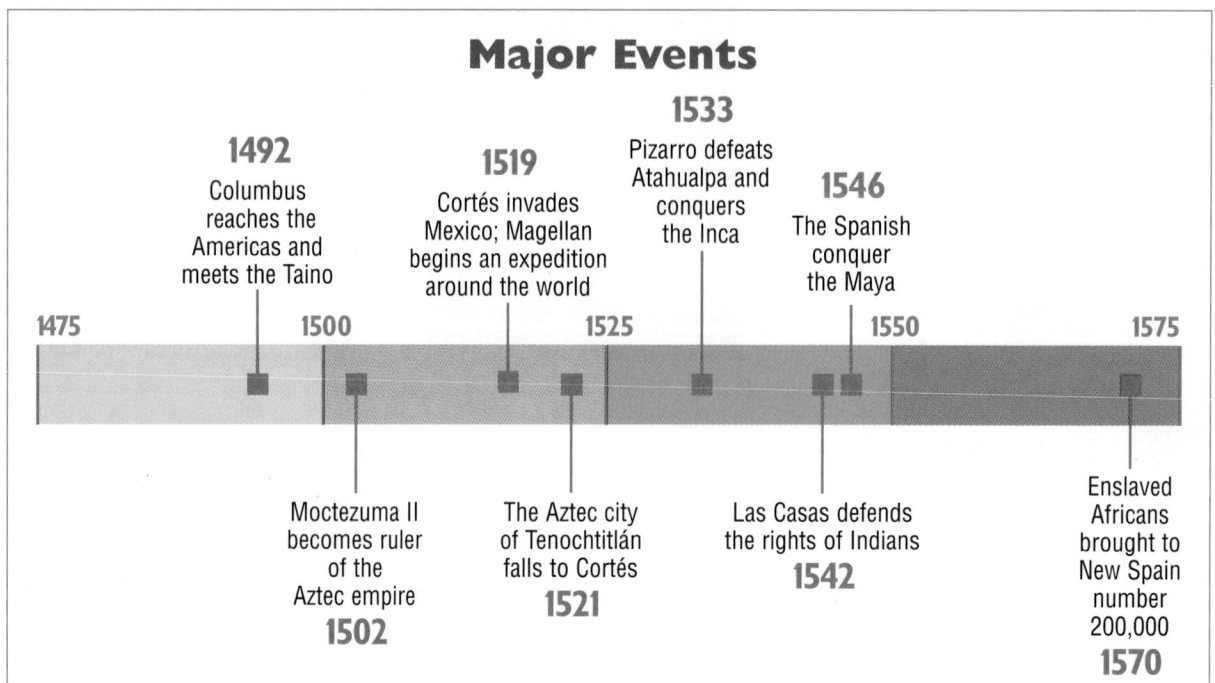

Major Events

1492
Columbus reaches the Americas and meets the Taino

1519
Cortés invades Mexico; Magellan begins an expedition around the world

1533
Pizarro defeats Atahualpa and conquers the Inca

1546
The Spanish conquer the Maya

1475   1500   1525   1550   1575

Moctezuma II becomes ruler of the Aztec empire
1502

The Aztec city of Tenochtitlán falls to Cortés
1521

Las Casas defends the rights of Indians
1542

Enslaved Africans brought to New Spain number 200,000
1570

THINKING ABOUT VOCABULARY

Number a sheet of paper from 1 to 5. Beside each number write the word or term from the list below that matches the description.

colony
Columbian exchange
conquistador
encomienda
expedition

1. a soldier who conquered lands for Spain
2. a journey made for a special purpose
3. a settlement that is ruled by another country
4. a system that gave Spanish colonists the right to use the labor of Native Americans
5. the movement of people, plants, animals, and germs across the Atlantic Ocean that began after Christopher Columbus arrived in the Americas

THINKING ABOUT FACTS

1. Who were the Taino? What had happened to them by the 1500s?
2. How did Christopher Columbus get the money he needed for his voyage?
3. Why do people remember Christopher Columbus today?
4. What was one good effect of the Columbian exchange for the peoples of the Americas? What was one bad effect?
5. What were Spanish troops looking for in Mexico?
6. How was Hernán Cortés able to conquer the Aztec on their own land?
7. What lands made up New Spain?
8. What is a missionary?
9. Why did Bartolomé de las Casas come to New Spain? What did he do there?
10. What events shown on the time line occurred in 1519?

THINK AND WRITE

WRITING A PARAGRAPH OF COMPARISON
Write a paragraph comparing Columbus's meeting with the Taino to Cortés's first meeting with Moctezuma.

WRITING A JOURNAL ENTRY
Suppose that you are either an Aztec or a Spanish soldier at the battle for Tenochtitlán. Write an entry in your journal in which you describe the experience.

WRITING A LETTER
Suppose that you are an Indian living in New Spain. Write a letter to the king of Spain describing the cruelty you believe your people have suffered under the Spanish colonists. Explain why you think the encomienda system should be ended.

APPLYING GEOGRAPHY SKILLS

HISTORICAL MAPS
To practice your skill in reading historical maps, answer the following questions about the map on page 149.

1. How do you know that the map on this page is an historical map?
2. What does the map key tell you?
3. Across which oceans did Magellan and his crew travel?
4. How many years did this journey around the world take?
5. What makes historical maps useful?

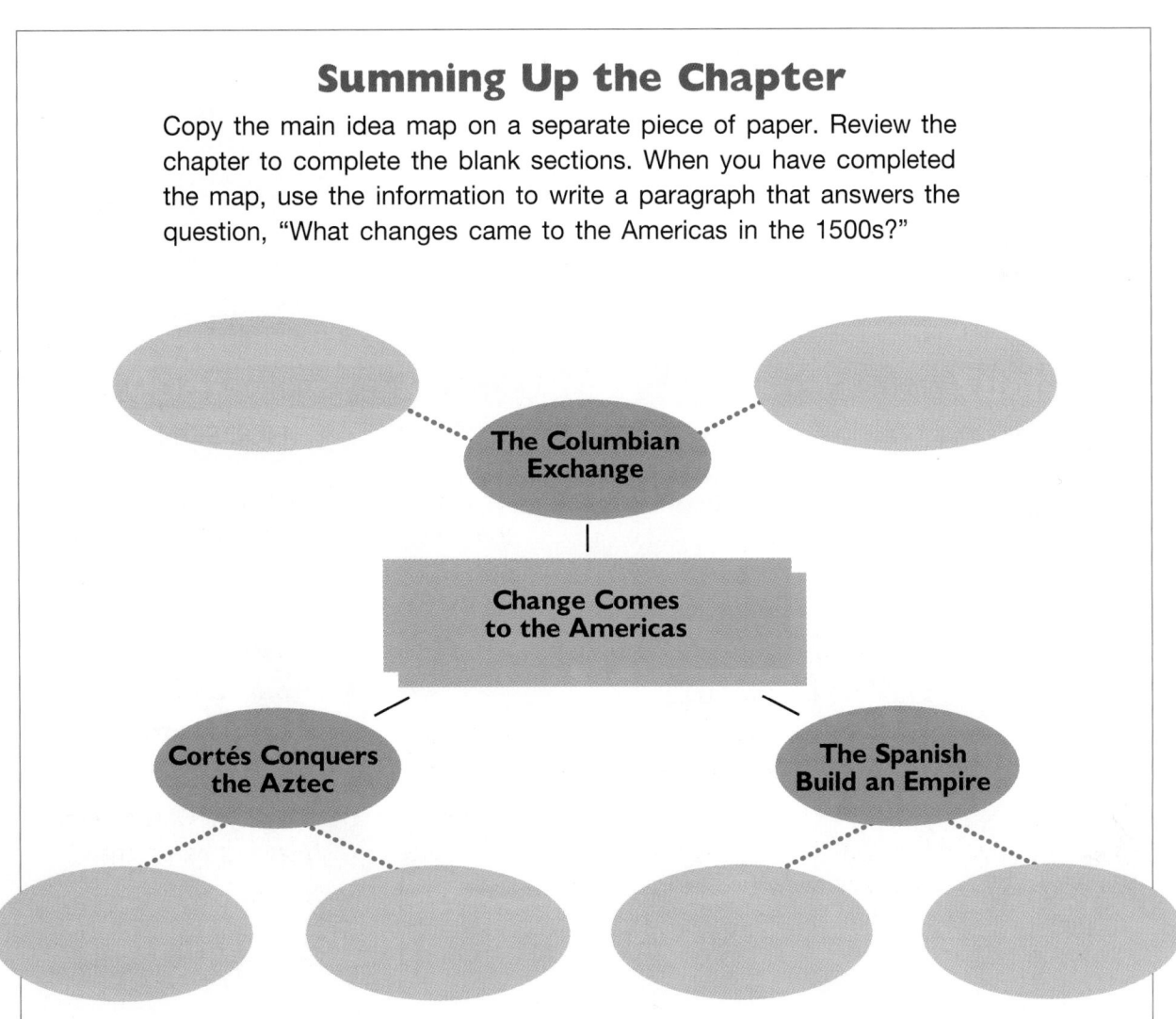

Summing Up the Chapter

Copy the main idea map on a separate piece of paper. Review the chapter to complete the blank sections. When you have completed the map, use the information to write a paragraph that answers the question, "What changes came to the Americas in the 1500s?"

The Columbian Exchange

Change Comes to the Americas

Cortés Conquers the Aztec

The Spanish Build an Empire

CHAPTER 6

Early English Settlements in North America

THINKING ABOUT HISTORY AND GEOGRAPHY

Chapter 6 covers the first English explorers and colonies in America. Starting in 1587, the English settled lands that long had been home to Native Americans. Soon after, captive and free Africans arrived. How these groups lived together is part of the story of our nation's beginning.

PACIFIC OCEAN

1587
ROANOKE ISLAND

John White leads English colonists to Roanoke Island

1607
JAMESTOWN

The English build a new settlement in Virginia

1609
HUDSON RIVER VALLEY

Henry Hudson explores North America for the Dutch

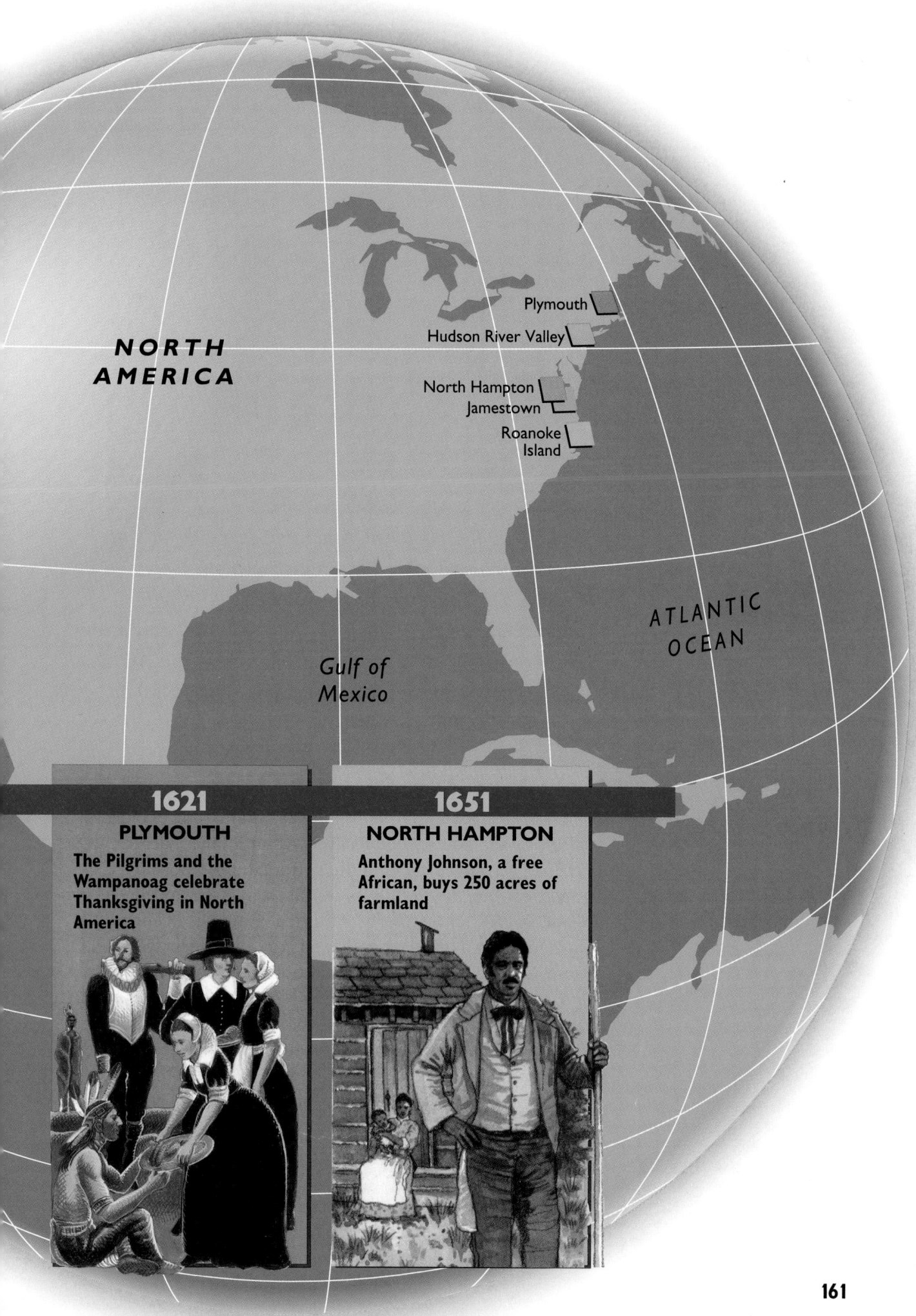

NORTH AMERICA

Plymouth

Hudson River Valley

North Hampton
Jamestown

Roanoke
Island

ATLANTIC
OCEAN

Gulf of
Mexico

1621

PLYMOUTH

The Pilgrims and the Wampanoag celebrate Thanksgiving in North America

1651

NORTH HAMPTON

Anthony Johnson, a free African, buys 250 acres of farmland

SEARCHING FOR A NORTHWEST PASSAGE

Focus Activity

READ TO LEARN
What did Henry Hudson's voyage gain for the Europeans who sent him?

VOCABULARY
Northwest Passage

PEOPLE
Henry Hudson
John Cabot
Giovanni da Verrazano
Jacques Cartier
Samuel de Champlain

PLACE
Hudson River

READ ALOUD

Some of the northern Atlantic Coast's great waterways are named after the English captain Henry Hudson. On Hudson's final expedition to North America, in 1611, his men set him, his son, and a few loyal crewmen adrift in a small boat near the Arctic Circle. They were never seen again. What mission drove Hudson so far north?

THE BIG PICTURE

You have read that in the 1500s Spain sent explorers to find a sea route between the Atlantic and Pacific oceans. Voyagers such as Juan Rodríguez Cabrillo hoped to find the Straits of Anián, a waterway they believed ran across North America. English, French, and Dutch explorers also looked for a western water route to Asia. They called this route the Northwest Passage. You can see what these explorers achieved on the Infographic on pages 164–165.

In 1609 Henry Hudson took his first voyage to North America. On this trip he believed at first that he had found the trade route he was looking for—the Northwest Passage.

THE VOYAGE OF HENRY HUDSON

Exploring the Americas was costly. Europe's rulers were not always willing to pay for expeditions. A group of merchants who wanted to trade with Asia formed the Dutch East India Company. The merchants agreed to pay for expeditions in return for the profits they might bring. In 1609 the Dutch East India Company hired Henry Hudson, an English sea captain, to search for a passage to Asia.

Exploring New York Harbor

That summer Hudson and his crew explored the coast of North America. In August Hudson saw the waters now known as Chesapeake Bay and Delaware Bay.

Thaw Collection, Fenimore House Museum, Cooperstown

The pouch above was made by the Lenape from leather, porcupine quills, and dyed hair. The painting below, *Hudson the Dreamer*, shows Hudson being met by the Lenape.

Continuing north, Hudson mapped what is today New York Harbor.

He traded with the local Native Americans, the Lenape, which means "the People" in Algonkian. Hudson's crew, however, also wrote of armed battles between the Dutch and the Lenape.

"Great River of the Mountains"

In September Hudson sailed north up the river that today is called the Hudson River. Certain the river was the Northwest Passage, Hudson called it the "Great River of the Mountains." After about 150 miles, the river narrowed and became shallow. Hudson realized that this was not the Northwest Passage. Near what is today Albany, New York, Hudson reached a large Lenape settlement. He traded for corn and beans with the Lenape and other groups, such as the Mahican and Mohawk.

Hudson the Dreamer, J. L. G. Ferris/Superstock Fine Arts Division

Infographic

The Search for a Northwest Passage

Europeans slowly explored the east coast of North America, searching for a Northwest Passage to Asia. The search failed. However, it did lead Europeans to begin colonies on the coast. Look at the map below and locate the Swedish, Dutch, English, French, and Spanish settlements.

Explorers

John Cabot, *an Italian who sailed under the flag of England, reached Newfoundland by way of Nova Scotia in 1497.*

Giovanni da Verrazano, *an Italian sailing under the flag of France, explored the Outer Banks of present-day North Carolina in 1524.*

Jacques Cartier, *who sailed under the flag of France, reached Newfoundland in 1534.*

Samuel de Champlain, *sailing under the flag of France, founded Port Royal in present-day Nova Scotia in 1604 and took colonists to Quebec in 1608.*

Henry Hudson, *an Englishman sailing under the flag of the Netherlands, explored the northern Atlantic Coast in 1609.*

Quebec (1608)

Montreal (1642)

Plymouth (1620)

Fort Orange (1624)

New Amsterdam (1624)

New Sweden (1638–1655)

Jamestown (1607)

Roanoke (1585–1587)

Verrazano 1524

Santa Elena (1566–1587)

Fort Caroline (1564)

St. Augustine (1565)

Cartier 1534

Cabot 1497

Port Royal
(1604)

Champlain 1604

Hudson 1609

● Swedish
● English   ● French
● Dutch   ● Spanish

WHY IT MATTERS

The search for a Northwest Passage continued for about another 200 years. It was not until the 1800s that Europeans finally carved a path through the frozen seas of the far north. However, in the 1600s the explorations made it possible for England, France, and the Netherlands to begin building colonies in North America. Like Spain, they also looked for ways to make a profit from their new colonies.

✓ Reviewing Facts and Ideas

MAIN IDEAS

- In the 1500s and 1600s, English, Dutch, and French explorers searched for a Northwest Passage to Asia.
- In 1609 Henry Hudson first sailed up the Hudson River, hoping it might be a waterway to Asia.
- During the search for a Northwest Passage, Europeans began to claim land and start colonies along the Atlantic Coast of North America.

THINK ABOUT IT

1. Why did European explorers want to find a Northwest Passage?

2. How did Dutch explorers pay for their explorations?

3. **FOCUS** What did Henry Hudson's 1609 voyage accomplish?

4. **THINKING SKILL** *Predict* how the Lenape reacted when increasing numbers of Europeans began to arrive.

5. **GEOGRAPHY** Use the Infographic on these pages to locate and list the explorers who journeyed to North America, the countries that sent them, and the colonies that each nation began.

Thaw Collection, Fenimore House Museum, Cooperstown

THE VIRGINIA COLONY

READ ALOUD

"We viewed the land about us, being . . . very sandy, and low towards the water side, but so full of grapes . . . that I think in all the world the like abundance is not to be found." This is how Arthur Barlowe, an English sea captain, described what is now Virginia. He was sent in 1584 to explore North America and find a good place for an English colony. The land Barlowe described was beautiful, but living there would not be easy.

Focus Activity

READ TO LEARN
Why did the English want to start colonies in North America?

VOCABULARY
charter
cash crop
indentured servant

PEOPLE
Queen Elizabeth I
Sir Walter Raleigh
John White
Powhatan
King James I
John Smith
Pocahontas
John Rolfe
Openchancanough

PLACES
Virginia
Roanoke Island
Jamestown

THE BIG PICTURE

By the late 1500s Spain's empire in North and South America was powerful and rich. Spanish rulers believed that the southern half of the North American coastline was rightfully theirs.

However, England began to challenge Spain in several ways. War at sea broke out as English captains called "sea dogs" seized and raided Spain's treasure ships. The English also planned to start colonies in North America. They claimed land near Chesapeake Bay that was home to several Native American groups and that had already been claimed by the Spanish. The English called the land Virginia. It included parts of modern-day Virginia and North Carolina.

166

ROANOKE

You can see on the map on this page that the Roanoac (ROH uh noh uk) were one of the peoples who already lived on the Atlantic coast. The word *roanoke* means "shell money" in Algonkian.

Queen Elizabeth I granted a charter to her trusted adviser Sir Walter Raleigh. A charter was a document that allowed colonists to settle on land claimed by a ruler. English explorers told Raleigh about Roanoke Island off the Atlantic coast of North America.

In 1585 about 100 men, mostly former soldiers, settled at Roanoke. Raleigh thought these men could best defend the colony against the Spanish. No women were sent because the first colonists planned to find land and wealth, not to raise families and build communities.

The English, however, met with hunger and hardship. In June of 1586, the colonists returned to England.

The Lost Colony

In 1587 Raleigh again sent colonists across the Atlantic. He chose John White to be the colony's governor. This time, men, women, and children came to farm the land and make a permanent colony.

White left for England in 1587 to gather needed food and supplies. A war between England and Spain kept White from returning to Roanoke until 1590.

Sir Walter Raleigh's (left) interests included military fighting, navigation, and writing history and poetry. (Below) Croatoan Island at dawn.

When he got to Virginia, White found no colonists, only a clue: the word *CROATOAN* carved into a tree trunk. *Croatoan* was the name of both an island south of Roanoke and a nearby Native American people. Were the colonists safely on Croatoan or had they fought with neighbors? White and his crew sailed toward Croatoan, but storms kept his ship from landing. Damage to the ships and low supplies forced White to return to England without solving the mystery of the "Lost Colony."

ROANOKE AND NEIGHBORING ISLANDS, Late 1500s

ATLANTIC OCEAN

Roanoke River

ROANOAC

Secotan

Roanoke Island

Pamlico River

Neuse River

HATTERAS

Hatteras Island

Croatoan Island (Ocracoke)

0   30   60 Miles

0   30   60 Kilometers   TUSCARORA

MAP WORK

Secotan was the name both of the village and of the people White met on his first voyage. Other Native American peoples are indicated by capital letters on the map.

Besides the Secotan people, which Native Americans lived near Roanoke Island?

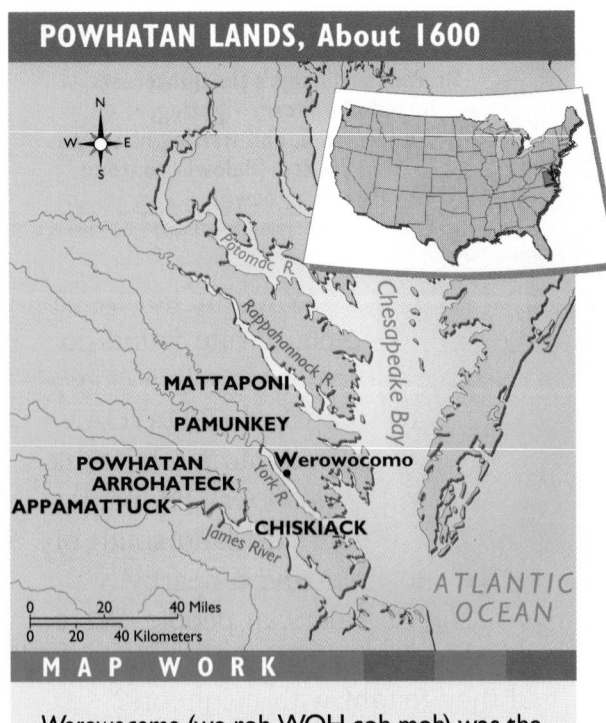

Werowocomo (we roh WOH coh moh) was the capital of the Powhatan chiefdom. Which peoples lived near the York River?

CHESAPEAKE BAY

The area around Chesapeake Bay had been home to Native Americans for more than 1,000 years. In the 1600s one important group, the Powhatan, joined together with 12,000 Native Americans—more than 30 groups—to form the Powhatan chiefdom, ruled by a single chief, who was called Powhatan (pow uh TAN). The map on this page shows the location of other Algonkian-speaking people in this area.

Powhatan

Powhatan was respected by all groups in the chiefdom. One colonist described him in the following passage.

His will is a law and must be obeyed: not only as a king, but as half a God they esteem him. . . . They pay tribute of skins, beads, copper, pearl, deer, turkeys, wild beasts, and corn. . . . It is strange to see with what great fear and adoration these people do obey this Powhatan.

The Jamestown Colony

English leaders were determined to build colonies in North America. In 1606 a group of London merchants received a charter from King James I for a colony in Virginia. This colony was called Jamestown, in honor of the king.

In England the Virginia Company offered to send colonists to North America and pay for seed and materials. Colonists agreed to repay the company with a share of their crops or of the gold that they found.

In 1607 three small ships entered Chesapeake Bay with more than 100 men and boys to search for gold in Virginia. They settled along the James River. Supplies could be brought from the sea to Jamestown by boat, and colonists could escape attack by sailing downriver.

This deerskin cloak, known as Powhatan's mantle, was taken to England in 1608.

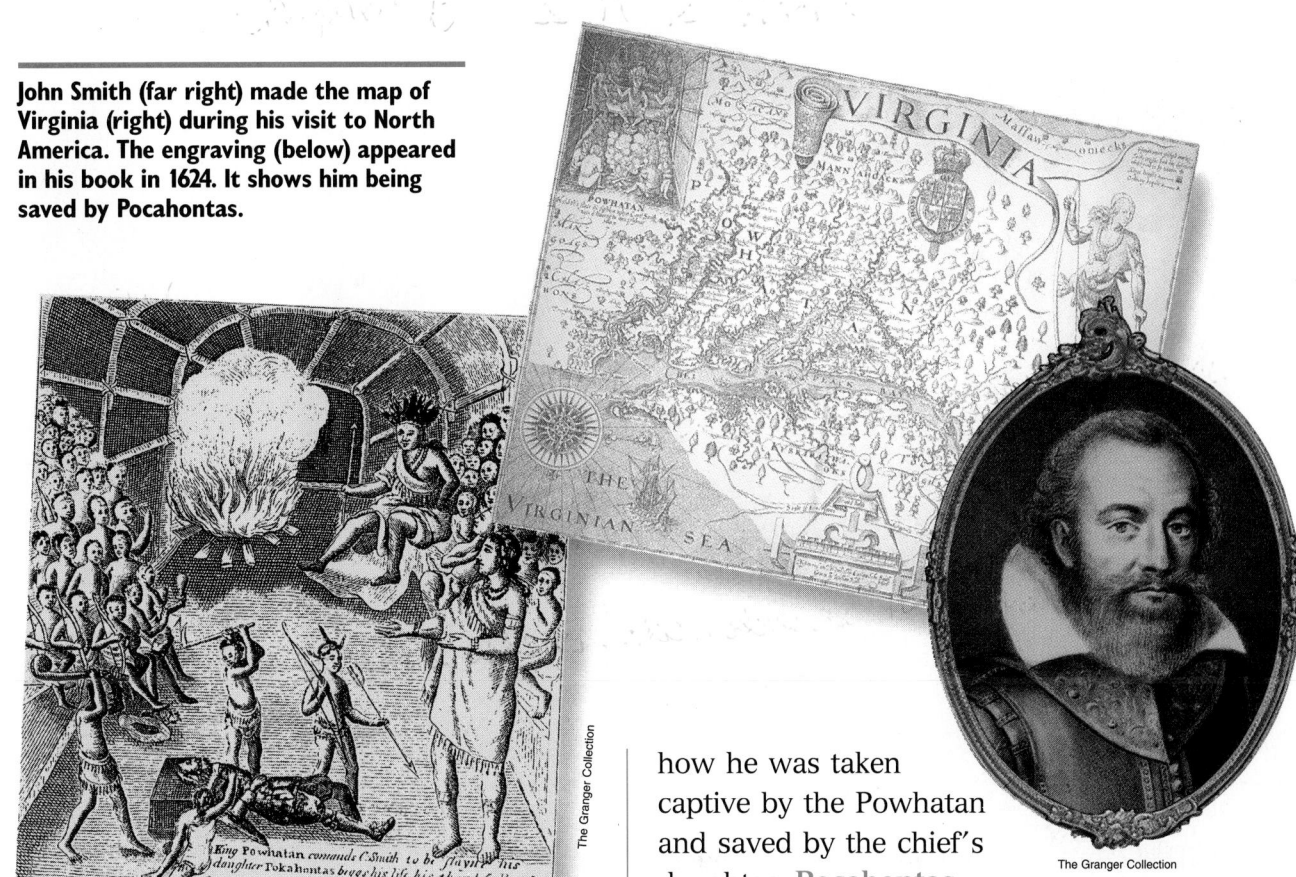

John Smith (far right) made the map of Virginia (right) during his visit to North America. The engraving (below) appeared in his book in 1624. It shows him being saved by Pocahontas.

The Granger Collection

The Granger Collection

The streams and meadows near Jamestown were full of fish and wildlife. However, the tide brought undrinkable salty seawater up the river. Also, the swampy riverbanks fed disease-carrying mosquitoes. Disease killed almost half of the settlers in the first summer.

John Smith Leads the Colony

The colonists all might have died without the leadership of Captain John Smith. They wanted to find gold and get rich quickly. Many were *gentlemen*, a word used in England then for a man who did not do physical labor. "He that will not work will not eat," Smith told them. He forced the colonists to build houses, plant crops, and raise livestock.

Some historians believe that Smith's writings about Virginia were not always accurate. For example, Smith described how he was taken captive by the Powhatan and saved by the chief's daughter, Pocahontas.

Some historians believe Smith did not understand that Pocahontas may have been taking part in a Powhatan ceremony to let Smith into the Powhatan community. Other historians think that Smith repeated a story a Spanish soldier had told him.

At times Smith traded with Powhatan for food. In his book about Virginia, Smith wrote down Powhatan's reaction to the colonists and the possibility of conflict:

Think you I am so simple not to know it is better . . . being your friend, than . . . being so hunted that neither can I rest, eat, nor sleep. . . . Every year our friendly trade shall furnish you with corn.

In 1609 Smith was hurt in a gunpowder explosion and he returned to England. Without his help, the colony again faced hard times. One colonist called the winter of 1609–1610 the "starving time."

CHANGE AND CHALLENGE

The Jamestown colony was in danger of failing like the Roanoke colony. In 1609 ships from England brought men, women, and children to Jamestown. Women made important contributions by working on the land, tending crops and animals. They also made and washed clothing and prepared meals. Women at one time were even offered free land to come to the English colonies.

John Rolfe settled in Virginia in 1610 and was successful growing a popular kind of tobacco that soon made Jamestown a wealthy colony. In 1617 almost 20,000 pounds of tobacco were shipped to England. Tobacco had become a cash crop, a crop grown to be sold for money.

Africans and Indentured Servants

Now colonists came to Jamestown hoping to become rich by raising tobacco. Many unable to afford the voyage agreed to work five to seven years as indentured (ihn DEN churd) servants for the person who paid their travel costs.

John Rolfe married Pocahontas (left) in 1614. The tobacco (above) Rolfe introduced to Jamestown made it a wealthy colony. The first Africans (right) were brought to Jamestown as captives in 1619.

In 1619 the first Africans arrived in Jamestown as captives on a Dutch ship. Forced to become indentured servants, they later became free farmers and planters. An African named Anthony Johnson arrived in Jamestown in 1621. He worked as an indentured servant and later owned 250 acres in what is now North Hampton County. Large Virginia farms required many workers, though. After 1661 laws allowed slavery. It became legal for most Africans in Virginia to be enslaved on large farms.

Conflict with the Powhatan

After 1619 the colonists faced the future with more hope. As English planters cleared more new land for tobacco, however, they took more and more Powhatan farms, villages, and hunting grounds.

Now, after years of small battles, many Native Americans determined to stop the colony's growth. Four years after Powhatan died in 1618, the new chief, his brother Openchancanough (oh pun CHAN kun awf) attacked the colonists early one March morning, killing about 350 colonists. The battle that resulted ended most Powhatan resistance to the spread of the English in Virginia.

WHY IT MATTERS

The English had a hard time establishing a successful colony in North America until 1607. Soon afterward, English colonists would set up new colonies north of Virginia.

Native Americans and the English colonists were friendly at first. As colonists began taking more and more land, though, distrust and fighting for many years replaced friendship.

Africans in early Virginia arrived as captives but were not forced into slavery. As tobacco farming increased, however, the practice of slavery grew gradually and would later lead to one of the bloodiest wars in our nation's history.

Reviewing Facts and Ideas

MAIN IDEAS

- In the late 1500s England challenged Spanish claims to North America by building colonies there.
- Two attempts to settle on Roanoke Island were unsuccessful.
- The first permanent English colony in North America was founded in Jamestown in 1607.
- The growth of tobacco as a cash crop helped Jamestown to grow wealthy and attract new colonists.

THINK ABOUT IT

1. Why is the second colony at Roanoke called the Lost Colony?

2. How did John Smith help Jamestown to succeed?

3. **FOCUS** Why did the English want to start colonies in North America?

4. **THINKING SKILL** What _effects_ did John Rolfe's success at growing tobacco have on the colonists? Explain.

5. **WRITE** Suppose that you are a newspaper reporter in London in 1607. Write an article about Jamestown. Give your article a headline.

THINKING SKILLS

Distinguishing Fact from Opinion

VOCABULARY
fact   opinion

WHY THE SKILL MATTERS

In Lesson 2 you read that John White searched for the "lost colonists" of Roanoke. White wrote about the **facts** of what he saw. A fact is a statement that can be checked and proved true. He also had an **opinion** about what happened to the missing colonists. An opinion is a personal view or belief. Being able to distinguish facts from opinions is important in the study of history.

USING THE SKILL

Many of the primary and secondary sources you read contain both facts and opinions. In statements that have both, you must first distinguish the facts from the opinions. Then check the facts before you decide whether or not the statement is correct.

An opinion is often based on a feeling or personal liking and, therefore, cannot be proved. One way to identify such opinions is to look for clue words like *I believe, I think,* or *it seems,* and descriptive words such as *good, the best,* or *wonderful.* These words express beliefs that cannot be proved. Therefore, they are clues that the writer is giving an opinion.

During the 1500s people in England were thinking about settling in Virginia. They needed to distinguish fact from opinion when they read explorers' accounts of the unfamiliar land. One of the most famous of these accounts was written by Thomas Hariot. Hariot spent the year of 1585 in Roanoke. During his stay, Hariot took notes on the plants, animals, and people that he found there. When he returned to England, he wrote *A Brief and True Report of the New Found Land of Virginia.* His book includes both facts and opinions about Virginia.

John White's paintings (far right and far left) show cooking methods of Native Americans of the Southeast. Books and advertisements encouraged people to come to Virginia.

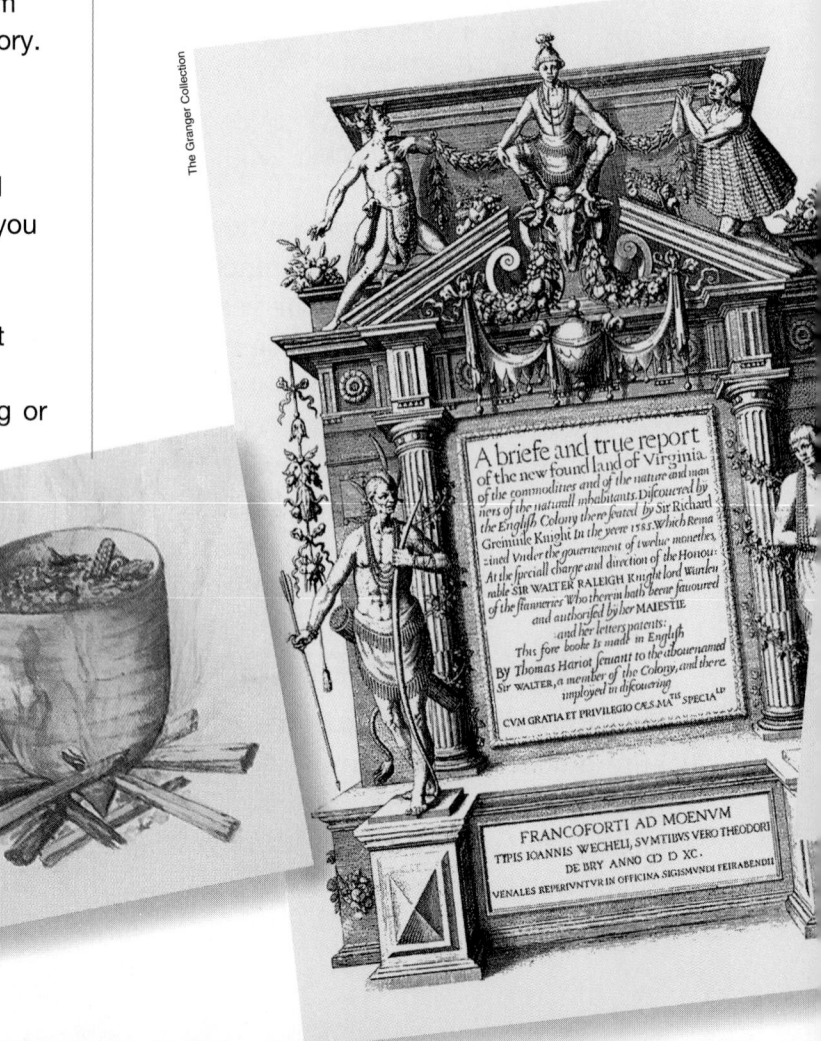

The Granger Collection

172

In the following excerpts Hariot talks about the Powhatan.

It remains for me to speak a word or two of the inhabitants of the country. They dress in loose mantles [capes] made of deerskins. They have no . . . tools of iron or steel. Their only weapons are bows made of witch-hazel [a kind of wood] and arrows of reeds.

[The Powhatan] seem very ingenious [good at inventing things]. For although they have no such tools, crafts, sciences, and arts as we, yet in those things they do, they show excellence of wit [they are very smart].

Which statements in the first paragraph present facts? What opinions can you find in the second paragraph? What word clues reveal that these are opinions?

HELPING Yourself

- **A fact can be proven true; an opinion cannot.**
- **Look for word clues that show an opinion, such as *believe* or *think*.**
- **Determine whether each statement is a fact or an opinion.**

TRYING THE SKILL

Read the following description of early Virginia by an English sea captain, Ralph Lane. Then use the Helping Yourself box to distinguish the facts from the opinions.

We have discovered the mainland to be the goodliest soil under. . . heaven. So abounding with trees . . . and. . . grapes that France, Spain nor Italy have no greater; so many kinds of apothecary drugs [medicines], several kinds of flax [a kind of plant] . . . Within these few days we have found here maize. . . whose ear yields corn. . . four hundred upon one ear.

Which statement is one that gives an opinion? How can you tell?

REVIEWING THE SKILL

1. What is a fact? What is an opinion?

2. What facts does Ralph Lane give to back up his opinion? How do you know?

3. What do you think Lane wants people in England to believe about Virginia?

4. Do you think the facts that Lane gives do back up his opinion? Explain.

5. Why is it important for you to be able to distinguish facts from opinions?

NOVA BRITANNIA.
OFFRING MOST
Excellent fruites by Planting in
VIRGINIA.
Exciting all such as be well affected
to further the same.

The Granger Collection

173

THE PILGRIMS COME TO PLYMOUTH

READ ALOUD

"All great and honourable actions are accompanied with great difficulties . . . overcome with answerable courages. The dangers were great, but not desperate." William Bradford, a colonist at Plymouth, wrote these words about the Pilgrims' decision to undertake the long and dangerous voyage to America.

THE BIG PICTURE

Early in the 1500s much of Europe was divided over religion. The king of England, Henry VIII, broke away from the Roman Catholic Church and set up another church called the Church of England. The members of the Church of England were called Protestants because they had protested against practices of the Catholic Church. Within England, however, some Protestants felt that the Church of England had kept too many Catholic ways. They set up their own Protestant churches.

In 1604 these Protestants asked King James I to grant them the freedom to worship as they chose. The King refused, forbidding religious services outside of the Church of England. A group known as the Separatists began to hold secret prayer meetings. They believed that it was necessary to separate from the Church of England in order to save their souls. In 1608 some of the Separatists left England. They became known as the Pilgrims. The word *pilgrim* is used to describe someone who travels to a faraway place for religious reasons.

Focus Activity

READ TO LEARN
What was life like for the Pilgrims in the Plymouth colony?

VOCABULARY
Separatist
Pilgrim
Mayflower Compact
sachem

PEOPLE
Miles Standish
John Carver
William Bradford
Samoset
Massasoit
Squanto

PLACES
Plymouth

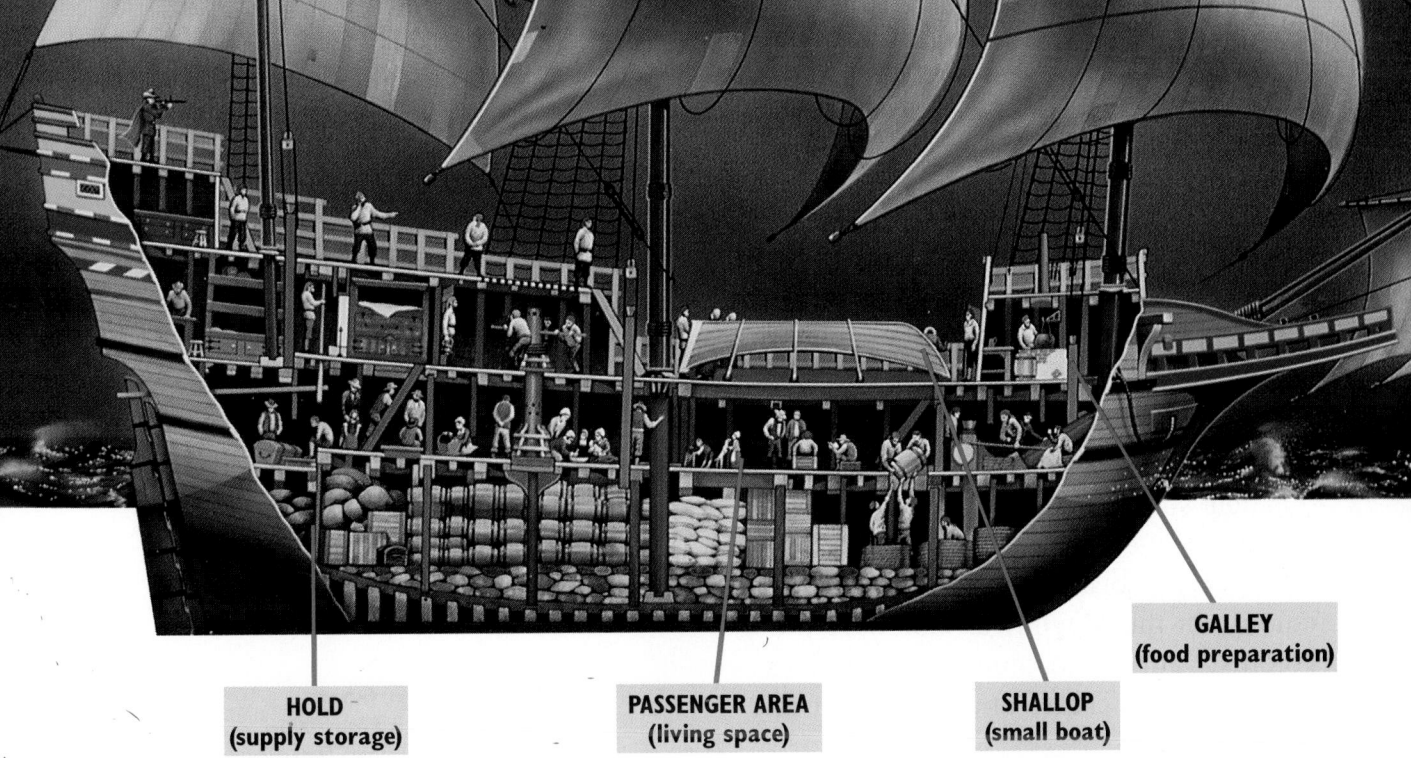

HOLD
(supply storage)

PASSENGER AREA
(living space)

SHALLOP
(small boat)

GALLEY
(food preparation)

SEARCHING FOR RELIGIOUS FREEDOM

In the spring of 1608, the Pilgrims made a trip to the Netherlands. They knew they would be able to practice their religious beliefs more freely there. However, life in the Netherlands was hard for the Pilgrims. They did not speak the language, and they had trouble finding jobs.

The Pilgrims were afraid that their children would lose their religion and culture. They decided to go to a new land, where they could create a community based on their own values.

The Voyage of the *Mayflower*

In 1619 King James I reluctantly allowed the Pilgrims in the Netherlands to settle in Virginia. A group of London businessmen and at least one woman paid for the voyage and the materials necessary to set up the colony. In return the Pilgrims agreed to give all profits at the end of seven years to those who had paid their way. On September 16, 1620, a ship called the *Mayflower* set sail from Plymouth, England.

Historians think that the *Mayflower's* deck was about 90 feet long and 21 feet wide. The living space —for over 100 people—was probably about 42 feet by 21 feet.

The Pilgrims sailed with other colonists who had special skills to help them. One such person was Captain Miles Standish, a soldier who had been hired to help the Pilgrims defend their colony. Standish would become an important member of the new community. In all, 102 passengers crowded into the ship for the long voyage. The diagram above shows what the cramped ship must have looked like.

For 65 days the *Mayflower* tossed in the stormy Atlantic. Then, on the morning of November 19, 1620, lookouts finally saw land. The *Mayflower* was far off course. The Pilgrims had not arrived in Virginia, as they had planned, but in Cape Cod, in the present-day state of Massachusetts. A small group went ashore to explore. One passenger wrote that they "fell upon their knees and blessed the God of Heaven who had brought them over the vast and furious ocean."

A NEW ENGLISH COLONY

The Pilgrims realized that they had landed far from Virginia and were in a completely new place with "no friends to welcome them." They knew that before they even left the ship, they would need to form some kind of government.

The Mayflower Compact

Their solution was to write a brief set of rules, called the Mayflower Compact, to bring order to the new colony. In the Mayflower Compact the colonists agreed to "combine ourselves together" and create and obey "just and equal laws."

Forty-one men signed the agreement, but no women did. Although women had certain rights, they could not take part in government. Everyone was expected to obey the laws, though, including men, women, and children. The Mayflower Compact was an important document in our history. It planted the idea of self-government among the colonists in North America.

After they signed the compact, the men on board the ship elected John Carver to be the first governor of the colony. Carver served until his death in 1621. After John Carver died, the colonists chose as governor William Bradford, whose words you read in the Read Aloud. Bradford served as governor or

This statue of William Bradford was sculpted by Cyrus Dalin.

assistant governor for 35 years. He wrote a book about the colony called *Of Plymouth Plantation*. Read his words below. Why was the fact that it was winter so important to the Pilgrims?

MANY VOICES
PRIMARY SOURCE

Excerpt from
Of Plymouth Plantation,
written by William Bradford
in 1646.

It was winter, and they that know the winters of the country know them to be sharp and violent, and subject to cruel and fierce storms, dangerous to travel to known places, much more to search an unknown coast.

*For summer being done, all things stand upon them with a weatherbeaten face. . . . If they looked behind them, there was the mighty ocean which they had passed and was now as a main bar and gulf to separate them from all the **civil** parts of the world. . . .*

What could now sustain them but the spirit of God and His grace?

---

civil: in this case, having a familiar social order and organized government

Plymouth

The Pilgrims gave the name Plymouth to the place where they finally decided to settle. A visitor from the Netherlands later wrote to a friend describing the Pilgrims' colony.

> New Plymouth lies on the slope of a hill stretching east towards the seacoast. . . . The houses are constructed of . . . planks, with gardens also enclosed behind and at the sides . . . so that their houses and courtyards are arranged in very good order, with a stockade [fort] against sudden attack. And at the end of the streets there are three wooden gates. In the centre . . . stands the Governor's house.

Inside their houses the Pilgrims lived simply. There was no room, for example, for a dining table. At mealtime a large board was brought out and set on top of barrels to act as a table. There might be one chair, and other members of the family would sit on a box or a chest. It was not unusual for children to eat standing up. The colonists ate roasted or preserved meat, such as pork or goat. Beef was rarely eaten, as the cows were needed for milk. When other foods were scarce, the colonists ate shellfish.

The Wampanoag

The Pilgrims settled on land already home to many Native Americans. The Wampanoag (wahm puh NOH ahg) lived in present-day Massachusetts and Rhode Island, as shown on the map on this page. In the Algonkian language, Wampanoag means "people of the east (or dawn)."

One morning, as the colonists were gathered, they were surprised by a Native American visitor. "He very boldly came all alone . . . saluted us in English and bade us 'Welcome!'"

This visitor was Samoset, an Abenaki from what is now Maine. Previously, he had met English sea captains and learned to speak their language. Samoset told the Pilgrims much about the history of the land at Plymouth.

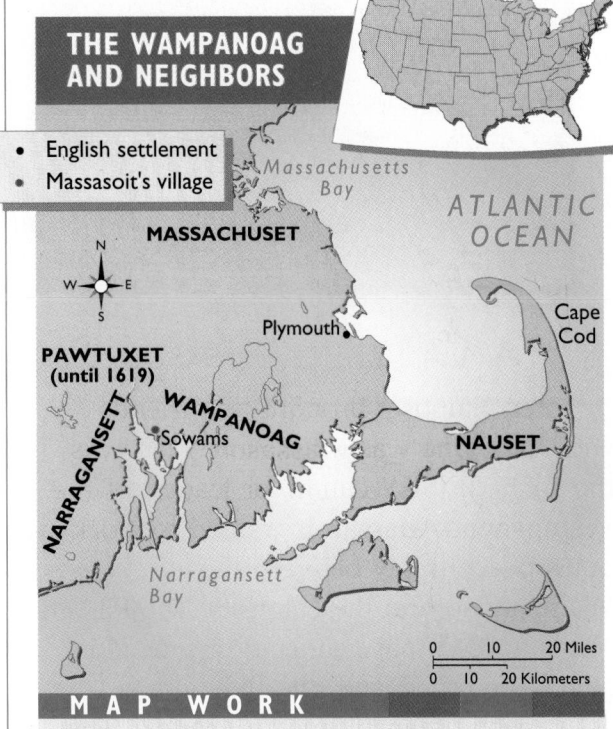

THE WAMPANOAG AND NEIGHBORS

- English settlement
- Massasoit's village

MASSACHUSET
Massachusetts Bay
ATLANTIC OCEAN
Plymouth
Cape Cod
PAWTUXET (until 1619)
WAMPANOAG
Sowams
NARRAGANSETT
NAUSET
Narragansett Bay

0   10   20 Miles
0   10   20 Kilometers

M A P   W O R K

The Native Americans of New England also included many smaller groups of peoples that are not shown on the map.

How many Native American peoples are shown on the map? Who are they?

According to popular belief, the Pilgrims stepped ashore on Plymouth Rock.

A LASTING PEACE

Later, Samoset brought two friends with him. One was Massasoit, who was the sachem (SAY chum), or leader, of the Wampanoag. Massasoit wanted to work out a peace treaty between the Wampanoag and the colonists. The Pilgrims agreed that neither group would attack the other, and that they would assist each other in times of trouble. This peace treaty was in effect for many years, until after Massasoit's death. Massasoit's son, however, would have a very different relationship with the English colonists.

Squanto Helps the Pilgrims

The other friend Samoset brought was Squanto. Squanto had been captured by an English fishing captain in 1614 and sold as a slave in Spain. When he returned to his home, Squanto found that all his people, the Patuxet (PAW tuk sut), had died from disease. Massasoit allowed Squanto to join the Wampanoag.

In their first winter at Plymouth, the Pilgrims suffered from disease, cold, and difficulties growing food. Half of the Pilgrims from the *Mayflower* died. Squanto stayed on with the Pilgrims and taught them to catch eels and fish and to make the soil rich for crops.

A Thanksgiving Feast

In 1621, probably in October, William Bradford sent Squanto to invite Massasoit and the Wampanoag to a feast of thanksgiving. The Pilgrims had suffered much hardship, but they still had good reason to thank God. The festivities lasted three days. The days were filled with feasting, games, and contests. This feast would later be viewed by many as our country's first Thanksgiving. Celebrating good harvests was not new, though. The English and the Wampanoag had each held such celebrations long before, but this time they feasted together.

In 1621 the Pilgrims celebrated Thanksgiving with the Wampanoag (above). The statue of Massasoit (left) stands today in Plymouth.

WHY IT MATTERS

Despite hardships, the Plymouth colony survived and grew. Friendly relations with the Wampanoag helped the Pilgrims to overcome early difficulties. Before long, other religious groups from Europe would seek freedom in North America.

The early colonists believed the right to govern themselves was very important. The Mayflower Compact served as a model for other colonists who wished to form a new government. This belief in self-government drove the later colonists to break away from England.

The Mayflower Compact was signed by men only. At the time married women had few legal rights. As you will later read, only single women over 21 were allowed to own property. It would be 300 years before women won the right to vote.

How did Thanksgiving become a national holiday?

For many years the United States as a country had no regular date on which to celebrate Thanksgiving. Then in 1863 President Abraham Lincoln officially made the last Thursday of November Thanksgiving Day. In 1941, the United States Congress made Thanksgiving the fourth Thursday of November. Thanksgiving also became a legal federal holiday.

✔️ Reviewing Facts and Ideas

MAIN IDEAS

- Religious conflict led the Pilgrims to leave England for the Netherlands and then to settle in North America.

- In 1620 the Pilgrims sailed for Virginia on the *Mayflower* but landed instead in New England. There they drew up the Mayflower Compact to set up a government for their colony.

- The Wampanoag were one of many Native American peoples living in New England. Their leader, Massasoit, became a loyal friend of the Pilgrims.

- In 1621 the Pilgrims and their Wampanoag friends celebrated a great harvest. Today many people in the United States count that feast as our country's first Thanksgiving.

THINK ABOUT IT

1. Why did the Pilgrims leave England?
2. Why did the Pilgrims write the Mayflower Compact?
3. **FOCUS** What was life like for the Pilgrims in the Plymouth colony in the first year? How did the Native Americans help the Pilgrims?
4. **THINKING SKILL** Read the excerpt on page 176 from *Of Plymouth Plantation*. Then list the *facts* Bradford gives in one column and his *opinions* in another.
5. **GEOGRAPHY** How did the New England climate affect the Pilgrims' attempt to settle there? How might the climate of Virginia have affected a settlement there?

Thanksgiving

How do you picture Thanksgiving? Perhaps you imagine a warm house filled with the delicious smell of turkey, where a family such as the one in this painting sits around the dinner table. Perhaps you think of it as a day on which to worship God and to help others. Both images of Thanksgiving have been around a long time.

Thanksgiving has been a national American holiday since 1863. The holiday's roots go back directly to the Pilgrims' feast in the fall of 1621.

Giving thanks is a legacy shared by many cultures. For hundreds of years people have come together for at least one day each year to give thanks for plentiful food and safe homes.

The Norman Rockwell Museum, Stockbridge

This painting, *Freedom from Want,* was created by Norman Rockwell in 1943.

This painting shows English colonists giving thanks to God for their safe arrival in Virginia on December 14, 1619. Similar ceremonies were held by the Pilgrims in Massachusetts, French colonists in Florida, and Spanish settlers in Texas. Many Native Americans in these places held thanksgiving celebrations long before Europeans arrived.

Thanksgiving reminds many people that their community is made up of more than family and friends. Every Thanksgiving state workers serve Thanksgiving dinner to homeless people in Austin, Texas.

Painting by Sidney King/Courtesy of the Berkeley Plantation and Bicast Publishing Co., Williamsburg

The people of Santa Clara Pueblo in New Mexico hold the ceremonial Rainbow Dance to show thanks for the season's corn crop.

181

CHAPTER 6 REVIEW

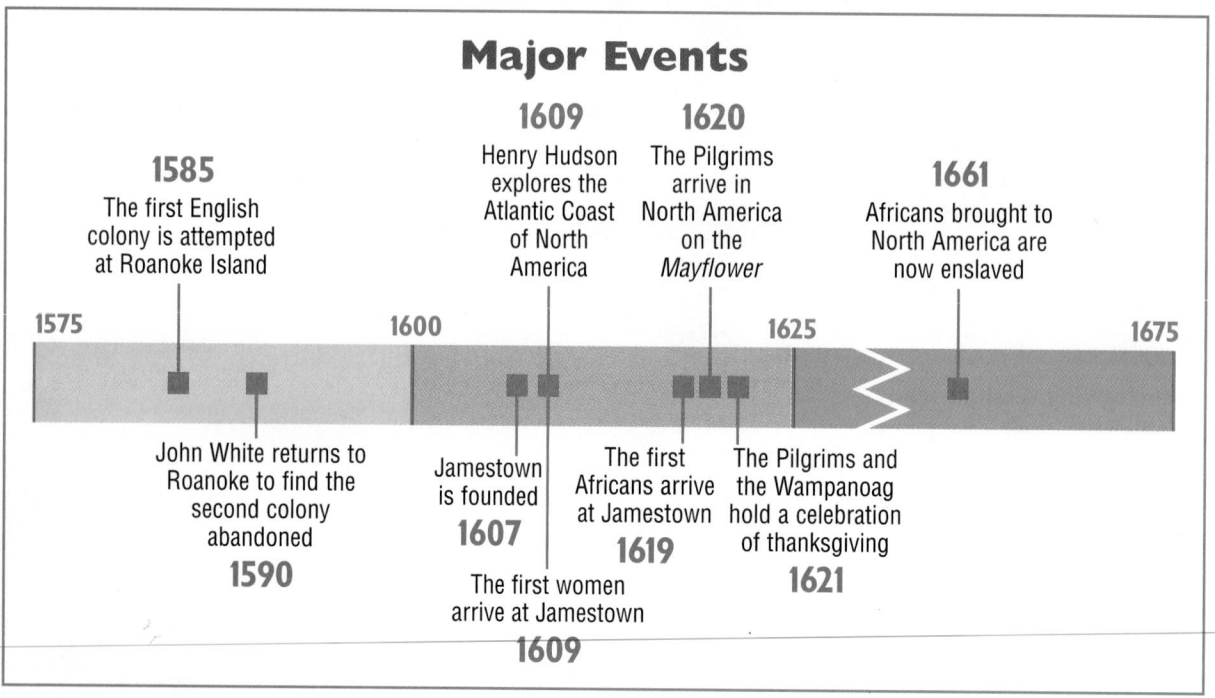

Major Events

1585
The first English colony is attempted at Roanoke Island

1609
Henry Hudson explores the Atlantic Coast of North America

1620
The Pilgrims arrive in North America on the *Mayflower*

1661
Africans brought to North America are now enslaved

1575   1600   1625   1675

John White returns to Roanoke to find the second colony abandoned
1590

Jamestown is founded
1607

The first women arrive at Jamestown
1609

The first Africans arrive at Jamestown
1619

The Pilgrims and the Wampanoag hold a celebration of thanksgiving
1621

THINKING ABOUT VOCABULARY

Number a sheet of paper from 1 to 10. Beside each number write the word or term below that best completes the sentence.

cash crop
charter
fact
indentured servant
Mayflower Compact

Northwest Passage
opinion
Pilgrim
sachem
Separatist

1. Henry Hudson sailed in search of the _____, a water route through North America to Asia.

2. When a sentence begins with "I believe," it may express an _____.

3. Each male _____ on the *Mayflower* signed a written set of rules to govern the Plymouth colony.

4. It is a _____ that John Carver was the first governor of the Plymouth colony.

5. Each of the Native American peoples had a _____, or leader.

6. Demand for tobacco in England made it a good _____ for the Virginia colonists.

7. The _____ governed the Plymouth colony.

8. The colonists got a _____ from their queen to let them settle in North America.

9. A person who believed that it was necessary to be apart from the Church of England was called a _____.

10. An _____ worked for the person who paid for his or her trip to North America.

THINKING ABOUT FACTS

1. What did Sir Walter Raleigh convince Queen Elizabeth to do in the late 1500s?

2. What was the purpose of Henry Hudson's explorations in 1609?

3. Who was John Rolfe?

4. Why did the Pilgrims come to North America?

5. Look at the time line above. How many years passed from the founding of Jamestown to the arrival of Africans?

THINK AND WRITE

WRITING AN EXPEDITION PROPOSAL
Write a proposal in which you attempt to convince a ruler or company to pay for your expedition across the Atlantic.

WRITING A DIARY
Suppose that you are Pocahontas, traveling in England for the first time. Write a series of diary entries in which you record your thoughts about the country.

WRITING A REPORT
Write a report in which you describe the various Native American peoples that Europeans met as they began colonies in North America. Include facts about their way of life and forms of government.

APPLYING THINKING SKILLS

DISTINGUISHING FACT FROM OPINION
Answer the following questions to apply the skill of distinguishing fact from opinion.

1. What is a fact? What is an opinion?
2. What are some clues that you can look for to help recognize an opinion?
3. Which of the following state a fact?
   a. John White returned to the Roanoke colony in 1590.
   b. The Pilgrims sailed on the *Mayflower*.
   c. The Roanoac were the most courageous people.
4. At first Henry Hudson believed that he had found the Northwest Passage as he sailed up the Hudson River. Was this a fact or an opinion?
5. Why is distinguishing facts from opinions an important skill?

Summing Up the Chapter

Copy the matrix chart on a separate sheet of paper. Fill in the blank sections to help summarize the information in this chapter. After you have finished, use the information in the chart to write a few paragraphs in which you answer the question "How would you compare and contrast the early European settlements and expeditions in the Americas?"

COLONY/EXPEDITION	YEARS	LEADER	RESULTS
Roanoke	1585 1587	Walter Raleigh John White	First colony fails. Second colony is lost.
Jamestown		John Smith John Rolfe	
Hudson's Expedition	1609	Henry Hudson	
Plymouth			Mayflower Compact; peaceful relations begin with the Wampanoag.

UNIT 3 REVIEW

THINKING ABOUT VOCABULARY

Number a sheet of paper from 1 to 10. Beside each number write the word or term from the list below that best completes the sentence.

cash crop

colony

Columbian exchange

conquistadors

expedition

historical map

indentured servant

Mayflower Compact

missionary

Northwest Passage

1. When the young woman agreed to work for a period of time in exchange for passage to the Americas, she became an _____.

2. The _____ was the movement of people, plants, animals, and germs across the Atlantic Ocean that began after Christopher Columbus arrived in the Americas.

3. European explorers from many countries began looking for a _____ to Asia.

4. The explorer's _____, or journey for a special purpose, took him through lands unknown to him.

5. The _____ came to New Spain to teach the Roman Catholic religion to the Indians of Mexico.

6. Only male Pilgrims could sign the _____ when they reached North America.

7. A _____ is a place ruled by another country.

8. Tobacco is an example of a _____.

9. The _____ came to the Americas to conquer land for Spain.

10. To find information about places where past events occurred, you can use an _____.

THINK AND WRITE

WRITING A SUMMARIZING PARAGRAPH

Write a summarizing paragraph that explains the cause-and-effect connections between Columbus's contact with the Taino in 1492 and the founding of European colonies in the Americas.

WRITING A DIALOGUE

Think about what the Wampanoag and the Pilgrims might have said to each other when they first met in the Plymouth Colony. Write a dialogue that you think could have taken place between one of the Pilgrims and one of the Wampanoag. For example, you might want to write a conversation between Samoset and William Bradford.

WRITING ABOUT PERSPECTIVES

Select a person you have read about in the unit. Compare what people thought about that person during his or her lifetime with what people may think about that person today. Explain why there might be differences between the two perspectives.

BUILDING SKILLS

1. **Historical maps** What does an historical map show?

2. **Historical maps** How can you tell if a map is an historical map?

3. **Fact and opinion** What are the clue words that help you know that something is an opinion?

4. **Fact and opinion** Is the following sentence a fact or an opinion? *Columbus made four voyages to the Americas.*

5. **Fact and opinion** What is one way to check the statement above?

YESTERDAY, TODAY &
TOMORROW

The explorers of the 1500s needed courage, knowledge, and creativity to invent new technology and to journey to places unknown to them. Would an explorer today need the same qualities? What kind of technology would he or she use? Where might an explorer of the future travel?

READING ON YOUR OWN

Here are some books you might find at the library to help you learn more.

HOW THE SEA BEGAN: A TAINO MYTH
by George Crespo, reteller
This myth tells about four boys who accidentally spill a sacred gourd that floods the land.

THE SPANISH PIONEERS OF THE SOUTHWEST
by Joan Anderson
This photographic essay shows the Latino culture of the Southwest region.

THREE YOUNG PILGRIMS
by Cheryl Harness
This story, based upon actual events, is about three Pilgrim children who sailed on the *Mayflower*.

UNIT REVIEW PROJECT

Make an Explorers' Map

1. Think about all the explorers you read about in this unit.

2. On a large piece of oak tag, trace a map that shows the Eastern and Western hemispheres.

3. Draw each explorer's route on the map. You can use a different colored marker for each one.

4. Present your map to the class.

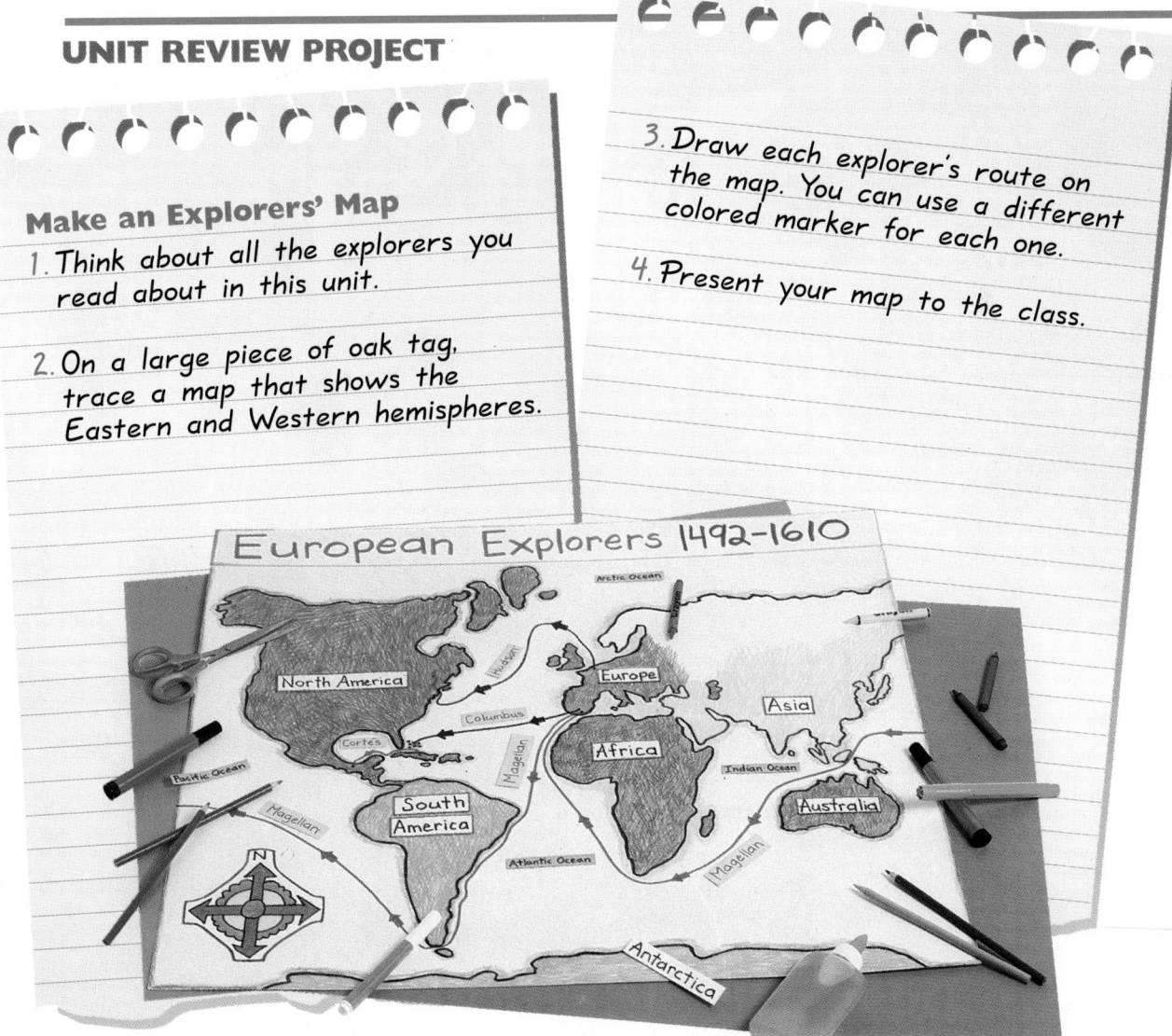

COLONIAL ROCKING HORSE;
MIDDLE COLONIES TAPESTRY;
PURITAN HORNBOOK

Colonial Williamsburg Foundation

The Granger
Collection

The 13 English Colonies

> "Early to bed, early to rise, makes a man healthy, wealthy, and wise."

from *Poor Richard's Almanack* by Benjamin Franklin
See page 283.

National Portrait Gallery, London

Metropolitan Museum of Art

BENJAMIN FRANKLIN; PEWTER CREAM PITCHER

WHY DOES IT MATTER?

In the 1500s and 1600s, explorers were coming to North America from Spain, France, and England. They all claimed the land that was first home to Native Americans. These countries established colonies, and settlers came to build new homes in North America. Some Native Americans who had been living on these lands found a way to live in peace with the colonists. Others fought to protect their way of life.

The colonists faced many hardships but worked hard to overcome them. The words above were written by a hard-working and wise colonist named Benjamin Franklin. In time, colonial settlements and cities developed and spread along the Atlantic Coast. With 13 thriving colonies, England became the major European power in North America.

The Granger Collection

SLAVE SHACKLES

Adventures with
with
NATIONAL
GEOGRAPHIC

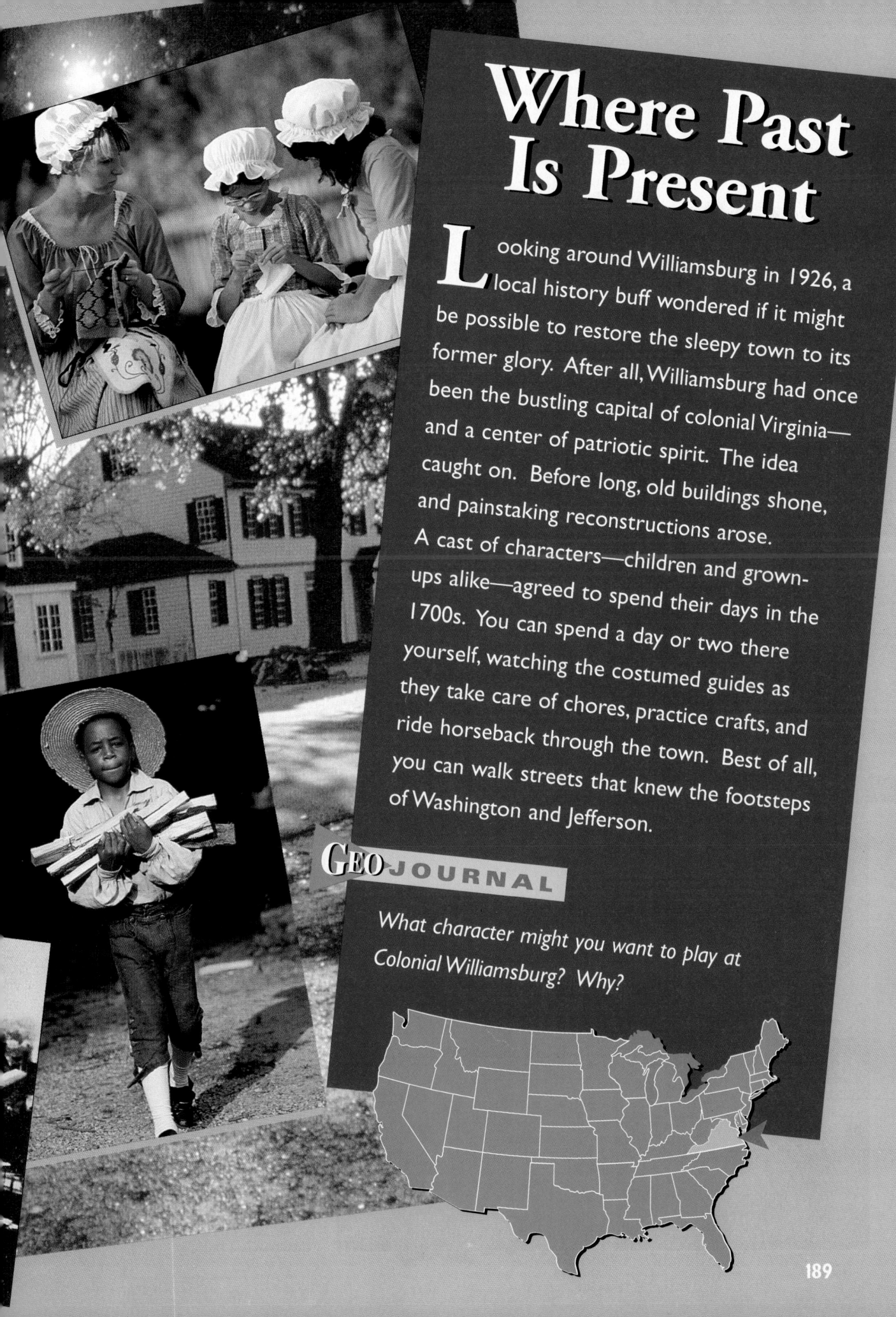

Where Past Is Present

Looking around Williamsburg in 1926, a local history buff wondered if it might be possible to restore the sleepy town to its former glory. After all, Williamsburg had once been the bustling capital of colonial Virginia— and a center of patriotic spirit. The idea caught on. Before long, old buildings shone, and painstaking reconstructions arose.

A cast of characters—children and grownups alike—agreed to spend their days in the 1700s. You can spend a day or two there yourself, watching the costumed guides as they take care of chores, practice crafts, and ride horseback through the town. Best of all, you can walk streets that knew the footsteps of Washington and Jefferson.

GEO JOURNAL

What character might you want to play at Colonial Williamsburg? Why?

CHAPTER 7

The New England Colonies

THINKING ABOUT
HISTORY AND GEOGRAPHY

From the time line you can see that Chapter 7 begins with the Puritans' arrival at Massachusetts Bay in 1630. Their colony quickly became one of the largest colonies of any European nation in North America. Out of this settlement grew the New England colonies. As you will read, the Puritans were strict and deeply religious. Their ways of life continue to influence our form of government, education system, and lifestyles even today.

1630
MASSACHUSETTS BAY

John Winthrop and the Puritans found a new colony

1638
RHODE ISLAND

Anne Hutchinson establishes the settlement of Portsmouth

1641
MASSACHUSETTS

The Puritans pass the first law that makes slavery legal

Massachusetts

Massachusetts Bay

Connecticut

Rhode Island

THE NEW ENGLAND COLONIES

NORTH AMERICA

ATLANTIC OCEAN

1675

CONNECTICUT

Chief Metacomet starts a war against the colonists

1692

MASSACHUSETTS

The Salem witch trials result in the deaths of innocent people

THE PURITANS BUILD A NEW SOCIETY

Focus Activity

READ TO LEARN
Who were the Puritans, and how did they differ from the Pilgrims?

VOCABULARY
common
grammar school
public school
town meeting
congregation

PEOPLE
King Charles I
John Winthrop
Cotton Mather

PLACES
Massachusetts
Boston

READ ALOUD

John Winthrop, the Puritan leader, saw Massachusetts for the first time from the ship Arbella. "We must be knit together as one," he said to the passengers. "We must rejoice together, mourn together, labor and suffer together." The year was 1630. These men and women had just completed the long voyage from England to North America.

THE BIG PICTURE

While the Pilgrims settled Plymouth, another group of English Protestants, the Puritans, were growing in numbers in England. The Puritans and the Pilgrims both disagreed with the practices of the Church of England. Both groups had been jailed for their belief in a plainer style of worship. Both were against stained-glass windows, statues, and fancy ceremonies in church. Unlike the Pilgrims, the Puritans never broke with the Church of England. They decided instead to build a model Puritan community 3,000 miles away.

In 1629 a group of Puritans formed the Massachusetts Bay Company. King Charles I of England gave them a charter to settle in North America. In 1630 the Puritans sailed there. They landed in an area that John Smith had reached in 1614. Smith later named the region New England. The Puritans settled in a part of New England called Massachusetts Bay. Their settlement later became known as Massachusetts.

192

THE PURITANS ARRIVE

Compared to the Pilgrims, the Puritans arrived in North America in great numbers. Instead of one ship, the Puritans sailed to North America in a fleet of 11 ships. Instead of 100 people, the Puritans brought close to 700. They also brought supplies, equipment, a herd of cows, and about 60 horses.

John Winthrop

The leader of the Puritans was a successful lawyer named John Winthrop. It was Winthrop who led the Puritans to Massachusetts Bay on the coast of New England in 1630. The word

Massachusetts means "at or near the great hill" in Algonkian, the language of the Native Americans who lived in the area.

The Puritans founded the Massachusetts Bay Colony along the Charles River. The colony's first settlement was named Boston. Find Boston on the map on this page. John Winthrop was elected the first governor by Puritan men, who were the only colonists allowed to vote.

The Geography of New England

At first life in the Massachusetts Bay Colony was hard. Much of the land was hilly. The soil was thin and rocky. These conditions made farming difficult.

Still, the area had many other natural resources that the Puritans needed to survive. The forests supplied the colonists with wood to make homes, fences, and tools. The Charles River and the Atlantic Ocean provided many kinds of fish. Although the land was not good for farming, New England had much to offer its colonists.

THE NEW ENGLAND COLONIES

Map labels:
St. Lawrence R. · 100 · 200 Miles · 0 · 100 · 200 Kilometers

NEW FRANCE · Lake Champlain · St. Croix River · MAINE (part of Massachusetts) · Kennebec River · VERMONT (claimed by New Hampshire & New York) · Connecticut R. · NEW HAMPSHIRE (1680) · Merrimac R. · ATLANTIC OCEAN · N W E S · MASSACHUSETTS (1630) · Boston · Salem · Massachusetts Bay · Plymouth · Cape Cod · CONNECTICUT (1636) · Providence · Cape Cod Bay · Hartford · Portsmouth · RHODE ISLAND (1636) · Long Island Sound · Long Island

M A P   W O R K

Dates after the names of New England colonies are the years they were founded.

1. Which colony was claimed by both New Hampshire and New York?
2. Which colonies were founded after 1630?

Metropolitan Museum of Art, NYC

Although the New England colonists lived off the land and sea, they also relied on supplies and household items like this jug (right) that they brought with them from Europe.

"A CITY UPON A HILL"

The Puritans wanted to create more than a colony. They wanted to set up a model community for all the world to follow. John Winthrop used words from the Bible to describe this community.

Consider that we shall be as a city upon a hill, the eyes of all people are upon us.

In many ways Winthrop's dream came true. Ten years after the Puritans arrived, the Massachusetts Bay Colony had grown from 700 people to more than 20,000. It had one of the largest populations of any colony in North America.

The Puritans had an easier time than the Pilgrims. They had studied the climate and geography of North America and came in spring, so there was time to clear land and build houses before winter. Most Massachusetts Puritans were merchants, craftworkers, and landowners, with more money than the Pilgrims.

The Puritan Way of Life

In the Puritan community each "free man," as a male colonist was called, promised that his family would live by the rules of the Puritan church. The Puritans believed that success was a result of their belief in their God and the Bible. They also believed in hard work and simple living.

The Puritans began to cut down the forests and build villages like ones in England. They built according to a plan. Look at the picture on page 195. The Puritan church, called a meetinghouse, was placed at the center of the village next to the village green, or common.

The Importance of Education

The Puritans valued education. Every member of the community had to be able to read the Bible. At first parents taught their children to read. In 1647 the Puritans passed laws setting up elementary schools in towns with 50 or more families, and secondary schools—called grammar schools—in towns with 100 or more families. These were the first public schools in the colonies. Public schools are ones open to all children and supported by people's taxes.

In 1636 the Puritans founded Newtowne College, the first college in the colonies. Soon the college's name was changed to Harvard, after John Harvard, a Puritan minister.

Massachusetts Historical Society

This tapestry shows Harvard College, founded by the Puritans in 1636.

A New England Village, 1630–1650

MILL

WOOD LOT

FIELDS

MINISTER'S HOUSE

SCHOOL

MEETINGHOUSE

INN

STOCKS

COMMON

WELL

SHOEMAKER

BLACKSMITH

BARREL MAKER

The Old Ship's Church (left) in Hingham, Massachusetts, is one of many surviving Puritan churches. New Englanders still hold town meetings (below).

PURITAN GOVERNMENT

The Puritans remembered how they had suffered under the English king. Instead of giving one leader all the power, they allowed certain people to have a say in their government. All issues affecting a town were discussed and voted on at town meetings. However, only white males who were members of the church, or congregation, had a vote. Women could not vote. They had few of the same rights as men.

Religion and the Law

For the Puritans, religion and government were not separate. Many of their laws strengthened Puritan religious practices. For example, a person could be punished for not attending church.

The Puritans were expected to follow the laws of the church and colony. The ministers had control over people's behavior. They encouraged colonists to report anyone who broke the rules. Those who went against Puritan beliefs could be publicly criticized and be forced to leave the church.

Africans Arrive in New England

As you read, the Puritans felt that they were creating an ideal community. Yet they were slave owners and slave traders. In 1638 the first captive Africans arrived in Boston. John Winthrop recorded the event.

> Mr. Pierce, in the Salem ship the Desire, returned from the West Indies after seven months. He had . . . bought some cotton, and tobacco, and negroes [Africans]. February 26, 1638

Slavery Is Made Legal

The first Africans in New England were indentured servants who could earn freedom after working a number of years. In 1641 the Puritans passed the first of several laws that made slavery legal. By 1670 Massachusetts law allowed the children of enslaved Africans to be sold into slavery.

The Puritans had different ideas about slavery than the Jamestown colonists. Jamestown slaves had no rights. In New

England enslaved Africans were sometimes treated as part of the family and had some of the same rights as Puritans. Enslaved men could testify in court, marry, own property, and become voting members of the church.

Puritans taught enslaved Africans to read and write. Many enslaved Africans learned a trade and held jobs in the community. However, enslaved people were still thought of as property, and some were treated cruelly.

The Negro Society

Cotton Mather, a Puritan minister, formed The Negro Society to improve the lives of enslaved people. He also set up a separate school for African Americans. Some free African Americans gained wealth and became respected members of their communities. In 1656 a freed slave named Bostian Ken became one of the first African American landowners. He owned a house and farm in Dorchester, Massachusetts.

Nantucket Historical Association

Many free and enslaved African Americans became seamen. This portrait of sailor Absalom Boston was painted in the 1700s.

WHY IT MATTERS

The Puritans valued hard work and simple living. Their way of life has had a lasting effect on our country. Some of our ideas about self-government and limiting the power of rulers can be traced back to the Massachusetts Bay Colony. In the next lesson you will learn about the growth of the New England colonies.

✓/ Reviewing Facts and Ideas

MAIN IDEAS

- The Puritans and the Pilgrims disagreed with practices of the Church of England.

- In 1630 a group of Puritans led by John Winthrop sailed to New England and founded the settlement of Massachusetts Bay.

- The Puritans believed in hard work and education. They built public schools and also founded Harvard College.

- The first Africans came to New England as indentured servants. In 1641 the Puritans began to make slavery legal in New England.

THINK ABOUT IT

1. Why did the Puritans disagree with the Church of England?

2. Why was education important to the Puritans?

3. FOCUS Who were the Puritans, and how were they different from the Pilgrims?

4. THINKING SKILL How did the Puritans _solve_ some of the _problems_ the Pilgrims had faced?

5. GEOGRAPHY Look at the map on page 193. Why was the Massachusetts Bay Colony a good location for trade?

STUDYSKILLS

Using Primary and Secondary Sources

VOCABULARY

primary source
secondary source

WHY THE SKILL MATTERS

When you become particularly interested in something that happened in the past, you probably want to learn all you can about it. Where do you look? There are two kinds of sources you need to check.

The first kind is called a primary source. Primary sources are accounts by people involved in the events being written about. They provide important, firsthand details that give you an idea of how people of the time thought and felt. Most of the "Many Voices" features in this book are from primary sources. Items such as letters, diaries, newspaper stories, speeches, and official documents are primary sources, as well. Photographs and paintings can also be primary sources since they tell us about the time during which they were created.

The second kind is called a secondary source. Secondary sources are written by people who were not there themselves.

Secondary sources are usually based on many primary sources. Thus they often provide useful summaries of historical events. They can also help you see how an event is part of larger trends or developments. This textbook is an example of a secondary source. Encyclopedias, atlases, and history books are also secondary sources.

In order to get the most complete information, you will want to use both primary and secondary sources. Primary sources give you an understanding of what a past event was like from the point of view of those involved in it or those who observed it. They express the view of one person. Secondary sources often compare, analyze, and combine different points of view. Together primary and secondary sources help you to form a more complete picture of an event.

USING PRIMARY SOURCES

The following passage is a primary source taken from *The Journal of Madam Knight*. Sarah Kemble Knight was born in Boston in 1666 and traveled to other parts of New England. She observed how some New Englanders treated enslaved African Americans. Treat this primary source the way a detective handles evidence. Look for clues that reveal Knight's feelings.

TO BE SOLD,
A likely ſtrong Negro Girl, about 17 Years of Age ; ſold by Reaſon that a Boy would ſuit the Owner better. Enquire at R. & S. Draper's Printing Office

[New Englanders are] too indulgent [soft] (especially the farmers) . . . with their slaves . . . permitting them to sit at table and eat with them . . . They told me there was a farmer lived near the town where I lodged who had some difference with his slave, concerning something the master had promised him and did not punctually perform; which caused some hard words between them; but at length they put the matter to arbitration [to be judged] . . . which done, the arbitrators [judges] . . . order[ed] the master to pay 40s [40 shillings].

Knight lets us know what one Puritan in the 1600s thought about how enslaved African Americans should be treated. She felt that New Englanders allowed enslaved people too much freedom.

USING SECONDARY SOURCES

Now read this excerpt from *In Freedom's Footsteps*, a book written by historian Charles H. Wesley in 1978. Notice the type of information Wesley presents.

Slaves were frequently treated as members of the family ... Slaves had recourse [could go] to the courts and, throughout the colonial period, could testify against whites. They were permitted to own property. Marital ties among the blacks were ordinarily respected, and their marriages were solemnly consecrated [viewed as godly] by the Puritan churches.

The Stratford Historical Society

Notice that Wesley does not limit his account of African Americans in Puritan society to one particular person or event. Wesley gives you information about how African Americans were treated in the New England colonies.

TRYING THE SKILL

Now reread each of the preceding passages. Which source would you use to learn about African Americans in the New England colonies in general? Which source tells you about how some Puritans might have felt about enslaved African Americans?

Finally, look at the 1763 advertisement reproduced on page 198 and the image on page 199 taken from a bill that accompanied the sale of an enslaved African American in 1796. Are they primary or secondary sources? Explain your answer.

REVIEWING THE SKILL

1. What is a primary source? What is a secondary source?
2. Which passage expresses the opinion of one person?
3. Which passage presents information based on the reports of more than one person?
4. Which passage gives a more factual account of the position of enslaved people in Puritan society? Explain.
5. How do both primary and secondary sources help you to understand history?

Enslaved Africans were sold through ads in newspapers (far left), just as goods are sold today. Sometimes images, such as the picture of Flora (left), accompanied the ads.

Architect of the Capitol, Washington, D.C.

Focus Activity

READ TO LEARN
What caused the New England colonies to grow?

VOCABULARY
tolerate

PEOPLE
Roger Williams
Anne Hutchinson
Thomas Hooker
Metacomet
Tituba
Samuel Sewall

PLACES
Providence
Rhode Island
Hartford
Connecticut
Portsmouth
New Hampshire
Vermont
Maine
Salem

THE NEW ENGLAND COLONIES GROW

READ ALOUD

Sometimes God gives them fish or flesh,
Yet they're content without.
And what comes in, they part [give] to friends
And strangers round about.

Roger Williams, a New England colonist who studied Native American cultures and languages, wrote this about New England's native people in the 1600s. As you will read, not all New Englanders agreed with Roger Williams.

THE BIG PICTURE

Shortly after the founding of the Massachusetts Bay Colony, some Puritans began to question the beliefs of their leaders. This caused them to leave Massachusetts to found colonies of their own. As new colonies were started, more people came to New England. However, the spread of the colonies eventually led to conflicts with Native Americans over land.

PURITANS SPEAK OUT

Puritans were not expected to question the actions of their leaders. Yet a few years after they arrived in Massachusetts, some Puritans began to speak out. Roger Williams, Anne Hutchinson, and Thomas Hooker were three Puritans who disagreed with the Puritan leaders. They founded their own colonies, which are shown on the map on page 193.

A Friend of Native Americans

Roger Williams had been a Puritan minister at Salem and at Plymouth. He left both places because his opinions made him unwelcome. Unlike most Puritans, he respected people of different faiths and backgrounds, including Native Americans.

Williams traded with the Wampanoag and Narragansett (nar uh GAN siht). He slept in their homes and ate their food. He also studied and wrote about their language and culture, as you read in the Read Aloud.

Williams shocked many Puritans, because he believed that people of different faiths should be free to practice their religion as they pleased. He also felt that the New England colonists should tolerate different religious beliefs. *Tolerate* means "allow people to have beliefs different from your own." He thought that it was wrong to make people go to church against their will.

Colonists such as Anne Hutchinson (right) disagreed with Governor John Winthrop (above). The scene below shows the coastal area where the Puritans settled.

PURITANS START NEW ENGLAND

Roger Williams shared his beliefs with other Puritans. For this he was brought to trial in 1635. The Puritan leaders tried to change his views. When they could not, they planned to send Williams back to England. He escaped from the colony in 1636. Williams and his followers founded a settlement called Providence. This settlement eventually became part of the new colony of Rhode Island. In Rhode Island people of all religions were welcome.

Connecticut Founder

The Puritan minister Thomas Hooker left Massachusetts by choice. He believed that each church should be independent and should choose its own leaders. In 1636 he and about 60 followers traveled 120 miles south to found the settlement of Hartford in the new colony of Connecticut.

A Spirited Woman

Another Puritan who disagreed with the Puritan ministers was Anne Hutchinson, mother of 15 children. The Puritans admired her ability to nurse the sick. Hutchinson had strong religious beliefs, but she found the sermons, or religious talks, of the Boston ministers too rigid.

Hutchinson began holding evening prayer meetings for women in her home. Soon men came as well. People liked her meetings because she was less strict and rigid in her teachings than the Puritan ministers.

Native Americans of Rhode Island helped Roger Williams when he fled from Massachusetts.

Anne Hutchinson used herbs such as chickweed (above) and borage (bottom right) as medicines. She stood trial and was banished from Massachusetts because she disagreed with Puritan leaders.

Hutchinson believed that holiness was a matter of inner faith, not good works. She told people that the Christian God revealed grace and love directly to them without the aid of ministers. The Puritan leaders decided that Hutchinson was a dangerous threat to their power. They brought her to trial in 1637. Governor Winthrop acted as one of the judges. He found Hutchinson to be a woman with "a nimble [quick] wit and active spirit," but he ordered her to leave the colony at the end of the trial. Winthrop said, "You have stepped out of your place, you have rather been a husband than a wife and a preacher than a hearer." Hutchinson stood before Winthrop and said, "I desire to know wherefore [why] I am banished." Winthrop said to her, "Say no more, the court knows wherefore, and is satisfied."

After Hutchinson left Massachsetts in 1638, she traveled south to Rhode Island. There her family and supporters started a new settlement. This community soon became known as Portsmouth.

TROUBLES IN NEW ENGLAND

The 1600s were not peaceful years in New England. Fighting occurred between colonists and Native Americans. Also a witch scare turned Puritans against one another.

Changes for the Native Americans

As the New England colonies grew, disagreements arose between colonists and Native Americans. In the Connecticut colony, bitter fighting broke out between the colonists and the Pequot (PEE kwaht). In the Pequot War of 1637, as a brutal attack on the Pequot was called, hundreds of Pequot, including women and children, were killed.

After the Pequot War, colonists were able to move further north to what is now New Hampshire. They also moved to the areas that later became Vermont and Maine.

Metacomet

By 1675 the Wampanoag leader Metacomet (met uh KAHM ut), whom the English called King Philip, was preparing to fight to keep Wampanoag lands and force the colonists out of New England. Many Native Americans joined Metacomet's forces.

During King Philip's War, as the struggle was called, fierce fighting took place. After first suffering losses, the colonists defeated the Native Americans.

Shelburne Museum, Vermont

In 1676 the Puritans captured and killed Metacomet. His family and other Native American families were sold into slavery in the West Indies. This defeat marked the end of strong Native American resistance in the New England colonies.

The Salem Witch Scare

After King Philip's War, New England colonists had another cause of unrest. Many Puritans believed in witches, people who were thought to have special powers that could cause harm to others. They believed that witches worked with the Devil, who was thought to be the chief spirit of evil and the enemy of their God. Witchcraft, the practice of putting spells on people, was a serious crime.

The home of Jonathan Corwin, a judge in the Salem witch trials (far right), has been made into a museum (right). Metacomet (above) led a war in which 12 colony towns were completely destroyed.

For no clear reason, several Puritan girls in Salem, Massachusetts, began to behave strangely in 1692. They screamed and fell to the ground. Soon it was said that they were victims of witchcraft. The girls accused Tituba, an enslaved African American woman, of practicing witchcraft. Tituba, in turn, accused one Salem girl of being a witch. The fear of witches spread quickly. Husbands accused wives of witchcraft. Neighbors accused one another. Witch trials were held, and by the fall of 1692, 19 people had been found guilty of witchcraft and hanged.

Some historians say that the girls were playing a terrible game. Others say that poor farmers accused wealthier neighbors to get their land. Some of the girls later admitted that they had lied.

Samuel Sewall was one of the judges who sentenced people to death for witchcraft. Five years after the trials, he said that he had made an awful mistake. In his diary he wrote that he, "Samuel Sewall . . . Desires to take the Blame and shame of it, Asking pardon."

WHY IT MATTERS

The New England Puritans disagreed about religion. This led to the founding of new colonies. Puritans who challenged their leaders spread new ideas about religious freedom. These ideas later became an important part of our government's laws.

✓ Reviewing Facts and Ideas

MAIN IDEAS

- In 1636, Roger Williams founded Providence, the first settlement in Rhode Island. In 1638 Anne Hutchinson founded Portsmouth, also in Rhode Island. Connecticut was founded in 1636 by Thomas Hooker.

- The Wampanoag leader Metacomet led King Philip's War against the English in 1675. He was defeated.

- The 1692 Salem witch trials led to the deaths of innocent people.

THINK ABOUT IT

1. Why were Roger Williams and Anne Hutchinson brought to trial?

2. Why did Metacomet fight the English?

3. **FOCUS** What caused the New England colonies to grow?

4. **THINKING SKILL** What *effects* did the New England colonists have on Native Americans?

5. **WRITE** Suppose that you are living in Massachusetts during Anne Hutchinson's time. Write a diary entry about your decision to join her new colony.

The Winterthur Museum

LIFE IN EARLY NEW ENGLAND

READ ALOUD

"I went to meeting [church] *and paid good attention to the sermon, came home and wrote down as much of it as I could remember. . . . I did everything before breakfast; endeavored* [tried] *to improve in school; went to the funeral in the afternoon, attended* [listened] *to what was said, came home and wrote down as much as I could remember . . . and after I was done I swept out the house and put the things to rights* [in order]*."* Mary Osgood Sumner was a Puritan girl who wrote down her duties in her diary in the 1700s.

Focus Activity

READ TO LEARN
How did Puritan religious beliefs affect how children were educated?

VOCABULARY
dame school
hornbook
The New England Primer
apprentice
journeyman

PEOPLE
John Cotton
Anne Bradstreet

THE BIG PICTURE

In an earlier lesson you learned how Puritan religious beliefs led to the creation of self-governing towns and public schools. Puritan religious beliefs also influenced every area of daily life. The Puritans believed that it was the duty of families to teach their children Puritan religious beliefs. Those who did not obey the rules were punished. Puritan families raised their children to become faithful church members and good citizens.

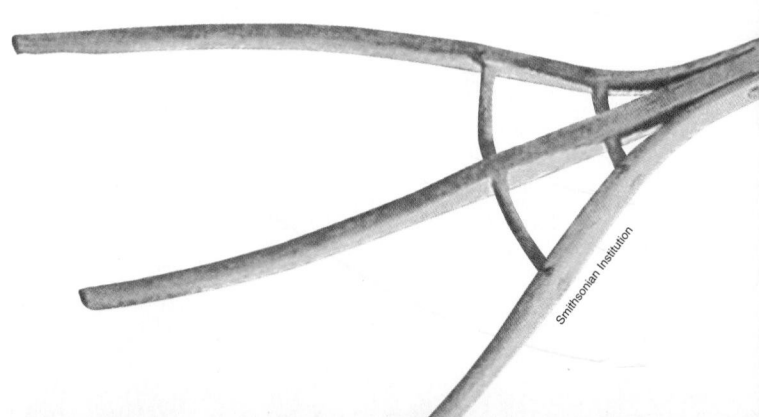

Smithsonian Institution

PURITAN FAMILIES

The early New Englanders lived in one-room wooden cabins. At first, the houses had straw roofs, chimneys made out of logs and clay, and frost-free cellars to store food. The first windows were made of paper coated with oil, waxed cloth, or scraped animal horn. Later houses had wooden shingles and lead-glass windows. A fireplace was the main source of heat.

Treatment of Children

The Puritans treated children as if they were little adults, expecting them to work hard and to respect others. Children could not play on the Sabbath, the period from sunset on Saturday to sunset on Sunday. They were told not to disobey their parents or act stubborn, lazy, or rude.

Puritans did not allow their children to waste time, but children were allowed to play games and have toys until the age of seven. John Cotton, a Puritan minister in Boston, wrote that children should spend much time playing, "for their bodies are too weak to labor." Puritan children had dolls, hoops, tops, and sleds. Both children and adults ice-skated.

Daily Chores

The New England colonists made many things by hand and grew their own food. Everyone in the family had jobs to do each day.

Women and girls took care of young children. They also cooked, cleaned, and made clothing. A Puritan girl knew how to spin wool into yarn, dye the yarn, and weave it into cloth. Girls and women also prepared family meals. They churned milk to make butter. They ground corn to make bread. They made candles and soap from animal fat and wax. They also helped with the farm chores.

Men and boys took care of the land and the cows, pigs, and sheep. They cleared rocks from the soil and built fences. They planted corn, squash, and other crops. They also hunted, fished, made furniture, and built houses.

Worcester Art Museum

Puritans used tools like this kettle and pitchfork (left). Adults and children dressed alike, as shown in the painting *Mrs. Freake and Baby Mary* (above).

Pilgrim Hall Museum

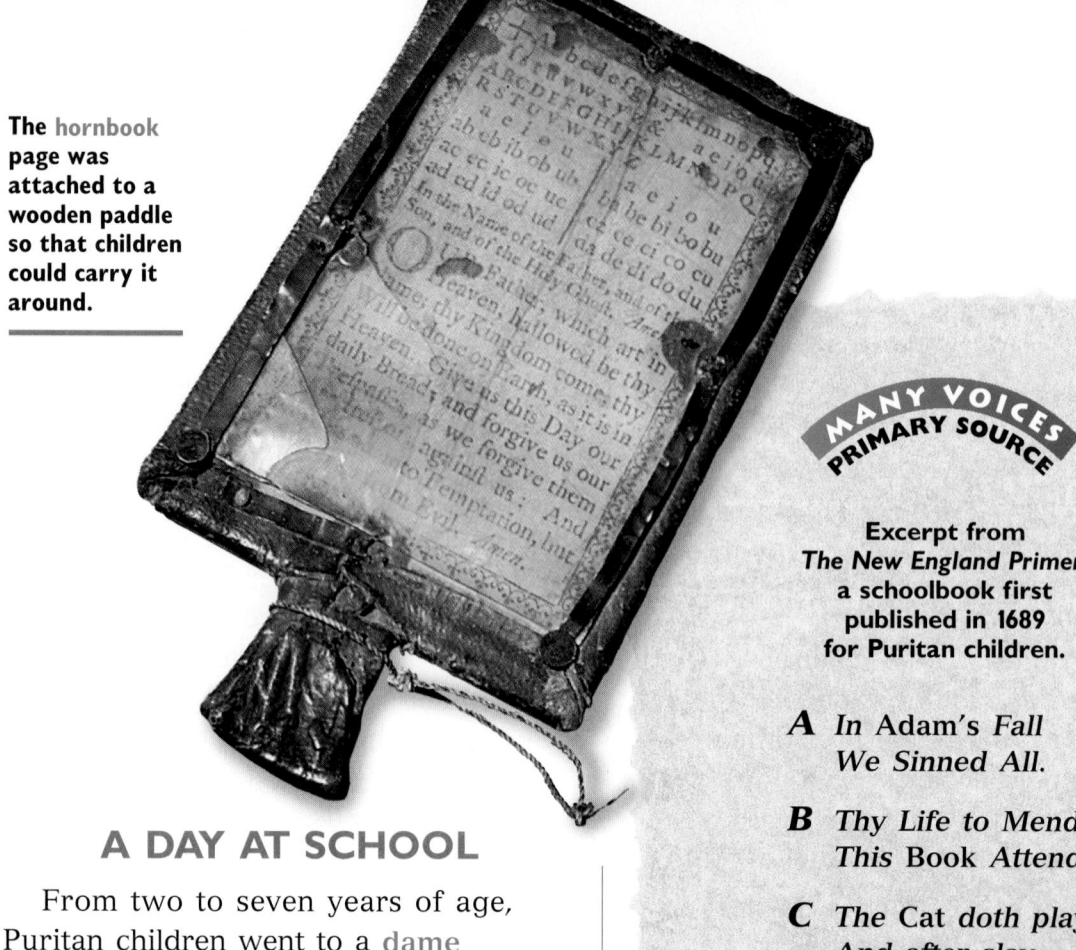

The **hornbook** page was attached to a wooden paddle so that children could carry it around.

Excerpt from *The New England Primer,* a schoolbook first published in 1689 for Puritan children.

A In Adam's *Fall* *We* Sinned All.

B Thy Life to Mend *This* Book Attend.

C The Cat *doth play* And after slay.

D A Dog *will bite* A Thief at night.

E An Eagle's *flight* Is out of sight.

F The Idle Fool Is whipt at School.

G As runs the Glass Man's life doth pass.

A DAY AT SCHOOL

From two to seven years of age, Puritan children went to a **dame school**. These elementary schools were often run by women in their homes. Enslaved African Americans also could attend these schools. Older children helped younger children with their school lessons.

Both boys and girls learned to read from a **hornbook**. This was not a book like the one you are reading now. It was a page placed under a sheet of clear animal horn with the alphabet, numbers, and a prayer printed on it. The hornbook was made to last a long time.

Once children could read the hornbook, they went on to study from **The New England Primer**. The primer taught spelling, vocabulary, and Puritan religious beliefs using simple rhymes. Around six million copies of *The New England Primer* were used between 1690 and 1830. To imagine what school was like then, read these lines from the primer. How does it compare to the books you are used to reading?

Skills They Needed

After students could read the primer, they learned how to read the Bible. In school Puritan children also learned how to add and subtract. After a girl was finished with dame school, she usually did not have any further schooling. The Puritans believed that girls should learn the many skills they would need as mothers and wives to manage their households.

For Boys Only

Around the age of seven, those boys who were preparing to become ministers went to grammar school. This was a school somewhat like our junior high school. Boys spent several hours a day, six days a week, learning rules and speaking their lessons out loud. They studied Latin and Greek, arithmetic, and religion.

Teachers were very strict. When a boy arrived at school, he had to take off his hat and bow to the teacher. Teachers punished students with a birch stick. Only boys who did well in grammar school could go on to college.

Learning a Trade

After the age of seven, boys who were going to learn a trade became apprentices. As an apprentice you would live with a master craftsman, such as a silversmith, blacksmith, or carpenter. Silversmiths made silver plates, cups, coins, and other objects. Blacksmiths made and repaired iron objects. The craftsman would teach you his skills.

At the end of the apprenticeship, you would hand in a project for approval. If you were an apprentice cabinetmaker, you would show your master a cabinet that you built yourself. If the master approved of your work, you would become a journeyman.

This was the next step toward becoming a master craftsman. As a journeyman you would receive a set of tools from your master. Then you would begin practicing your trade at home or in a shop. Some women helped their husbands or ran the family business when their husbands were away.

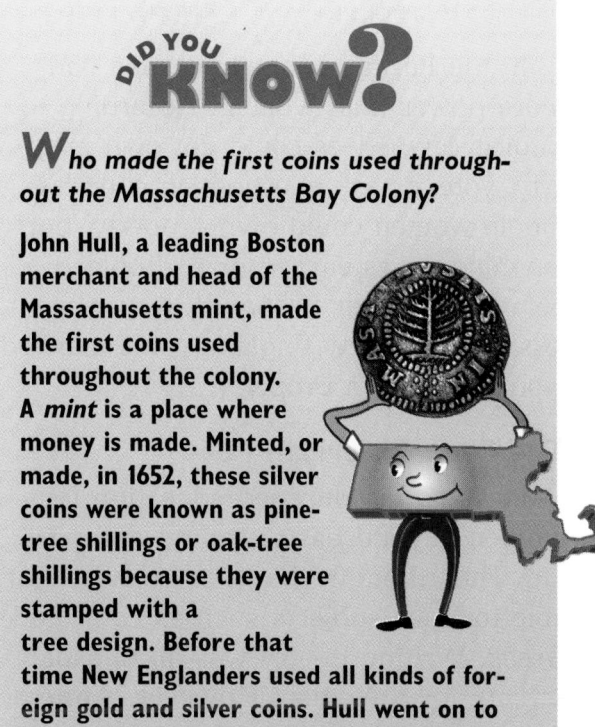

DID YOU KNOW?

Who made the *first coins used throughout the Massachusetts Bay Colony?*

John Hull, a leading Boston merchant and head of the Massachusetts mint, made the first coins used throughout the colony. A *mint* is a place where money is made. Minted, or made, in 1652, these silver coins were known as pine-tree shillings or oak-tree shillings because they were stamped with a tree design. Before that time New Englanders used all kinds of foreign gold and silver coins. Hull went on to become the colony's treasurer and one of the richest men in Massachusetts.

Craftsmen made many of the items used by the Puritans, even small items such as this hinge (right). Their saws were kept in cases (below) when not in use.

The Winterthur Museum

The Pilgrim Society

209

THE PURITAN COMMUNITY

In the Puritan community men had more power than women. According to English law, wives could not own property, vote, or ask questions in church. Single women could own property, but anything wives earned or had owned belonged to their husbands. Nevertheless, in early New England some married women did own property.

The First American Poet

Puritans discouraged education for women beyond basic reading and writing. They thought that women were not able to learn subjects such as Latin and Greek. Writing poetry was an unusual activity for a woman. However, Anne Bradstreet became the first important poet in the colonies.

Bradstreet was among the first Puritans to arrive in Massachusetts on the *Arbella*. She led a busy life as the wife of a Puritan leader and mother of eight. However, she still found time to write poems. In one poem she says that some people thought she would be better off sewing and knitting than writing. Bradstreet ignored her neighbors' disapproval. She continued to write of life in colonial Massachusetts. In 1650 a collection of Bradstreet's poems was printed in England.

Read this excerpt from a later Bradstreet poem about the fire that destroyed her house. What were her feelings when she saw the fire?

Parish of Boston, Lincolnshire, U.K.

Excerpt from "Upon the Burning of Our House, July 10th 1666," a poem by Anne Bradstreet.

*I wakened was with thund'ring noise
And piteous shrieks of dreadful voice.
That fearful sound of "Fire!" and "Fire!"
Let no man know is my desire.
I, starting up, the light did spy,
And to my God my heart did cry....*

*Here stood that trunk, and there
    that chest,
There lay that store I counted best.
My pleasant things in ashes lie.*

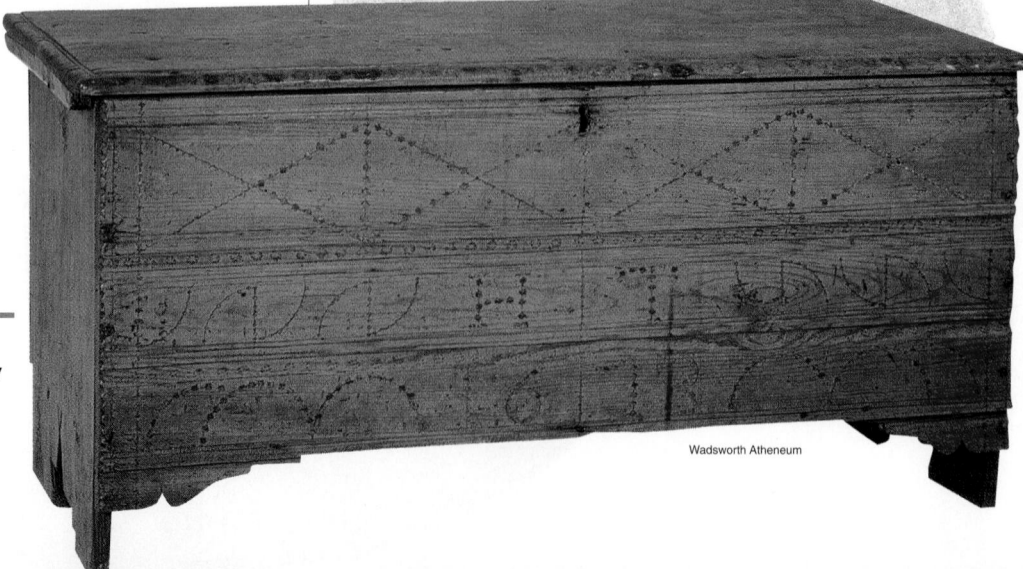

The chest Bradstreet mentions in her poem may have looked like this one.

Wadsworth Atheneum

Sunday Worship

Every Sunday at nine o'clock, Puritans would be called to church by a drum or horn. The meetinghouses were simple and bare inside with no heat or lights. The minister stood on a raised square platform. He faced the benches where the congregation sat.

From sunset on Saturday to sunset on Sunday, Puritans could not work or play. They were expected to attend both morning and afternoon religious services. The services lasted from three to five hours. Sometimes people fell asleep. To awaken the sleepers, a foxtail or feather hanging from a long stick was used to tickle their faces. The ministers often frightened church members with stories of things that would happen to them when they died if they did not follow the Puritan faith.

Museum of Fine Arts, Boston

The Puritan beliefs that death comes quickly and that people should be prepared to be judged by God are shown on this 1681 gravestone.

WHY IT MATTERS

Families played an important part in Puritan religious life, work, and schooling. The Puritans taught their children and passed on values such as hard work. This value, along with the Puritans' many skills, helped to build a strong New England economy.

Reviewing Facts and Ideas

MAIN IDEAS

- New England colonists led lives ruled by their Puritan religious beliefs.
- The Puritans made almost everything they needed by hand. Everyone in a Puritan family had daily chores.
- Puritan boys and girls attended dame schools. Some boys went to grammar schools, while others became apprentices. Girls usually helped to run the house and take care of the younger children.
- Puritan men could take part in government, while Puritan women's rights were limited.

THINK ABOUT IT

1. How did Puritan children learn to read?
2. What is an apprentice?
3. **FOCUS** How did Puritan religious beliefs influence how children were raised?
4. **THINKING SKILL** *Compare* the roles of men and women in Puritan New England. How were they the same? How were they different?
5. **WRITE** Suppose you were a Puritan child living in colonial New England. Write a poem or song that describes your daily chores.

CITIZENSHIP VIEWPOINTS

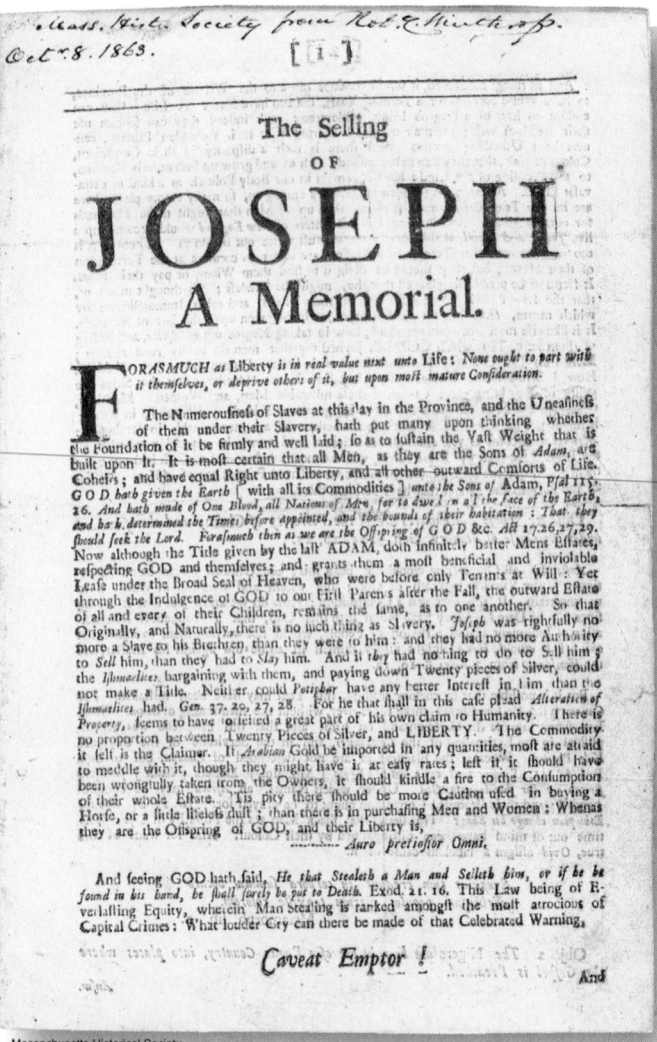

The Selling
OF
JOSEPH
A Memorial.

Massachusetts Historical Society

This is the first page of *The Selling of Joseph*, published by Samuel Sewall in 1700. In this paper Sewall explains his opposition to the enslavement of Africans.

1700S: HOW DID THE PURITANS FEEL ABOUT SLAVERY?

In 1641 the Massachusetts Puritans wrote the "Body of Liberties," one of the first sets of laws in America. It said that it was legal to enslave "strangers [who] . . . willingly sell themselves or are sold unto us." Enslaving Africans or Native Americans became legal. At the same time, the "Body of Liberties" contained laws to protect indentured servants and enslaved people against harsh treatment. Enslaved people also had a right to trial by jury.

Captive Africans were treated more equally in the New England colonies than in the South. Still, few Puritan leaders spoke out against slavery. Even the minister Cotton Mather, who opened schools for enslaved African Americans, did not seek their freedom. Instead he advised captive Africans to accept their position and to serve their owners better.

In Lesson 2 you read about Samuel Sewall's part in the Salem witchcraft trials. In 1700 Sewall published one of the first papers against slavery written in the colonies. John Saffin, a merchant and judge, attacked Sewall's stand on slavery. He argued that ending slavery would upset the natural order of the world. Read and consider these three viewpoints. Then answer the questions that follow.

Three DIFFERENT Viewpoints

1 COTTON MATHER
Puritan minister
Excerpt from his diary, June 18, 1723

[There] can be nothing more . . . reasonable than for us to consider whether our conduct [toward] . . . our African slaves [is something] . . . for which our God may . . . [be angry] with us. Are they always treated according to the rules of humanity? . . . Are they made to know such things [that would make] . . . them blessings in the families they belong unto? . . . [Slaves should try] to study a dutiful behavior unto their superiors . . . to be patient in their low and hard conditions.

"Are they always treated according to the rules of humanity?"

2 JOHN SAFFIN
Puritan merchant and judge
Excerpt from *A Brief and Candid Answer to a late Printed Sheet, Entitled,* The Selling of Joseph, 1701

To prove that all men have equal right to Liberty . . . seems to [overturn] the order that God has set in the world, who has [made] different . . . orders of men, some to be high . . . some to be low . . . some to be born slaves, and so to remain during their lives. . . . They are all of use, but not equal.

" . . . some to be born slaves, . . . "

3 SAMUEL SEWALL
Puritan merchant and judge
Excerpt from *The Selling of Joseph,* 1700

Liberty is in real value next unto life: None ought to part with it themselves, or deprive others of it. All men as they are the sons of Adam, . . . have equal right unto liberty . . . and all other outward comforts of life. The [rights] of all and every of [Adam and Eve's] children, remains the same as to one another. So that originally, and naturally, there is no such thing as slavery.

"All men . . . have equal right unto liberty."

BUILDING CITIZENSHIP

1. What was the viewpoint of each person? How did each support his view?

2. In what ways were some of the viewpoints alike? In what ways were they different?

3. What other viewpoints might Puritans have had on this issue?

SHARING VIEWPOINTS

As a class, discuss the viewpoints and decide which is closest to the class's feelings on the issue. Is there any statement that all three writers would agree with? If so, what would the statement be? Then work with a partner to rewrite, in your own words, the viewpoint that you find most reasonable.

CHAPTER 7 REVIEW

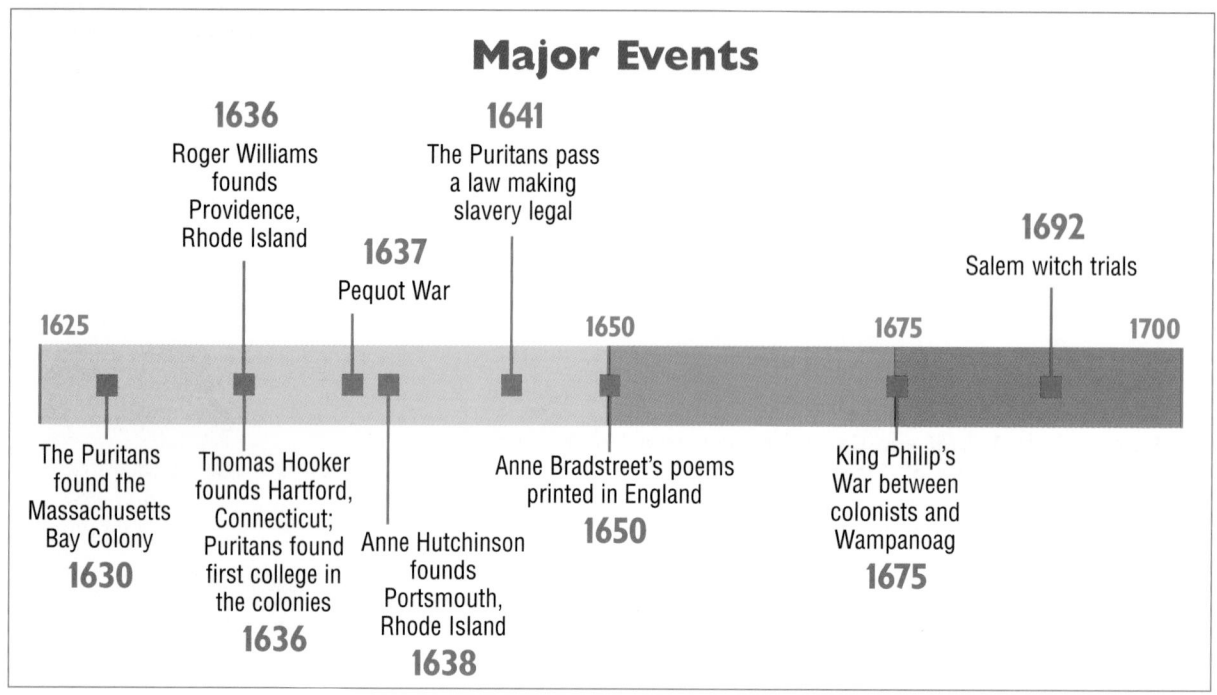

Major Events

1636 — Roger Williams founds Providence, Rhode Island

1637 — Pequot War

1641 — The Puritans pass a law making slavery legal

1692 — Salem witch trials

1625   1650   1675   1700

The Puritans found the Massachusetts Bay Colony **1630**

Thomas Hooker founds Hartford, Connecticut; Puritans found first college in the colonies **1636**

Anne Hutchinson founds Portsmouth, Rhode Island **1638**

Anne Bradstreet's poems printed in England **1650**

King Philip's War between colonists and Wampanoag **1675**

THINKING ABOUT VOCABULARY

Number a sheet of paper from 1 to 10. Beside each number write the word or term below that best completes each sentence.

apprentice
common
congregation
dame school
grammar school

hornbook
journeyman
primary source
tolerate
town meeting

1. Most Puritans did not _____ religions different from their own.

2. A _____ was held to discuss a new church.

3. A _____ was used in early school to teach people to read.

4. An _____ begins to learn a trade from a craftworker.

5. Only male members of the church _____ were allowed to vote.

6. Children from ages 2 to 7 attended a _____.

7. A secondary school was called a _____.

8. A _____ received a set of tools with which to practice his trade.

9. Townspeople met on the grassy _____ at the village's center.

10. An eyewitness account of the meeting is described in a _____.

THINKING ABOUT FACTS

1. Why did Roger Williams, Anne Hutchinson, and Thomas Hooker leave the Massachusetts Bay Colony? What did they each do?

2. Why was education so important to the Puritans? How did the Puritan colonists provide for education in a new way?

3. What was the status of the first Africans in the colonies? How did their status change?

4. Give two reasons that the 1600s were not a peaceful time in the New England colonies.

5. Look at the time line. Which colony was founded last? How many years after the Pequot War did King Philip's War begin?

THINK AND WRITE

WRITING A NEWSPAPER ARTICLE

Suppose that you are a newspaper reporter in the Massachusetts Bay Colony. Write an article about the trial of Anne Hutchinson.

WRITING A PARAGRAPH OF COMPARISON AND CONTRAST

Write about a Puritan child's upbringing and compare and contrast it to your own. What would seem strange to you? What might be familiar?

WRITING A DIARY

Imagine that you live in Salem during the time of the witch trials. Write a series of diary entries that tell about a trial.

APPLYING THINKING SKILLS

USING PRIMARY AND SECONDARY SOURCES

To apply the skill of recognizing primary and secondary sources, answer the questions below.

1. What is the difference between a primary source and a secondary source?

2. Why are secondary sources useful?

3. Which of the following is a secondary source?

    a. A speech about Puritan values

    b. *A History of the Wampanoag*

    c. A diary written by Samuel Sewall

4. Reread the sources on pages 198 and 199. What information did you learn in Knight's primary source that you did not find in Wesley's secondary source?

5. Why is it important to use both primary and secondary sources?

Summing Up the Chapter

Copy the comparison chart on a sheet of paper. Review the chapter to find details to complete the chart. After you have finished, use the information in the comparison chart to write a paragraph that answers the question "What did each of the colonies have in common?"

FOUNDER/ COLONY	REASON FOUNDER LEFT FORMER PLACE OF RESIDENCE	OCCUPATION	RESULTS
John Winthrop, Massachusetts Bay			Puritan; people should be free to choose their own religious leaders
Roger Williams,	To escape being sent to England by Puritans		
Anne Hutchinson,		Mother, nurse	

CHAPTER 8

The Middle Colonies

THINKING ABOUT HISTORY AND GEOGRAPHY

Chapter 8 begins in 1621 when a Dutch company plans to develop trade in the Americas. In the chapter you will learn about the people who settled the land between the New England Colonies and Virginia. This land would become known as the Middle Colonies. You will also learn about the early government of Pennsylvania, which later influenced the founders of a new nation.

1624

NEW NETHERLAND

The Dutch West India Company sends colonists to America

1626

NEW YORK

Peter Minuit buys the island of Manhattan from the Lenape

1681

PENNSYLVANIA

William Penn forms a new colony

216

NORTH
AMERICA

New
Netherland

New
York

Pennsylvania

THE MIDDLE
COLONIES

ATLANTIC
OCEAN

1700s
NEW YORK

**Martha Turnstall Smith
runs a successful
company on Long Island**

1700s
PENNSYLVANIA

**Philadelphia becomes the
largest city in the North
American colonies**

NEW NETHERLAND

Focus Activity

READ TO LEARN
How and why were the colonies of New York and New Jersey founded?

VOCABULARY
patroon

PEOPLE
Peter Minuit
Meijeterma
Seyseys
Peter Stuyvesant
James, Duke of York
Martha Turnstall Smith
Sir George Carteret
Lord John Berkeley
Philip Carteret

PLACES
New Netherland
Manhattan Island
New Amsterdam
New Sweden
New York
Middle Colonies
New Jersey

READ ALOUD

Father Isaac Jogues, a French Catholic priest, visited the Dutch colony of New Netherland in 1646 and wrote: " . . . the Director General told me that there were men of eighteen different languages. . . . " How did these immigrants from many cultures come together to form a colony?

THE BIG PICTURE

In addition to the Spanish and the English, the Dutch, French, Swedish, and Portuguese all wanted a share of the Americas' land and resources.

In 1621 a group of Dutch merchants formed the Dutch West India Company to develop trade in the Americas and along the west coast of Africa. This company sent colonists to a region along the Hudson River that had been named New Netherland. The company hoped that their settlement, the first European colony in the region, would grow and earn profits through trade and farming.

In 1624, about 30 families sailed to New Netherland. These colonists were Dutch, French, Spanish, Italian, and people from other European countries. Under Dutch rule, they came to build new lives and homes in America.

Westmoreland Museum of American Art

EUROPEANS ARRIVE

Most of these newcomers followed the routes taken by earlier Dutch explorers. They traveled up the Hudson River and built Fort Orange, which we know today as Albany. The explorers had exchanged goods with the Lenape, Pequot, and Mahican in the area. They had traded knives, kettles, and other goods for pelts—animal skins with fur—which were highly valued in Europe. The Dutch colonists hoped to build a profitable fur trade as well.

Geography of the Colony

Unlike much of New England, New Netherland had plentiful fresh water, rich soil, and a mild climate. Forests and meadows surrounded the rivers. Animals and fish filled the many woods and streams. In time, colonial settlements would grow up on either side of the Hudson River. This land is known as the Hudson River valley.

Settling the Colony

The Dutch West India Company offered land to Dutch men wealthy enough to send 50 adults to live and farm along the Hudson. These new landowners were called patroons. Colonists who lived on the patroons' properties had the hard job of clearing land for farming. They also had to give the patroon part of their harvests and livestock, which left them with little to

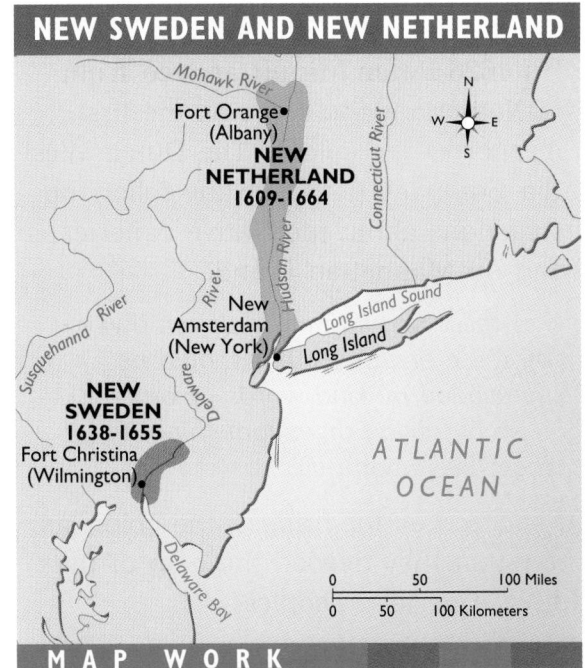

NEW SWEDEN AND NEW NETHERLAND

Mohawk River
Fort Orange (Albany)
NEW NETHERLAND 1609-1664
Connecticut River
Susquehanna River
Hudson River
Mohawk River
New Amsterdam (New York)
Long Island Sound
Long Island
NEW SWEDEN 1638-1655
Fort Christina (Wilmington)
Delaware River
ATLANTIC OCEAN
Delaware Bay

0   50   100 Miles
0   50   100 Kilometers

MAP WORK

New Sweden extended from the mouth of the Delaware Bay north along the Delaware River. New Netherland stretched along the banks of the Hudson River.

How many miles along the Hudson River did New Netherland stretch?

sell. In 1640 the Dutch company changed its rules, making it easier for people to own land. Settlements along the Hudson slowly grew.

Some settlers remained on an island they called Manhattan Island. They mistakenly thought that this was the Native Americans' name for it. As the settlement grew, its name was changed to New Amsterdam.

New Amsterdam (below) on Manhattan Island later became New York City.

SUCCESSES AND DEFEATS

In 1626 Peter Minuit arrived from The Netherlands to serve as the first governor of the colony. The Dutch West India Company gave him the following instructions about the Native Americans living on Manhattan Island:

> . . . these should not be driven away by force or threats, but should be persuaded by kind words or otherwise by giving them something, to let them live among us.

To succeed as fur traders, the colonists knew that they needed the help of the Native American peoples.

The Lenape Sell Their Land

The Lenape had lived along the Hudson River for hundreds of years. Several smaller Lenape groups lived on Manhattan Island. In 1626 Peter Minuit met with two of their sachems, or leaders, named Meijeterma (ME he ter mah) and Seyseys (SE ses). For 60 Dutch guilders, or about $24, and goods that probably included knives, axes, and clothing, Minuit bought the whole island of Manhattan. The Lenape, however, believed that the land could be used but not owned. They may not have meant to give the Dutch ownership of the land itself.

New Amsterdam

Ships from the West Indies and Europe made many stops in New Amsterdam's port and brought people and goods. One Dutch colonist wrote that Manhattan Island was "like a great natural pier ready to receive the commerce [trade] of the world." Trade of European-made products for beaver pelts thrived in taverns, inns, and in the Dutch West India Company's store.

At first Native Americans and colonists got along well. Later, when a new Dutch governor tried to force the Native Americans to give him furs, fighting broke out. Conflicts lasted until 1645, when the Dutch forced the local Native Americans to sign a peace treaty. In 1647 Peter Stuyvesant took over as the new governor of New Netherland.

Stuyvesant Captures New Sweden

Sweden had settled a small colony, New Sweden, in the present-day states of Delaware, New Jersey, and Pennsylvania in 1637. Its woods and streams were full of mink, otter, and beaver. These animal pelts, along with crops from the fields, brought rich profits.

Beaver was valued for its fur, and colonists traded pelts for cloth and lace.

Museum of the
City of New York

Dutch guilders (left) were part of the trade for Manhattan Island. Peter Stuyvesant (above) was enraged when English ships arrived off New Amsterdam in 1664.

Stuyvesant believed that Sweden had taken lands covered by the Dutch charter for New Netherland. In 1651 he built a fort on Swedish land, near what is now New Castle, Delaware. Three years later the colonists of New Sweden destroyed it. The Dutch government then ordered Stuyvesant to capture the lands of New Sweden. Stuyvesant sent 650 soldiers and seven ships to North America—New Sweden quickly fell to the Dutch. Now the Swedish colonists were governed by the Dutch, but that would soon change.

The English Take Over

The English claimed that their early explorations had given them the right to settle all of North America. The English king, Charles II, gave his brother James, Duke of York, land between the Hudson and Delaware rivers. In 1664 the Duke of York sent English ships to New Amsterdam.

The British sent a message to Stuyvesant that read, "His majesty [the king] of Britain . . . requires a surrender of all such forts, towns, or places of strength, which are now possessed by the Dutch." Furious, Stuyvesant threatened to fight a war against the English. The Dutch West India Company was having money problems, and did not come to the aid of the colonists. More importantly, the colonists did not want to fight. Although Stuyvesant had brought order to New Amsterdam, many Dutch colonists disliked his bad temper and harsh rule. They believed that life under the English would be easier.

Stuyvesant was forced to surrender, but he said, "I would rather have been carried to my grave." The English brought in a new government and renamed the colony New York, after the Duke of York. They also renamed New Amsterdam. It became New York City.

221

The Granger Collection

Along the Atlantic Ocean, whaling grew into a vital industry. The Montauk and Shinnecock, who lived on what is now Long Island, taught what they knew about whales and whale-hunting to many Europeans. One of these colonists was Martha Turnstall Smith. In the early 1700s Smith was one of the few women to run a business, selling whale oil for lamps and whale bones for buttons.

Almost one-quarter of New York's population was from Africa or the West Indies. Africans had lived in the colony since 1626, arriving first as indentured servants. They earned their freedom and plots of land when they completed their

THE MIDDLE COLONIES

When the English claimed New York in 1664, they gained control of all of the land between the New England colonies and Virginia. The colonies of New York and New Jersey eventually became part of a region known as the Middle Colonies.

The New York Colony

The English allowed the Dutch to keep their land and continue to practice their own religions. Although they replaced the Dutch governor, mayor, and sheriff, they allowed colonists to elect lower government officers.

New York continued to be home to many different groups of people. The Dutch and English colonists lived alongside other people, including many Native Americans and French, Jewish, German, and Swedish colonists. New farms filled in the landscape.

THE MIDDLE COLONIES

FRENCH TERRITORY

Lake Champlain

Lake Ontario

Lake Erie

Albany

NEW YORK (1664)

PENNSYLVANIA (1681)

Susquehanna River

New York City

Long Island Sound

Trenton

Philadelphia

NEW JERSEY (1664)

DELAWARE (1704)

Dover

Delaware Bay

ATLANTIC OCEAN

0   100   200 Miles

0   100   200 Kilometers

MAP WORK

Some colonies were smaller than the present-day states of the same name.

Which city was located farthest north?

work term. Some were laborers. Others were skilled craftworkers. By the late 1600s, though, most Africans in New York were enslaved. Some New Yorkers spoke of ending slavery there in the late 1700s, but it continued until 1827.

New York City

Unlike the rest of the New York colony, New York City developed rapidly as a port, soon becoming a center of business and culture. In 1664 about 10,000 people lived there. By 1700 the population had doubled. In the city the lives of traders, craftworkers, and servants differed from those of the wealthy, who kept fine houses and servants. Poor people shared roughly built houses and encountered street garbage, rowdy pirates, and crime.

Poor and rich New Yorkers socialized by playing and listening to music, dancing, and sharing news of other colonies.

At least 1,000 people in the city were enslaved workers from Africa. Free blacks also lived in New York, including one man who saved the city from burning down in 1689. His name is unknown.

New Jersey

JAMES, DUKE OF YORK

James, the Duke of York, gave a large portion of land west of the Hudson River to two of his friends, Sir George Carteret and Lord John Berkeley. Because Carteret had been born on England's Isle of Jersey, they called their colony New Jersey. In 1665 the two men sent Sir George's cousin, Philip Carteret, to govern the region.

WHY IT MATTERS

England's power in North America grew to include settlements all along the Atlantic coast. Before long, all of these settlements would become British colonies. New York City became one of the major trade centers of the colonies and, later, of the United States.

Reviewing Facts and Ideas

MAIN IDEAS

- In 1626 the governor of New Netherland, Peter Minuit, "bought" Manhattan Island from the Lenape.

- Peter Stuyvesant conquered New Sweden for the Dutch in 1651. In 1664 the English forced him to surrender all of New Netherland.

- The land between New England and Virginia became known as the Middle Colonies.

- The English became the major power on North America's Atlantic coast after they took over New Netherland.

THINK ABOUT IT

1. Why did the Dutch West India Company want a colony in North America?

2. Who were the patroons?

3. **FOCUS** How and why did New Netherland become New York and New Jersey?

4. **THINKING SKILL** _Compare and contrast_ the population of colonial New Netherland with that of the Massachusetts Bay Colony. How were they similar? How were they different?

5. **GEOGRAPHY** Look at the map on page 222. What geographic features made the Middle Colonies so desirable to European rulers?

223

1600   1630   1644   1730

The Granger Collection

THE FOUNDING OF PENNSYLVANIA

Focus Activity

READ TO LEARN

How did William Penn's religious beliefs affect the colony of Pennsylvania?

VOCABULARY

Quaker
Walking Purchase
Holy Experiment

PEOPLE

William Penn

PLACES

Pennsylvania
Delaware
Philadelphia
Schuylkill River

READ ALOUD

"I found Love and Respect enough where I came; a universal kind Welcome, every sort in their way. For here are some of several Nations, as well as divers[e] Judgments [different ways of thinking]: Nor were the Natives wanting [lacking] in this, for their [leaders] both visited and presented me; to whom I made suitable Returns." This letter, written by William Penn in 1683, describes the warm welcome he received from the Native Americans who lived on the land on which he would found his colony.

THE BIG PICTURE

You have read about how the Pilgrims and Puritans came to America in search of religious freedom. Other Protestant groups who had separated from or disagreed with the Church of England also faced hardship in the 1600s. The Quakers were one such group. Their name comes from their belief that people should "quake before the power of the Lord." Some Quakers settled in the Massachusetts Bay Colony. However, they were punished by the Puritans for their different beliefs.

William Penn, a Quaker, decided to form a colony in North America where people of all religious beliefs would be allowed to live and worship. As you will read, Penn's plan led to the establishment of both Pennsylvania and Delaware.

Historical Society of Pennsylvania

William Penn made a treaty with the Lenape (above) and built the Pennsylvania colony. The wampum belt (left) was made in honor of the treaty.

WILLIAM PENN

William Penn was born to a rich family in London, England, in 1644. He joined the Quakers as a young man and was imprisoned four times for disagreeing with the Church of England. When Penn heard about the growing Quaker settlements in New Jersey, he dreamed of starting a new Quaker colony nearby. The British royal family owed money to Penn's father. In 1681 Penn made a deal with King Charles II. The king would pay back the debt by giving Penn a royal charter to land west of New Jersey. In honor of Penn's father, the king named the colony Pennsylvania, which means "Penn's Woods."

The Pennsylvania Colony

Penn wrote a plan to govern the new colony. His "Frame of Government of the Province of Pennsylvania" guaranteed religious freedom for all persons who believed in God. The document also gave the colonists a voice in their government. They would have an elected assembly as well as a governor and a council appointed by the king.

Peace with the Lenape

Penn wished to treat the Native Americans of his colony fairly. Instead of taking land from the Lenape, Penn bought each piece with money and goods. The Lenape were also friendly. They wrote, "We will live in love with [Penn] and his children as long as the creeks and rivers run and while the sun, moon, and stars endure [last]." Peace between the Lenape and the Pennsylvania colonists lasted for many years.

However, in 1737 the Lenape lost the last of their Pennsylvania land under an agreement that became known as the Walking Purchase. Fifty years earlier, Penn had bought Lenape land "as far as a man can go in a day and a half." Penn had meant walking distance, but his son now hired the colony's fastest runners to measure the land. This dishonesty destroyed the trust that the colony had earned from the Lenape.

THE RESIDENCE OF DAVID TWINING 1787.

Colonial Williamsburg Foundation

The painting (left) shows an early farm in the Middle Colonies. These Philadelphia homes (bottom right) were built in the 1700s.

A HOLY EXPERIMENT

William Penn planned the colony around his religious beliefs. He wrote, "Government seems to me a part of religion itself. . . . Let men be good and government cannot be bad." Penn even called the new colony a Holy Experiment.

Quaker Beliefs

The Quakers called themselves the Society of Friends. They believed in the equality of all people. Quaker women under Penn's government had more freedom and power than women in most other European colonies. Quakers thought of women and men as equals in most matters, and as able partners in the new colony. Some Quaker women became leaders of their own meetinghouses.

However, the early Quakers in America did not always practice their belief in equality. The Middle Colonies allowed slavery, and even William Penn owned enslaved Africans. Still, many Quakers were against slavery. By 1696, they had forbidden people from bringing enslaved Africans to Pennsylvania. The colony then became a place where freed Africans and escaped slaves from other colonies came to live in freedom.

In Search of Freedom

As Penn's belief in freedom of religion became well known, more people journeyed to his colony. Swedish Protestants had been moving to the region since 1644. They were called Lutherans because they were followers of the German religious leader Martin Luther. A community of Scots-Irish colonists settled between the

Susquehanna and Ohio rivers in the 1720s. By 1730 Jewish people from Poland, Germany, and central Europe had also made new homes in Pennsylvania's cities and towns. In the mid-1700s a French Protestant group called the Huguenots [HYOO guh nahtz] also settled in Pennsylvania.

Many of the German and Swiss colonists belonged to Protestant groups such as the Mennonites or the Amish. They lived simply and were sometimes called the plain people. German colonists are sometimes called Pennsylvania Dutch because Pennsylvanians mispronounced Deutsch [DOYCH], the German word for "German."

The City of Brotherly Love

Penn wanted a beautiful city to be the capital of his colony. He called this city Philadelphia, after an ancient city in the Bible whose Greek name means "brotherly love."

Penn designed Philadelphia while he was still in England. The location of the city, where the Schuylkill [SKOO kul] River meets the Delaware River, was important for shipping and trade. Penn planned to have wide, straight streets and room for trees and gardens.

Many Pennsylvanians were hardworking business people who soon became successful. Wealthy Quaker merchants and farmers helped Philadelphia grow quickly. Silversmiths, bankers, insurance agents, paper makers, and furniture makers all set up businesses there. By 1718 about 10,000 people lived in Pennsylvania's capital. In the late 1700s it would be the largest city in the American colonies and a great center of culture, learning, and ideas.

The Many Voices excerpt below was written by Gabriel Thomas, a Welsh Quaker who spent about 15 years in Pennsylvania. Thomas described Philadelphia's attractions to draw Europeans to Penn's colony. What features of Philadelphia would attract people from as far away as Europe?

MANY VOICES
PRIMARY SOURCE

Excerpt from
An Historical and Geographical Account of the Province and Country of Pennsylvania and of West-New-Jersey in America
by Gabriel Thomas,
published in 1698.

*The . . . **inhabitants** have built a Noble and Beautiful City, and called it Philadelphia, which contains above two thousand Houses . . . of Brick, generally three stories high. . . . It hath in it Three Faires every Year, and Two Markets every Week. . . .*

In the said City are several good Schools of Learning for Youth. . . . Here is to be had on any Day in the Week, Tarts, Pies, Cakes, etc. . . . All sorts of very good Paper are made in the German-Town, as also very fine German Linen, such as no Person of Quality need be asham'd to wear.

inhabitants: people who live permanently in a place

227

DELAWARE IS FORMED

William Penn wanted his colony to have a port on the Atlantic Ocean. He asked the Duke of York for rights to the Delaware colony, an area by the sea that was governed by New York. The Duke agreed, and Delaware became part of Pennsylvania. Delaware and Pennsylvania were each allowed three votes in the assembly in Philadelphia. In 1704 Delaware and Pennsylvania agreed to separate. Delaware was still officially part of the Pennsylvania colony, but now it could make its own laws.

WHY IT MATTERS

Although William Penn spent only three and a half years in the new colony, his beliefs about religious freedom and equality would one day help shape our country's government. The Pennsylvania and Delaware colonies grew quickly because of the freedom Penn's charter offered.

Museum of Fine Art, Boston

MAIN IDEAS

- William Penn received a charter for Pennsylvania from King Charles II of England in 1681.

- Penn based the government of Pennsylvania on such Quaker beliefs as the equality of all people and freedom of religion.

- In the 1600s people from many different cultures lived in Pennsylvania—African, Native American, French, Swedish, Jewish, Scots-Irish, German, as well as English.

- Delaware gained the right of self-government in 1704, but it remained part of Pennsylvania.

THINK ABOUT IT

1. How did Penn feel about the Lenape?

2. Where did newcomers to Pennsylvania come from in Europe?

3. **FOCUS** How did Penn's beliefs affect the colony of Pennsylvania?

4. **THINKING SKILL** Reread Penn's statement on page 226 about government. Is Penn stating *facts* or expressing *opinions*? Explain the reasons for your answer.

5. **WRITE** Suppose that you are a colonist who has just moved to Philadelphia. Write a letter home describing what you think about the city.

Both men and women attended Quaker meetings.

Getting Out the News

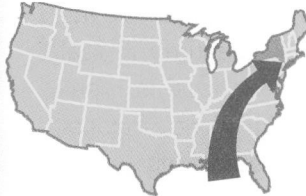

NEW YORK, NEW YORK. Meet 16-year-old Scarlett Arias and 18-year-old Osiris Adorno. When these two teen-agers talk, people listen—about 3 million of them.

Scarlett and Osiris work for the New York office of *Children's Express*. You will read about Ben Franklin's newspaper, the *Pennsylvania Gazette*. Instead of writing stories for one newspaper, the students at *Children's Express* gather and write news stories that appear weekly in newspapers across the country.

Children's Express reporters are 8 to 13 years old. The editors range in age from 14 to 18. Teenagers at news offices in Indianapolis, Indiana, Washington, D.C., and New York City work without pay to research and write news stories for a variety of news sources.

Children's Express calls itself the "news service by children for everybody." Explains Scarlett, "Our stories give a young person's point of view on issues from government to life in homeless shelters. Stories spotlight whatever affects children." The *Children's Express* news teams know that citizens need to be informed about many issues. Their readers have followed *Children's Express* stories on elections for President of the United States since 1976. News teams have also interviewed people running for other offices, local voters, and such elected officials as senators and mayors.

"We also talk to kids about the issues that concern them directly," says Osiris. "We cover the things that kids hear about or see around them every day. We try to find out what kids are thinking about—that includes school dropouts and gang members." In 1997 *Children's Express* editors traveled to Dhaka, Bangladesh, to report on children in the work force. These interviews were later published in a book. Scarlett believes her years of working on the news stories have helped her in another way. "What I've gained the most is confidence that my voice can be heard."

". . . my voice can be heard."

Scarlett Arias

GEOGRAPHYSKILLS

Reading Elevation and Relief Maps

VOCABULARY

elevation
relief

WHY THE SKILL MATTERS

As you saw on the map of the Middle Colonies on page 222, Delaware and New Jersey lie along the Atlantic Coastal Plain, which is mostly flat. Colonists arriving in the Middle Colonies often used maps to study the geography of a place.

Different kinds of maps used today can show different kinds of geographical information. The elevation of a place, for example, is shown on an elevation map. Elevation is the height of land above sea level. Mountain climbers often use maps that show elevation. Why do you think they need them?

USING ELEVATION MAPS

Elevation maps show how high, or elevated, the land is. Elevation is measured in feet or meters above sea level. Sea level is measured as 0 feet all around the world. Places close to sea level have low elevations.

Elevation maps use color to show the difference in height of land areas. In the elevation map of New York on this page, red shows areas with the highest elevation. The key tells you that red represents areas higher than 2,000 feet, or 600 meters, above sea level. Each of the other colors on the map shows a different elevation.

You know that as you travel east from the Appalachian Mountains to the coast, the land drops suddenly in elevation. The drop in elevation from the foothills of the Appalachians

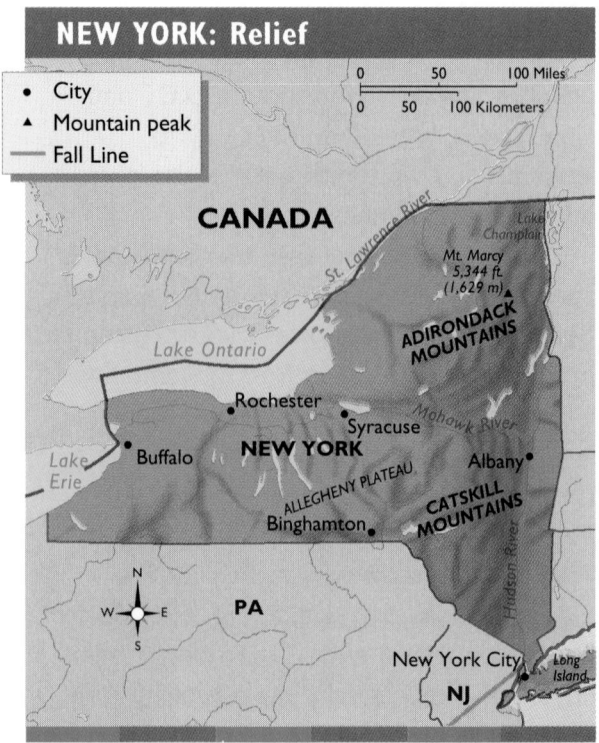

NEW YORK: Elevation

FEET | METERS
2,000 | 600
1,500 | 450
1,000 | 300
500 | 150
0 | 0
BELOW SEA LEVEL

0   50   100 Miles
0   50   100 Kilometers

CANADA

St. Lawrence River

Lake Champlain

Mt. Marcy 5,344 ft. (1,629 m)▲

ADIRONDACK MOUNTAINS

Lake Ontario

Rochester

Buffalo

Syracuse

Mohawk River

NEW YORK

Albany

Lake Erie

ALLEGHENY PLATEAU

CATSKILL MOUNTAINS

Binghamton

Delaware R.

Hudson River

PENNSYLVANIA

• City
▲ Mountain Peak

New York City

Long Island

NJ

NEW YORK: Relief

• City
▲ Mountain peak
— Fall Line

0   50   100 Miles
0   50   100 Kilometers

St. Lawrence River

CANADA

Lake Champlain

Mt. Marcy 5,344 ft. (1,629 m)▲

ADIRONDACK MOUNTAINS

Lake Ontario

Rochester

Buffalo

Syracuse

Mohawk River

NEW YORK

Albany

Lake Erie

ALLEGHENY PLATEAU

CATSKILL MOUNTAINS

Binghamton

Hudson River

PA

New York City

Long Island

NJ

to the flatter land along the coast is called the fall line. On the relief map on page 230, the fall line is east of the foothills.

USING RELIEF MAPS

Elevation maps show the height of land areas. A relief map shows how elevation changes from place to place. Relief is the difference in height between land areas. Level, or flat, land that stretches for long distances has low, or little, relief. Land that rises and then drops off within short distances has high, or more, relief. Mountains are landforms with both a high elevation and high relief. Plains and plateaus are landforms with low relief.

On a relief map the difference in height between land areas is shown by using light to heavy shading. Look at the relief map on page 230. The heavy shading shows high elevation areas. The light shading indicates low elevation.

The relief map on page 230 tells us the Adirondack Mountains have high relief because they are heavily shaded.

TRYING THE SKILL

Look at the map of the Middle Colonies on this page. It shows both elevation and relief. Both color and shading are used to show what the landforms in the Middle Colonies are like. The highest mountains are heavily shaded and colored red. What does this map tell about these mountains?

Look at the area around the Appalachian Mountains. What does the map tell you about the elevation as you move east or west of the mountains? How do you think elevation affected the settling of this region?

THE MIDDLE COLONIES: Elevation and Relief

FEET	METERS
2,000	600
1,500	450
1,000	300
500	150
0	0
BELOW SEA LEVEL	

REVIEWING THE SKILL

1. What is elevation? What is relief?

2. Which map is better for showing the height of a mountain above sea level—an elevation map or a relief map? Why?

3. Suppose you were planning a bicycle trip. Which kind of map would you use to avoid pedaling up steep hills? Why?

4. Using the map on this page, compare the elevation and relief of the Middle Colonies. Which colony do you think would have the best land for farming? Explain.

5. How would you use an elevation and relief map to find a place in which to settle?

1600   1626   1700   1720

DAILY LIFE IN THE MIDDLE COLONIES

Focus Activity

READ TO LEARN
What was everyday life like for people who lived in the Middle Colonies?

VOCABULARY
Kentucky rifle
Conestoga wagon

PLACES
Lancaster County
Conestoga Valley

READ ALOUD

You that will seek a Country strange,
   Attend [pay attention] *to what is true,*
All that are willing to exchange
   An Old place for a New.
We that our Country did forsake [give up],
   And leave our Native Land,
Will do the best we can to make
   Our Neighbors understand.

This verse about Pennsylvania was written by Richard Frame in 1692. Understanding new neighbors was very important for the early colonists.

THE BIG PICTURE

If you had just arrived in the Middle Colonies in the early 1600s, what would you expect to find? You might expect to meet the Susquehannock [sus kwuh HAN uk], Native Americans who lived in villages there and who grew corn and squash—foods you had never tasted before. You might hope to see the great forests filled with deer, wild turkeys, bears, wolves, foxes, and rattlesnakes. When you arrived, though, you would also find other people who were newcomers. Some would speak languages you had never heard before and practice religions you did not know. Some would be rich landowners. Others would be indentured servants or enslaved people. You would all have to work together to survive the first, hard years of starting a new colony.

NATIVE AND FOREIGN WAYS

The colonists learned from each other, and from their Native American neighbors, the best ways to feed and shelter themselves. The Middle Colonies were ideal for farming. Underneath plentiful oak and hickory forests, the soil was rich and deep. However, clearing the land was slow, hard work because most families had few tools other than axes. It might take a year to clear enough land for a profitable farm. Meanwhile, everyone needed shelter and food to eat. Fortunately, people in the Middle Colonies could often count on neighbors to help them build their first homes.

Building Homes

In both New York and Pennsylvania, some of the earliest colonists made their homes in caves. Later they built homes made of long poles covered with tree bark that were like the longhouses of the Lenape and Susquehannock. Some Native American longhouses were 100 feet long. Twenty-nine of the 30 colonial houses on Manhattan Island in 1626 were made of poles and tree bark.

Colonists in Delaware and Pennsylvania learned to build log cabins from the Swedish settlers. Whole logs were cut with notches and then fitted together. Log cabins became very popular in the colonies because they could be put up quickly with available materials. In the countryside, nails, cut lumber, and bricks were hard to get and expensive. Newcomers in German and Swedish communities could build a house or even a barn quickly because all of the neighbors pitched in. Everyone celebrated with a large feast when the work was done.

As the colonists settled in, they built homes like the ones they had left behind in Europe. The English built brick houses. Dutch farmhouses were one story high and had steep, curved roofs. In the cities Dutch homes looked like those in Amsterdam. They were made of colored brick and had high, "gabled" roofs. These roofs had steps like a staircase.

Swedish colonists who came to Delaware in 1638 built the first log cabins (below) in America. Dutch farmhouses (right) in cold climates had many chimneys.

THE BREADBASKET OF THE COLONIES

In 1698 the Welsh Quaker Gabriel Thomas, comparing Pennsylvania to England, concluded that colonial life was better for poor people. Colonists, Thomas pointed out, could eat much more fresh meat. They could hunt deer "most delicious, far exceeding [more than] that in Europe," and "vast Numbers of . . . Beasts, Fowl, and Fish" that were "free and common to any Person who can shoot or take them." Also, many colonists had brought hogs and cattle with them from Europe, so pork and milk became plentiful.

Colonists could gather wild berries and nuts in the woods. They also collected maple syrup from the forests. Native Americans taught the colonists how to cut a hole in the bark of a maple tree and gather the sap, or juice, from inside. When the sap was boiled for a long time, it turned into sweet syrup. It was often used in place of sugar to sweeten their desserts.

Farming in the Woods

By the middle 1700s people in Pennsylvania and New Jersey were raising so much wheat, corn, barley, and rye that colonists in New England and the South began to call the Middle Colonies the "breadbasket" of the colonies.

Farmland, however, took a long time to cultivate. Most of the land was covered with woods. Some newcomers could plant crops on land that had already been cleared by the Susquehannock. Others learned Susquehannock and Chesapeake methods of farming without chopping down the trees. One way was to "girdle" a tree, which meant cutting out chunks of bark all the way around the tree's trunk. The tree would then die and its leaves would fall off. Through the empty branches, the sun could shine through onto the crops. Native Americans also taught the colonists how to plant squash, beans, and corn. The colonists grew corn by following Native American practices. They placed one herring (a small fish used to fertilize the soil) and five corn seeds, in each mound of soil. The colonists made up a rhyme to explain the five seeds:

One for the blackbird;
One for the crow;
One for the cutworm;
And two to grow!

In the fall, after crops were collected, farmers burned the dead trees. The ashes fertilized the soil.

tobacco

smokehouse

kitchen garden

The **Kentucky rifle** (above) was designed by German colonists.

Better Guns and Wagons

As farmers and hunters began trading more goods in the port towns, they started to design better tools for their work. German craftworkers in Lancaster County, Pennsylvania, developed a new, light rifle that could be reloaded quickly. Today, this gun is called the Kentucky rifle.

Carrying goods and passengers to port towns became safer and easier in 1750s when Germans in Conestoga Valley, near Lancaster, designed a large, canvas-topped wagon. The Conestoga wagon rode high above the ground on large wheels that could roll over ruts and potholes. The floor curved up at both ends to keep goods from falling out on steep hills.

Words from Many Languages

Many words from other cultures became part of everyday speech in the Middle Colonies. The words *skunk* and *toboggan,* for example, are Algonkian. When colonists could not pronounce a long Native American word, they shortened it. The words *squash* and *raccoon* are short forms of Algonkian words.

The words *prairie, bureau,* and *chowder* came from the French language. *Boss, Yankee,* and *cookie* came from the Dutch language. Colonists sometimes combined two English words to name something they had not seen before. Such new compound words included *groundhog, bullfrog, garter snake, catfish,* and *backstreet.*

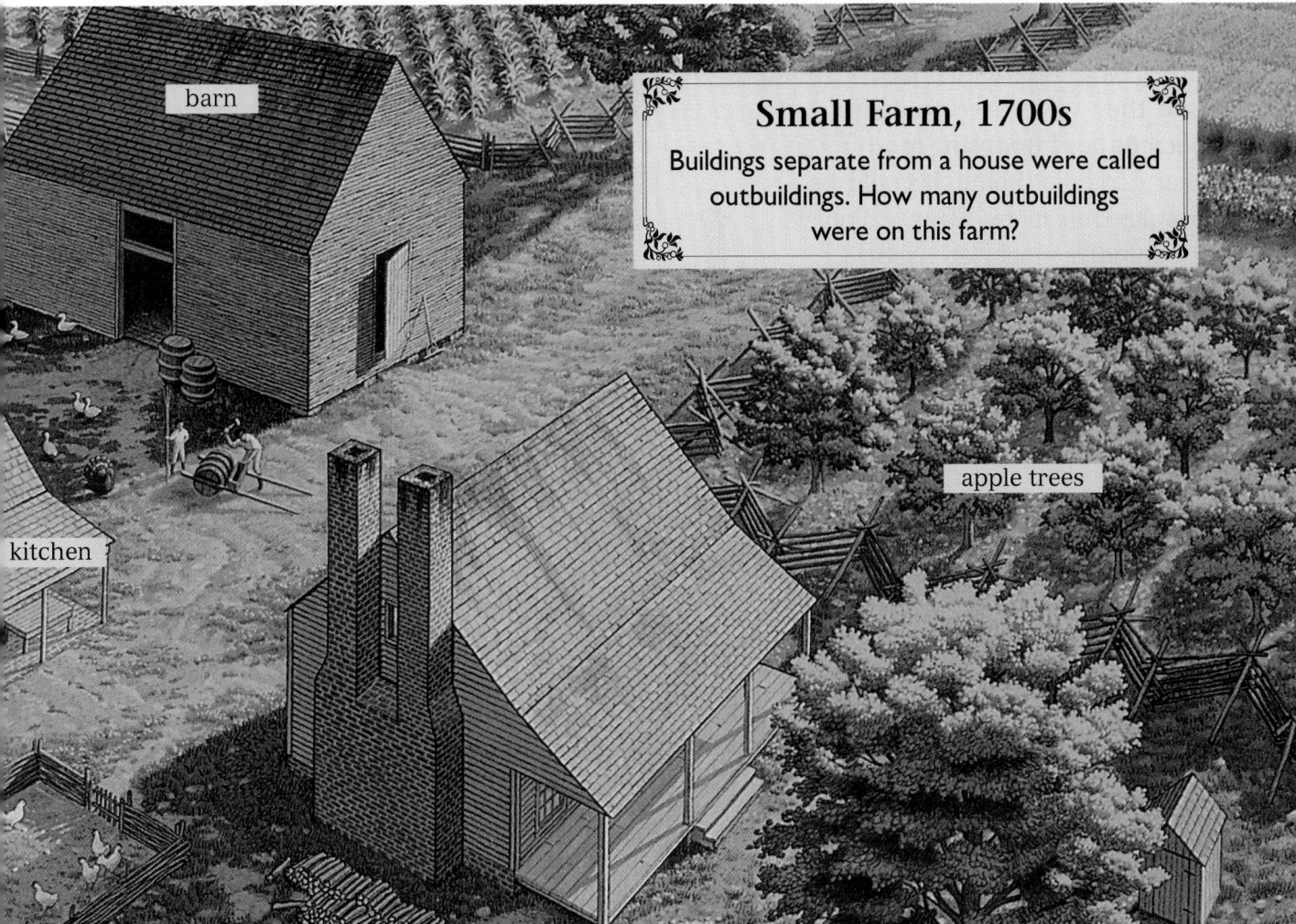

barn

Small Farm, 1700s

Buildings separate from a house were called outbuildings. How many outbuildings were on this farm?

apple trees

kitchen

DAILY LIFE

Most Middle Colonists were farmers who worked hard for a living. Both men and women worked in the fields. Men hunted, fished, and made furniture. Women spun, wove, and made clothes. They also made their own soap and candles, and cooked, baked, and preserved food. Children grew up fast because they had to help on the farm.

Africans in the Middle Colonies—whether free or enslaved—worked to keep their families together and hold on to their traditions. In Philadelphia's public parks many Africans held parades celebrating their culture. Despite Pennsylvania's laws, however, free Africans were not always safe. There was always the danger that slave traders would kidnap them to other states where they could be legally sold into slavery.

Foods from Near and Far

At first, European colonists preferred the stews and well-cooked vegetables that they were used to. Corn, however, became an important food in every colonial home. It could be prepared in many ways. Colonists made corn mush, or hasty pudding, a Native American dish with cornmeal. Dutch colonists in New York added beef and vegetables to the mixture and then cooked it for three days. Every household had its favorite recipes for corn bread and corn pancakes. The newcomers soon grew fond of the local wild berries and nuts.

The Dutch in New York brought the first cookies and crullers (braid-shaped

doughnuts) to the Middle Colonies. Germans introduced their cabbage dishes, such as coleslaw and sauerkraut.

Education in the Middle Colonies

Many children in early New York never went to school. Those who did learned only a little reading, writing, and arithmetic. Quakers and other Pennsylvania colonists paid church groups and private schools to teach their children to read, to write, to do arithmetic, and to know the Bible. However, children did not study for very long—they had to help do the work necessary for survival. As one colonist wrote:

*Book learning gets the upper hand and work is slow and slack,
And they that come long after us will find things gone to wrack [ruin].*

Colonial Williamsburg Foundation

Collection of the New York Historical Society

The Dutch children (above) dressed up in their best for this portrait. They ate butter made at home with a churn (left) like this one.

Many colonial boys learned how to farm and hunt, but not how to read or write.

Places of Worship

The Middle Colonies contained many different houses of worship. Followers of the Church of Sweden built the first church in Philadelphia. Quakers in Pennsylvania built meetinghouses, plain wood-and-stone buildings with white walls. The first synagogue in North America was built by a Jewish community in the New York colony in 1730.

WHY IT MATTERS

The Middle Colonies allowed people of many different backgrounds and cultures to live together and share ideas. It was not always easy for people from different countries or religions to learn to respect others' beliefs. By trying to live together in peace, however, the settlers in the Middle Colonies were creating a new way of life that would become important when their children formed a new nation.

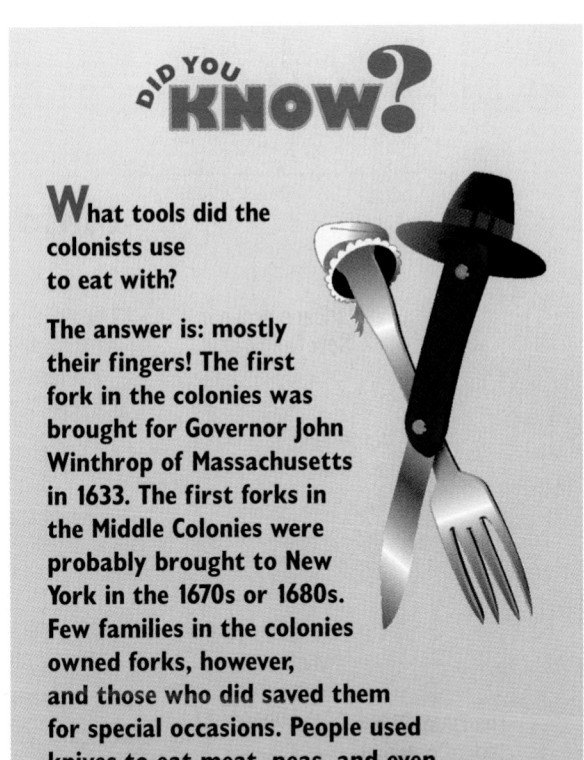

DID YOU KNOW?

What tools did the colonists use to eat with?

The answer is: mostly their fingers! The first fork in the colonies was brought for Governor John Winthrop of Massachusetts in 1633. The first forks in the Middle Colonies were probably brought to New York in the 1670s or 1680s. Few families in the colonies owned forks, however, and those who did saved them for special occasions. People used knives to eat meat, peas, and even ice cream! Spoons were used to eat soup and stews. If you couldn't eat it with a knife or spoon, you used your fingers.

✓ Reviewing Facts and Ideas

MAIN IDEAS

- Language, food, and religion in the Middle Colonies were influenced by people from many different backgrounds.
- Native Americans helped colonists learn how to farm, prepare meals, and build homes.
- Pennsylvania colonists created the Conestoga wagon and the Kentucky rifle to make life in the Middle Colonies easier.
- Some children in New York and Pennsylvania learned to read and write in school, but many left school to work, helping their families to survive.

THINK ABOUT IT

1. What were some words that the colonists created by combining other words?

2. Describe the way Native Americans taught the Middle Colonists to farm in the woods.

3. **FOCUS** What was daily life like for people in the Middle Colonies?

4. **THINKING SKILL** What _effects_ did the geography of the Middle Colonies have on the way people lived?

5. **WRITE** Suppose that you are a child in the Middle Colonies. Describe the dinner you will serve tonight.

CHAPTER 8 REVIEW

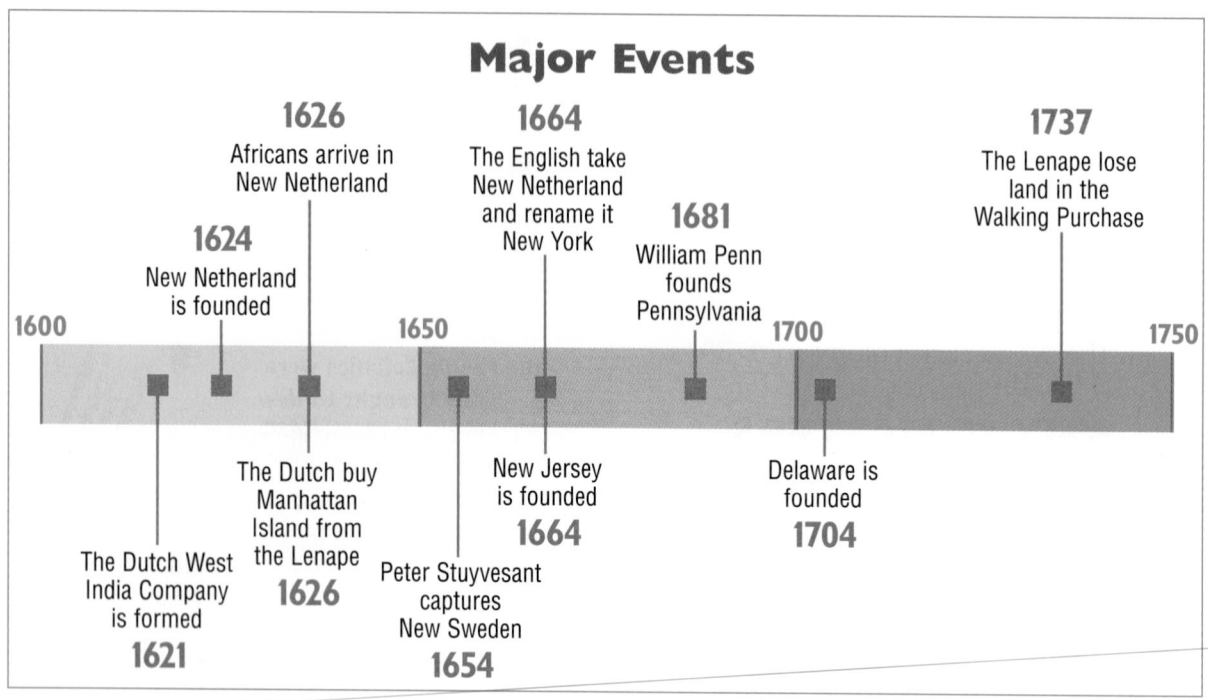

Major Events

1626
Africans arrive in
New Netherland

1624
New Netherland
is founded

1664
The English take
New Netherland
and rename it
New York

1681
William Penn
founds
Pennsylvania

1737
The Lenape lose
land in the
Walking Purchase

1600   1650   1700   1750

The Dutch buy
Manhattan
Island from
the Lenape
1626

New Jersey
is founded
1664

Delaware is
founded
1704

The Dutch West
India Company
is formed
1621

Peter Stuyvesant
captures
New Sweden
1654

THINKING ABOUT VOCABULARY

Number a sheet of paper from 1 to 5. Beside each number write the word or term below that best completes the sentence.

Conestoga wagon   Quaker
Holy Experiment   Walking Purchase
patroon

1. The _____ was an agreement that cost the Lenape the remainder of their land.

2. William Penn called his colony a _____.

3. A _____ believes in the equality of all people and in freedom of religion.

4. The _____ was designed to travel through muddy, uneven terrain.

5. Farmers in New Netherland paid their _____ a portion of their crops.

THINKING ABOUT FACTS

1. Who established the first settlements in New Netherland? Where was the colony located?

2. Who were the Lenape? What deal did they make with Peter Minuit?

3. What goods were traded by the early colonists in New Amsterdam?

4. Who was Peter Stuyvesant? What was his greatest disappointment?

5. How did James, Duke of York, help to form the Middle Colonies?

6. What Quaker ideas made Pennsylvania attractive to many new colonists?

7. How did Native Americans help the early colonists?

8. Why were the Middle Colonies a good place for poor people to settle?

9. Why did people from so many lands settle in the Middle Colonies? What different groups of people lived there?

10. Look at the time line above. How long did the colony of New Netherland belong to the Dutch?

THINK AND WRITE

WRITING A REPORT

Write a report describing the treaties made by the Lenape in New Amsterdam and in Pennsylvania, and the results of those agreements.

WRITING JOURNAL ENTRIES

Suppose that you are a resident of New Amsterdam in the years from 1625 to 1664. Write two or three short journal entries describing the changes in your community over time.

WRITING A POEM

Suppose that you have moved to one of the Middle Colonies. Write a short poem describing your new home.

APPLYING GEOGRAPHY SKILLS

USING ELEVATION MAPS AND RELIEF MAPS

Answer the questions below to apply the skill of using elevation maps and relief maps.

1. How is elevation shown on a map? How is relief shown?

2. How is color used on an elevation map? On a relief map?

3. What does a fall line show?

4. Look at the elevation map of New York on page 230. What is the highest point in New York?

5. If you led a colony and were in search of good farmland, how might a map that showed both elevation and relief help you?

Summing Up the Chapter

Copy the flow chart on a separate sheet of paper. Then review the chapter to complete this chart about the founding of New York. After you have finished, use the chart to write a paragraph that answers the question, "Which event, had it not occurred, might have allowed New Amsterdam to remain Dutch?"

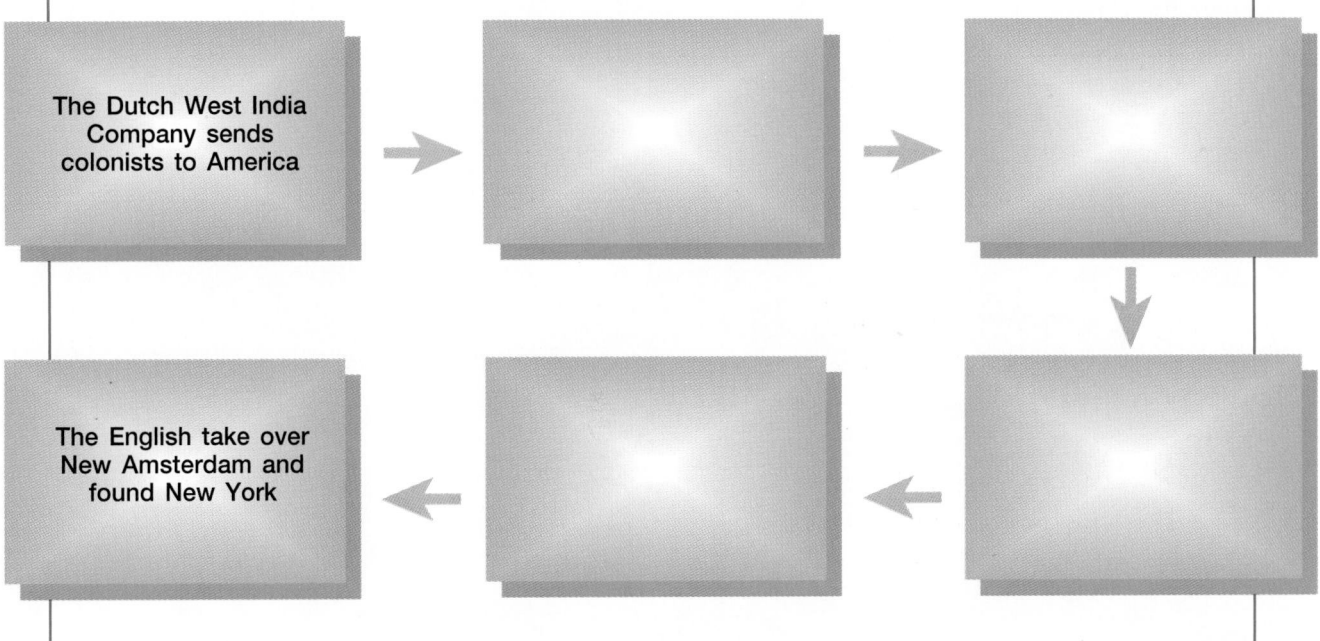

The Dutch West India Company sends colonists to America →

The English take over New Amsterdam and found New York ←

The Southern Colonies

THINKING ABOUT HISTORY AND GEOGRAPHY

Chapter 9 tells how the Southern Colonies were founded and how the different people there lived. The natural resources of the region attracted many colonists. At first the newcomers settled near the coast. But as they spread inland, Native Americans resisted the colonists' efforts to push them farther west. Read the time line below to follow some major events of this chapter.

1634	1660s	1711
MARYLAND	**VIRGINIA**	**NORTH CAROLINA**
Leonard Calvert and 150 colonists arrive to start a new colony	Laws are passed allowing slavery	Native Americans and colonists fight in the Tuscarora War

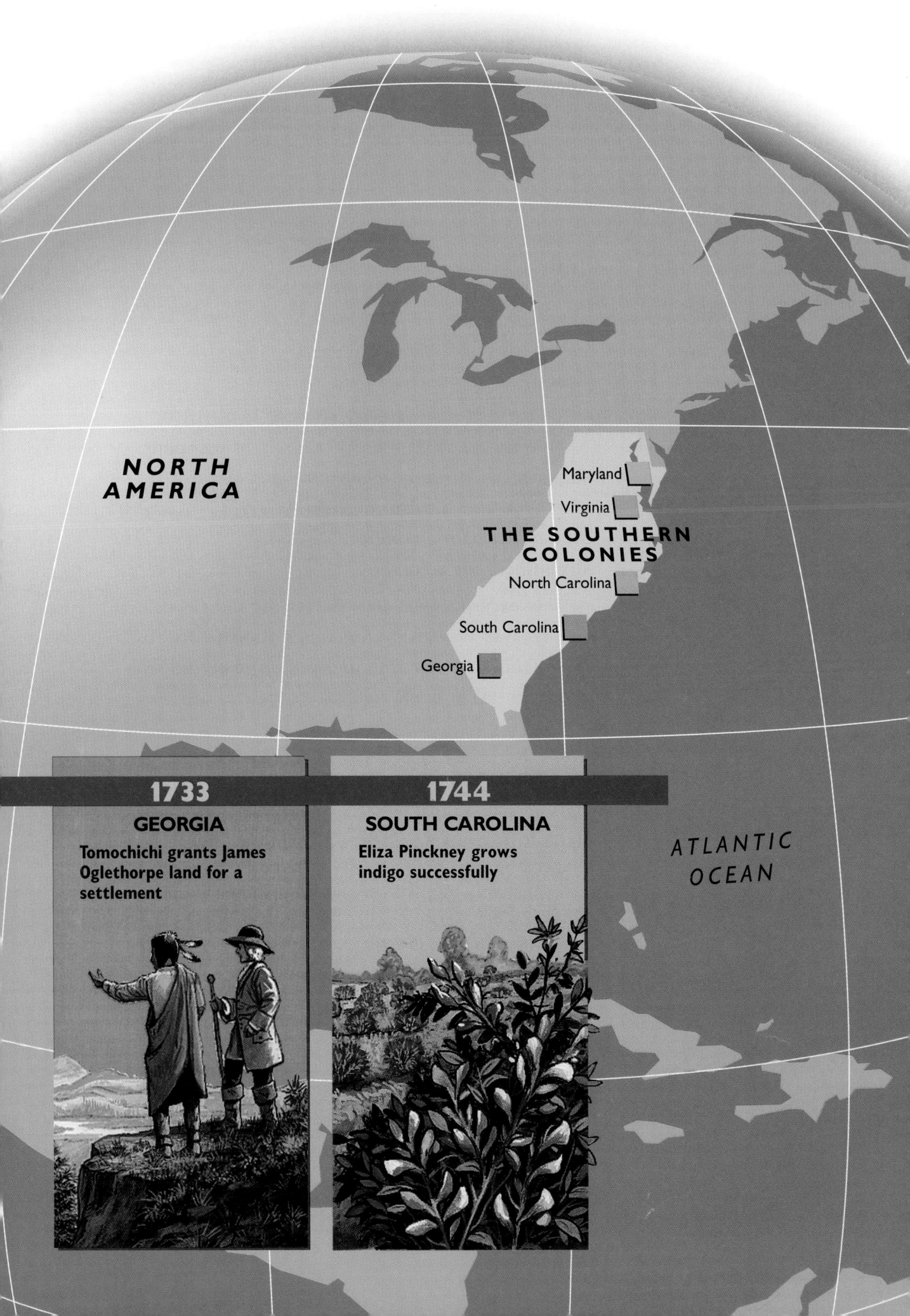

NORTH
AMERICA

Maryland

Virginia

THE SOUTHERN
COLONIES

North Carolina

South Carolina

Georgia

ATLANTIC
OCEAN

1733

GEORGIA

Tomochichi grants James Oglethorpe land for a settlement

1744

SOUTH CAROLINA

Eliza Pinckney grows indigo successfully

New York Public Library

THE GROWTH OF THE SOUTHERN COLONIES

READ ALOUD

"We are . . . informed that many of our poor subjects . . . through misfortune and want of employment . . . wish to go to America . . . where they might gain a comfortable [living] . . . and also strengthen our colonies."

This excerpt, from the charter for the Georgia colony, was written by England's King George II. It explains why the king allowed so many English people to leave home and go to the colonies.

Focus Activity

READ TO LEARN
How were the Southern Colonies founded?

VOCABULARY
House of Burgesses
Act Concerning Religion
established church
proprietor
debtor

PEOPLE
George Calvert
Margaret Brent
James Oglethorpe
Tomochichi

PLACES
Maryland
North Carolina
South Carolina
Georgia
Southern Colonies
Williamsburg
Savannah

THE BIG PICTURE

The success of Jamestown proved that English colonies could do well in North America. The money made from growing tobacco convinced English merchants that new colonies could make England wealthier.

English rulers gave several Englishmen permission to start colonies to the north and south of Virginia. Thousands of settlers were encouraged to cross the ocean. You have read about those who settled in the New England and Middle Colonies. To the south, Virginia was settled. Soon Maryland, then Carolina—later divided into North Carolina and South Carolina—and Georgia were growing settlements. They became known as England's Southern Colonies.

As in the New England and Middle Colonies, many of the colonists came because they hoped to make better lives for themselves. Some had other reasons for risking the long journey. They came to practice their religions freely. Some also came hoping to find adventure.

242

VIRGINIA'S SUCCESS

One of the reasons Virginia succeeded was its strong government. The leaders of the Virginia Company decided that its colony needed a new kind of government to help guide it. They gave the colony an assembly with two branches. The members of one branch were appointed by the Virginia Company. The members of the other branch were elected.

The House of Burgesses

In 1619 colonial America's first election of lawmakers took place. All free male colonists who owned land in Virginia were allowed to vote for a new assembly, the House of Burgesses. Two representatives, or burgesses, were elected for each of the colony's settlements. The House of Burgesses established taxes, made laws, and set the price of tobacco. They also presented the colonists' views to the governor.

In 1624 King James I made Virginia a royal colony. He appointed a royal governor and said the House of Burgesses could keep some powers, such as calling for taxes. However, it was not until the mid-1700s that the House of Burgesses was allowed any real self-government.

The first male landowners at Jamestown (top) learned how to govern themselves in the House of Burgesses. The College of William and Mary (above) was founded in Williamsburg in 1693.

Williamsburg

In 1698 Virginia's capital was moved away from Jamestown. Williamsburg, about 5 miles upriver from Jamestown, was picked as the new location. Williamsburg already had a church and a college, and the region was not swampy like Jamestown, so there were fewer insects. Williamsburg was the capital of Virginia from 1699 until 1780.

The city became a center for education and religion, as well as government. The College of William and Mary, founded in 1693, was the second oldest college in the colonies after Harvard.

243

Lord Baltimore (below) founded the colony of Maryland. Margaret Brent (right) managed Calvert property and her own plantation.

THE FOUNDING OF MARYLAND

George Calvert, an English noble with the title of Lord Baltimore, wanted to start a colony where Catholics like himself could practice their religion openly. In 1632 he was given a large area of land north of Virginia by his friend King Charles I.

Lord Baltimore's Colony

George Calvert died before he could carry out his plans. His son Cecilius inherited the title of Lord Baltimore and the land in America. He named the future colony Maryland, after the English king's wife, Queen Henrietta Maria.

About 150 colonists, both Catholics and Protestants, landed in Maryland in 1634. Governor Leonard Calvert, the new Lord Baltimore's brother, met with local Native American groups, such as the Yaocomico. He exchanged axes, blankets, and other items for land.

Lord Baltimore made generous offers of land to attract colonists. Most colonists used their land for raising crops. As in Virginia, enslaved Africans were brought to the colony.

Before Governor Leonard Calvert died in 1647, he chose plantation owner Margaret Brent to be in charge of his land and money. However, as a woman she was not allowed to vote in the colony's assembly. By 1657 Brent had become one of the largest landowners in Maryland. She argued that she should actually have two votes: one as a landowner and one as the representative of the brothers Calvert and Baltimore. Brent's request was denied.

Changes in Maryland

Maryland's charter allowed people of all Christian faiths to settle there. By the middle of the 1600s the colony had more Protestants than Catholics. To help keep the peace between Catholics and Protestants, Maryland's assembly created the Act Concerning Religion. It stated that no Christian person should be in "any ways troubled . . . for or in respect of his or her religion." Even so, the Church of England eventually became the colony's established church, or official church.

THE CAROLINAS

Carolina was the next Southern colony to be settled. In 1663 King Charles II gave huge parcels of land to eight of his friends. They became Carolina's proprietors. A proprietor is a business or property owner. In this case, the proprietors owned the entire colony.

Early Problems

At first, the colony grew slowly. Settlers were given very small pieces of land. By 1688 larger areas of land were offered as in Maryland, and new colonists arrived. Freedom of religion was guaranteed. In the early 1700s, though, people who were not members of the Church of England had to pay a tax.

Carolina's Native Americans

As more colonists arrived in Carolina, Native Americans lost more land. Some were also captured and enslaved. In 1711 the Tuscarora, members of the Iroquois Confederacy, began a war in the north of the colony. After two years, the Tuscarora were defeated.

In the south the Yamasee also fought to stop their villages from being raided by slave traders. Native Americans of many different nations took part in the Yamasee War of 1715. After the Cherokee joined the English colonists, the Yamasee were defeated.

North and South

Most of the colonists in the north of Carolina had come from Virginia and Maryland to find land for their new farms. In the south new colonists came from France, Germany, and Switzerland. They were wealthier and owned more enslaved Africans. They traded in crops and furs.

The proprietors had not helped the colonists in the wars against the Native Americans. They also provided no support against pirates and Spanish settlers from Florida. In 1719 they refused to pass laws that the colonists had requested. The colonists finally rebelled. As a result, King George I bought back southern Carolina. Ten years later, he bought back the rest of the Carolina land and made two colonies: North Carolina and South Carolina.

Charles Town (below) was the capital of South Carolina from 1670 until 1790.

Colonial Williamsburg

THE THIRTEENTH COLONY

James Oglethorpe was a wealthy member of the English government. In 1729 he was on a committee formed to examine England's prisons for debtors. A debtor is a person who owes money. Oglethorpe was shocked by the conditions of the prisons and by the number of debtors locked away. He asked King George II for a charter to start a colony for debtors and the poor. "England will grow rich by sending her poor abroad," Oglethorpe explained. The king had little pity for the poor, but he was concerned about the Spanish settlements in what is now Florida. He granted Oglethorpe a charter for the land between present-day Florida and South Carolina. In the charter the king demanded that every male colonist fight the Spanish if it became necessary.

In 1732 Oglethorpe and about 120 followers sailed from England and landed in the new colony, which they called Georgia after King George II. Their first settlement was Savannah.

The Granger Collection

James Oglethorpe (above) and Chief Tomochichi met in London, England (below), to sign a treaty giving the English land on which to build Savannah.

The Muscogee and the English

The area the English called Georgia was home to the Muscogee, Cherokee, Choctaw, and Chickasaw. The Muscogee were the largest of these Native American nations. Most Muscogee villages were located along rivers and streams. Because of this, the English called the Muscogee "Creek." Before the arrival of the Europeans, the Muscogee villages had joined together to form the Muscogee Confederacy to protect their lands from other Native Americans.

Chief Tomochichi

One Muscogee group, the Yamacraw, were not part of the confederacy. They lived along the Savannah River near where Oglethorpe's group settled.

The chief of the Yamacraw at the time was named Tomochichi (toh mah CHEE chee). Tomochichi gave the colonists advice on their dealings with the Native American people of the region. He also sent runners to every Muscogee town inviting the chiefs and leaders to meet with James Oglethorpe and to welcome him and his followers.

Georgia grew slowly. Very few debtors moved to the colony. Farmers could not get enough workers, and Oglethorpe did not allow slavery. Also, he had insisted that colonists start a profitable silk trade, but silkworms could not survive in Georgia's climate. In addition, Oglethorpe did not allow colonists to own more than 500 acres. By 1752 the colony had less than 5,000 people. Oglethorpe then returned the colony to the king.

WHY IT MATTERS

Georgia became the thirteenth English colony. From the forests of present-day Maine in the North to the coastal plains of Georgia in the South, each of the 13 English colonies was developing in its own way. Over 100 years had passed since England established its first colony in North America. In less than 50 years time, the 13 English colonies would become the United States of America.

Links to MATHEMATICS

Savannah's Squares

How did Oglethorpe plan the first settlement in Georgia? Savannah was laid out on Yamacraw Bluff as a series of squares. Each square measured 1 mile by 1 mile. Some squares were broken up into rectangular farms. There were 12 rectangular farms in each square mile.

Oglethorpe laid out 23 of the square miles with rectangular farms. How many such farms did Savannah have?*

Reviewing Facts and Ideas

MAIN IDEAS

- The colony of Maryland was founded in 1634 by Lord Baltimore as a place for Catholics to worship in freedom.

- In 1663 the English established what would become the colonies of North Carolina and South Carolina.

- Before the arrival of Europeans, the Muscogee, one of the largest Native American groups in Georgia, formed a confederacy.

- In 1732 James Oglethorpe, an English general, established Georgia as a colony for debtors and poor people.

THINK ABOUT IT

1. What was the House of Burgesses?

2. Why did George Calvert want to start a colony in North America?

3. **FOCUS** How did the Southern Colonies come to be founded?

4. **THINKING SKILL** The proprietors refused to pass the laws that the Carolina colonists requested. What *effect* did this have on the colony?

5. **WRITE** Suppose you are a colonist in Carolina. Write a letter to the newspaper explaining what you think about the tax placed on all people who are not members of the Church of England.

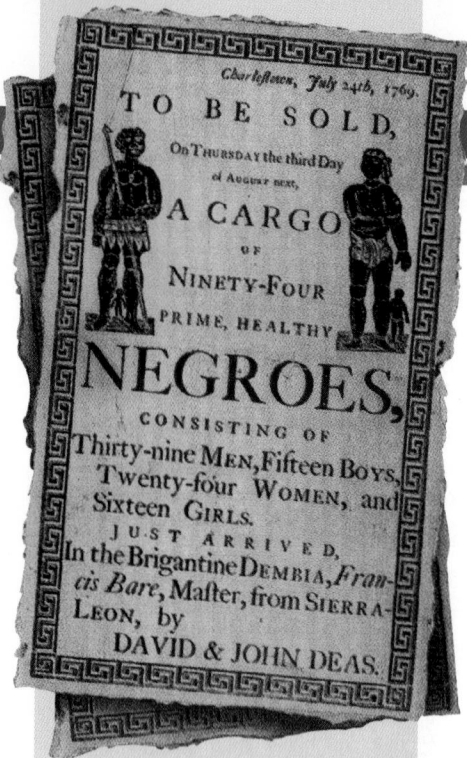

SLAVERY ON SOUTHERN PLANTATIONS

Focus Activity

READ TO LEARN
What was the plantation system, and how did it affect blacks and whites in the Southern Colonies?

VOCABULARY
indigo
backcountry
plantation
overseer
slave code

PEOPLE
Eliza Lucas Pinckney
John Punch

PLACES
Tidewater
Piedmont

READ ALOUD

"Before I'd be a slave,
I'd be buried in my grave,
And go home to my Lord and be saved."

These are the words of a hymn sung by enslaved African Americans. Many enslaved workers felt that if they could not be free, they did not want to live.

THE BIG PICTURE

Slavery was not a new practice in the 1600s—it had existed for thousands of years. The Maya and Aztec, whom you read about in Chapter 3, had enslaved workers. People in Europe, Africa, and Asia also forced people to work as slaves. Before the 1500s, however, most enslaved people were prisoners of war. They lost their freedom when they lost in battle.

Slavery in colonial America was different. The colonists did not enslave their enemies—they enslaved people of a different skin color. African captives were bought and sold like property. They had no rights. Families of enslaved workers could be broken up, and individual members sold to different colonists.

Captured Africans were brought to all the colonies in North America. However, most of them worked in the Southern Colonies. The large farms in the South raised crops that needed a lot of workers. In time most of these workers became enslaved.

THE GEOGRAPHY OF THE SOUTHERN COLONIES

Southern colonists who settled along the coast and on the higher plateau to its west found rich land suitable for raising crops.

The Coast

The Tidewater is a 75-mile-wide strip along Virginia's coast that is often flooded. Despite the salt water, the land is fertile. There, in the early 1600s, the first settlers planted tobacco.

The coast south of the Tidewater has swamps. Captive Africans knew how to plant rice in swampland. Colonists soon began to raise a lot of rice. Then, white colonists used more enslaved workers to raise the crops.

At 17, Eliza Lucas Pinckney managed her father's farms. She experimented with indigo—a plant used to make blue dye. In 1744 she found a way to grow it successfully in land too dry for rice. Indigo became a main cash crop for the Southern Colonies.

The Backcountry

The rocky land between the coastal plain and the Appalachian Mountains was often called the backcountry. It included the Piedmont—a plateau

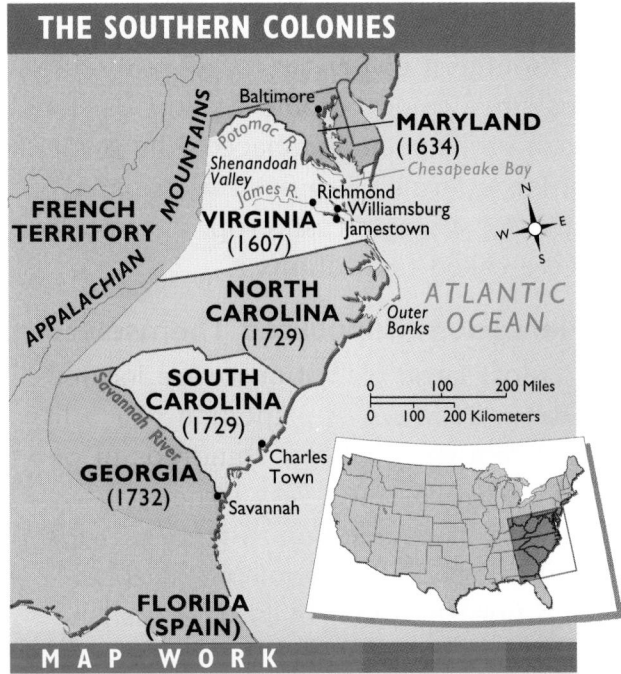

THE SOUTHERN COLONIES

Baltimore
MARYLAND (1634)
Potomac R.
Shenandoah Valley
Chesapeake Bay
James R.
Richmond
Williamsburg
FRENCH TERRITORY
VIRGINIA (1607)
Jamestown
APPALACHIAN MOUNTAINS
NORTH CAROLINA (1729)
Outer Banks
ATLANTIC OCEAN
Savannah River
SOUTH CAROLINA (1729)
0   100   200 Miles
0   100   200 Kilometers
GEORGIA (1732)
Charles Town
Savannah
FLORIDA (SPAIN)

MAP WORK

The Southern Colonies were located between the French territory to the west and Spanish Florida to the south. Which Southern colonies were founded after 1607 and before 1732?

higher than the coastal plain stretching through the Middle and Southern colonies. Most backcountry settlers lived on small farms. They raised food for their families, and small cash crops like tobacco, apples, or peaches.

This farmland (below left) is located in the Tidewater. The house (below right) was built in the backcountry.

THE PLANTATION SYSTEM

Southern colonists quickly realized that they could become wealthy raising cash crops such as tobacco. The owners of large farms often used most of the land for a single cash crop. These farms were called plantations.

Plantations Supported Themselves

Most large plantations were located near waterways. A plantation was a little like a small village. Hundreds of people might live on a very large plantation. In addition to raising crops and livestock, the people on a plantation operated flour mills. They had a blacksmith's forge and a carpenter's shop.

The diagram on the next page shows a large Colonial Southern plantation. The plantation owner and his family lived in the "big house" which you can see at the top of the diagram. Some enslaved people worked there as "house slaves." Others toiled in the fields or were skilled workers who made furniture, shoes, or glass. The enslaved workers' cabins were usually near the crop fields.

Plantation Workers

At first, plantation owners relied on indentured servants to work the land. These European and African servants usually received their freedom after a certain number of years. However, as the plantation system grew, the number of indentured servants decreased.

Many plantation owners had European luxuries like this two-handled silver cup (above) in their homes.

The Introduction of Slavery

The first Africans brought to Virginia arrived as indentured servants in 1619. Plantation owners needed many workers and wanted to pay as little as possible. Some planters thought that one solution was to use enslaved people as plantation workers.

Even in the early 1600s black and white servants were treated differently. In 1640 John Punch, a black indentured servant, and two white servants escaped from their owner. The three runaways were soon captured. The two white servants had several years added to their period of service. Punch, however, became a "servant for life." He was the first colonist to be enslaved. Gradually, indentured servants were replaced by captive Africans. These captives were bought for their lifetimes and were considered the property of the people who had purchased them.

Wealth for a Few Planters

Most farmers in the Southern Colonies did not own plantations. In the late 1700s almost 80 percent of the colonists in South Carolina lived in the backcountry and had small farms.

Those who did own large plantations, though, usually lived a rich lifestyle. Most plantation owners were men, but some women also owned plantations. These people held important positions in the colonies. The courts as well as government and business leaders accepted the planters' view that the economy of the South would grow weak without slavery.

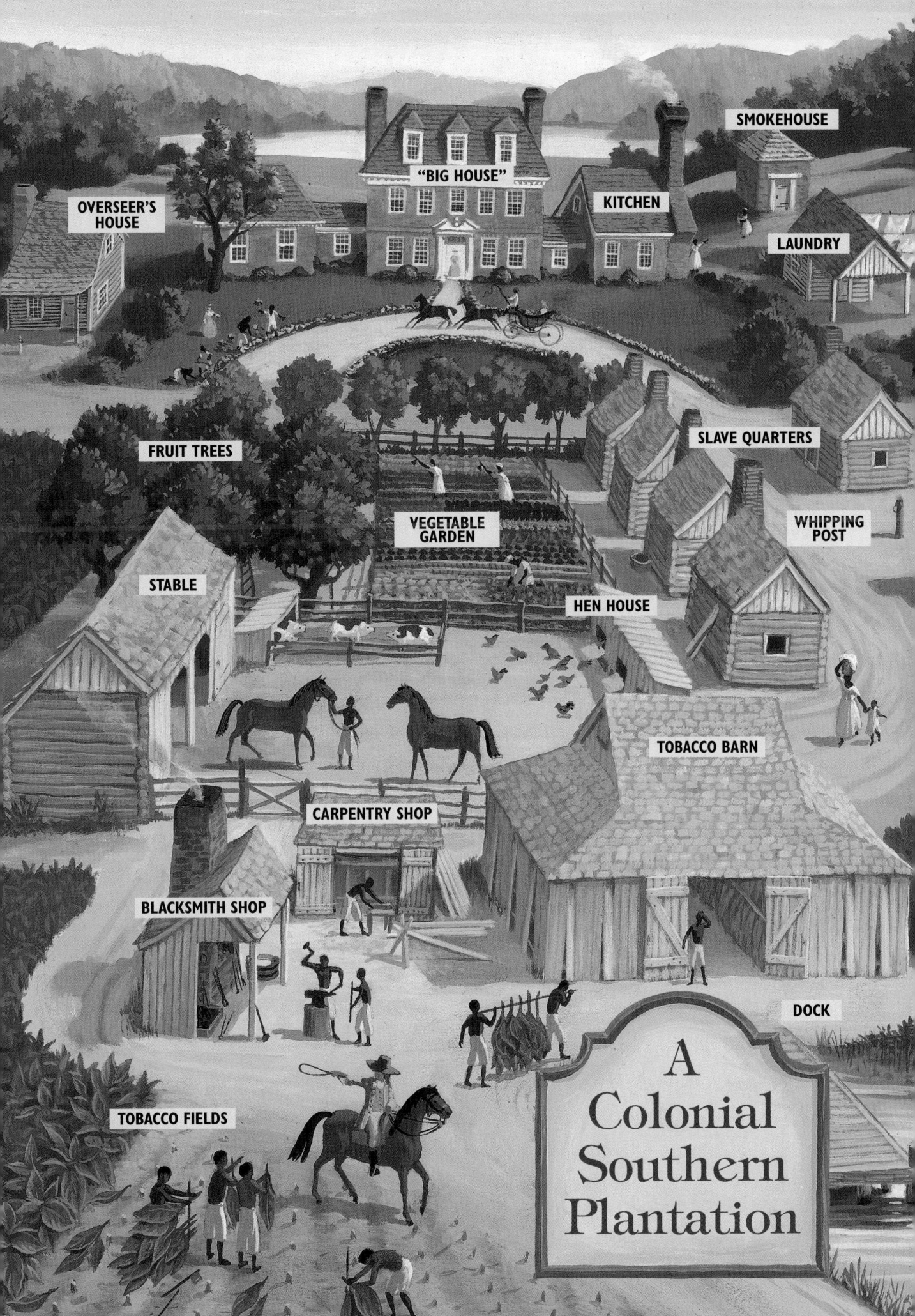

OVERSEER'S HOUSE

"BIG HOUSE"

KITCHEN

SMOKEHOUSE

LAUNDRY

FRUIT TREES

VEGETABLE GARDEN

SLAVE QUARTERS

WHIPPING POST

STABLE

HEN HOUSE

TOBACCO BARN

CARPENTRY SHOP

BLACKSMITH SHOP

DOCK

TOBACCO FIELDS

A Colonial Southern Plantation

SLAVERY

In the 1660s new laws in Virginia and Maryland allowed the enslavement of Africans. By 1710 there were about 50,000 enslaved workers in the colonies. By 1770 the number was half a million.

A Life of Suffering

Enslaved Africans had to endure terrible conditions and physical hardship. On a plantation their day began early and ended late. In the fields they did the work of planting and harvesting tobacco, rice, and indigo. They also took care of animals and repaired tools.

The overseer—often an indentured servant or an enslaved person—told the enslaved people what to do. He was usually the one who punished the workers. Overseers or planters sometimes killed enslaved people, by accident or on purpose. Under a 1669 Virginia law, even a person who killed an enslaved person would not be punished. Read the following excerpt by Solomon Northup. Northup was kidnapped and enslaved in 1841. If the overseer Northup writes about was also enslaved, why do you think he was so cruel?

MANY VOICES PRIMARY SOURCE

Excerpt from *Twelve Years a Slave*, the autobiography of Solomon Northup, published in 1853.

The overseer or driver follows the slaves on horseback with a whip. . . . The faster hoer takes the lead row. . . . If one [of his companions] passes him, he is whipped. If one falls behind or is a moment idle, he is whipped. In fact, the lash is flying from morning until night.

Slave Codes

As the numbers of enslaved Africans grew, the planters became afraid that they would rebel. Many of the Southern Colonies passed slave codes. These laws took even more rights away from enslaved people, such as the rights to practice their own religions or to marry.

Stratford Hall (below) in Virginia was built with the help of enslaved African workers. An enslaved African created this sculpture in the eighteenth century (right).

Smithsonian Institution

Some enslaved Africans continued to follow traditions of music and dance that they had brought with them from Africa.

Rebellion

From the beginning, captured Africans fought against slavery. Many enslaved people refused to work. Some worked slowly or purposely broke tools, while others escaped. If caught, they could be beaten or killed.

What the planters feared most was an uprising. In 1700, 6,000 enslaved people lived in Virginia. There had already been nine uprisings in that colony. Sometimes enslaved people organized raids. In the Stono Rebellion of 1739, a captive named Jemmy led a rebellion in which 30 colonists of South Carolina were killed.

WHY IT MATTERS

Although some people believed slavery was wrong, others thought that the Southern economy would not work without enslaved workers. Historians think that overall more than half a million enslaved Africans were brought to North America. This forced immigration has had a tremendous and lasting effect on the history and culture of our country.

✔️ Reviewing Facts and Ideas

MAIN IDEAS

- Most Southern colonists settled along the coast and on the Piedmont.
- Slavery was practiced throughout North America, but most enslaved people worked on large plantations in the Southern Colonies.
- A plantation was a large farm on which cash crops were grown.
- African captives rebelled against slavery in many ways.

THINK ABOUT IT

1. How did slavery in colonial America differ from slavery among the Aztec?

2. What is a plantation?

3. **FOCUS** How did the plantation system affect African American indentured servants in the Southern Colonies?

4. **THINKING SKILL** What were the *cause* and *effect* connections between the plantation system and slave rebellions? Use a cause-and-effect chain to trace these connections.

5. **GEOGRAPHY** How did the geography of the Southern Colonies affect the crops colonists grew?

THINKINGSKILLS

Evaluating the Credibility of a Source

VOCABULARY
credibility

WHY THE SKILL MATTERS

In Chapter 7 you learned about primary and secondary sources. We use primary and secondary information to understand history. In this chapter, on page 242, for example, you read an excerpt from a primary source—the charter for the Georgia colony.

An engraving, from the time, can be a primary source of information.

When reading such sources, how can you tell whether you should believe them? Are they accurate? Asking a few key questions will help you to evaluate the credibility, or believability, of a source's information.

USING THE SKILL

To determine whether a source is credible, first consider the professional background of the author. Is the author well informed about or an expert on the subject? Does he or she have anything to gain by not being truthful?

Reread this excerpt from page 252, taken from the autobiography of Solomon Northup, written in 1853. He describes the punishment of field workers.

> *The overseer or driver follows the slaves on horseback with a whip. . . . The faster hoer takes the lead row. . . . If one [of his companions] passes him, he is whipped. If one falls behind or is a moment idle, he is whipped. In fact, the lash is flying from morning until night.*

Was the author in a position to describe his subject accurately? If we know Northup actually experienced these events, the answer is yes. What did Northup have to gain by giving an untruthful account? He may have wanted freedom and justice for enslaved people.

To check the source's credibility, you could also locate and compare the facts with another account of the same situation. Because many accounts of the cruelty of overseers were written by many formerly enslaved people you can easily check this source's credibility.

TRYING THE SKILL

Now read the quotation below by William Byrd. How credible is Byrd's statement? Use the Helping Yourself box as a guide. Byrd was a Virginia planter who was traveling through the backcountry in 1710. In this excerpt he describes the types of skills a backcountry woman possessed.

She will carry a gun in the woods and kill deer, turkeys . . . shoot down wild cattle, catch and tie hogs, knock down beeves [cows] with an ax, and perform the most manful Exercises as well as most men in those parts.

Ask yourself about Byrd. Was he in a position to tell the truth about the subject? Did he have anything to gain by not being truthful? Based on your answers to these questions, is he a credible source about backcountry women in colonial America?

REVIEWING THE SKILL

1. What does *credibility* mean?
2. What questions should you answer to help you determine if a source is credible?
3. How can a second source be useful in establishing a document's credibility?
4. Given the following two choices, which would be a more credible source? Why?
   a. The journal entries written in 1717 by a South Carolina planter
   b. An historical novel written in 1950 about a planter's daughter in Virginia
5. Why is it important to establish the credibility of any source?

Solomon Northup may have lived in slave quarters like these.

1600   1642   1750   1800

DAILY LIFE IN THE SOUTHERN COLONIES

Focus Activity

READ TO LEARN
What was life like for the different people of the Southern Colonies?

VOCABULARY
extended family

PEOPLE
Robert "King" Carter

READ ALOUD

Devereux Jarratt was born into a backcountry family in the Piedmont in 1732. He described his home life, which was shared by many people in the region, as follows: "Our food was altogether the produce of the farm, or plantation, except a little sugar, which was rarely used; and our raiment [clothing] was altogether my mother's manufacture, except our hats and shoes, the latter of which we never put on but in the winter season. We made no use of tea or coffee for breakfast, nor at any other time; nor did I know a single family that made any use of them."

THE BIG PICTURE

Daily life in the Southern Colonies depended greatly on who you were and where you lived. If you were a craftworker in the backcountry, your life was much harder than that of a wealthy plantation owner. If you were an enslaved African, you had little control over your life. If you were a Cherokee, your way of life was changed by the colonists' arrival.

Geography also shaped daily life in the South. Great distances between small Southern settlements made it hard to unite communities.

LIFE ON SMALL FARMS

As you have read, most Southern colonists lived with their families on small farms. Sometimes they had a few indentured servants or enslaved workers. More often the family, which included many children and close relatives, did the work.

Farms in the Backcountry

Many backcountry farmers lived in rough log cabins, some of which were open in the front to let in cooling breezes. A backcountry home would typically be furnished with homemade three-legged stools, tables, and straw mattresses. The family made nearly everything themselves, and they did without things they could not make. A visitor to the backcountry in the mid-1700s said, "Not half the homes had kitchen utensils, only about a third had beds, and only one family in six had chairs and tables."

Native Americans in the Backcountry

As colonists came to the backcountry, they forced Native Americans from their homes. Peoples such as the Cherokee and the Chesapeake suffered more than the loss of their lands. They had no resistance to diseases that the colonists brought with them, and many died.

Some colonists did more than force Native Americans to leave their land. In 1642 Maryland's government encouraged colonists to shoot on sight any member of the Wiccomiss, a native people of the eastern Maryland shore. In Virginia the Assateague and Pocomoke were wiped out.

New ideas and goods also changed Native Americans' ways of life. Read the following excerpt from Robert Beverly's study of the Chesapeake. How might the new goods brought by the colonists have hurt Native Americans?

Excerpt from a study of the Chesapeake culture published by Robert Beverley, a burgess of Virginia, in 1705.

The English have taken away [a] great part of their country and consequently made everything less plenty amongst them. They have introduced . . . luxury . . . [that has] multiplied their wants and put them up to desiring a thousand things they never dreamt of before.

Colonists in the backcountry played musical instruments such as the handmade fiddle and dulcimer.

This tapestry shows the "big house" of a plantation.

PLANTATION LIFE

The plantation was a community much like a small town. Most planters and their families lived in large homes.

A Planter's Life

A planter's house was usually built with between four and seven rooms. As the planter got wealthier, he or she would use enslaved Africans to build more rooms. Planters imported furniture, china, silver, and clothing from England.

Many planters had very large families. Robert Carter, who owned Nomini Hall in Virginia, had 17 children. His grandson was one of the South's most wealthy men—Robert "King" Carter. He had owned about 1,000 enslaved workers.

Aunts, uncles, and other relatives also often lived on the plantation. This kind of large family is called an extended family.

Male family members helped the planter manage the land and crops. The women of the family worked hard to feed and care for everyone on the plantation. They had to plan the raising or buying of meat, fruits, and vegetables; the baking of breads; and the serving of meals.

In the evening family members on rich plantations often played games. They also read books aloud, or played music and sang together.

Read the Primary Source describing one planter's home. What kind of work would the servants, hired workers, and slaves have done here?

Excerpt from a letter written by Virginia planter William Fitzhugh in 1686.

*The plantation where I now live contains a thousand acres . . . three-quarters is well furnished with all necessary houses; grounds and fencing, together with a . . . crew of [blacks] at each plantation . . . with stocks of cattle and hogs at each quarter, upon the same land, is . . . a very good **dwelling house** with rooms in it . . . nine of them plentifully furnished with all things necessary and convenient, and all houses for use furnished with brick chimneys, four good cellars, a dairy, **dovecote**, stable, barn, hen-house, kitchen . . . a large orchard, of about 2,500 [apple] trees.*

dwelling house: home
dovecote: house built for doves or pigeons

The Metropolitan Museum of Art, NY

AFRICAN FAMILIES ON THE PLANTATION

As you have read, the planters hoped to grow vast amounts of crops to become rich. Over time most of the region's African Americans, including children, became enslaved by law.

By about age ten, enslaved children were usually thought to be strong enough to work in the fields. Enslaved field workers tended the plantation crops for 12 or 13 hours a day.

For enslaved people the day "never really ended" on the plantation. A typical day might begin at four o'clock in the morning. The workers would already be in the fields by sunrise and would work until dark, with only two short breaks. Some also had to weave the baskets used on the plantations for the harvest and make dugout canoes for transportation on rivers and waterways. After work was done, enslaved workers had their own chores.

Despite the long hours and not being allowed to read, write, or go to school, enslaved Africans managed to keep alive much of their culture through music, dancing, cooking, and storytelling.

Free Blacks in the South

Not all blacks in the South were enslaved. On the eastern shore of Virginia, for example, a free black community grew. They won their freedom in several ways. In North Carolina some were freed as rewards for acts of bravery, such as rescuing persons in danger. Others were freed through the terms of their owners' wills. Some former slaves were able to purchase their children's or spouses' freedom.

Many free blacks farmed plots of land or became craftworkers such as carpenters or blacksmiths. They earned a living from the same skills they had once used as enslaved workers.

Many laws made it hard, or even impossible, for African Americans to live free in the South. Blacks had few rights. They could not vote or serve on juries or bear arms. Whites did not invite free blacks into their homes. Those who were not enslaved were often encouraged to leave the region.

This slave house has been restored to show a part of the way of life of enslaved workers.

LIFE OUTSIDE WORK

The wealthy planter had plenty of free time, but most colonists in the South were kept very busy staying alive. They had few opportunities for relaxation.

Education

Most white children in the Southern Colonies learned some reading, writing, and arithmetic, either at school or at home. The sons of wealthy planters might attend private schools, where they learned Latin and Greek, and from there go on to college. There were private schools for girls, too, that taught languages, math, history, sewing, music, and dancing. Some children of wealthy families were often taught by tutors, or private teachers.

As in the New England and Middle Colonies, the sons of many colonists often became apprentices. Apprentices learned trades such as carpentry from skilled craftworkers.

Free African Americans often learned skills from their parents. Enslaved children were not allowed to attend school. They started working at an early age. There was no time for learning. Many planters did not want their enslaved workers to know how to read or write.

Recreation

People found ways to enjoy life during their free time. Southern children, to a greater degree than Puritan children in

Metropolitan Museum of Art, Gift of Mr. and Mrs. Samuel Schwartz, 1979

the North, were allowed to play, have toys, run, and make noise. Planters often hunted and enjoyed horse races, plays, and large parties or balls.

Enslaved workers did not have parties. At night in their cabins, African Americans told stories, sang, and played music together.

Religion

The Southern colonists were more tolerant of different religions than the Puritans or Quakers in the North. South Carolina allowed public worship by all, including Jews and other non-Christians. The Church of England was the established church in the Southern Colonies, and many planters attended with their families on Sundays. However, the church did not hold much power anywhere except in Virginia. Southern colonists lived far apart and did not meet regularly to worship.

Enslaved Africans were not allowed to practice their native religions. Some were introduced to Christianity and the Bible by planters. Many planters used

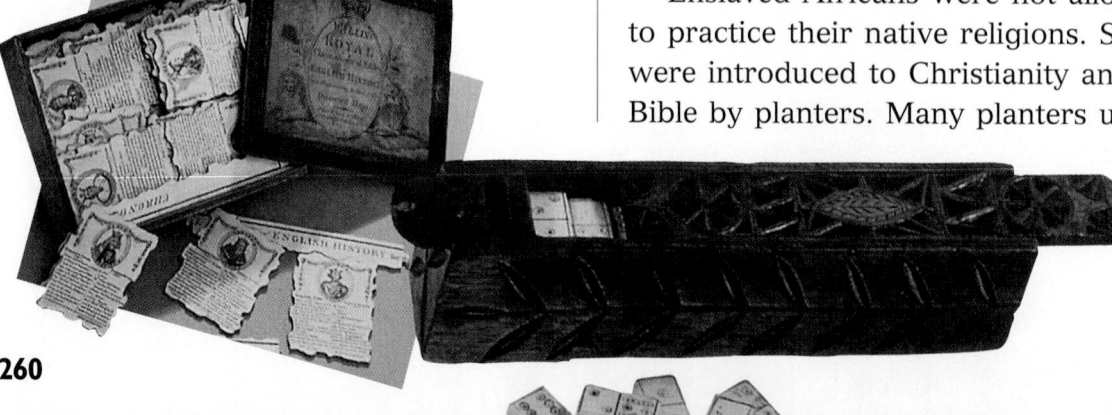

only the Old Testament, because they thought it contained justifications for slavery. Some enslaved workers compared stories of the Old Testament, such as Exodus, to their own experiences.

WHY IT MATTERS

As the plantation system spread in the South, wealthy landowners, with their position and power, became involved with the government of the colonies. Many of the first leaders of the United States were to come from this class of planters.

When and where did the marriage license first appear?

Marriage in England and in the colonies was originally licensed by the Church. In the Southern Colonies, however, settlements were far from one another, and there was often no local church. Weddings were held in people's homes. In the 1600s a new way of giving permission to wed was created: the county clerk issued a civil marriage license. The use of this marriage license spread to the Middle Colonies by 1700.

Marriage License

✓// Reviewing Facts and Ideas

MAIN IDEAS

- Most Southern colonists lived on small farms. As more colonists settled, clashes between colonists and Native Americans increased.

- Wealthy planters lived comfortably on plantations, unlike servants and enslaved African Americans.

- Wealthy planters had plenty of free time for recreation. Most other colonists and enslaved African Americans had little time to have fun.

THINK ABOUT IT

1. In what way were Southern families large?

2. What made life difficult for free African Americans in the South?

3. **FOCUS** How was life different for different groups of people in the South?

4. **THINKING SKILL** *Compare* how religion affected life in Puritan New England and in the Southern Colonies.

5. **WRITE** Suppose you are visiting the Southern Colonies from England. Write a letter home describing what you see.

Legacy

LINKING PAST AND PRESENT

AMERICAN MUSIC: AFRICAN ROOTS

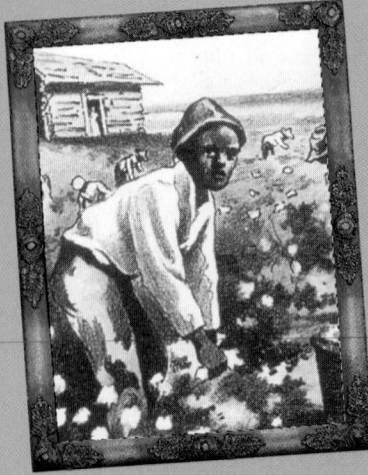

Rock-and-roll, hip-hop, blues, and jazz grew out of African musical traditions.

Enslaved Africans were not allowed to sing African music. However, they mixed their musical traditions with colonial folk songs and church hymns to create work songs and spirituals.

The blues developed from "field hollers," or calls used on plantations, and also from work and sorrow songs. The blues, in turn, influenced jazz and rock-and-roll. Rap and hip-hop have developed from African "boasting" songs and a mixture of blues, jazz, and rock-and-roll.

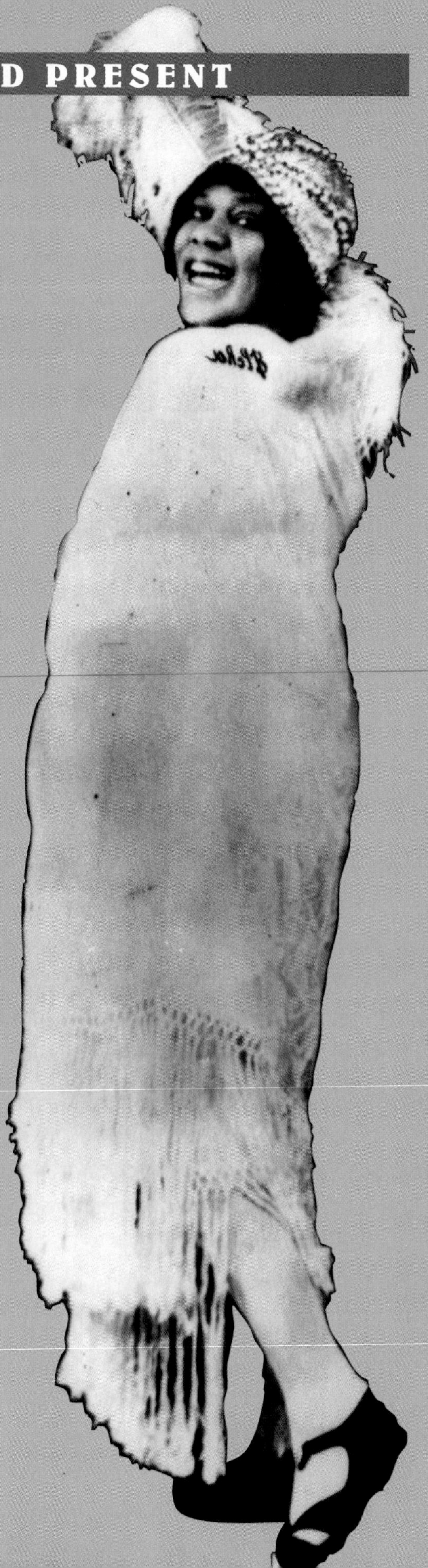

Blues lyrics grew out of songs about loneliness and suffering sung in the cotton fields (above). When Bessie Smith (right) sang the blues, she attracted people of all ages and ethnic groups.

Marian Anderson, pictured at the Lincoln Memorial, was the first African American opera singer to perform at Carnegie Hall in New York. Her singing of spirituals made them popular throughout our country.

Wynton Marsalis, a gifted trumpeter, has mastered both classical music and jazz. In 1984 he became the first musician to win Grammy awards for jazz and classical solo performances in the same year. His music style is inspired by earlier jazz greats such as Duke Ellington and Louis Armstrong.

New Orleans is famous as the birthplace of jazz and one of jazz's most famous musicians. The trumpeter and singer Louis Armstrong, known as "America's Ambassador," popularized jazz all around the world.

CHAPTER 9 REVIEW

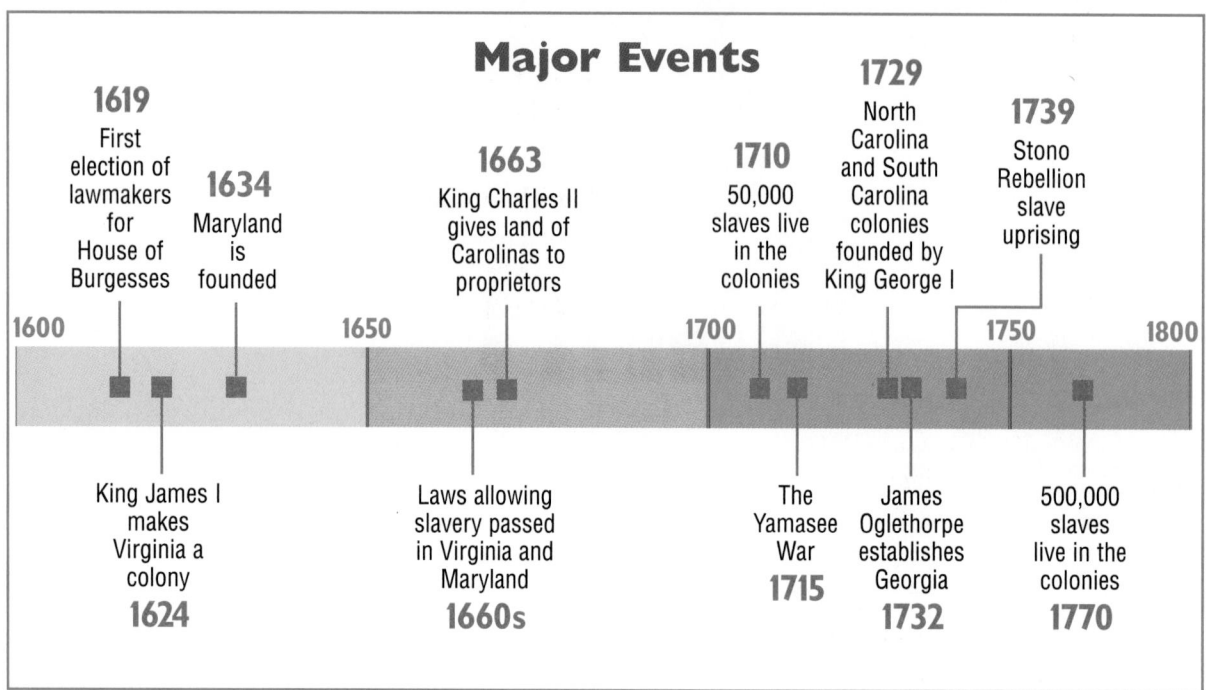

Major Events

1619 First election of lawmakers for House of Burgesses

1634 Maryland is founded

1663 King Charles II gives land of Carolinas to proprietors

1710 50,000 slaves live in the colonies

1729 North Carolina and South Carolina colonies founded by King George I

1739 Stono Rebellion slave uprising

1600   1650   1700   1750   1800

King James I makes Virginia a colony **1624**

Laws allowing slavery passed in Virginia and Maryland **1660s**

The Yamasee War **1715**

James Oglethorpe establishes Georgia **1732**

500,000 slaves live in the colonies **1770**

THINKING ABOUT VOCABULARY

Number a sheet of paper from 1 to 5. Beside each number write the word or term below that best completes each sentence.

debtors
extended family
overseer

proprietor
slave codes

1. A _____ is a business or property owner.

2. An _____ supervised the work of enslaved Africans on a plantation.

3. The _____ were laws that took away the human rights of enslaved people.

4. An _____ includes aunts, uncles, and other relatives.

5. England had prisons for _____, people who owed money.

THINKING ABOUT FACTS

1. Who founded the colony of Maryland? What persecuted religious group did the founder want to protect?

2. Why did Margaret Brent argue that she should have a vote in Baltimore's assembly?

3. Why was the Yamasee War fought? How were the Yamasee defeated?

4. What was the thirteenth colony? Why was it founded?

5. What is indigo? Who succeeded in growing it?

6. Where is the backcountry? Why did colonists settle there?

7. Who was John Punch? What happened to him in 1640?

8. What were some of the main features of the plantation system?

9. What were some things that were forbidden by the slave codes? Why were the slave codes written?

10. Look at the time line above. Which of the events shown accounts for the tremendous growth of slavery during this period?

THINK AND WRITE ◂ ▭▭▭▭ ◗

WRITE AN ORAL HISTORY

Suppose you are a writer who visits a Southern plantation to find out about the lives of enslaved Africans. Write down an oral history given by an African woman. Include information about her family, work, and treatment on the plantation. Write in the first person.

WRITE A CHART

In one column, list the names of Native American peoples who lived in the Southern Colonies. In a second column, write a fact about each group you listed. Tell how contact with the colonists changed the lives of the Native American peoples.

WRITE A DESCRIPTION

Suppose that you are a young person living in the backcountry. Write a description of your family's way of life.

APPLYING THINKING SKILLS

DETERMINING THE CREDIBILITY OF A SOURCE

1. What does *determining the credibility of a source* mean?

2. How can knowing an author's reputation help you decide if a source is credible?

3. How can comparing two historic accounts of the same event help you decide if a source is credible or not?

4. Which would be a more credible source about the lives of slaves on a plantation?
   a. A planter's letter in support of slavery written to a colonial assembly.
   b. An autobiography written by a young female slave.

5. If a person has something to gain by giving an untruthful account, is the source more likely to be credible or not credible?

Summing Up the Chapter

Copy the conclusion chart on a separate sheet of paper. Then review the chapter to complete the chart. After you have finished, use the information in the chart to answer the question, "What are the differences and similarities in the lives of colonists, plantation owners, slaves, and Native Americans in the Southern Colonies?"

TOPIC	CONCLUSION	EVIDENCE
The Southern colonists and Native Americans	The colonists and Native Americans are often in conflict.	
Plantation owners and Africans	The plantation owners used enslaved Africans as workers.	
The colonists and the plantation owners	Not all newcomers to the Southern Colonies lived or thought alike.	

CHAPTER 10

Life in the 13 English Colonies

THINKING ABOUT HISTORY AND GEOGRAPHY

The story of Chapter 10 takes place in the growing English colonies. Since the early 1600s people had been arriving from all over the world. Some came as colonists. As you can see on the time line, others came as captives. As you read the chapter, you will learn more about the people who came to the 13 English colonies and their ways of life.

1740s
CHARLES TOWN

The Southern Colonies depend on trade for goods and income

1740s
MIDDLE PASSAGE

African captives are brought to the 13 colonies

1740s
PHILADELPHIA

Ben Franklin writes *Poor Richard's Almanack*

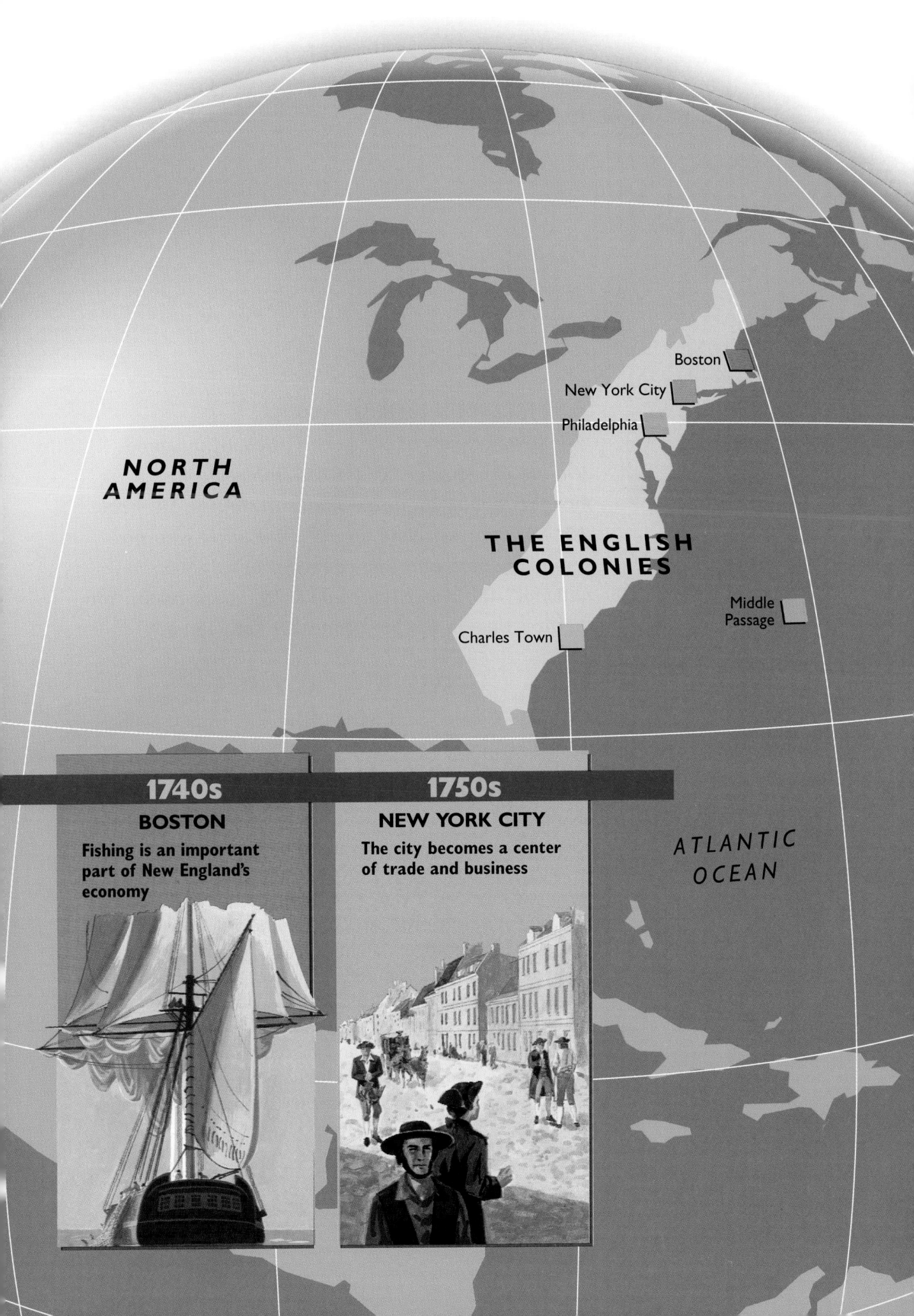

NORTH
AMERICA

THE ENGLISH
COLONIES

Boston

New York City

Philadelphia

Charles Town

Middle
Passage

ATLANTIC
OCEAN

1740s

BOSTON

Fishing is an important part of New England's economy

1750s

NEW YORK CITY

The city becomes a center of trade and business

The Granger Collection

HOW THEY CAME

READ ALOUD

In 1782 a Frenchman named Michel-Guillaume Jean de Crèvecoeur (krev KUR) published his thoughts about life in the English colonies. He wrote that Europe was made up of "great lords who possess everything and [the common] people who have nothing." The American colonist, by comparison, "for the first time in his life counts for something."

Focus Activity

READ TO LEARN
How did different groups of people come to the 13 colonies?

VOCABULARY
steerage
autobiography

PEOPLE
Olaudah Equiano
Jane Hoskens

THE BIG PICTURE

Life in England was hard. There was trouble with government, conflict over religion, and spreading poverty. In contrast, life in the colonies seemed attractive. Many people decided to travel to North America, and people said that "colony fever" had hit England. By 1760 about 1.5 million people lived in the colonies.

What kind of people moved to the colonies? Some were wealthy. Most were not. Many people sold everything they had in order to pay for the voyage. Others could not afford to pay for the trip. They wanted to come so badly that they agreed to become servants in exchange for the cost of the voyage. Still others came against their will. Thousands of Africans were kidnapped from their homes and forced to come to the English colonies as slaves. Whether people came as free persons, captives, or servants, they all made the dangerous voyage across the Atlantic Ocean.

THE VOYAGE TO AMERICA

The voyage to the English colonies lasted from six weeks to five months, and the Atlantic Ocean was often rough. Sometimes food ran out. People were trapped in crowded conditions. Sicknesses spread quickly. Two Dutchmen who made the voyage wrote that "the meat was old and tainted . . . the bread moldy or wormy . . . the water smelled very bad."

Poor people traveled in steerage, the part of the ship for the passengers paying the lowest fare. Inside there was little air or light. The ceiling measured only 4 1/2 feet in height.

Traveling in Chains

Africans sold into slavery suffered greatly on the voyage to North America. They were branded with hot irons and chained so they could not escape. Often, there were so many Africans on a boat that they had no room to move and were forced to lie on top of each other. If they refused to eat, they were whipped or burned.

Although most enslaved workers were from West Africa, they came from many different kingdoms. Slave owners tried to separate Africans who spoke the same language so they could not communicate with each other.

Olaudah Equiano was an Ibo born in the kingdom of Benin. One day in the mid-1700s, the 11-year-old Equiano was playing outside with his sister. Suddenly they were captured and carried away. Read this excerpt from Equiano's autobiography. An autobiography is the story of a person's life, written by that person. What was life like for captives aboard a slave ship?

MANY VOICES
PRIMARY SOURCE

Excerpt from the autobiography of Olaudah Equiano, published in 1789.

The sight of the slave ship amazed me. This amazement turned to terror when I was carried on board. . . . We were packed together in chains so tightly we could hardly move or turn over. . . . Many slaves fell sick and died—a result of being packed so closely. The only reason they were packed so closely was to increase the profits of the slave dealers.

National Maritime Museum, London

Enslaved Africans made the long voyage to the colonies packed tightly in the holds of ships.

269

A NEW LIFE IN THE COLONIES

Some people came to the colonies to increase their wealth and also to improve their position. In the Southern Colonies the more servants people brought, the more land they received. As the new landowners made money and bought more servants, they received still more land. In this way, some achieved positions that a farmer in England never could.

Indentured Servants

Most free colonists owned land and used indentured servants to work on it. In the early 1700s, more than half of the Europeans in the Southern Colonies were indentured servants. Many came by choice, but others were criminals sent to the colonies instead of being jailed or hanged.

Some servants were able to buy land and farm animals as they worked. When they finished their service, they became landowners themselves. In the Carolinas men were given 50 acres of land at the end of their service. Women servants also were given 50 acres.

Other indentured servants were treated terribly. Their employers did not care if the servants were completely worn out at the end of their service. Jane Hoskens was treated well as an indentured servant. She arrived from London in 1710. Read this excerpt from her autobiography. How did Hoskens feel about her position?

MANY VOICES PRIMARY SOURCE

Excerpt from the autobiography of Jane Hoskens, published in 1837.

*The [heads] of four families living in Plymouth, who had several children, agreed to **procure** a sober young woman, as a school-mistress to instruct them in reading. . . . I was recommended for that service. . . . I bound myself to them by indenture for three years, and went cheerfully with them. . . . The children learned very fast, which afforded comfort to me and satisfaction to their parents.*

procure: get

Many people worked as indentured servants in exchange for the cost of the voyage to the colonies.

The Granger Collection

Some Suffered as Others Prospered

As you can see in the graph, the colonies grew quickly between 1660 and 1760. But not everyone did well. Native Americans suffered as the colonies grew. They lost their homes, most of their land, and their ways of life. Smallpox and other diseases brought by Europeans to North America killed thousands of Native Americans.

In the early years of the colonies, many Africans were indentured servants. However, some of them had no end date for their service. They might be servants all their lives. This practice led to slavery in the colonies. By 1760 about 284,000 enslaved Africans lived in the Southern Colonies. About 41,000 enslaved Africans lived in the Middle Colonies and the New England Colonies.

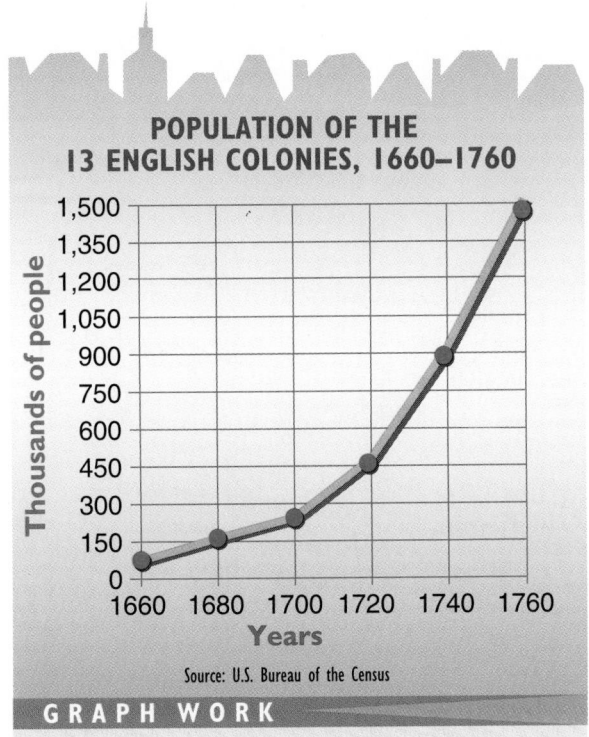

POPULATION OF THE 13 ENGLISH COLONIES, 1660–1760

Thousands of people

1,500
1,350
1,200
1,050
900
750
600
450
300
150
0

1660 1680 1700 1720 1740 1760
Years

Source: U.S. Bureau of the Census

GRAPH WORK

The colonies grew quickly. How many more people were living in the colonies in 1740 than in 1720?

WHY IT MATTERS

People came to the colonies for many reasons, some by choice and some in chains. The resulting diversity of peoples in North America was unique in the world at that time. By the mid-1700s each of the 13 colonies had its own identity. Patterns of life and government were established that would last until the colonies became states.

✓ Reviewing Facts and Ideas

MAIN IDEAS

- The trip across the Atlantic Ocean was hard on all travelers, but it was hardest on captive Africans.

- Landowners had unique opportunities in the colonies, while servants, enslaved Africans, and Native Americans generally suffered.

THINK ABOUT IT

1. What hardships did people suffer to reach the English colonies?

2. What was life like for indentured servants in the colonies?

3. **FOCUS** How did some people come to North America?

4. **THINKING SKILL** Reread the excerpt from the autobiography of Olaudah Equiano. Is this a _credible source_? Give reasons for your answer.

5. **WRITE** Suppose that you are an indentured servant in the 13 colonies. Write an essay called "How My Life Has Changed."

STUDYSKILLS

Writing an Outline

VOCABULARY

outline

WHY THE SKILL MATTERS

In the last lesson you learned how different groups of people came to the 13 colonies. You read how free people, captives, and indentured servants made the voyage. If you were asked to write a report on this subject, it might seem difficult at first to organize the information. Making an outline helps you to group facts into broad categories and to see how the facts are related. An outline is a plan that presents ideas about a subject in an organized way.

USING THE SKILL

One good way to start an outline is to state clearly the topic of the report. Then choose two or three main ideas about the topic. As you complete your research, add details to each main idea.

You can use Roman numerals to identify the main ideas of your outline. Under each Roman numeral, list the related details using capital letters to show the order.

Suppose that you were asked to write a report on how people came to the 13 colonies. The topic covers a lot of information. An outline can help you to organize all of the facts that you find.

You might begin your outline with three main ideas: "Free People," "Captives," and "Indentured Servants." During your research you can determine which details should support each of these main ideas. Eventually, your outline might look like the one at right.

How does the outline make it easier to understand the three groups of people who came to the colonies? What other information could you have included?

How People Came to the 13 Colonies

I Free People
   A. Some were wealthy and came with servants.
   B. Many were poor and traveled in steerage.

II Captives
   A. Came as indentured servants but were later enslaved
   B. Brought against their will and enslaved

III Indentured Servants
   A. Poor people who exchanged their labor for the price of the voyage
   B. Prisoners who were sent as indentured servants instead of being jailed or hanged

TRYING THE SKILL

Now suppose that you have been asked to write an outline on the reasons for Germans moving to Pennsylvania. Read the excerpt below from a history of immigration.

[Until 1871] the region we call Germany was a collection of independent states. . . . Each [state's] ruler taxed his subjects what he wished and chose the official religion. . . . As a result, many Germans were faced with crushing taxes and religious persecution. . . .

In the seventeenth century Germans suffered a series of long and bloody wars. . . . If a German was lucky enough to survive . . . he often became the victim of the starvation and disease that followed on the heels of battle. . . .

German immigrants settled in farm communities (above left) in Pennsylvania. Ships like these (below) carried immigrants across the Atlantic Ocean.

Against this backdrop, William Penn's promise of land and a fresh start in Pennsylvania, free from war, religious persecution, and high taxes, seemed like a gift from heaven.

What steps would you take to create an outline? Use the Helping Yourself box, and list two or three main ideas. How does listing the ideas help you to organize the information?

REVIEWING THE SKILL

1. What is an outline?

2. Which are the main ideas in the outline on how people came to the 13 colonies?

3. Where would you place this fact in that outline? Most enslaved people came from West Africa.

4. Could an outline about the voyage across the Atlantic Ocean be organized in more than one way? Explain.

5. How can writing an outline help you to understand historical information?

THE COLONIAL ECONOMY

READ ALOUD

"Whosoever commands the sea commands the trade; whosoever commands the trade of the world commands the riches of the world," said Sir Walter Raleigh. His words explain why England controlled the trade of its colonies.

Focus Activity

READ TO LEARN
How did people in the 13 English colonies make their living?

VOCABULARY
export
import
free enterprise
industry
triangular trade
Middle Passage

PEOPLE
Britton Hammon

PLACE
West Indies

THE BIG PICTURE

As more people arrived in the English colonies, their economy grew. During this time, England's rulers said that colonists could export certain items, such as tobacco and sugar, only to England or another English colony. To export means "to send goods to other countries to be sold or traded."

The colonists also imported goods such as cloth, metal, and glass from England. To import means "to bring goods from another country to be sold or traded."

The English paid low prices for colonial goods. However, they did not have complete control over colonial trade. Some colonies were able to trade with other countries and make a profit.

DIFFERENT ECONOMIES

In the early 1700s about nine out of ten colonists made a living from agriculture. By selling crops and other products, colonists were following a system of free enterprise. In a free enterprise system, people decide what to make, how much to produce, and what price to charge.

The Southern Colonies

The Southern Colonies had the right climate and soil to grow tobacco, rice, and indigo. These cash crops, often harvested by enslaved African workers, were then exported to England. Merchants in the South built large businesses by exporting crops and importing goods from England. They sold the goods to shopkeepers and Native American traders.

The Middle Colonies

Farmers in the Middle Colonies grew so much wheat and corn that people called their region the "breadbasket of the colonies." These farmers looked south to the English colonies in the West Indies for a place to sell their grain.

The colonists of the West Indies needed to import grain to feed the people they held in slavery. Little land was available to grow food because the colonial planters used most of it for cash crops such as sugarcane.

The Middle Colonies also had many small businesses. New York City, for example, had a flour-packing business. Philadelphia had so many leather shops that it became known for the smell of leather being prepared. In the Middle Colonies women owned some of these small businesses.

This oil painting of a colonial farm (below) was done about 1732. The indigo plant (right) probably came from South Carolina.

New England harbors in the 1700s (left) were busy fishing centers. Today (below) their beauty attracts many tourists.

NEW ENGLANDERS AND THE SEA

In the rocky soil of New England, farmers barely grew enough crops to feed themselves. As a result, many New Englanders turned to the region's thick forests or to the sea to make a living. In the 1700s waters off the coast of Massachusetts were among the richest fishing areas in the world. Some New Englanders fished for a living, while others built ships.

Profits from the Sea

English ships were too expensive for the colonists to buy. So workers began cutting down trees from New England's forests to build their own ships. By 1741 New England had a fleet of more than 800 fishing boats. New England ships were built so well that soon the English companies were buying them.

New Englanders used their own sturdy boats to catch fish and whales, and their fishing and whaling industries made large profits. An industry is a group of businesses that all make the same kind of product or provide the same kind of service.

The Triangular Trade

Many colonial merchants and sea captains also became rich in the triangular trade. The map on page 277 shows how the colonial trade routes formed a triangle. The first leg of the triangle started at such ports as Boston and New York. Traders sailed from these ports to the coast of West Africa, where they traded rum and guns for gold, ivory, and captive Africans.

The second leg of the triangle led from Africa to the West Indies. This part of the voyage was called the Middle Passage because it was the middle part of the triangular trade route. On this voyage thousands of Africans died from lack of water, tainted food, or disease. Olaudah Equiano, whom you read about in the last lesson, was sold into slavery in the West Indies before he arrived in North America. He wrote, "It was very common in several of the islands . . . for the slaves to be branded . . . and a load of heavy iron hooks hung about their necks."

In the West Indies the sea captains traded Africans for molasses, a thick syrup made from sugarcane. Then they returned to the northern ports, completing the third leg of the triangular trade route. In the northern colonies the molasses was made into rum, which began a new round of triangular trade. Many of the Africans sold in the West Indies also traveled this last leg and were resold in the 13 colonies. Equiano, for example, was sold to a Virginia plantation owner in 1756.

This drawing (below) shows how captive Africans were crowded into ships on the Middle Passage.

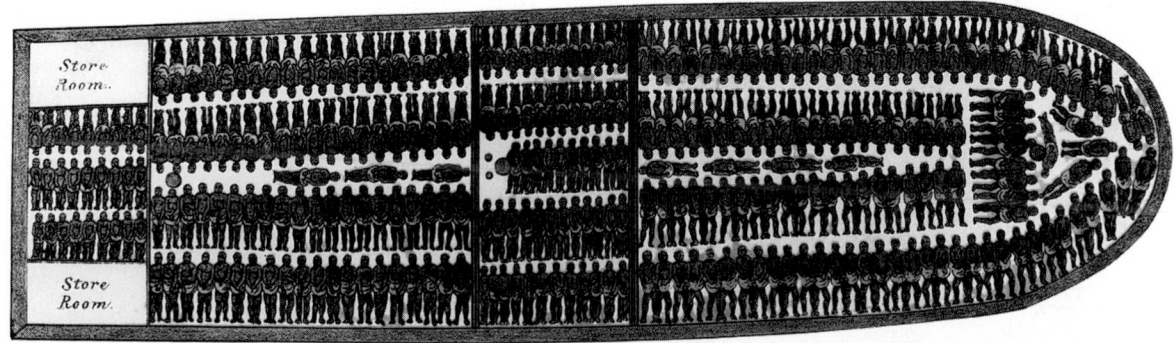

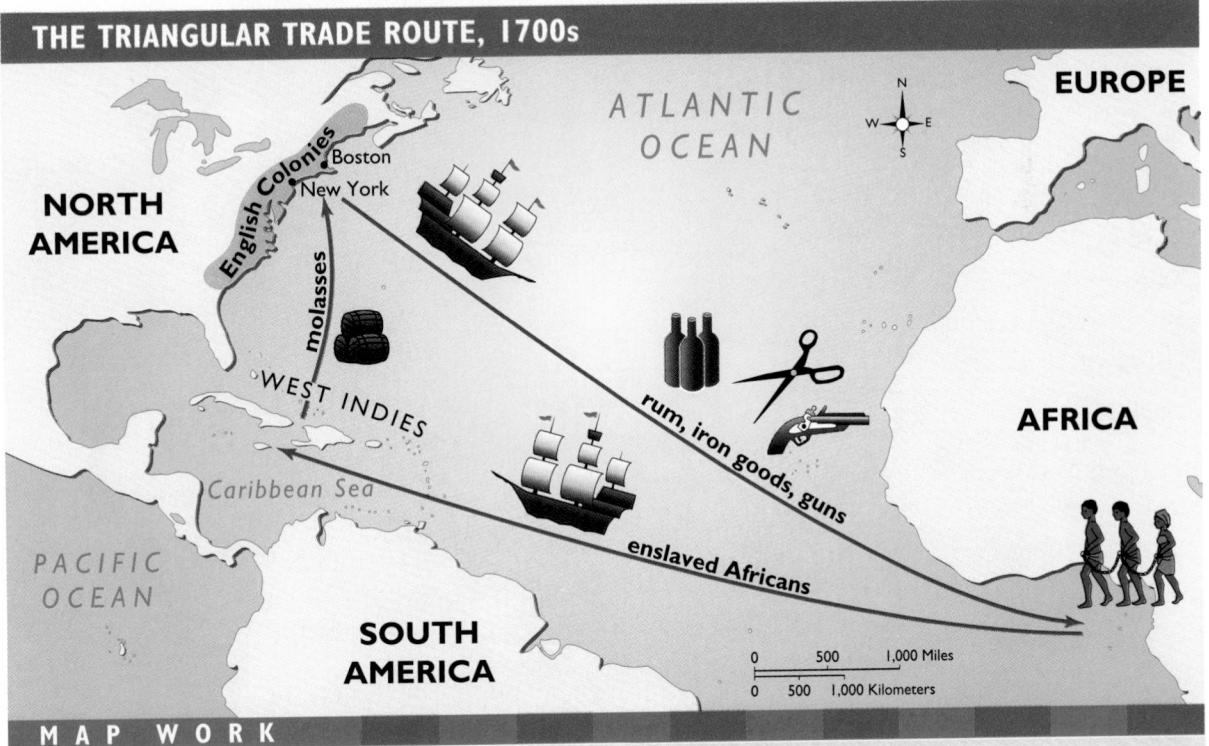

THE TRIANGULAR TRADE ROUTE, 1700s

MAP WORK

Trace the colonial routes of the triangular trade on the map.

1. How long was the route between Africa and the West Indies?

2. What was the destination of most of the enslaved Africans?

3. What products were shipped from New England to Africa? From the West Indies to Boston and New York?

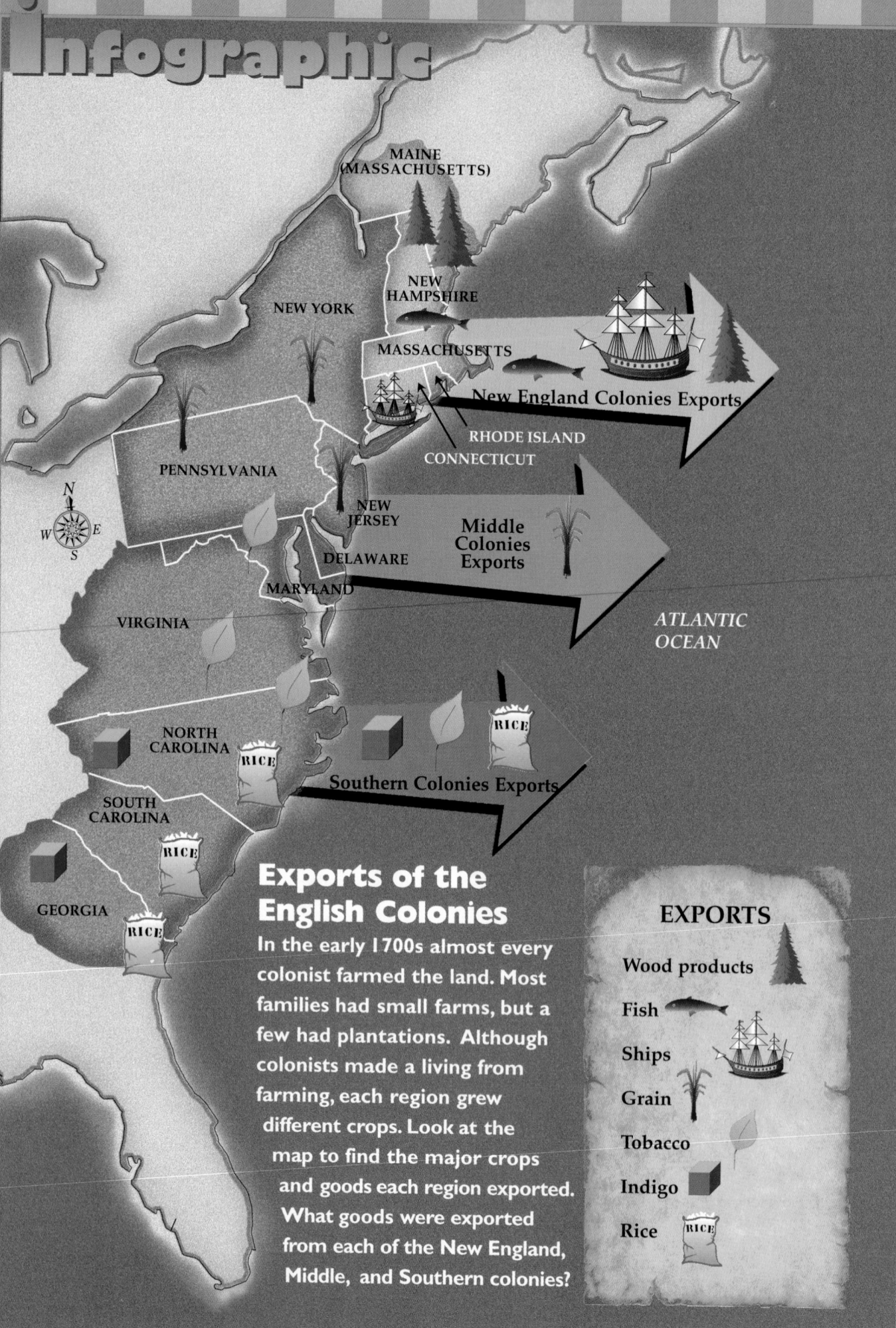

infographic

MAINE (MASSACHUSETTS)

NEW HAMPSHIRE

NEW YORK

MASSACHUSETTS

New England Colonies Exports

RHODE ISLAND
CONNECTICUT

PENNSYLVANIA

NEW JERSEY

DELAWARE

Middle Colonies Exports

MARYLAND

VIRGINIA

ATLANTIC OCEAN

NORTH CAROLINA

RICE

Southern Colonies Exports

SOUTH CAROLINA

RICE

GEORGIA

RICE

RICE

N W E S

Exports of the English Colonies

In the early 1700s almost every colonist farmed the land. Most families had small farms, but a few had plantations. Although colonists made a living from farming, each region grew different crops. Look at the map to find the major crops and goods each region exported. What goods were exported from each of the New England, Middle, and Southern colonies?

EXPORTS

Wood products

Fish

Ships

Grain

Tobacco

Indigo

Rice

FREEDOM AT SEA

During the colonial period some free Africans lived in North America. A small number of Africans who were enslaved found some freedom at sea. Equiano became one of these enslaved sailors, and later wrote, "I was extremely well-treated by all on board; and had leisure to improve myself in reading and writing." Other Africans used the sea to escape slavery completely. In 1747 an enslaved African in Massachusetts named Britton Hammon found work on a ship going to Jamaica. There he began a new life as a free sailor. By the end of the 1700s, more black sailors were free than enslaved. There were about 59,000 free Africans living in the United States in 1790.

WHY IT MATTERS

Farming, fishing, and trading were a few of the ways colonists made their living. Craftworkers produced all kinds of goods. As the colonial economy grew, colonists were more and more able to support themselves without importing goods from England. The colonists' desire to run their own economy eventually led to conflict with England.

Winterthur Museum

MAIN IDEAS

- By the middle of the 1700s, English colonists in the Americas were following a free enterprise system.
- The different colonies had different resources and different economies. Agriculture was important to all three regions.
- Some New Englanders relied on fishing, shipbuilding, and trading. The triangular trade of the 1700s made many New Englanders wealthy.
- During colonial times, both free and enslaved Africans lived in North America. A few Africans—some free, some enslaved—found greater freedom at sea.

THINK ABOUT IT

1. What kinds of resources did the Southern Colonies have?

2. Select three crops or products shown on the Infographic on page 278. Explain how each contributed to the economy of the English colonies.

3. **FOCUS** How did the Atlantic Ocean help New England to grow and become successful?

4. **THINKING SKILL** What caused English colonists in North America to begin looking for new places to trade their goods? What were some of the effects of the new trade?

5. **GEOGRAPHY** Look at the map of triangular trade on page 277. Compare the distance of the Middle Passage with the lengths of the other legs of the route.

This scrimshaw was carved from walrus ivory by a sailor during a long voyage.

FREE ENTERPRISE

Do you know someone who owns a business? Business owners in the United States take part in our country's system of free enterprise. Since colonial times, people here have worked hard in their own businesses, making and selling goods.

Colonial businesspeople strained their eyes to see in the flickering candlelight. Through patience and determination, they built a legacy of independence and hard work—a legacy that is still an important part of our country's free enter-prise economy.

Museum of Fine Arts, Boston

These houses of Cornhill Street (bottom) in Annapolis, Maryland, were the homes and businesses of such colonial trades-people as the tinsmith, the carpenter, the blacksmith, and the shoemaker.

National Geographic

280

Mary Provoost Alexander (below) had a shop in New York City. It was crammed with goods from Europe and the colonies. It probably looked like this one (left) in colonial Williamsburg.

Museum of the City of New York

Colonial craftworkers such as Paul Revere (far left) took great pride in their work. Revere is famous for his skill in silversmithing, as the teapot (near left) shows. His shop also produced iron products, such as cannons, bells, Franklin stoves, and bolts for ships.

The Minneapolis Institute of the Arts

COLONIAL CITIES GROW

READ ALOUD

Andrew Burnaby, an Englishman traveling in North America in 1760, was surprised at the bustling cities he visited. He wrote: "Philadelphia, if we consider that not eighty years ago the place where it now stands was a wild . . . desert . . . must certainly be the object of everyone's wonder and admiration. . . . The city is in a very flourishing state, and inhabited by merchants, artists, tradesmen, and persons of all occupations."

THE BIG PICTURE

By the time Burnaby was traveling through the colonies, several cities were growing rapidly. There were no large inland cities, but those that were ports were actively trading with the West Indies, Europe, and each other. These cities grew according to the amount of goods they exported. Philadelphia grew fastest. Its population increased from 4,000 people in 1690 to 40,000 people in 1775. It was bigger than any English city except London. Boston, which mostly imported goods, did not grow much in the early 1700s. Charles Town and New York got bigger, but not as much as Philadelphia.

Benjamin Franklin, Philadelphia's most famous citizen, helped it become the largest city in the 13 colonies. He grew up at a time when the colonies were changing rapidly. Before 1700, eight out of ten colonists were English or had English parents. By 1750 colonists from Germany, Ireland, France, and other countries had begun to shape the 13 colonies.

Focus Activity

READ TO LEARN
How did colonial cities grow?

VOCABULARY
almanac
Great Awakening

PEOPLE
Benjamin Franklin

PLACES
Philadelphia
Boston

Cigna Museum and Art Collection

282

BENJAMIN FRANKLIN

Ben Franklin, the grandson of an indentured servant, grew up to become the most famous person in the colonies. Born in 1706 into a large Boston family, Franklin learned at a young age that reading was a key to success. He read everything he could get his hands on.

At age 16 he wrote funny stories for his brother's newspaper under the name Mrs. Silence Dogood. His brother published them, not knowing that Ben had written them. This was the beginning of Franklin's work as a writer.

Franklin the Writer

In 1729 Franklin founded Philadelphia's first newspaper, the *Pennsylvania Gazette*. As a writer, one of Franklin's greatest successes was *Poor Richard's Almanack*. Now spelled without a *k*, an almanac is a reference book that contains information about the stars and the weather. Franklin added jokes and sayings to his almanac. From 1732 to 1757, Franklin's almanac sold more copies than any other book in the colonies except for the Bible.

The Granger Collection

Franklin also wrote clever sayings to fill the blank spaces in his newspaper. Many of the sayings are still popular. Read some of them on this page. What is Franklin trying to teach us?

Excerpts from
Poor Richard's Almanack
by Benjamin Franklin, published from 1732 to 1757.

Early to bed, early to rise, makes a man healthy, wealthy and wise.

Little strokes fell great oaks.

Glass, china, reputation, are easily cracked, and never well mended.

An open foe may prove a curse; but a pretended friend is worse.

One today is worth two tomorrows.

Haste makes waste.

Franklin the Scientist

As a scientist Franklin is best known for his experiments with electricity and his invention of the lightning rod. Among his other inventions that are still used today are bifocal eyeglasses and a wood-burning stove called the Franklin stove.

Franklin received many honors and prizes. His writings and experiments made him the best-known North American in Europe. When he visited Europe, people crowded in the streets to get a glimpse of him.

The Franklin stove heated rooms and tea kettles during the cold winters.

The Library Company of Philadelphia

PHILADELPHIA GROWS AND CHANGES

In the history of the English colonies, no city grew as quickly as Philadelphia did in the 1700s. The city met the needs of its growing population with streetlights, brick sidewalks, and public water pumps. You can find Philadelphia on the map on page 286.

Philadelphia was a city of great ethnic and religious diversity. By 1790 doctors, lawyers, business owners, and craftworkers from many different backgrounds lived in Philadelphia.

Benjamin Franklin started the colonies' first public library as well as their first newspaper. He also started the colonies' first hospital and the world's first volunteer fire department.

Franklin also played a role in the government. He served as Postmaster General and as Philadelphia's official printer. The postmaster is an official in charge of a post office.

Education in the Colonies

During much of the 1700s, schooling was mainly for the wealthy. Women and African Americans were usually not allowed to attend school. Abigail Smith (who later married John Adams) was born in 1744. She wrote, "Female education, in the best families, went no further than reading and arithmetic; in some few and rare instances, music and dancing."

Franklin wanted to help more people get an education. He himself had gone to school only until the age of ten. "It would be well," he wrote, "if students could be taught everything that is useful."

284

Philadelphia (above) was growing in 1730. The College of Philadelphia (below left) became the University of Pennsylvania in 1791. Deborah Franklin (right) ran a business and a home.

American Philosophical Society

Franklin founded the college that became the University of Pennsylvania. He also helped start a school for African Americans at the end of the 1700s.

Each of the early colleges was founded to support the established church of its colony. During the middle of the 1700s, a religious movement known as the Great Awakening spread throughout the colonies. The Great Awakening's goal was to strengthen people's religious beliefs and feelings. It widened the differences between several Protestant groups. Each group wanted to start a college for members of its church. This led to the founding of new colleges such as Princeton and Rutgers in New Jersey, Brown in Rhode Island, and Dartmouth in New Hampshire.

Women in Colonial Cities

The wives of wealthy men in colonial cities lived comfortable lives. Yet they also had many responsibilities. Franklin had little time to give to his printing shop because of his many other activities, so Deborah Franklin, his wife, ran much of the business. She also ran the busy Franklin household and took care of their three children.

Some of the newspaper publishers in the colonial cities were women. Not all of them were wives or widows of printers. The shortage of labor in the colonies resulted in women having more opportunities than they would in Europe. Other colonial women were shopkeepers and pharmacists, or practiced medicine. A number of these colonial women became highly successful.

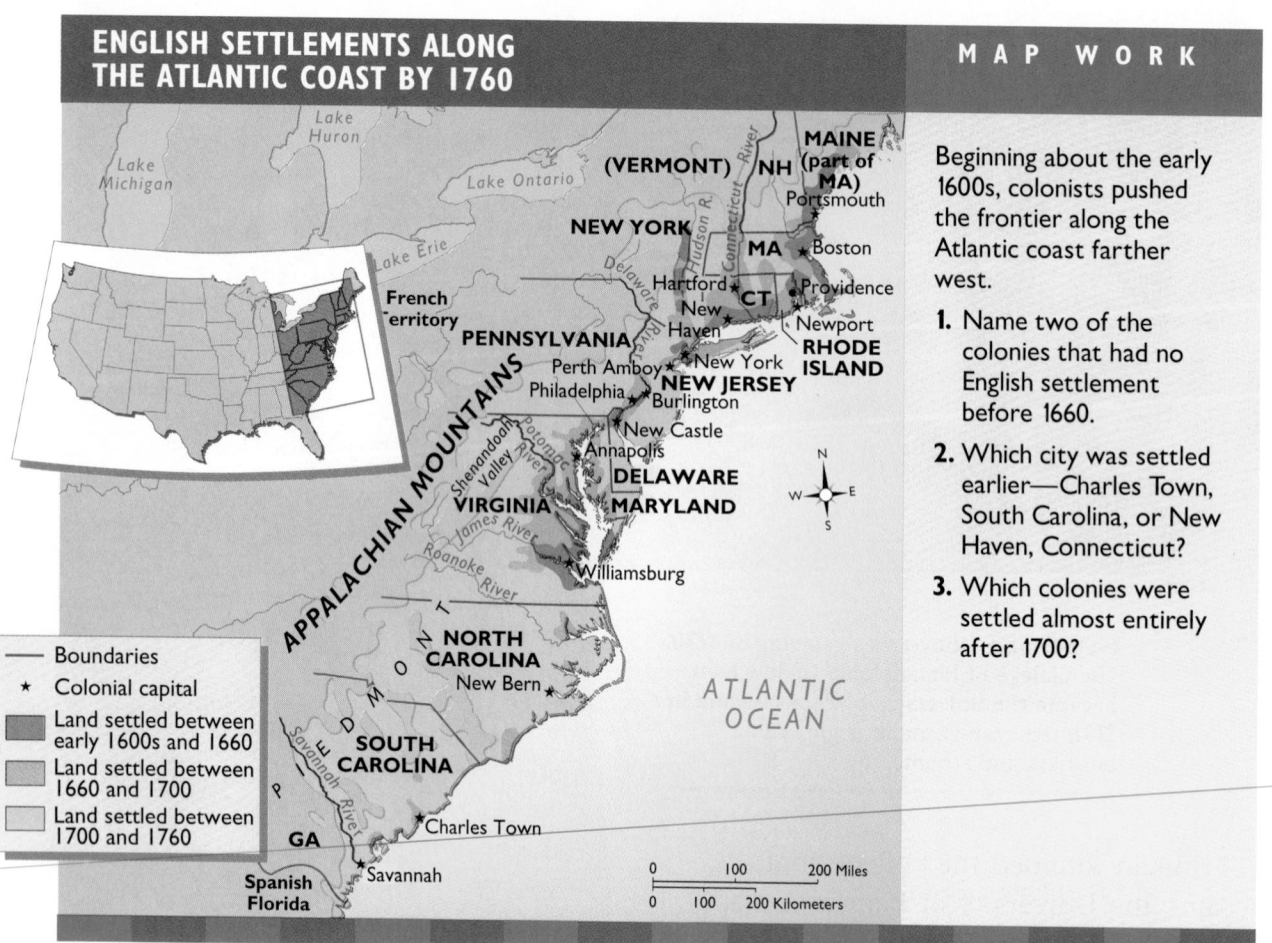

Boundaries
★ Colonial capital
Land settled between early 1600s and 1660
Land settled between 1660 and 1700
Land settled between 1700 and 1760

0   100   200 Miles
0 100   200 Kilometers

Beginning about the early 1600s, colonists pushed the frontier along the Atlantic coast farther west.

1. Name two of the colonies that had no English settlement before 1660.

2. Which city was settled earlier—Charles Town, South Carolina, or New Haven, Connecticut?

3. Which colonies were settled almost entirely after 1700?

GROWING CITIES

As you read, Philadelphia changed even faster than ports such as Newport and New York in the 1770s. The oldest large city in the colonies was Boston. Although its population did not increase very much in the mid-1700s, Boston remained New England's center for trade, business, and education. It sold more English books than any other city except London. In the Southern Colonies, Charles Town was the only large city. Find these cities on the map above.

Boston

Merchants and tradespeople from all over the English colonies came to Boston to trade. As in most cities of the time, the gap between the rich and the poor was greater than it was in the country. In Boston in the 1700s, five percent of the people owned nearly half of the wealth.

Boston was a busy port with 40 wharves—piers for unloading goods or passengers from ships. Most of the trading involved goods that arrived at Boston's docks and were then sent throughout the New England colonies.

Boston had several newspapers and an art academy. One of the colonies' first major portrait painters was Joseph Blackburn, who moved from England to Boston in 1753. In the mid-1700s he was one of many professional artists in the colonies. Most were portrait painters. They moved to the cities, where they could find a lot of wealthy customers for their work.

Charles Town

Charles Town was the center of trade for the Southern Colonies. By 1742 it did six times as much trade with England as all of the Northern colonial cities.

The streets of Charles Town were laid before any houses were built. Some streets were paved with cobblestones that ships carried to keep them low in the water. Once they had loaded rice, deerskins, and indigo in Charles Town, the ships did not need the weight of the stones. They left the stones on shore, where they were used for the roads.

Charles Town had many wealthy planters. No other city in the colonies was as elegant. It had a theater and the colonies' first museum—now called the Charleston Museum—founded in 1773.

WHY IT MATTERS

By the mid-1700s several colonial cities had become centers of trade and government. British laws about trade in the colonies became one of the causes of the American Revolution. Benjamin Franklin was a key figure in both of these events.

Reviewing Facts and Ideas

MAIN IDEAS

- Cities in the colonies grew very quickly in the 1700s.
- Philadelphia was the fastest-growing city. One of its citizens, Benjamin Franklin, helped it to grow.
- Boston and Charles Town were important Atlantic coast cities.

THINK ABOUT IT

1. What were some of Ben Franklin's contributions to Philadelphia?

2. What was Boston known for?

3. **FOCUS** What caused colonial cities such as Charles Town to grow?

4. **THINKING SKILL** What was Franklin's *point of view* about education?

5. **WRITE** Choose a saying from *Poor Richard's Almanack* on page 283 and write a paragraph about its meaning.

Boston in the 1700s served as New England's business and cultural center. The wealth produced from its trade supported professional artists and craftspeople.

CHAPTER 10 REVIEW

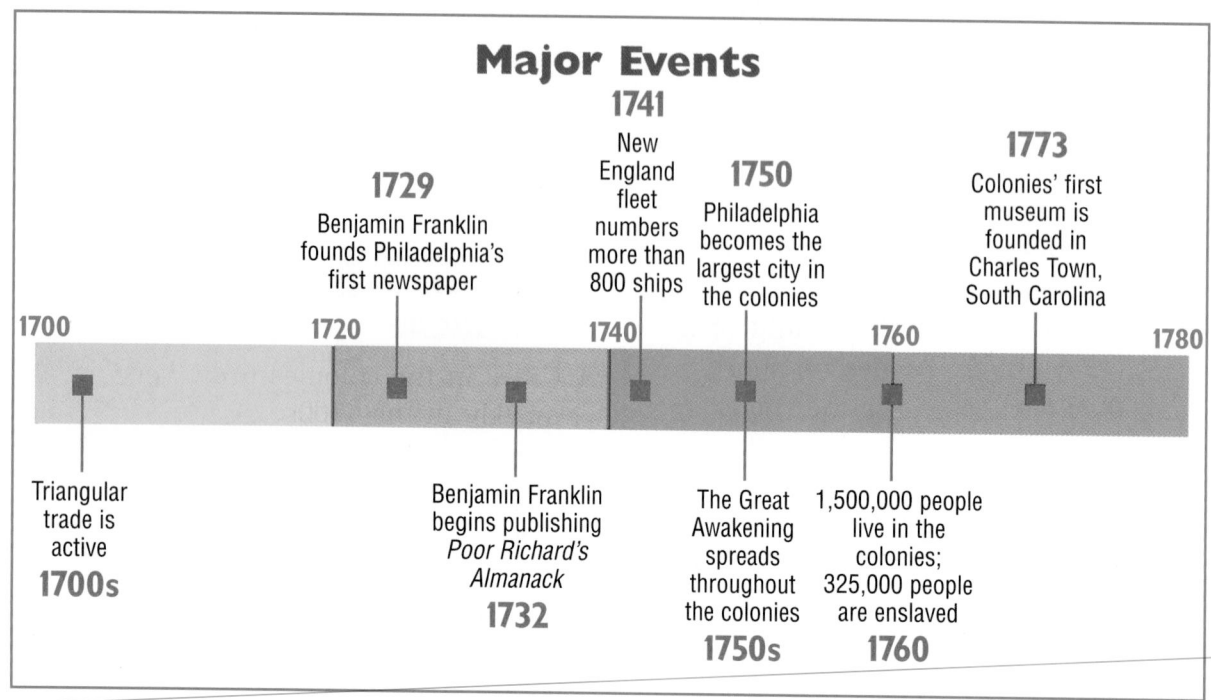

Major Events

1741
New England fleet numbers more than 800 ships

1729
Benjamin Franklin founds Philadelphia's first newspaper

1750
Philadelphia becomes the largest city in the colonies

1773
Colonies' first museum is founded in Charles Town, South Carolina

1700 1720 1740 1760 1780

Triangular trade is active
1700s

Benjamin Franklin begins publishing *Poor Richard's Almanack*
1732

The Great Awakening spreads throughout the colonies
1750s

1,500,000 people live in the colonies; 325,000 people are enslaved
1760

THINKING ABOUT VOCABULARY

Number a sheet of paper from 1 to 10. Beside each number write the word or term below that best completes the sentence.

almanac
autobiography
export
free enterprise
Great Awakening

import
industry
Middle Passage
steerage
triangular trade

1. In an _____ a person writes the story of his or her own life.

2. An _____ is a reference book that gives information about the stars and the weather.

3. The _____ was the second part of the triangular trade route.

4. To _____ means to bring goods from another country to be sold or traded.

5. An _____ is a group of businesses that all make the same kind of product.

6. _____ is the part of a ship for passengers paying the lowest fare.

7. Sea captains sailed three separate voyages on the _____ route.

8. Colonists could _____ tobacco only to England or other English colonies.

9. In a system of _____, people make their own decisions about how to run many kinds of businesses.

10. The _____ was a religious movement that strengthened people's religious beliefs.

THINKING ABOUT FACTS

1. Why did so many people go to the colonies as indentured servants?

2. How did England try to control trade in the colonies?

3. During what part of the triangular trade route were African captives transported? To what place were enslaved people taken?

4. What were some of the major cities in the colonies? In what way did geography affect their growth?

5. Look at the time line above. How many years after Benjamin Franklin published a newspaper did he publish *Poor Richard's Almanack*?

288

THINK AND WRITE

WRITING A REPORT

Write a report on the triangular trade. Identify the goods and people involved as well as the routes that the trade followed.

WRITING INTERVIEW QUESTIONS

Suppose that you have been assigned by a newspaper to interview people who arrived in the colonies in steerage. Write a series of questions that you would like to ask about where people have come from, why they came to the colonies, their experiences on the journey, and their impressions of colonial life.

WRITING A LIST

Suppose that you live in the colonies and work as a farmer or a trader. Make a list of the goods you produce or trade over the course of one week.

APPLYING STUDY SKILLS

WRITING AN OUTLINE

1. How does writing an outline help you organize information?

2. After identifying the topic, what should your next step be in making an outline?

3. Under which heading on the outline on page 272 would you place a detail about the families of wealthy colonists?

4. What three headings for main ideas might you use if you were writing an outline about the growth of cities in the 1700s?

5. When might writing an outline be helpful?

Summing Up the Chapter

Copy the main idea map on a separate sheet of paper. Then review the chapter to complete the main ideas. After you have finished, answer the following question about one region in the colonies: "How did the people in the _____ live?"

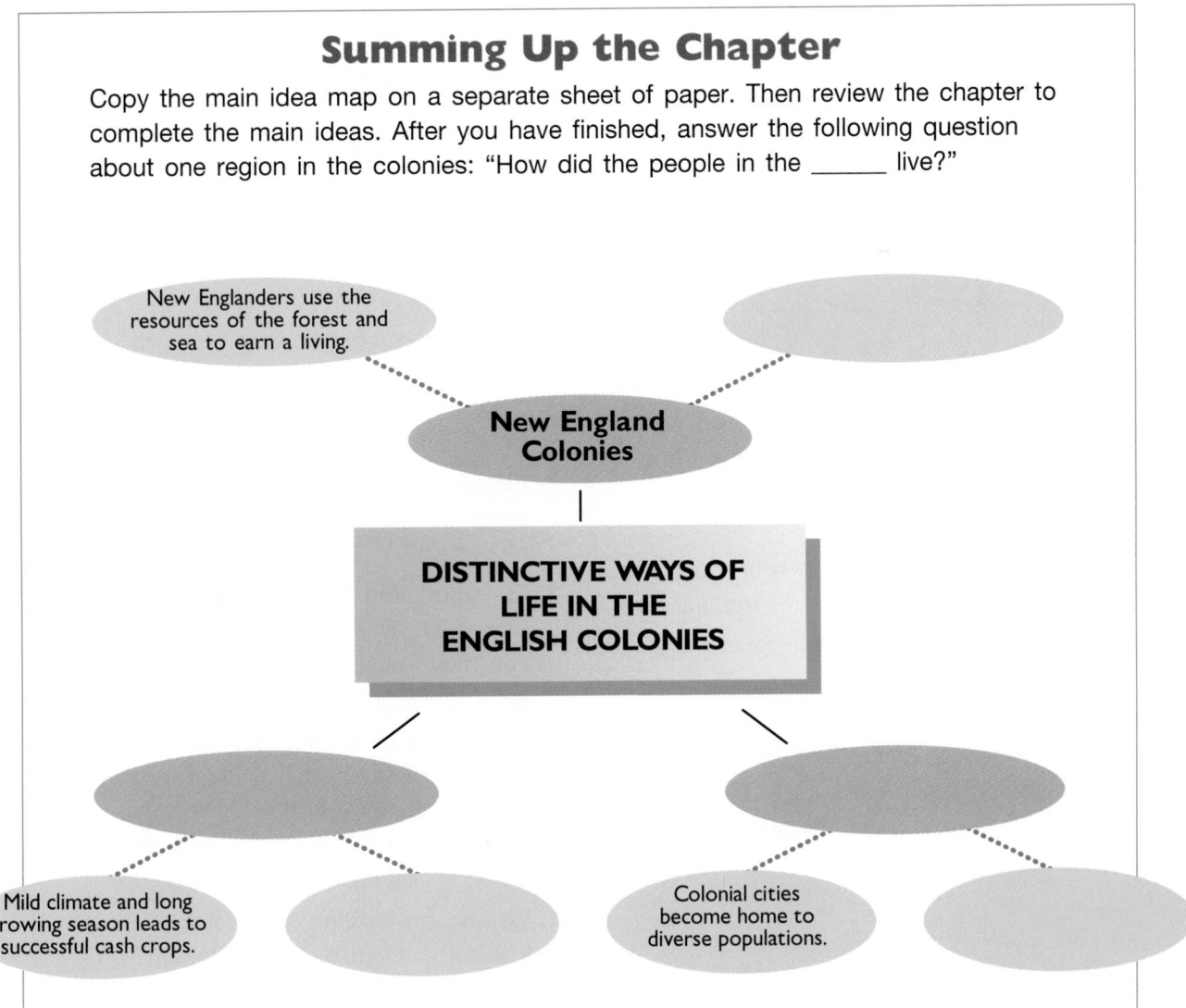

New Englanders use the resources of the forest and sea to earn a living.

New England Colonies

DISTINCTIVE WAYS OF LIFE IN THE ENGLISH COLONIES

Mild climate and long growing season leads to successful cash crops.

Colonial cities become home to diverse populations.

UNIT 4 REVIEW

THINKING ABOUT VOCABULARY

Number a sheet of paper from 1 to 10. Beside each number write the word or term from the list below that best completes the sentence.

Act Concerning
  Religion
apprentice
common
established church
export

House of
  Burgesses
plantation
Quaker
slave codes
triangular trade

1. William Penn, a _____, was imprisoned for his religious beliefs.

2. The _____ met to discuss the Virginia colony's taxes.

3. A master craftsperson taught the _____ who worked for her.

4. In Maryland, Protestantism became the official religion, or _____.

5. On a Southern _____, there was usually one main cash crop.

6. The _____ was a law stating that Christian people should not be mistreated because of their religious beliefs.

7. _____ were laws passed in the 1700s that took away the rights of African captives.

8. To _____ means to send goods to other countries to be sold or traded.

9. At the center of the Puritan town there was a village green, or _____.

10. The three-sided trade route between North America, Africa, and the West Indies was known as _____.

THINK AND WRITE ◄ ⟩

WRITING A DESCRIPTION

Suppose you are a visitor to Philadelphia in 1775. Write a description of some of the people and things that you find there. Include information about the goods that are produced and traded.

WRITING A PARAGRAPH OF COMPARISON AND CONTRAST

Compare and contrast the lives of plantation owners with the lives of other colonists in the Southern Colonies.

WRITING ABOUT PERSPECTIVES

Many early colonists came to America to find religious freedom, but some people did not find as much freedom as they expected. Suppose that you are a follower of Roger Williams of Massachusetts. Write a diary entry in which you tell why you have decided to follow Williams to Providence.

BUILDING SKILLS

1. **Primary and Secondary Sources** Is the autobiography of Olaudah Equiano a primary source or a secondary source? Why?

2. **Elevation and Relief** Look at the map on page 230. What is the elevation of the city of Buffalo?

3. **Elevation and Relief** Look at the map on page 231. What does the map show as you move east of the Appalachian Mountains towards the ocean?

4. **Credibility of a Source** Who would be a more credible source of information about conditions of life in the first colonies: a Quaker from Pennsylvania or a newspaper reporter visiting from England?

5. **Writing an Outline** What part of an outline is identified by capital letters?

YESTERDAY, TODAY &
TOMORROW

In this unit you learned about people who moved to new lands for a variety of reasons. Why did the Puritans sail to North America? Why did some colonists move from the coast to the backcountry? What are some reasons that people move today? Will there be different reasons for people to move to new homes in the future?

READING ON YOUR OWN

Here are some books you might find at the library to help you learn more.

ANNE HUTCHINSON: RELIGIOUS LEADER
by Elizabeth Ilgenfritz
The biography describes a leader who raised the question of religious tolerance.

COLONIAL PEOPLE
by Sarah Howarth
The pictures and text about daily life in the colonial period make you feel as though you are there.

BENJAMIN FRANKLIN:
PRINTER, INVENTOR, STATESMAN
by David A. Adler
This fascinating biography is filled with stories and other accounts of Franklin's many outstanding accomplishments.

UNIT REVIEW PROJECT

Make a Colonial Collage

1. Work with a partner. Make a list of the colonies you learned about in this unit.
2. Choose one colony. List people, places, objects, and events that were important in the establishment of the colony.

3. For each item on your list, think of artwork to illustrate it. You can make drawings, cut out pictures from magazines, draw maps, create crafts, or design documents.
4. Make the artwork that you will include in your collage. Then glue or tape the different pieces to a large piece of oak tag.
5. Make a title for your collage and include a date. Exhibit your work in a class art show, and explain how each item tells something about your colony.

SPANISH MISSION IN CALIFORNIA

MINUTEMAN OF CONCORD;
THE DECLARATION OF INDEPENDENCE

PATRIOT DRUM

IN CONGRESS, JULY 4, 1776.

The unanimous Declaration of the thirteen united States of America,

The Fight for Independence

"This is a glorious day for our country."

George Washington, after the Battle of Trenton.
See page 359.

WHY DOES IT MATTER?

Washington's first major victory in the American Revolution was at the Battle of Trenton in December of 1776. As you can tell from his words, the separate colonies had started to think of themselves as one nation.

At this time, Britain was the major power in North America. It ruled the colonies and had gained Florida and won the vast land claimed by the French in North America. Spain controlled California and the Southwest, but was no longer a threat to the British.

When the American Revolution was finally over, the rest of the world accepted the United States of America as an independent country.

**GEORGE WASHINGTON;
REVOLUTIONARY TEAPOT**

Colonial Williamsburg
Foundation

Adventures
with
NATIONAL
GEOGRAPHIC

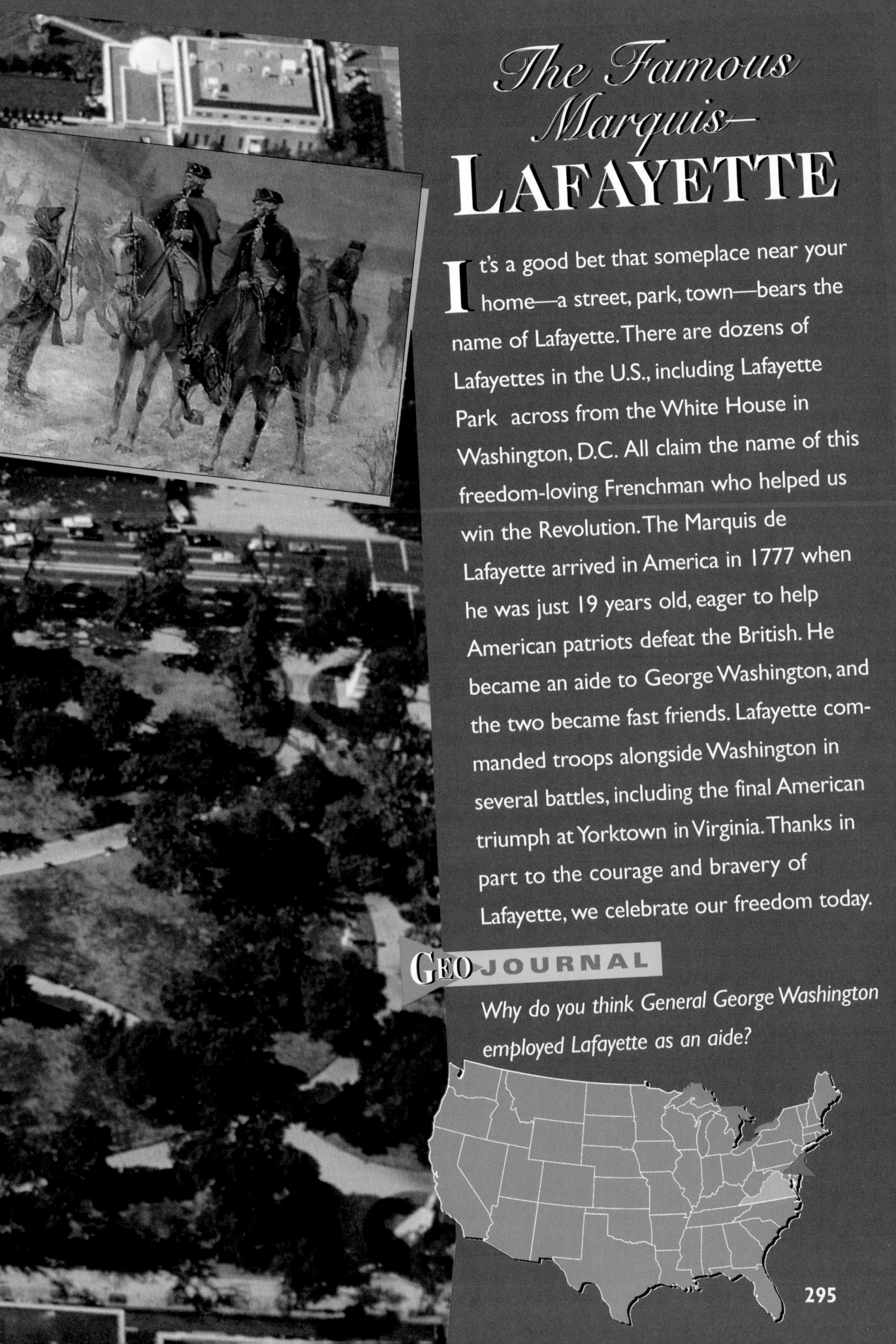

The Famous Marquis—
LAFAYETTE

It's a good bet that someplace near your home—a street, park, town—bears the name of Lafayette. There are dozens of Lafayettes in the U.S., including Lafayette Park across from the White House in Washington, D.C. All claim the name of this freedom-loving Frenchman who helped us win the Revolution. The Marquis de Lafayette arrived in America in 1777 when he was just 19 years old, eager to help American patriots defeat the British. He became an aide to George Washington, and the two became fast friends. Lafayette commanded troops alongside Washington in several battles, including the final American triumph at Yorktown in Virginia. Thanks in part to the courage and bravery of Lafayette, we celebrate our freedom today.

GEO JOURNAL

Why do you think General George Washington employed Lafayette as an aide?

CHAPTER 11

The Struggle for North America

THINKING ABOUT HISTORY AND GEOGRAPHY

Chapter 11 takes place west of the Appalachian Mountains. On the map you can see that the British were not the only Europeans in North America. From the time line and the map you can see how the French and Spanish also claimed lands that had long been home to Native Americans. In time the British would challenge other European powers for control of North America.

San Diego

PACIFIC OCEAN

1682	1754	1763
MISSISSIPPI RIVER DELTA	**OHIO RIVER VALLEY**	**OHIO RIVER VALLEY**
Robert La Salle claims Louisiana for France	George Washington leads Virginia colonists in the French and Indian War	Pontiac's War forces the British to defend their territory

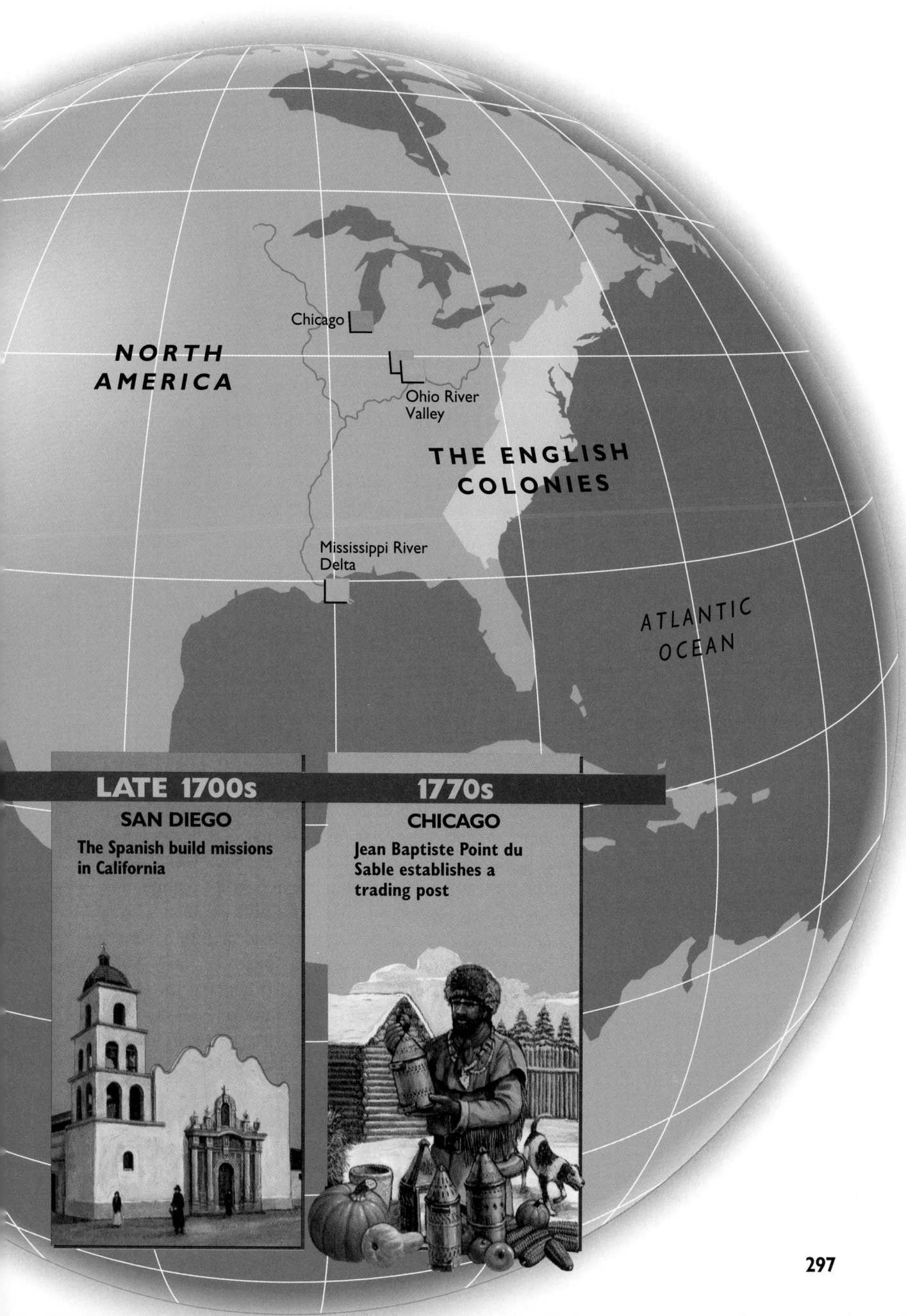

NORTH AMERICA

THE ENGLISH COLONIES

Chicago

Ohio River Valley

Mississippi River Delta

ATLANTIC OCEAN

LATE 1700s

SAN DIEGO

The Spanish build missions in California

1770s

CHICAGO

Jean Baptiste Point du Sable establishes a trading post

SPANISH MISSIONS

Focus Activity

READ TO LEARN
Why did the Spanish build missions in the West and the Southwest?

VOCABULARY
mission
missionary
presidio

PEOPLE
Popé
Junípero Serra

PLACES
California
New Mexico
St. Augustine
Santa Fe
El Camino Real
San Diego
San Francisco

READ ALOUD

In 1599 Don Juan de Oñate [don wahn de on YAH te], a Spanish explorer, wrote a letter describing the Native Americans who lived in what is now New Mexico. "In their temples, after their own nature, they worship. . . . In their government they are free." Not long after this letter was sent, Spanish priests brought a new religion to the area. How would life change for the Native Americans?

THE BIG PICTURE

As you read in Chapter 5, the Spanish had settled in North America long before the English formed the 13 colonies. You have read about how Francisco Coronado explored the Southwest from 1540 to 1542 in search of the Seven Cities of Gold. By the late 1500s New Spain included most of present-day Mexico, the Caribbean islands, Central America, and the Southwestern United States. The Spanish also claimed parts of South America.

Mountains and deserts made it hard for early Spanish settlers to reach areas north of Mexico. However, New Spain gradually expanded. Many of New Spain's settlements were missions. A mission is a religious outpost where missionaries live and work. Missionaries are people who teach their religion to others who have different beliefs. One purpose of the Spanish missions was to convert Native Americans to the Roman Catholic religion. The missions that spread through California and New Mexico had devastating effects on the Native Americans who lived there.

THE SPANISH COLONIES

In 1565, to protect their sea routes from the English "sea dogs" and their lands from French traders, Spain founded St. Augustine. It was Spain's first settlement in what is now the United States. St. Augustine was founded on the Atlantic Coastal Plain in the colony of Florida, 20 years before the English came to Roanoke, and over 40 years before the founding of Jamestown.

Spanish explorers continued to search for gold in the American Southwest. In 1595 King Philip III of Spain gave them permission to build a settlement in the lands the Spanish called New Mexico. In 1609 Spanish colonists founded Santa Fe and made it the capital of New Mexico.

The Spanish Missions

A Catholic Church was the center of mission life. The mission also included farms, ranches, orchards, workshops, and sleeping quarters.

There were Spanish towns and ranches in northern New Spain. But missions became the center of life. The Spanish forced Native Americans to work inside the missions. Native Americans raised sheep and cows, wove cloth, tanned leather, butchered meat, worked metal, and built wood furniture. You can see a diagram of a Spanish mission on page 300.

The Spanish built presidios near some missions. A presidio was a fort in which Spanish soldiers lived. The soldiers protected the missions and other Spanish settlements.

Spain's northern colonies were connected to Mexico City by El Camino Real (EL kah MEE noh RAY ahl), which means "the royal road" in Spanish. Parts of it began as Native American trails. Find El Camino Real on the map on page 302.

Today Santa Fe is the capital of New Mexico. It is famous for its mix of Native American and Spanish cultures.

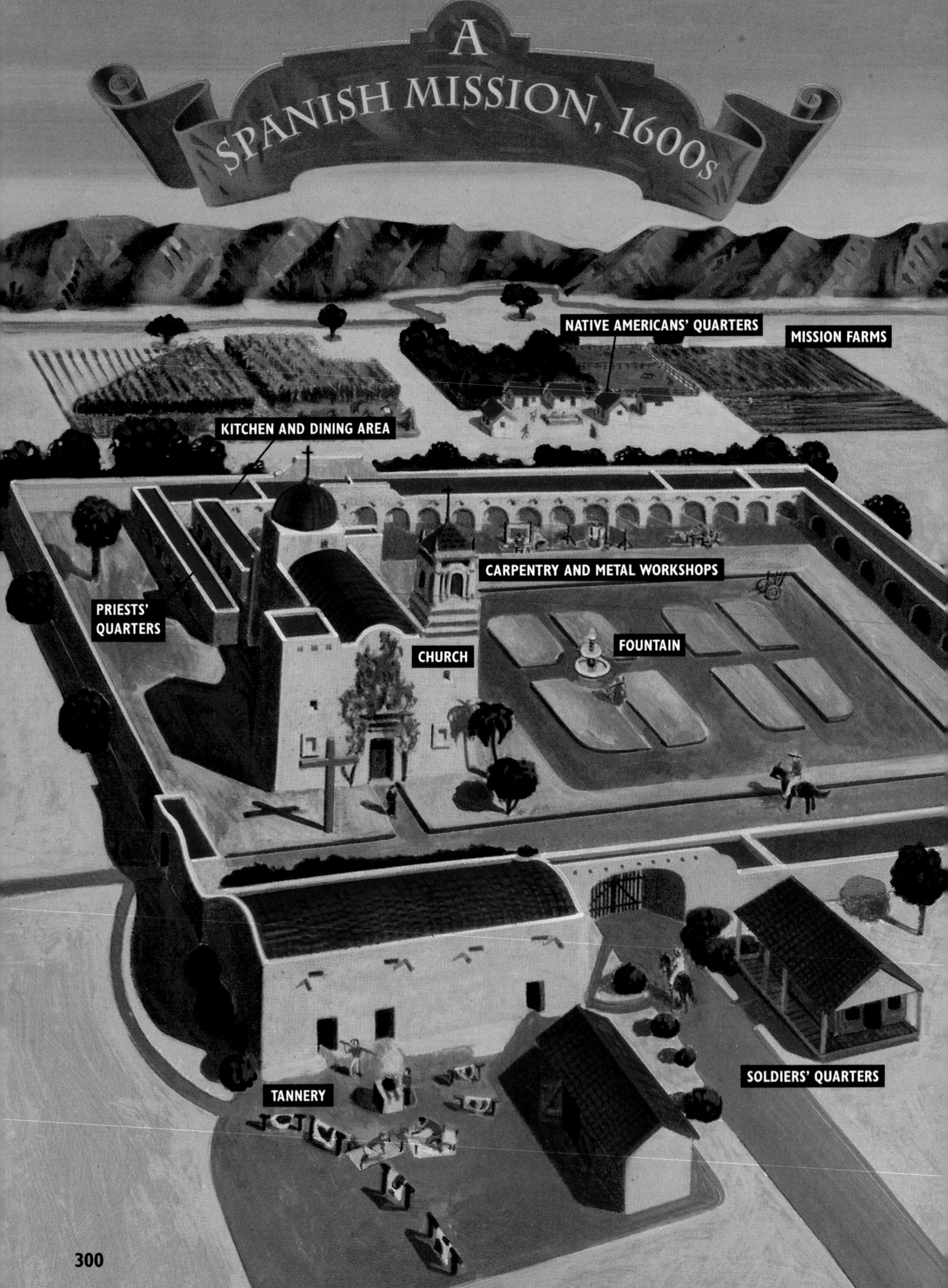

A

SPANISH MISSION, 1600s

NATIVE AMERICANS' QUARTERS

MISSION FARMS

KITCHEN AND DINING AREA

CARPENTRY AND METAL WORKSHOPS

PRIESTS' QUARTERS

CHURCH

FOUNTAIN

SOLDIERS' QUARTERS

TANNERY

LIFE IN THE MISSION

Native Americans in northern New Spain were expected to follow a new way of life. Many of them were forced to live and work in the missions.

Mission Days

If you were a Native American child living in a mission, you would have no opportunities to study your own religion or language. Each morning you would learn about the Christian religion and the Spanish language. After lessons you would help the priests by working on the farms with the animals. If your work was not satisfactory, you might be whipped.

Those who worked in the missions got food to eat and a place to live. But they had to follow all of the mission rules. Those who tried to escape were punished or killed. Many Native Americans were angry at this new life.

The Pueblo Revolt

Many Pueblo people refused to give up their beliefs. In 1675 the Spanish governor of New Mexico put 47 of their religious leaders in jail. When the Pueblo threatened to leave the missions, the religious leaders were released.

Among them was a man named Popé (poh PAY).

Popé persuaded other leaders that the Pueblo peoples should unite to force the Spanish from Native American lands. On August 10, 1680, the Pueblo and Apache people joined forces and attacked Spanish settlements all across New Mexico.

The Spanish had to flee. They were amazed that the Pueblo people had organized the revolt. Read the description in Many Voices describing the plan of attack that the Pueblo peoples used.

MANY VOICES
PRIMARY SOURCE

Excerpt from the statement of Pedro Naranjo, as recorded by Spanish questioners, 1680.

He said that the cord was passed through all the pueblos of the kingdom so that those which agreed to it [the rebellion] might untie one knot in sign of obedience. . . . As a sign of agreement . . . they were to send up smoke signals to that effect in each one of the pueblos singly. The said cord was taken from pueblo to pueblo by the swiftest youths under the penalty of death if they revealed the secret.

The Granger Collection

Taos Pueblo in New Mexico has changed very little in the past 300 years. Don Juan de Oñate (inset) was a Spanish explorer.

SPANISH MISSIONS IN CALIFORNIA AND THE SOUTHWEST, LATE 1700s

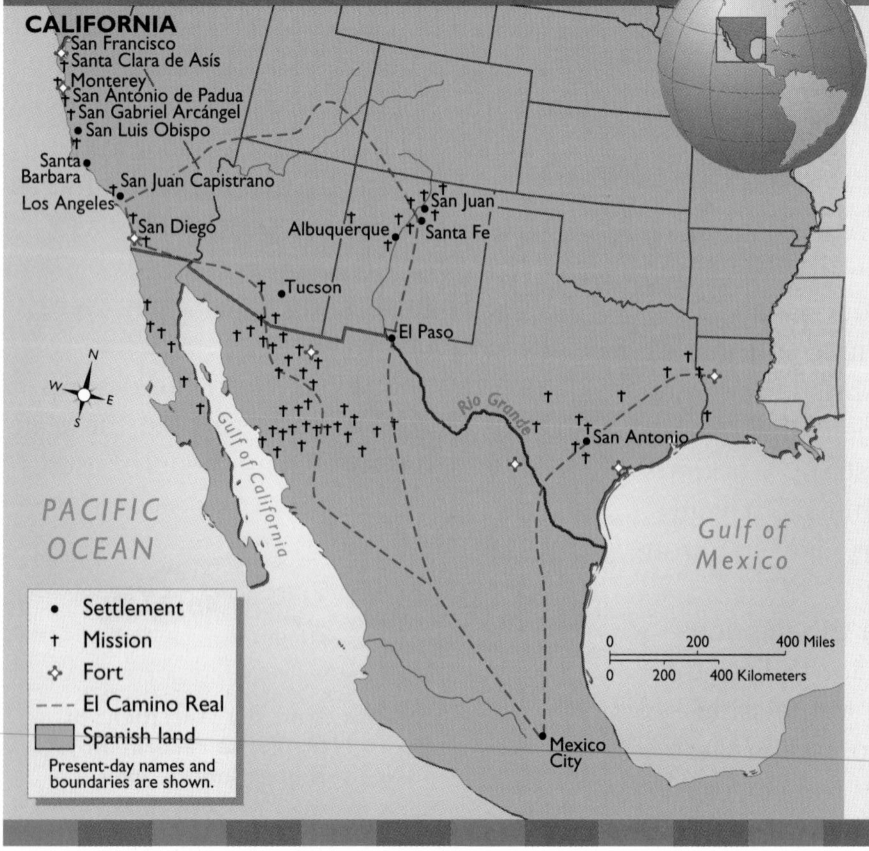
CALIFORNIA
San Francisco
Santa Clara de Asís
Monterey
San Antonio de Padua
San Gabriel Arcángel
San Luis Obispo
Santa Barbara
San Juan Capistrano
Los Angeles
San Diego
Albuquerque
San Juan
Santa Fe
Tucson
El Paso
Rio Grande
San Antonio
Gulf of California
PACIFIC OCEAN
Gulf of Mexico
Mexico City
N
W
E
S
0 200 400 Miles
0 200 400 Kilometers
Settlement
Mission
Fort
El Camino Real
Spanish land
Present-day names and boundaries are shown.

MAP WORK

The Spanish built **missions** throughout California and the Southwest. Many of them, such as Los Angeles, are large cities today.

1. Which missions in the Southwest were also settlements?
2. In which present-day states were most of the missions built?

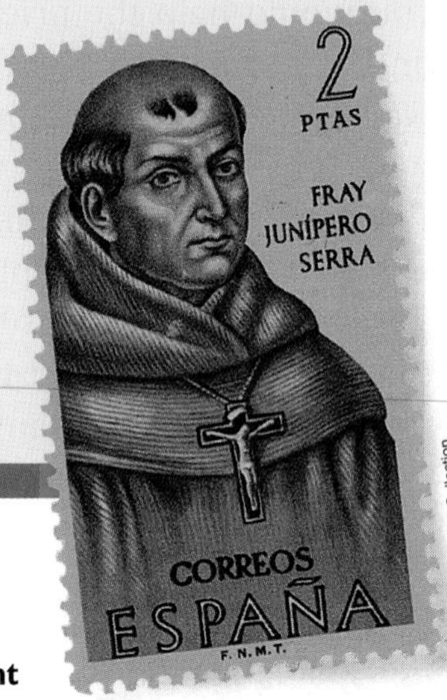
2
PTAS
FRAY JUNÍPERO SERRA
CORREOS
ESPAÑA
F. N. M. T.

The Granger Collection

Father Serra tried to treat the Native Americans fairly. Later, he also fought to end slavery.

THE SPANISH RETURN

In 1692, without firing a shot, the Spanish took back Santa Fe. Popé and many other leaders of the Pueblo revolt had died. After four years of fighting the Spanish regained control of New Mexico. However, the Pueblo agreed to Spanish rule only if they could live apart from the Spanish and practice their own religion.

California Missions

In 1765, José de Gálvez (DAY GAHL vez), a Spanish official, was put in charge of New Spain. He picked a missionary named Father **Junípero Serra** (hoo NEE pair oh SE rah) to establish missions in the land the Spanish called California. In 1769, Father Serra walked to **San Diego** and founded the first mission in California.

Serra founded eight missions after San Diego, and after he died, Father Fermín Lasuén (fer MEEN lahs WEN) founded nine more. By 1823 there was a chain

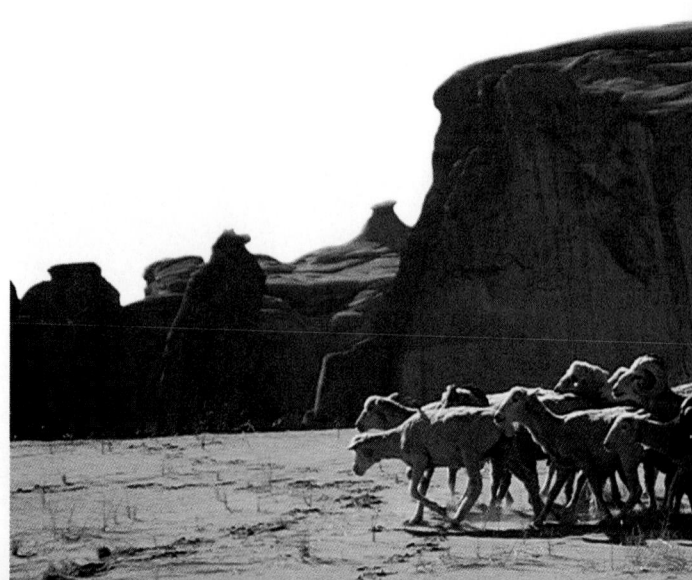

of 21 missions stretching as far north as San Francisco.

Father Serra believed that the Native Americans should "have their own lands and crops so that poverty will not make them [leave the mission]." Many Native Americans, though, did not believe the missions gave them anything of "their own." Instead, they felt that all their hard work helped the Spanish and harmed their own people. Native Americans became sick from European diseases, lack of food, and poor conditions. They were often beaten or whipped for even the slightest mistake.

Resentment against the missions grew. Although no rebellion in California was as successful as the Pueblo revolt, there was constant resistance to the Spanish. In 1775 Native Americans attacked the mission at San Diego. In 1785 a woman shaman, or religious leader, named Toypurina led an attack on San Gabriel. Even so, Native Americans in northern New Spain lost their freedom.

Today many Navajo raise sheep, an animal that the Spanish introduced in what is now the American Southwest.

WHY IT MATTERS

By 1800 the Spanish controlled much of the land in what is now the United States. Most of the early Spanish colonists in North America came without families. Unlike English colonists, the Spanish allowed Native Americans to live in their settlements.

Both Native American and Spanish influences can still be seen in many parts of the United States. Many cities, like Taos, New Mexico, have Pueblo names. Others, like Los Angeles, California, have Spanish names.

✓// Reviewing Facts and Ideas

MAIN IDEAS
- From the 1500s to the 1800s, the Spanish built many missions in what is today the United States.
- The Pueblo people organized a successful revolt against Spanish rule in 1680. In 1692 the Spanish returned and regained control of New Mexico.
- In 1769 the Spanish priest Father Junípero Serra began building a series of missions in California.

THINK ABOUT IT
1. Where in our present-day country did the Spanish build missions?
2. What is a presidio? Why were presidios often built near missions?
3. **FOCUS** How did the missions change the lives of Native Americans in the West and Southwest?
4. **THINKING SKILL** Place the following events in the correct *sequence*: San Diego is founded; St. Augustine is founded; Santa Fe is founded.
5. **WRITE** Write a diary entry about working in a mission from the point of view of a Native American. Include details shown in the diagram on page 300.

VAQUEROS AND COWBOYS

The Granger Collection

When the Spanish came to what is now the United States, they brought some of their most valuable animals with them—the horse and the cow. They also brought the skill, developed over many generations in Spain and Mexico, of herding cattle on horseback.

Spanish-speaking and Native American vaqueros (vah KE rohz) soon worked the ranches and rode the plains of the West and Southwest. In Spanish the word *vaquero* means "a person who works with cows." The English word for vaquero—*cowboy*—is probably one you know well. As you look at the pictures on these pages, you will see examples of how the vaqueros' legacy lives on today.

A vaquero (top left) shows his roping skills. Frederic Remington painted *Turn Him Loose, Bill* (above) in the late 1800s. Remington is known for his paintings of cowboys and Native Americans. Today women also work as cowhands (right).

Vaqueros caught cattle by using a braided rope called *la reata* (LAH ray AH tah). This rope came to be called a lariat in the United States. Vaqueros wore wide-brimmed hats to keep out the sun and the rain.

THE FRENCH COLONIES

READ ALOUD

They first arrived on fishing ships. Yet they soon "threw up their old [jobs] . . . for bear skins and beaver skins," wrote historian Francis Parkman. They "followed the Indians . . . , lived with them, [and] grew familiar with their language." Who were these Europeans who chose to live deep in the forests of North America?

Focus Activity

READ TO LEARN
Why did France build colonies in North America?

VOCABULARY
portage
voyageur
coureur de bois

PEOPLE
Samuel de Champlain
Jacques Marquette
Louis Jolliet
Robert La Salle
Jean Baptiste Point
   du Sable

PLACES
St. Lawrence River
Canada
New France
Quebec
Louisiana
St. Louis
Detroit
Chicago

THE BIG PICTURE

While Spain was founding colonies in Mexico and the Caribbean islands in the early 1500s, France was claiming land farther north in North America. As you read in the Infographic on pages 164–165, French explorers such as Jacques Cartier (kahr TYAY) first came to North America in search of a Northwest Passage to Asia. Then, in 1534, the French reached what is now Newfoundland and claimed the land along the St. Lawrence River. The French called it Canada, after the Huron word *kanata*, which means "village." Later the name of New France was given to France's lands along the St. Lawrence River and the Great Lakes.

For more than 60 years, few French people settled in New France. Religious wars in Europe between Catholics and Protestants took up much of France's attention. However, some of the French did begin fishing off the coast of New France. They also began a fur trade with the Native Americans. This fur trade would soon bring wealth and power to France.

FRENCH TRADERS

Furs were in great demand in France. New France's forests were filled with fur-bearing animals. So in the early 1600s France began to think about starting a colony there to help its fur-trading business. A colony would also make it easier to continue its search for a Northwest Passage, which you read about in Chapter 6.

In 1608 a French geographer and explorer named Samuel de Champlain (DUH sham PLAYN) founded a trading post called Quebec (kuh BEK) on the St. Lawrence River. Quebec was the first permanent French settlement in North America.

The Huron and the French

Champlain knew that France's success in the fur trade depended on its Native American trading partners. Champlain made friends with the Huron near Quebec. He learned their language and respected their ways.

The French also sent missionaries to New France. Unlike most of the Spanish, the French did not, for the most part, force Native Americans to work

Champlain (top) is called the Father of New France. The Huron tray (above) was stitched with moosehair.

for them or to live in French missions. Instead, the black-robed French missionaries lived in Huron villages in order to convert them to the Roman Catholic religion.

In 1609 the Huron agreed to supply Champlain with furs if he would help them defeat their rivals in the fur trade, the Iroquois. The French agreed. In return, the Huron helped the French increase their fur-trading business and remained their allies for many years. However, the Iroquois never forgot their defeat at the hands of the Huron and the French.

307

NEW FRANCE

France's attempts to encourage settlement in New France during the 1600s were not successful. French colonists were not allowed to own land, and farming in Canada's cold climate was difficult. In addition, only Catholics were allowed to settle in New France. As a result, the French who did come to New France were mainly fur traders and missionaries. By 1660 there were fewer than 3,000 French colonists living in Canada.

Marquette and Jolliet

Although Champlain made many explorations into Canada, he failed to find a Northwest Passage. Many other French explorers had also tried. One of them was Jacques Marquette (ZHAHK mahr KET). While working as a missionary in what is today the state of Michigan, Marquette heard Native Americans tell of a mighty river to the west. Could this river be the long-sought after Northwest Passage?

In 1673 Marquette and a former fur trader named Louis Jolliet (LOO ee JOH LEE et) set out together to find the river Marquette had heard about—the Mississippi River. Marquette told of entering its waters "with a joy I cannot express." You can trace the route of Marquette and Jolliet on the map below. After a long while, when they had reached the Arkansas River, they saw that the Mississippi flowed south. Since the river did not flow west toward the Pacific Ocean, Marquette and Jolliet realized it could not be a Northwest Passage. They decided to return to Lake Michigan.

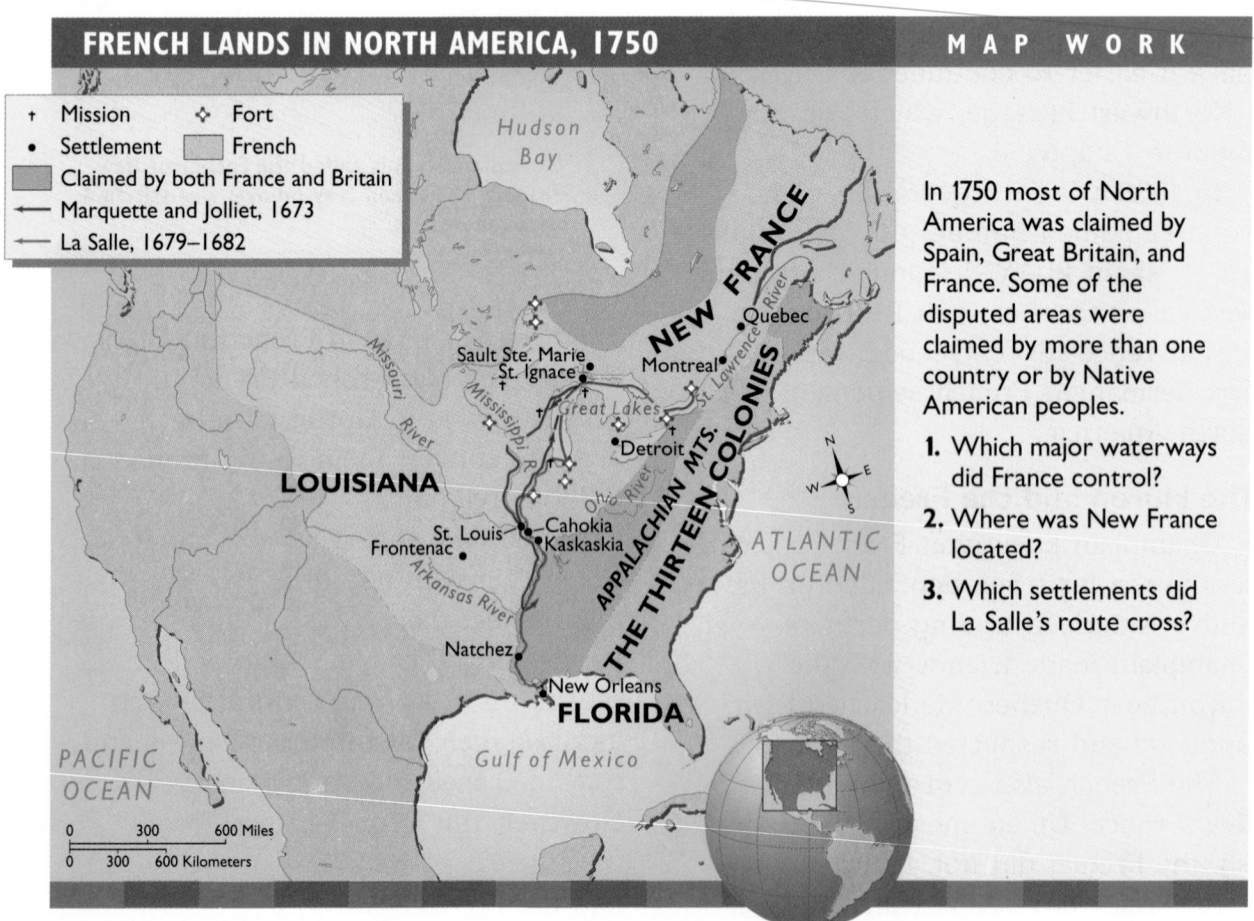

FRENCH LANDS IN NORTH AMERICA, 1750

MAP WORK

Legend:
- † Mission
- ◇ Fort
- • Settlement
- ▫ French
- ▫ Claimed by both France and Britain
- ← Marquette and Jolliet, 1673
- ← La Salle, 1679–1682

Map labels: Hudson Bay, NEW FRANCE, Quebec, Sault Ste. Marie, St. Ignace, Montreal, Great Lakes, Detroit, Missouri River, Mississippi R., LOUISIANA, Ohio River, St. Louis, Cahokia, Frontenac, Kaskaskia, Arkansas River, APPALACHIAN MTS., THE THIRTEEN COLONIES, ATLANTIC OCEAN, Natchez, New Orleans, FLORIDA, PACIFIC OCEAN, Gulf of Mexico

0 300 600 Miles
0 300 600 Kilometers

In 1750 most of North America was claimed by Spain, Great Britain, and France. Some of the disputed areas were claimed by more than one country or by Native American peoples.

1. Which major waterways did France control?

2. Where was New France located?

3. Which settlements did La Salle's route cross?

The Granger Collection

National Postal Museum

Jean Baptiste
Pointe Du Sable
22

Black Heritage USA

Because of its easy access to the Mississippi River and the Great Lakes, Chicago (left and below), founded by Du Sable, grew to become a major transportation center.

Robert La Salle

The French explorer Robert La Salle (LAH SAHL) learned of Marquette and Jolliet's journey. In 1682 he set out to find the mouth of the Mississippi River. Near the Arkansas River, La Salle met the Quapaw (KWAH pah). With their help he reached the Gulf of Mexico. La Salle became the first European to see the mouth of the Mississippi River. La Salle claimed the Mississippi River valley for France. He named it Louisiana after King Louis XIV of France. Find Louisiana on the map on page 308.

Settlements in New France

During the late 1600s and early 1700s, the French built forts, missions, and other settlements in New France. Some were built to keep the English from moving into French lands. Some settlements later became major cities.

In 1700 French priests built a mission along the Mississippi River in what is today Missouri. A trading post was soon added. Over the years it grew into the city of St. Louis. In 1701 the French built a trading post along the Detroit River between Lake Huron and Lake Erie. This trading post later became the city of Detroit.

On their return trip, Marquette and Jolliet had used a *portage* that connected the Mississippi River to the Great Lakes. A portage is a land route from one body of water to another. In the 1770s a Haitian fur trader named Jean Baptiste Point du Sable (ZHAHN bap TEEST PWAN DOO SAH bluh) built a trading post along this portage. He became friendly with the Potawatomi who lived around the Great Lakes. The trading post Du Sable built grew to become the city of Chicago.

309

Buffalo Bill Historical Center

THE FUR TRADE

The fur trade was important to New France. In Europe the forests had been overhunted for many years, which made fur-bearing animals rare. Beaver hats had become popular in Europe. As a result, the money to be made from furs attracted many trappers and traders to North America.

Trading Posts

By the early 1700s the French had built a vast network of forts and trading posts throughout New France. Trappers who often lived in the region's forests for months at a time came to the trading posts to sell or trade furs and other goods as well.

Fur traders went to the forests and bought furs from both French and Native American trappers. The furs were then transported to Quebec by *voyageurs*

The Granger Collection

(vwah yah ZHURZ). The voyageurs were people who carried furs and other goods from post to post by canoe. From Quebec the furs were shipped to France.

The Coureurs de Bois

France granted only a few people the right to trap and trade in its American colonies. As a result, many trappers became *coureurs de bois* (koo RUR DUH BWAH), which means "woods runners" in French.

The coureurs de bois trapped furs without permission from the French government.

Because colonists could not own land, becoming coureurs de bois was the only way many of the colonists could earn a living.

The furs transported by the voyageurs (above) were made into hats like this one worn by Benjamin Franklin (left).

People such as the Huron, Chippewa, and Ottawa taught many French trappers to use lightweight birchbark canoes and to survive in the forests.

An adventurous life attracted many voyageurs and coureurs de bois. According to one voyageur:

> There is no life so happy as a voyageur's life; none so independent; no place where a man enjoys so much variety and freedom.

WHY IT MATTERS

By building settlements throughout New France, the French surrounded English lands in North America. The 13 English colonies had no way to expand. By the mid-1700s, the French had won many Native American allies. The voyageurs and coureurs de bois helped to form strong partnerships with them.

Links to LANGUAGE ARTS

Parlez-vous français?

Parlez-vous français? (PAHR lay VOO frahn SAY) means "Do you speak French?" You may know more French words than you think. As you learned in Chapter 3, the Iroquois call themselves the Hodenosaunee. The French called them the Iroquois, and that name stuck. The Wyandot are also generally known by their French name—Huron. Until recently, most people called the Lakota by their French name—the Sioux.

Other French words are now part of the English language. Among them are *glacier*, *plateau*, *lacrosse*, and *prairie*.

Bonjour! I'm a prairie dog!

✓ Reviewing Facts and Ideas

MAIN IDEAS

- Samuel Champlain built the first permanent French settlement in North America, called Quebec, in 1608.

- Explorations by Marquette and Jolliet in 1673, and by La Salle in 1682, led to French control of the entire Mississippi River valley.

- By the early 1700s France had a vast network of forts and trading posts throughout North America.

- The fur trade became a source of wealth for the French, who developed good relations with their Native American trading partners.

THINK ABOUT IT

1. Who were some of the French explorers who came to North America? Why did they come?

2. How did Native Americans such as the Huron help the French?

3. **FOCUS** How did the fur trade shape the growth of New France?

4. **THINKING SKILL** *Compare* and *contrast* the French and the English colonies of North America.

5. **GEOGRAPHY** Look at the map of New France on page 308. Plot a route that a voyageur might have taken from St. Louis to Quebec. Then list the trading posts where a fur trapper might have stopped.

THINKINGSKILLS

The Granger Collection

Making Conclusions

VOCABULARY
conclusion

WHY THE SKILL MATTERS

As you read in the previous lesson, the explorer Robert La Salle reached the mouth of the Mississippi River with the help of the Quapaw people. The Quapaw needed to know if La Salle was friendly or not. His face did not look angry. He did not reach for a weapon. There was a peace pipe in his hand. From what they saw, the Quapaw made a conclusion that La Salle was friendly.

When you make a conclusion, you pull together all the pieces of information you have and tell the result in a single sentence. Making conclusions is often the final step in solving a problem. You have "tied up" all the facts and come up with a final answer.

USING THE SKILL

Here is an example of how conclusions are made: you have read about two other French explorers, Marquette and Jolliet, who searched for a Northwest Passage to the Pacific Ocean. Marquette and Jolliet had heard about a river that the Native Americans called "big river," or "Mississippi." They thought that this river might flow into the Pacific Ocean. They paddled down the Mississippi and realized that it became wider as it flowed south. They concluded that the river was probably not the Northwest Passage. Marquette and Jolliet turned back at the mouth of the Arkansas River and headed north.

Before they made a conclusion, the explorers identified their topic—whether the river that they were on could be the Northwest Passage. Then they collected facts about the topic. Next, they looked for what the facts had in common. All the facts seemed to show that the river would continue to flow south. From all the information, the explorers made the conclusion that the Mississippi River was not the Northwest Passage.

TRYING THE SKILL

Now that you have learned how, make a conclusion on your own. Marquette and Jolliet paddled down the Mississippi for two months. Finally the speed of the water slowed. They tasted the water and found it salty.

What conclusion do you think they made once they tasted the water? Explain how

and why they might have made this conclusion. If you need help answering this question refer to the Helping Yourself box on this page.

REVIEWING THE SKILL

1. What is a conclusion?
2. Suppose a fourth grader has asked for help making a conclusion. Write the steps that you would suggest.
3. Reread the Legacy on pages 304–305 and choose three facts about the topic. Then make a conclusion, and explain how you made it.
4. Was La Salle expecting to meet Native Americans when he met the Quapaw people? How did you make your conclusion?
5. How can making conclusions help you?

Marquette and Jolliet (right) were the first Europeans to reach the Mississippi. In the painting by George Catlin (top left), La Salle feasts with Native Americans in what is now Illinois.

1600   1640   1680   1720   1754 1763

THE FRENCH AND INDIAN WAR

Focus Activity

READ TO LEARN
What were the results of the French and Indian War?

VOCABULARY
French and Indian War
Treaty of Paris
Proclamation of 1763

PEOPLE
George Washington
Edward Braddock
Pontiac
King George III

PLACES
Ohio River valley
Fort Duquesne
Fort Necessity
New Orleans

READ ALOUD

George Washington, a 21-year-old lieutenant, looked out over his troops. British and Virginian soldiers marched stiffly in neat rows in red and blue coats. Washington was worried. The troops were an awesome sight. However, they also made an easy target for the enemy. The enemy was not marching in neat rows or wearing bright uniforms. Scattered throughout the forests, the enemy was hard to find.

THE BIG PICTURE

The enemy that George Washington worried about was the French. During the 1700s, England, now part of Great Britain, fought several wars with France over control of Europe. By the middle 1700s this struggle had spread to North America.

As you read in Chapter 10, the British colonies in North America were thriving. By the 1750s there were nearly 2 million colonists living there. Yet France had difficulty getting colonists to come to North America. Only about 60,000 French colonists lived in New France.

Trouble began when British colonists started moving into lands claimed by the French. In 1754 this conflict led to what the British called the French and Indian War. The war got its name from the people the British colonists were fighting—the French and their Native American allies.

THE OHIO RIVER VALLEY

The Ohio River valley lies mostly in what is now the Middle Western region of the United States. Both Britain and France claimed the land in the Ohio River valley. Until the middle of the 1700s, the Native Americans who lived there had kept both groups of colonists from settling in the valley. Then disputes among themselves and with the colonists led some Native Americans in the valley to sell their land to the British colonists. Fearing the loss of the fur trade, the French began building a series of forts in the valley to keep the British out.

Fort Duquesne and Fort Necessity

In 1754 young George Washington was sent by the British to force the French to leave the Ohio River valley. There the French had built Fort Duquesne (doo KAYN), where the city of Pittsburgh, Pennsylvania, stands today. The British colony of Virginia also claimed this land in the valley.

When Washington arrived, his troops attacked and defeated a small force of French soldiers in the woods near the fort. This short battle marked the beginning of the French and Indian War. An excited Washington wrote home, "I heard the bullets whistle; and believe me, there is something charming in the sound."

Washington's troops quickly built a temporary fort out of logs and called it Fort Necessity. Soon a larger French army arrived and attacked the fort, and Washington's men were defeated.

General Braddock's Defeat

In 1755 the British tried again to capture Fort Duquesne. This time General Edward Braddock led the troops. Braddock's soldiers were well trained. He felt they would easily win the battle. Yet as the British neared the fort, the bullets seemed to come from out of nowhere. Braddock's troops "broke and ran as sheep pursued by dogs," Washington wrote. Braddock himself died four days later from wounds he had received.

Washington learned an important lesson from Braddock's defeat. The French were using Native American methods of warfare. They made surprise attacks on the British from behind trees, large rocks—anywhere they could hide. The British and colonial soldiers' brightly colored jackets only made it easier for the French to take aim.

A young lieutenant in 1754, George Washington later would become one of our country's best known generals.

315

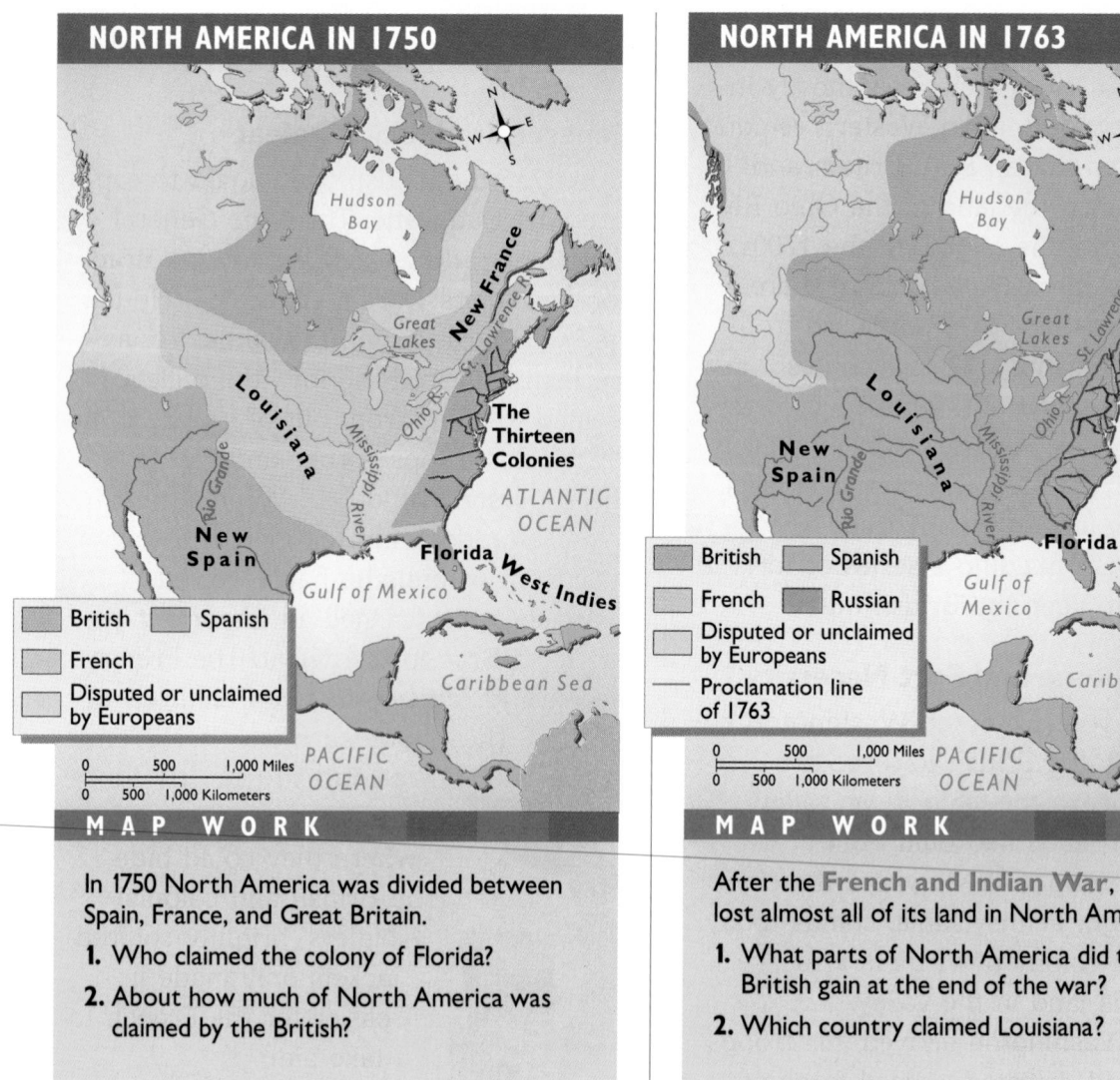

NORTH AMERICA IN 1750

Hudson Bay

New France

Great Lakes

St. Lawrence R.

Louisiana

Ohio R.

Mississippi River

Rio Grande

New Spain

Florida

Gulf of Mexico

West Indies

ATLANTIC OCEAN

The Thirteen Colonies

Caribbean Sea

PACIFIC OCEAN

Legend: British • Spanish • French • Disputed or unclaimed by Europeans

0   500   1,000 Miles
0   500   1,000 Kilometers

MAP WORK

In 1750 North America was divided between Spain, France, and Great Britain.

1. Who claimed the colony of Florida?

2. About how much of North America was claimed by the British?

NORTH AMERICA IN 1763

Hudson Bay

Great Lakes

St. Lawrence R.

Louisiana

New Spain

Ohio R.

Mississippi River

Rio Grande

Florida

Gulf of Mexico

West Indies

ATLANTIC OCEAN

The Thirteen Colonies

Caribbean Sea

PACIFIC OCEAN

Legend: British • Spanish • French • Russian • Disputed or unclaimed by Europeans • Proclamation line of 1763

0   500   1,000 Miles
0   500   1,000 Kilometers

MAP WORK

After the French and Indian War, France lost almost all of its land in North America.

1. What parts of North America did the British gain at the end of the war?

2. Which country claimed Louisiana?

THE TIDE TURNS

Because British colonists greatly outnumbered them, French colonists had welcomed the help of the Huron. Washington had seen what valuable allies Native Americans could be. The British decided to ask the Iroquois for help.

The Iroquois were not eager to side with the British. While French settlements were few and scattered, British colonists had taken over much Iroquois land. "You have disregarded us, thrown us behind your back," said Tiyanoga (tih an OH guh), a Mohawk leader. Still, the Iroquois decided to join the British against their old enemies, the Huron and the French. In return the British

promised to keep colonists away from Iroquois lands.

Britain Wins the War

The French won victory after victory over the British until 1758. Then Britain began to pour money into winning the war. It bought new equipment and sent more troops and its best generals to the colonies. These resources helped Britain to win the war.

In 1762, as the war was ending, France gave Spain much of Louisiana to keep it out of Britain's hands. This agreement included the city of New Orleans, an important port in the French fur trade.

In 1763 Britain and France signed the Treaty of Paris, which officially ended the French and Indian War. The maps on page 316, show that Great Britain gained almost all of the land in North America. Because Spain had been France's ally in the war, Britain also gained the Spanish colony of Florida.

Pontiac's War

When the war ended, British colonists again began moving west into the Ohio River valley. An Ottawa chief named Pontiac (PAHN tee ak) urged the Native Americans of the Ohio Valley to unite against the British. In 1763 they captured and burned British settlements, but were soon defeated by the British army.

WHY IT MATTERS

Pontiac's War made King George III realize that avoiding conflict with Native Americans would be costly. As a result, he issued the Proclamation of 1763. This proclamation, or official announcement, gave all land east of the Appalachians to the colonists. Lands west of the mountains would be set aside for Native Americans. This would give control of the fur trade there to Britain. The colonists did not like being closed off from the western lands and the fur trade. They ignored the proclamation and continued to move onto Native American lands west of the Appalachians.

Reviewing Facts and Ideas

MAIN IDEAS

- In 1754 Britain and France began fighting for control of the Ohio River valley in the French and Indian War.

- By winning the war in 1763, Britain gained control of Florida, the colony of Canada, and almost all of New France.

- The Proclamation of 1763 granted the rights to lands in the Ohio River valley to Native Americans, but this did not stop colonists from trying to take these lands.

THINK ABOUT IT

1. Why were the British soldiers easy targets at Fort Duquesne?

2. Why did Native Americans unite under Pontiac to fight the British?

3. **FOCUS** How did the French and Indian War change North America?

4. **THINKING SKILL** Look at the maps on page 316. What *conclusions* can you make about France's influence in North America?

5. **WRITE** Write a letter to a relative from the point of view of a British colonist in 1754. Explain how the French and Indian War is affecting your life.

Pontiac urged Native Americans in the Ohio River valley to "drive off your land those . . . who will do you nothing but harm."

CHAPTER 11 REVIEW

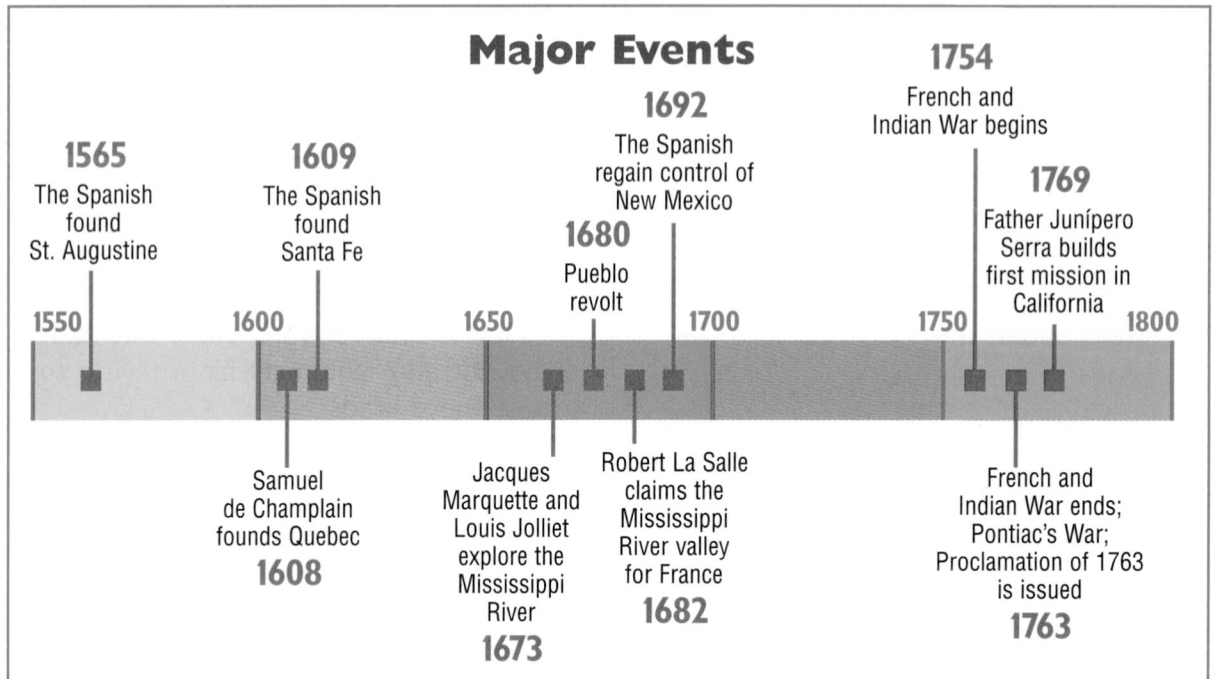

Major Events

1565
The Spanish found St. Augustine

1609
The Spanish found Santa Fe

1692
The Spanish regain control of New Mexico

1680
Pueblo revolt

1754
French and Indian War begins

1769
Father Junípero Serra builds first mission in California

1550   1600   1650   1700   1750   1800

Samuel de Champlain founds Quebec
1608

Jacques Marquette and Louis Jolliet explore the Mississippi River
1673

Robert La Salle claims the Mississippi River valley for France
1682

French and Indian War ends; Pontiac's War; Proclamation of 1763 is issued
1763

THINKING ABOUT VOCABULARY

Number a sheet of paper from 1 to 5. Beside each number write the word or term from the list below that matches the description.

mission   Proclamation of 1763
portage   voyageurs
presidio

1. a religious settlement where missionaries lived and worked

2. people who transported furs by canoe for shipment to France

3. a fort where Spanish soldiers lived

4. an official announcement that gave all the land east of the Appalachian Mountains to the British colonists and set aside land west of the mountains for the Native Americans

5. a land route from one body of water to another

THINKING ABOUT FACTS

1. What was the purpose of the Spanish missions?

2. What route connected Spain's colonies in the Southwest to Mexico?

3. Who was Popé and why was he important?

4. What was the most important economic activity of the French in New France? Which Native American people helped them?

5. Why were the settlements that later became St. Louis and Chicago founded?

6. What skills did coureurs de bois learn from Native Americans?

7. Which peoples fought in the French and Indian War? Why was the war fought?

8. How was Louisiana claimed at the end of the French and Indian War?

9. What did the British gain by the Treaty of Paris in 1763?

10. Look at the time line above. How were the events that happened in 1763 related?

WRITING A LIST

Suppose that you are a soldier defending either Fort Duquesne or Fort Necessity during the French and Indian War in 1754. Write a letter to someone at home describing the actions taking place.

WRITING A TRAVEL LOG

Suppose that you are joining Marquette and Jolliet on their explorations. Write a log entry about what you might expect to find in your travels. Then write a log entry about what you actually find.

WRITING A SPEECH

Suppose that you are a Pueblo leader who agrees with the ideas of Popé. Write a speech telling why you think that the Pueblo should join forces and resist the Spanish.

MAKING CONCLUSIONS

Answer the questions below to practice the skill of making conclusions.

1. What is a conclusion?

2. After identifying the topic of information, what should your next step be in making a conclusion?

3. Suppose that you have not heard the weather report for the day, but you see everyone on your street is carrying an umbrella. What conclusion would you make about the weather forecast?

4. From the information about the Pueblo revolt in this chapter, what conclusion can you make about the importance of Pueblo culture and independence to the Pueblo?

Summing Up the Chapter

Copy the conclusion chart on a separate sheet of paper. Then review the chapter to complete the chart. After you have finished, use the information in the chart to answer the question, "What are the differences and similarities between how the Spanish, French, and English settled in North America?"

TOPIC	CONCLUSION	EVIDENCE
The Spanish and the Pueblo	The Spanish and the Pueblo are often in conflict.	
French relations with Native Americans		The French trade with Native Americans, learn their language and many of their customs, and often live with them.
The French and Indian War	The French and Indian War has a major influence on the history of North America.	

CHAPTER
12

Breaking Ties with Great Britain

THINKING ABOUT
HISTORY AND GEOGRAPHY

The conflict in Chapter 12 begins in New York City in 1735. John Peter Zenger, a printer, was one of the first colonists to help establish freedom of speech and freedom of the press, important rights. For the next 50 years, colonists in North America moved slowly toward independence from Great Britain. The time line shows some of the events that led eventually to the birth of the United States of America.

1735	1770	1773
NEW YORK CITY	**BOSTON**	**BOSTON HARBOR**
The trial of printer John Peter Zenger establishes freedom of speech and the press	Protests by Crispus Attucks and other colonists lead to the Boston Massacre	Colonists dressed as the Mohawk take part in the Boston Tea Party

NORTH
AMERICA

THE BRITISH
COLONIES

Boston
Harbor

Lexington

Boston

New York City

Williamsburg

ATLANTIC
OCEAN

1775

WILLIAMSBURG

Patrick Henry urges the
House of Burgesses to
vote for war with Britain

1775

LEXINGTON

Paul Revere warns colonists
of a British attack

THE ROAD TO SELF-GOVERNMENT

READ ALOUD

In 1741 angry members of the Massachusetts assembly tried to remove Governor Jonathan Belcher from office. The king of England had appointed Belcher, but the assembly members did not like him. The governor, in turn, complained about the members. They think, he said, "that they are as big as the Parliament of Great Britain."

THE BIG PICTURE

As you read in Chapter 10, the population of the colonies grew dramatically in the 1700s. As the colonies grew, they gained experience in governing themselves. The colonists had been creating their own governing bodies and laws since the early 1600s. Some followed their own written arrangement for governing, such as the Mayflower Compact. Most used the unwritten English common law, which includes the idea "innocent until proven guilty." They modeled their colonial assemblies, or lawmaking bodies, on Parliament. Parliament is Britain's lawmaking body.

As you read in Chapter 9, the first meeting of Virginia's assembly, the House of Burgesses, took place at the church in Jamestown in 1619. This first colonial assembly served as a model for other colonial assemblies. In this lesson you will read about the colonists' growing desire for self-government. You will also read about how this desire led to the founding of some of the important rights that we enjoy in our country today.

Focus Activity

READ TO LEARN
How did the colonists begin to govern themselves?

VOCABULARY
assembly
town meeting
militia
delegate

PEOPLE
Thomas Jefferson
Richard Henry Lee
John Adams
John Peter Zenger
Phillis Wheatley

PLACES
Williamsburg

COLONIAL GOVERNMENT

Laws affecting each colony were made by the colonial assemblies. In the New England Colonies, the town meeting was the earliest form of self-government. The town meeting was a group of male colonists who got together to solve local problems.

In other colonies men created written plans for government. These plans spelled out important rights that the colonists would have. The chart on this page lists some of these plans for government in the colonies.

Royal Governors

Eight of the 13 colonies were ruled by royal governors. A royal governor was not elected by the colonists. Instead he was chosen by the king of England. Royal governors saw that the colony obeyed British laws. Sometimes the governor and the assembly disagreed on which laws had to be obeyed. If the governor found the assembly unwilling to support him, he could dissolve, or shut down, the assembly.

Assembly members could, in return, refuse to vote for the money needed for the governor's plans. "Let us keep the dogs poor and we'll make them do what we please," one New Jersey assembly member said of the governors. The royal governors did not always have the same view as the assembly members.

PLANS FOR GOVERNMENT IN THE COLONIES, 1600s

Date	Plan	Description
1620	*Mayflower Compact*	A written agreement to make laws for the Plymouth colony
1639	*Fundamental Orders of Connecticut*	A written plan for government that gave the right to vote to free men who owned property in Connecticut
1649	*Maryland Toleration Act*	A law giving religious freedom to all Christians in Maryland
1682	*Pennsylvania Frame of Government*	A written plan for government that granted religious freedom to colonists in Pennsylvania

City of Norfolk, VA/The Chrysler Museum

CHART WORK

At right is a 1753 mace from Norfolk, Virginia. The mace, a club-shaped staff, has been used by law-making bodies since the 1300s to call an assembly to order. A mace is still used today in the United States House of Representatives.

1. Which plans for government granted colonists freedom of religion?
2. Which plans for government were written for New England colonies?

THE VIRGINIA HOUSE OF BURGESSES

In 1624 King James of Britain had made Virginia a royal colony and appointed a royal governor to rule the colony. The House of Burgesses still had some power. It could, for example, decide whether to divide large counties into smaller ones. It could also make laws about the sale of tobacco. By the middle of the 1700s, the colonial burgesses had gained much valuable experience in self-government.

The Talented Burgesses

On a spring day in 1769, Thomas Jefferson traveled to Williamsburg, Virginia's capital. Only 26 years old, the young planter and lawyer had just been elected burgess. Jefferson judged the House of Burgesses to be "the most dignified body of men ever assembled to [make laws]."

Most of the burgesses were wealthy planters. George Washington and Richard Henry Lee served as burgesses. They felt it was their duty to help govern the colony. But sometimes the assembly could try their patience. Lee, who served from 1758 to 1776, admitted to his brother his disappointment about not getting much work done:

> I find the attendance on Assemblies so expensive, and the power of doing good so rarely occurring, that I am determined to quit.

Many burgesses also tired of the many procedures connected to government. Formal ceremonies took up most of Jefferson's first day in office.

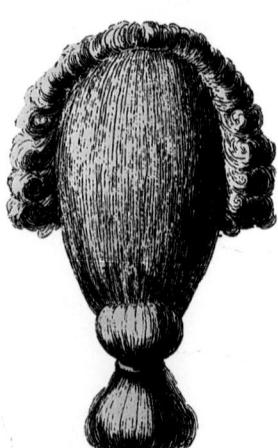

Members of the Virginia House of Burgesses met in this room (left) in the 1700s. They wore wigs like the ones below.

The House of Burgesses did make some important laws for the colony. The burgesses had the power to print money, call for taxes, build roads, and make land laws. They also had the power to prepare for war and raise money to support the colony's militia. A colonial militia was a military force made up of volunteers. The militia was similar to today's National Guard, which is made up of citizen soldiers.

Thomas Jefferson (left) was painted by the artist C. W. Peale. Richard Henry Lee (below) was also a strong supporter of the colonies' rights.

A Model for the Colonies

By 1760 Virginia's assembly was the model for colonial government. Every colony had elected an assembly like the House of Burgesses. To be elected, a delegate, or member of the assembly, had to meet several requirements. A delegate had to be an adult white male. In most colonies he also had to own a certain amount of land and follow the Protestant faith. Thus in most colonies, women, African Americans, Catholics, Jews, and Native Americans could not be elected.

Most of the delegates were wealthy merchants or lawyers. In 1770 a lawyer named John Adams was elected to the Massachusetts assembly. Benjamin Franklin was pleased to serve in the Pennsylvania assembly. Franklin wrote that he was "flattered."

Early Colonial Elections

Elections in the 1600s and 1700s were noisy, social occasions. An election "causes a Hubbub for a week or so," wrote one Virginia colonist. He explained that to Virginians, used to "dull barbecues and yet duller dances," an election was quite an event.

On election day men from all over the county gathered at the courthouse or village common. Voters looked forward to the punch, cookies, and cakes given by the candidates. George Washington provided similar food and drink during his first election to the Virginia House of Burgesses in 1758.

Unlike today's secret voting, each voter spoke his choice in front of a large crowd. Loud cheers or boos followed each vote. The candidates often personally thanked a voter for his vote.

ESTABLISHING FREEDOMS

In their assemblies colonial delegates spoke up for the freedom to rule themselves. The growing spirit of freedom also influenced the press, or news publications, in the colonies.

John Peter Zenger

In 1733 a few members of the New York assembly started a newspaper called the *New York Weekly Journal*. They hired John Peter Zenger, a German immigrant, as its printer. Zenger printed stories that criticized New York's royal governor, William Cosby. One story in the newspaper accused Cosby of being dishonest.

In 1734 the New York sheriff, who supported the governor, burned copies of the paper and put Zenger in jail. The governor accused Zenger of publishing remarks attacking the government.

A lawyer named Andrew Hamilton defended Zenger at his trial in 1735. He argued that Zenger could not be punished for printing stories that were true, even if they were about the governor. Every person had a right, Hamilton said, "publicly to [oppose] the abuses of power . . . of men in authority."

The jury agreed with Hamilton and found Zenger not guilty. Zenger's victory helped establish important rights— freedom of the press and freedom of speech. This meant that colonists could speak or print the truth without fear of being put in jail.

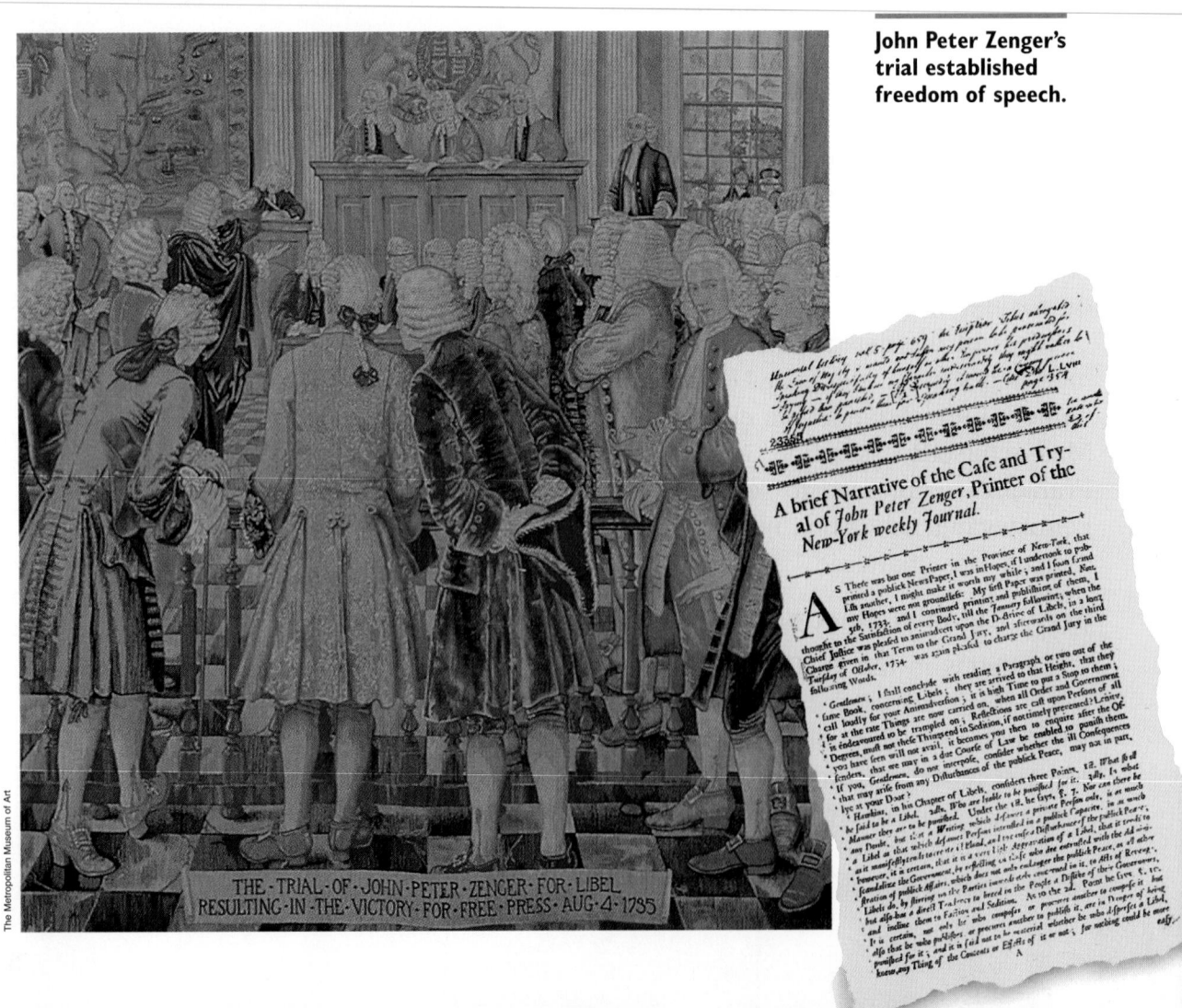

John Peter Zenger's trial established freedom of speech.

THE·TRIAL·OF·JOHN·PETER·ZENGER·FOR·LIBEL RESULTING·IN·THE·VICTORY·FOR·FREE·PRESS·AUG·4·1735

The Metropolitan Museum of Art

Phillis Wheatley urged colonists to end slavery.

African Americans Speak Out

Enslaved African Americans took special note of the growing calls for freedom in the colonies.

One African American who wrote of liberty was Phillis Wheatley. Born in what is now the country of Senegal in West Africa, she was kidnapped and brought to the colonies at the age of eight. Wheatley was then sold as a slave to John Wheatley in Boston. It was common for enslaved people to be given the last name of their owner.

Mr. and Mrs. Wheatley taught young Phillis to read and write English. In 1773 she published a book of poetry while she was still enslaved. Wheatley urged the colonists to free their slaves. "In every human . . . God has implanted a principle, which we call love of freedom," she wrote. "The same principle lives in us."

WHY IT MATTERS

Since their beginnings the 13 colonies practiced some form of self-government. Far from the king of England, the colonists held town meetings and assemblies. They created their own laws, showing their desire to be free to live as they chose. These beliefs in freedom and self-government would later shape the new government of the United States.

Links to LANGUAGE ARTS

The Power of Poetry

Why are Phillis Wheatley's poems remembered today?

People who are not free to do or say what they want sometimes write down their feelings to make them known. Phillis Wheatley was enslaved, and she could not vote. She used poetry to express her opinions about slavery. Find a poem at home or in your library that you think has a message. Share the poems aloud in class and talk about their meanings.

✔ Reviewing Facts and Ideas

MAIN IDEAS

- The colonial assemblies helped establish self-government in the colonies.
- Assemblies such as the House of Burgesses made laws to print money, collect taxes, build roads, make land laws, and organize colonial militias.
- John Peter Zenger's trial in 1735 won support for the rights to freedom of speech and freedom of the press in the colonies.

THINK ABOUT IT

1. What were some of the colonies' earliest written plans for government?

2. Who could be elected to serve in the colonial assemblies?

3. **FOCUS** What were the major duties of the colonial assemblies?

4. **THINKING SKILL** How would you decide which parts of John Peter Zenger's stories contain *facts* and which contain *opinions*?

5. **WRITE** Write a short speech that a British colonist might have written in support of self-government.

THE 13 COLONIES REBEL

READ ALOUD

Hanging from the Liberty Tree, a tall elm in the center of Boston, was a straw puppet of a British tax collector. The colonists were furious about a new tax the British government wanted them to pay. Many conflicts arose between Britain and the 13 colonies after the French and Indian War.

THE BIG PICTURE

What is liberty? The word *liberty* means "freedom." To the colonists liberty came to mean freedom to govern themselves.

After the French and Indian War, British lawmakers passed new taxes for the colonists. Some voted against the taxes. "The Kingdom has no right to lay a tax upon the colonies," declared English legislator William Pitt. Edward Burke said, "Leave America . . . to tax herself." But the majority of British lawmakers continued to vote in favor of new colonial taxes.

The colonists angrily told the British that Parliament had no right to tax them without the vote of the delegates in the colonial assemblies. Cries of "Taxation without representation is tyranny!" filled the streets. Tyranny is the cruel and unfair use of force or power.

These and other conflicts would lead the colonies to rebel against the British. To rebel is to follow one's own beliefs and refuse to obey those in charge.

Focus Activity

READ TO LEARN
What led the colonies to rebel against Great Britain?

VOCABULARY
liberty
rebel
Stamp Act
treason
Sons of Liberty
repeal
Townshend Acts
boycott
Committee of
    Correspondence
Boston Tea Party
Intolerable Acts

PEOPLE
Patrick Henry
Samuel Adams
Mercy Otis Warren
Crispus Attucks
Abigail Adams

ENGLAND TIGHTENS ITS GRIP

After the French and Indian War, the British found that governing and defending its new, larger empire was expensive. Taxing the colonists seemed like an easy solution to the problem.

The Stamp Act

The Stamp Act of 1765 was one of the first British laws placing taxes on the colonies. The colonists had to pay a tax every time they bought a newspaper or pamphlet or signed a legal document. These items had to have a stamp on them to show that the tax had been paid.

In Virginia a burgess from the backcountry named Patrick Henry spoke to the assembly. He said that anyone who paid the stamp tax was an enemy of Virginia. Another burgess accused Henry of treason. Treason is the betrayal of one's country by giving help to one of its enemies. "If this be treason,"

Henry replied, "make the most of it." Henry's speeches were later published in colonial newspapers. His words inspired many colonists to protest the Stamp Act.

The Colonists Fight Back

To fight the Stamp Act, some colonists formed the Sons of Liberty. The Sons of Liberty were groups of colonists who organized protests against the British government. One member, Samuel Adams, wrote articles for Boston newspapers attacking the Stamp Act. Sam Adams was a cousin of John Adams.

In other cities the "liberty boys," as they were called, attacked British tax agents. These protests forced some stamp-tax agents to quit their jobs.

In October 1765 delegates from nine colonies attended a Stamp Act Congress. They decided that Parliament could not tax the colonies without their consent. They demanded that the Stamp Act be repealed, or canceled. A year later, Parliament repealed the Stamp Act. "I rejoice that America has resisted," said William Pitt.

The Sons of Liberty set up a rally (below) to protest the use of tax stamps like this one (right).

The Granger Collection

The Granger Collection

TROUBLES IN BOSTON

The repeal of the Stamp Act did not end the troubles between Britain and the 13 colonies. Barely a year after the Stamp Act was repealed, Parliament passed another law taxing the colonies. The city of Boston became the center of protest against the new tax.

The Townshend Acts

Charles Townshend (TOWN zend), the treasurer of the British government, called for new taxes in 1767. Parliament then passed the Townshend Acts, which said the colonists had to pay taxes on all the tea, paper, glass, lead, and paint that they imported from Britain.

In Boston the colonists held a town meeting to protest the new taxes. The colonists decided to make a list of all the British goods they would boycott, or refuse to buy. To *boycott* means "to refuse to do business or have contact with a person, group, or country."

Women formed groups called the Daughters of Liberty to support the boycott. The Daughters of Liberty held "spinning bees" to spin thread so that they would not have to import clothes from Britain. The women, wrote one colonial newspaper, act "with the men in contributing to . . . their country and equally share in the honor of it."

Poet and playwright Mercy Otis Warren encouraged women to give up tea and the other goods from Britain. We should make "a small sacrifice," she wrote. "We'll quit the useless vanities [luxuries] of life."

Colonists opposing the British often met in Mercy Otis Warren's home. She later wrote a history of how the colonies rebelled.

The Boston Massacre

Boston soon faced even bigger conflicts. Warren and other Bostonians expected trouble when British troops marched into town in October 1768. That was the first time soldiers had been sent to control the colonists.

Boston residents grew angry as soldiers began their noisy drills and set up guard posts around the city. Some colonists picked fights with the soldiers. Young boys called the soldiers "lobsters" because of their red uniforms and threw snowballs at them.

The growing anger finally boiled over on March 5, 1770. Church bells rang as a large group of colonists met outside the Customs House. Crispus Attucks, a former slave, yelled to the crowd, "The way to get rid of these soldiers is to attack the main guard." In the confusion that followed, the British soldiers fired. Five men were killed, including Attucks.

Sam Adams (left) and John and Abigail Adams (above right) led the colonists' early struggles. The Boston Massacre (above left), engraved by Paul Revere, horrified many colonists.

The people of Boston were horrified at the killings. The soldiers were arrested. John Adams agreed to defend them. Although he did not want British soldiers in Boston, Adams believed the soldiers should have a fair trial.

The Committees of Correspondence

John Adams feared that defending British soldiers would make him unpopular. But in fact, the opposite was true. John Adams, his wife Abigail Adams and Samuel Adams became the center of political events in Boston.

In October 1772 Sam Adams asked 21 colonists at a Boston town meeting to form a committee "to state the rights of the colonists." Boston's Committee of Correspondence sent reports to similar committees in other colonies. By 1774 all of the colonies except Pennsylvania had their own Committees of Correspondence. This communication helped to unite the colonies toward action.

John Adams wrote some of the most important correspondence in the colonies. In one paper he wrote:

Either the Colonies are Vassals [slaves] of the Parliament, or . . . they are totally independent.

331

COLONISTS REBEL

After the Boston Massacre some colonists wondered whether they would have to defend their liberty in battle. Although Parliament agreed to repeal the Townshend Acts, it kept the tax on tea. The colonies began to unite in order to fight this hated tax.

The Boston Tea Party

In 1773 British ships carrying thousands of pounds of tea sailed across the Atlantic Ocean to Boston and other colonial ports. In early December, Abigail Adams reported that the colonists were preparing a protest:

> The Tea . . . is arrived. . . . I hope [effective] opposition had been made to the landing of it. . . . The flame is kindled [lit] and like Lightning it catches from Soul to Soul.

In fact, on a quiet December night, a group of colonists disguised as Mohawks crept toward Boston Harbor. "Boston Harbor will be a teapot tonight!" they shouted. They then boarded a ship and dumped 342 chests of valuable tea into the harbor.

John Adams wrote about the Boston Tea Party in his diary.

American Nathaniel Currier later painted the Boston Tea Party in his work *The Destruction of Tea at Boston Harbor* (above). The Boston Tea Party led King George III (above right) to blockade Boston Harbor (right).

The people should never rise without doing something to be remembered— something notable and striking. This destruction of the tea is so bold, so daring . . . that I can't but consider it as a [new and important period] in history.

Because the men were disguised, the governor did not know whom to charge for destroying the tea. When King George III learned of the "tea party" he demanded that Boston be punished.

In early 1774 Parliament decided to close the port of Boston until the colonists paid for the tea. Town meetings were banned. Parliament also ordered colonists to feed and house British soldiers in the colonies. The colonists called Parliament's actions the Intolerable Acts.

Unknown to the British, the Committees of Correspondence sent food and money to Boston. "Don't pay for an ounce of the . . . tea," they wrote. The committees then worked to decide on a united response to the Intolerable Acts.

WHY IT MATTERS

The colonists learned about the power of writing and organizing in the Committees of Correspondence, which helped them become more united. The committees saw that they could make Britain repeal some of its taxes. John Adams felt that the Committees of Correspondence had become "a great political engine" that would move the colonies closer toward liberty.

✓ Reviewing Facts and Ideas

MAIN IDEAS

- To raise money after the French and Indian War, Parliament passed the Stamp Act in 1765 to collect taxes from the colonies.
- The Townshend Acts of 1767 made colonists pay taxes on many everyday products. After the Boston Massacre in 1770, the Committees of Correspondence were formed to tell colonists of important events.
- The Boston Tea Party led to Britain's strongest actions against the colonies, the Intolerable Acts of 1774.

THINK ABOUT IT

1. What kinds of taxes were included in the Stamp Act?

2. How did the Daughters of Liberty oppose the Townshend Acts?

3. **FOCUS** What acts of the British Parliament caused the colonists to rebel?

4. **THINKING SKILL** What *effects* did the Committees of Correspondence have? Explain your answer.

5. **WRITE** Suppose you were a member of the Massachusetts Committee of Correspondence. Describe the Boston Tea Party and Intolerable Acts.

STUDYSKILLS

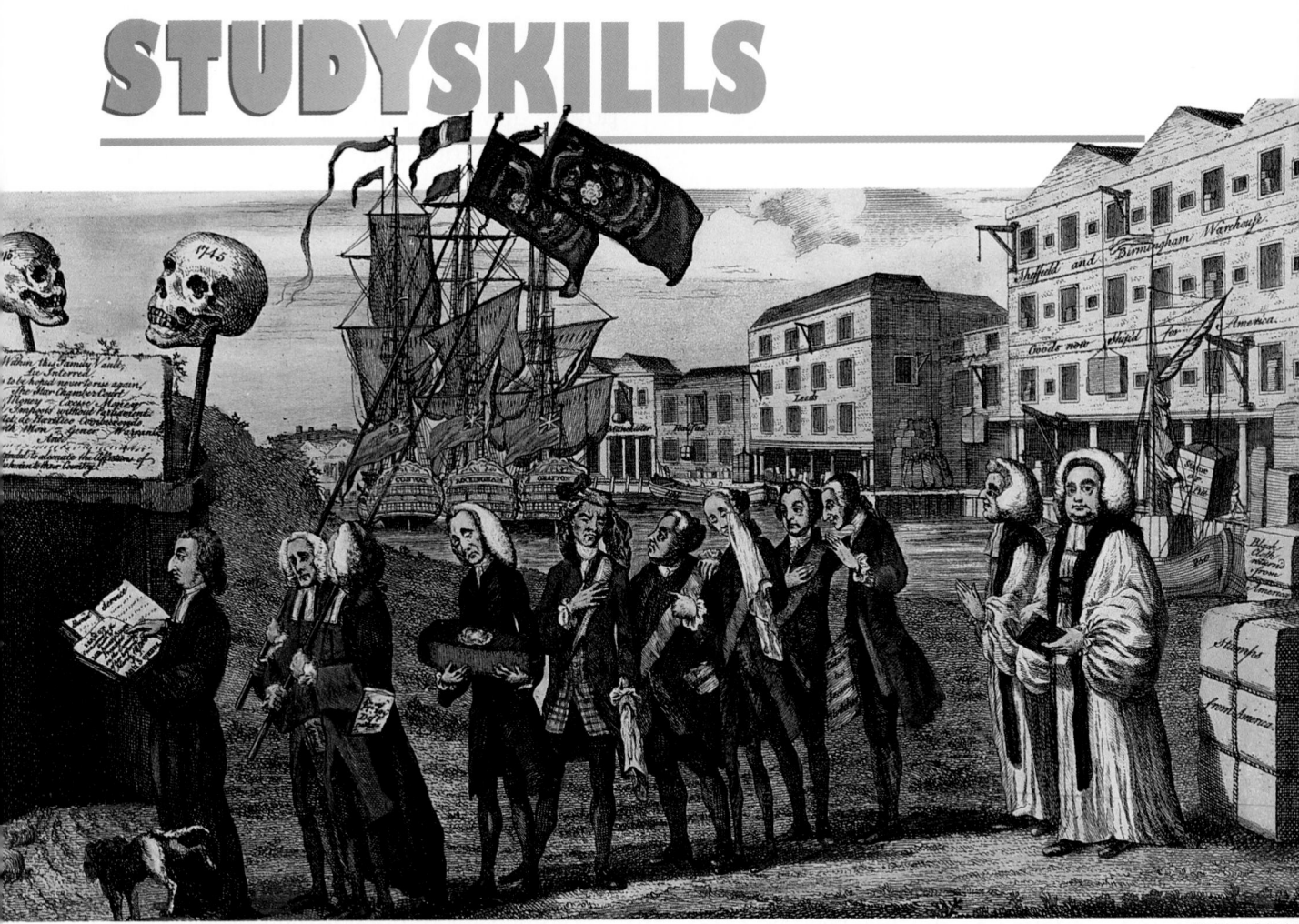

The Granger Collection

Reading Political Cartoons

VOCABULARY

political cartoon   symbol

WHY THE SKILL MATTERS

The trial of John Peter Zenger helped to establish freedom of speech and freedom of the press. One way that people in the 13 colonies expressed this freedom was through political cartoons that were printed in newspapers and pamphlets. A political cartoon is a drawing that expresses a cartoonist's opinion about people, political events, or newsworthy issues.

Have you ever drawn a picture to express how you feel about something? That is what a political cartoon does. Political cartoons deal with very serious issues, such as taxes and elections. Yet cartoonists often treat these issues in a humorous way.

Reading political cartoons can help you learn about the important issues of a particular time or of a particular city or country. Political cartoons give readers something to think and even laugh about.

USING THE SKILL

Political cartoons often contain symbols that help get their message across to readers. A symbol is something that stands for something else. You know, for example, that the 50 stars on the flag of the United States stand for the 50 states.

Symbols can be hard to understand. Look at the cartoon on page 334. It is about the repeal of the Stamp Act in 1766. The small coffin one man is carrying is a symbol for the Stamp Act that has just been repealed, or "killed." The skulls are symbols for other taxes that the colonies had repealed. The sad men are British leaders who supported the Stamp Act. In the background the ships stand for the trade that will begin again between Great Britain and America.

To help readers understand their drawings, some cartoonists use captions. Or they may use dialogue (DĪ uh lahg) in order to express their opinions in words. Dialogue is conversation. The cartoon about the Stamp Act on page 334 uses captions and symbols rather than dialogue to make its point. The cartoon below, on the other hand, uses only dialogue.

HELPING Yourself

- **A political cartoon shows a cartoonist's opinion about a person, an event, or an issue.**

- **To understand a political cartoon, look for symbols and other clues. If there is dialogue, determine who is speaking.**

TRYING THE SKILL

Look at the cartoon on this page, from an American newspaper in the 1990s. It is like many cartoons that praise or find fault with people or events. What is this cartoon about? What point is this cartoonist trying to make? Is this cartoon praising or finding fault with something?

REVIEWING THE SKILL

1. What is a political cartoon?
2. How does a political cartoon express its meaning?
3. What kinds of issues does a political cartoon cover?
4. Do you think political cartoons influence people? Explain your answer.
5. If you had to draw a political cartoon, what issue or person would you picture? What symbols would you use to express your opinion? Why?

The political cartoon from the late 1700s shows the funeral of "Miss Stamp" (left). Today, political cartoons appear in a wide variety of magazines and newspapers (right).

THE REVOLUTION BEGINS

READ ALOUD

"The colonies must either submit or triumph," said King George III. *The king was sure that the colonies would submit, or surrender, to the authority of the British government. But many colonists felt the time had come to stand up to Britain and to unite the colonies.*

Focus Activity

READ TO LEARN
What happened in the first battles of the American Revolution?

VOCABULARY
First Continental Congress
petition
minuteman
American Revolution
Battle of Bunker Hill

PEOPLE
John Hancock
Paul Revere
William Dawes
John Parker
Ethan Allen
Israel Putnam
Peter Salem

PLACES
Lexington
Concord
Fort Ticonderoga
Charlestown

THE BIG PICTURE

On September 5, 1774, delegates from every colony except Georgia met at Carpenter's Hall in Philadelphia. At this First Continental Congress, delegates wrote a petition to send to King George III asking for repeal of the Intolerable Acts. A petition is a written request signed by many people. The delegates argued that the Intolerable Acts were illegal and unfair. They also claimed that they had the right to make their own laws without Britain's approval.

To fight the Intolerable Acts, the delegates agreed to stop trade with Britain. They also asked the colonists to gather minutemen to defend the cities. Minutemen had to be ready for battle at a minute's notice. They were usually the best trained or most experienced soldiers.

The colonists felt that they needed the minutemen because the conflicts between the colonies and Britain might explode into war at any time. They were right. Within a year the colonists and the British would be fighting a war called the American Revolution. A revolution is a sudden, violent, or very great change.

PREPARING FOR WAR

By 1775 every able-bodied man in every colonial town was required to join the militia. Most of the militia members were farmers, craftworkers, business owners, or wealthy men. Early in the revolution some militias allowed both free and enslaved African Americans to join. Later most colonial militias refused to accept any African Americans.

The militias near Lexington were given orders "to be ready at the beat of the drum." The rumor was that the British were going to arrest Sam Adams and John Hancock, a leading Boston patriot. Then the British would march to Concord to capture weapons the militia had stored there.

Paul Revere

On the night of April 18, a silversmith named Paul Revere learned that the British were leaving Boston and heading for Concord. Revere mounted his horse and rode to Lexington to warn Adams and Hancock. Revere's friend William Dawes, a shoemaker, joined him on the way to Concord. Trace the routes of Revere and Dawes on the map below.

They were joined by a doctor named Samuel Prescott. All three carried one message, "The British are coming!" A British patrol caught up with the men. The patrol took Revere's horse, but Dawes escaped. Only Prescott reached Concord.

Revere is remembered today because of the lines of the poem "Paul Revere's Ride." Henry Wadsworth Longfellow wrote it in 1863:

Listen, my children, and you shall hear
Of the midnight ride of Paul Revere,
On the eighteenth of April, in
*   Seventy-five;*
Hardly a man is now alive
Who remembers that famous
*   day and year.*

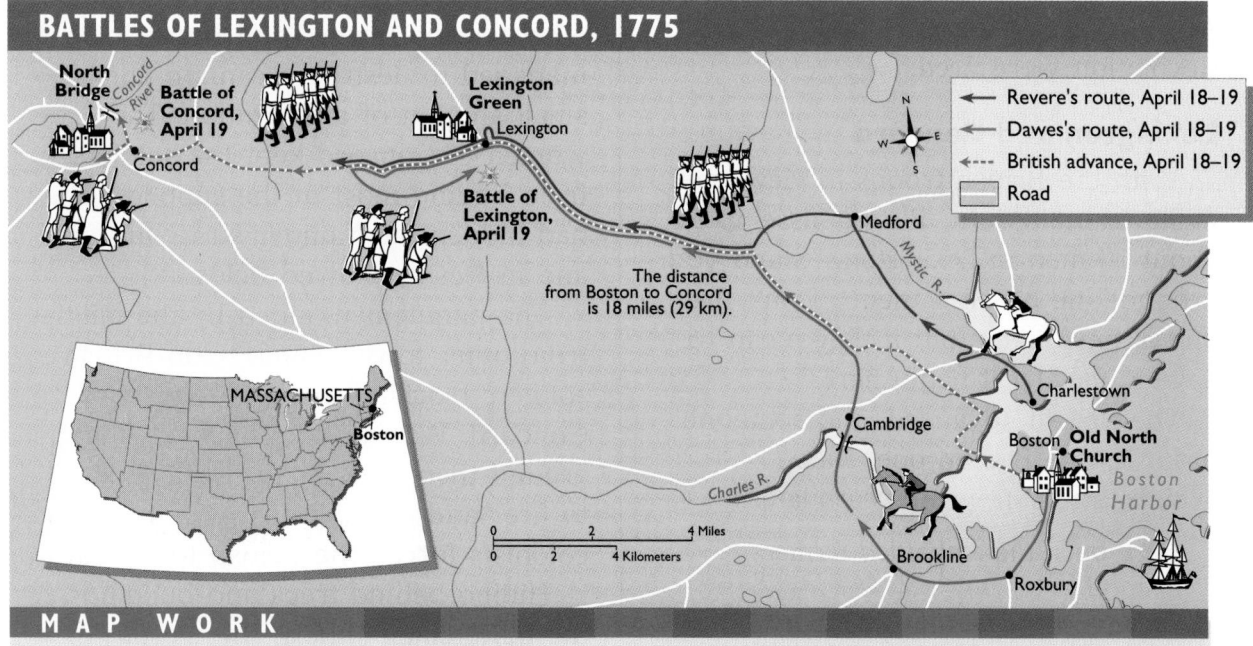

BATTLES OF LEXINGTON AND CONCORD, 1775

North Bridge
Concord River
Battle of Concord, April 19
Concord
Lexington Green
Lexington
Battle of Lexington, April 19
The distance from Boston to Concord is 18 miles (29 km).
Medford
Mystic R.
Charlestown
MASSACHUSETTS
Boston
Cambridge
Boston — Old North Church
Boston Harbor
Charles R.
Brookline
Roxbury

Revere's route, April 18–19
Dawes's route, April 18–19
British advance, April 18–19
Road

0 2 4 Miles
0 2 4 Kilometers

MAP WORK

Lexington and Concord were the first major battles of the American Revolution. Because of the warnings provided by Revere and Dawes, the colonists were able to move the weapons they had stored at Concord.

1. Through which cities did Revere ride? Dawes?
2. In which direction did the British travel?
3. About how far is the city of Lexington from Concord?

THE FIRST SHOTS ARE FIRED

The night buzzed with activity after Paul Revere's ride. Minutemen galloped from their farms to Lexington. About 700 British redcoats marched toward the town. In the early morning hours of April 19, the first shots of the American Revolution were fired.

Lexington and Concord

With the British troops in view, the militia captain John Parker assembled about 70 men in Lexington. "Stand your ground!" he ordered them. "Don't fire unless fired upon, but if they mean to have a war, let it begin here."

The British advanced, and someone fired. As the Boston poet Ralph Waldo Emerson wrote years later:

Here once the embattled farmers
  stood,
And fired the shot heard round
  the world.

In the battle that followed, eight militiamen were killed, and ten were wounded. Only one British soldier was hurt.

A farmer at the Battle of Lexington (above) said, "We always had governed ourselves, and we always meant to."

The British then marched 5 miles to Concord. Knowing that they were badly outnumbered, the 250 militiamen waited for reinforcements as the British searched the town. The British only managed to destroy a cannon and a small amount of ammunition. The women of Concord kept the soldiers from finding most of the supplies. They had hidden them under straw in barns and in freshly plowed fields.

The minutemen, aided by the militias from other towns, came upon British soldiers blocking the bridge west of Concord. With musket balls whistling around them, the militia were ordered to fire "and not kill our own men." The colonists forced the British to retreat.

Hiding behind trees and buildings, the minutemen shot at the weary British soldiers who were retreating back toward Boston. More than 70 British soldiers were killed, and 174 were wounded.

"Liberty or Death"

Muskets were not the only weapons used against the British. In Virginia the fiery speeches of Patrick Henry convinced many in the House of Burgesses that a final break with Great Britain was near.

On March 23, 1775, Henry gave one of the most famous speeches in our country's history. He argued that the British troops were in Boston to take away the colonists' rights. "And what have we to oppose them?" he asked. Read the following excerpt from Henry's speech. What course of action did he suggest the colonies take?

The Granger Collection

Excerpt from a speech by Patrick Henry before the Virginia House of Burgesses, Williamsburg, 1775.

There is no retreat but in submission and slavery! Our chains are forged. Their clanking may be heard on the plains of Boston! The war is **inevitable**—and let it come!! I repeat it, sir, let it come!!!

It is vain, sir, to **extenuate** the matter. Gentlemen may cry, peace, peace; but there is no peace. The war is actually begun! The next **gale** that sweeps from the north will bring to our ears the clash of **resounding** arms! Our **brethren** are already in the field! Why stand we here idle? What is it that gentlemen wish? What would they have? Is life so dear or peace so sweet as to be purchased at the price of chains and slavery?

Forbid it, Almighty God—I know not what course others may take; but as for me, give me liberty, or give me death!

---

inevitable: impossible to avoid
extenuate: excuse
gale: strong wind
resounding: echoing
brethren: brothers

Patrick Henry's speeches inspired colonists to take action. As a result of the speech he gave in 1775, the Virginia House of Burgesses voted to organize a militia for Virginia's defense.

CANNONS ROAR

Henry's powerful speech predicted the battles of the coming war. After Lexington and Concord, the Massachusetts minutemen kept up their attack on the British around Boston.

"Let the cannon roar," said an English lord. Then the colonists will run away "as fast as their feet will carry them." He was wrong.

The Fall of Fort Ticonderoga

While the minutemen surrounded Boston, a militia leader from Vermont named Ethan Allen set his sights on Fort Ticonderoga. This fort on Lake Champlain was one of the main supply posts for the British army.

The Green Mountain Boys served in the militia under Allen. The band of farmers who mostly made up this group included both blacks and whites.

Near dawn on May 10, 1775, the Green Mountain Boys crept past the

fort's light defenses. Allen woke the commander and demanded his surrender. "Come out of there, you old rat," he shouted. Without any bloodshed, the Americans had captured British cannons and cut off British support from Canada.

The Battle of Bunker Hill

In June some 1,200 militiamen around Boston were sent across the bay to Charlestown. Whoever controlled the

This painting, *Battle of Bunker Hill*, is by John Trumbull. Most of the fighting took place on nearby Breed's Hill.

Items carried by men in the colonial militia (left) included a flask, spoon, and plate for meals. They also used a lantern (center) for sending messages.

The Granger Collection

hills surrounding Charlestown would be able to fire cannons on Boston.

Through the night the colonists dug out a rough fort near Breed's Hill. By dawn the soldiers "began to be almost beat out," remembered one colonist, "being tired by our labor and having no sleep the night before." Then a British ship in the harbor began to fire its cannons at the exhausted men.

British troops marched on the fort after noon. "Don't fire till you see the whites of their eyes," ordered the colonial general Israel Putnam. The colonists bravely fought off two charges. But they ran out of ammunition, and a third charge forced them to retreat to nearby Bunker Hill. The British commander, Colonel Pitcairn, who had fought the colonists at Lexington, leaped upon a wall of the fort to declare victory. Peter Salem, a former slave, killed him with a single shot.

In what was later called the Battle of Bunker Hill, the British "victory" cost them the lives of more than 1,000 soldiers. Although more than 400 colonists were also killed, they had proven their willingness to put up a hard fight.

WHY IT MATTERS

In the First Continental Congress, the colonists gained experience in forming a government for a new country. In the first battles between colonists and British troops, the colonial militias learned some of the skills they would need in the American Revolution.

By 1775 the final break between Britain and its colonies had not yet come. Some colonists still hoped the British would repeal the Intolerable Acts and restore peace. Already colonial unity and military readiness showed the beginning of a new country—a country separate from Britain.

✔/// Reviewing Facts and Ideas

MAIN IDEAS

- The First Continental Congress met in 1774 to discuss the colonies' response to the Intolerable Acts.
- The first battles of the American Revolution were fought in Lexington and Concord on April 19, 1775.
- The capture of Fort Ticonderoga and the Battle of Bunker Hill in 1775 proved that the colonists were serious in their struggle against the British.

THINK ABOUT IT

1. What actions did the First Continental Congress decide to take?

2. Who fought to defend the colonies?

3. **FOCUS** What happened at the battles of Lexington and Concord?

4. **THINKING SKILL** List in *sequence* the events leading to the "shot heard round the world."

5. **GEOGRAPHY** Look at the map on page 337. What waterways did Paul Revere and William Dawes cross?

341

CHAPTER 12 REVIEW

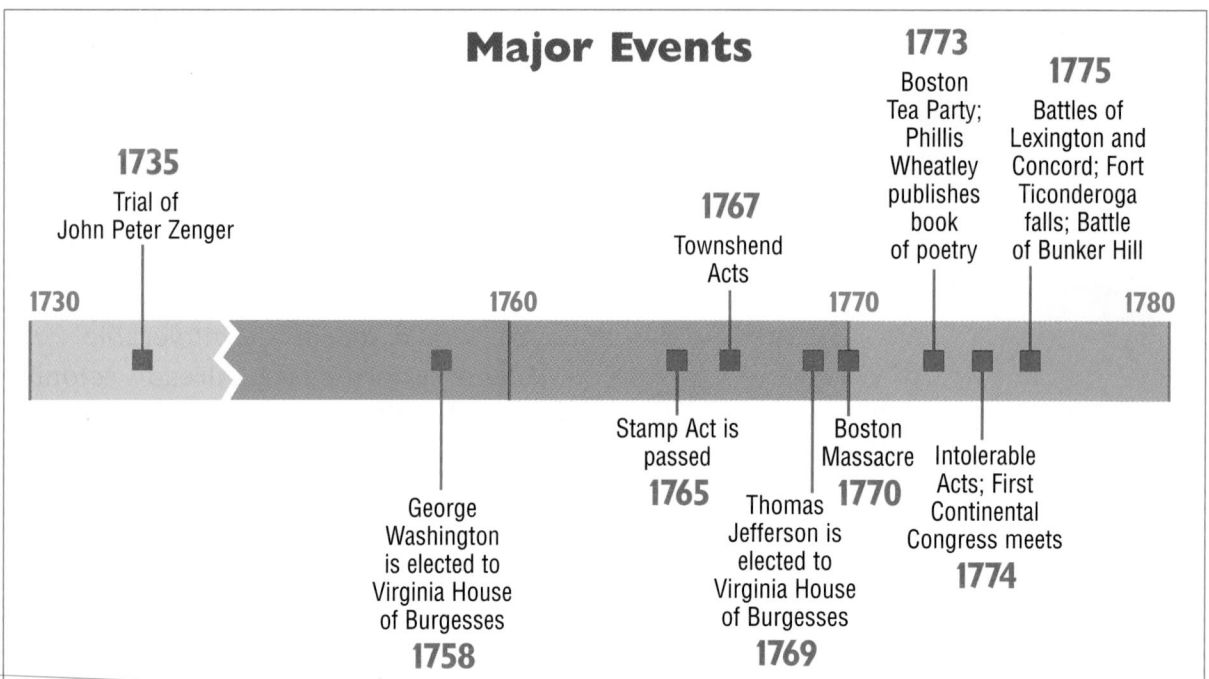

Major Events

1735
Trial of
John Peter Zenger

1767
Townshend
Acts

1773
Boston
Tea Party;
Phillis
Wheatley
publishes
book
of poetry

1775
Battles of
Lexington and
Concord; Fort
Ticonderoga
falls; Battle
of Bunker Hill

1730   1760   1770   1780

Stamp Act is
passed
1765

Boston
Massacre
1770

Intolerable
Acts; First
Continental
Congress meets
1774

George
Washington
is elected to
Virginia House
of Burgesses
1758

Thomas
Jefferson is
elected to
Virginia House
of Burgesses
1769

THINKING ABOUT VOCABULARY

Number a sheet of paper from 1 to 5. Next to each number write the two words or terms from the list below that best complete the sentence.

American Revolution
assembly
Battle of Bunker Hill
boycott
delegate

militia
minutemen
rebel
Stamp Act
treason

1. The male colonists elected a _____ to represent them in the _____ .
2. The _____ was one of the first battles of the _____ .
3. The _____ volunteered to serve in the colonial _____ .
4. The _____ was one reason that the colonists decided to _____ British goods.
5. The British thought it was _____ when the colonists decided to _____ against Great Britain's authority.

THINKING ABOUT FACTS

1. Give an example of an early form of self-government in the colonies.
2. How did the trial of John Peter Zenger become important to the colonists?
3. Why did the colonies rebel against the British government?
4. Describe the role Samuel Adams played during the conflict between Parliament and the English colonies.
5. Who was Mercy Otis Warren?
6. Who was Crispus Attucks? In which event did he play a key role?
7. How did the Committees of Correspondence help to unify the colonies?
8. What was unusual about the capture of Fort Ticonderoga?
9. What did the Battle of Bunker Hill accomplish?
10. In the time line above, study the dates for the Boston Tea Party and the Intolerable Acts. Which was a cause for the other? Which was an effect?

THINK AND WRITE

WRITING A POEM

Reread the section on Phillis Wheatley and the power of poetry on page 327. Think about what freedom meant to Wheatley. Then write a poem in which you express what freedom means to you.

WRITING A SPEECH

Reread the excerpt of Patrick Henry's speech to the House of Burgesses on page 339. Suppose that you are a Son or Daughter of Liberty. Write a speech trying to convince others to join your cause.

WRITING A BATTLE REPORT

Suppose that you are assigned to report on the activities of the Patriot forces. Describe the battles of Lexington and Concord and Bunker Hill. Include the basic facts and conclusions about the outcome.

APPLYING STUDY SKILLS

READING POLITICAL CARTOONS

Answer the questions below to practice the skill of reading political cartoons.

1. What is a political cartoon?
2. Look at the political cartoon from 1766 on page 334. What symbols does the cartoonist use? What do they mean?
3. How do you think this cartoon might have influenced a colonial reader?
4. Why does the cartoon on page 335 need the dialogue that it includes?
5. Do political cartoons express facts or opinions?

Summing Up the Chapter

Copy the cause-and-effect chart on a separate piece of paper. Then review the chapter to complete the chart, showing some of the causes and effects that led to the Revolutionary War. After you have finished, use the chart to answer the question, "How can an effect sometimes become the cause of other effects?"

CAUSE	EFFECT
Colonists have a strong belief in freedom and self-government.	
	Colonists protest; Sons of Liberty is formed.
	Colonists boycott British goods.
Boston Tea Party takes place.	
	Colonists stop trading with Britain; minutemen begin defending the colonies.
	Colonists prove the seriousness of their beliefs.

CHAPTER 13

The American Revolution

THINKING ABOUT HISTORY AND GEOGRAPHY

Chapter 13 begins with the signing of the Declaration of Independence on July 4, 1776. For the next several years the British colonists fought to win independence from Great Britain. Read the time line to follow some of the events of the American Revolution. Almost 300 years after Columbus first reached the Americas, the British colonists began forming their own country, free from European control.

1776
PHILADELPHIA

Thomas Jefferson writes the Declaration of Independence

1776
TRENTON

George Washington crosses the Delaware River to attack the British

1778
VALLEY FORGE

Martha Washington helps wounded soldiers through a terrible winter

NORTH
AMERICA

Fort
Vincennes

Valley Forge

Trenton

Philadelphia

Yorktown

THE BRITISH
COLONIES

ATLANTIC
OCEAN

1779

FORT VINCENNES

**George Rogers Clark
captures British forts in
the Ohio River valley**

1781

YORKTOWN

**The British surrender to
George Washington**

THE DECLARATION OF INDEPENDENCE

Focus Activity

READ TO LEARN
What was the purpose of the Declaration of Independence?

VOCABULARY
Second Continental Congress
Continental Army
traitor
Declaration of Independence

PEOPLE
Thomas Paine
William Howe
Henry Knox
Thomas Jefferson
John Locke

PLACE
Monticello

READ ALOUD

Benjamin Franklin had hoped that Britain and the colonies would make peace. After the Battle of Bunker Hill, Franklin gave up this hope. He wrote to a friend who was a member of the British Parliament, "You have begun to burn our Towns, and murder our People. Look upon your Hands! They are stained with the Blood of your Relations! You and I were long Friends: You are now my Enemy, and I am, Yours, Benjamin Franklin."

THE BIG PICTURE

News of the Battle of Bunker Hill had made Franklin break with a good friend. Yet not all Americans were ready to break completely from Britain in 1775. Many still wanted Britain and the colonies to compromise. Some felt that the colonies were not strong enough to govern themselves. Most colonists spoke English, shared English customs and laws, and had relatives in Britain. The British were the colonists' major trading partner. British ships protected colonial trade routes.

One fact, however, could not be forgotten. Colonists had lost their lives at Lexington, Concord, and Bunker Hill. The fight for liberty had begun.

King George III did not think much of the colonists' will to fight. He was sure that once they "have felt a small blow, they will submit." In this lesson you will see how the colonists proved the king's prediction wrong.

THE REBELLION CONTINUES

By 1776 more and more colonists wanted to declare independence immediately. "We must be content to wait till the fruit is ripe," Sam Adams told them, "before we gather it."

Common Sense

A talented writer helped to ripen the "fruit" of independence. He was Thomas Paine, an Englishman who had settled in Pennsylvania in 1774.

In January 1776 Paine published a pamphlet entitled *Common Sense*. In it Paine argued that the colonists owed no loyalty to an unjust ruler. It made no sense, Paine wrote, for "a continent to be perpetually [forever] ruled by an island . . . Tis time to part."

Paine used language most people could easily understand. In three months, more than 100,000 copies of his pamphlet were sold. "I find *Common Sense* is working a powerful change in the minds of many men," observed George Washington.

The British Leave Boston

Meanwhile, 15,000 American soldiers surrounded the British troops in Boston. When British General William Howe showed no signs of leaving Boston, Washington sent Henry Knox, a former bookseller, to Fort Ticonderoga. Knox and his men dragged cannons from the New York fort more than 250 miles over frozen rivers and snowy hills to Boston. When the British awoke on March 5, 1776, they saw the cannons staring down at them.

The showdown was over. As George Washington told his brother, the British soldiers, along with some 1,000 colonists loyal to Britain, retreated "in a shameful and precipitate [hurried] manner." The colonists had retaken Boston.

Ticonderoga Museum

Common Sense (left) inspired support for independence. Cannons from Fort Ticonderoga (above) helped the Patriots retake Boston.

SECOND CONTINENTAL CONGRESS

In May 1775, soon after the battles of Lexington and Concord, the Second Continental Congress had begun to meet. Colonists cheered the delegates as they arrived in Philadelphia. However, these men faced tough issues. The year before, the delegates had decided on a peaceful protest. Now British and American soldiers were fighting. The Congress had to respond.

Preparing for Defense

The delegates did not agree on what path to take. They knew that any actions they took must help protect the colonies against future attacks. John Adams suggested that the Congress form a "Grand American Army," with troops from every colony.

Adams nominated Virginian George Washington to be commander in chief of the new Continental Army. He praised Washington as "a gentleman whose skill as an officer . . . would command the respect of America." Washington accepted and promised to use "every power I possess . . . for the support of the glorious cause."

The Second Continental Congress, headed by John Hancock (below right), met in Independence Hall (right) in Philadelphia. Today, thousands visit the site of our country's beginnings (below).

The Congress also started a post office so that all the colonies could share news. Benjamin Franklin, a new delegate, was appointed Postmaster General. Afraid that Native Americans would side with the British, the Congress set up a committee to make peace with them. The Congress also asked foreign countries for support against Britain. The Second Continental Congress had begun to act like the central government for a new country.

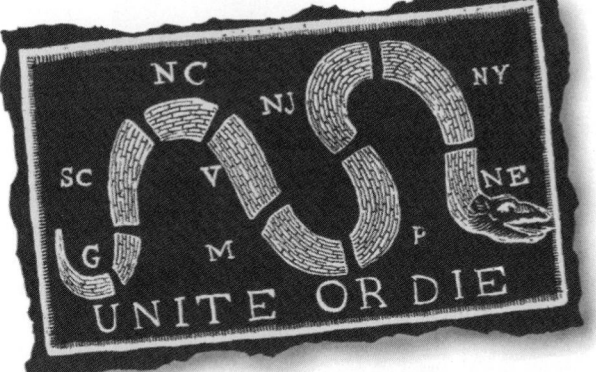

A Last Chance for Peace

"The war is now heartily entered into," wrote Thomas Jefferson of Virginia, a new delegate. Many agreed with him, including John Hancock.

Hancock, a Massachusetts delegate, was president of the Congress.

In July 1775 the Congress agreed to try one last time to make peace. The delegates sent what they called the "Olive Branch Petition" to King George. The olive branch is a symbol of peace. The petition assured Britain of American loyalty. It also asked for the repeal of the Intolerable Acts and an end to the fighting.

Declaring Independence

The king refused to read the petition from what he called an "illegal congress." He threatened to "bring the traitors to justice." A traitor is someone who turns against his or her country. The king's angry words shocked many of the colonists.

The delegates then took a big step. Early in June 1776 Virginia delegate Richard Henry Lee proposed "that these United colonies are, and of right ought to be, free and independent States." Many agreed. The Congress named a committee to write a statement of independence.

At first, six men—including John Adams, Benjamin Franklin, and Thomas Jefferson—were asked to write the Declaration of Independence. But Adams convinced Jefferson to draft the document. "You can write ten times better than I can," he argued. Jefferson was only 33 years old at the time.

Jefferson's love of architecture and European culture can be seen in his design for Monticello, his home near Charlottesville.

JEFFERSON WRITES THE DECLARATION

Despite his youth, Jefferson was a perfect choice to write the Declaration. He had served in Virginia's government, and although he rarely took part in debates, he wrote brilliantly.

A Man of Many Talents

Jefferson was born in 1743. He studied at the College of William and Mary in Williamsburg, and later practiced law.

Jefferson designed Monticello (mahn tih CHEL oh), the beautiful home he had built near Charlottesville, Virginia. Jefferson also designed the Virginia Capitol building and the University of Virginia, which he founded.

Jefferson owned several slaves in his lifetime and lived in a slave-owning colony. Yet he often spoke out against slavery. "Nothing is more certainly written in the book of fate than that these people are to be free," he wrote.

Writing the Declaration

When Jefferson sat down to write the Declaration, he was well prepared. As a law student he had heard Patrick Henry speak against the Stamp Act. He had read Thomas Paine's *Common Sense*. He had also studied the ideas of John Locke, an English philosopher from the late 1600s. Locke wrote that all people are born with certain rights, including life, liberty, and the right to own property. Locke believed that it was the responsibility of governments to protect these rights.

Jefferson wrote his draft in two days and then showed it to Franklin and Adams. They made a few changes, but agreed the Declaration was ready to be shown to the Congress. Jefferson was proud of his work. He felt that it was "an expression of the American mind."

The Granger Collection

Debating the Declaration

On a hot July day the Congress began debating the content of the Declaration. The draft included a list of angry complaints against King George. In one fierce passage, Jefferson accused the British King of promoting the slave trade in the English colonies. "He has waged cruel war against human nature itself," Jefferson wrote, "violating . . . sacred rights . . . of a distant people . . . carrying them into slavery." Adams considered Jefferson's writings on slavery some of the best work in the Declaration. But Southern and Northern delegates who owned slaves felt uncomfortable. The passage on slavery was cut, along with some of the angrier accusations against King George.

The Declaration Is Finished

For three days Franklin whispered reassuring words to Jefferson, who fumed as the delegates changed his work. Afterward, Richard Henry Lee told Jefferson that they had mangled his draft. "However," he added, "the [Declaration] in its nature is so good that no cookery can spoil the dish."

On July 4, 1776, the Declaration of Independence was approved. John Hancock was the first delegate to sign it. He wrote his name in large letters, "so the king doesn't have to put on his glasses," he is supposed to have said.

Signing the document took courage. The British would consider those who signed traitors. British soldiers could seize the delegates at any time. They had already chopped down Hancock's fences and thrown rocks through his windows. "We must all hang together," said Benjamin Franklin, "or [else] we shall all hang separately."

In the painting (above) Jefferson, right, works with John Adams, center, and Ben Franklin, left, on a draft of the Declaration of Independence (left).

THE DECLARATION OF INDEPENDENCE

What made the Declaration so powerful? No other colony had declared independence in writing before. As one President said many years later, the Declaration gave "hope to the world, for all future time."

Basic Principles of the Declaration

When Jefferson wrote, "We hold these truths to be self-evident," he meant that there are truths that should be clear to everyone. The first is that "all men are created equal." Men have the right given by God to "Life, Liberty, and the pursuit of Happiness."

The second truth is that people establish governments in order to "secure these rights." As you have read in Chapter 1, these governments get their power, or authority, from "the consent of the governed."

Jefferson then listed the colonists' grievances, or complaints, against King George. The king had, for example, dissolved the colonial assemblies, kept soldiers in the colonies, and taxed the colonies without their consent. King George, in short, was "unfit to be the ruler of a free people."

To conclude the Declaration, Jefferson echoed the words of Richard Henry Lee. It was time, he argued, for the colonists to declare "that these United Colonies are, and of Right ought to be, Free and Independent States."

Read the following excerpt from the Declaration. How might the British react to this document?

Thomas Jefferson presented the Declaration of Independence to the Second Continental Congress.

Yale University Art Gallery

*When in the Course of human
events, it becomes necessary for one
people to dissolve the political bands
which have connected them with
another, and to assume, among the
powers of the earth, the separate and
equal station to which the Laws of
Nature and Nature's God entitle them,
a decent respect to the opinions of
mankind requires that they should
declare the causes which* **impel** *them
to the separation.*

*We hold these truths to be self-
evident, that all men are created
equal, that they are* **endowed** *by their
Creator with certain* **unalienable**
*Rights, that among these are Life,
Liberty, and the pursuit of Happiness.*

*That to secure these rights, Gov-
ernments are* **instituted** *among Men,
deriving their just powers from the
consent of the governed.*

*That whenever any Form of Gov-
ernment becomes destructive of these
ends, it is the Right of the People to
alter or to abolish it. . . .*

---

impel: inspire   **instituted:** created
endowed: given
unalienable: cannot be taken away

WHY IT MATTERS

After the Declaration was approved,
copies were sent throughout the
colonies. Bells rang, cannons roared,
and colonists cheered when the Declaration was read.

The Declaration proclaimed independence, but not all people in the new
country were free. What would the new
government have to say about slavery,
and the rights of Native Americans and
women? In later chapters, you will read
about how the phrase "all men are created equal" was expanded to include
all people.

The Declaration of Independence was
one of the most important documents in
history. It was the first to set out the
rights and responsibilities of people in a
democracy. Over the years peoples of
other countries have used the Declaration as a model for their own statements
of independence.

✓// Reviewing Facts and Ideas

MAIN IDEAS

- Published in January 1776, Thomas
  Paine's *Common Sense* inspired many
  colonists to break with Britain.

- In 1775 the Second Continental Congress established the Continental
  Army and chose George Washington
  as its commander. The Congress also
  sent the Olive Branch Petition to King
  George of Britain.

- Thomas Jefferson wrote the Declaration of Independence, which explained
  why the colonies were breaking away
  from Britain. The Second Continental
  Congress approved it July 4, 1776.

THINK ABOUT IT

1. How did Henry Knox help to force
   the British to leave Boston?

2. What act did the Second Continental
   Congress make in 1775? In 1776?

3. **FOCUS** What was Thomas Jefferson's
   purpose in writing the Declaration of
   Independence?

4. **THINKING SKILL** Read the excerpt
   from the Declaration of Independence
   on this page. Are the statements *facts*
   or *opinions*? How do you know?

5. **WRITE** Write a pamphlet like
   Common Sense on a subject you
   would like to inspire others about.

The Fourth of July

When the colonists celebrated the signing of the Declaration of Independence in July, 1776, a new legacy was created. Today, Independence Day, or the Fourth of July, remains one of our country's most important holidays.

Like the colonists, today we celebrate with parades, picnics, barbecues, bell ringing, patriotic music, cannon salutes, speeches, fireworks, and games. In the photos on these pages, you can see some of the different ways that some Americans celebrate Independence Day. How does your community honor the legacy of independence on the Fourth of July?

Watching fireworks over the Capitol Building (above) is one way Americans celebrate the Fourth.

The Independence Day Parade (top), by Jane Wooster Scott, portrays people enjoying the day in the 1800s. Today, paraders in Revolutionary War uniforms (left) get into the spirit of 1776. This greeting card (above) shows Uncle Sam, who is always dressed for the Fourth.

THE CONTINENTAL ARMY

READ ALOUD

"I only regret that I have but one life to lose for my country." These were the dying words of Captain Nathan Hale. At the age of 21, Hale was hanged by the British while in the service of the Continental Army. In this lesson, you will read the story of Hale and many others who made independence possible for the United States of America.

Focus Activity

READ TO LEARN
How did the leadership of George Washington help the Continental Army?

VOCABULARY
mercenary
Loyalist
Patriot

PEOPLE
Nathan Hale
Martha Washington
John Burgoyne
Thaddeus Kosciuszko
Marquis de Lafayette
Friedrich von Steuben
Benedict Arnold

PLACES
Mount Vernon
Trenton
Saratoga
Valley Forge

THE BIG PICTURE

The dying words of Nathan Hale proved his loyalty to the new United States of America. At the time things had not been going well for George Washington and the Continental Army. The British had hired German mercenaries to fight the Americans. A mercenary is a soldier paid to fight for another country. In August 1776 these mercenaries, called Hessians after their home in the German state of Hesse, helped the British capture Long Island near New York City.

The British continued to gain territory in New York. In December Washington and his last 3,000 men retreated to Pennsylvania. "I think the game is pretty near up," the tired commander wrote.

Only a few thousand poorly equipped soldiers stood between the British and the home of the Continental Congress in Philadelphia. How would the Americans keep the British from crushing their revolution, once and for all?

THE CONTINENTAL ARMY

The winter of 1776 was a sad time for the soldiers of the Continental Army. The winter winds chilled them to the bone. Some fought in their own clothes because uniforms were in short supply. Food and ammunition were running low. Most soldiers joined the army for only a certain amount of time and looked forward to leaving as soon as that time was over. As Thomas Paine wrote:

These are the times that try men's souls. The summer soldier and the sunshine patriot will, in this crisis, shrink from the service of their country; but he that stands it now, deserves the love and thanks of man and woman.

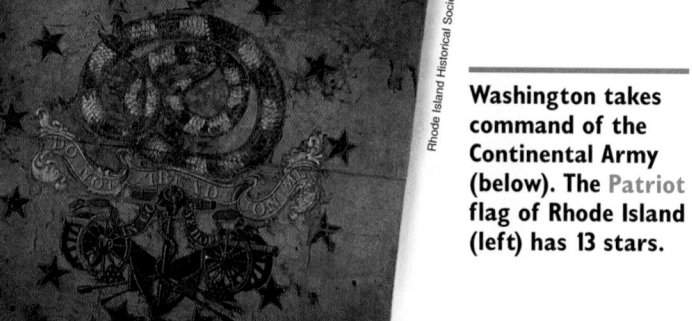

Washington takes command of the Continental Army (below). The Patriot flag of Rhode Island (left) has 13 stars.

Redcoats and Continentals

In contrast the British soldiers in their fine red uniforms were well trained and well supplied. Britain had the strongest navy in the world and the money to hire mercenaries. The Americans, however, had some strengths. They were defending their homes, and unlike the British, they knew the land well.

Another advantage the Americans had was that it was slow and very costly for Britain to ship troops and supplies across the Atlantic Ocean. As the war dragged on, many British people began to wonder whether the war was worth it.

Patriots and Loyalists

Not all Americans supported the American Revolution. About one out of three of the colonists were Loyalists.

Loyalists were people who remained loyal to Britain.

Another third supported the fight for independence. These Americans were known as Patriots. The remaining one-third of Americans did not take sides. This group included many Quakers, who oppose all wars.

GEORGE WASHINGTON TAKES COMMAND

The Patriots had strong leadership. George Washington had been commander of the Virginia militia during the French and Indian War. Now he faced a much greater responsibility. Who was this man who led an untrained army against a major world power?

The Life of a Leader

George Washington was born in 1732 in Virginia. Washington was good in mathematics, but he never went to college.

In 1752 the young Washington joined the Virginia militia. He became angry when he learned that colonial soldiers were paid less than British soldiers. Then, during the French and Indian War, the British lowered Colonel Washington's rank because they did not want colonists to rise above captain. Washington left the militia in protest. He later returned when the governor of Virginia restored his original rank.

In 1758, while still in the military, Washington was elected to the Virginia House of Burgesses. There he met Thomas Jefferson and Patrick Henry, and later joined colonial protests against the British.

In 1759 Washington retired from military life to manage his lands. By then he had become the most famous American in the military. That same year he married a wealthy widow named Martha Custis. George and Martha Washington moved to Mount Vernon, the plantation he owned on the Potomac River in Virginia. Martha Washington also supported the Patriots.

Victory in Trenton

Martha Washington often joined George Washington in the field, where things were going badly for the Continental Army at the end of 1776. Washington was discouraged. He wrote, "Such is my situation that if I were to wish the bitterest curse to an enemy on this side of the grave, I should put him in my [place] with my feelings."

Certain of future victories, General Howe decided to rest for the winter in New York City. Washington knew that

George Washington married Martha Custis in 1759 (left). The young couple went to live on Washington's Virginia plantation, Mount Vernon (below).

the British would not try to advance again until the spring. So he planned a surprise attack on the 1,400 Hessian troops in Trenton, New Jersey. The password Washington gave his soldiers was "Victory or Death!" After nightfall on Christmas Day, 1776, Washington and his troops crossed the Delaware River into New Jersey. The next morning, they surprised the Hessians, who quickly surrendered. "This is a glorious day for our country," said Washington.

African Americans and the War

Among the soldiers that crossed the Delaware with Washington were Prince Whipple and Oliver Cromwell. Whipple was an enslaved worker from New Hampshire. He was freed after the war. Cromwell, who fought with the New Jersey troops, lived to be one hundred

years old—one of the last living Revolutionary soldiers. These men were two of many African American Patriots.

In 1775 Americans had debated whether to allow enslaved men to be soldiers. Many were afraid that enslaved African Americans might rebel if given guns. Washington agreed not to allow any more African Americans to join the army.

In 1776, however, Washington changed his mind. The reason was that British rulers were promising freedom to all enslaved persons in the colonies who fought on the British side.

By 1778 about 750 African Americans, both free and enslaved, were soldiers in 14 divisions of the American army. Agrippa Hull, a free man from Massachusetts, joined the American troops when he was 18 years old. Hull served for six years and fought in some of the most famous battles of the war. James Forten, born free in Philadelphia, was captured at the age of 15 while serving aboard an American ship. British soldiers offered Forten a life of freedom in England. He replied, "No, I'm a prisoner for my country, and I'll never be a traitor to her."

Freedom for Some

Many African Americans served bravely under Washington at a time when thousands of white men chose not to fight. How could the colonies continue to enslave African Americans who were willing to die for the freedom of all Americans? Some states began to answer that question. In 1780 Pennsylvania adopted a plan for abolishing, or ending, slavery. Many northern states soon followed. In other states, such as Virginia, those who fought as Patriots were freed.

TURNING POINTS

In June 1777 a British general named John Burgoyne (bur GOYN) set out to capture the Hudson River valley. This would cut New England and New York off from the rest of the colonies.

The Battle of Saratoga

From Canada, Burgoyne headed south toward Albany, New York. Then Patriots attacked from the woods and forced Burgoyne's men to cut through forests and swamps. It took them all day to travel one mile.

The Americans had time to prepare. Thaddeus Kosciuszko (THA dee us kahs ee US koh), a Polish engineer serving with the Americans, placed cannons on a cliff overlooking the road to Albany. Local farmers with excellent shooting skills poured into the area to help the Patriots. By the time Burgoyne reached Saratoga, New York, the Americans vastly outnumbered the British. Burgoyne surrendered on October 17, 1777. This helped convince France to send soldiers, gunpowder, and ships to America until it won independence.

Marquis de Lafayette

Kosciusko was not the only European who helped the American Patriots. The Marquis de Lafayette (mar KEE de la fay ET) was a wealthy French nobleman. In 1777 Lafayette wrote to John Hancock asking to serve as a volunteer. Hancock made him a major general on George Washington's staff. Lafayette and Washington became like father and son.

The Winter at Valley Forge

While Burgoyne was marching to Saratoga, General Howe captured Philadelphia. The Continental Congress fled to York, Pennsylvania, and Washington set up camp at Valley Forge, near Philadelphia.

Supplies were dangerously low. Many soldiers went home. At least 2,500 died of disease. Martha Washington helped nurse the sick. One out of three soldiers had no shoes at all. Washington noted bitterly that "you might have tracked the army . . . by the blood of their feet" upon the snow.

Friedrich von Steuben (FREED rihk vahn STOO bun), an energetic soldier from the German state of Prussia, helped train the ragged troops. Von Steuben taught them the latest

At Valley Forge (left) Lafayette joins Washington. Von Steuben trains the troops (above right).

European fighting methods. Under his watchful eyes, storekeepers, farmers, and others became a powerful army.

Heroes and Traitors

You read Nathan Hale's words earlier in this lesson. Hale spied for the Patriots. Dressed as a teacher, Hale slipped into British-held New York. In September 1776 the British arrested Hale and hanged him. He met his death with great bravery, and is still considered an American hero.

Benedict Arnold was a Patriot general. In 1778 he married a Loyalist. Soon in debt, Arnold made plans to sell defense secrets to the British. When his plans were found out, Arnold fled and joined the British army. Today, a "Benedict Arnold" has come to mean a traitor to one's country.

WHY IT MATTERS

The Battle of Saratoga was a turning point. It showed Europeans that the Patriots could beat the British. The resulting French support would help America win the war.

✔️ Reviewing Facts and Ideas

MAIN IDEAS

- Britain had a strong navy and excellent troops. The American soldiers had little training, but they were fighting on their home ground.
- The Patriot victory at Saratoga won the Americans European support.
- American troops survived a difficult winter at Valley Forge in 1777 and trained to become a strong army.

THINK ABOUT IT

1. What were the strengths and weaknesses of the British and American forces at the start of the Revolution?

2. How did the Patriots and Loyalists feel about the war for independence?

3. **FOCUS** How did George Washington help the Continental Army?

4. **THINKING SKILL** Based on the events in this lesson, what _predictions_ would you make about the rest of the war? Explain your answer.

5. **GEOGRAPHY** What role did climate play in the American victories?

CITIZENSHIP
VIEWPOINTS

Spirit of '76, the famous painting by Archibald M. Willard, was unveiled at our country's Centennial Exposition in Philadelphia in 1876.

1776: WHAT DID COLONISTS THINK ABOUT SEPARATING FROM GREAT BRITAIN?

By 1776 many Patriots believed independence was the only answer to their conflicts with Great Britain. As Sarah Morris Mifflin expressed in her viewpoint, the Patriots saw only disadvantages in being ruled by Britain.

The Loyalists were against separating from Great Britain. Many of them agreed that the colonists had not always been treated fairly. Still, they believed that strong advantages remained in being connected to Britain. According to William Franklin, they did not feel the colonies' economy and military could stand on their own.

Many African Americans refused to take sides. As the unsigned newspaper letter in the third Viewpoint explained, slavery was an exception to the Patriots' call for liberty. Some African Americans joined the Patriot cause hoping that the Revolution would result in the end of slavery. Others supported the British because of the British promise to free any enslaved African Americans who joined their side. Many wondered if either side would end slavery when the war was over.

Read and consider the three viewpoints on the issue of separating from Great Britain. Then answer the questions that follow.

Three DIFFERENT Viewpoints

1 WILLIAM FRANKLIN
Governor of the New Jersey Colony
Excerpt from a letter to the New Jersey Legislature, 1776

Depend upon it, you can never place yourselves in a happier situation than in your dependence on Great Britain. Independence has not even a chance of being gained, without the loss of the lives and properties of many thousands of the honest people of this country—yet *these,* it seems, are as nothing in the eyes of the patriots! But remember, Gentlemen, that I now tell you, that should they by chance achieve their purpose, yet their government will not be lasting.

" . . . their government will not be lasting."

2 SARAH MORRIS MIFFLIN
Wife of General Thomas Mifflin of the Continental Army
Excerpt from a letter to a friend in Boston, 1776

I know this, that as free I can die but once; but as a slave [to British rule] I shall not be worthy of life. I have the pleasure to assure you that these are the [feelings] of my sister Americans. They have sacrificed [gatherings], parties of pleasure . . . and finery, to that great spirit of patriotism which [moves] . . . people throughout this . . . country.

Pennsylvania Historical Society

" . . . that great spirit of patriotism which [moves] . . . people throughout this . . . country."

3 "A SON OF AFRICA"
Excerpt from a letter written by an enslaved or free African American published in *Massachusetts Spy,* February 10, 1774

You are taxed without your consent, (I grant that a grievance,) and have petitioned for relief, and cannot get any. Are not your hearts also hard, when you hold men in slavery who are entitled to liberty by the law of nature, equal as yourselves? When the eyes of your understanding are opened, then will you see clearly between your case and Great Britain, and that of the Africans. If so, is it lawful for one nation to enslave another?

" . . . is it lawful for one nation to enslave another?"

BUILDING CITIZENSHIP

1. What was the viewpoint of each person? How did each support his or her view?

2. In what ways were some of the viewpoints alike? In what ways were they different?

3. What other viewpoints might people have on this issue? What are some ways in which the issue of colonies separating from their ruling country might be discussed today?

SHARING VIEWPOINTS

Suppose you were a colonist during the American Revolution. Why might you have expected the speakers to have the viewpoints they did? As a class discuss which viewpoints you would have agreed or disagreed with. Are there any statements you could make about the separation from Great Britain with which all speakers could agree?

INDEPENDENCE AT LAST

READ ALOUD

The minutemen had left Groton, Massachusetts, for the battlefield. Yet the town was still protected. "Armed with muskets, pitchforks, and such other weapons as they could find," Prudence Wright, Sarah Shattuck, and some 30 other women guarded the town bridge.

Focus Activity

READ TO LEARN
Who helped the Patriots win the Revolution?

VOCABULARY
Treaty of Paris

PEOPLE
George Rogers Clark
John Paul Jones
Haym Salomon
Deborah Sampson
Mary Ludwig Hays
Francis Marion
Nathanael Greene
Charles Cornwallis
Bernardo de Gálvez
James Armistead
Joseph Brant

PLACES
Fort Vincennes
Yorktown

THE BIG PICTURE

You have read about the hardships endured by the Continental Army and about such leaders as Thomas Jefferson and George Washington. Yet the war could not have been won without the help of ordinary citizens like the women of Groton, Massachusetts.

Farmers, craftworkers, and merchants left their families to join the army. Women like Abigail Adams kept the farms and businesses running in addition to raising their families. She wrote to her husband that she was "sometimes thrown into an agony of distress" trying to get everything done.

Some colonists joined the army as cooks and servants. Others raised money, sewed clothes for the soldiers, and nursed the wounded. It was this quiet work that often made the difference between victory and defeat in the Revolution.

Both the Americans and the British had expected the struggle for independence to end quickly. Instead it was eight years before a peace treaty would be signed. In this lesson you will read about some of the men and women who helped bring the war to a victorious end.

PATRIOTS IN THE WEST AND ON THE SEAS

In the early days of the American Revolution, much of the fighting took place in the Northeast. However, brave Patriots in the Middle West and on the high seas also fought the British.

Patriots Fight in the West

George Rogers Clark was living in Kentucky when the Revolution began. In 1778 he set out to drive the British out of the Ohio River valley, which was then called "the West."

One of the forts Clark captured, Fort Vincennes (vihn SENZ), was soon retaken by the British. Clark refused to give up. He knew that the British would not expect an attack in the winter. So in February 1779, Clark's men marched to the fort again, wading waist-deep through icy, flooded swampland. At night the soldiers slept in mud, covering themselves with wet blankets. "Our suffering is too terrible for any person to believe," Clark said.

By having his men yell and scream as they attacked the fort, Clark tricked the British into believing that he had a large army. The British quickly surrendered. As Clark wrote, "great things" have been done "by a few men." Americans now controlled the Ohio River valley. Clark became known as the "Washington of the West."

Patriots Fight on the Seas

Like the Continental Army, the American navy was also poorly equipped in comparison to the British. However, an American sea captain, John Paul Jones, proved that a strong fighting spirit can make a difference. Some historians have called Jones our country's first naval hero.

In the battle between the *Bonhomme Richard* and the *Serapis*, the United States defeated the great British navy.

In September 1779 Captain Jones's ship, the *Bonhomme Richard*, faced the British warship *Serapis*. Jones's ship had originally been French and he had given it a French name that honored Benjamin Franklin, the author of *Poor Richard's Almanack*. The British pounded the *Bonhomme Richard* with cannon fire, leaving it in ruins. When the British captain asked Jones if he was ready to surrender, Jones yelled back, "I have not yet begun to fight."

After three hours of close fighting, it was the *Serapis* that surrendered. One of Jones's men called the battle "the most bloody, the hardest fought . . . between two ships of war of any nation under heaven."

Patriot women who fought the British included Mary Ludwig Hays (left), Nancy Hart (top), and Deborah Sampson (above), who is disguised as a man.

PATRIOTS IN THE COLONIES

Patriots like George Rogers Clark and John Paul Jones led the Americans to victories over the British. Other men and women also played important roles in the fight for independence. The businessman Haym Salomon (HI am SAL uh mun) spied for the Patriots when the British captured New York City. A Jew who had fled Poland when it was invaded by Russia, he believed strongly in the cause of independence and freedom. Salomon gave so much money to the Patriots that when he died in 1785, he was penniless.

Women and War

Women served the American cause both on and off the battlefield. Some women disguised themselves as men and fought as soldiers. One of these women, Deborah Sampson, won the admiration of her fellow soldiers when she fought in battle. When Sampson was wounded, the doctor revealed her secret to her commanding officers. Sampson received an honorable discharge. Historians are not sure how many women served as disguised soldiers. Some others include Mary Ritchie, Eliza Veach, and Sally St. Clair.

About 20,000 women traveled with the soldiers to cook, clean, wash clothes, and nurse the ill. These women were not paid. Some of them helped on the battlefield when the fighting became fierce. Mary Ludwig Hays went to war along with her husband. She was called

"Molly Pitcher" because she brought pitchers of water to soldiers in battle. Hays also loaded cannons and even took up her husband's gun when he was wounded.

At home, women had to hold their families and farms together even as British soldiers moved in. Some women formed groups to raise money and make clothing and bandages for the Patriot troops. Sarah Franklin Bache, Ben Franklin's daughter, helped organize these activities.

Patriots Fight in the South

The British headed south after the Patriot victories in Saratoga and Vincennes kept them from advancing in the North and the West. In South Carolina, however, the British were stopped by Captain Francis Marion.

Marion's small band of soldiers made lightning-quick attacks on the British before fading back into the Carolina swamps. Because of this, Marion became known as the "Swamp Fox." Years later the poet William Cullen Bryant wrote:

Our band is few, but true and tried,
Our leader frank and bold;
The British soldier trembles
When Marion's name is told.

Marion's men also fought in North Carolina under General Nathanael Greene. Greene's approach was simple: "We fight, we get beat, rise, and fight again." By the spring of 1781, British commander Charles Cornwallis declared he was "quite tired of marching about the country" chasing Greene. Instead, Cornwallis decided to head north to Virginia. You can see some of the major battles fought in the South in the Infographic on page 368.

The Spanish Help the Patriots

A year after France joined the war, Spain followed suit. Many Spanish soldiers, like Jorge Ferragut (HOR hay FAIR uh gut), fought with the Patriots. Women in Cuba sold their jewelry to raise money for the American cause.

In 1777 Bernardo de Gálvez (bair NAHR doh de GAHL vez) became Governor of Spanish Louisiana. He opened up the port of New Orleans to American ships and ended British trade with Louisiana. Gálvez also sent money and supplies to George Rogers Clark. As a commander of Spain's troops in America, Gálvez won control of several key cities along the Gulf Coast including Pensacola, Florida.

Valentine Museum, Richmond

James Armistead spied for the Patriots and was one of many enslaved African Americans who aided the Revolution.

Infographic

Battles of the American Revolution

The map on this page shows the major battles of the American Revolution. The Revolution began in the New England Colonies. As the map shows, the fighting shifted south during the long war. It moved first to the Middle Colonies and then to the Southern Colonies. The time line can help you follow the sequence of the major battles and events of the Revolution.

MAINE (part of Mass.)

Fort Ticonderoga 1775

NEW HAMPSHIRE

Saratoga 1777

Bennington 1777

Bunker Hill 1775

Oriskany 1777

Concord and Lexington 1775

BOSTON

MASSACHUSETTS

NEW YORK

CONNECTICUT

RHODE ISLAND

PENNSYLVANIA

Hudson R.

Delaware R.

NEW YORK CITY

Long Island 1776

Princeton 1777

Monmouth Courthouse 1778

Germantown 1777

VALLEY FORGE

Trenton 1776

Brandywine 1777

PHILADELPHIA

MARYLAND

NEW JERSEY

DELAWARE

Cahokia 1778

Vincennes 1779

Kaskaskia 1778

VIRGINIA

James River

WILLIAMSBURG

Yorktown 1781

ATLANTIC OCEAN

Guilford Court House 1781

NORTH CAROLINA

Kings Mountain 1780

Cowpens 1781

Camden 1780

Savannah River

SOUTH CAROLINA

Eutaw Springs 1781

Charles Town 1780

GEORGIA

Savannah 1778

Legend

American Victory	★
British Victory	✸
13 English Colonies	☐
British	☐
Spanish	☐
Proclamation Line of 1763	- - -

Time Line

1775 1776 1777 1778 1779 1780

1775

April Battles of Lexington and Concord

May Battle of Fort Ticonderoga

June Battle of Bunker Hill

1776

March British leave Boston

August British invade Long Island

December Battle of Trenton

1777

June–October Battle of Saratoga

December 1777– March 1778 Winter spent at Valley Forge

1778

December British troops move south to Georgia

1779

February Final battle of Fort Vincennes

September Battle of *Serapis* v. *Bonhomme Richard*

The three-cornered hat worn by American soldiers during the Revolution came to be seen by Europeans as a symbol of liberty.

The first United States military medal was created by George Washington. Known as the Purple Heart, it is still given to soldiers who are wounded in battle.

1781

October
Battle of Yorktown

1783

November
Treaty of Paris

BATTLES IN THE SOUTHERN COLONIES

As the Infographic on these pages shows, the fighting of the Revolution moved to the South. Before heading north to Virginia, General Cornwallis had taken his forces to the Carolinas where he won a series of battles. Cornwallis counted on support from the southern Loyalists. But although some Loyalists joined British troops, they were a small part of the British force.

The vast majority of southerners supported the Patriots. They fed and clothed the American troops that marched through the countryside. Still, from 1778 to 1781, the outnumbered and poorly equipped Patriots were defeated at Savannah, Charles Town, Eutaw Springs, and Camden. At Kings Mountain, North Carolina, in October 1780 the Patriots achieved one of their few victories in the South.

The Battle of Guilford Court House

As you have read, the British Army marched its men shoulder to shoulder toward the enemy's fire, which made the soldiers easy targets. Cornwallis continued to use this traditional European style of fighting despite warnings from his men.

In March 1781 at Guilford Court House, North Carolina, the strategy proved costly once again. Cornwallis lost one-fourth of his men during the fierce battle. The British were able to claim victory only because the Patriot forces led by Nathanael Greene had retreated.

"Another such victory," one British officer said, "would destroy the British army." Although Cornwallis won most of the battles in the South, he left the Carolinas with his forces greatly weakened and in need of supplies.

THE END OF THE WAR

When Nathanael Greene forced the British to retreat north, General Cornwallis went as far as Yorktown, Virginia. This was to be his last stand.

Victory at Yorktown

When General Cornwallis asked his servant James Armistead to spy *on* the Americans, he did not realize that Armistead was already spying *for* them. Armistead alerted Lafayette to Cornwallis's plans. He also gave Cornwallis false information about the Americans.

Washington could thus trick Cornwallis into thinking he was going to attack New York. Instead, more than 17,000 American and French soldiers surrounded Yorktown. French warships blocked the harbor and prevented the British from retreating. The map on page 373 shows the positions of the troops. Realizing that he was outgunned and outnumbered, Cornwallis surrendered on October 19, 1781. The Battle of Yorktown was the last major battle of the Revolution.

After the Battle of Yorktown, a disappointed King George III wanted to continue the fight. The British House of Commons, however, was tired of the war. It wanted to make peace.

In the Treaty of Paris of 1783, Britain finally recognized the independence of the United States. The land west of the Appalachian Mountains that had been won by George Rogers Clark became part of the United States. Florida, which had come under British control, was returned to Spain, an ally of the Patriots.

This painting by artist John Trumbull shows the British surrendering to the Americans at Yorktown in 1781.

Yale University Art Gallery

The Iroquois Confederacy

At the end of the war, many Loyalists left the United States for good. Joining them were Britain's allies among the Iroquois Confederacy.

During the Revolution, both the Americans and the British tried to win the support of Native Americans. In the Iroquois Confederacy, the Tuscarora and Oneida chose not to take sides. The Mohawk, Cayuga, Seneca, and Onondaga fought with the British. Their leader, Joseph Brant, had hoped that the British would protect Iroquois lands from settlement by the colonists. When the British lost the war, many Iroquois moved north to Canada.

WHY IT MATTERS

The United States was now independent. Some years later, John Adams was asked about the meaning of the American Revolution. He replied that there had been two revolutions. One was the war itself. The other "was in the minds and hearts of the people."

Indeed, by the end of the war many Americans like John Adams wanted more than independence. They wanted the chance to form a new kind of government. In the next chapter, you will read about how this was done.

How did the colonists celebrate their victory?

After the Battle of Yorktown, bells all across the country rang out to announce the victory. Everywhere Washington went, crowds lined the roads to see him. "With a heart full of love and gratitude, I now take my leave of you," Washington told his troops at a farewell dinner in Fraunces Tavern in New York City. Tears were streaming down his cheeks as he hugged each soldier and said goodbye. One soldier wrote, "such a scene of sorrow and weeping I have never before seen."

Reviewing Facts and Ideas

MAIN IDEAS

- In 1779 George Rogers Clark won control of the Ohio River valley. Later that year John Paul Jones won a victory over the mighty British navy.

- Americans supported the Patriots by running farms and businesses, serving as spies and nurses, and raising money for the cause.

- Francis Marion, Nathanael Greene, and Bernardo de Gálvez helped stop the British advance in the South.

- The Battle of Yorktown in 1781 was the last major battle of the war. The Treaty of Paris of 1783 recognized American independence.

THINK ABOUT IT

1. How did the capture of Fort Vincennes help the Americans?

2. How did colonists who stayed home support the Patriot cause?

3. **FOCUS** Name some of the people who helped win the Revolution and list their contributions.

4. **THINKING SKILL** What were the goals of France and Spain in _deciding_ to help the Patriots?

5. **GEOGRAPHY** Look at the map of the Battle of Yorktown on page 373. Why was it a good location for the Patriots and their allies to trap Cornwallis?

GEOGRAPHYSKILLS

Comparing Maps of Different Scales

VOCABULARY

map scale
large-scale map

small-scale map

WHY THE SKILL MATTERS

As you have read, the battles of the American Revolution were fought in different parts of the United States. A map such as the one on page 368 can give you a great deal of information about the major battles of the Revolution. By looking at that map you can find out in which state a particular battle was fought.

Most of the time you only need one map to give you all the information you need about

a topic. Yet sometimes you may want to find more detailed information. The map of major battles, for example, does not give you information about the route George Washington took to reach Trenton. If you were writing a report on the Battle of Trenton, you would need a map that showed a smaller area—Trenton—in greater detail.

USING THE SKILL

No map can be as large as the part of Earth it shows. So all maps are drawn to scale. A map scale uses a small unit of measure, such as an inch, to represent a real distance on Earth. Each map has its own scale depending on the size of the area and the amount of information that needs to be shown. A large-scale map, like the one you would need to show the Battle of Trenton, shows a smaller area in greater detail. A small-scale map, like the map of major

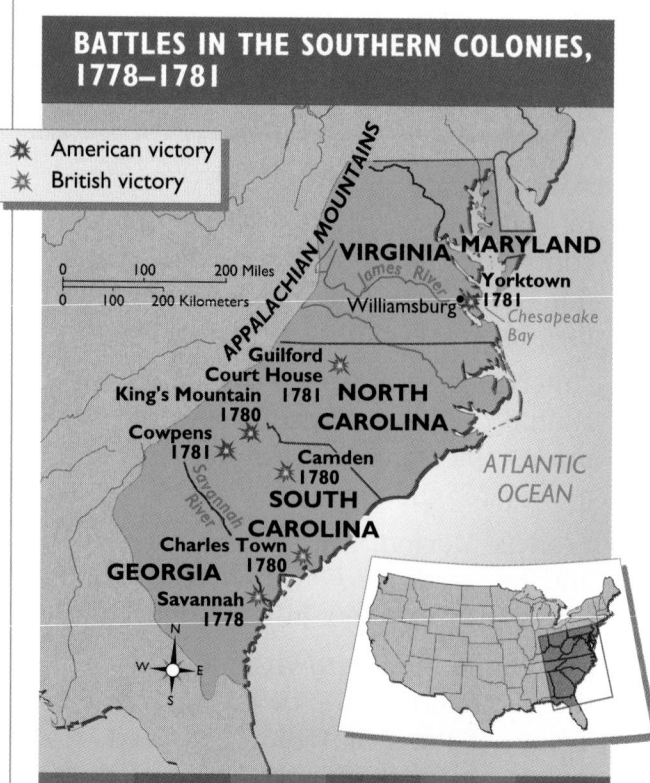

BATTLES IN THE SOUTHERN COLONIES, 1778–1781

American victory
British victory

battles, shows a large area without much detail.

Look at the map of the Southern Colonies on page 372. Note the scale. It shows the entire South and the major battles that were fought there during the American Revolution. In order for you to locate each of the battles, the map has to show almost the entire geographical area of the Revolution-era South. On this map, 1 inch stands for about 200 miles. Using the map scale, you can determine the distance Cornwallis had to cover between the Battle of Charles Town and the Battle of Camden that followed it.

Now find the location of the Battle of Yorktown on the same map. Can you see the exact route American forces took to

Yorktown? No, because this is a small-scale map. It is not detailed enough to give you this information. You would need a large-scale map that focuses on the area around Yorktown to show the Americans' exact route. A large-scale map helps make some information easier to read and interpret.

TRYING THE SKILL

Look at the map of the Battle of Yorktown on this page and find the map scale. Now, look again at the map of the Southern Colonies on page 372. How many miles does 1 inch represent on the map of the Battle of Yorktown? Which map scale is larger? How can you tell?

As you can see from the Helping Yourself box on this page, different map scales give you different types of information. First you have to determine which map scale would best give you the information you are looking for. Which map would you use if you want to find out the distance between Yorktown and Savannah? The areas in the Southern Colonies that the British controlled? The positions of the troops around Yorktown? Why?

REVIEWING THE SKILL

1. What is a map scale? How is it used?

2. When would it be better to use a small-scale map? A large-scale map?

3. What information can you find on the Southern Colonies map that you cannot find on the Yorktown map?

4. Which map would help you understand the plan of the Americans at the Battle of Yorktown? How do you know?

5. When might you need to compare maps of different scales in your own life?

BATTLE OF YORKTOWN, 1781

York River · Williamsburg · Jamestown · Yorktown · Chesapeake Bay · CAPE CHARLES · James River · Norfolk · Portsmouth · ATLANTIC OCEAN

British forces
American forces
French forces
British fleet
French fleet
• City

0   5   10 Miles
0   5   10 Kilometers

CHAPTER 13 REVIEW

Major Events

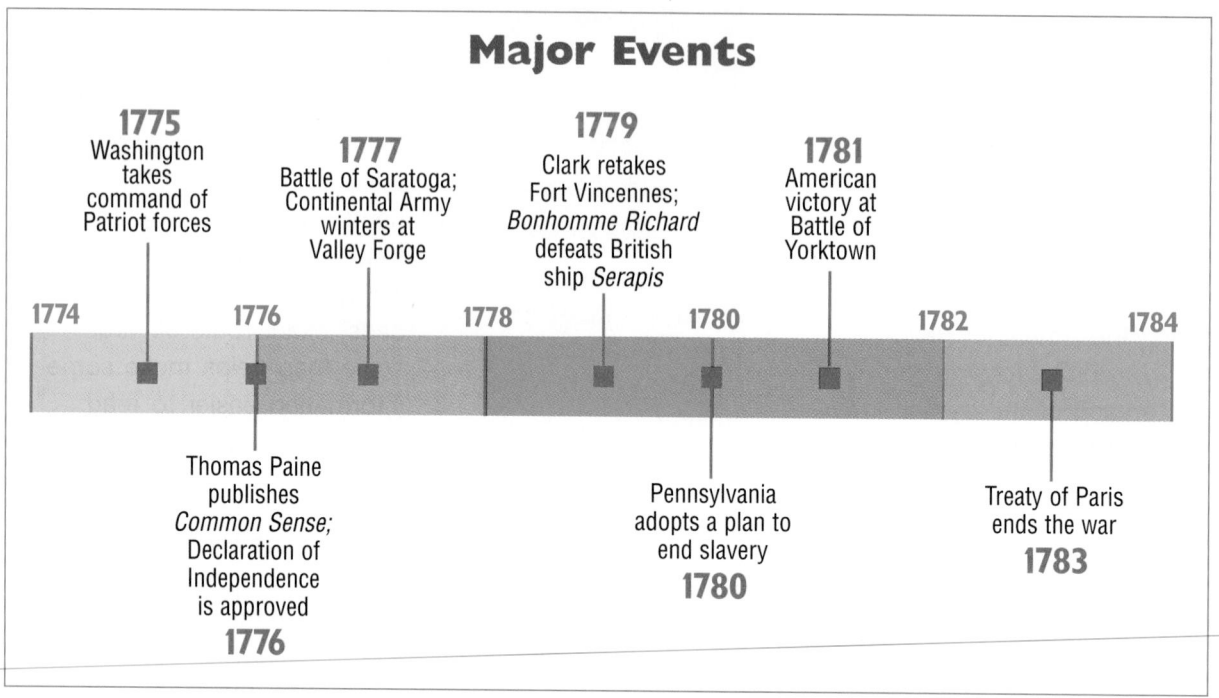

1775 Washington takes command of Patriot forces

1777 Battle of Saratoga; Continental Army winters at Valley Forge

1779 Clark retakes Fort Vincennes; *Bonhomme Richard* defeats British ship *Serapis*

1781 American victory at Battle of Yorktown

1774 1776 1778 1780 1782 1784

Thomas Paine publishes *Common Sense;* Declaration of Independence is approved **1776**

Pennsylvania adopts a plan to end slavery **1780**

Treaty of Paris ends the war **1783**

THINKING ABOUT VOCABULARY

Number a sheet of paper from 1 to 10. Beside each number write the word or term from the list below that best completes the sentence.

Continental Army

Declaration of Independence

large-scale map

Loyalist

map scale

mercenary

Patriot

Second Continental Congress

traitor

Treaty of Paris

1. Colonists cheered the delegates of the _____ when they met in May 1775.

2. A _____ was someone who supported the fight for independence.

3. A _____ is a soldier paid to fight for another country.

4. If your map shows great detail of a small area, it is a _____.

5. Thomas Jefferson wrote the _____ in Philadelphia in 1776.

6. Britain agreed to the colonies' independence in the _____ in 1783.

7. You must look at the _____ to calculate real distances on a map.

8. John Adams named George Washington as commander in chief of the _____.

9. King George III thought that anyone who supported the colonies' independence was a _____.

10. One out of three colonists was a _____, and supported Britain.

THINKING ABOUT FACTS

1. Why was *Common Sense* important to the cause of independence?

2. Why did the issue of slavery come up during the American Revolution?

3. What advantages did the Patriots have in the war?

4. How did Bernardo de Gálvez help the Patriot cause?

5. Look at the time line above. Compare and contrast the events that occurred in 1777.

THINK AND WRITE

WRITING A DIALOGUE

Write a dialogue in which a Loyalist and a Patriot discuss their opinions about the American Revolution.

WRITING A DIARY ENTRY

Suppose that you are a female camp follower during the Revolutionary War. Give a date and location, tell what happened during the day, and record your impressions.

WRITING A NEWSPAPER ARTICLE

Write an article in which you describe one of the battles you have read about in this chapter. Include dates, events, and people who played a key role in the battle. Write a headline for your article.

APPLYING GEOGRAPHY SKILLS

COMPARING MAPS AT DIFFERENT SCALES

Answer the questions below to practice the skill of comparing maps at different scales.

1. What is a map scale?
2. What is the difference between large-scale and small-scale maps?
3. How do you decide whether to use a large-scale map or a small-scale map?
4. Look at the map of the Southern Colonies on page 372. What is the distance between Yorktown and Savannah, Georgia?
5. What kind of information could you see on a large-scale map of Savannah that is not on this map?

Summing Up the Chapter

Copy the main idea map on a separate sheet of paper. Then review the chapter to complete the map. After you have finished, choose two of the events shown on the map and answer the question, "How are these events related?" For example, how did the approval of the Declaration of Independence lead to the debate over slavery?

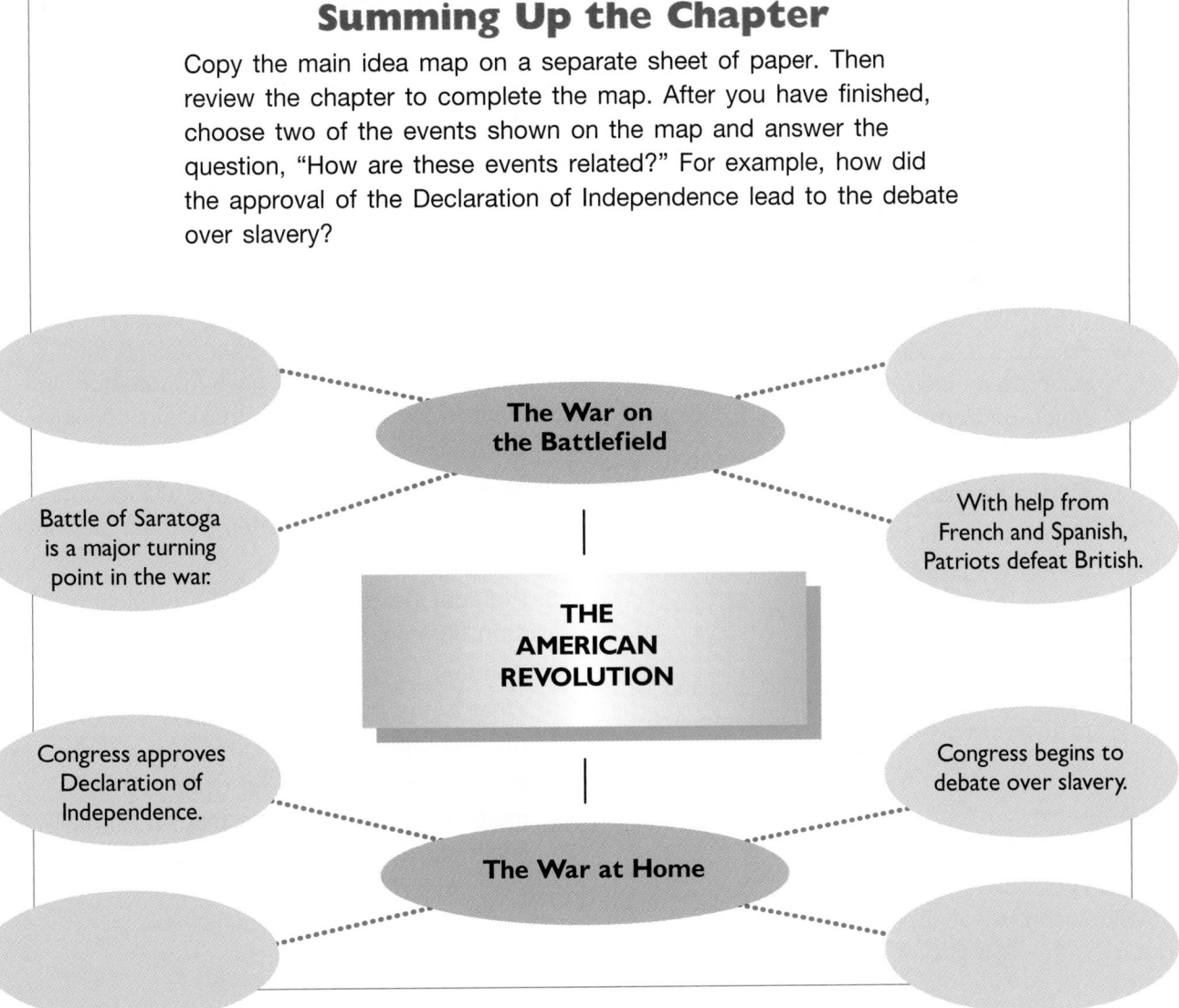

The War on the Battlefield

Battle of Saratoga is a major turning point in the war.

With help from French and Spanish, Patriots defeat British.

THE AMERICAN REVOLUTION

Congress approves Declaration of Independence.

Congress begins to debate over slavery.

The War at Home

UNIT 5 REVIEW

THINKING ABOUT VOCABULARY

Number a sheet of paper from 1 to 10. Beside each number write the word or term from the list below that best completes the sentence.

Boston Tea Party   map scale
coureur de bois   petition
First Continental Congress   repeal
French and Indian War   town meeting
liberty   Townshend Acts

1. The _____ was fought between the British and French in 1754.

2. In New France, many trappers worked as _____ or "woods runners."

3. The _____ was the earliest form of self-government in the colonies.

4. The _____ said the colonists had to pay taxes on tea, paper, glass, lead, and paint.

5. Delegates from many colonies met at the _____ in 1774 and agreed to stop trade with Britain.

6. A _____ uses a unit of measure, such as an inch, to represent a real distance on Earth.

7. A _____ is a written request signed by many people.

8. Rebel colonists protested the tax on tea during the _____.

9. _____ is another word for freedom.

10. The colonists demanded that England _____ or cancel, the Stamp Act.

THINK AND WRITE

WRITING A DIALOGUE

Suppose that in the early 1700s there was a meeting between a French trader from New France and a Spanish missionary from the Southwest. Write a dialogue in which the two men give their impressions about America and its peoples.

WRITING A LETTER

Suppose that you are an African American patriot who decides to fight with George Washington's troops. Write a letter to your parents in which you explain your reasons for joining the American Revolution.

WRITING ABOUT PERSPECTIVES

Although the colonists named them the Intolerable Acts, these laws had different names in the British Parliament. Suppose that you are a British government official. Write a speech to your fellow citizens explaining why it is necessary to pass these tax laws.

BUILDING SKILLS

1. **Making Conclusions** After looking for what the related facts have in common, what is the final step in making a conclusion?

2. **Making Conclusions** Why is using facts to make conclusions often the final step in solving a problem?

3. **Political Cartoons** How is a political cartoon different from other cartoons?

4. **Political Cartoons** What is dialogue? What is the purpose of dialogue in some political cartoons?

5. **Map Scales** Which kind of map shows more detail, a large-scale map or a small-scale map?

376

YESTERDAY, TODAY &

TOMORROW

The Declaration of Independence expressed the idea that "all men are created equal." Today, the Declaration is still a model for countries from all parts of the world who seek their own freedom. Why do you think the idea of equality is so important? Do you think it will continue to be important in the future?

READING ON YOUR OWN

Here are some books you might find at the library to help you learn more.

PHOEBE THE SPY
by Judith Berry Griffin
Based on a true story, this book tells the tale of a young African American girl who uncovers a plot against George Washington.

IF YOU WERE THERE IN 1776
by Barbara Brenner
This book is full of information about daily life at the time of the Revolution.

THE FIGHTING GROUND
by Avi
In this story a 13-year-old boy who joins the Revolution finds out what war is like.

UNIT REVIEW PROJECT

Organize a Living Time Line

1. Have each group member choose an event from this unit to research, such as the Boston Tea Party or the Treaty of Paris.
2. List several facts about each event.
3. Write the name and date of your event on a large piece of oak tag. Decorate it with glitter, colorful markers, and colored tissue paper.
4. On another piece of oak tag, write several facts about your event. Make a border for your facts with ribbon and paint.
5. Tie together the left sides of the oak tag with a piece of string. Then tie together the right sides.
6. Place the pieces of oak tag over your head so that you are wearing one piece in front of you and one piece behind you.
7. Participate in a living time line with your group.

377

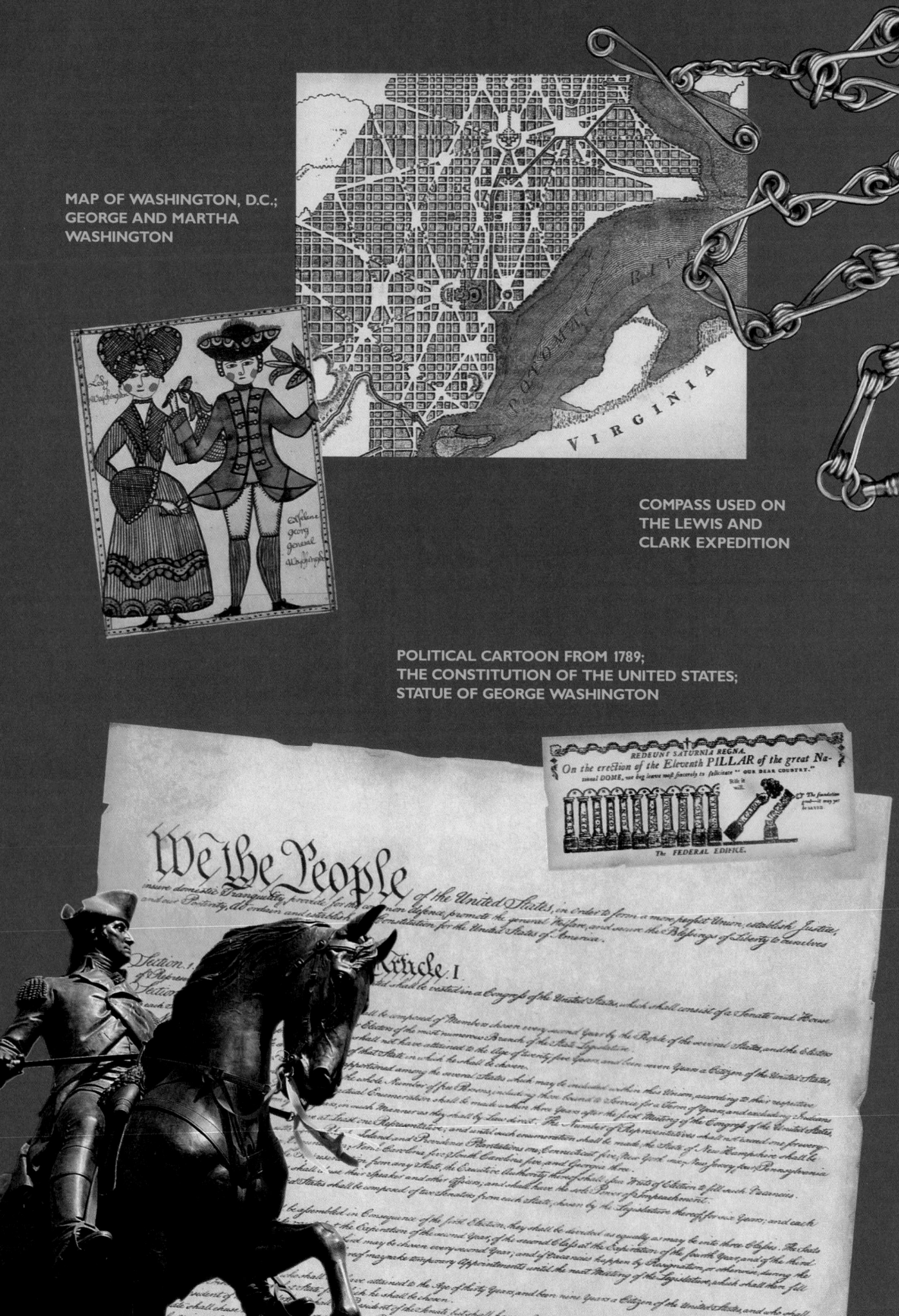

MAP OF WASHINGTON, D.C.;
GEORGE AND MARTHA
WASHINGTON

COMPASS USED ON
THE LEWIS AND
CLARK EXPEDITION

POLITICAL CARTOON FROM 1789;
THE CONSTITUTION OF THE UNITED STATES;
STATUE OF GEORGE WASHINGTON

Building the United States

"We the People of the United States . . ."

from the Preamble to the Constitution
of the United States.
See page 397.

WHY DOES IT MATTER?

After winning the Revolutionary War, the colonies became the United States. The new states needed a new government—one that stood not only for independence, but also for unity. Delegates from the states worked together to create a document that would describe how the new nation would be governed. It was no easy task, but in 1787 the delegates signed the Constitution of the United States. In 1781 the Bill of Rights was added. These two documents set down the responsibilities of the government and the rights of the people. A new government began working to build a young but growing United States.

THOMAS JEFFERSON

SILVER INKSTAND AND QUILL
SET USED BY DELEGATES TO
SIGN THE CONSTITUTION

Adventures with NATIONAL GEOGRAPHIC

We the People of the...

Upper–class woman   Quaker merchant   Shopkeeper   German housewife   Journeyman printer

Philadelphia— 1787

Y ou have just arrived by coach in the bustling city of Philadelphia in the summer of 1787. Here, within the chambers of the Pennsylvania State House (now called Independence Hall), a group of delegates labor over an historic document, the Constitution of the United States. Outside on the broad brick streets, somber Quakers jostle with elegantly dessed French visitors and frontier scouts in buckskin. Past white-spired Christ Church, you wander into one of the city's many bookshops. At the riverfront, dockworkers unload China silk and French soaps from newly arrived sailing ships. There are not enough hours in the day to take in all the city has to offer.

GEOJOURNAL

List some reasons why Philadelphia was one of the new nation's major cities in the late 1700s.

CHAPTER 14

The Constitution of the United States

THINKING ABOUT HISTORY AND GEOGRAPHY

As you can see on the time line, Chapter 14 tells the story of settlers from the eastern United States moving west. It also describes the establishment of the United States government. The Articles of Confederation set up our first central government but did not succeed in uniting the country. In 1787 the Constitution presented a new system of government. Later, the Bill of Rights was added to the Constitution.

PACIFIC OCEAN

1780s
CINCINNATI

Colonists begin moving west into the Northwest Territory

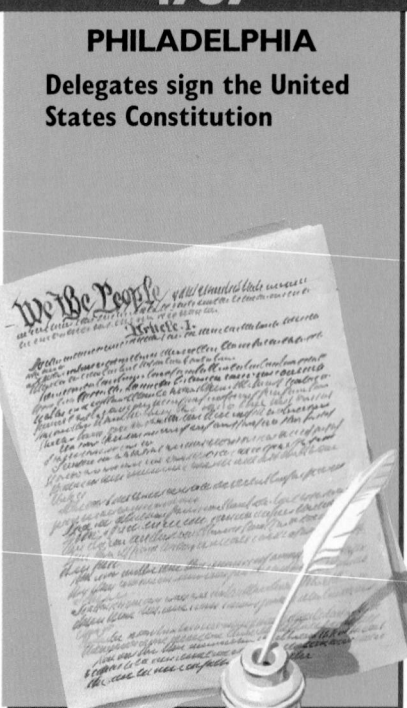

1787
PHILADELPHIA

Delegates sign the United States Constitution

1787
PHILADELPHIA

Richard Allen begins movement for equal rights by African Americans

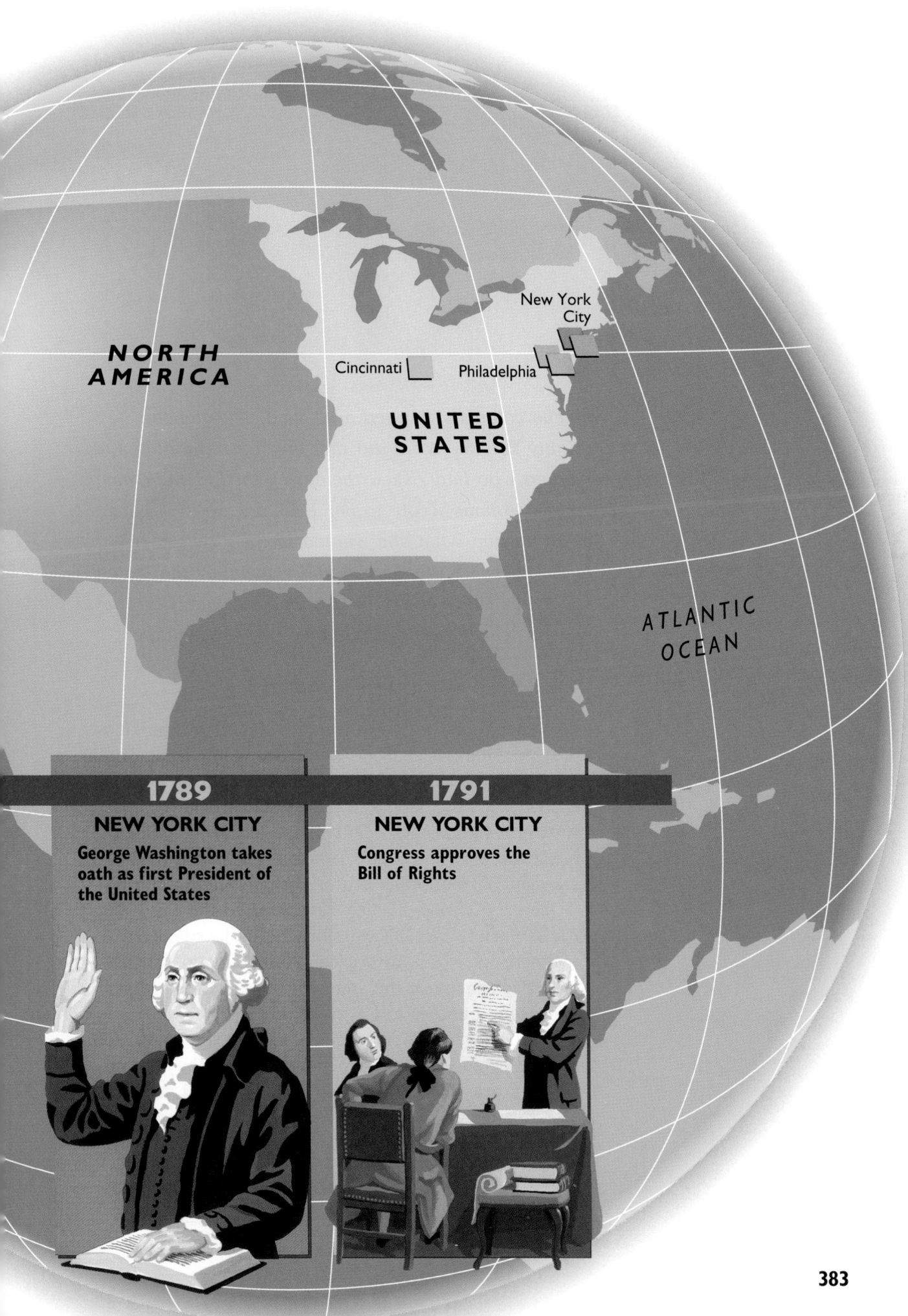

NORTH
AMERICA

Cincinnati

New York
City

Philadelphia

UNITED
STATES

ATLANTIC
OCEAN

1789

NEW YORK CITY

**George Washington takes
oath as first President of
the United States**

1791

NEW YORK CITY

**Congress approves the
Bill of Rights**

THE ARTICLES OF CONFEDERATION

Focus Activity

READ TO LEARN

What kind of government did the Articles of Confederation create?

VOCABULARY

Articles of Confederation
Shays's Rebellion
Northwest Ordinance
territory
statehood

PEOPLE

Richard Allen
Daniel Shays

PLACES

Northwest Territory
Indiana
Ohio
Wisconsin
Michigan
Illinois
Minnesota

READ ALOUD

The colonists' ragged army had defeated the mighty British. What did that mean for the men and women who had risked their lives for independence? Abigail Adams wrote to her husband, John Adams, and told him what she wanted in the new government. "I desire that you would remember the ladies," she said. "We will not hold ourselves bound to obey laws in which we have no voice or representation."

THE BIG PICTURE

Abigail Adams was not the only American thinking about the changes that independence from Great Britain might bring. Encouraged by their victory over a great European power, people in the 13 states believed that anything was possible. Many of the enslaved African Americans who had fought against the British in the American Revolution asked for their freedom—and got it. Richard Allen, a former slave, started the Free African Society in 1787, possibly the first organized movement for rights by African Americans in North America. In many of the states of the North, slavery began to be outlawed.

Everyone was thinking about change. The states, too, began to explore their independence. First they set up their own governments. By 1777, 10 of the 13 states had adopted constitutions. Soon, however, there were conflicts between the states. In 1783 George Washington wrote, "It is yet to be decided whether the Revolution [was] a blessing or a curse." The states were independent, but they were not fully united.

THE FIRST CENTRAL GOVERNMENT

The Second Continental Congress adopted the Articles of Confederation in 1781. The Articles set up our country's first central government. British rule made many Americans distrust strong central power. The Articles of Confederation gave most powers to state governments.

A Weak Government

Under the Articles of Confederation, each state made its own laws. States collected their own taxes and printed their own money, which was not always accepted in another state.

Women could not vote or be elected to public office. They were excluded from all state constitutions except New Jersey's, where they could vote after 1783.

Most people thought of themselves only as citizens of the state in which they lived and not as citizens of the United States. The Congress could do little to settle conflicts between the states or to enforce the laws it passed.

Congress did not even have money to pay soldiers who had fought in the Revolution. Many farmers were owed money by Congress. This caused serious problems in Massachusetts. It charged heavy taxes on land. Its courts began jailing farmers and taking their land when they could not pay the taxes.

In 1786 a Massachusetts farmer named Daniel Shays organized farmers to protest against the courts. Over 1,000 farmers battled against the local militia. Eight men were killed before the uprising, called Shays's Rebellion, was stopped.

Shays's Rebellion led Patrick Henry to conclude, "Our body politic is dangerously sick." Things would never improve, said George Washington, under the "half-starved, limping government" of the Articles of Confederation.

Shays's Rebellion (left) showed that the central government was weak. Neither paper money from Massachusetts nor coins from New Jersey (below) could buy goods in other states.

THE NORTHWEST ORDINANCE

In spite of its weaknesses, Congress passed some important laws under the Articles of Confederation. The Northwest Ordinance, passed in 1787, provided a way for new territories to become states. A territory is an area of land belonging to a government.

The Northwest Territory

After the American Revolution the United States claimed all land from the Atlantic Ocean to the Mississippi River. This land had been inhabited for generations by Native Americans. It included an area called the Northwest Territory.

Use the map on this page to locate this area. The Northwest Territory was the home of the Cherokee, Delaware, Miami, and other tribes. Their lands became the future states of Indiana, Ohio, Wisconsin, Michigan, Illinois, and parts of Minnesota.

Before Congress passed the Northwest Ordinance, the states quarreled over control of the Northwest Territory. The ordinance divided this huge territory into smaller territories. The people who lived in a territory could apply for statehood, or to be a state, when the territory had 60,000 people. The Northwest Ordinance did not allow an existing state to claim any part of the new territories.

The Nation Grows

Under the British, the Northwest Territory had been set aside for Native Americans. Now, with the promise of land, thousands of United States citizens began crossing over treaty boundaries onto Native American lands. Many arrived in covered wagons with all their belongings. They were not supposed to bring enslaved Africans along because the Northwest Ordinance outlawed slavery.

To control settlement of the Northwest Territory, Congress divided the land into townships of 6 square miles each. Each township then became a self-governing part of the territory.

THE NORTHWEST TERRITORY, 1787

CANADA (GREAT BRITAIN)

United States
Northwest Territory
Present-day state boundary

Lake Superior

N W E S

Mississippi River

WISCONSIN

MICHIGAN

Lake Michigan

Lake Huron

Lake Ontario

NEW YORK

Lake Erie

LOUISIANA (SPAIN)

ILLINOIS

INDIANA

OHIO

PENNSYLVANIA

MD

0   150   300 Miles
0   150   300 Kilometers

Ohio River

VIRGINIA

(Claimed by VA)

(Claimed by NC)

NORTH CAROLINA

(Claimed by GA)

SOUTH CAROLINA

GEORGIA

MAP WORK

Ohio was the first territory to join the United States under the Northwest Ordinance.

1. Which territories do you think would become states after Ohio?

2. What effects do you think settlement of the Northwest Territory had on Virginia and Pennsylvania?

E PLURIBUS UNUM

This is a later version of the Great Seal of the United States.

The Northwest Ordinance gave new settlers in the territories the same rights citizens had in the 13 states. It outlawed slavery and the hiring of indentured servants, and required that each township set aside land for public schools. Members of Congress believed that if people were going to govern themselves, they had to be educated.

WHY IT MATTERS

One important legacy of the Articles of Confederation was the Northwest Ordinance. It would serve as a model for creating new territories from Native American lands for more than 100 years. Although slavery was as strong as ever in the South, the ordinance outlawed it in the Northwest Territory. However, the weaknesses of the Articles of Confederation created problems for the new country. Many Americans concluded that the United States needed a stronger central government.

How was the Great Seal of the United States chosen?

In the 1700s most countries had a seal that they used to stamp official documents. When our country won its independence, our leaders decided to create a Great Seal to represent the new country. Benjamin Franklin suggested a picture of a wild turkey on the seal. It was not a bad choice—turkeys are one of the few large birds that are native to North America. However, in 1782 Franklin, Thomas Jefferson, and John Adams settled on a seal that showed an eagle with a ribbon in its mouth. On the ribbon is the Latin phrase e *pluribus unum*. This motto, as you read in Chapter 1, means "Out of many, one."

✓✓ Reviewing Facts and Ideas

MAIN IDEAS
- The Articles of Confederation, adopted in 1781, set up the first central government for the 13 states.
- The weaknesses of the central government under the Articles of Confederation made it hard to settle conflicts between the states.
- The Northwest Ordinance was passed under the Articles of Confederation in 1787. It provided a way for territories to become states and outlawed slavery.
- The Articles of Confederation and the Northwest Ordinance both provided models for the rights and treatment of citizens.

THINK ABOUT IT
1. Why did the Articles of Confederation give most powers to the states?
2. Under the Northwest Ordinance, when could a territory get statehood? How did this affect Native Americans?
3. **FOCUS** How did the Articles of Confederation treat the role of a central government?
4. **THINKING SKILL** Was Patrick Henry stating a *fact* or an *opinion* when he said that the government was "dangerously sick"?
5. **GEOGRAPHY** Which rivers form the western and southern borders of the Northwest Territory?

1775　　　1780　　　1786 1787　1790　　　1795

THE CONSTITUTIONAL CONVENTION

Focus Activity

READ TO LEARN
What was the result of the Great Compromise?

VOCABULARY
Constitutional Convention
Virginia Plan
legislative branch
executive branch
judicial branch
Supreme Court
New Jersey Plan
Great Compromise
House of Representatives
Senate

PEOPLE
Alexander Hamilton
James Madison
George Mason
Roger Sherman

READ ALOUD

In 1786 George Washington opened a letter from Congress asking him to attend a meeting. It said, "Commissioners to meet at Philadelphia on the second Monday in May next, to take into consideration the situation of the United States." Four years before, Washington had said he had "retired forever" from public life. Yet his country needed him again.

THE BIG PICTURE

In September 1786 the lawyers Alexander Hamilton from New York and James Madison from Virginia attended a meeting held in Annapolis, Maryland. The purpose of the meeting was to discuss trade problems between the states. The longer the meeting went on, the more everyone agreed that a second meeting was needed.

The delegates asked Hamilton to write a letter inviting delegates from all 13 states to this second meeting, supported by Congress. As you read in the Read Aloud above, George Washington was invited to this meeting, which became known as the Constitutional Convention.

Hamilton had to be careful about what he said in the letter. The government under the Articles of Confederation was not working. Still many leaders were not ready to get rid of the Articles. So the letter talked about changing the Articles of Confederation. What actually happened, as you will see, was very different.

THE DELEGATES MEET

In May 1787 the delegates began arriving in Philadelphia for the meeting. Newspapers called it "The Grand Convention." Fifty-five delegates came. They represented the "wisdom of the continent," wrote one newspaper.

The Constitutional Convention

The meeting could not begin until delegates from at least seven states arrived. The meeting finally began, almost two weeks late, on May 25, 1787, in the Philadelphia State House.

The delegates included Hamilton and Madison. At age 81, Benjamin Franklin of Pennsylvania was the oldest delegate. Other delegates included George Mason, who had helped to write Virginia's constitution, and Gouverneur Morris, who was from New York.

Absent from the convention were Thomas Jefferson and John Adams, who were serving as ambassadors abroad. An ambassador is an official representative sent to another country. Patrick Henry refused to attend the convention, believing the delegates would try to take power away from the states.

The delegates had many things in common. All 55 were white men who owned property. More than half of them were lawyers. Most had fought beside Washington in the Continental Army. Many had also helped write the constitutions of their own states.

The delegates elected Washington president of the convention. He insisted that what went on in the meeting be kept secret. So the windows were nailed shut and the doors closed, even in the terrible summer heat.

Washington Addressing the Constitutional Convention, by Junius B. Stearns, includes portraits of 1. Gouverneur Morris, 2. Benjamin Franklin, 3. James Madison, 4. John Rutledge, 5. Alexander Hamilton, and 6. George Washington.

MADISON AT THE CONVENTION

James Madison was only 36 years old when he came to the convention, but he would play a major part in this important event. He arrived 11 days early. This was not surprising to those who knew him. Madison liked to be prepared. Long before the meeting, he had asked his friend Thomas Jefferson for books about the governments of other countries. Jefferson sent back trunkloads of books from his library in Paris, France.

Madison spent all of his daylight hours reading what he called his "literary cargo." Delegate William Pierce of Georgia wrote that Madison was "the best informed man on any point in a debate."

Today we know a great deal about what happened at the Constitutional Convention because of the notes kept by James Madison. He chose a seat in front so he could hear and write down everything that was said. "I was not absent a single day," wrote Madison, "nor more than a fraction of an hour in any day."

The Virginia Plan

Madison left nothing to chance. He arrived at the meeting with a plan of government already written. He made sure his plan was discussed first. Presented by Virginia's popular governor, Edmund Randolph, it came to be called the Virginia Plan. The plan would establish a republic. A republic is a nation in which the government is managed by people who were elected by citizens. One part of the plan said "that a national government ought to be established." Madison fought for a strong central government.

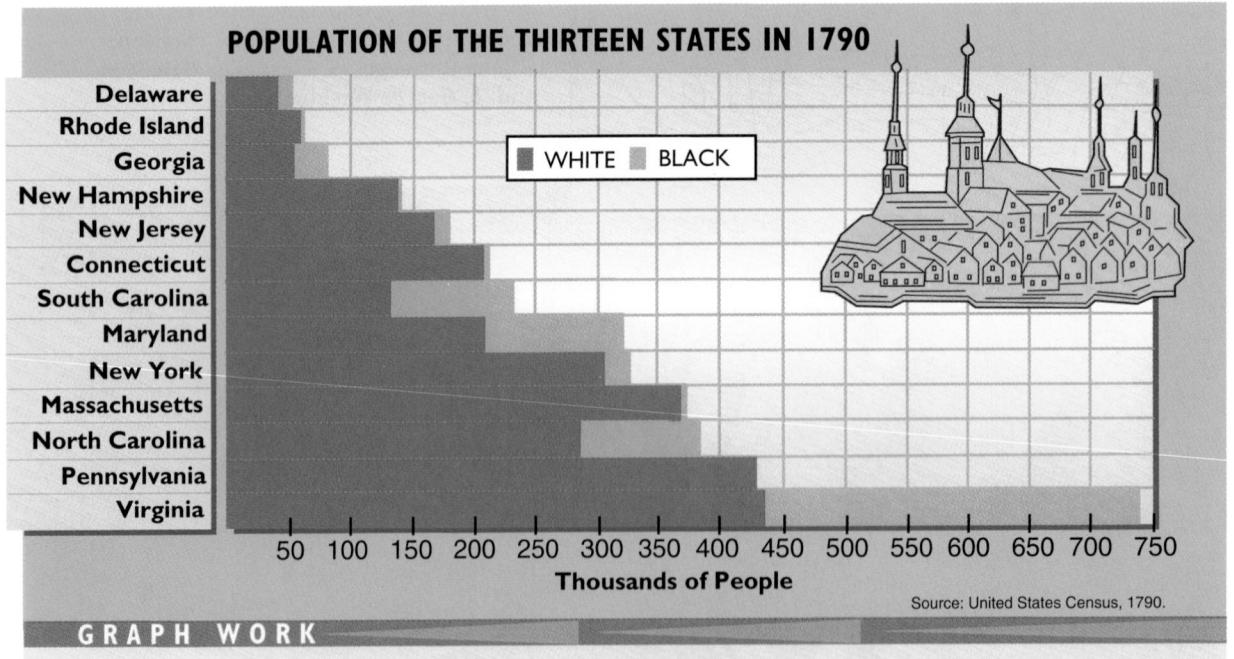

POPULATION OF THE THIRTEEN STATES IN 1790

WHITE   BLACK

Delaware
Rhode Island
Georgia
New Hampshire
New Jersey
Connecticut
South Carolina
Maryland
New York
Massachusetts
North Carolina
Pennsylvania
Virginia

50 100 150 200 250 300 350 400 450 500 550 600 650 700 750
Thousands of People

Source: United States Census, 1790.

GRAPH WORK

The year 1790 was the date of our country's first census.

1. In which states were black and white populations almost the same?

2. Which states had populations between 300,000 and 450,000?

3. Why do you think Virginia had the largest population?

This portrait of James Madison, made when he was 23 or 24 years of age, is set in a brooch now kept in the Library of Congress in Washington, D.C.

The Library of Congress

The Virginia Plan said that the central government should have three branches, or parts. A legislative (LEJ ihs lay tihv) branch, or law-making body, called the Congress, would make laws for the country and raise money for the central government. The executive (eg ZEK yuh tihv) branch would be headed by the person who had been elected President of the United States. The role of the President would be to carry out the laws made by Congress. The third branch of government was a judicial (joo DIHSH ul) branch that would decide the meaning of laws. It would be headed by a body of judges called the Supreme Court. Most states had already adopted this three-part model of government. It was based on the system of government that was followed by Great Britian.

On May 30 the delegates voted to accept part of the Virginia Plan. This decision was important to Madison because it meant that many delegates were not trying to change the Articles of Confederation. Instead, they wanted to form a new central government. From that point on, the meeting in Philadelphia was a Constitutional Convention. James Madison later became known as the Father of the Constitution.

The New Jersey Plan

Two weeks later, delegates from large states and small states were locked in a heated debate. The Virginia Plan called for one house of Congress that would be based on population. The large states liked this plan, because it would give them more representatives than the smaller states. The small states did not like this plan. If they had fewer representatives than the large states, they would have less power and little influence in the Congress.

Under the Articles, all of the states had equal power. The small states wanted to keep it that way. They presented the New Jersey Plan, which gave all states the same number of representatives. As the graph on page 390 shows, Virginia, with a population of more than 700,000, would have the same number of representatives as the state of Delaware, which had a population of about 59,000.

This picture of the signing of the Constitution was painted by Howard Chandler Christy in 1940. It hangs in the Capitol Building in Washington, D.C.

MANY COMPROMISES

The debate between large states and small states threatened to end the convention. So the delegates decided to work out a compromise. Each side gave up something it wanted to reach an agreement. It took the delegates two months to find a solution.

The Great Compromise

Roger Sherman from Connecticut proposed what became known as the Great Compromise. The new Congress would have two separate houses. In the House of Representatives, the number of each state's representatives would be based on population, which favored the large states. In the Senate, each state would have two representatives, which favored the small states.

Other Compromises

Some delegates did not want the people to vote directly for the President. They were afraid that people could easily be fooled into voting for an unacceptable candidate. Finally, the delegates decided that the people would vote for members of an Electoral College, who would then vote for a President. However, as in most European countries at that time, only white men who owned property would be able to vote in the United States. That left out all women, Native Americans, and enslaved people.

Slavery and the Constitution

Should enslaved people be counted in a state's population? Many northern states had few slaves. They felt slavery was wrong and wanted to end it. Most southern states, which had many slaves on their farms and plantations, wanted slavery to continue. They felt it was necessary to their society.

Finally, a compromise was reached. Every five slaves, or people "bound to service," would be counted as three. The delegates agreed to end slave trading with other countries in 1808.

Many delegates were unhappy with this compromise. Without it, however the Southern states might have left the convention.

On September 17, 1787, the delegates finally signed the Constitution of the United States. Before the Constitution was approved, the states would debate yet another compromise, one that added protection for individual rights.

WHY IT MATTERS

When Ben Franklin came out of the convention hall for the last time, Eliza Powel stopped him. Although as a woman she could not vote or be elected to office, she asked him what kind of government the country would have. "A republic, if you can keep it," he told her.

Franklin, Madison, and the other delegates had created a complex written plan of government. You can read the Constitution on pages R26–R49 in the back of this book.

Writing the Constitution involved many compromises. The hard job of keeping the republic alive continues today.

Eliza Powel (above right) was among those who greeted the convention delegates. The delegates used this silver inkstand and quill set (below) to sign the Constitution.

✓ Reviewing Facts and Ideas

MAIN IDEAS

- Delegates gathered in Philadelphia in May 1787 for the Constitutional Convention.
- The Constitution set up a central government with legislative, executive, and judicial branches.
- The delegates signed the Constitution of the United States of America on September 17, 1787.

THINK ABOUT IT

1. How did James Madison prepare for the Constitutional Convention?

2. What did the delegates to the Constitutional Convention have in common?

3. **FOCUS** On what issues did the delegates compromise to get the Constitution signed?

4. **THINKING SKILL** *Compare* the Virginia Plan with the New Jersey Plan. Who favored each plan? Why?

5. **WRITE** Write an outline for a film about the Constitutional Convention. Focus on the Great Compromise debate.

393

THINKINGSKILLS

The Granger Collection

Recognizing Point of View

The Granger Collection

Delegates William Paterson (left) and James Wilson (above) debated how many representatives the states should have.

VOCABULARY

point of view

WHY THE SKILL MATTERS

In the last lesson you read about the Constitutional Convention. The delegates from each state had disagreed about how representatives should be chosen for the United States Congress. They had different points of view. A point of view is the position from which a person looks at something.

The delegates' opinions were shaped by the positions or points of view from which they viewed certain issues. Delegates from small states were concerned about protecting their states from large states. From their point of view, it was important for small states to have representation equal to the states with large populations. Delegates from

large states were concerned about losing their power. From their point of view, it was important for representation in Congress to be based on population.

Recognizing a person's point of view is a useful skill. It will help you determine the accuracy of what he or she is writing about.

USING THE SKILL

Read the following statement by William Paterson. He presented the New Jersey Plan to the Constitutional Convention.

There is no more reason that a large state should have more votes than a small one, than that a rich individual citizen should have more votes than a [poor] one. . . . Give the large states an influence in proportion to their [size], and what will be the consequence? Their ambition will be . . .

increased, and the small states will have everything to fear.

Paterson's statement reflects the point of view of the small states. There are several ways you can tell what a person's point of view is. First, identify that person's position. Paterson was against basing a state's representation on population.

Next, think about the information a person gives. Identify which statements are facts and which are opinions. Paterson used the word *should*, which is a clue that he was expressing an opinion. He was giving his view of what was the "right" thing to do. He also used the words *rich* and *poor* when he compared the number of votes a citizen should have. These words let you know that Paterson is using an example to describe less wealthy people as small states.

TRYING THE SKILL

Now try identifying the point of view of another delegate from the Constitutional Convention. James Wilson of Pennsylvania said:

> *As all authority is derived from the people, equal numbers of people ought to have an equal number of representatives, and different numbers of people different numbers of representatives.*

In other words, representation should be based on population, which would give large states more votes than small states.

HELPING Yourself

- **A point of view is the position from which a person looks at something.**

- **To recognize a point of view, identify statements of fact and opinion.**

- **Next, identify words or phrases that tell how the person feels about the subject.**

What position did Wilson support in his statement? Is Wilson expressing a fact or an opinion? How do you know? What words or phrases tell you about Wilson's point of view? Why did Wilson have the point of view he had on this topic?

REVIEWING THE SKILL

1. What is a person's point of view?

2. What kinds of clues tell you about a person's point of view?

3. Why is it important to be able to recognize a person's point of view?

4. Georgia, then a small southern state, depended on the large southern states for trade. It voted with the large states. What shaped Georgia's point of view? Why do you think it voted with the large states?

5. Historians often present different versions of the same event. How can knowing their points of view help you to understand their accounts of what happened in the past?

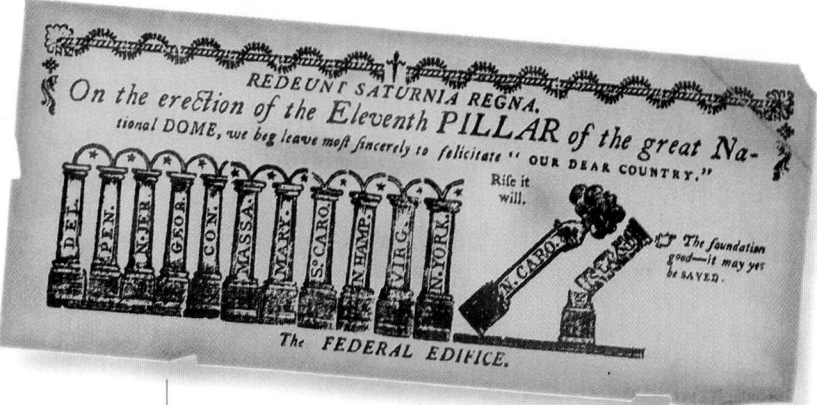

This political cartoon shows that North Carolina and Rhode Island had not yet adopted the Constitution.

HOW THE CONSTITUTION WORKS

Focus Activity

READ TO LEARN
What kind of government did the United States Constitution create?

VOCABULARY
amendment
Preamble
federal system
checks and balances
veto

READ ALOUD

Tears streamed down Benjamin Franklin's face as he signed the Constitution. He looked once again at the carving of the sun on the back of George Washington's chair. "I have often looked at that sun behind the president of the convention without being able to tell whether it was rising or setting," he said, "but now, I have the happiness to know that it is a rising and not a setting sun." The rising sun that Franklin spoke of was the new central government of a very young country, the United States of America.

THE BIG PICTURE

The Constitution of the United States is many things. It is a code of laws and a framework for government. It is also a piece of history—the world's oldest written plan of government still in use. How is it that a document written over 200 years ago remains meaningful today?

The Constitution still works because the people who wrote it made sure that it could change with the needs of a growing country. They provided for amendments, or additions, to the Constitution. They knew that the Constitution needed to be permanent, but at the same time it needed to allow for change. It also had to protect the rights of both individuals and states. In this lesson you will learn why the Constitution has been able to work for more than 200 years.

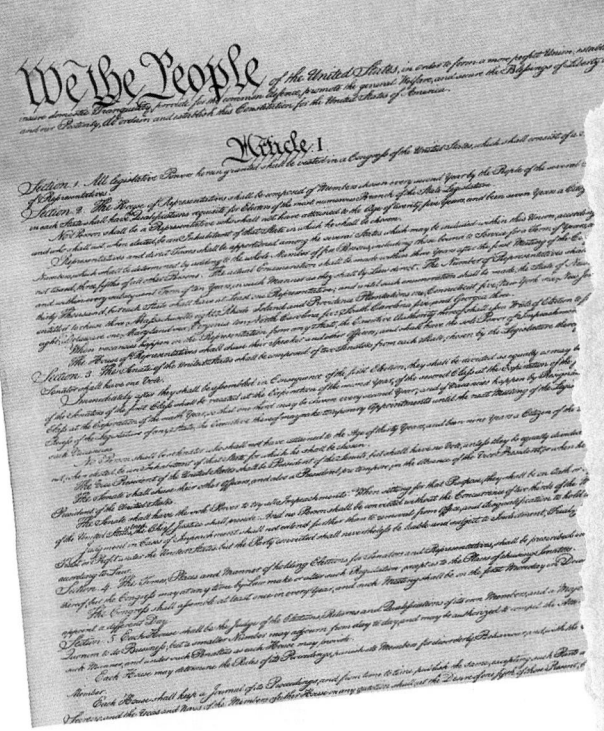

THE UNITED STATES CONSTITUTION

As the delegates wrote the Constitution, they chose every word carefully. Their struggle with Great Britain had made them distrust living under a powerful central government. Yet they agreed that government under the Articles of Confederation had not been strong enough. They worked for a balance. As James Madison wrote, "Every word [of the Constitution] decides a question between power and liberty."

The Preamble

The introduction, or the Preamble (PREE am bul), to the Constitution begins with the words "We the People." The authors of the Constitution wanted to show that the people held the power in this country. The three main branches of government—legislative, executive, and judicial—had to answer to the people and no one else. Read the Preamble to the Constitution on this page. What other goals does the Preamble list?

Preamble to the Constitution of the United States, approved by the states in 1789.

*We the People of the United States, in Order to form a more perfect Union, establish Justice, insure **domestic Tranquility**, provide for the common Defense, promote the general Welfare, and secure the blessings of Liberty to ourselves and our **Posterity**, do **ordain** and establish this Constitution for the United States of America.*

domestic tranquility: peace within the country
posterity: future generations
ordain: make legal

A Federal System of Government

The Constitution set up a federal system of government. In a federal system, the states and the central government share power. Some powers are given only to the states. Others are given only to the central government, which is also known as the federal government. For example, only the federal government has the power to declare war, print or create money, make treaties, run the post office, and settle disputes between states.

The states have power to set up public schools and local governments and run elections. Both state and federal governments have the right to collect taxes and pass laws.

CHECKS AND BALANCES

After years of living under British rule, the authors of the Constitution had seen what happened when one branch of government gained too much power. They did not want any branch of the federal government to become too powerful. So they set up a system of checks and balances. In this system the powers of one branch of government are balanced by the powers of another. Each branch can check, or stop, another branch. If one branch tried to use its powers wrongly, the other two could keep it under control.

The flow chart below shows how this system works. For example, under the Constitution, the President is allowed to order the army into battle. Yet only Congress can declare war. So Congress has a check on the President's powers. Although the Congress may pass any law, the President can veto, or refuse to approve, that law. The Supreme Court can check the powers of both the Congress and the President. It can put

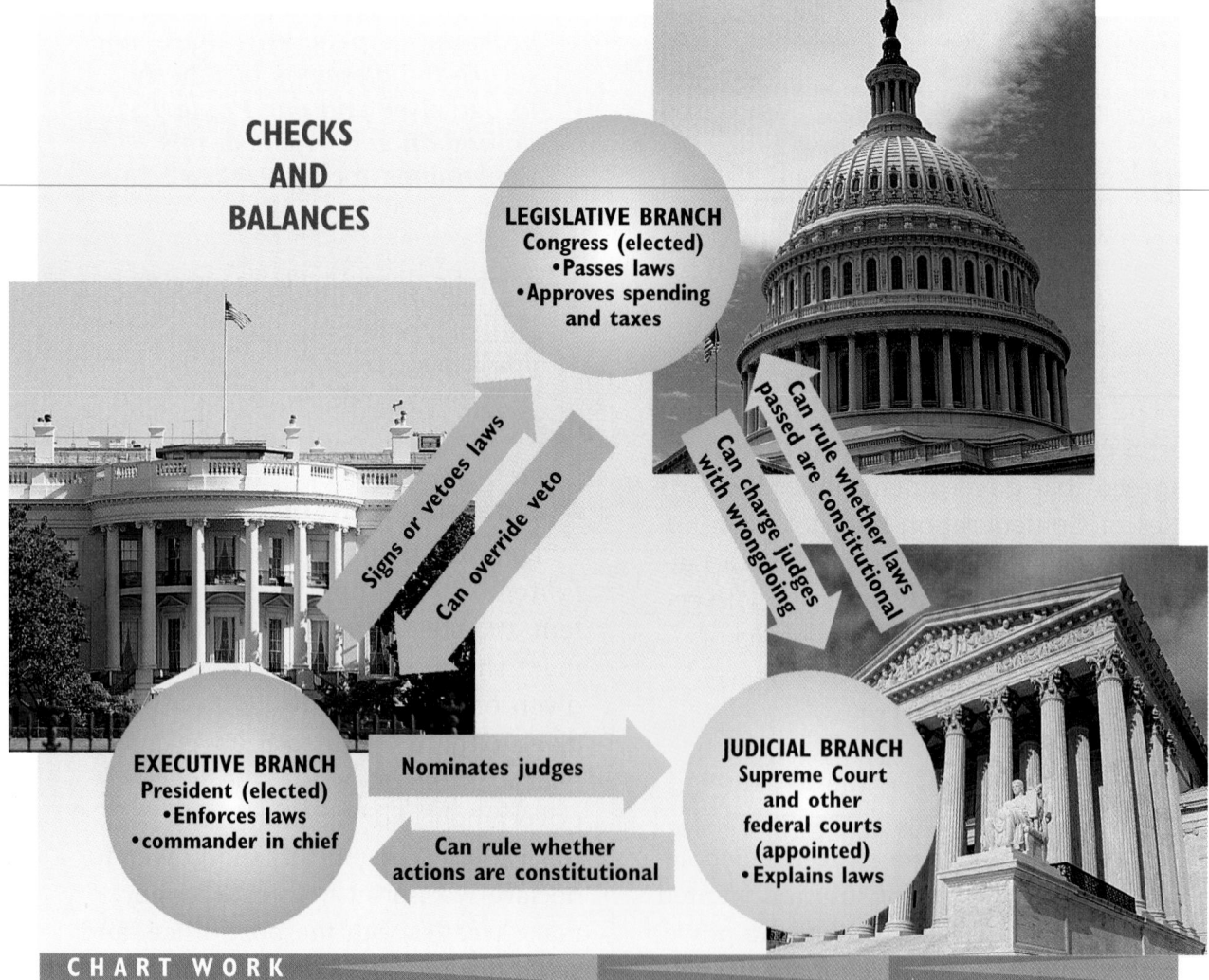

CHECKS AND BALANCES

LEGISLATIVE BRANCH
Congress (elected)
• Passes laws
• Approves spending and taxes

Signs or vetoes laws
Can override veto

Can rule whether laws passed are constitutional

Can charge judges with wrongdoing

EXECUTIVE BRANCH
President (elected)
• Enforces laws
• commander in chief

Nominates judges

Can rule whether actions are constitutional

JUDICIAL BRANCH
Supreme Court and other federal courts (appointed)
• Explains laws

CHART WORK

The delegates also debated how many people should head the executive branch. By compromise, the delegates decided on one President.

1. What are the powers of the executive branch?

2. How can Congress check the powers of the executive branch?

3. How can the judicial branch check the powers of both the executive and legislative branches?

a stop to any law passed by Congress or signed by the President. To do this, the Supreme Court must decide whether such a law is allowed by the Constitution.

Amending the Constitution

The Constitution includes rules for adding amendments. However, the writers of the Constitution did not want people to be able to change it without serious debate. They made changing the Constitution a long, slow process. Before the states can vote on an amendment, it must be approved by two-thirds of both houses of Congress. Or two-thirds of the states can request that Congress call a special convention. Then, three-quarters of all the states must approve the amendment. You will read about the first amendments in the next lesson, and you can read all the amendments on pages R39–R49.

WHY IT MATTERS

The Constitution balances freedom and power by creating a federal system of government. That government unites the states while sharing power with them. The Constitution has been able to work for more than 200 years because of the system of checks and balances and its rules for adding amendments.

✓ Reviewing Facts and Ideas

MAIN IDEAS

- The government set up by the Constitution is a federal system in which the states and the central government share power. The Constitution is the "supreme law of the land," as stated in the Constitution.

- The Constitution may be amended by the people.

- The system of checks and balances prevents any one branch of government from gaining too much power.

THINK ABOUT IT

1. What is a federal system of government?

2. What are some of the powers that the federal government and the states have under the Constitution?

3. **FOCUS** How does the system of checks and balances keep one branch of the government from gaining too much power?

4. **THINKING SKILL** What was Benjamin Franklin's *point of view* on the carving of the sun on Washington's chair? Explain how you identified Franklin's point of view.

5. **WRITE** Write a description of how a law vetoed by the President can still become a law.

Focus Activity

READ TO LEARN
How was the Constitution adopted by the states?

VOCABULARY
ratify
Federalist
Antifederalist
Bill of Rights
secretary
Cabinet
political party

PEOPLE
George Washington

PLACE
New York City

RATIFYING THE CONSTITUTION

READ ALOUD

In 1787 feelings were running high as the states decided whether or not to approve the new Constitution. Some state leaders, like Amos Singletary of Massachusetts, were against it. "If anybody had proposed such a Constitution as this in 1775," said Singletary, "it would have been thrown away at once." Robert Livingston of New York had a different view. "A vote against the Constitution is a vote for mystery and nonsense," Livingston said. "A vote for it is a vote for clarity and sense."

THE BIG PICTURE

In the autumn of 1787, the Constitutional Convention closed its doors. Yet the debate over the Constitution was not over. In fact, it had only started.

The approval of nine states—two-thirds of the 13 states—was needed before the Constitution could go into effect. Each of the states held a convention to decide whether or not to ratify, or officially approve, the Constitution.

The responses of the citizens varied. The idea of a central government troubled some people. Many, like Amos Singletary, worried that the states would lose their rights. Others, like Robert Livingston, felt that the new country's problems could be solved only by a strong central government. The debates over the Constitution had begun.

THE NEW GOVERNMENT

Two days after the Constitutional Convention ended, a Philadelphia newspaper called the *Pennsylvania Packet* published a complete copy of the Constitution. Many other newspapers soon did the same. Within weeks, leaders in the 13 states had taken sides in the debate about the Constitution. They gave speeches, published pamphlets, and wrote newspaper articles supporting their cause.

Federalists and Antifederalists

Supporters of the Constitution were called Federalists because the Constitution called for a federal system of government. Opponents, like Virginia's Patrick Henry, were called Antifederalists. Henry was afraid the states would lose their freedom under the Constitution. "Liberty," Henry said, "give us that precious jewel, and you may take everything else!"

The Federalists included such people as Edmund Pendleton of Virginia, James Madison, and Alexander Hamilton. "There is no quarrel between government and liberty," Pendleton said. Yet Antifederalists, like the Massachusetts writer Mercy Otis Warren, were not convinced. Warren saw efforts to ratify the Constitution as "dark, secret" plots of men who were "growing rich" while "lovers of freedom" suffered.

In a series of 85 articles published in New York newspapers, Madison, Hamilton, and John Jay, a lawyer from New York, built a strong case for the Constitution. These articles became known as *The Federalist Papers.* They argued that a weak government actually threatened people's freedoms. Only the strong government provided by the Constitution could protect the rights of all.

Alexander Hamilton (top) wrote articles in *The Federalist Papers* (center) supporting the Constitution. Patrick Henry (bottom) was a leading Antifederalist.

Shelburne Museum

THE BILL OF RIGHTS

By January 9, 1788, five states—Delaware, Pennsylvania, New Jersey, Georgia, and Connecticut—had already ratified the Constitution. Only four more states were needed to approve it. Then, as the debate heated up, the process slowed down.

"There Is No Declaration of Rights!"

The Antifederalists complained that the Constitution did not contain a bill of rights. A bill of rights is a document that describes the basic rights of the people. It also says that the government cannot take away these rights. Some people called this document a "declaration of rights" because it contained rights that were listed in the Declaration of Independence.

Almost every state constitution included a bill of rights. Many people felt strongly that the United States Constitution should also have one. When it was his turn to sign the United States Constitution, George Mason, who wrote Virginia's bill of rights, refused, saying, "There is no declaration of rights!"

Conflict in Massachusetts

As the delegates gathered in Boston to debate ratifying the Constitution, many in Massachusetts took up Mason's cry. John Hancock, who had become governor of Massachusetts, told the delegates that a bill of rights could be added to the United States Constitution as amendments. This promise persuaded the Massachusetts delegates to ratify the Constitution.

Other states followed Massachusetts. On June 21, 1788, New Hampshire became the ninth state to ratify the document. Now the Constitution was law. By 1790, all 13 states had ratified it. A year later Congress added the ten amendments to the Constitution that are known as the Bill of Rights. You can read the Bill of Rights on pages R39–R41.

Starting at the top of the page with Delaware and ending at the bottom with Connecticut (left), these seals are those of the first five states to ratify the Constitution.

WASHINGTON AS PRESIDENT

Every member of the Electoral College voted for George Washington as President. The Electoral College never again reached a decision so easily.

On April 14, 1789, Washington set out from Mount Vernon for the country's capital, New York City. Parades and cheering crowds greeted him all along the way.

Eight days later, he arrived in New York City. Dressed in a plain brown suit made of American cloth, Washington placed his left hand on an open Bible and took the President's oath of office on April 30, 1789. He swore to "preserve, protect, and defend the Constitution of the United States."

The President's Cabinet

To help the President run the government, Congress set up three government departments. Each was headed by an official called a secretary.

The Secretary of the Treasury, Alexander Hamilton, made decisions about how the federal government spent money. Thomas Jefferson, the Secretary of State, handled the country's dealings with other countries. The Secretary of War, Henry Knox, took charge of the country's defense. The Attorney General made sure that the country's laws were obeyed. Together these officials were called the Cabinet.

Political Parties

Disagreements arose within Washington's Cabinet. Alexander Hamilton believed the country's future lay in trade and industry. He argued for a strong federal government. Thomas Jefferson saw a country of self-sufficient farmers. He argued that the best government was one that governed the least.

Washington (above) arrived in New York City to be sworn in as President at Federal Hall. This statue of Washington (left) is part of a monument in Boston, Massachusetts.

This watercolor shows President Washington and the First Lady, Martha Washington.

These opposing views led to the first political parties. A political party is a group of people who share similar ideas about government. Followers of Hamilton later organized the Federalist Party. Jefferson's followers formed the Democratic-Republican Party.

First in War and Peace

George Washington served two terms, or eight years, as President. In 1797 he retired from office. In his farewell speech, Washington praised the "influence of good laws under a free government." He then returned to Mount Vernon. The country was greatly saddened by Washington's death in 1799. Virginia's United States Representative Henry Lee expressed the feelings of many people in the United States. During a meeting of Congress, he said that Washington was "first in war, first in peace, and first in the hearts of his countrymen."

WHY IT MATTERS

The debate over ratifying the Constitution helped establish the tradition of fighting with words rather than with weapons. Each side presented its views in pamphlets, newspapers, and speeches.

The Constitution has become one of the world's most important documents. The United States was the first nation to have a constitution written by the people. The United States seemed to be a great experiment. Most people now agree the experiment succeeded.

✓ Reviewing Facts and Ideas

MAIN IDEAS

- In 1787 the debate over the Constitution began when the states voted whether or not to ratify it. By 1788, 9 of the 13 states, or two thirds, had ratified the Constitution.

- The Bill of Rights was ratified by the states in 1791.

- George Washington was elected the first President of the United States.

THINK ABOUT IT

1. Describe the Federalists' and the Antifederalists' point of view about ratifying the Constitution.

2. How did the views of Thomas Jefferson and Alexander Hamilton on the future of the United States differ?

3. **FOCUS** What compromise did the Federalists make to get enough states to ratify the Constitution?

4. **THINKING SKILL** Name one _cause_ and one _effect_ of the publication of _The Federalist Papers_.

5. **WRITE** Write a short speech an Antifederalist might have given in support of adding the Bill of Rights.

Getting Out the Vote

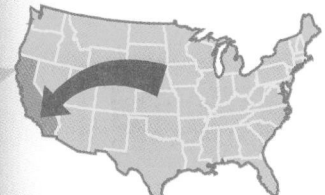

WALNUT, CALIFORNIA— Students in Alan Haskvitz's class at Suzanne Middle School are using their Internet connections to get Californians to the election polls. Though too young to vote, the students know that voting is a constitutional right and part of being a good citizen. They made a year-long study of how to encourage voter participation. "Originally," admits Emily Zeller, "I thought voting wasn't important. Now I realize voting is a major part of what America is."

Students wrote to the United Nations, government officials, college professors, and teachers in Denmark, Singapore, and Australia, where voter turnout is high. They asked for suggestions to get more people to vote, and received almost 100 replies. "We heard from the governors of New Jersey and New Hampshire, Hawaii's secretary of state, members of Congress, and election boards," said Karly Edwards.

From the responses and their research, the class made a list of 12 ideas. The ideas included having two days to vote, moving election day to the weekend, or making it a national holiday. Other suggestions included making the voter registration form easier to understand and allowing people to register or vote by computer, telephone, or mail.

"We put all 12 ideas on the Internet, so that we can share with other people what we have learned," explains Sumudu Dissanayake, who designed the class's Web site. Voter education is vital because, as Emily says, "People don't understand that their one vote can make a difference."

In July 1997, Los Angeles County held a meeting for election officials from the 88 cities in the county. Everyone got a copy of the students' research. "If you try hard enough," Sumudu says, "you can get people excited about voting, so that they see it is not just a duty but a privilege."

" . . . it is not just a duty but a privilege."

Karly A. Edwards

Emily Zeller

Sumudu Dissanayake

CHAPTER 14 REVIEW

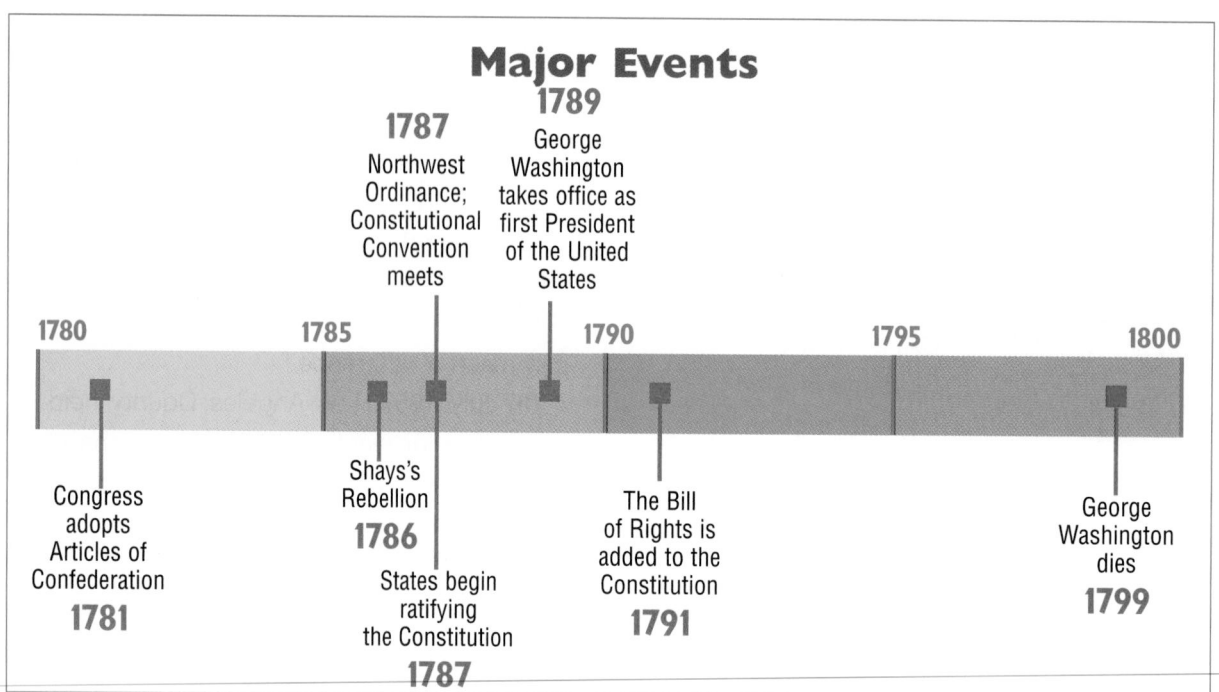

Major Events

1787
Northwest Ordinance; Constitutional Convention meets

1789
George Washington takes office as first President of the United States

1780   1785   1790   1795   1800

Congress adopts Articles of Confederation
1781

Shays's Rebellion
1786

States begin ratifying the Constitution
1787

The Bill of Rights is added to the Constitution
1791

George Washington dies
1799

THINKING ABOUT VOCABULARY

Number a sheet of paper from 1 to 5. Beside each number write the word or term from the list below that matches the description.

judicial branch   territory
Preamble   veto
ratify

1. refuse to approve
2. an area of land that belongs to a government
3. the introduction to the Constitution of the United States
4. the branch of government that decides on the meaning of laws
5. officially approve

THINKING ABOUT FACTS

1. What were the weaknesses of the Articles of Confederation?
2. What was the Northwest Ordinance? What states did it help to create?
3. What was the original purpose of the Constitutional Convention?
4. What three branches of government does the Constitution set up? What does each one do?
5. What was the Great Compromise of the Constitutional Convention? What was decided in the compromise?
6. How did the issue of slavery enter into the Constitutional Convention? What did the delegates vote to do on this issue?
7. What is an amendment? Why is it important that the Constitutional Convention provided for amendments?
8. What is the purpose of the system of checks and balances?
9. What is the Bill of Rights? What role did the Bill of Rights play in convincing the states to ratify the Constitution?
10. Look at the time line above. What events in the chapter could you add to the time period?

THINK AND WRITE ⬿

WRITING A DIALOGUE
Write a dialogue between two members of the Constitutional Convention with opposing views about ratifying the Constitution.

WRITING ABOUT COMPROMISE
Write a paragraph about the compromises made in the Constitutional Convention and why compromise was needed to help the delegates reach an agreement. Then write another paragraph explaining how compromise might be useful in your own life.

WRITING A REPORT
Choose one branch of the United States government, and write a report on it. Describe the responsibilities of this branch. Include, if possible, the names of government officials who now serve in this branch.

APPLYING THINKING SKILLS

RECOGNIZING POINT OF VIEW
To apply the skill of recognizing point of view, answer the questions below.

1. What is point of view?
2. What are some steps you can take to recognize a point of view?
3. Look at page 385. What was Patrick Henry's point of view about the government under the Articles of Confederation?
4. What words did Patrick Henry use that helped you to identify his point of view?
5. Why is recognizing point of view especially important when studying history?

Summing Up the Chapter

Copy the main idea pyramid on a separate sheet of paper. Then review the chapter to complete the pyramid. After you have finished, use the information in the pyramid to write a paragraph explaining, "How did the Articles of Confederation compare with the Constitution?"

The weaknesses of the Articles of Confederation lead to the writing of a new Constitution for the United States.

The Constitution creates a strong central government and protects people's rights.

- Cannot tax people
- Cannot raise army
- No power to carry out or enforce laws

CHAPTER 15

The Young Nation

THINKING ABOUT
HISTORY AND GEOGRAPHY

Chapter 15 describes a time of both growth and change in the United States. In the East the new capital—Washington, D.C.—became a symbol of the growing country. Follow the time line below to learn more about the young country and the people who helped to develop it.

PACIFIC OCEAN

1775
KENTUCKY

Daniel Boone cuts the Wilderness Road from Native American trails

1791
WASHINGTON, D.C.

Benjamin Banneker helps survey and plan the country's new capital

1804
ST. LOUIS

Lewis and Clark begin their exploration of the Louisiana Territory

UNITED STATES

Tippecanoe

St. Louis

Washington, D.C.

Kentucky

ATLANTIC
OCEAN

1811

TIPPECANOE

Tecumseh speaks to Native
American leaders

1814

WASHINGTON, D.C.

Dolley Madison rescues
George Washington's
portrait during the
War of 1812

THE PATHFINDERS

READ ALOUD

"Now, brothers, go home and stay there. Don't come here any more, for this is the Indians' hunting ground, and all the animals, skins, and furs are ours; and if you are so foolish as to venture [come] here again you may be sure the wasps and yellow-jackets will sting you severely." This Shawnee warning was given to Daniel Boone and his companions, who were hunting deer in Kentucky in 1769.

THE BIG PICTURE

After the American Revolution, thousands of people moved to the lands west of the Appalachians. We often call these early settlers pioneers. A pioneer is a person who leads others into areas new to them.

Why did Eastern colonists decide to move west? In 1770 the 13 colonies had a population of a little more than 2 million. By 1790 the number of settlers in the United States had reached nearly 4 million. Most of these people were farmers, but farmland in the original 13 states had become scarce and expensive. Many farmers viewed the fertile valleys just west of the mountains as an unsettled land, full of promise. They wanted to claim the land for themselves. However, the land already belonged to Native American groups such as the Cherokee and the Shawnee, who had lived there for years.

Focus Activity

READ TO LEARN
Why did European settlers begin moving west of the Appalachians?

VOCABULARY
pioneer

PEOPLE
Daniel Boone
John Findley
Abraham Lincoln

PLACES
Kentucky
Cumberland Gap
Boonesborough
Wilderness Road

GEOGRAPHY OF A GROWING NATION

As you can see on the map on this page, the young country in 1800 stretched from the 13 original states along the Atlantic Coast to the Mississippi River. The United States was bordered by British Canada to the north and Spanish Florida and French Louisiana to the south. Louisiana also bordered the nation to the west, across the Mississippi.

Beyond the Appalachians

The Appalachians were rugged and difficult to farm. Beyond the mountains lay the Central Plains, where the rich soil was ideal for farming. The woodlands sheltered deer, bears, buffalo, turkeys, and ducks. South of the Central Plains was the Gulf Coastal Plain. Its dense forests, grassy marshes, and tree-shaded swamps were filled with such wildlife as opossums and muskrats.

Native Americans had long farmed these lands. The Miami had been growing corn in the Ohio River valley for hundreds of years. Along the Gulf Coast the Choctaw lived in villages and on farms. The Cherokee lived along the slopes of the Appalachian Mountains. Many Shawnee lived north of the Ohio River, though their hunting grounds were to the south. These groups fought against whites who tried to move into the dense forests that would one day become the state of Kentucky. Locate the Ohio River on the map below.

People called trailblazers marked paths by notching trees with an ax.

THE UNITED STATES, 1800

Map legend:
- States
- Territories

Map labels: Lake Superior, Lake Michigan, Lake Huron, Lake Ontario, Lake Erie, Susquehanna River, Hudson R., CENTRAL PLAINS, Indiana Territory, Terr. NW of Ohio R., APPALACHIAN MOUNTAINS, Mississippi River, Missouri River, Ohio River, Potomac River, Savannah River, ME (part of Mass.), VT 1791, NH, MA, NY, RI, CT, NJ, PA, DE, MD, VA, KY 1792, TN 1796, NC, SC, GA, Terr. South of Ohio R., Mississippi Territory, GULF COASTAL PLAIN, ATLANTIC COASTAL PLAIN, ATLANTIC OCEAN, Gulf of Mexico

Scale: 0 200 400 Miles / 0 200 400 Kilometers

MAP WORK

Once the Constitution was ratified, Vermont, Kentucky, and Tennessee were the first three states to join the original thirteen.

1. In which years did Vermont, Kentucky, and Tennessee become states?

2. Which lands were part of the United States but were not yet states?

3. Which was the only state that lay along both the Gulf and Atlantic coastal plains?

THE ROAD TO KENTUCKY

The trails that the pioneers followed to the West began as Native American paths. The trailblazers marked these paths with piles of stones or notches cut into trees so that later travelers could find their way. Daniel Boone, who explored, hunted, and trapped in the Appalachians, may have been the most famous trailblazer of all.

"Pathfinder" Boone

Asked if he had ever been lost, Daniel Boone once replied, "No, but I was bewildered [confused] once for three days." His skill at finding trails earned Boone the nickname "the pathfinder." Like other great trailblazers, Boone loved the outdoors. He sometimes fought the Native Americans he met in his travels, but he also respected them. The Shawnee eventually adopted Boone because they thought he was so brave.

Boone was born in 1734 to a Quaker family in Pennsylvania. He became an expert at hunting and shooting after his family moved to the frontier in North Carolina. Boone helped support his family by hunting and trapping animals. Animal furs and skins could be traded or sold to merchants.

Rumors About Kentucky

Boone heard about the land called Kentucky in 1755 from a hunter named John Findley. Findley had explored the waters of the Kentucky River and traded with the Native Americans along its banks. Boone and Findley met while driving wagons for the militia during the French and Indian War. At night they sat around the campfire,

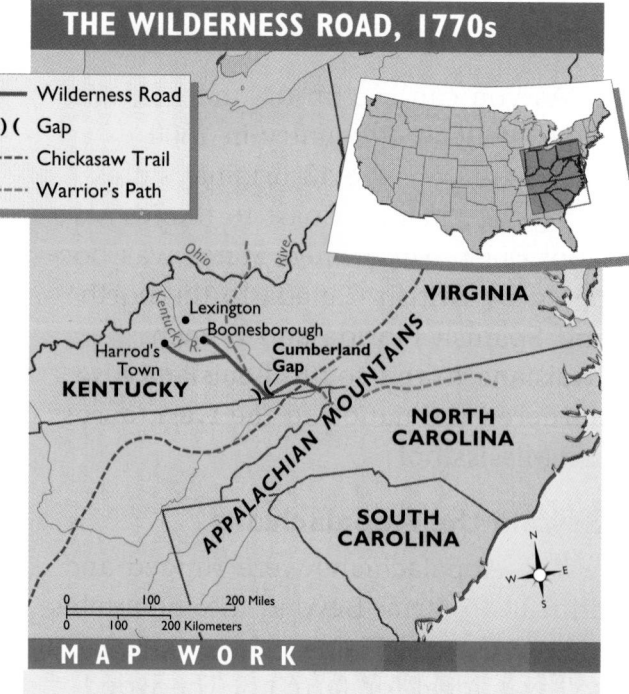

THE WILDERNESS ROAD, 1770s

— Wilderness Road
) (Gap
--- Chickasaw Trail
--- Warrior's Path

Ohio River
Kentucky R.
Lexington
Boonesborough
Harrod's Town
Cumberland Gap
KENTUCKY
VIRGINIA
APPALACHIAN MOUNTAINS
NORTH CAROLINA
SOUTH CAROLINA

0   100   200 Miles
0   100   200 Kilometers

MAP WORK

The Cumberland Gap led to the fertile meadows of central Kentucky.

1. How far is the Gap from Boonesborough?
2. Why might the distance traveled be greater than the distance represented on the map?

and Findley told amazing tales of a rich land for hunters called Kentucky. He described forests and plains filled with buffalo, deer, wild turkey, and other game. Boone decided he had to go and see Kentucky.

Fort Boonesborough State Park

412

Findley told Boone that there was one problem. To pass through the Appalachians, they had to find the Warriors' Path. This path had been used by Native Americans for centuries. The path led to a "gap" in the mountains that made a natural passageway to the West. It later became known as the Cumberland Gap.

Boone Heads for Kentucky

Boone had married Rebecca Bryan in 1756, and they had a growing family to support. He thought they could have a better life in Kentucky. In 1767 Boone first reached Kentucky, but a snowstorm forced him to turn back. In 1769 Boone headed west again. On May 1st, Boone, Findley, and four other men packed a team of horses and went in search of the gap in the mountains.

Five weeks later they found the Cumberland Gap and entered Kentucky. Boone later described what he had seen:

We had passed through a great forest on which stood myriads [a great number] *of trees, some gay with blossoms, others rich with fruits.*

Boone and his companions were struck by the land's beauty. The fertile soil meant that settlers could grow crops. There was plenty of wild game to hunt for meat. The dense forests could provide fuel and building materials.

Settling in Kentucky would not be easy, though. The Cherokee and the Shawnee did not want to lose their land to settlers. Boone also had to break British law. As you read in Chapter 11, the British Proclamation of 1763 did not allow colonial settlements west of the Appalachians. The British did not want to pay the cost of sending troops to defend colonists if there were conflicts over land. They also wanted to trade for fur with the Native Americans in the area.

The Granger Collection

Daniel Boone led families into Kentucky (left). The grinding stone (far left) is typical of the kinds of tools used by pioneers.

PIONEERS IN KENTUCKY

"Pathfinder" Boone was among the first to disobey the Proclamation of 1763. He persuaded people in a few Cherokee villages to sell their land to the Transylvania Company. This colonial company bought land for white settlements.

Building Boonesborough

On March 10, 1775, Boone led a group of pioneers to a site near the Kentucky River. Boone and the pioneers built a fort and named their settlement Boonesborough. Boone returned to North Carolina and brought his family to Boonesborough. He said, "My wife and daughter . . . [were] the first white women that ever stood on the banks of the Kentucky river."

On their way to Kentucky, Boone and his companions widened the old Warriors' Path leading to the Cumberland Gap. The new trail became known as the Wilderness Road. It became one of the main routes pioneers used to travel west.

Moving Families

By 1776 about 200 people were living in Boonesborough. The new settlers found life there hard. They were 300 miles from the nearest colonial town so they could not depend on anyone else to help them if they were attacked. To make their community more secure, the pioneers built cabins close together. With few rules to govern the settlement, tensions between neighbors arose. Some people became greedy and fought over who owned the land.

Disputes about ownership of the land existed between the settlers and the Native Americans. Dragging Canoe, a Cherokee, had warned Boone: "Brother, we have given you a fine land, but I believe that you will have much

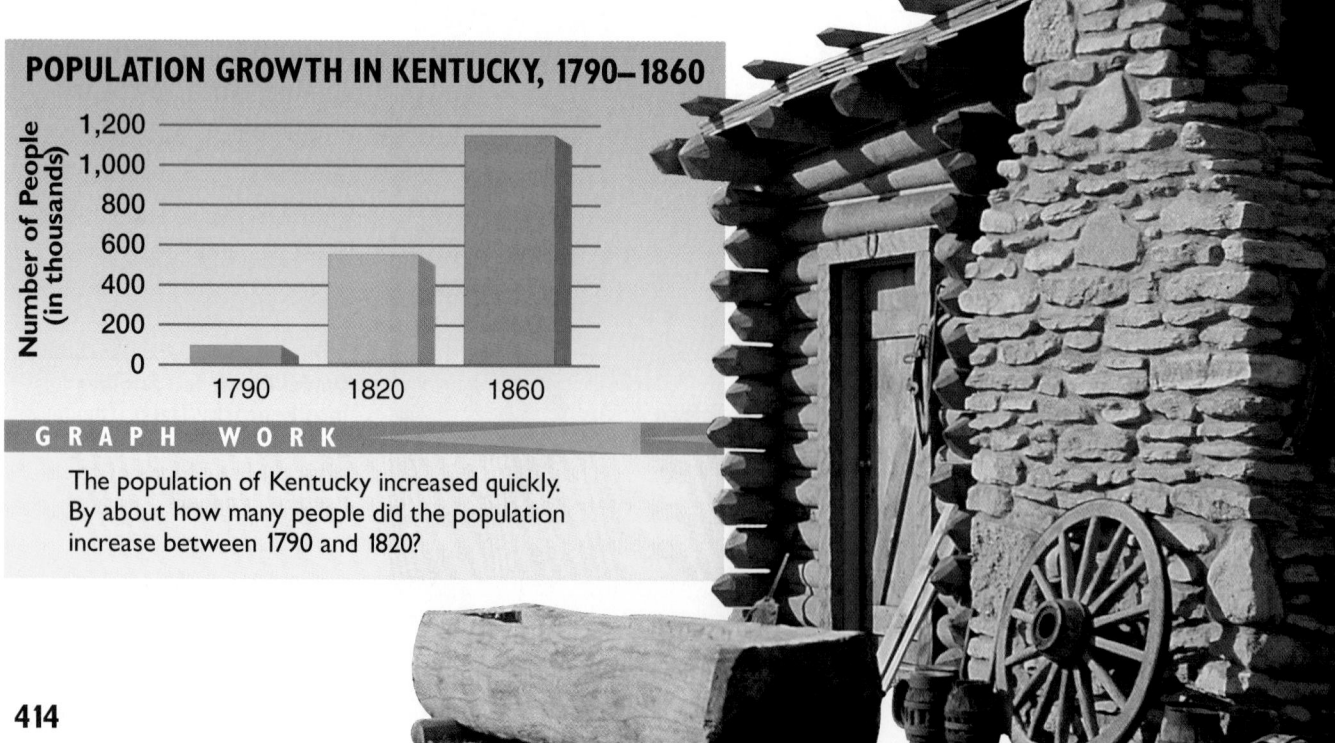

Fort Boonesborough State Park

This Boonesborough cabin was reconstructed to preserve its original appearance.

POPULATION GROWTH IN KENTUCKY, 1790–1860

Number of People (in thousands)

1,200 / 1,000 / 800 / 600 / 400 / 200 / 0

1790   1820   1860

GRAPH WORK

The population of Kentucky increased quickly. By about how many people did the population increase between 1790 and 1820?

trouble in settling it." The few Cherokee who had sold land to the Transylvania Company treated the new settlers well, but other native peoples in the area did not. The Shawnee felt that the white settlers were trespassing and unlawfully hunting the wildlife that the Shawnee needed. People in Boonesborough lived in fear of Native Americans. After several Native American raids, many settlers returned to the East or moved to safer settlements.

However, white settlers continued to move to Kentucky. You can see from the population chart on page 414 how quickly Kentucky's population grew.

A Pioneer Childhood

A young pioneer child who would later become famous was born in Kentucky in 1809. His name was Abraham Lincoln. Lincoln's grandfather had been a friend of Daniel Boone. Like other pioneer children, young Lincoln weeded crops, collected nuts and berries for family meals, and fed the farm animals. Later his family moved farther west into the Indiana Territory. Young Abraham grew up to become our country's sixteenth President.

WHY IT MATTERS

Daniel Boone and other pioneers played a key part in starting white settlements in the West. Boone became one of our country's first folk heroes. Throughout the 1800s people from the United States continued to move farther and farther west. In 1792 Kentucky became the 15th state, the first state west of the Appalachian Mountains.

The painting *Boyhood of Lincoln* shows Lincoln reading. On the frontier, books were precious.

Reviewing Facts and Ideas

MAIN IDEAS

- Many new settlers moved west of the Appalachians in the late 1700s.

- Daniel Boone led pioneers west on trails such as the Wilderness Road.

THINK ABOUT IT

1. What lands were new settlers moving to in the 1790s?

2. What was life like for a young pioneer boy like Abraham Lincoln?

3. **FOCUS** Why did settlers begin moving west in the late 1700s?

4. **THINKING SKILL** What different *points of view* might pioneers and Native Americans in Kentucky have had?

5. **GEOGRAPHY** Use the map on page 411 to list the states that joined the country in the late 1700s.

JEFFERSON PLANS FOR GROWTH

READ ALOUD

In 1800 John Adams spent his first night in the newly built President's house. "May none but wise and honest men ever rule under this roof," he said. One day the building would be known as the White House, the home of the President of the United States and the President's family.

THE BIG PICTURE

By 1790 many new settlers were building homes in the West. At the same time the federal government was making plans for its new home. Each state wanted to be the site of the country's new capital. The country's leaders decided to compromise. They agreed to build the capital on land that would not be part of any state.

In 1791 President Washington began making plans for the District of Columbia. The district is named after Christopher Columbus. The city within the District of Columbia is called Washington, after George Washington. Washington hired Benjamin Banneker to help lay out the city. Banneker was a writer, an inventor, and a scientist. He was also one of the first African Americans appointed by a President to work for the federal government. Banneker began with plans for the capital already created by a French architect named Pierre L'Enfant (pee AIR LAHN fahn).

The capital city was still unfinished when Thomas Jefferson became President in 1801. Jefferson influenced the design of many of its buildings—but he would affect far more than the new capital.

Focus Activity

READ TO LEARN
What was the Louisiana Purchase?

VOCABULARY
Louisiana Purchase

PEOPLE
Benjamin Banneker
Pierre L'Enfant
Thomas Jefferson
Napoleon Bonaparte
Meriwether Lewis
William Clark
York
Sacajawea

PLACES
District of Columbia
Missouri River
Snake River
Columbia River

416

THOMAS JEFFERSON BECOMES PRESIDENT

Thomas Jefferson became the third President of the United States after defeating President John Adams in a bitter election. John Adams belonged to the Federalist party. As you read in Chapter 14, the Federalists believed in a strong central government. Jefferson and his supporters belonged to the Democratic-Republican party. This party's followers believed that the government in Washington, D.C. should let the people in each state govern themselves as much as possible.

Jefferson wanted citizens to feel that the new government belonged to them. Each morning Jefferson opened the White House to visitors and warmly shook their hands.

A Threat from France

In 1801 the United States had 16 states. Settlers were pouring into the Ohio and Indiana territories. Louisiana, the land west of the Mississippi, kept changing hands between France and Spain as a result of several wars. In 1800 Louisiana returned to France.

At the time, a general named Napoleon Bonaparte (nuh POH lee un BOH nuh pahrt) ruled France. During the early 1800s Napoleon took over much of Europe. Jefferson feared that Napoleon wanted to expand the French empire in the Americas as well.

President Thomas Jefferson, shown in Gilbert Stuart's painting (above right), presided over great changes in our country, including the completion of Washington, D.C., which Benjamin Banneker (below) helped to lay out.

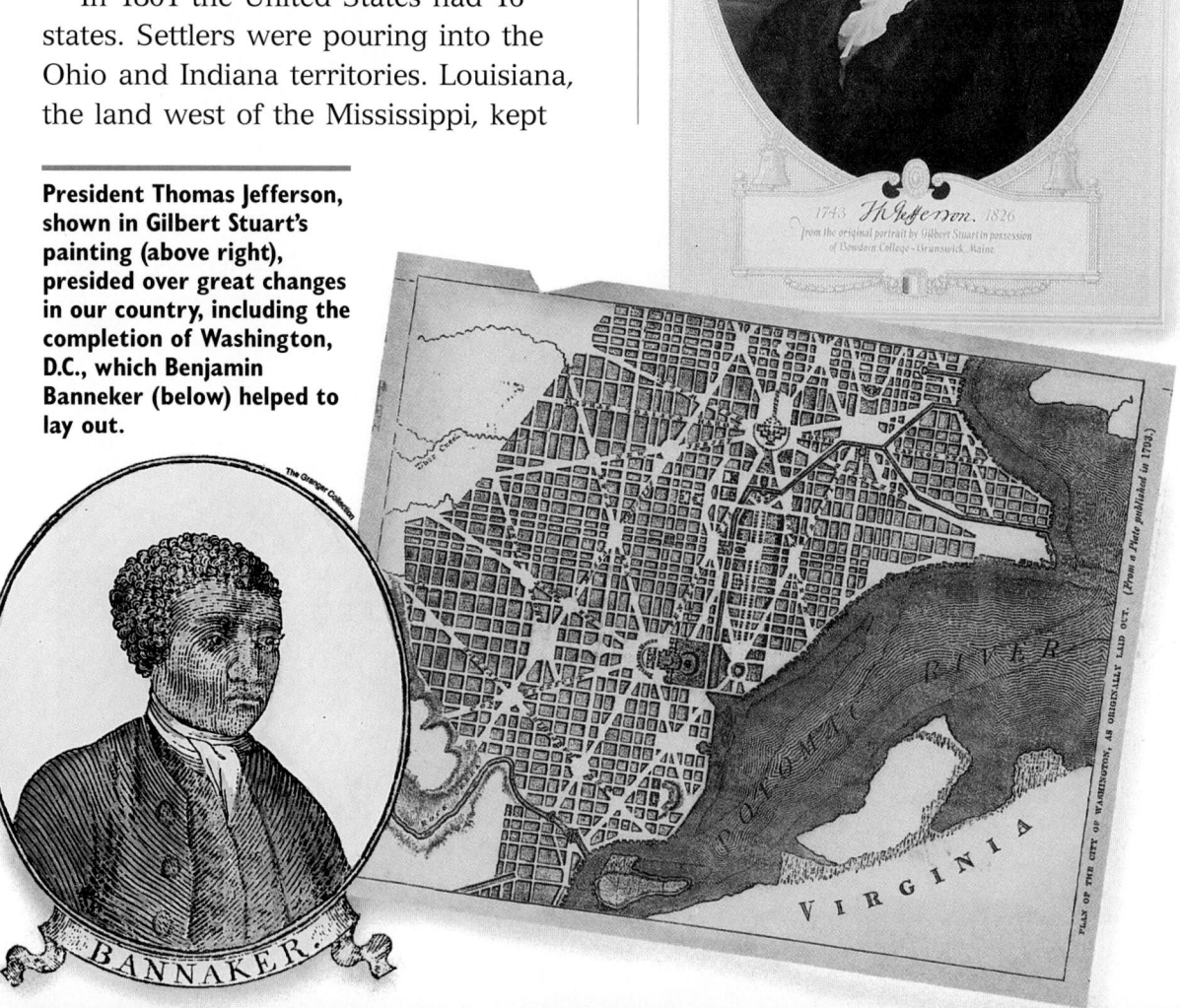

THE LOUISIANA PURCHASE

President Jefferson was especially worried that France might close Louisiana's main port, New Orleans, to the United States. Farmers from Kentucky, Tennessee, and the territories shipped their goods down the Mississippi River to be sold in that busy port city. Whoever blocked the mouth of the Mississippi, Jefferson declared, was "our natural enemy." Jefferson was also worried that France might stop American settlers from moving west. Rather than start a costly war, he decided to try to buy New Orleans from France.

James Monroe Goes to France

In 1803 Jefferson sent his friend James Monroe to Paris, France with an offer to buy New Orleans. Monroe was surprised when a French official asked, "How much will you give for

The French beginnings of New Orleans, shown in 1803 (bottom), can be seen today in the city's old French Quarter (below).

UNDER MY WINGS EVERY THING PROSPERS

Chicago Historical Society

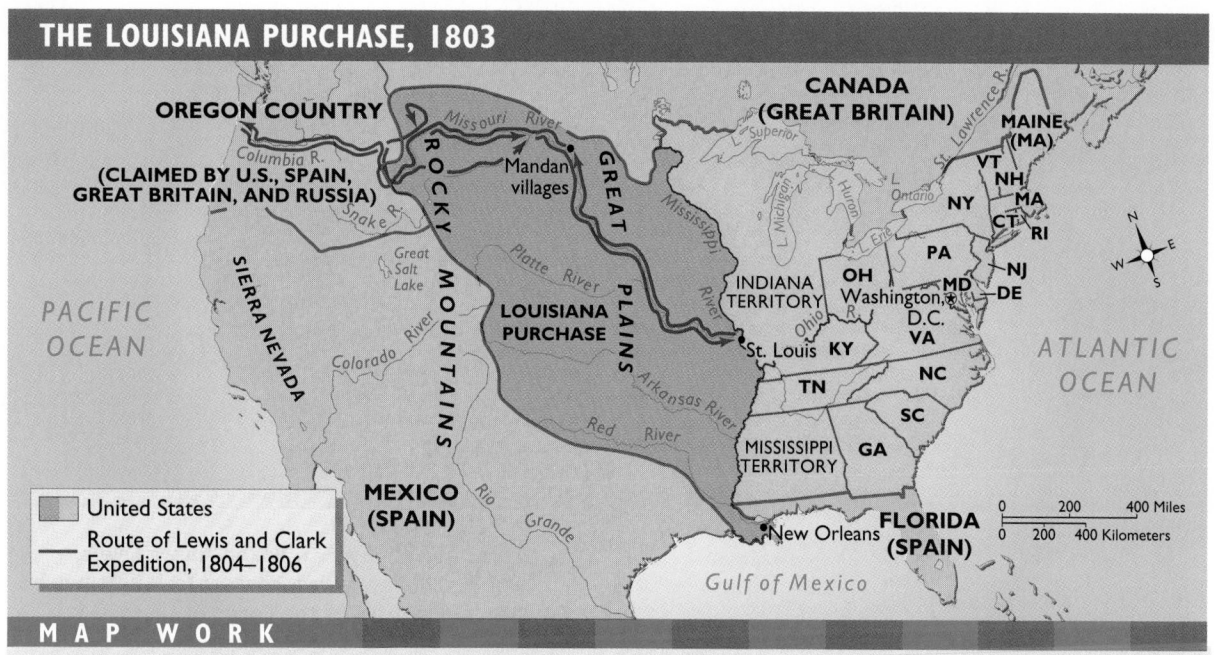

THE LOUISIANA PURCHASE, 1803

OREGON COUNTRY

(CLAIMED BY U.S., SPAIN, GREAT BRITAIN, AND RUSSIA)

CANADA (GREAT BRITAIN)

MAINE (MA)

Columbia R.

Missouri River

Mandan villages

Snake R.

ROCKY MOUNTAINS

GREAT PLAINS

Mississippi R.

PACIFIC OCEAN

SIERRA NEVADA

Great Salt Lake

Platte River

LOUISIANA PURCHASE

Colorado River

Arkansas River

Red River

MEXICO (SPAIN)

Rio Grande

INDIANA TERRITORY

Ohio R.

St. Louis

MISSISSIPPI TERRITORY

New Orleans

Gulf of Mexico

L. Michigan

L. Superior

L. Huron

L. Erie

L. Ontario

St. Lawrence R.

VT NH MA CT RI

NY

PA

OH MD DE

Washington, D.C.

VA

KY

TN

NC

SC

GA

NJ

FLORIDA (SPAIN)

ATLANTIC OCEAN

United States

Route of Lewis and Clark Expedition, 1804–1806

| 0 | 200 | 400 Miles |
| 0 | 200 | 400 Kilometers |

MAP WORK

Like other early explorers, Lewis and Clark found no direct water route to the Pacific Ocean. However, they did answer many questions Americans had about the West.

1. Which rivers did Lewis and Clark travel?
2. During which years did they explore?
3. Which European counties claimed areas that eventually became the United States?

the whole of Louisiana?" Napoleon badly needed money for France's war.

An agreement was soon reached. For $15 million the United States bought a huge piece of land stretching west from New Orleans to the border of what is now Idaho and north to Canada. The Louisiana Purchase, as shown on the map on this page, doubled the size of the United States at a very low price—about four cents per acre.

Jefferson Looks to the West

Jefferson knew very little about this huge territory. However, he was excited to find out more. In 1804 Jefferson sent an expedition to explore Louisiana and all the land to the Pacific Ocean. He chose his assistant Meriwether Lewis to lead the trip. Lewis had served as an army officer in the Northwest Territory.

Jefferson told Lewis to write down everything he saw—people, landforms,

plants, and animals. Lewis sent a letter to his friend William Clark, an army officer, asking him to help lead the expedition. "My friend," Clark wrote back, "I join you with hand and heart."

Clark's compass guided the expedition 8,000 miles, from St. Louis to the Pacific Ocean and back.

Missouri Historical Society

419

Montana Historical Society

THE LEWIS AND CLARK EXPEDITION

Lewis and Clark were given another important job: to explore the Missouri River and find a safe route to the Pacific. Follow the route that Lewis and Clark took on the map on page 419.

The group called itself the "Corps of Discovery." A corps is a group of people working together toward a common goal. Of the 42 men, about half were soldiers. One, Clark's servant, was an enslaved African American named York. The rest were trappers or scouts.

On May 14, 1804, the explorers set out from St. Louis in three boats. The men took tools, clothing, and weapons with them. They also took such things as eyeglasses, mirrors, fishhooks, and beads. These goods would be used as gifts for Native Americans whom the expedition might meet. Lewis and Clark gave out peace medals with a likeness of Jefferson on one side and an image of a peace pipe and a tomahawk on the other. They also handed out American flags. With these objects the explorers would mark and claim the regions they passed through for the United States.

Sacajawea

The Corps of Discovery spent its first winter in a Mandan village in present-day North Dakota. There they hired a French fur trapper named Toussaint Charbonneau (too SAHN SHAHR buh noh) as a guide. Charbonneau brought his wife, Sacajawea (sah kah jah WEE uh), along. Sacajawea had lived in the West with her people, the Shoshone, as a child. When she was still young, a rival group had stolen her. She had been separated from her family ever since.

Lewis and Clark knew how lucky they were to have Sacajawea along when the expedition reached the Rocky Mountains. Winter was coming and they needed horses. A group of Shoshone approached them. Clark wrote that Sacajawea began "to dance and show every mark of joy." The Shoshone chief turned out to be her long-lost brother Cameauhwait (KAH moh wayt). Sacajawea convinced him to give the expedition the horses it needed to cross the Rockies.

Reaching the Pacific Ocean

From the Rockies, Lewis and Clark followed the Snake River and then took the Columbia River to the Pacific Ocean. In November 1805 they arrived at what the Shoshone called the "great shining lake." It had taken them 18 months to reach the Pacific Ocean. Read an excerpt from William Clark's journal below. How do you think Clark felt when he finally reached the Pacific Ocean?

MANY VOICES
PRIMARY SOURCE

Excerpt from the journal of William Clark, written on November 7, 1805.

The morning was rainy, and the fog so thick that we could not see across the river.

*We had not gone far from . . . [a small] village when the fog cleared off, and we enjoyed the delightful **prospect** of the ocean—that ocean, the object of all our labors, the reward of all our anxieties. This cheering view **exhilarated** the spirits of all the party, who were still more delighted on hearing the distant roar of the **breakers**.*

prospect: view
exhilarated: excited
breakers: waves that break on a shore

WHY IT MATTERS

Lewis and Clark returned to Washington, D.C., in 1806. They had explored, mapped, and claimed land that stretched more than 3,000 miles. The maps that Lewis and Clark drew made it easier for new settlers to follow the way west. The United States, President Jefferson said, was "a rising nation, spread over a wide and fruitful land." In the next lesson you will see how the United States continued to grow.

✓ Reviewing Facts and Ideas

MAIN IDEAS

- In 1791 work began on plans for the new capital of the United States, the District of Columbia.

- Thomas Jefferson became President in 1801. In 1803 the United States purchased Louisiana from France for $15 million.

- From 1804 to about 1806, Lewis and Clark explored the Louisiana Purchase. With help from Sacajawea and others, they crossed the Rocky Mountains and reached the Pacific Ocean.

THINK ABOUT IT

1. What concerns did Jefferson have about French control of Louisiana?

2. What goals did Lewis and Clark have for their expedition?

3. **FOCUS** Where were the lands that the United States bought under the Louisiana Purchase.

4. **THINKING SKILL** What could you *predict* about the history of the United States if the Louisiana Purchase had not been made? Explain.

5. **GEOGRAPHY** In 1801 Washington, D.C., was located in the center of the country. Where is the center now?

AMERICAN Wildlife ARTISTS

As long as people have lived in this country, they have used artwork to celebrate the variety and abundance of wildlife. Native Americans and early explorers made drawings of the animals they saw. When Lewis and Clark returned from their expedition, they brought with them drawings of animals that most people in the United States had never seen.

Today, as in the past, artists travel from the hottest deserts to the coldest reaches of our country. They take photographs—and now videos, too—of animals most people would otherwise never get to see.

Whether they draw, paint, photograph, or create sculptures, wildlife artists provide a lasting legacy of the natural beauty of the United States.

John James Audubon is known for his skill in portraying the birds of our country. The work above is titled *Bald Eagle*.

Wildlife such as the owl (right) has long been the subject of Native American art. The trout (far right) was one of the fish that William Clark drew during his expedition.

Smithsonian Institution

The New York Historical Society

This mountain lion, also called a cougar or puma (PYOO muh), was photographed by Renee Lynn.

The Granger Collection

THE WAR OF 1812

READ ALOUD

In 1811 talk of war was in the air. In Congress, Senator John Calhoun of South Carolina spoke out against the British: "Which shall we do," he asked, "abandon or defend our rights?" As you will see, President James Madison agreed that it was time to fight Great Britain once again.

Focus Activity

READ TO LEARN
What were the results of the War of 1812?

VOCABULARY
neutral
War Hawks
War of 1812
national anthem
Battle of New Orleans
Era of Good Feelings
nationalism
Monroe Doctrine

PEOPLE
James Madison
Henry Clay
Oliver Hazard Perry
Tecumseh
Tenskwatawa
William Henry Harrison
Andrew Jackson
Dolley Madison
Francis Scott Key
James Monroe

PLACES
Baltimore

THE BIG PICTURE

When James Madison became President of the United States in 1809, Great Britain and France had been fighting a long, costly war. Like earlier Presidents, Madison tried to keep the United States neutral (NOO trul). *Neutral* means "not taking sides." Great Britain and France did not respect the decision of the United States. They both began to take American ships by force. The British also kidnapped American sailors and forced them to serve in the British navy.

People in the United States were angered over Great Britain's actions. American ships needed to travel safely to trade goods. "Free trade and seamen's rights!" cried a Kentucky senator named Henry Clay. Clay was the leader of the War Hawks, or members of Congress who wanted to declare war against Great Britain. The War Hawks disliked the British for trading guns to Native American groups such as the Seneca and Shawnee. They also disagreed with the British about United States borders to the north. Many War Hawks hoped to drive the British out of Canada and the Spanish out of Florida. Senator Clay urged the United States to "take the whole continent."

The USS *Constitution* (left) is still a symbol of American might on the seas. Commodore Perry (below) led the United States to one of the greatest victories in the Navy's history.

THE WAR AT SEA

The War Hawks convinced Congress to declare war on Great Britain in June 1812. In the United States the fighting became known as the War of 1812. Former President Thomas Jefferson claimed that the capture of Canada would be "just a matter of marching." He and the War Hawks were mistaken. The United States was not prepared for war.

"Old Ironsides"

Even the War Hawks feared the mighty British navy. Yet it was the war at sea that brought the United States its early victories. One of the most famous battles in United States naval history took place on August 19, 1812. Off the coast of Nova Scotia in Canada, the USS *Constitution* sank the *Guerrière* (ger ee YAIR), one of Britain's finest warships. After the fierce battle, sailors nicknamed the *Constitution* "Old Ironsides" because cannonballs seemed to bounce off its tough oak sides.

In 1813 United States Commodore Oliver Hazard Perry fought the British navy on Lake Erie. His ship flew a flag that read, "Don't give up the ship." These had been the dying words of Captain James Lawrence of the USS *Chesapeake*. The *Chesapeake* had been sunk by the British earlier that year.

Perry kept fighting until most of his crew lay wounded or dead. Perry and a few men then rowed out under heavy fire to a second ship and went on to defeat the British. After the victory, Perry said, "We have met the enemy and they are ours."

425

The Granger Collection

A British view of the invasion (left) incorrectly shows the White House on a hill. First Lady Dolley Madison (below) barely escaped.

THE WAR ON LAND

The war was more difficult for the United States on land than at sea. Many Native Americans sided with the British because they thought that the United States would take more of their land.

In the North and Middle West, the United States Army battled Native American forces led by Tecumseh, a Shawnee chief. His brother Tenskwatawa (tens kwah TAH wah) was a popular religious leader known as the "Prophet." Tecumseh warned many Native American communities against adopting the white man's ways and selling their land to new settlers. "Why not sell the air, the clouds, and the great sea?" he asked. Tecumseh and the British successfully fought American troops in several battles near the Great Lakes. In 1813, however, soldiers under General William Henry Harrison killed Tecumseh in battle.

In Tennessee an American commander named Andrew Jackson defeated the Muscogee at the Battle of Horseshoe Bend and took nearly all of their lands. Many Muscogee fled to Florida to live with the Seminole.

The War Nears the Capital

In 1814 British troops marched on Washington, D.C. The capital had few troops to defend it, and many fled as the British set fire to the buildings. The First Lady, Dolley Madison, was able to race through the White House and save important state papers and a famous painting of George Washington.

"Our Flag Was Still There"

After burning Washington, the British moved on to Baltimore and attacked Fort McHenry. A lawyer named Francis Scott Key watched as British cannon fire lit up the night sky.

The battle continued through the night. As dawn broke, Key saw that "our flag was still there." The British attack had failed. The battle inspired Key to write the words for "The Star-Spangled Banner," shown on the next page. In 1931 it became our country's national anthem. A national anthem is a nation's official song that expresses patriotism and celebrates the nation.

MANY VOICES MUSIC

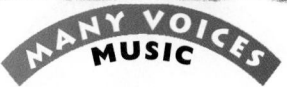

THE STAR-SPANGLED BANNER

Music attributed to J. S. Smith

Words by Francis Scott Key

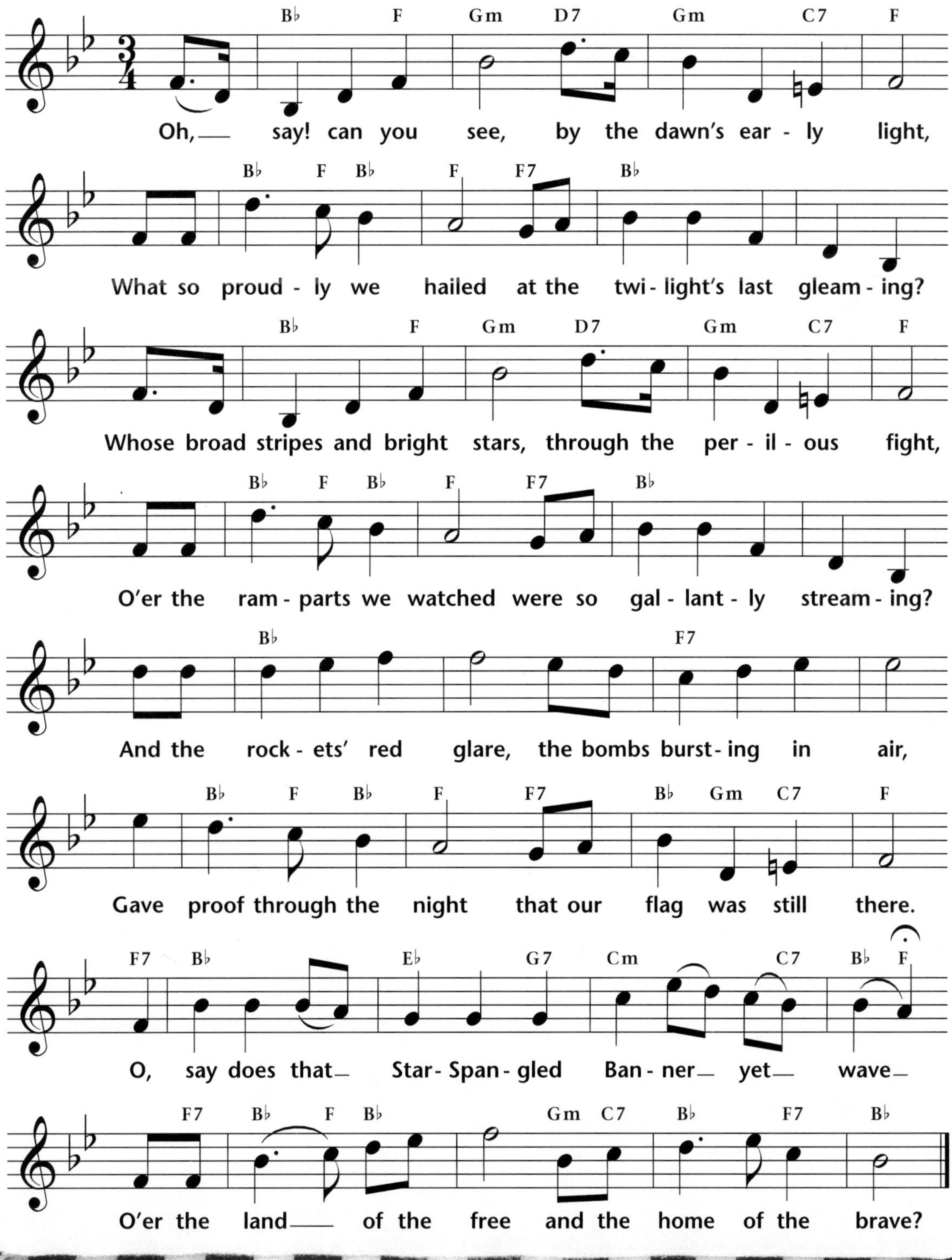
B♭ F Gm D7 Gm C7 F
Oh, say! can you see, by the dawn's ear - ly light,
B♭ F B♭ F F7 B♭
What so proud - ly we hailed at the twi - light's last gleam - ing?
B♭ F Gm D7 Gm C7 F
Whose broad stripes and bright stars, through the per - il - ous fight,
B♭ F B♭ F F7 B♭
O'er the ram - parts we watched were so gal - lant - ly stream - ing?
B♭ F7
And the rock - ets' red glare, the bombs burst - ing in air,
B♭ F B♭ F F7 B♭ Gm C7 F
Gave proof through the night that our flag was still there.
F7 B♭ E♭ G7 Cm C7 B♭ F
O, say does that Star - Span - gled Ban - ner yet wave
F7 B♭ F B♭ Gm C7 B♭ F7 B♭
O'er the land of the free and the home of the brave?

THE ERA OF GOOD FEELINGS

In 1815 Andrew Jackson, now a general, led Americans to an important victory in the land battle shown in the painting on this page. The Battle of New Orleans, as it became known, marked the end of the War of 1812. Neither army knew that, six days before the battle took place, leaders from England and the United States had signed a peace treaty.

After the war, the United States enjoyed a time of peace and economic

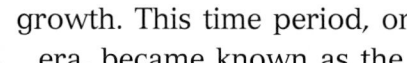

National Portrait Gallery/Smithsonian Institute

growth. This time period, or era, became known as the Era of Good Feelings. The people were "one great family with common interest," said James Monroe, the new President of the United States.

Soon after Monroe took office in 1817, he toured the country to promote nationalism (NASH uh nuh lihz um). Nationalism is a strong loyalty to one's own country and culture.

The Monroe Doctrine

James Monroe believed that all of the Americas, North and South, should be free from European control. After the War of 1812, settlers in Latin America began to break free of Spanish rule. Several independent republics were created. Monroe worried that Spain and

Black, white, and Native American troops cheered Andrew Jackson in his historic victory at the Battle of New Orleans (below). Soon after the war, President Monroe (above) warned Europeans to stay out of American affairs.

Historic New Orleans Collection

France might try to take over these small republics.

In 1823 Monroe issued a statement saying that the United States was against "future colonization by any European powers" in the Americas.

Monroe warned that any invaders would risk war with the United States. He promised that the United States would stay out of European affairs if Europe left the American continents alone. This historic statement became known as the Monroe Doctrine.

WHY IT MATTERS

Although neither side really won the War of 1812, the United States had become stronger and more successful. Great Britain and France had been forced to respect America's independence. Today we celebrate our country's hard-won freedom each time we sing our national anthem.

✔ Reviewing Facts and Ideas

MAIN IDEAS

- Britain's taking of American ships and sailors led Congress to declare war on Great Britain in 1812.

- In 1814, after the British burned much of Washington, D.C., they moved on to Fort McHenry, where they were stopped. Francis Scott Key wrote "The Star-Spangled Banner" about this battle.

- Although neither side really won the War of 1812, the Battle of New Orleans in 1815 marked the end of the war.

- The Era of Good Feelings followed the end of the War of 1812 as Americans felt great pride in their country and hope for its future.

THINK ABOUT IT

1. What reasons did the United States have for entering the War of 1812?

2. Describe some of the major American victories in the War of 1812.

3. **FOCUS** What did the United States gain from the War of 1812?

4. **THINKING SKILL** What was Tecumseh's *point of view* on the War of 1812? What might have led him to look at the war in this way?

5. **GEOGRAPHY** In 1815 news of the peace treaty arrived from Washington, D.C., too late to stop the Battle of New Orleans. Using the map on page 419, plot a route showing how news of the treaty might have reached Jackson and his troops by river.

GEOGRAPHYSKILLS

Comparing Maps

VOCABULARY

political map

WHY THE SKILL MATTERS

In this chapter you have used maps to find out historical information. The maps you used are called historical maps. In this lesson you will learn about maps that communicate other kinds of information. For example,

a political map shows the boundaries of states or countries. Relief and elevation maps show what the land is like and how high it is. Sometimes you need information that cannot be obtained from one map alone. In this case you need to compare different kinds of maps.

USING THE SKILL

The map on the left of this page is an historical map. It shows the location of several towns and some of the Native American peoples that Tecumseh visited between 1811 and 1813. The map on the right is a political map. It shows state boundaries for a section

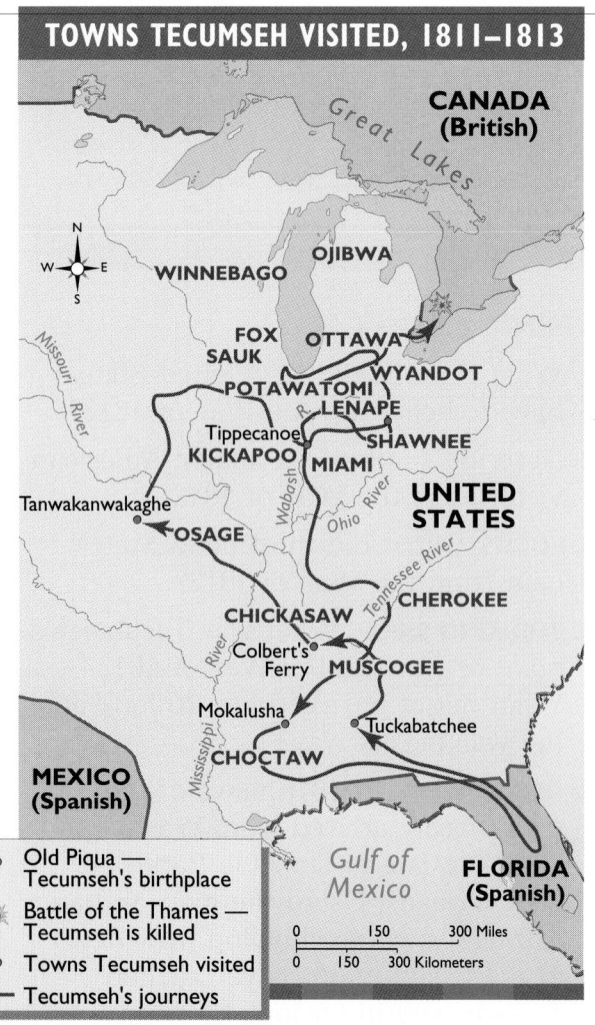

TOWNS TECUMSEH VISITED, 1811–1813

- Old Piqua — Tecumseh's birthplace
- Battle of the Thames — Tecumseh is killed
- Towns Tecumseh visited
- Tecumseh's journeys

THE EASTERN UNITED STATES

of the United States today. Suppose you wanted to identify the present-day state where the Native American town of Tanwakanwakaghe was located. What would you do?

Alone, neither of the two maps will give you the answer. Using both maps together, however, you can find the state in which Tanwakanwakaghe is located. On the historical map, use landmarks such as the Missouri and Mississippi rivers. Now find the same location on the political map. Use the map scale to make sure your location is about the same distance from these rivers. You will find that Tanwakanwakaghe was located in present-day Missouri.

TRYING THE SKILL

The towns shown on the historical map are just a few of those that were visited by Tecumseh as he tried to form a confederacy of Native American nations. In what present-day state was the town of Tuckabatchee located?

Now find the state of Mississippi on the political map. What Native Americans lived in this area? What landmarks did you use to help you find out?

HELPING Yourself

● **When comparing two or more maps, locate the position you need on the first map. Note the landmarks.**

● **Use the landmarks to locate the same position on the second map.**

● **Look at both maps together to find the information you need.**

REVIEWING THE SKILL

1. What does a political map show?

2. How can you locate the same position on two maps?

3. Tecumseh founded a huge community called Tippecanoe as the center of his operations. In what present-day state does the land that Tippecanoe once occupied lie?

4. Why do people often need more than one map to obtain information?

5. Suppose you wanted to find out which people lived in the different mountain ranges of the world in 1776. Which two kinds of maps would you use? Explain.

This portrait is believed by historians to be of Tecumseh.

CHAPTER 15 REVIEW

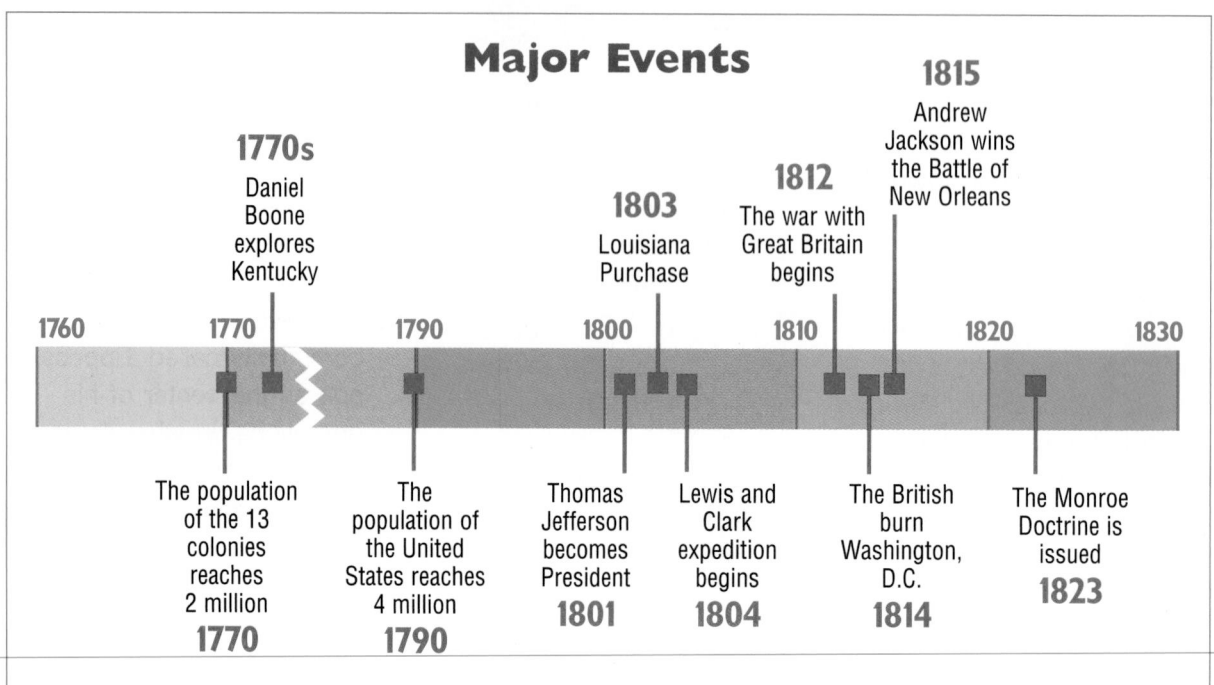

Major Events

1770s
Daniel Boone explores Kentucky

1803
Louisiana Purchase

1812
The war with Great Britain begins

1815
Andrew Jackson wins the Battle of New Orleans

1760 — 1770 — 1790 — 1800 — 1810 — 1820 — 1830

The population of the 13 colonies reaches 2 million
1770

The population of the United States reaches 4 million
1790

Thomas Jefferson becomes President
1801

Lewis and Clark expedition begins
1804

The British burn Washington, D.C.
1814

The Monroe Doctrine is issued
1823

THINKING ABOUT VOCABULARY

Number a sheet of paper from 1 to 5. Beside each number write the word or term below that best completes the sentence.

Louisiana Purchase   neutral
Monroe Doctrine   pioneers
nationalism

1. Early _____ led other settlers from the East into newly claimed areas of the West.

2. The new territory that doubled the size of the United States in 1803 was known as the _____.

3. President Madison wanted the United States to remain _____ in the war between Great Britain and France.

4. The _____ stated that America would stay out of Europe's affairs if Europe did not interfere with America.

5. Pride in one's own country is called _____.

THINKING ABOUT FACTS

1. Who was Daniel Boone?

2. What Native American peoples lived in Kentucky? Why did white settlers want to go there?

3. Name two things Thomas Jefferson did that helped the United States to grow.

4. What was the goal of Lewis and Clark's expedition?

5. Give two reasons the War Hawks wanted to battle Great Britain.

6. Explain the roles of these people in the War of 1812: Oliver Hazard Perry, Tecumseh, and Andrew Jackson.

7. Why did many Native Americans join with the British in the War of 1812?

8. What did Francis Scott Key write? What event inspired him to write it?

9. What was the Era of Good Feelings?

10. Look at the time line above. About when was Boonesborough founded?

THINK AND WRITE

WRITING A TRAVEL LOG
Suppose that you are a trailblazer who traveled with Daniel Boone and John Findley in 1769. Write several entries in a log describing your journey. Include observations about the people you are with.

WRITING A LETTER
Suppose that you are President Jefferson. Write a letter to James Monroe explaining why you want him to go to Paris to buy New Orleans.

WRITING A LIST
Write a list of people who played a part in the War of 1812, with a fact about each.

APPLYING GEOGRAPHY SKILLS

COMPARING MAPS
Answer the questions below to apply the skill of comparing maps.

1. What kinds of maps appear on page 430? What other kinds of maps do you know how to read?
2. What kind of information might you find by comparing an historical map with a political map?
3. What kinds of landmarks can help you locate a position on two maps?
4. What are some of the steps involved in comparing maps?
5. Why is it helpful to compare maps?

Summing Up the Chapter

Copy the spider map on a separate sheet of paper. Review the chapter to fill in the blank sections on the map. When you have finished, choose one event from the map and write a paragraph that answers the question "How did this event help the United States to grow?"

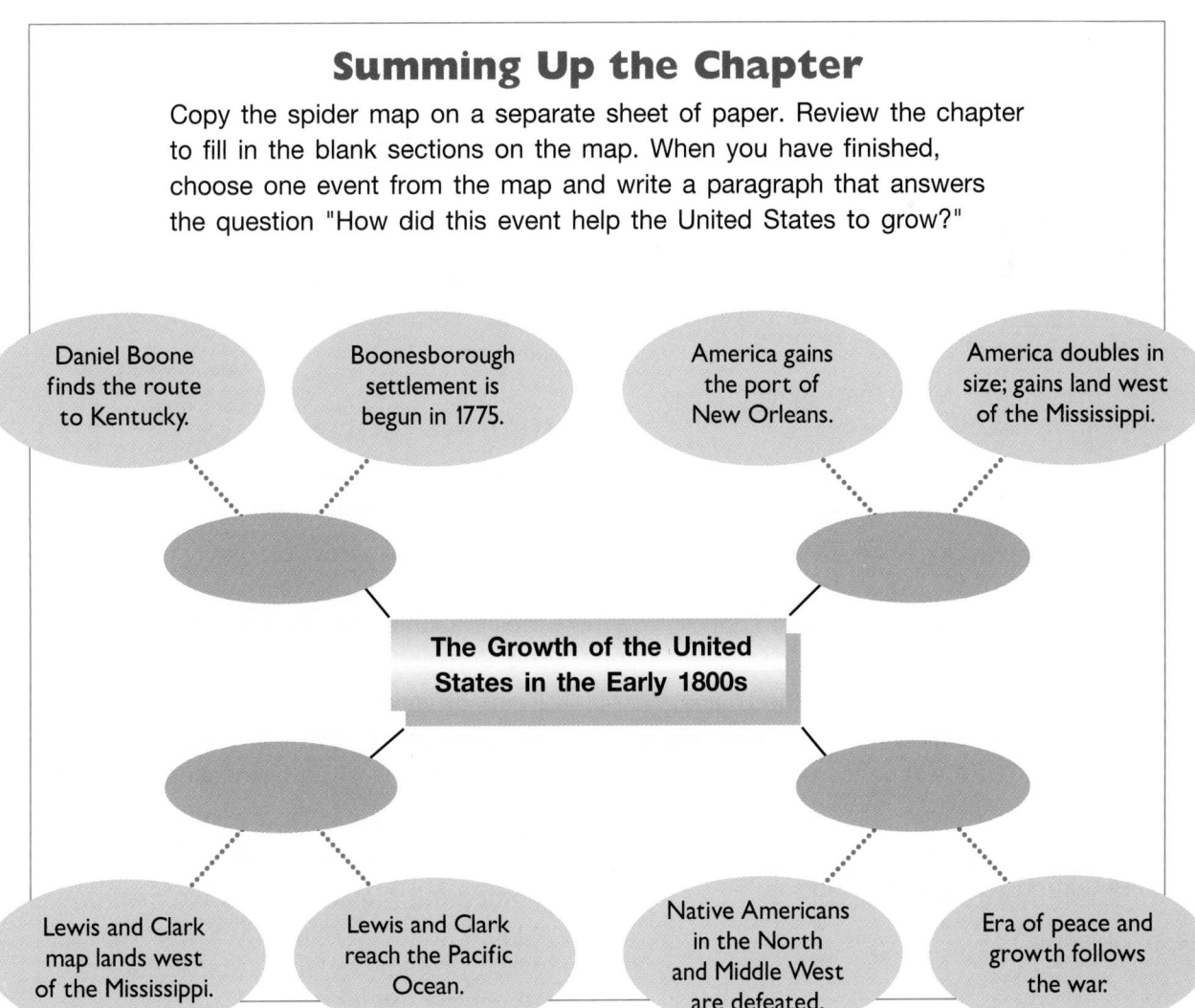

Daniel Boone finds the route to Kentucky.

Boonesborough settlement is begun in 1775.

America gains the port of New Orleans.

America doubles in size; gains land west of the Mississippi.

The Growth of the United States in the Early 1800s

Lewis and Clark map lands west of the Mississippi.

Lewis and Clark reach the Pacific Ocean.

Native Americans in the North and Middle West are defeated.

Era of peace and growth follows the war.

UNIT 6 REVIEW

THINKING ABOUT VOCABULARY

Number a sheet of paper from 1 to 10. Beside each number write the word or term from the list below that best completes the sentence.

Battle of New
   Orleans
Bill of Rights
Constitutional
   Convention
federal system

national anthem
Northwest Ordinance
pioneer
Monroe Doctrine
War Hawks
War of 1812

1. Under a _____, the state and the central government share power.

2. A _____ is a song celebrating a country.

3. The _____ was a law that provided a way for territories to become states.

4. The people that argued for war with Great Britain were known as the _____.

5. Delegates from 13 states attended the _____ to write a plan of government for the United States.

6. A person who leads the way into areas that are new to him or her is a

   _____.

7. The _____ are the ten amendments to the Constitution that describe people's rights.

8. Andrew Jackson won the final fight of the War of 1812 in the _____.

9. The _____ stated that the United States would stay out of European affairs if Europe left the American continents alone.

10. The _____ was fought against Britain on sea and on land.

THINK AND WRITE

WRITING A SKIT

Choose one of the events you have read about in this unit, and write a skit about it. For example, you might write a skit about pioneers and the Wilderness Road or about Tecumseh as he talked to other Native Americans about the settlers. Remember to include several characters in your skit as well as facts about the real-life events.

WRITING A NEWSPAPER ARTICLE

Suppose that you have been assigned to report on the Constitutional Convention. Write an article about one of the events that takes place there. Include a headline for your article and information about the setting.

WRITING ABOUT PERSPECTIVES

This unit describes the building of the United States as it developed its government system and acquired and explored lands. How might the perspective of a Native American living west of the Mississippi have changed from 1770 to 1830? Write a paragraph to explain your views.

BUILDING SKILLS

1. **Point of view** What can you look for to tell what a person's point of view is?

2. **Point of view** How can recognizing point of view help you to understand historical topics such as the debate over ratifying the Constitution?

3. **Point of view** How is it possible that two historical documents would have two different versions of an historical event?

4. **Comparing maps** How is an historical map different from a political map?

5. **Comparing maps** Look at the map on page 419. How would you find out in which present-day states the Appalachian Mountains are located?

YESTERDAY, TODAY &
TOMORROW

Although the Constitution was written over 200 years ago, it remains the law of our country today. How does the amendment process keep the Constitution useful in the present? What main ideas of the Constitution do you think will continue to make it an important document in the future?

READING ON YOUR OWN

These are some books you might find at the library to help you learn more.

THE GREAT LITTLE MADISON
by Jean Fritz
This is the biography of James Madison, our fourth President and a framer of the Constitution.

A MORE PERFECT UNION: THE STORY OF OUR CONSTITUTION
by Betsy and Giulio Maestro
This well-illustrated story describes how the Constitution was drafted and ratified.

LEWIS AND CLARK, EXPLORERS OF THE AMERICAN WEST
by Steven Kroll
This picture book tells the story of these two explorers' famous journey to reach the Pacific Ocean.

UNIT REVIEW PROJECT

Organize a Living Time Line

1. Have each group member choose an event from this unit to research, such as the Lewis and Clark expedition or the British invasion of Washington, D.C.
2. List several facts about each event.
3. Write the name and date of your event on a large piece of oak tag. Include a lively illustration that tells more about the event. Make drawings, cut out magazine pictures, or make a collage.
4. On another piece of oak tag, write several interesting facts about your event. Paint or draw a border around the oak tag.
5. Tie together the left sides of the oak tag with a piece of string. Then tie together the right sides.
6. Place the pieces of oak tag over your head so that you are wearing one piece in front of you and one piece behind you.
7. Participate in a living time line with your group.

435

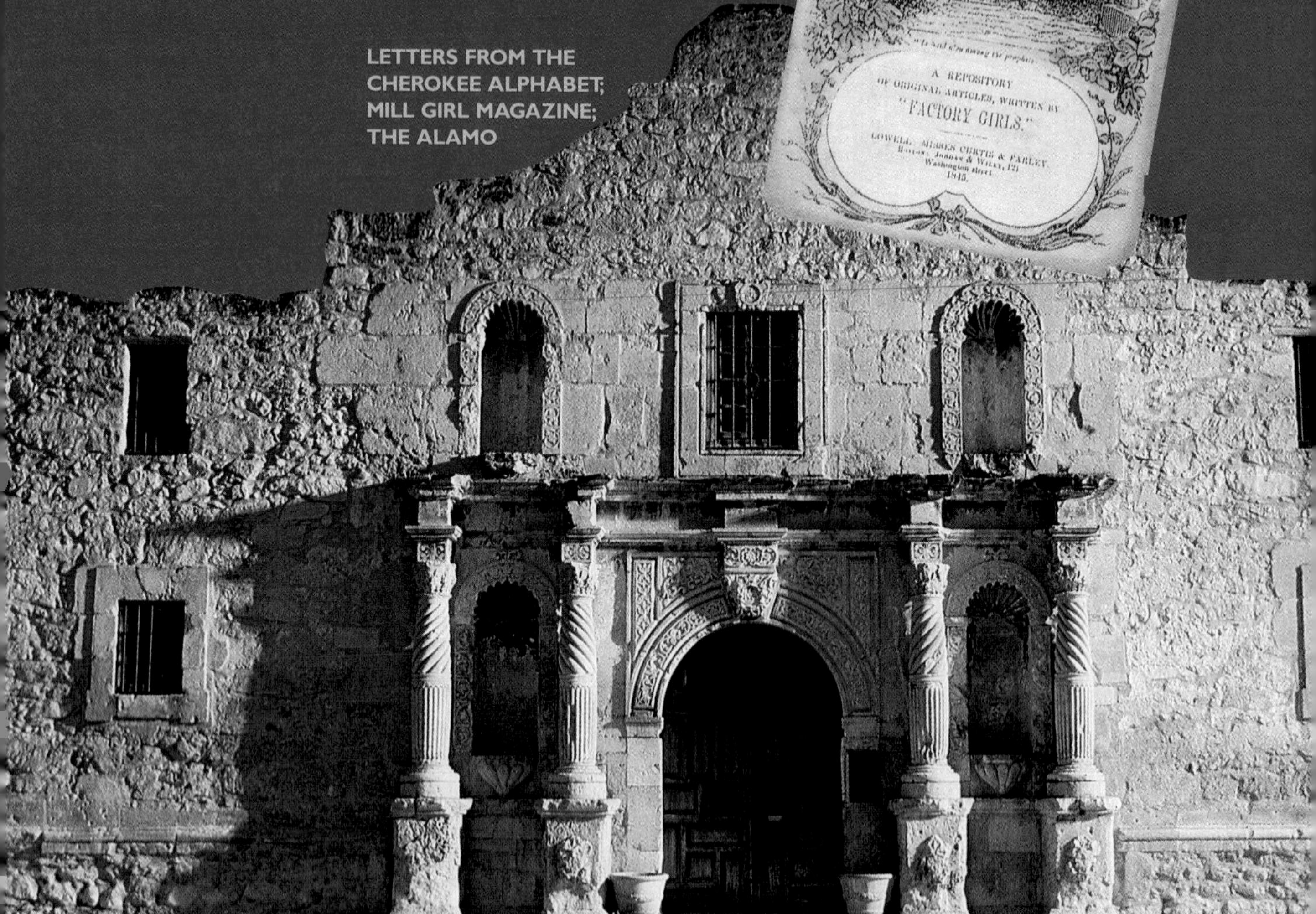

ᎠᎠᎠᏴᎳᏅᏀ

LETTERS FROM THE
CHEROKEE ALPHABET;
MILL GIRL MAGAZINE;
THE ALAMO

LOWELL
OFFERING

December, 1845.

A REPOSITORY
OF ORIGINAL ARTICLES, WRITTEN BY
"FACTORY GIRLS."

LOWELL, MISSES CURTIS & FARLEY.
Boston: Jordan & Wiley, 121
Washington street.
1845.

GOLD NUGGETS;
WAGON TRAIN HEADED WEST

Westward Expansion and Change

"The whole population is in motion."

from an observer in 1828.
See page 448.

ANDREW JACKSON

WHY DOES IT MATTER?

During the first half of the 1800s, the United States was growing and changing rapidly. After winning much of the West and Southwest from Mexico, the nation stretched from the Atlantic Ocean to the Pacific Ocean. New land and the discovery of gold in California caused a mass migration of people moving westward. New roads, canals, and railroads crossed the land. New technology and inventions changed life on farms and in the cities.

Adventures
with
NATIONAL
GEOGRAPHIC

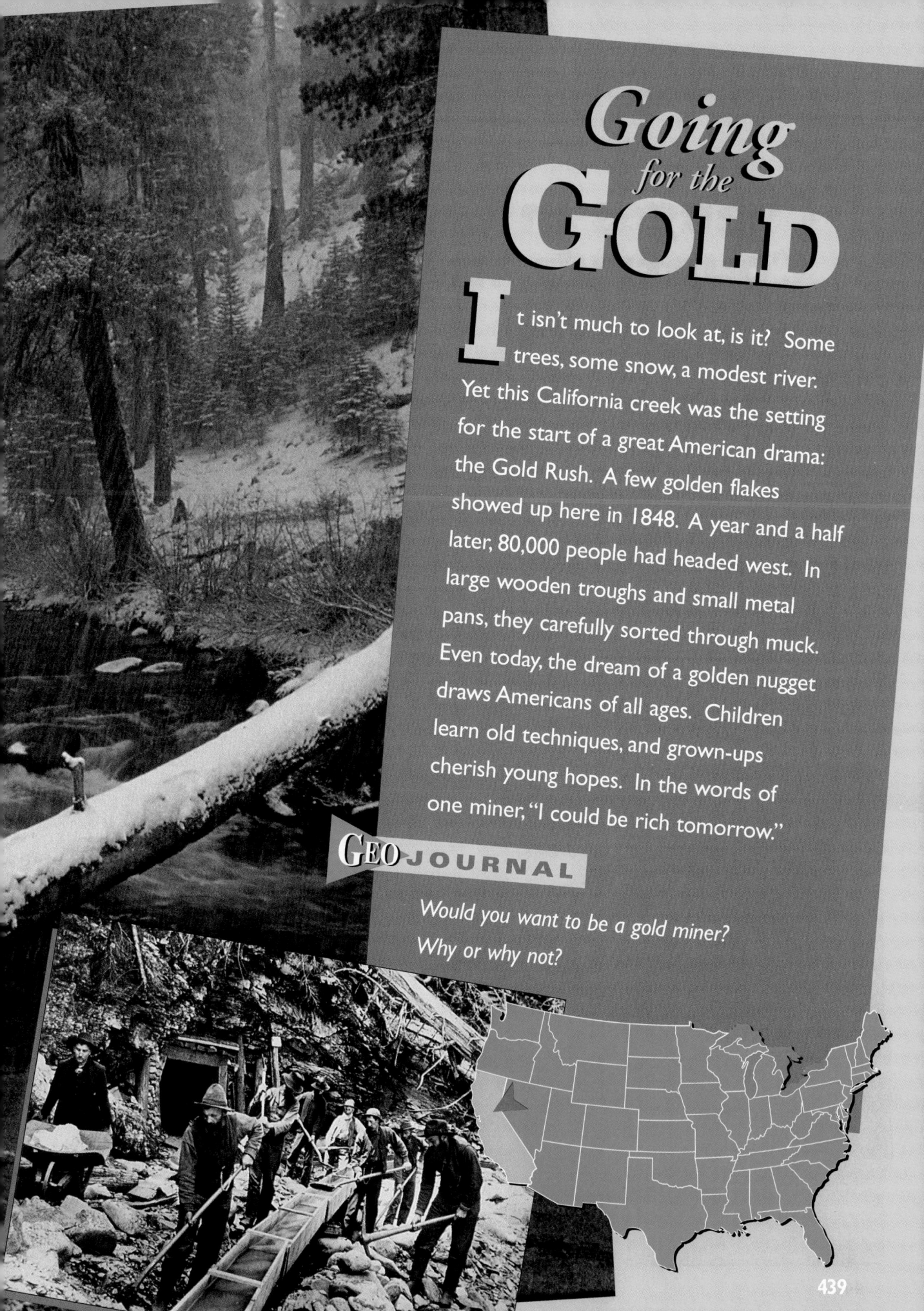

Going
for the
GOLD

It isn't much to look at, is it? Some trees, some snow, a modest river. Yet this California creek was the setting for the start of a great American drama: the Gold Rush. A few golden flakes showed up here in 1848. A year and a half later, 80,000 people had headed west. In large wooden troughs and small metal pans, they carefully sorted through muck. Even today, the dream of a golden nugget draws Americans of all ages. Children learn old techniques, and grown-ups cherish young hopes. In the words of one miner, "I could be rich tomorrow."

GEO JOURNAL

Would you want to be a gold miner?
Why or why not?

CHAPTER 16

Changes in Our Country's Way of Life

THINKING ABOUT HISTORY AND GEOGRAPHY

Chapter 16 begins with the Industrial Revolution in the early 1800s. During this period new inventions changed businesses and farms. At the same time, steam engines and new roads allowed people to move west of the Appalachians into lands that are now the Midwest. Free African Americans and immigrants moved to new farmlands and to the rapidly growing cities that were the centers of industry. As the new settlers moved westward, Native Americans were forced from their homes.

PACIFIC OCEAN

1793
SAVANNAH, GEORGIA

Eli Whitney invents the cotton gin

1807
NEW YORK, NEW YORK

Robert Fulton's steamboat makes travel upriver much easier

1817
LOWELL, MASSACHUSETTS

The town of Lowell is built as a textile center

UNITED
STATES

Lowell

New York City

Baltimore

Indian Territory

Savannah

ATLANTIC
OCEAN

1830

**BALTIMORE,
MARYLAND**

**Peter Cooper demonstrates
his steam locomotive**

1838

**INDIAN
TERRITORY**

**Thousands of Cherokee
die during their forced
march on the Trail of Tears**

THE INDUSTRIAL REVOLUTION

Focus Activity

READ TO LEARN
What were the effects of the Industrial Revolution?

VOCABULARY
Industrial Revolution
cotton gin
interchangeable parts
reaper

PEOPLE
Samuel Slater
Eli Whitney
Francis Cabot Lowell
Cyrus McCormick
John Deere

PLACE
Lowell, Massachusetts

READ ALOUD

A few miles outside of Boston, a new brick building stood beside the Charles River. Inside, a few people watched as a machine wove yarn into cloth far more swiftly than a person could weave it by hand. The year was 1814. "We sat by the hour," Nathan Appleton, a merchant, remembered, "watching the beautiful movement of this new and wonderful machine."

THE BIG PICTURE

Before the mid-1700s craftworkers made goods by hand in their workshops and homes. By the end of the century British business owners had factories like the one that Appleton described. They bought machines like the yarn-spinner, opened cloth factories, and hired workers to operate the machinery.

American business people encouraged new inventions because they saw the profit the British had gained by producing goods with machines. As more machine-made goods were produced, people's lives changed. Many moved from farms and small towns to cities to find work in factories. Machine-made goods were cheap, and people began buying goods rather than making them. The result of these changes was that the United States began to change from an agricultural to an industrial country. These large-scale changes in industry and technology became known as the Industrial Revolution

SPINNING COTTON

The British made cloth more cheaply than any other country in the world. They wanted to keep their profitable technology a secret, so they passed laws making it illegal to export machines or machine plans. The people who operated machines in cotton factories were not even allowed to leave the country.

In 1789 a British mechanic named Samuel Slater memorized the plans of the British spinning machines. He had heard that people in the United States wanted to start their own businesses making cloth and would pay for this new technology.

Slater left Great Britain and came to the United States. He was soon hired to build spinning machines by a merchant in Rhode Island. In 1790 Slater completed the first American machines to spin cotton into yarn.

The Cotton Gin

Slater had to pay a high price for the cotton he used in his factory. This limited his profits. In 1793, however, an American inventor built a machine that made cotton cheaper to produce. His name was Eli Whitney.

Whitney heard planters talk about how long it took enslaved workers to remove the stubborn seeds stuck to cotton. Whitney invented the cotton gin in ten days. Whitney's gin, which is short for "engine," helped workers clean up to 50 times more cotton than they could by hand. As you can see from the bar graph, cotton production boomed after the invention of the cotton gin.

Together, slave labor and the cotton gin made growing cotton more profitable. Many planters became more determined to keep slavery alive.

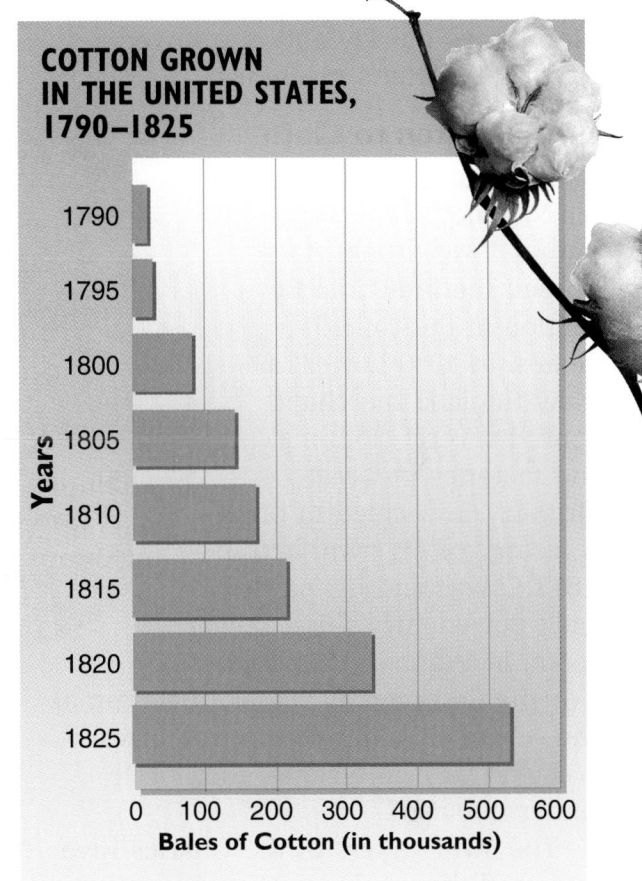

COTTON GROWN IN THE UNITED STATES, 1790–1825

Years (vertical axis): 1790, 1795, 1800, 1805, 1810, 1815, 1820, 1825

Bales of Cotton (in thousands): 0, 100, 200, 300, 400, 500, 600

Source: U.S. Bureau of Census

GRAPH WORK

Cotton was a major cash crop in the 1800s.

1. In which year did the largest increase in cotton production occur?
2. What factors other than the cotton gin might have caused this large increase?

Whitney's original cotton gin is kept today in the National Museum of History in Washington, D.C.

443

TEXTILE MILLS

The cotton gin helped create a plentiful supply of cotton. However, the United States did not have Great Britain's water-powered machines, called "power looms." These looms spun and wove cloth more quickly and at a lower cost than Slater's machines.

From Cotton to Cloth

Like Samuel Slater and Eli Whitney, Francis Cabot Lowell helped spread the Industrial Revolution in the United States. In 1810 Lowell, a New England merchant, toured several cloth-making factories in Great Britain. He decided to build a factory of his own, and in 1813 Lowell and his partners built our country's first power loom, in Waltham, Massachusetts. For the first time all stages of cloth-making—from spinning cotton into thread to weaving yarn into cloth—took place under one roof.

The swift waters of the Charles River powered the machines. The diagram on the next page shows how the water-wheel spun big leather belts. The belts, in turn, kept the machines moving.

After Lowell died in 1817, his partners built several textile mills next to the Merrimack River in Massachusetts. They also built a town around the mills for the workers. Lowell, as the partners named the new town, was the first planned town for workers in the United States.

Working at Lowell

Most of the workers at the mills in Lowell and other towns were unmarried women between the ages of 15 and 19. Few jobs were open to women then, and many were glad to get the work. They had long and tiring days, however, and lived apart from their families.

The women from New England who worked at Lowell were called "mill girls." They lived in boarding houses built by the mill owners. A mill girl spent 12 to 14 hours a day working at her machine, six days a week. The noise was often deafening. Lucy Larcom complained of "the buzzing and hissing of pulleys and rollers and spindles." Read the following excerpt from a Lowell mill girl's letter home to her father. What rule did she have to follow? Why do you think that rule was important?

MANY VOICES
PRIMARY SOURCE

**Excerpt from
a letter written by Mary S. Paul
on April 12, 1846.**

I am at work in a spinning room and tending four sides of warp which is one girl's work. The overseer tells me that he never had a girl get along better than I do and that he will do the best he can by me. . . . I have a very good boarding place [and] have enough to eat. . . . The girls are all kind and obliging. The girls that I room with are all from Vermont and good girls too. Now I will tell you about our rules at the boarding house. We have none in particular except that we have to go to bed about 10 o'clock. At half past 4 in the morning the bell rings for us to get up and at five for us to go into the mill.

---

warp: lengthwise threads of the spinning machine
obliging: helpful

444

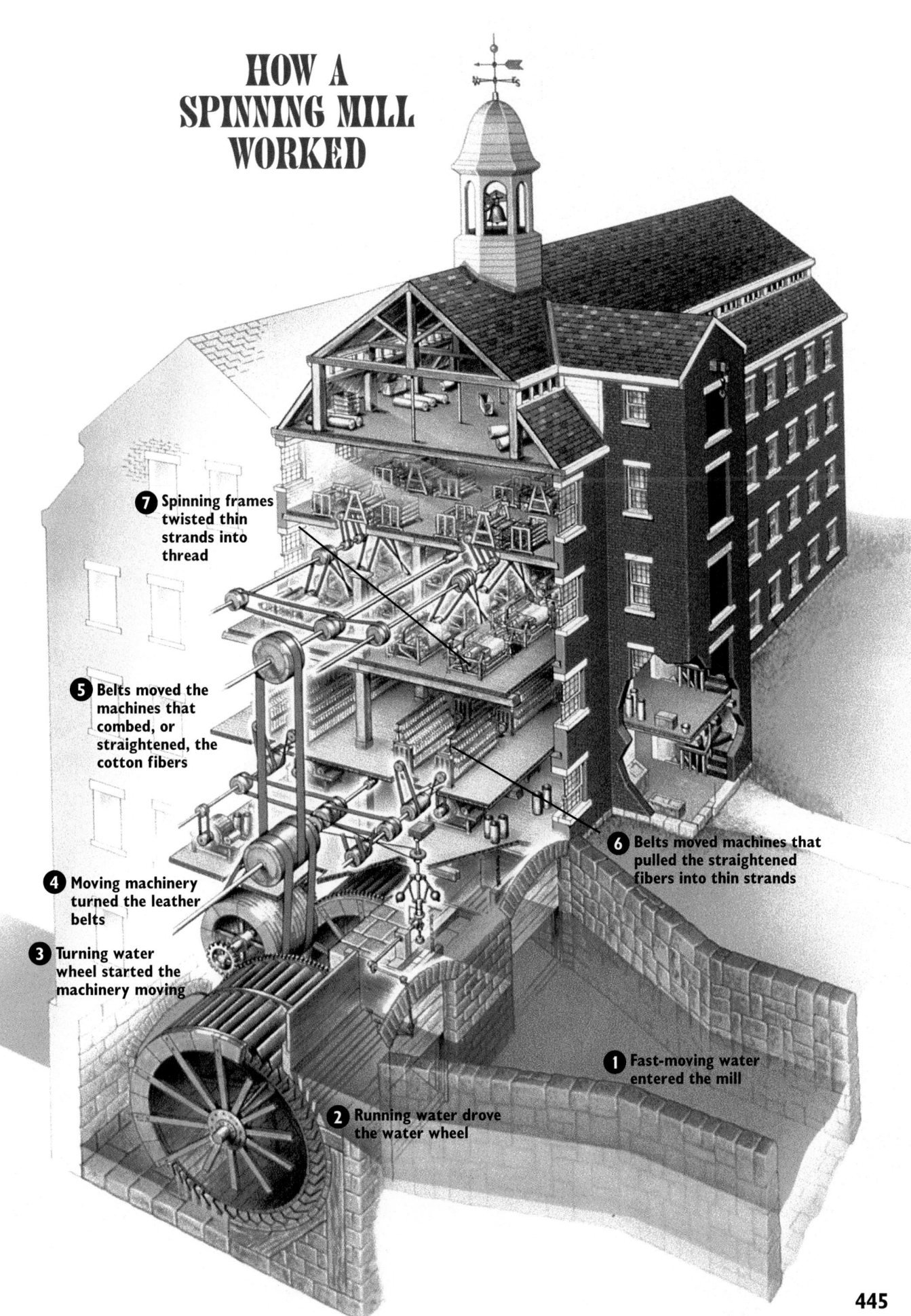

HOW A SPINNING MILL WORKED

7 Spinning frames twisted thin strands into thread

5 Belts moved the machines that combed, or straightened, the cotton fibers

6 Belts moved machines that pulled the straightened fibers into thin strands

4 Moving machinery turned the leather belts

3 Turning water wheel started the machinery moving

1 Fast-moving water entered the mill

2 Running water drove the water wheel

TOOLS FOR CHANGE

In addition to the cotton gin, Eli Whitney introduced another idea that helped spread the Industrial Revolution. The idea came from a French inventor, but Whitney was the first to use it in the United States.

In 1798 Whitney got a contract to make 10,000 muskets for the United States Army. Muskets—early kinds of rifles—were among the many items that were still being made by hand. If a musket broke, a gun maker had to make a new part to fit that particular gun.

Whitney said that he could make the 10,000 muskets in only two years. Many people doubted that he could deliver them in time. But Whitney had an idea. He planned to create tools that could make thousands of each part of a musket. A part from one of his muskets would fit any of his other muskets. In addition, all these identical parts would be made at once, which also saved time. These standard-sized parts were called interchangeable parts

At his factory near New Haven, Connecticut, Whitney slowly brought together machines and workers. In the end, he did not deliver the muskets in time. But his efforts led the way for the new advances that would be made in the Industrial Revolution.

Changes on the Farm

In 1832 the Industrial Revolution came to the farm. A Virginia farmer named Cyrus McCormick improved the horse-drawn reaper. A reaper is a machine that uses sharp blades to cut and harvest grain. By hand, farmers could only cut 2 or 3 acres of wheat a day. Using McCormick's reaper, they could cut up to 12 acres a day.

In his factory in Chicago, McCormick made reapers with interchangeable parts. This meant that broken reapers could be repaired quickly. McCormick even sent agents to make on-the-spot repairs during the harvest season.

In the Middle West, farmers complained that they were unable to cut through the tough roots of the prairie grass with their plows. In 1837 an Illinois blacksmith named John Deere made a better plow. He started with an old steel saw which he bent over a log. The soil fell cleanly off the new steel plow. Soon many farmers were using Deere's new plow. Later, historians called it "the plow that broke the plains" of the West.

Thanks to interchangeable parts, people can replace brakes, handle bars, tires—practically every part of a bicycle.

The old horse-drawn reaper (top) and the modern gasoline-powered reaper (above) have both been labor-savers for American farmers.

WHY IT MATTERS

The Industrial Revolution brought great wealth to some business owners. The lives of people who could buy factory goods improved. However, a price was paid for these gains. In the South, slavery was strengthened. In the North, many factory workers labored long hours for low wages.

In 1790 only one person in 20 lived in cities. By 1860 one of every six people did. By the end of the 1800s workers in the United States were producing more factory-made goods than workers in any other country, including Britain.

Reviewing Facts and Ideas

MAIN IDEAS

- The Industrial Revolution came to America in 1790 when Samuel Slater began building spinning machines.
- In 1793 Eli Whitney invented the cotton gin, and in 1798 he introduced the idea of interchangeable parts.
- In 1813 Francis Cabot Lowell built the first mill that handled all stages of cloth production under one roof.
- Cyrus McCormick's reaper of 1832 and John Deere's steel plow of 1837 made work on farms easier.

THINK ABOUT IT

1. How were Slater and Lowell important to the Industrial Revolution?

2. In what ways did the Industrial Revolution change farming?

3. **FOCUS** What were the effects of the Industrial Revolution?

4. **THINKING SKILL** What were some *effects*—positive and negative—of the invention of the cotton gin?

5. **WRITE** Suppose you are a mill girl in New England. Write a few paragraphs that explain what you like and dislike about your work.

ROADS, RIVERS, AND RAILS

READ ALOUD

In 1788 a French traveler named Brissot de Warville (bree SOH duh vahr VEE yuh) boarded a stagecoach in Fairfield, Connecticut. The coach clattered over the steep and rocky road to New York. Warville could not understand how the driver avoided "dashing the carriage to pieces."

Focus Activity

READ TO LEARN
What inventions improved transportation across the country?

VOCABULARY
stagecoach
steam engine
steamboat
canal
investor
lock

PEOPLE
Robert Fulton
DeWitt Clinton
Peter Cooper

PLACES
National Road
Erie Canal

THE BIG PICTURE

In 1800 the best roads in the United States were paved with rocks or logs. Most roads were narrow dirt trails filled with roots and tree stumps that could break wagon wheels. When it rained, deep puddles and sticky mud slowed the wagons and horses even more. It took a stagecoach, for example, four days to cover the 215 miles between Boston and New York. A stagecoach was a large, horse-drawn carriage for passengers, baggage, and mail. It was called a "stagecoach" because it had to stop frequently to pick up passengers or change horses, and trips were broken up into stages.

In 1811 the federal government started building the National Road. When it was finished, the road stretched from Cumberland, Maryland, all the way west to Vandalia, Illinois, linking the East with what was then the West. The National Road was made of stone and gravel, and was a big improvement in transportation. "The whole population is in motion," wrote one observer in 1828. Soon, however, the steam engine—an engine powered by steam pressure—would make travel even easier over both land and water.

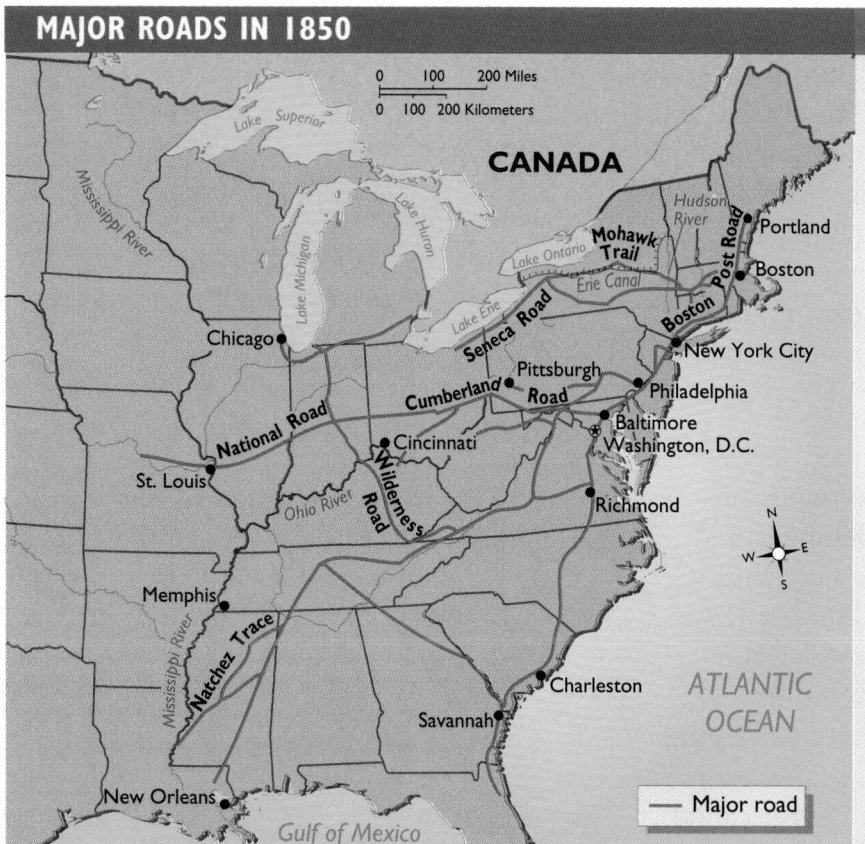

Roads of the mid-1800s had improved greatly since the beginning of the century. Even so, they were nothing like today's highways.

1. What state did travelers on the Mohawk Trail pass through?

2. How many miles long was the National Road?

MOVING WEST OF THE APPALACHIANS

In 1790 the population of the United States was growing rapidly. Most of its 4 million people lived within 50 miles of the Atlantic coast. During the next 50 years, transportation improved and people found ways to cross the Appalachian Mountains. By 1840 nearly one fourth of the population of 17 million people lived west of the Appalachians.

The people moving west traveled by river or road. Families who went by road carried as many of their belongings as they could. Pack horses, light carts, stagecoaches, and wagons crowded the roads.

New Englanders took the Mohawk Trail from Albany, New York, and headed toward Lake Erie. There, some people sailed across the lake to Ohio, or, in winter, walked across the ice.

By the 1840s these stagecoach passengers could expect improved roads.

People from the mid-Atlantic states often took the National Road from Maryland to Missouri. To reach the Ohio River valley they took the Pennsylvania Road to Pittsburgh and crossed the Ohio River on flatboats. In 1818 an English traveler, William Tell Harris, complained, "the number of wagons, horses, and passengers crossing and wading across the Ohio, was so great, that a great part of the morning was spent in waiting for my turn. . . ."

Southerners took the Wilderness Road to Kentucky and Tennessee. It had been improved since Daniel Boone's time, but one traveler called it "the worst on the whole continent even in the best weather."

STEAM POWER

Traveling by river was not always easy. However, because river travel was cheap, canoes, flat-bottomed boats, and even log rafts carried many goods and passengers down the country's rivers. Going upstream, against the current, was much harder. The steam engine solved this problem.

Full Steam Ahead!

An American artist named Robert Fulton learned of a powerful steam engine that had been developed in Scotland. In 1793 he gave up painting and began to design a steamboat. As its name suggests, a steamboat is a boat powered by a steam engine.

After years of work, Fulton designed a boat that used a steam engine and two large paddle wheels. Fulton called his steamboat the *Clermont*.

In August 1807, the *Clermont* was ready for a run from New York City north to Albany. Crowds cheered as the steamboat paddled upriver. The 150-mile trip took only 32 hours, a record time in those days. A flat-bottomed boat took as much as 11 days for the same trip. The *Clermont* proved that steamboats could move people and goods quickly and at a low cost. Soon tourists began taking the *Clermont* for pleasure, and merchants used it to transport their goods.

While people like Fulton built better boats, other people built better waterways. The governor of New York, DeWitt Clinton, dreamed of linking the Hudson River with Lake Erie through a canal, or human-built waterway.

Robert Fulton (below) and his *Clermont* (bottom) proved that steamboats were an easier way to travel upstream.

INVENTOR OF THE STEAMBOAT. IN 1807 HIS FIRST STEAMBOAT THE CLERMONT APPEARED ON THE HUDSON

ROBERT FULTON

BORN IN PENNSYLVANIA

HIGHER LEVEL

LOCK GATES BEING CLOSED

CANAL TOWPATH

HORSES AND MULES TOW BOATS ALONG CANAL

STONE WALL OF CANAL

LOCK GATES BEING OPENED

LOWER LEVEL

HOW A CANAL LOCK WORKS

What do you think happens as a boat travels through each lock of the canal?

THE ERIE CANAL

Most canals in the early 1800s were only a few miles long. Clinton's canal would be 350 miles long. "It is little short of madness to think of it!" said Thomas Jefferson.

Clinton asked investors from Europe for money. An investor is a person who uses money to buy or make something that will make him or her a profit. By 1817, Clinton had raised $7 million—an astonishing amount at the time.

Digging the Canal

In a ceremony on July 4th, 1817, Clinton broke ground on the Erie Canal. Local farmers were hired to dig, but there weren't enough of them. So European immigrants were hired, too.

Lake Erie is 565 feet higher than the Hudson River. To solve this problem, the workers built canal locks. A canal lock is like a water elevator that moves boats up and down. Review the diagram above to see how a lock works.

The Completed Canal

In 1825, after eight years of hard work, the Erie Canal was finally finished. Cannons roared and people cheered as Clinton sailed into New York Harbor from Lake Erie. "They have built the longest canal in the world in the least time, with the least experience, for the least money, and to the greatest public benefit," reported one newspaper in Buffalo, New York.

Before the canal was built, shipping goods between Buffalo and New York City took 20 days and cost $100 a ton. The Erie Canal brought the price down to $10 a ton and cut travel time to eight days. This helped increase trade between the East and the West.

The *Tom Thumb* marked the first use of steam engines on our country's railroads.

THE "IRON HORSE"

Railroads were also improved during the 1800s. The first railroad cars were pulled along iron rails by horses. The nation's first steam-powered locomotive was built by John Stevens in 1825. But today, a New York businessman named Peter Cooper is best remembered in connection with the steam-powered engine. In 1830 Cooper suggested that the Baltimore & Ohio Railroad Company use steam power instead of horses. "I will knock an engine together in six weeks that will pull carriages 10 miles an hour," he said. Peter Cooper named the engine *Tom Thumb*, after a character in a children's story.

When a Baltimore stagecoach company challenged the *Tom Thumb* to a race, Cooper eagerly accepted. The *Tom Thumb* had an engine problem and lost the race, but it still proved that steam engines could haul large loads long distances.

WHY IT MATTERS

Improvements in transportation allowed Americans to move farther west and businesses to ship more products. Building roads, canals, and railroads also created jobs. All of these new jobs attracted many immigrants to the United States.

 Reviewing Facts and Ideas

MAIN IDEAS

- Improved transportation allowed more people to move westward.
- The Erie Canal increased trade between the East and the West.
- Peter Cooper built the Tom Thumb in 1830 and showed that it could haul large loads over long distances.

THINK ABOUT IT

1. What were some of the problems of our country's early roads?

2. What did the *Clermont* prove?

3. **FOCUS** How did inventions improve transportation in our country?

4. **THINKING SKILL** Name two *points of view* on the Erie Canal in the lesson.

5. **GEOGRAPHY** What kind of maps would a canal builder use? Explain.

CITIZENSHIP
MAKING A DIFFERENCE

Cleaning Up Lake Pontchartrain

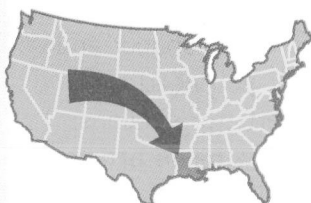

NEW ORLEANS, LOUISIANA Lake Pontchartrain is the largest body of water in Louisiana and a popular place for boating and picnics. But Lake Pontchartrain has a problem—pollution.

Since 1990, teacher Sue Ellen Lyons and the students in Project FUR have been hard at work attacking this problem. FUR stands for Fight Urban Runoff. "Sometimes," says Mrs. Lyons, "city dwellers throw used motor oil, old paint, and other dangerous chemicals down the storm drains. Water that goes into the drains flows into the drainage canals and then into Lake Pontchartrain. Many people just don't make the connection between dumping trash down the storm drains and lake pollution."

The pollution in Lake Pontchartrain hurts shrimp, crab, fish, and other marine and plant life. "To fight this problem," says Mrs. Lyons, "FUR members go storm drain stencilling." Several times a year, 20 to 30 students spread out through city neighborhoods with spray paint and stencils. The volunteers stencil the warning "Dump No Waste—Drains to Lake" on drain covers or on the curb near the drain. This helps remind residents that dumping dangerous material into drains hurts Lake Pontchartrain. Charles Childress, age 12, says he became a volunteer because, "I wanted to make people aware of what we're doing to the earth, how we might be harming it when we could be helping it."

The students encourage people to recycle used motor oil by bringing it to service station collection centers. "Every time a person sees our spray-painted warning on a storm drain and decides not to throw their trash into the drain, we're making a difference," says Charles. "I think everyone should care about this. The future depends on it. After all, if we abuse our natural resources now, they might not be there when we grow up."

" . . . everyone should care about this."

Charles F Childress III

453

STUDYSKILLS

Reading a Newspaper

VOCABULARY

dateline	feature article
editor	headline
editorial	news article

WHY THE SKILL MATTERS

In the nineteenth century, newspapers were people's main source of information. There was no television or radio. There were no computers. People relied on newspapers to find out what was happening in their town, city, or country, as well as in the world.

Today, people can get news from television or radio. Still, many read newspapers to find out what is going on in the country and in the world. For example, if you follow sports, you read the sports section to find out about the previous day's sporting events. If you want to see a film, you look at the entertainment page in your local paper to find out what is playing.

USING THE SKILL

In order to understand a newspaper and to make the best use of it, you need to know about its different parts, or sections. The first part usually contains **news articles**. A news article describes an important event that has recently taken place. News articles can be about local, state, national, or international events.

A news article always begins with a **headline**, a sentence or phrase printed in

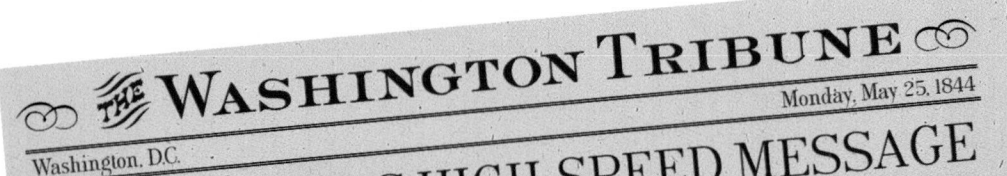

THE WASHINGTON TRIBUNE

Monday, May 25, 1844

Washington, D.C.

MORSE SENDS HIGH-SPEED MESSAGE

Washington D.C., May 23—On Saturday evening Samuel Morse successfully demonstrated his electric telegraph before a large audience of Congressmen and curious onlookers in the Capitol building. Mr. Morse had strung electric wire from the Capitol to Baltimore, Maryland. Telegraph devices connected to the wire at each end received and sent messages. On his telegraph Mr. Morse tapped out a coded message of dots and dashes. The dots and dashes represent letters of the alphabet. Electrical current carried the message to Baltimore, where a pencil attached to the telegraph printed the codes. Then a telegraph operator translated the

"News Worth Reading" **The Cascade T**

★ California ★ Wednesday ★ October

ARCHAEOLOGISTS RUINS OF ANCIENT

By Vince Ito

DEATH VALLEY, October 2 –A team of archaeo University of California announced today that t ered the remains of a city in Death Valley that 1000 B.C. The team, headed by Dr. Walter Jones, ing views of a people whose culture revolved arou tural life long extinct within the now harsh en desert.

large type across the top of the news article. Headlines, like the ones on the previous page, are meant to catch the reader's attention. Usually a news article also has a dateline. A dateline tells when and where the story was written. The dateline on one of the news articles on page 454 is DEATH VALLEY, October 2.

The first paragraph of a news article should catch the reader's interest and tell the most important facts in the story. Usually the first paragraph answers the questions *Who? What? When?* and *Where? Who* is the story about? *What* is it about? *When* did the events take place? *Where* did they take place? The rest of the article gives more facts. It generally does not give the writer's opinions.

Many newspapers also offer feature articles. A feature article is a detailed report on a person, an issue, or an event. For example, the newspaper containing the article about Samuel Morse on page 454 might also have included a feature article about inventions that change the way people live.

In most newspapers you might also find an editorial page. An editorial is an article in which the editors, or people who run the newspaper, give their opinions on important issues. The editorial page might also contain letters to the editors which are written by the newspaper's readers to tell how they feel about certain issues. For example, a week after Samuel Morse's demonstration, the

Washington Tribune might have published letters that voiced opinions about the new invention.

TRYING THE SKILL

Why do news articles often tell the *who, what, where,* and *when* of an event in the first paragraph? Before computers were used, newspapers were typeset and laid out by hand. But editors could not predict what each day's news would be. If more news arrived as the day's deadline drew near, long articles were cut to make room. Editors cut the ends of articles to save time. To make sure that the important facts were printed, news writers made a practice of telling *who, what, where,* and *when* at the beginning of a news story.

Suppose you were writing a newspaper article about Morse's demonstration. Whom would you identify in your first paragraph? What would you say had happened? What headline might you write for your article?

REVIEWING THE SKILL

1. What is a headline of a news article? A dateline? An editorial?

2. What is the purpose of the first paragraph of a news article?

3. Compare a newspaper to a news show on television. List three ways they are the same. List three ways they differ.

4. What would be some topics for at least two feature articles in an edition of the *Washington Tribune* today?

5. How can knowing how to read a newspaper help someone to be a better citizen?

- **A news article** tells about important events. A **feature article** gives details about a person, issue, or event. The **editorial** page has opinions written by the **editors.**

- **Decide which part of the newspaper you want or need to read.**

NEW PEOPLE AND NEW IDEAS

Focus Activity

READ TO LEARN
How did life in the United States change in the early 1800s?

PEOPLE
Richard Allen
Absalom Jones
Andrew Jackson

READ ALOUD

In the early 1800s the historian Thomas B. Searight wrote about the newly built National Road: "As many as twenty-four coaches have been counted in line at one time on the road, and large, broad-wheeled wagons, covered with white canvas . . . laden with merchandise and drawn by six Conestoga horses were visible all the day long at every point."

THE BIG PICTURE

In the previous lesson you read how transportation improved in the 1800s. This caused great changes in the early United States. People were able to move from one part of the country to another more easily than ever before. Many of them moved from the East to the lands between the Appalachians and the Mississippi River. Today, that's part of what we call the Middle West, but to those early travelers it was the western frontier.

Many other changes were occurring in the United States at this time. The northern states abolished slavery, and thousands of African Americans were creating new, free lives there. Improved transportation allowed many more immigrants to come to this country, settling in the East and along the frontier.

In the city, the Industrial Revolution created new jobs. On the farm, it provided new ways to grow, harvest, and transport crops. In both places, it changed many aspects of Americans' everyday lives. And as people changed the way they lived, they changed the way they viewed the government.

CHANGES FOR AFRICAN AMERICANS

By 1820 about one eighth of all African Americans were free. The Northern states had outlawed slavery. As you have read, many free African Americans were creating new lives. Some stayed with their former owners and worked for wages. Others worked for themselves as blacksmiths and carpenters, or became farmhands, or sailors on merchant ships. Free African Americans also went west to find better lives. They started farms and raised crops or livestock.

However, all African Americans still faced discrimination from white settlers. Even those African Americans in the North who had gained their freedom were often treated badly. In most states, they had no legal rights.

In the West, many had their land taken from them. For example, John Randolph had freed his slaves and left them land in Ohio in his will. In 1832, 385 free African Americans traveled to Ohio to claim the land. When they arrived, they found that Randolph's relatives had taken all of the land.

The A.M.E. Church

With little help from whites, African Americans had to help each other. They did this through societies and churches. The earliest of these was established in the 1790s by Richard Allen and Absalom Jones, African American leaders in Philadelphia. When the two men were ordered to sit in a separate area of a white church, Allen said they "thought it necessary to provide for ourselves [African Americans] a house separate from our white brethren [brothers]."

Allen and Jones established the Bethel African Methodist Episcopal (A.M.E.) Church. A group of A.M.E. churches was formed in 1816, with Richard Allen as their bishop. By 1820, the A.M.E. Church had 4,000 members in Philadelphia and almost 2,000 in Baltimore.

In addition to the A.M.E. Church, Richard Allen (above) started the Free African Society in 1787. "Leaving the Old Homestead" (below) was painted by J. Wilkins.

Many of the immigrants from Europe in the 1800s arrived in New York City (above).

IMMIGRANTS TO THE UNITED STATES
1845-1850

All other
95,877

Canada and
Newfoundland
33,621

West Indies
11,425

Great Britain
206,068

Germany
363,693

Ireland
638,795

Source: U.S. Bureau of the Census

GRAPH WORK

Between 1845 and 1850 more than 1,300,000 immigrants came to the United States.

1. Which country was the third-largest source of immigrants during these years?

2. How many immigrants came from Ireland between 1845 and 1850?

THE CHANGING POPULATION

The population of the United States was changing in the 1800s. The free African American community was growing. Another change involved immigrants. In the early 1800s a new wave of immigrants arrived. During the 1820s nearly 500,000 people left Europe for the United States. By 1850, 2.5 million more immigrants had arrived.

Some came to escape crop failures, food shortages, and unemployment in their own countries. Many came from Great Britain, the Netherlands, and Scandinavia. Beginning in the 1840s, the largest numbers of immigrants came from Ireland and Germany. Look at the graph on this page to see some of the other countries from which immigrants arrived.

Irish immigrants often settled in port cities such as Boston and New York. They worked mainly as laborers. Many of the German immigrants were farmers. Most of them settled in Missouri, Ohio, Wisconsin, and Illinois.

458

A CHANGING NATION

The United States was a country that contained two different worlds. One was the world of the farm and the small town. The other was the world of the big city. In the early 1800s both of these worlds were changing.

Growing Cities

An Englishwoman named Frances Trollope wrote in 1832 that Americans were a "busy, bustling, industrious population." Much of this activity took place in the growing cities. In the early 1800s the ports of Boston, Philadelphia, Baltimore, New York, and New Orleans became major centers for trade and industry. To the west, St. Louis, Cincinnati, Cleveland, and Chicago became early centers of trade.

Owners of factories and textile mills hired men, women, and children to run their machines. These new jobs attracted immigrants and rural Americans to the cities. As the population of the cities grew, craftworkers and merchants hired more people to make goods to sell to all these new customers. Larger cities also needed more doctors, lawyers, and teachers. Port cities needed workers to load and unload ships.

Life in the Cities

As the cities grew, new buildings went up. Wealthy merchants built themselves fine townhouses. But housing for workers was built in a hurry, and very cheaply.

Cities offered plenty of work and entertainment. But they were often dirty because there was no organized system for removing garbage. People simply threw it into the street, and animals wandered by and ate it.

As the 1800s progressed, more boys and girls in cities attended grammar school. Because there were more printing presses, textbooks became more widely available. Still, many city children missed school because they worked such long hours in factories and mills.

Changes in the West

Improvements in transportation made it easier for people to move west. New technology also made it possible for many farmers to prosper. For example, inventions such as the McCormack reaper helped farmers plant more crops. Steam-powered ships carried wheat to Europe faster. Wheat became the major cash crop of the Ohio River valley.

The people who moved west founded new communities, which gradually grew into towns. The towns attracted skilled workers such as furniture makers, blacksmiths, and storekeepers. Churches and schools were built.

As areas became crowded, new towns were started. Gradually, settlements pushed farther and farther west.

This factory in Staten Island, New York, was built in the mid-1800s.

This painting shows an early nineteenth-century election. The portrait of President Andrew Jackson (below) was painted by Thomas Sully about 1829.

CHANGES IN DEMOCRACY

You have been reading about how life in the United States changed during the 1800s. The nation itself changed, too. In its first 50 years, 12 new states— Alabama, Arkansas, Illinois, Indiana, Kentucky, Louisiana, Michigan, Mississippi, Missouri, Ohio, Tennessee, and Vermont—joined the country. Look at a political map of the United States on pages R4–R5 to find them.

A Change in Voters

In the original 13 states only white men who owned property could vote. The people in the new states, though, had different ideas about democracy. They passed laws allowing all white men over the age of 21 to vote. The original states soon changed their voting laws. In the Presidential election of 1828, almost three times as many people voted as had in 1824.

What were these new voters like? Most of them did not have great wealth or education. Many of them had experienced great hardships. Some had braved journeys across the ocean or the mountains to start new lives—which were usually not easy. So many new people competed for jobs that employers did not have to pay high wages. Almost all workers' earnings were spent on housing and food.

Many working people in the United States came to believe that they wanted the country to be run by someone like themselves. So when they voted for the first time in 1828, the majority of people helped elect a President unlike anyone who had served before him.

A President for the People

Andrew Jackson was from Tennessee. He was the first President to be elected from a state west of the Appalachians. He was the first President who was not from a wealthy family, and he had never gone to college. His opponent, John Quincy Adams, described him as a man "who can scarcely spell his own name."

Jackson did not have much formal education, but he learned a great deal from experience. He had been a lawyer, a judge, a Congressman, and a rich landowner. He became a national hero after he led his troops to victory against the British in the Battle of New Orleans in 1815. On the march from Tennessee to New Orleans, Jackson gave his horse to a wounded soldier. He then walked nearly 500 miles on foot, causing his soldiers to name him "Old Hickory," after the toughness of hickory wood.

Jackson thought of himself as a common man. He ran for President in 1828; his motto was, "Let the people rule."

During his eight years as President, Jackson supported reforms that helped workers and poor people. However, African Americans, Native Americans, and women continued to have few or no political rights. During Jackson's presidency, the nation began to divide over slavery and the removal of Native Americans from their lands.

WHY IT MATTERS

The United States of the 1700s was made up mostly of farmers. In the early 1800s immigrants from many countries came to the United States. Cities grew larger and ideas about government began to change. Many people started to think ordinary people should have a greater say in the nation's government.

DID YOU KNOW?

What did students read in the early 1800s?

Like you, students read textbooks about reading, writing, and math. The most important textbooks of the 1800s were the *McGuffey Readers*. Most of them were written by William McGuffey, one of the people who moved out west and settled in Ohio. McGuffey Readers were so popular that schools were still using them in the 1900s.

Reviewing Facts and Ideas

MAIN IDEAS

- The Northern states outlawed slavery. Freed African Americans learned trades and started new lives. Still, they had few rights, if any.

- European immigrants flocked to the growing cities of the United States.

- Voters elected Andrew Jackson, the "People's President," in 1828.

THINK ABOUT IT

1. Why were black churches like the A.M.E. Church formed?

2. Where did most of the immigrants of the early 1800s come from?

3. **FOCUS** How did life in the United States change in the early 1800s?

4. **THINKING SKILL** Make a flow chart showing a chain of *causes* and *effects* linking the Industrial Revolution with the election of Andrew Jackson.

5. **WRITE** If you had lived in the early 1800s, would you have preferred to live in a growing city or on a farm? Explain your choice.

Legacy

Tall Tales

Have you ever stretched the truth when telling your friends about an adventure you or someone you know had? Just to amaze your listeners, did you make the hero of your story braver, faster, or more clever than in real life? In the 1800s, Americans in frontier towns loved to tell amazing tales about real people. They stretched the truth so much that the stories became known as tall tales.

Famous tall tale characters tell us much about the qualities that were admired then.

Tall tales are a valuable link to America's past. Not only do they remind us of character traits that we admire, but they also tell how our country developed.

According to legend, Johnny Appleseed gave apple seeds to every man, woman, and child he ever saw. The man behind the tall tales, John Chapman, was born in Massachusetts in the late 1700s. The Shawnee named him the "Appleseed Man" because he planted apple orchards throughout Ohio, Indiana, and Illinois. Today he is a symbol of American cooperation and generosity.

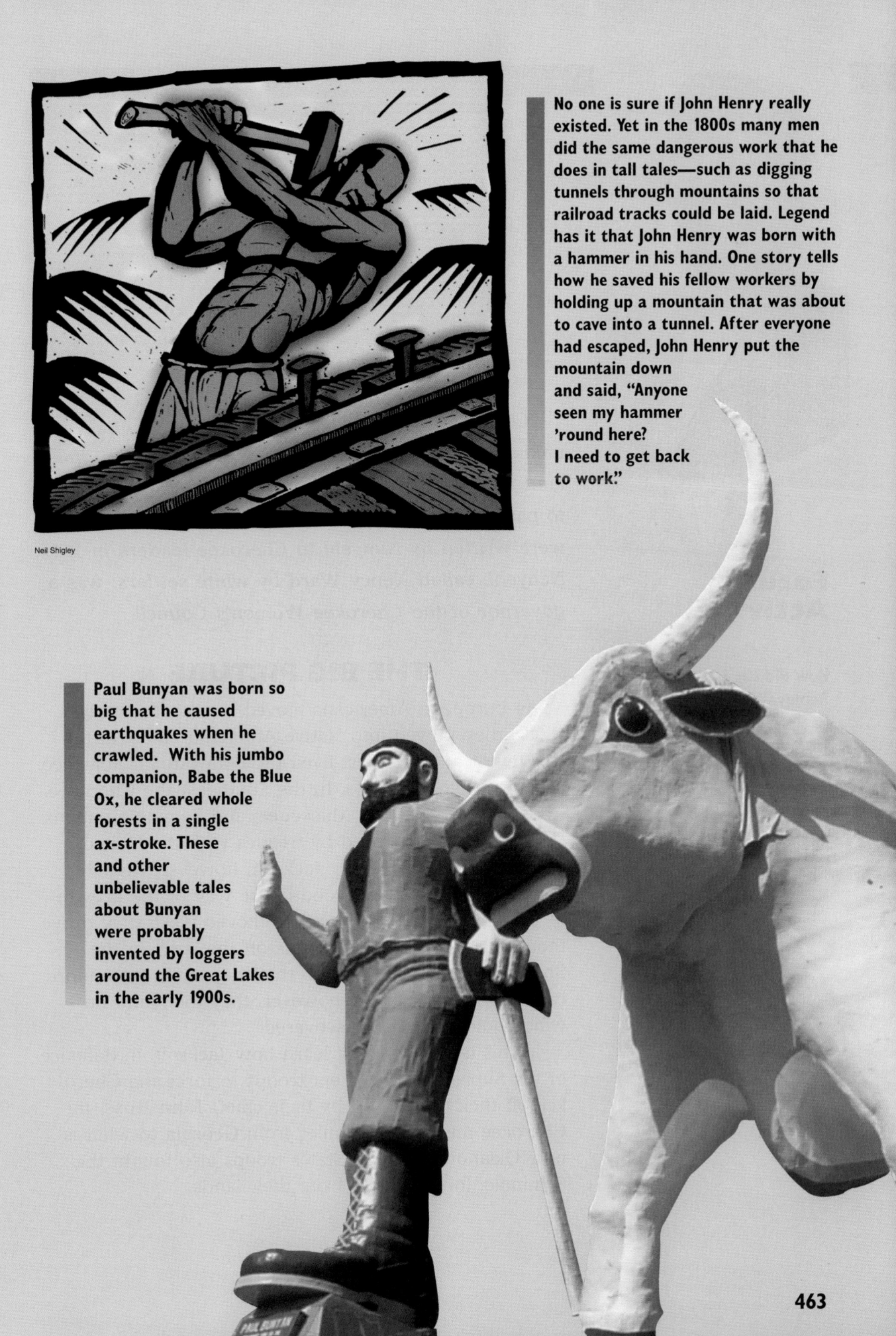

No one is sure if John Henry really existed. Yet in the 1800s many men did the same dangerous work that he does in tall tales—such as digging tunnels through mountains so that railroad tracks could be laid. Legend has it that John Henry was born with a hammer in his hand. One story tells how he saved his fellow workers by holding up a mountain that was about to cave into a tunnel. After everyone had escaped, John Henry put the mountain down and said, "Anyone seen my hammer 'round here? I need to get back to work."

Neil Shigley

Paul Bunyan was born so big that he caused earthquakes when he crawled. With his jumbo companion, Babe the Blue Ox, he cleared whole forests in a single ax-stroke. These and other unbelievable tales about Bunyan were probably invented by loggers around the Great Lakes in the early 1900s.

463

CONFLICTS OVER LAND

Focus Activity

READ TO LEARN

How did the Indian Removal Act affect Native Americans of the Southeast?

VOCABULARY

Indian Removal Act
Trail of Tears

PEOPLE

John Ross
Sequoyah
Osceola

PLACE

Indian Territory

READ ALOUD

"Cherokee mothers do not wish to go to an unknown country. We have raised all of you on the land which we now inhabit. . . . We beg of you not to part with any more of our land." These words were written by Nanyehi to Cherokee leaders in 1817. Nanyehi, called Nancy Ward by white settlers, was a governor of the Cherokee Women's Council.

THE BIG PICTURE

As European Americans moved west in the early 1800s, they moved into Native American lands. In the Northwest and Midwest lived the Potawatomi, Shawnee, and many other groups. In the Southeast the Cherokee, Chocktaw, Chickasaw, Muscogee, and Seminole nations lived on lands protected by treaties with the United States. President Andrew Jackson, however, thought that Native Americans stood in the way of the growth of the United States. As settlers moved west, they drove thousands of Native Americans off the land. In the Southeast, they took land so that they could raise more cash crops. In Georgia, however, they took land on which gold had been discovered.

In this lesson you will learn how Jackson, in defiance of the Supreme Court, sent troops to force the Cherokee off their lands. Led by their chief, John Ross, the Cherokee marched 800 miles from Georgia to what is now Oklahoma. United States troops also fought the Seminole, forcing them from their lands.

INDIAN REMOVAL

Andrew Jackson believed in a simple government, "protecting all and granting favors to none." He fought any law that he believed would harm American farmers, new settlers on the frontier, or working people. Not everyone, however, was protected by President Jackson.

Native Americans of the Southeast

In the early 1800s, some Native American communities in the Southeast were growing. These groups included the Cherokee, Choctaw, Chickasaw, Muscogee, and Seminole. These groups farmed the land and had organized governments.

The Cherokee had the first written Native American alphabet. It was developed by Sequoyah, a Cherokee silversmith. Sequoyah worked for 12 years to create this alphabet, using Greek, Hebrew, and English symbols to stand for the sounds of the Cherokee language. Sequoyah compared the job to "catching a wild animal and taming it."

Thousands of Cherokee men, women, and children learned to read and write in their own language. In 1828, Sequoyah published the first Native American newspaper, the *Cherokee Phoenix,* which is still printed today. Sequoyah remained a respected leader until his death in 1843. The giant California redwood tree is named *Sequoia* in his honor.

In the early 1800s, some Cherokee learned European ways so that they might get along with their new neighbors. Cherokee children learned to read and write English. Some Cherokee became merchants and cattle ranchers. A few owned large plantations with slaves. Even so, tensions between white settlers and the Cherokee increased.

Sequoyah (above) holds a sample of the Cherokee alphabet. The Council House (right) in New Echota served as the Cherokee national capital until 1838.

New Echota State Historic Site

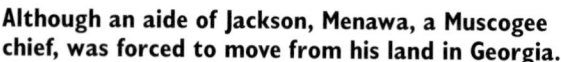
Although an aide of Jackson, Menawa, a Muscogee chief, was forced to move from his land in Georgia.

Removal Begins

In 1831 United States troops began forcing Native Americans to leave their homes. The Choctaw left first, then the Chickasaw and the Muscogee. In Alabama, some of the Muscogee who refused to leave were forced into slavery. Finally, the Georgia government gave away the Cherokee farms to white settlers. The Cherokee still refused to leave.

The Cherokee, led by their chief, John Ross, took their case to the Supreme Court. Ross had a Cherokee mother and a Scottish father. Read Ross's point of view on the Indian Removal Act in the excerpt on this page. How would you describe his attitude toward the United States government?

Excerpt from the Papers of Chief John Ross, 1807–1839

*I am still in the midst of efforts to **prevail** on the United States Government to turn aside, as far as may now be possible, the ruin they are bringing upon my native Country; yes . . . the ruin—and for what? Have we done any wrong? We are not charged with any. We have a Country which others **covet**. This is the only offense we have ever yet been charged with.*

---

prevail: to use persuasion
covet: to desire something that belongs to someone else

THE INDIAN REMOVAL ACT

The United States government had signed treaties with the Cherokee and the other Native Americans who lived in the Southeast, protecting their lands from white settlers. However, the demand for cotton had increased because of the growing textile industry, and planters wanted more land. In 1830 gold was discovered on Cherokee land. Thousands of gold miners trespassed to hunt for riches. Soon, states such as Georgia began to force Native Americans to leave. The Cherokee asked the United States government to protect them. Jackson's solution to the problem was to make Native Americans move to lands west of the Mississippi.

In 1830 Congress passed the Indian Removal Act. This law allowed the President to remove Native Americans from their homelands. In return for the land they lost, they would receive land in Indian Territory, which is now Oklahoma and parts of Kansas.

In 1832 the Court ruled that "the laws of Georgia can have no force" on Cherokee lands. The decision meant that Georgia could not force the Cherokee from their land.

President Jackson refused to enforce the Court's decision. "[Supreme Court Justice] John Marshall has made his decision; now let him enforce it," he said. In 1838, United States soldiers rounded up the Cherokee, burning their houses. They then forced the Cherokee to march 800 miles to Indian Territory.

"The Place Where They Cried"

The march took over a year. They trekked from their fertile mountain homelands to much less desirable territory. About 4,000 of 15,000 Cherokee people died along the way. Among them was Quatie, the wife of Chief John Ross. She had given her only blanket to a sick child.

A soldier named John Burnett, who was an interpreter on the march, wrote many years later:

> [I] witnessed the execution [carrying out] of the most brutal order in the History of American Warfare. I saw helpless Cherokees arrested and dragged from their homes. . . .
> I saw them loaded like cattle or sheep into six hundred and forty-five wagons and started toward the west.

The Cherokee called this march to Indian territory "the place where they cried." Over time, this bitter journey has come to be known as the Trail of Tears. On the map on page 468, you can follow the route of this and other journeys that Native Americans of the Southeast were forced to make.

One of every four Cherokee people died on the Trail of Tears (below).

The Granger Collection

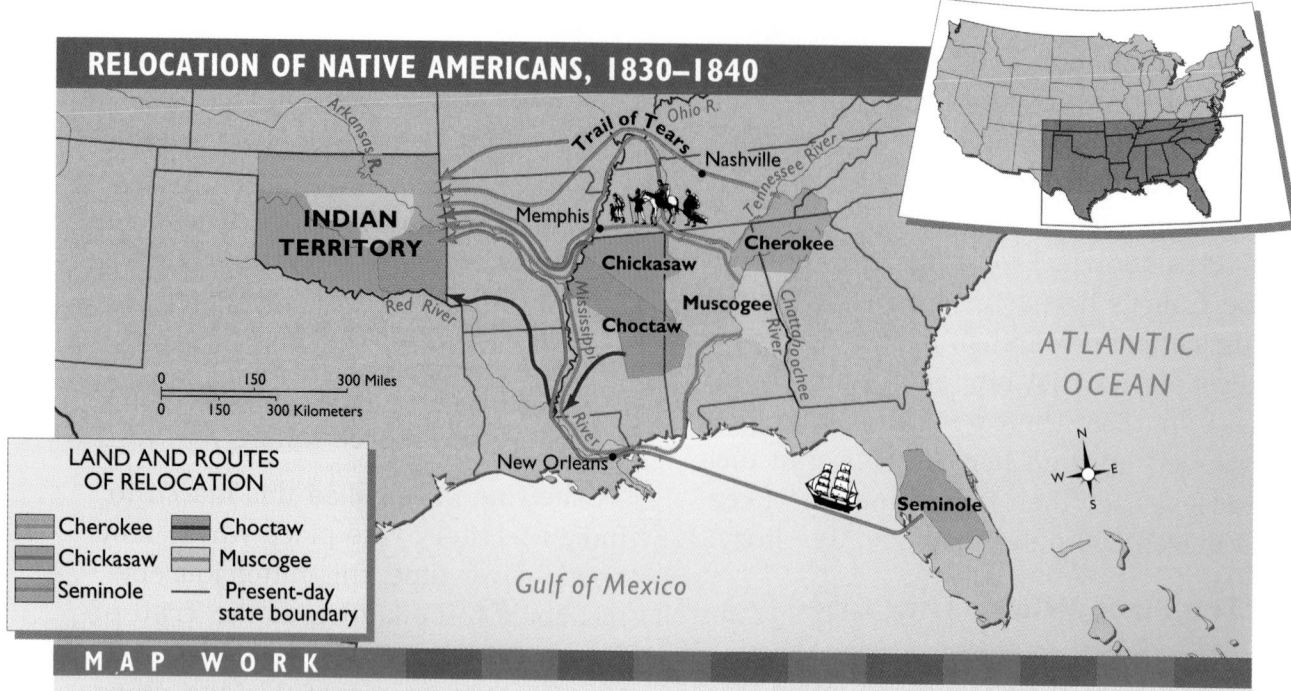

Arkansas R.

Ohio R.

Trail of Tears

Nashville

Memphis

INDIAN TERRITORY

Tennessee River

Cherokee

Chickasaw

Red River

Mississippi River

Muscogee

Choctaw

Chattahoochee River

ATLANTIC OCEAN

0   150   300 Miles
0   150   300 Kilometers

New Orleans

Seminole

Gulf of Mexico

N W E S

LAND AND ROUTES OF RELOCATION

Cherokee — Choctaw
Chickasaw — Muscogee
Seminole — Present-day state boundary

MAP WORK

The Trail of Tears is now a national historic trail. From Georgia, it leads to Tahlequah, Oklahoma, today's Cherokee national capital.

1. Which Native Americans traveled by water?
2. Which Native Americans were relocated along the Red River?

The Seminole Fight Back

In Florida, the Seminole, led by Osceola, fought two wars against the United States to try to keep their lands.

The First Seminole War lasted from 1816 to 1818. Plantation owners in northern Florida wanted Seminole lands. They also resented the Seminole protecting run-away slaves.

Osceola, Seminole Chief

When the first war ended, the United States took over 24 million acres of Seminole land.

The Second Seminole War began in 1835, when the Seminole refused to move to Indian Territory. After several victories, the Seminole faced an army of 4,000 men led by General Thomas S. Jesup. Thousands of Seminole died in battle or from disease or starvation.

In 1837, Osceola agreed to discuss peace. Even though he was carrying a white flag of peace, Jesup put Osceola in prison, where he died. Among his last words were: "I have done nothing to be ashamed of; it is for those to feel shame who entrapped me." By 1842 most Seminole had surrendered and had been moved to Indian Territory.

Many Americans did not approve of the Seminole Wars. A newspaper editor in New York wrote: "We commenced the war without cause, other than the desire to rob the Indians of their lands . . .

with no purpose, it would seem, but to allow an army of speculators to 'pick and steal,' and to sink the nation deeper into its ignominy [disgrace]."

WHY IT MATTERS

Jackson encouraged greater participation in government by the average citizen. Even so, Jackson's treatment of Native Americans had cast a cloud over the country.

Today, many native Americans have reestablished their tribal governments. Many Cherokee still live in northeastern Oklahoma. In 1970, the United States government agreed to pay the Seminole over $12 million for land that had been taken from them.

Before the relocation of the mid-1800s, the Seminole people (above) lived in Florida, which is where this Seminole artifact (right) was found.

✔️ Reviewing Facts and Ideas

MAIN IDEAS

- In the early 1800s Americans wanted to expand into rich Native American lands in the Southeast.

- In the 1800s the Cherokee in the Southeast created a Cherokee alphabet.

- In 1830 Congress passed the Indian Removal Act, forcing Native Americans to move to Indian Territory.

- The Seminole fought two wars against the United States and lost. They had to give up much of their land.

THINK ABOUT IT

1. Who was Sequoyah? What were his achievements?

2. Why did some Americans want the Seminole lands in Florida?

3. **FOCUS** How did the Indian Removal Act affect Native Americans?

4. **THINKING SKILL** Describe steps you might have taken to _solve_ the _problem_ of land ownership in the Southeast?

5. **WRITE** Write a letter to President Jackson from your own point of view about the Indian Removal Act.

CHAPTER 16 REVIEW

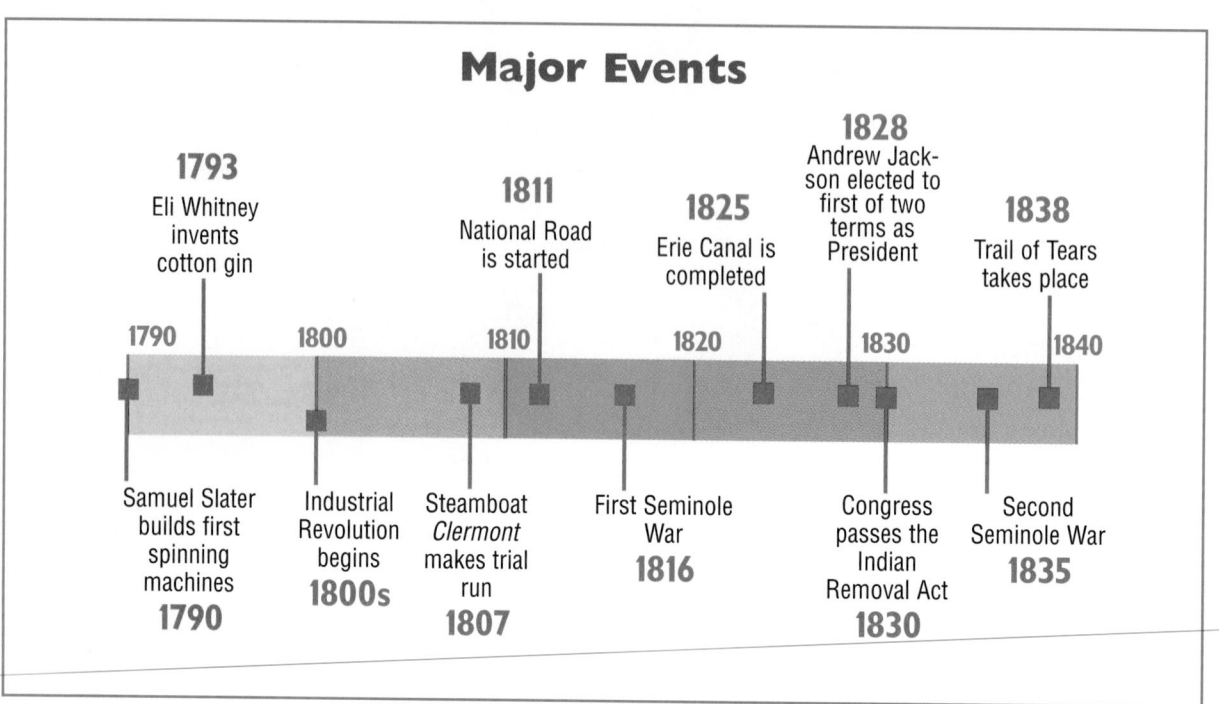

Major Events

1793 Eli Whitney invents cotton gin

1811 National Road is started

1825 Erie Canal is completed

1828 Andrew Jackson elected to first of two terms as President

1838 Trail of Tears takes place

1790 — 1800 — 1810 — 1820 — 1830 — 1840

Samuel Slater builds first spinning machines **1790**

Industrial Revolution begins **1800s**

Steamboat *Clermont* makes trial run **1807**

First Seminole War **1816**

Congress passes the Indian Removal Act **1830**

Second Seminole War **1835**

THINKING ABOUT VOCABULARY

Number a sheet of paper from 1 to 5. Next to each number write the word or term below that best completes the sentence.

Industrial Revolution   investor
lock   Trail of Tears
steam engine

1. A canal _____ moves boats from one water level to another.

2. A _____ uses the energy from steam to power a piece of machinery.

3. The large-scale change in industry and technology in the 1800s is known as the _____.

4. Someone who uses money to buy or make something that will make them a profit is an _____.

5. The forced march of the Cherokee to the Indian territory is known as the _____.

THINKING ABOUT FACTS

1. What did the cotton gin do? How did it change the economy of the South?

2. What were some of the first machines that had interchangeable parts?

3. How did the National Road improve transportation in the United States?

4. From which two countries did the largest number of immigrants come in the 1800s?

5. How was the growth of cities and rural farms affected by the Industrial Revolution?

6. How was Andrew Jackson different from Presidents elected before him?

7. What were some of the achievements of the Cherokee culture?

8. Why did Jackson want the Indian Removal Act to be passed?

9. Who was Osceola? What did he try to achieve?

10. Which events listed on the time line made it easier for settlers to move to the West?

THINK AND WRITE

WRITING A NEWSPAPER ARTICLE

Suppose that you are a newspaper reporter assigned to write an article about work in the mills in the early 1800s. Include observations about the machinery, workers, and working conditions.

WRITING A REPORT

Write a report describing the situation of free African Americans in the North and middle Atlantic states in the early 1800s. Include facts about daily life and organizations that helped African Americans.

WRITING A DIALOGUE

Write a dialogue between a person who supports the Indian Removal Act and a representative of the Cherokee nation.

APPLYING STUDY SKILLS

READING A NEWSPAPER

Answer the following questions to practice the skill of reading a newspaper.

1. What are three different kinds of articles that can be found in a newspaper?
2. What appears on the editorial page of a newspaper?
3. Reread the article from the *Washington Tribune* on page 454. What is the dateline for that article?
4. Using the same article, answer the questions: Who? What? When? and Where?
5. Why is knowing how to read a newspaper an important skill?

Summing Up the Chapter

Copy the matrix chart on a separate sheet of paper. Then review the chapter to fill in the blank sections. After you have finished, use the information in the chart to write a paragraph that answers the question, "How did the United States change in the early 1800s?"

Event	Years	Location	Results
		Georgia	Southern economy booms; plantations need slave workers
The Industrial Revolution		Northeast, Middle America	
Transportation improves		From the East to the Midwest	
Cotton planters want more land; gold discovered on Cherokee land	1816–1830s		

CHAPTER 17

In Search of Better Lives

THINKING ABOUT HISTORY AND GEOGRAPHY

The story of Chapter 17 takes place in the first half of the 1800s. During this time, the high cost of land in the eastern United States encouraged people to move west where land was easy to get. Later, the discovery of gold in California and Oregon helped begin the greatest movement westward in our nation's history. In the process, Native Americans, who had built many of the trails that led the eastern settlers west, lost much of their land. Read the time line below to follow some events from this period.

PACIFIC OCEAN

1820s
TEXAS

"Texas Fever" causes people from the United States to settle in Texas

1840s
OREGON TERRITORY

Pioneers travel to the West on the Oregon Trail

1848
MEXICO CITY

Mexico loses half of its territory in the Treaty of Guadalupe Hidalgo

Oregon
Territory

Sutter's Mill

California

UNITED
STATES

Texas

Gulf of
Mexico

MEXICO

Mexico City

1849

SUTTER'S MILL,
CALIFORNIA

Forty-Niners rush west
after the discovery of
gold in California

1850

CALIFORNIA

California is admitted
to the Union

CALIFORNIA REPUBLIC

TEXAS AND THE MEXICAN WAR

READ ALOUD

Mary Austin Holley was impressed with the rich lands of Texas. In 1831 she wrote to her friends in the United States, "The newcomer has but to plant his seeds in the ground, and the increase is astonishing." Holley was one of the many people who had left the United States to start a new life in the West.

THE BIG PICTURE

In the early 1500s, Spanish explorers became the first Europeans to set foot in Texas. As you read in Chapter 5, Spain was building a colonial empire in the Americas, called New Spain. By 1540 this empire had spread North to the present-day boundaries of Texas and New Mexico.

For many years the Spaniards had heard stories of "the great kingdom of the Tejas (TAY hahs)." These stories described Native American people, the Caddo, who called themselves *tejas*, or "friends." The Spanish explored the region occupied by the Caddo, and claimed it for their empire.

In 1821 Mexico won independence from Spain, and Texas became part of Mexico. Mexican leaders worried that the United States might try to take control of Texas. Since the Louisiana Purchase, people from the United States had been moving steadily west. They believed that it was obvious, or manifest, that their nation was fated to grow west to the Pacific Ocean and south to the Rio Grande. This belief became known as Manifest Destiny. The Mexican government began looking for settlers to occupy Texas, so that they would not lose their land to the Manifest Destiny of the United States.

Focus Activity

READ TO LEARN
How did the United States expand into western lands controlled by Mexico?

VOCABULARY
Manifest Destiny
Mexican War
Treaty of Guadalupe Hidalgo

PEOPLE
Stephen F. Austin
Antonio López de Santa Anna
Juan Seguín
Sam Houston
Lorenzo de Zavala
Zachary Taylor

PLACES
The Alamo
San Jacinto River

474

TEXAS FEVER

One of the first Americans to move to Texas was Stephen F. Austin, a Missouri merchant, who brought about 300 families from the United States in 1822. He offered the families cheap, fertile land. Soon "Texas fever" swept through the United States. Americans also began moving to Oregon, Utah, and California. By the 1820s land in the eastern part of the United States was crowded and expensive. Some people moved west for cheap land and open spaces. Others moved west for religious freedom.

Gone to Texas

All across the South the sign "G.T.T." hung on abandoned cabins and houses. The letters stood for "Gone to Texas." In the 1820s and 1830s, many United States farm families moved to Texas, where land was being offered for free.

The woodlands and coastal plains of Texas were perfect for growing corn and cotton and for raising cattle. Many of the planters who moved into Texas brought enslaved African Americans with them. Mexico had made slavery illegal in 1829. However, Mexican leaders decided to allow slavery in Texas in order to encourage American immigration.

In exchange for the right to settle in Texas, the Mexican government required that American settlers become Mexican citizens and join the Roman Catholic church. The American settlers were also expected to speak Spanish, the official language of Texas. Mexico's leaders hoped these rules would make the Americans loyal to Mexico rather than to the United States.

Yet most Americans did not learn Spanish or change their religion. They were able to ignore the laws because the newly formed government in Mexico City was far away and too weak to enforce them.

This oil painting of Stephen F. Austin (below) hangs in the Texas Capitol in Austin. The longhorn (bottom) was one of the first breeds of cattle to come through Texas.

475

WAR WITH MEXICO

By 1830 English-speaking settlers in Texas outnumbered Mexican residents, or Tejanos, by three to one. Worried that they might lose Texas, Mexican leaders decided to stop all immigration from the United States. They also made slavery illegal in Texas, as it was in the rest of Mexico.

In 1833 the Texans sent Stephen F. Austin to the capital, Mexico City, to explain why the recent laws angered the Texans, and why Texas should be separate from Mexico. Accused of starting a rebellion, Austin was jailed for nearly two years.

The Texas Rebellion

In 1835 about 1,400 Mexican troops rode north toward Texas, sent by Mexico's president Antonio López de Santa Anna, to take control of Texas. This led to war for independence.

Tejanos joined with English-speaking settlers to fight the Mexican Army. A Tejano leader, Juan Seguín (HWAHN say GEEN), organized volunteers. David Crockett, a former United States congressman recently arrived from Tennessee, joined up. William Travis, a lawyer from Alabama, was commander of the Texas army.

In December 1835 about 150 Texans led by Travis occupied a San Antonio mission called The Alamo. On February 23, 1836, Santa Anna surrounded The Alamo with 1,000 troops. During the next eleven days, 3,000 more Mexican soldiers joined Santa Anna. On March 6 Santa Anna's army attacked, killing nearly all the Texas rebels. In spite of this defeat, the Texas army did not give up.

Texas State Library

Texas rebels, including David Crockett (top) and Juan Seguín (left) fought to defend The Alamo. The Texas rebels finally defeated Santa Anna (bottom) at the San Jacinto River.

On April 21, 1836, General Sam Houston surprised Santa Anna near the San Jacinto (sahn hah SEEHN toh) River. Shouting, "Remember The Alamo!" the Texans defeated the Mexican force in only about 18 minutes, ending the war. In exchange for his freedom, Santa Anna signed a treaty granting Texas independence.

Sam Houston was elected the first president of the new Republic of Texas. Lorenzo de Zavala, a Tejano, became the republic's first vice president.

THE UNITED STATES DECLARES WAR

The new republic of Texas had spent and borrowed a great deal of money to fight for independence and now had little left. The Texans also faced wars with Comanches and other Native Americans on whose lands they had settled. In 1837 Sam Houston asked President Andrew Jackson to allow the Republic of Texas to become part of the United States.

President Jackson refused Houston's request because he was afraid that acquiring Texas could lead to war with Mexico. He was also worried because Texas permitted slavery, which the Northern states opposed.

However, by the 1840s, the belief in Manifest Destiny was sweeping the United States. This belief was that our country was destined to spread west to the Pacific coast and south to the Gulf of Mexico. James K. Polk ran for President promising the American people "all of Texas." After Polk won the 1844 election, he persuaded Congress to admit Texas as a slave state. On December 29, 1845, Texas became the twenty-eighth state.

The Texas–Mexico border, however, became a source of bitter dispute. The United States claimed the Rio Grande as the Texas border. Mexico wanted the border to be farther north, at the Nueces (NWAY sus) River.

On May 13, 1846, a large majority of Congress voted for war with Mexico. The Mexican War lasted from 1846 to 1848. General Zachary Taylor led American troops into Mexico. His troops called him "Old Rough and Ready" because of his preparedness for battle. Taylor's troops captured cities in northern Mexico including Matamoros and Monterrey.

Western Revolt

The Mexican War soon spread. In the 1840s, some Americans had moved to the Mexican province of California. You will learn more about these settlers in Lesson 4. After the settlers rebelled against Mexico in June 1846, the United States Navy arrived and claimed California for the United States. Most of the Spanish-speaking residents, known as Californios, were loyal to Mexico and fought against the Americans. Californio General Andrés Pico won an important battle against the American General Stephen Kearney's troops at the Battle of San Pascual, near San Diego. Outnumbered and short of supplies, however, the Californios surrendered in January.

This print of General Zachary Taylor includes a scene of the Battle of Monterrey in the bottom left corner.

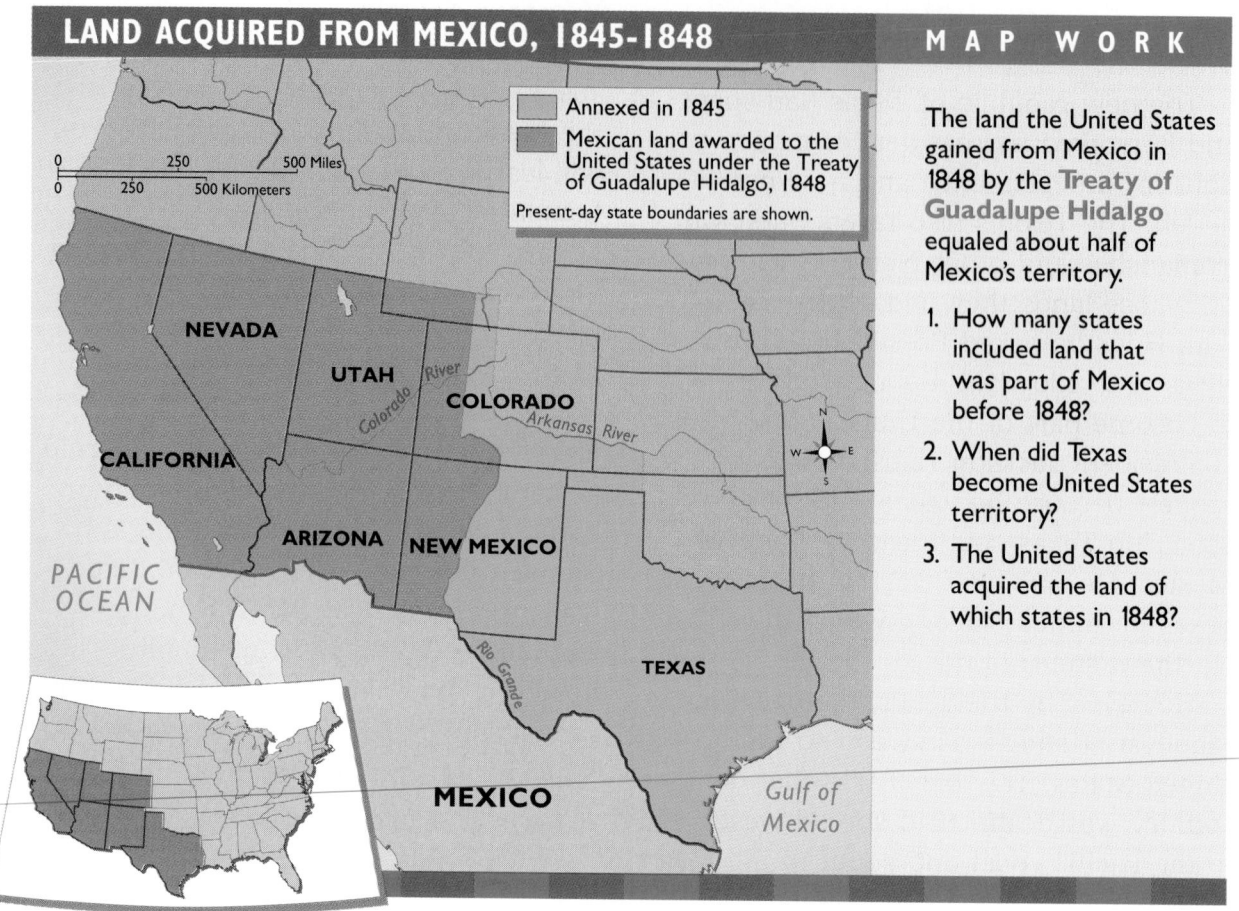

LAND ACQUIRED FROM MEXICO, 1845-1848

MAP WORK

Annexed in 1845

Mexican land awarded to the United States under the Treaty of Guadalupe Hidalgo, 1848

Present-day state boundaries are shown.

NEVADA

UTAH

Colorado River

COLORADO

Arkansas River

CALIFORNIA

ARIZONA

NEW MEXICO

PACIFIC OCEAN

Rio Grande

TEXAS

MEXICO

Gulf of Mexico

The land the United States gained from Mexico in 1848 by the **Treaty of Guadalupe Hidalgo** equaled about half of Mexico's territory.

1. How many states included land that was part of Mexico before 1848?

2. When did Texas become United States territory?

3. The United States acquired the land of which states in 1848?

VICTORY AT CHAPULTEPEC

By early 1847 the United States Army held key parts of northern Mexico, including New Mexico and California. Under the command of General Winfield Scott, the army landed on Mexico's coast and fought its way to Mexico City, Mexico's capital.

A fortress called the castle of Chapultepec (chuh PUL tuh pek) guarded the entrance to Mexico City. In September, the walls of the fort fell, and Scott's troops moved into Mexico City.

Peace Treaty with Mexico

In 1848 the Treaty of Guadalupe Hidalgo (GWAH dal oo pe hih DAL goh) ended the war. Mexico had to accept the Rio Grande as its border with Texas.

As the map above shows, Mexico had to give up half of its territory to the United States. In exchange, the United States paid Mexico $15 million.

The treaty gave the 80,000 Mexicans living in this territory the choice of remaining Mexican citizens or becoming citizens of the United States. All except 2,000 chose to become United States citizens. They were guaranteed the same rights as other Americans, including the right to keep their property. However, many Mexican Americans were unfamiliar with the English language and with American courts of law. In spite of the treaty, many Mexican Americans lost their lands and many rights.

Native Americans were not granted United States citizenship. Many suffered slavery, land theft, and starvation. California's Native American population declined by more than 100,000 between 1848 and 1868.

The Southwest now belonged to the United States. Even though Mexican Americans made up the majority of people there, some towns passed laws outlawing Mexican fiestas, or festivals. Mexican Americans were not allowed in certain restaurants and stores. Manuel Crescion wrote of the people of the United States that "their future expansion begins with the territory they take from us . . . pushing aside our citizens who inhabit the land." Pablo de la Guerra spoke before the California Senate and explained that the "conquered" Mexicans did not understand the new language—English—that was spoken on "their native soil." The Mexican Americans had become "foreigners in their own land."

WHY IT MATTERS

After the Mexican War, the borders of the United States stretched to the Pacific Ocean. The successes of the Mexican War helped General Zachary Taylor become President of the United States in 1848. Although the Treaty of Guadalupe Hidalgo guaranteed Mexicans the same rights as Americans, many Mexicans lost their land and their way of life.

Bayard Taylor wrote in 1849 that the Californios "witnessed the immediate extinction of their own political importance, and the introduction of a new language, new customs, and new laws."

Reviewing Facts and Ideas

MAIN IDEAS

- The Mexican War started over a dispute between the United States and Mexico about the border between Texas and Mexico.

- The 1848 Treaty of Guadalupe Hidalgo forced Mexico to give half of its territory to the United States.

THINK ABOUT IT

1. How did Stephen F. Austin help Texas to grow?

2. How did Texas win its independence from Mexico?

3. **FOCUS** How did the United States expand into lands in the West?

4. **THINKING SKILL** How did the governments of Mexico and Texas differ in their *points of view* regarding the border between Mexico and Texas?

5. **GEOGRAPHY** Using the map on page 478, give two reasons why the United States wanted to acquire Mexico's northern territory.

MOVING TO OREGON AND UTAH

Focus Activity

READ TO LEARN
What was life like traveling on the westward trails?

VOCABULARY
mountain men
wagon train

PEOPLE
James Beckwourth
Jesse Applegate
Brigham Young

PLACES
Oregon Territory
Oregon Trail
Mormon Trail
Great Salt Lake
Salt Lake City

READ ALOUD

In the middle 1800s thousands of people were traveling to the same place, but they called it by different names. To the Native Americans who lived there, it was home. United States citizens called it the West—the land of opportunity. Some Americans thought of it as the "Promised Land," where they could find freedom from slavery and from religious prejudice. What exactly was this place? Why were so many people going there?

THE BIG PICTURE

As you read, in the early 1800s many people in the United States believed that it was the Manifest Destiny of the country to stretch from sea to sea. During this time, many people from the Southern states moved to Texas to take advantage of the cheap, fertile land. At the same time, groups of families and individuals in the East moved to the Oregon Territory, Utah, and other parts of the West. They came mostly from the upper Southeast and the Middle West. As the newcomers arrived, thousands of Native Americans lost their lands and freedom. Many died from violence and disease.

Why did the newcomers risk the dangerous trip west? Some people sought religious freedom. Others wanted to make their fortunes in gold. Many, perhaps most, wanted to find cheap land where they could build new lives as farmers or ranchers. As you have read, African Americans came to escape slavery.

LOOKING WEST

During the early 1800s the land to the south of Oregon was Spanish territory. In 1818 Great Britain and the United States signed a treaty that allowed them to occupy the Oregon Territory jointly.

After the Lewis and Clark expedition, people in the United States began to make their way west. British, Americans, Canadians, and Russians had already started fur-trading posts in the Pacific Northwest.

Mountain Men

In the early 1800s mountain men trapped beavers along the rivers and streams of the Pacific Northwest and the Rocky Mountains. Around 1820, the wearing of beaver hats became a popular fashion in Europe. The demand for furs and fur trappers skyrocketed. In 1832 fur companies, such as John Jacob Astor's American Fur Company, employed about 1,000 trappers along the Missouri River and in the Rocky Mountains. Native American guides, interpreters, and teachers helped the mountain men survive their journeys. Mountain men followed old Native American trails and discovered new paths through the steep mountains that blocked their way to the Pacific Coast. Later, these routes helped travelers heading west. In 1850 James Beckwourth, a runaway slave who became a mountain man, discovered a major route to California through the Sierra Nevada, later known as Beckwourth Pass.

After months of lonely trapping, mountain men greatly looked forward to their yearly gathering—a rendezvous (RAHN duh voo). At an agreed-upon place, they met to trade with other trappers, Native Americans, and fur companies. Wagon trains also came with needed supplies, such as traps, guns, and ammunition. A wagon train is a group of covered wagons that follow one another like the cars of a railroad train.

The European demand for beaver pelts gave work to thousands of trappers and mountain men (left). Beaver was used for hats (below) that were fashionable in the early 1800s.

Museum of the City of New York

OREGON FEVER

In 1836 two missionary couples set out for Oregon through a pass in the Rocky Mountains. Marcus and Narcissa Whitman and Henry and Elizabeth Spalding hoped to teach the Cayuse, a native people in the Oregon Territory, about Christianity. After traveling about six months, the Whitmans set up their mission near the Columbia River. In 1839 only about 100 Americans lived in Oregon. Yet in the 1840s the United States government offered free land to settlers willing to make the journey to Oregon. Jesse Applegate led 900 people to Oregon from the Middle West in 1841. Two years later Dr. Whitman led a wagon train of 1,000 eager settlers over the long path known as the Oregon Trail.

Heading West

To make the long trip safer, groups of travelers formed wagon trains. The "jumping off" point for the Oregon Trail was in Independence, Missouri, where people met to organize the trip.

Travelers used small, light wagons called Prairie Schooners, pulled by four to six oxen. These wagons could carry as much as 2,500 pounds of supplies, enough for a five-month journey.

The Oregon Trail

The travelers had to start their four- to six-month journey to Oregon no later than April or May in order to cross 2,000 miles of prairie, desert, and mountains before the winter snows. Jesse Applegate described how early the travelers' days began:

> It is four o'clock A.M.; the sentinels [guards] on duty have discharged [shot] their rifles—the signal that the hours of sleep are over.

Covering 12 to 15 miles a day, the travelers stopped in the evening and placed their wagons in a circle for protection. Traveler Martha Morrison recalled that "the women helped pitch the tents, helped unload the wagon, and helped…[handle] the cattle." Next, women began preparing for dinner over a campfire. Boys and girls collected materials to make a fire. They ate the same meal every night— dried beef or cod, rice, and tea.

Travelers sometimes fought Native American groups along the trail who feared that they would lose their land. They also encountered buffalo stampedes, dangerous river crossings, and wagon breakdowns.

Narcissa Whitman (above) traveled to Oregon to set up a mission. Today stone markers (far right) point out the path travelers took as they moved west on the Oregon Trail loaded with supplies (near right).

Supplies to Bring West

200 pounds of flour
150 pounds of bacon
10 pounds of coffee
20 pounds of sugar
10 pounds of salt

OLD OREGON TRAIL 1843-57

Many settlers traveled the Oregon trails in wagon trains.

The Granger Collection

Many of the diaries and letters written by travelers on the Oregon Trail told of experiences that would help make the journey easier for friends and relatives who might follow. Read the following excerpt written by 13-year-old Lucy Hall Bennett about her trip to Oregon. What information did she give that might have helped other travelers?

MANY VOICES
PRIMARY SOURCE

Excerpt from the diary of Lucy Hall Bennett written in 1845.

We came across Steve Meek, [who] told us of a better road to Willamette Valley. . . . The road we took had been traveled by the Hudson Bay Fur traders, and while it might have been all right for pack horses, it was certainly not adapted to immigrants traveling by ox train. The water was bad. . . . There was little grass and before long our cattle all had sore feet from traveling over hard sharp rocks.

A New Home in Oregon

Some travelers left the wagon train at Fort Walla Walla near the Columbia River in Oregon. They then journeyed down the river by boat to the Willamette Valley. Others continued on by wagon to The Dalles, and then traveled by raft, boat, and canoe to Fort Vancouver.

George and Abigail Malick and their six children arrived in the Willamette Valley in 1850. They filed a claim, a legal document naming the owner of a piece of land. Abigail wrote, "We got a beautiful claim near Fort Vancouver . . . and there ships are sailing every day on the great Columbia right before our door." George cleared the land, sold the timber, built a home, and planted crops.

Oregon and the United States

Between 1840 and 1860, almost 300,000 people followed the Oregon Trail. In 1846 the United States and Britain signed the Oregon Treaty, setting the boundary between their territories.

Two years later Oregon officially became a territory of the United States. The discovery of gold in southern Oregon in 1851 led to a very fast increase in population, and to statehood in 1859.

Moving West, Mid-1800s

By 1850, well-traveled wagon trails snaked across the United States to the west coast. These trails paved the way for Americans to move west across North America. They had been developed in the early 1800s from Native American trails by fur trappers called mountain men. Look at the map on the next page.

Wyoming Division of Cultural Resources

Fort Bridger

This fort, south of the Mormon and California trails, was a stopping off point for many settlers moving west. There they traded goods and repaired their wagons and tools. The fort was established by a mountain man named Jim Bridger in 1843.

Nebraska Game and Parks Division

Chimney Rock

Settlers traveling on the Oregon Trail probably reached this landmark as their supplies began to run low. At this point the oxen that had pulled their heavily loaded wagons would also have grown weak. To lighten the load, settlers tossed out furniture they had planned to use in their new homes in the West.

Trails to the West

= Mountain Pass   ● City
🏠 Fort   ～ Trail

Ft. Vancouver   Ft. Walla Walla
Whitman's Mission
Oregon Trail
Ft. Boise
Bozeman Trail
Ft. Hall
SODA SPRINGS
South Pass
SACRAMENTO   Beckwourth Pass
Ft. Laramie
Castle Rock
Independence Rock   Chimney Rock
Red Buttes
California Trail   SALT LAKE CITY   Split Rock
Mormon Trail
Donner Pass   Ft. Bridger   Oregon Trail   OMAHA
Sutter's Fort
SAN FRANCISCO   NAUVOO
Santa Fe Trail   INDEPENDENCE
Old Spanish Trail   ST. LOUIS
LOS ANGELES   SANTA FE
El Camino Real (from Mexico)
EL PASO

James Beckwourth

A runaway slave, Beckwourth became a mountain man and was hired as a trader by the American Fur Company. In 1850 he reached a gap in the northern Sierra Nevada Mountains, now called Beckwourth Pass. Beckwourth, like many mountain men, got along with Native Americans. He was made chief of the Crow people and was buried on their lands.

485

WEST TO UTAH

The Oregon Trail was not the only route to the West. Early in 1847 more than 14,000 travelers left from Nauvoo, Illinois, along a route called the Mormon Trail. The trail got its name from the people who traveled it. They were part of a religious group called the Church of Jesus Christ of Latter-Day Saints, or Mormons. Because of mistreatment in Nauvoo, some of the Mormons decided to move west. On the Infographic on pages 484–485, you can see that the Mormon Trail closely follows the Oregon Trail through the Great Plains.

Settling by the Great Salt Lake

The Mormon leader Brigham Young led the long march. The Mormons' wagons crossed ice-covered rivers as they followed the Oregon Trail. Near Fort Bridger the group left the trail and headed south into lands claimed by Mexico. Finally, in July 1847, the first group of Mormons reached a large lake now known as the Great Salt Lake. The region's inhabitants included the Ute (YOOT) and Shoshone peoples. The present-day state of Utah got its name from the Ute.

"Everything looked gloomy, and I felt heartsick," wrote a Mormon traveler

Brigham Young (left) led the Mormons to Utah. Salt Lake City (right) was the destination chosen by many Mormon settlers.

named Harriet Young after her first view of the dry land.

The Mormons decided to use irrigation to grow potatoes, grain, and apples. Because of the limited water supply, the land and water had to be carefully divided among the settlers. However, the Mormons did not rely on farming alone. They built small factories to make such things as pottery, leather goods, textiles, paper, guns, and soap.

Mormon missionaries tried to convert people and urge them to move to Salt Lake City. The Mormons established a special fund for those who could not pay their own expenses. Brigham Young also came up with a plan to cut down on the cost of wagontrain travel. Church members built two-wheeled handcarts that travelers pushed with their belongings along the Mormon Trail to Salt Lake City.

Salt Lake City, one of the first Mormon settlements, grew rapidly. By 1850 there were about 5,000 Mormons living in the town. Utah became a state in 1896.

WHY IT MATTERS

The 1840s to the 1860s was one of the great periods of movement in the history of the United States. People kept moving west, forever changing the lands between the Mississippi River and the Pacific Ocean. However, the time of the wagon trains did not last long. By 1860 war would interrupt most of the traffic. By 1869 the railroad lines would connect the two coasts, making it easier to cross the country.

✔ Reviewing Facts and Ideas

MAIN IDEAS

- From 1840 to 1860 almost 300,000 people traveled to the West.
- Travelers followed the Oregon Trail, Mormon Trail, California Trail, and other trails established by the Native Americans and by mountain men.
- Brigham Young led a religious group called the Mormons into Utah in 1847.

THINK ABOUT IT

1. What religious group moved to Utah in early 1847?

2. What were wagon trains?

3. **FOCUS** Why did so many people travel to the West in the 1800s?

4. **THINKING SKILL** What *effects* did the discovery of gold in Oregon have?

5. **GEOGRAPHY** Name two landforms that the Oregon Trail crossed.

NATIVE AMERICANS AND NEWCOMERS CLASH

Focus Activity

READ TO LEARN
How did Native Americans' way of life change as newcomers traveled to the West?

PEOPLE
White Cloud

PLACES
Fort Laramie

READ ALOUD

In the 1850s a Navajo told a United States Army major: "The water there is mine, not yours, and the same with the grass. Even the ground it grows from belongs to me, not to you. I will not let you have these things."

THE BIG PICTURE

Travelers crossing the Great Plains knew little about the Native Americans they encountered. The Pawnee, Lakota, Cheyenne, Blackfoot, Crow, and other Plains peoples each had different ways of life. Some were farmers while others hunted game. The Plains peoples had their own beliefs and governments, their own songs, dances, and languages. The newcomers took over land and hunting grounds, which led to great conflict between new settlers and native groups.

NEW WAYS OF LIFE

The arrival of the Spanish and English had changed life for Native Americans. The Plains peoples, whom you read about in Chapter 3, had been greatly influenced by the introduction of the horse in the 1500s. Some Plains people who had been farmers now depended on buffalo meat and hides for food and clothing. Hunting groups often traded their goods with those who farmed. For example, the Cheyenne traded their buffalo meat for corn and beans the Arikara grew.

By 1845 several thousand settlers had traveled along the Oregon Trail. As the fur trade grew, Native Americans traded less with one another and more with white settlers for items such as knives, guns, and tobacco. Native peoples who once relied on fishing, hunting, and farming for food, often bought and sold for their livelihood.

Loss of the Buffalo

During the 1840s, as white settlers took over many Native American lands, they also began to kill huge numbers of the estimated 40 million buffalo on the plains for food, for sport, and for profit. One hunter might kill 150 buffalo a day.

Animal skins were turned into coats and blankets. Buffalo tongues were smoked and shipped east to be sold as food. A Lakota chief, White Cloud, said, "Wherever the whites are established, the buffalo is gone, and the red hunters must die of hunger." By 1890, only about 1,000 buffalo had survived.

This Lakota beadwork (above right) shows a hunting scene. The Lakota depended on the buffalo (below).

489

CONFLICT IN THE WEST

At first many Native Americans and travelers tried to get along. Wagon trains hired native people to work as scouts and guides. They also traded with Native Americans along the way. Amelia Stewart Knight, one westward settler, wrote:

This afternoon we passed a large village of Sioux [Lakota] Indians. Numbers of them came round the wagons. Some of the women had moccasins and beads, which they wanted to trade for bread.

One of the many groups of Native Americans who were pushed off their land were the Lakota. They hunted buffalo on the plains south of the Crow. Now they were forced to move farther north into Crow country. Crowding led to fighting among the Lakota, the Crow, and other groups.

Government Treaties

In 1851, to protect settlers going west, the United States government asked the chiefs of many Plains groups to meet at Fort Laramie in present-day Wyoming. Cheyenne, Arapahoe, Crow, Shoshone, Lakota, Assiniboin, Arikara, and Atsina chiefs came. Each of the chiefs signed the Treaty of Fort Laramie in 1851. Some Native Americans said the chiefs who signed the treaty did not represent the views of all of the people.

According to the treaty, the government promised to pay the Native Americans $50,000 worth of goods each year for 50 years. In return, the Native Americans said that they would not harm white settlers along the Oregon Trail. They agreed to let the government build roads and forts on their land. The treaty also marked new land boundaries that

Fort Laramie, in Wyoming, has been restored both inside and out.

told the different native groups where they could now live and hunt. This treaty and those that followed failed to bring lasting peace.

In the following excerpts, an Oglala chief, Black Hawk, and a Cheyenne chief, Old Bark, give their opinions about the Fort Laramie treaty. Read the following excerpts. How are the viewpoints of the two men different?

MANY VOICES PRIMARY SOURCE

Remarks of the Oglala chief, Black Hawk, to other Oglala chiefs at Fort Laramie, 1851.

You have split the country and I don't like it. . . . These lands once belonged to the Kiowas and Crows, but we whipped these nations out of them, and in this we do what the white men do when they want the lands of the Indians.

From a speech given by the Cheyenne chief, Old Bark, to the treaty council at Fort Laramie, September 1851.

If all the nations here were willing to do what you tell them, and do what they say as we are, then we could sleep in peace; we would not have to watch our lodges in the night.

WHY IT MATTERS

The Treaty of Fort Laramie did not solve the problems between the United States government and the Plains peoples. Many settlers continued to move west across their lands. Native Americans lost much of their land and many of their rights.

Reviewing Facts and Ideas

MAIN IDEAS

- Arrival of settlers from the East and Middle West caused the lives of Native Americans of the Plains to change. It also led to increased conflict on the Plains.

- Many Native Americans were forced to move off their land to escape the white settlers.

- The Treaty of Fort Laramie marked new boundaries for Native Americans living on the Plains.

THINK ABOUT IT

1. What effects did growth of the fur trade have on the Plains peoples?

2. Why did the United States government want the Plains peoples to sign the Fort Laramie treaty?

3. **FOCUS** How did Native Americans' way of life change as newcomers traveled to the West?

4. **THINKING SKILL** Why did the United States government and the Plains peoples have different *points of view* about the Treaty of Fort Laramie?

5. **WRITING** Write a short story about a Lakota brother and sister whose lives change when white settlers cross their lands.

THE CALIFORNIA GOLD RUSH

READ ALOUD

In 1849 the Reverend Walter Colton wrote this to describe the California Gold Rush: "The blacksmith dropped his hammer, the carpenter his plane, the mason his trowel, the farmer his sickle, the baker his loaf, and the tapster his bottle. All were off for the mines."

Focus Activity

READ TO LEARN
How did the Gold Rush change life in California?

VOCABULARY
emigration
Gold Rush
Forty-Niner

PEOPLE
Jedediah Smith
John C. Frémont
James Wilson Marshall
John Sutter

PLACES
Sutter's Mill
San Francisco
Mother Lode Country

THE BIG PICTURE

In Chapter 11 you read about the building of Spanish missions in California. The missions were the main European settlements. In 1821, after Mexico gained its independence from Spain, California became part of Mexico. The Mexicans closed the missions and gave the land to the Californios, who started huge cattle ranches, or ranchos.

Soon after, California's ports opened up to United States and European trade. The hide-and-tallow trade began with New England. Clipper ships from Britain, New England, and South America brought manufactured goods to exchange for cowhides and beef tallow, or fat. Hides and tallow were produced from the cattle raised on California ranchos. This trade helped spark American interest in California, and it paved the way for later emigration. Emigration is the movement of people to a new place.

It was not long, however, before an event happened that changed the history of California. In 1848 gold was discovered at Sutter's Mill. As news of the discovery spread across the world, people made their way to "the golden state" in one of the greatest rushes in history.

EXPLORING CALIFORNIA

In the early 1800s explorers carved routes to California. The first was mountain man Jedediah Smith. In 1826 Smith and his group crossed the Mojave Desert and the Sierra Nevada. Through 60 days of hunger, thirst, heat, and exhaustion, they traveled all the way to Mission San Gabriel, near Los Angeles. Smith described California as a "country where the creator has scattered a more than ordinary share of his bounties." The Mexican authorities were very surprised to see them.

The second explorer was the scientist John C. Frémont. From 1843 to 1844 Frémont traveled out west mapping western routes for the United States government. He crossed the Sierra Nevada and ended up at Sutter's Fort in the Sacramento Valley.

Sutter's Fort was a bustling trading post near the American and Sacramento rivers in California. When Frémont reached Yerba Buena, it had only 12 houses and 50 inhabitants. In 1847 it became part of San Francisco.

John C. Frémont explored routes to California, and led the short-lived Bear Flag Republic.

California and the United States

Frémont departed California with the feeling that war would soon break out between the United States and Mexico. In 1845 he returned to California without official permission.

Frémont knew that tension existed between American settlers and Californios. This time Frémont took along 60 well-armed men. He then dug in on top of Hawk's Peak near Monterey and raised the American flag. After three days he fled to the mountains of Oregon. Just a few months later, a group of American settlers seized the area near Sonoma, declaring it a republic. One of the settlers hastily raised a flag with a grizzly bear on it. Frémont rushed back to claim command of the new republic.

However, the Bear Flag Republic, as it became known, lasted only a month. As you read, the United States declared war on Mexico on May 13, 1846, and American naval units were ordered to occupy California's ports. On July 7, 1846, United States Commodore Sloat sailed into Monterey and raised the American flag. He declared that California had become part of the United States.

When the Mexican War ended in 1848, the United States formally received California in the Treaty of Guadalupe Hidalgo.

GOLD FEVER

One January morning in 1848 near Sutter's Mill, a sawmill on the American River, a carpenter named James Wilson Marshall found something lying in a ditch. "I reached my hand down and picked it up," remembered Marshall. "It made my heart thump, for I was certain it was gold."

Marshall rushed to report his discovery to Captain John Sutter, a Swiss immigrant and the mill's owner. Sutter tested the shiny stone and concluded that it truly was gold.

Forty-Niners

All over the world people got the "gold fever" and headed to California, the homeland of 125,000 Native Americans. Many came by wagon on the California Trail, the Santa Fe Trail, the Mormon Trail, and the Oregon Trail.

"As far as [the] eye can reach . . . you see nothing but wagons," wrote Sally Hester, one of the emigrants along the California Trail. So many people came that this event became known as the California Gold Rush. The new arrivals became known as Forty-Niners, for the year in which many reached California.

From the eastern states and Europe, people sailed by ship around South America's Cape Horn. Many Chinese sailed across the Pacific Ocean from Asia. Experienced miners from Peru and Mexico made the trip, too. By 1849 more than 80,000 people had arrived in California.

On the western face of the Sierra Nevada, known as Mother Lode Country, the richest deposit of gold was discovered. It was on the lands taken from peoples such as the Pomo and Yokuts. With no government to keep order, miners often fought over claims, settling arguments violently.

Chinese, Irish, African American, and Native American miners panned for gold in California's many rivers and streams (below). New stores (above right) sprang up to meet the demands of the increased population.

CALIFORNIA GROWS

After the discovery of gold, California grew rapidly. The population of San Francisco jumped from 812 in 1848 to 25,000 in 1850. Businesses other than mining also prospered from the Gold Rush. For example, Levi Strauss, a Jewish immigrant, took heavy canvas and made sturdy pants, which we know as "Levis," for miners. Storekeepers, barbers, doctors, lawyers, and saloon keepers made huge profits from the gold miners.

Thousands of Chinese arrived during the Gold Rush. Many worked in the mines, facing hostile behavior from whites. Some were merchants who brought grain, rice, sugar, tea, and dried fruits to sell to the miners.

Not many women came to California in this period. Some of those who did started businesses such as laundries for the miners. What kind of business did Luzena Stanley Wilson run?

Excerpt from *Luzena Stanley Wilson, Forty-Niner,* an autobiography published in 1937.

*As always occurs to the mind of a woman, I thought of taking boarders. There was a hotel nearby and the men who ate there paid $1 a meal . . . . With my own hands I chopped [tent] stakes, drove them into the ground, and set up my table. I bought **provisions** at a neighboring store and when my husband came back at night he found . . . twenty miners eating at my table. Each man as he rose put a dollar in my hand and said I might count on him as a permanent customer. I called my hotel "El Dorado."*

provisions: a stock of food
El Dorado: a mythical land of great riches.

Californios and Native Americans

As you read in Lesson 1, the Treaty of Guadalupe Hidalgo guaranteed to protect the rights of Californios. However, state laws did not uphold Californios' rights, and many lost their lands—and even their lives—to the new settlers.

Some Californios owned large cattle ranches. During the Gold Rush, many newcomers settled unlawfully on Californio land. These settlers drove the Californios off their land by burning their crops and shooting their cattle.

Some Native Americans, such as the Choctaw, Cherokee, and Wyandot, moved to California in search of better lives. However, other groups that were native to California often had their ways of life destroyed.

Some Native Americans, including children, were kidnapped for slave labor in the mines. Thousands were murdered, or died from starvation or diseases such as smallpox, measles, and pneumonia. By the 1860s only about 30,000 remained of the 125,000 Native Americans that had lived in California in 1849. An observer, E. A. Stevens, wrote, "The poverty and misery that now exists among these Indians is beyond description."

Californians in San Francisco celebrate the admission of California into the Union in 1850 (above). Before long, the new state had many new towns, such as Iowa Hill (left).

CALIFORNIA BECOMES A STATE

The invasion of Forty-Niners during the Gold Rush increased California's population quickly. This helped California become a state in a very short time. By 1850 California had a population of about 100,000. A territory could apply for statehood when its population reached 60,000. First, the people of California wrote a constitution to set up a government and establish laws. It was written in both Spanish and English. In the Spanish legal tradition, the constitution gave married women the right to own property. It also outlawed slavery. Then, in 1850, California asked Congress to be admitted to the United States as a state.

The Compromise of 1850

At this time, both Northerners and Southerners in Congress were debating a solution to the question of whether new territories should be admitted to the United States as free states or slave states. Free states did not permit slavery within their borders. Slave states did. A solution called the Compromise of 1850 was reached. In this compromise, California was admitted as a free state. In return, the Northern states would agree to obey the Fugitive Slave Law. This law would require free states to help capture slaves escaping from slave states. The other territories that had been gained from Mexico in 1848 would decide for themselves whether or not to allow slavery. Peter Burnett became California's first governor. John Frémont and William M. Gwin became California's first United States senators.

From Sea to Sea

With California's statehood, the United States now had states that bordered on both the Atlantic and the Pacific oceans. America's idea of Manifest Destiny was now a reality. But many people, especially Native Americans and Californios, lost land that they had held for generations. Californios such as Mariano Vallejo lost their land because the authorities did not uphold their claims. In the following quote Mariano Vallejo expresses his feelings about why he lost his land.

These legal thieves, clothed in the robes of law, took from us our lands and our houses, and without the least scruple enthroned themselves in our homes like so many powerful kings. For them existed no law but their own will.

WHY IT MATTERS

The Forty-Niners searched for gold using picks, axes, shovels, and pans. For all their hard work, most returned home broke. Although the Gold Rush did not make many miners rich, it brought many people to California and helped make it a state.

The issue of slavery that the Congress debated when California asked to become a state would continue to divide the country. The divisions between the Northern states and the Southern states over slavery would became deeper and would finally erupt into a war.

This trunk carried a family's treasured possessions to their new home in the West.

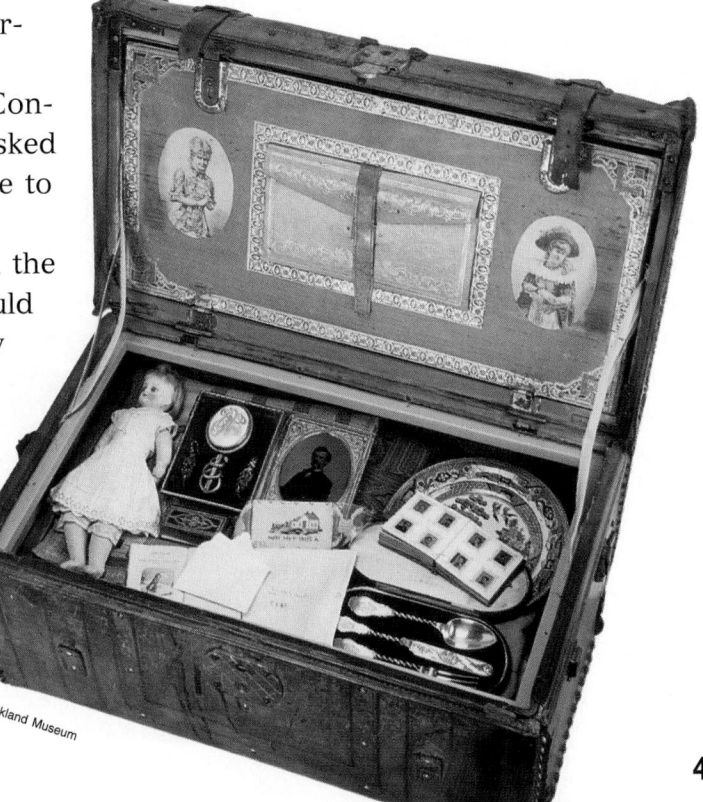

The Oakland Museum

THINKINGSKILLS

Identifying Stereotypes

stereotype

WHY THE SKILL MATTERS

In Lesson 2 you read that the Mormons left Illinois to find a peaceful life in Utah. You read about the conflict created when white settlers moved into Native American lands in Lesson 3. Later you learned how the Californios were stripped of their land, and about the poor relations between whites and Chinese.

In each of these situations, some people had **stereotypes** about another group of people. A stereotype is an idea that all the people in a group are the same in some way. For example, the idea that all immigrants share the characteristic of being poor is a stereotype.

Suppose someone says, "All fifth graders are too lazy to do their homework." The statement is unfair to fifth graders as a group, even though it may be true that some fifth graders don't do their homework. The fact that part of a group shares a trait or characteristic can make it difficult to recognize a stereotype. However, to say that all fifth graders are lazy about their homework is a stereotype.

Stereotypes often, but not always, express prejudice or dislike of a particular group. Identifying stereotypes helps us to recognize people as individuals, not as part of a particular group. This helps us to treat people fairly.

Understanding stereotypes also helps us identify statements or classifications that are unfair and/or untrue.

USING THE SKILL

Stereotypes are often expressed with authority. You can sometimes recognize a stereotype by words such as "always," "every," "none," or "all." Look for the clue words in the following statements. Also identify the group about which the statement is being made.

- *Every fifth grader is more interested in math than in English.*
  Can you find an example that does not fit the stereotype? Do you have a classmate who likes English more than math? If so, you know that every fifth grader is not more interested in math than in English.
- *Tall boys are all great basketball players.*
  The idea that all tall boys are great basketball players stereotypes tall boys. This is unfair to tall boys who are uninterested in basketball, or who are not skilled athletes.
- *Some girls are better readers than boys.*
  This is not a stereotype because it is only about some girls. Some girls are better readers than boys, some are not.

498

TRYING THE SKILL

Use the hints in the Helping Yourself box to help you determine if the following statements include stereotypes. Remember that a stereotype doesn't always say something bad about a group. Some stereotypes say good things about people.

- *Some Native Americans wanted to make peace with the settlers.*
- *Women on the frontier were all skilled nurses, cooks, and hunters.*
- *All Californios were successful ranchers.*
- *The Chinese who joined the Gold Rush preferred to live separately.*

As you read each of the statements above, ask yourself whether a whole group is being

HELPING Yourself

- **A stereotype is an idea that all people in a group are the same in some way.**

- **A stereotype may or may not express a prejudice against a group of people.**

- **To identify a stereotype, look for words such as "always," "every," "none," or "all."**

- **Look also for examples that do not fit the stated trait or characteristic.**

identified as having a certain trait or characteristic. If a statement doesn't contain one of the clue words, does that mean it isn't a stereotype? Based on your answers to these questions, decide whether each of the statements includes a stereotype.

REVIEWING THE SKILL

1. What is a stereotype?

2. Why are stereotypes inaccurate?

3. Can stereotypes be positive as well as negative? Give an example.

4. Why is it important to identify stereotypes?

5. When or where might you find examples of stereotypes?

What would you say about these groups of people (left and right)? Can you identify any of your statements as stereotypes?

CITIZENSHIP
VIEWPOINTS

Henry Clay presents his compromise bill in Congress, urging Congress to accept California as a free state.

1850: SHOULD CALIFORNIA BE ADMITTED TO THE UNION?

California's request for admission to the Union fueled the heated debate in the nation's capital over slavery. Most Southern lawmakers strongly opposed making California a state because they feared it would enter the Union as a free state. In Congress Southerners were already a minority in the House of Representatives, but in the Senate in 1850 the two sides were equally balanced—15 slave states and 15 free ones. If California entered the Union as a free state, the balance would be upset.

Southern Senators like John Calhoun warned that admitting California as a free state might force the Southern states to leave the Union. However, Northerners were equally determined to see California enter the Union as a free state.

President James Polk, a Southerner, helped make California a United States territory. Unlike many Southerners at this time, he wanted to see California become a state. Consider three viewpoints on this issue and answer the questions that follow.

Three DIFFERENT Viewpoints

1 JOHN CALHOUN
Senator from South Carolina,
Speech to Congress, March 4, 1850

The [President] . . . asks you to admit [California] into the union as a State. . . . If you admit her, under all the difficulties that oppose her admission, you [force] us to [assume] that you intend to exclude us from the . . . territories, with the intention of destroying [forever] the [balance] between the two sections *[North and South]*. We would be blind not to [see], in that case, that your real objects are power and [glory].

" . . . you intend to exclude us . . . "

2 JAMES POLK
President of the United States
Diary entry, January 20, 1849

[The] only hope of providing a government for California . . . was to admit her as one of the States of the Union . . . all the . . . Cabinet [agreed]. . . . I expressed my strong desire that California be admitted . . . I believe if this was not done . . . the danger was that the inhabitants of [California] would . . . set up an independent government for themselves and . . . be lost to the Union.

" . . . be lost to the Union."

3 WILLIAM SEWARD
Senator from New York
Speech to Congress, March 11, 1850

Indeed, our revolutionary [forefathers] had . . . the same question before them in establishing a law under which . . . Ohio, Indiana, Michigan, Illinois, and Wisconsin, have since come into the union, and they . . . excluded slavery from those states forever . . . I shall vote for the admission of California . . . without conditions . . . and without compromise.

"I shall vote for the admission . . ."

BUILDING CITIZENSHIP

1. What is the viewpoint of each person?
2. In what ways do some of the viewpoints agree? In what ways do they disagree?
3. What other viewpoints might people have on this issue? What are some issues about which Americans feel strongly today?

SHARING VIEWPOINTS

Discuss reasons why Northerners and Southerners had such strong opinions about this issue. As a class discuss which viewpoints you agree or disagree with. What are some statements, if any, that all three speakers could have agreed on?

CHAPTER 17 REVIEW

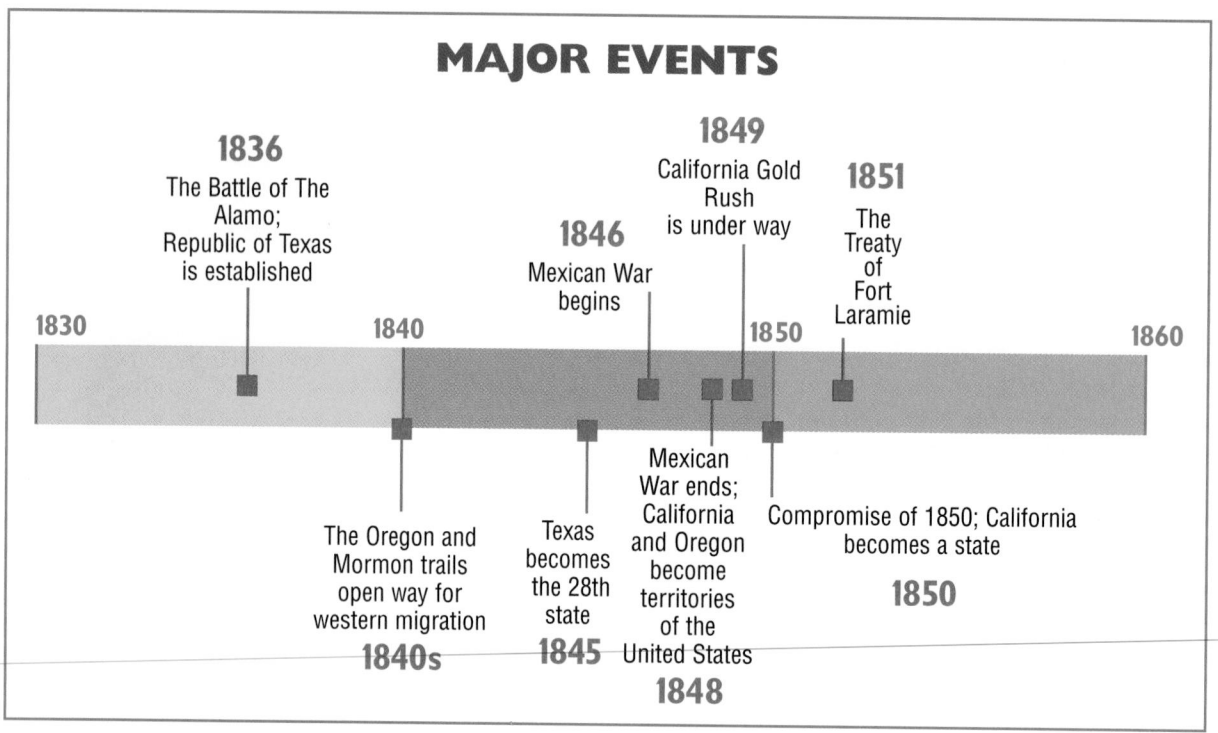

MAJOR EVENTS

1836
The Battle of The Alamo; Republic of Texas is established

1849
California Gold Rush is under way

1846
Mexican War begins

1851
The Treaty of Fort Laramie

1830   1840   1850   1860

The Oregon and Mormon trails open way for western migration
1840s

Texas becomes the 28th state
1845

Mexican War ends; California and Oregon become territories of the United States
1848

Compromise of 1850; California becomes a state
1850

THINKING ABOUT VOCABULARY

Number a sheet of paper from 1 to 5. Beside each number, write the word or term from the list below that best completes the paragraph.

Forty-Niner
Gold Rush
Manifest Destiny
Mexican War
Treaty of Guadalupe Hidalgo

_____1_____ was the idea that the borders of the United States should reach west to the Pacific and south to the Rio Grande. The idea became a reality in 1848, at the end of the conflict known as the ____2____. The United States and Mexico signed the ____3____, which made California a territory of the United States. A year later, James Marshall's discovery at Sutter's Mill led to the California ____4____. Thousands of people took their axes and supplies and headed west. A person who mined gold at that time was known as a ____5____.

THINKING ABOUT FACTS

1. Why did people migrate west in the early 1800s?

2. Who fought in the battle at The Alamo? What was the outcome?

3. What was the outcome of the Mexican War?

4. Why did settlers head for Oregon in the 1840s? What route did they follow?

5. The Compromise of 1850 made California a free state. What does that mean?

6. Who were some of the groups of people who arrived in California in the 1850s?

7. Where did the Mormons settle? Why?

8. Name three ways white settlers affected Native Americans.

9. How did the issue of slavery that the Congress debated when California asked to become a state further divide the North and the South?

10. Use the time line above to find how long California was a territory.

THINK AND WRITE

WRITING COMPARE AND CONTRAST PARAGRAPHS
Write several paragraphs comparing and contrasting how Texas and California joined the United States. Include important dates.

WRITING A REPORT
Write a report on the Oregon Trail. Show the route and give details about the geography. Also, describe a wagon train and tell about the people and goods along the route.

WRITING A LETTER
Suppose you are a woman from Virginia who settled in San Francisco in the 1850s. Write a letter about your new life to a friend in the East.

APPLYING THINKING SKILLS

IDENTIFYING STEREOTYPES

1. Define the word *stereotype*.
2. What words may help you identify a stereotype?
3. How do words such as "always," "every," "none," and "all" help you identify a stereotype?
4. How can thinking of examples help you decide if a statement is a stereotype or not?
5. Why is it important to identify stereotypes in the information you read?

Summing Up the Chapter

Copy the matrix chart on a separate sheet of paper. Then review the chapter to fill in the blank sections. After you have finished, use the information in the chart to write a paragraph that answers the question, "How did the movement west change the lives of different peoples?

EVENT	PERSON	LOCATION	RESULT
	Tejanos, Californios		Tejanos and Californios lost most of their land and rights despite the laws that were to protect them
Compromise of 1850		California	
Treaty of Fort Laramie		Plains states	
Discovery of gold	settlers/ miners		

UNIT 7 REVIEW

THINKING ABOUT VOCABULARY

Number a sheet of paper from 1 to 10. Beside each number write the word or term from the list below that best matches each description.

canal
emigration
Gold Rush
Indian Removal Act
interchangeable parts

investor
Manifest Destiny
mountain men
stagecoach
wagon train

1. a person who uses money to buy or make something that will make a profit

2. a large, horse-drawn carriage that carried passengers and mail

3. a group of covered wagons that follow one another while traveling

4. same-sized parts of a machine that could be replaced with identical parts

5. the event that brought people to California after the discovery at Sutter's Mill

6. the movement of people to a new place

7. the act of Congress that forced Native American peoples to leave their land

8. the belief that the United States was fated to grow west to the Pacific Ocean and south to the Rio Grande

9. men who learned Indian ways, working as traders and guides in the West

10. a waterway that is built by people

THINK AND WRITE

WRITING A BIOGRAPHY

Choose one of the individuals you read about in this unit and, after doing further research, write a short biography about the person. Try to include facts or quotes about how the individual viewed the changes that were occurring in America during his or her time.

WRITING A JOURNAL ENTRY

Suppose you are moving from one part of the United States to another in the 1800s. Write a journal entry telling where you are going, what route or trail you are taking, and the transportation you are using to get there. You can also include a list of things you are carrying with you on your journey.

WRITING ABOUT PERSPECTIVES

Although the expansion into the West in the 1800s meant great changes for the United States, these changes did not have the same meaning for everybody. Suppose you are a Native American in Indian Territory or a Mexican in the Southwest. Write a speech to your community telling your thoughts about recent events.

BUILDING SKILLS

1. **Reading a Newspaper** In which part of a newspaper do the editors give their opinions about important issues?

2. **Reading a Newspaper** What kinds of events are described in a news article?

3. **Reading a Newspaper** What questions should be answered in the first paragraph of a newspaper article?

4. **Identifying Stereotypes** What is a stereotype?

5. **Identifying Stereotypes** If a statement about a group of people does not apply to every person in the group, what can you tell about the statement?

YESTERDAY, TODAY & *TOMORROW*

Our country did not just grow geographically in the 1800s. New inventions and new ideas led to people changing their ways of life. What were some of these inventions? How did they affect the way we live now? Can you think of discoveries happening today that will change the way we live in the future?

READING ON YOUR OWN

Here are some books you might find at the library to help you learn more.

THE BOBBIN GIRL
by Emily Arnold McCully
This lively story tells of a 10-year-old girl's experience working in a textile mill in Lowell, Massachusetts, in the 1830s.

THE AMAZING IMPOSSIBLE ERIE CANAL
by Cheryl Harness
This detailed account describes the building of the Erie Canal in 1825.

THE GOLD RUSH OF 1849
by Arthur Blake and Pamela Dailey
This book describes the events of the Gold Rush, and tells of their effects on the rest of the country.

UNIT REVIEW PROJECT

Role Play an Interview

1. Working in groups of three, each member chooses one of the following people from the unit.
   - a pioneer moving west of the Appalachian Mountains in the early 1800s
   - a Southerner moving to Texas in the 1830s
   - a "Forty-Niner" looking for gold in California in 1849

2. Write an interview. Be sure to include questions about the individuals, their travels, what each expects to find, and the purpose of the journey.
3. Take turns role-playing each interview.

NAT LOVE

ITALIAN IMMIGRANT'S PASSPORT

CESAR CHAVEZ AND DOLORES HUERTA LEAD A PROTEST

The United States, Past and Present

"I have a dream."

from a 1963 speech by Martin Luther King, Jr.
See page 558.

WHY DOES IT MATTER?

Martin Luther King, Jr.'s dream is shared by many in the United States. It is the dream that all Americans might enjoy freedom and equality. The fight to reach these goals has been a long one, supported by many.

As new immigrants arrived, they too joined the struggle to end unfair treatment, outlaw unsafe working conditions, and gain civil rights for all Americans. From far and wide, newcomers continue to look at the United States as a symbol of liberty, economic opportunity, and hope for world peace. Now, as then, the future of liberty, equality, and democracy lies in the hands of the people of the United States.

IMMIGRANTS FROM ASIA TODAY

CIVIL WAR CAP AND BUGLE; MARTIN LUTHER KING, JR., LEADING A MARCH

Adventures
with
NATIONAL
GEOGRAPHIC

Cesar Chavez

When you eat a salad or bite into a peach, you probably don't think about how these foods were harvested. Most likely, migrant farmworkers were involved. For decades these hardworking laborers have traveled from region to region, earning as little as 30 cents a day in the fields. Cesar Chavez, a former farm laborer, felt that migrant workers deserved better pay and working conditions. In 1962 he founded the first farmworkers' union in California to fight for these goals. He led several successful strikes against powerful vineyard and farm owners. Chavez dedicated his life to the farmworkers' cause. So the next time you munch on some vegetables or fruit, think about Cesar Chavez!

GEOJOURNAL

Can you imagine devoting your life to a cause? Which one and why?

CHAPTER 18

The End of Slavery

THINKING ABOUT HISTORY AND GEOGRAPHY

By the middle of the 1800s, the land area of the United States was almost its present size. The country, however, was increasingly divided by one issue—slavery. As each new state joined the Union, this conflict grew. Eventually, the North and the South fought each other in the Civil War, or the War Between the States. After the war ended, slavery was abolished in the reunited nation. African Americans gained citizenship, and began the struggle for equal rights under the law.

PACIFIC OCEAN

1838
NEW YORK

Frederick Douglass reaches freedom after escaping from slavery in Baltimore

1850s
MARYLAND

Harriet Tubman leads captives to freedom along the Underground Railroad

1861
SOUTH CAROLINA

The Civil War begins with the Confederate attack on Fort Sumter

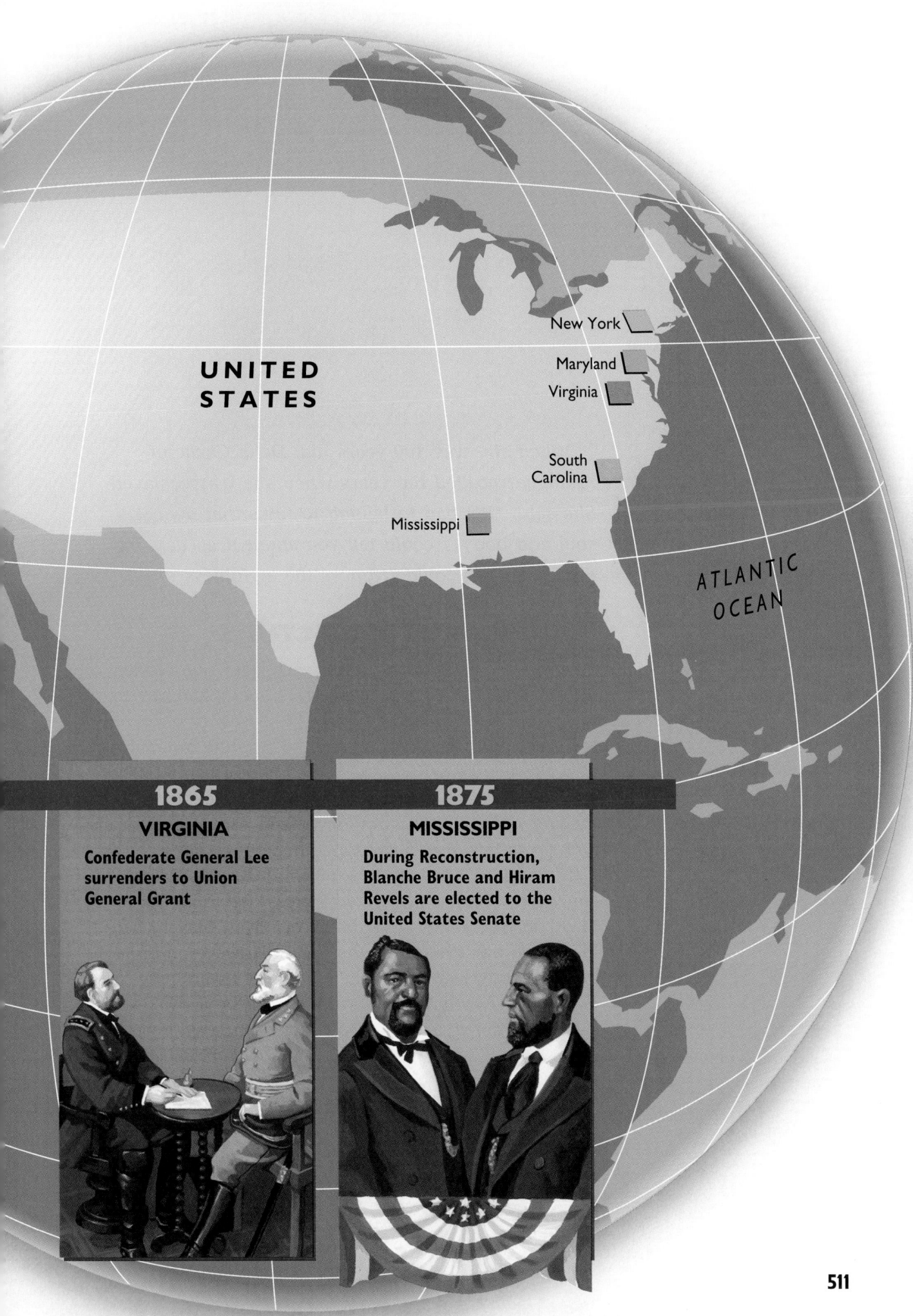

UNITED
STATES

New York

Maryland

Virginia

South
Carolina

Mississippi

ATLANTIC
OCEAN

1865

VIRGINIA

Confederate General Lee surrenders to Union General Grant

1875

MISSISSIPPI

During Reconstruction, Blanche Bruce and Hiram Revels are elected to the United States Senate

A COUNTRY DIVIDED

READ ALOUD

When she was 100 years old, Delia Garlic of Alabama recalled the years when she was enslaved. She said, "It's bad to belong to folks that own you soul and body. I could tell you about it all day, but even then you couldn't guess the awfulness of it."

THE BIG PICTURE

After the Revolutionary War, each state had decided if it would allow slavery. Slave states permitted slavery while free states did not.

Laws had been passed in 1808 to stop the bringing of slaves to the United States. Even so, more than 50,000 enslaved Africans were smuggled into the country after the laws were passed. Also, millions of African Americans were born into slavery with little hope of escape.

In the mid-1800s nearly 4 million enslaved African Americans lived in the United States. Like Delia Garlic, they had little control over their own lives. Slavery had long been a part of life in the South. However, a great many Northerners and some Southerners were now questioning whether the practice should be allowed to continue. How could America be the "land of the free" when so many of its people were without the most basic of human rights: freedom?

Focus Activity

READ TO LEARN
Why did the issue of slavery divide the country?

VOCABULARY
slave state
free state
Missouri Compromise
Compromise of 1850
Kansas-Nebraska Act
abolitionist
Underground Railroad
Dred Scott Decision

PEOPLE
Frederick Douglass
William Lloyd Garrison
Sojourner Truth
Angelina and Sarah Grimké
Harriet Tubman
Harriet Beecher Stowe
John Brown

512

SLAVERY IN THE NORTH AND SOUTH

In the early 1800s most people in the North and the South were farmers, but the two regions had different economies. Most farms in the North were small, but the South depended on its large plantations for wealth. Manufacturing was becoming very important in the North.

After the Revolutionary War, northern states had passed laws to gradually free enslaved African Americans there. In 1830 there were still more than 3,500 enslaved workers in the North.

In the South, some enslaved Africans had been freed after the Revolutionary War because fewer workers were needed to care for the cotton and tobacco crops. Then, in 1793, Eli Whitney invented the cotton gin. This machine allowed workers to remove the seeds from cotton 50 times more quickly than they could by hand. That made cotton more profitable for growers.

The cotton gin made cotton the main source of wealth in the South. It also increased the plantations' use of enslaved workers. Compare the graphs showing the production of cotton and the number of enslaved African workers in the United States in the 1800s.

Even Southerners who did not own slaves defended the practice as being fair. For example, Alexander Stephens, a Georgia slaveowner, said, "the Negro is not equal to the white man; that slavery . . . is his natural and normal condition." After about 1830 the argument over slavery became more heated. Eventually, those who argued against slavery in the South were likely to be beaten and driven away.

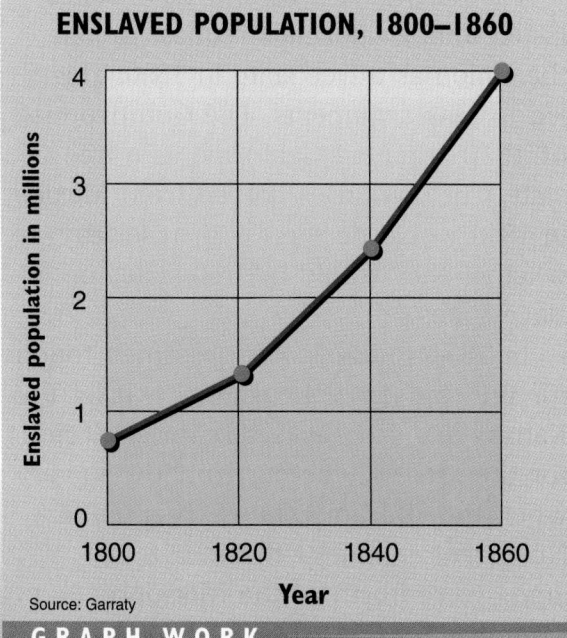

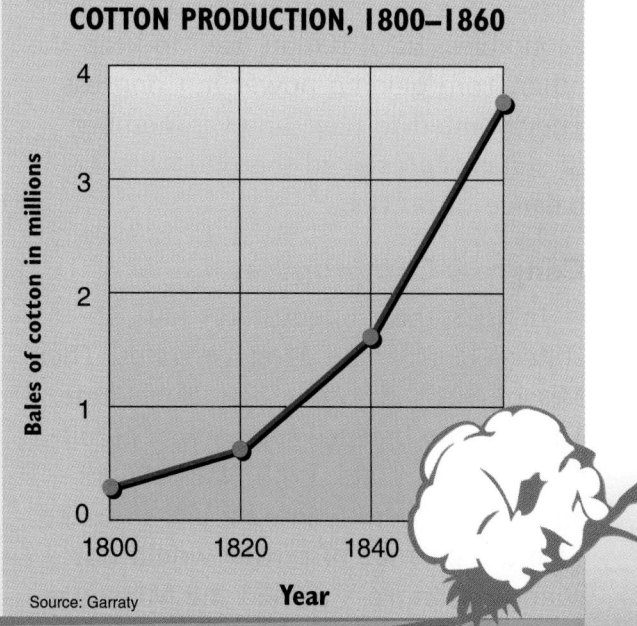

GRAPH WORK

The graphs show the enslaved population and cotton production in the United States from 1800 to 1860.

What do the graphs tell you about the amount of labor needed to grow and harvest cotton?

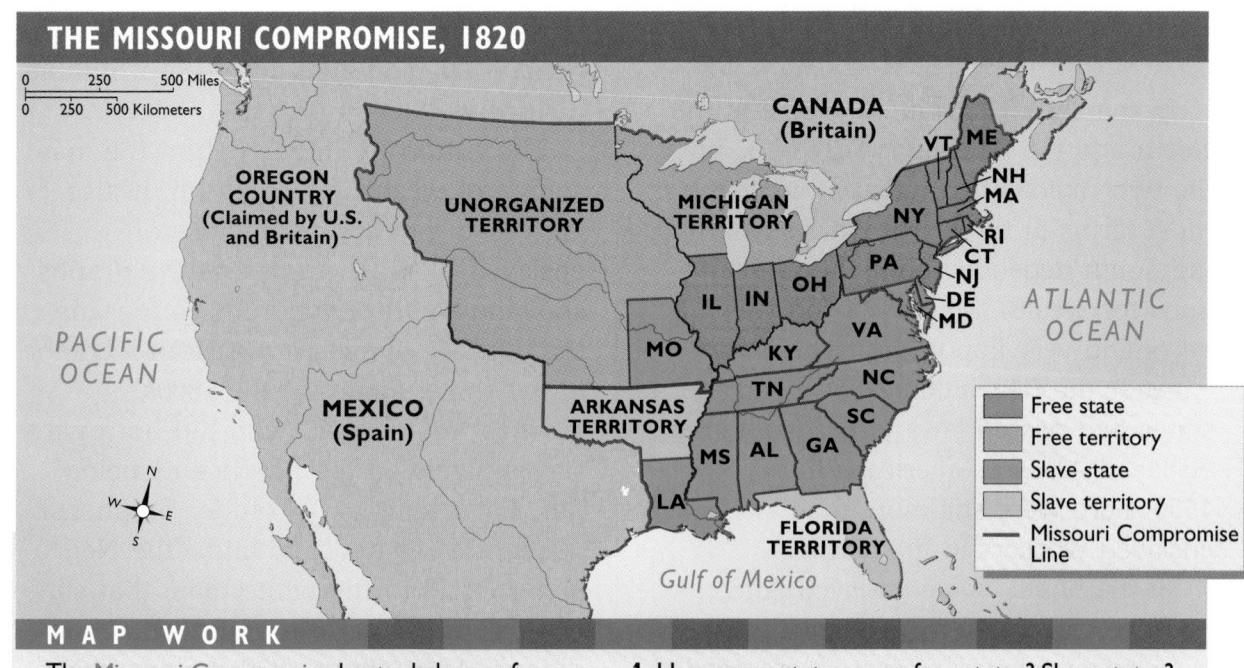

THE MISSOURI COMPROMISE, 1820

0   250   500 Miles
0   250   500 Kilometers

CANADA (Britain)

OREGON COUNTRY (Claimed by U.S. and Britain)

UNORGANIZED TERRITORY

MICHIGAN TERRITORY

PACIFIC OCEAN

MEXICO (Spain)

ARKANSAS TERRITORY

ATLANTIC OCEAN

VT ME
NH
MA
NY
RI
CT
NJ
DE
MD

PA
OH
IL IN
MO
KY
TN
MS AL GA
LA

VA
NC
SC

FLORIDA TERRITORY

Gulf of Mexico

Legend:
- Free state
- Free territory
- Slave state
- Slave territory
- Missouri Compromise Line

MAP WORK

The Missouri Compromise kept a balance of power in Congress for 30 years.

1. How many states were free states? Slave states?
2. In which territories was slavery allowed?

SLAVERY AND THE STATES

Northern and southern states had different needs. Both regions wanted laws passed in Congress that would help their economies. Each region tried to keep the other from gaining power in Congress. They wanted to have an even number of states represented there to keep a balance of power.

Congress Compromises

In 1819 the United States had 22 states—11 free and 11 slave states. Then Missouri asked to join as a slave state. To keep the balance Maine was admitted as a free state. Both Northerners and Southerners wanted a law to make sure the balance of power would not change. Congress passed the Missouri Compromise. This law created an imaginary line, shown on the map on this page. Slavery would be allowed in states south of the line and forbidden in states north of the line—except for Missouri.

The balance of free and slave states lasted until California's request to join the Union as a free state in 1850. This led to new arguments. The Compromise of 1850 admitted California as a free state. The territories gained from Mexico in 1848 would decide for themselves whether they would be free states or slave states.

In 1854 southern congressmen fought for the Kansas-Nebraska Act. It let the Kansas and Nebraska territories decide for themselves whether to allow slavery when they became states. This made Northerners angry—these lands were north of the Missouri Compromise line.

Shackles like these were used on slaves in the 1800s.

514

SLAVERY AND THE INDIVIDUAL

While lawmakers fought about slavery in Congress, some individual citizens decided to become involved in the struggle. Opposition to slavery had existed long before the United States won independence. Quakers were among the first abolitionists, those who wanted to abolish, or end, slavery. Abolitionists were both northern and southern, male and female, white and black. In the early 1800s there were more than 50 African American anti-slavery societies.

Frederick Douglass

One of the most well known abolitionists was Frederick Douglass. As an enslaved child in Baltimore, Maryland, Douglass was taught to read by his owner's wife. She taught him for a while even though it was against the law.

Douglass escaped from Baltimore in 1838, at the age of 21, wearing a borrowed sailor suit and carrying false identification papers. He settled in Massachusetts, where his skills as a speaker attracted the attention of the Massachusetts Anti-Slavery Society. The society hired Douglass to speak about his experience as a slave at meetings all over the country.

In 1845 Douglass wrote his autobiography, *Narrative of the Life of Frederick Douglass, An American Slave.* He also wrote newspaper articles. Read the excerpt from a speech Douglass made at an Independence Day picnic. Why did people respond to his words?

MANY VOICES
PRIMARY SOURCE

**Excerpt from
a speech by Frederick Douglass
in Rochester, New York,
July 4, 1852.**

Fellow citizens—Pardon me, and allow me to ask, why am I called upon to speak here today? What have I, or those I represent, to do with your national independence? . . . This Fourth of July is yours, not mine. You may rejoice, I must mourn . . .

*[Why should I have] to argue that it is wrong to make men **brutes**, to rob them of their liberty, to work them without wages, to keep them ignorant of their relations to their fellow-men, to beat them with sticks, to **flay** their flesh with the lash, to load their limbs with irons, to hunt them with dogs, to sell them at auction, to **sunder** their families, to knock out their teeth, to burn their flesh, to starve them into obedience and submission to their masters?*

brutes: animals
flay: strip away
sunder: break apart

TAKING SIDES

In 1831 Bostonian William Lloyd Garrison began publishing an anti-slavery newspaper called *The Liberator*. He demanded that slaves be freed immediately and treated as equals. In his paper he said: "I will not retreat a single inch—and I will be heard."

The Abolitionists

Soujourner Truth was born into slavery about 1797 and freed when she was 30 years old. Throughout the 1840s and the 1850s, Sojourner Truth gave speeches about the evils of slavery. After one of her speeches an angry listener shouted, "I don't care any more for your talk than I do for the bite of a flea." Truth answered, "Perhaps not, but, the Lord willing, I'll keep you scratching."

A few Southerners spoke out against slavery. Among them were Angelina and Sarah Grimké, daughters of a wealthy South Carolina plantation owner. Their hatred of slavery drove them from their home state to the North. In an open letter to other southern women, Angelina Grimké called for action: "The women of the South can overthrow this horrible system of oppression and cruelty."

The Underground Railroad

Abolitionists also fought slavery by helping enslaved people escape on the Underground Railroad. This was not a real railroad but a network of secret routes to the North. "Conductors" on the railroad guided African Americans escaping from the South. The places where they hid along the way—houses, barns, attics—were called "stations."

Of about 3,200 conductors, the best known was Harriet Tubman. She had escaped to the North as a "passenger" on the Underground Railroad. She then helped others as a conductor. Tubman later recalled how she felt when she planned to escape slavery: "No man should take me alive. I should fight for my liberty as long as my strength lasted." After safely making her way to the North, Tubman risked great danger returning to the South 19 times, guiding more than 300 fugitives to freedom.

Decade of Trouble

In the 1850s the argument about slavery became even more heated. Then Harriet Beecher Stowe published *Uncle Tom's Cabin*, a novel that showed the horrors of slavery. Over 300,000

The Granger Collection

copies were sold. It moved many people throughout the country to join the fight against slavery.

By late 1856 more than 200 people in the Kansas Territory had been killed fighting about slavery. Newspapers called the territory "Bleeding Kansas."

Then in 1857 the Supreme Court handed down the Dred Scott Decision. The justices ruled against an enslaved man named Dred Scott. The decision said that slaves were property. The justices also said the Constitution protected the right of slave owners to take their "property" into free territories. Many Northerners believed that Scott should be free, because his owner had moved to a free territory.

In October 1859 a white abolitionist named John Brown led a raid on a building in Harper's Ferry, Virginia, where the federal government stored weapons. He hoped to arm enslaved African Americans and start a revolt. Brown was found guilty of treason and hanged.

Garrison's paper *The Liberator* called Brown's plan "insane," but people around the world thought Brown was a hero.

WHY IT MATTERS

The events of the 1850s pushed the people of the North and the South farther apart. "On the subject of slavery," said a South Carolina newspaper, "the North and South . . . are not only two Peoples, but they are rival, hostile Peoples." Many feared the United States would be destroyed by this division.

✓ Reviewing Facts and Ideas

MAIN IDEAS
- By 1850 the northern economy was based on manufacturing. The South depended on cotton and slave labor.
- Former slaves and white Northerners led the fight against slavery.
- In the 1850s *Uncle Tom's Cabin,* the Dred Scott Decision, and John Brown's raid deepened the conflict between North and South.

THINK ABOUT IT
1. Why did more Southerners than Northerners want slavery?
2. Why did Congress pass the Missouri Compromise?
3. **FOCUS** What events of the 1850s caused the country to pull apart?
4. **THINKING SKILL** List at least five events involving slavery from this lesson. *Classify* them into at least two groups.
5. **WRITE** Write a few lines describing what an abolitionist might have thought about the Dred Scott Decision.

WORDS OF FREEDOM

The printed word played a key role in convincing people to join the fight against slavery. By 1860 about 17 African American newspapers were printed in the United States. These newspapers were read by both whites and blacks.

The most famous and influential was the *North Star*, started by Frederick Douglass in 1847. There were others, such as *Freeman's Advocate*, *Freedom's Journal*, and *The Mirror of Liberty*. They included news of speeches, reports of meetings, notices of upcoming activities, and articles related to ending slavery. The legacy of these newspapers can be seen in today's many African American publications.

The *North Star* was read by people all over the country. Douglass named the paper after the star that many escaping slaves used to guide themselves to the North.

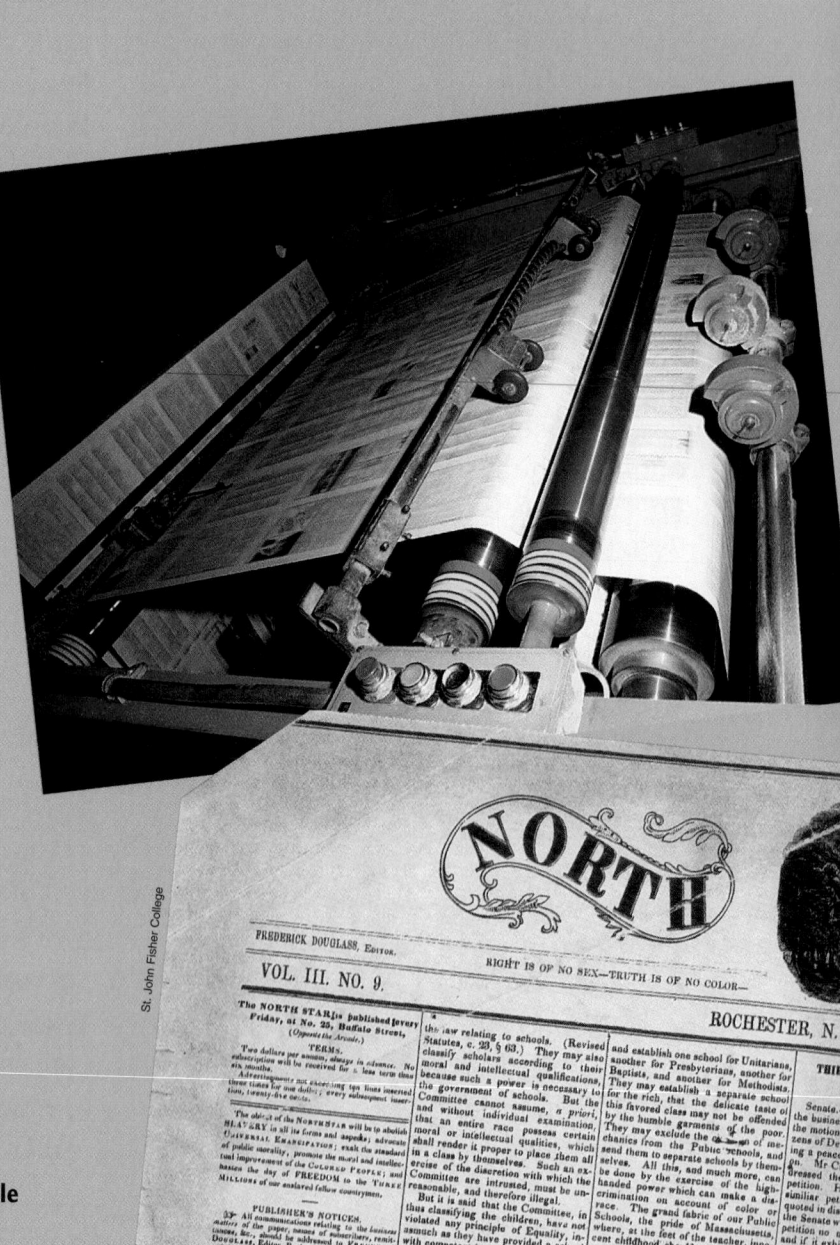

St. John Fisher College

518

John Russwurm (left) and Samuel E. Cornish founded *Freedom's Journal*, the first African American-owned newspaper in the United States, in 1827. One of its goals was to "arrest the progress of prejudice." The journalist Ida Wells (below left) was an owner of the Memphis paper *Free Speech* in the early 1900s. Today several publications are owned by African Americans (below).

Ida B. Wells

25

Black Heritage USA

National Postal Museum,
Smithstonian Institution

NEW YORK Amsterdam News

Vol. 86 No. 39 Saturday, September 30, 1995
© 1995 The Amsterdam News

New York City
Outside N.Y.C.

CELEBRATING OUR 25TH ANNIVERSARY YEAR

ESSENCE

OCTOBER 1995
$2.25

50 YEARS AS THE NO. 1 BLACK MAGAZINE

EBONY

OCTOBER 1995 USA $2.25/CANADA $2.95

BLACK ENTERPRISE

MONEY MANAGEMENT SPECIAL

OCTOBER 1995

GET MORE FOR YOUR

BARBARA McKNIGHT'S MONEY MANAGEMENT STRATEGIES HELP HER MAKE THE MOST OF HER RETIREMENT

Can Myrlie Evers-Williams Save The NAACP?

Annual Roundup: Gone? New? Back?

STAR.

GOD IS THE FATHER OF US ALL, AND ALL MEN ARE BRETHREN.

JOHN DICK, Printer.

FRIDAY, FEBRUARY 22, 1850.

WHOLE NO. 113

The Granger Collection

CIVIL WAR ENDS SLAVERY

Focus Activity

READ TO LEARN
How did the Civil War affect slavery?

VOCABULARY
secession
Confederate States of America
Civil War
states' rights
Emancipation Proclamation

PEOPLE
Jefferson Davis
Ulysses S. Grant

PLACES
Vicksburg
Appomattox Court House

READ ALOUD

"A house divided against itself cannot stand. I believe this government cannot endure half slave and half free." Abraham Lincoln had given this warning to Americans in 1858 when he ran—unsuccessfully—for the United States Senate. By the time he ran for President in 1860, Lincoln's prediction was proving to be correct.

THE BIG PICTURE

In his campaign for President, Abraham Lincoln promised to leave slavery alone in the slave states. He also promised that he would not allow it to spread. The slave states held a lot of power in the government. However, they would lose that power if every territory joined the Union as a free state. Some Southern states talked about secession, or leaving the Union, if Lincoln won the election.

Lincoln did win the election in 1860, and South Carolina voted to secede. When Lincoln took office in March of 1861, he warned that "no state can lawfully get out of the Union." However, Alabama, Arkansas, Florida, Georgia, Louisiana, Mississippi, North Carolina, Tennessee, Texas, and Virginia joined South Carolina in secession and started taking over federal property in the South. They called themselves the Confederate States of America. They drafted a constitution and named Jefferson Davis, a United States Senator from Mississippi, as president of the Confederacy.

WAR BREAKS OUT

In April 1861, Confederate troops captured the Union-held Fort Sumter in Charleston, South Carolina. The Civil War, a war between people of the same country, had begun. Lincoln called for 75,000 volunteers for the Union army. However, African Americans who rushed to join were told that "this is a white man's war."

At first, the Union was fighting to save the nation. The Confederacy was fighting for states' rights—the right of each state to make its own decisions on most issues.

Northern and Southern Resources

Each side also believed that it would win the war. The chart shows that the North had ten times the production of goods, more factories for making weapons, more railroads, and most of the nation's farmland. It would be better able to feed, arm, and move a large army.

The South hoped for a quick victory. It had experienced officers, and it had the wealth gained from cotton. On both sides, people worked hard for the war effort. Many women ran their family businesses and farms by themselves, and made ammunition, uniforms, and bandages for the soldiers.

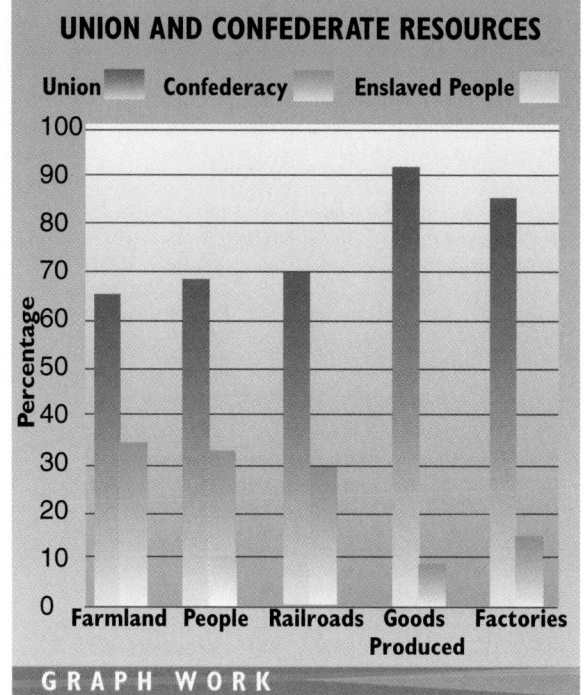

UNION AND CONFEDERATE RESOURCES

Union Confederacy Enslaved People

(Bar graph showing Percentage from 0 to 100 for categories: Farmland, People, Railroads, Goods Produced, Factories)

GRAPH WORK

The Union and the Confederacy went into the Civil War with unequal resources.

Which resources of the North were greater compared to the South?

The Start of the War

The first year of the war went in the South's favor. Confederate forces won the First Battle of Bull Run, near a stream in Virginia, and sent Union troops in retreat towards Washington, D.C. The Union Army won a victory at Antietam, Maryland, in September 1862, but nearly as many Union soldiers as Confederates were killed in the fighting.

Abraham Lincoln (right) was elected President in 1860. A few months later Confederate troops attacked Fort Sumter (left).

521

The sculptor Augustus Saint Gaudens created this tribute to the 54th Massachusetts Regiment. The inscription reads "Americans of African descent possess the pride, courage and devotion of the patriot soldier." It is in Boston, Massachusetts.

THE WAR OVER SLAVERY

Five days after the battle of Antietam, Lincoln issued the Emancipation Proclamation. It said that on January 1, 1863, "all persons held as slaves within …the United States, shall be then, thenceforth and forever free." Emancipation means freeing people. What had been a war to preserve the Union was now a war to end slavery.

The Proclamation actually freed only those slaves on Confederate land that the Union controlled. Reverend Henry Turner read it to a crowd in Washington, D.C. "Men squealed," he recalled. "Women fainted, dogs barked, white and colored people shook hands, songs were sung…nothing like it will ever be seen again in this life."

African Americans in the War

African Americans began to serve as soldiers for the Union. One celebrated unit was the 54th Massachusetts Colored Regiment. This all-volunteer regiment fought bravely at Fort Wagner in South Carolina in 1863, despite losing many men. More than 180,000 African American soldiers fought in more than 200 battles in the war.

The Confederate government used enslaved African Americans for warwork in railroad construction, weapons factories, mines, and hospitals. Many of these workers rebelled by slowing down their work or damaging products.

Behind Confederate lines, enslaved African Americans guided Union scouts. In South Carolina, some were part of a spy network organized by Harriet Tubman.

The Union Plan

A key part of the Union strategy was to gain control of the Mississippi River. That would split the Confederacy in two. Then, by controlling the Mississippi River, Union ships would prevent the movement of Confederate troops and supplies, and destroy the South's economy by stopping its cotton trade.

By June 1863, Union General Ulysses S. Grant had nearly achieved the goal. One city —Vicksburg, Mississippi— stood in his way. Grant's army trapped the Confederates in the city and pounded them with cannon fire. After 47 days, the Confederates surrendered. Later Grant said, "The fate of the Confederacy was sealed when Vicksburg fell."

The War Comes to an End

Over the next two years, the South began to weaken, and some of its soldiers deserted. Some Southerners who were not slaveowners resented fighting for people richer than themselves.

In 1864, General William Tecumseh Sherman led an army through Georgia to South Carolina. The army destroyed nearly every building and farm in its path, and burned the city of Atlanta.

Finally, after four terrible years, the war came to an end. Confederate forces surrendered at Appomattox Court House, Virginia, on April 9, 1865. Almost 620,000 people had died in the war.

WHY IT MATTERS

The Civil War reunited North and South and put an end to the debate over slavery. However, African Americans continued to be treated unfairly. In the next lesson you will see how African Americans fought for their rights.

Union General William Tecumseh Sherman (right) led a campaign that was called "the March to Sea" (below). It destroyed the Confederacy's last source of supplies.

The Granger Collection

Reviewing Facts and Ideas

MAIN IDEAS

- The Civil War began on April 12, 1861, when Confederates fired on Union forces occupying Fort Sumter.
- The Emancipation Proclamation freed African Americans in the Confederacy.
- Over 380,000 African Americans were part of the Union Army.

THINK ABOUT IT

1. What were the strengths and resources of the North and South when the Civil War began?

2. How did African Americans contribute to the Union war effort?

3. **FOCUS** How did the Civil War affect enslaved people in the United States?

4. **THINKING SKILL** *Compare* how African Americans in the North and in the South helped the Union war effort.

5. **WRITE** Write a newspaper article describing the end of the Civil War from the point of view of a slaveowner or newly freed slave.

STUDY SKILLS

Using Reference Sources

VOCABULARY

reference source   CD-ROM
encyclopedia   Internet
atlas   card catalog
historical atlas   call number

WHY THE SKILL MATTERS

You have read about Frederick Douglass and the abolitionist movement. If you wanted to write a report about the events in Douglass's life, you could try to find information in a reference source. A reference source is a book or other source that contains facts about many different subjects. Reference sources are mostly found in a special section of the library. Knowing the different types of reference sources and the kinds of information each contains will help you to find information quickly and easily.

USING REFERENCE SOURCES

One of the best places to start looking for information about a particular subject is in an encyclopedia. Encyclopedias provide very general information about important people, places, topics, and events. The subjects are arranged in alphabetical order in a series of books.

To learn more about Frederick Douglass, you need the encyclopedia volume that includes the letter *D*. Often a bibliography at the end of each entry will give you titles of books

The Library of Congress's reading room (right) is a quiet place to review reference sources. A computer disk (above right) is the latest way to store information.

524

about related subjects. You might also look in the encyclopedia's main index to see if Douglass is discussed under another subject heading.

If you already know the names of some places that were important in Douglass's life, an atlas will help you locate these places. The reference section of your textbook contains an atlas. Historical atlases include maps of important events and changes over time that affected political boundaries.

A CD-ROM is another kind of reference source. A CD-ROM is a computer disk that can contain as much information as a set of encyclopedias. In fact some encyclopedias are stored on CD-ROMs. Other CD-ROMs contain geographical and historical information, as well as photographs and paintings from museums.

You might also use the Internet as a reference source. The Internet is a computer network. With a computer that has an Internet connection, you can "visit" sources of information such as libraries, schools, or government offices.

USING THE CARD CATALOG

What if you need more specific information about Douglass's life but you do not know the title of a book on this subject? The card catalog will help you find it. A card catalog is a listing of all the books a library contains. The catalog is arranged alphabetically by author, title, and subject. Each card has a call number listed on it. The call

number is a series of letters and numbers that tells you the exact location of the book on the shelf.

Many libraries now have their card catalogs stored on computers. The computer can help you search for a book more quickly. For example, if you type in Douglass's name as a subject, then biographies and other reference sources about him soon appear on the screen. Which related subjects do you think might help you find other useful books?

TRYING THE SKILL

Historians do not always agree on how to interpret history, so it is always best to look at different sources to compare their points of view.

What do you think would be the best source to find out about Douglass's work? If you wanted to find out how the nation was divided between slave states and free states, where would you look?

REVIEWING THE SKILL

1. What kinds of reference sources are available in most libraries?

2. Where would you find the most complete information about historical events? Explain your answer.

3. In what ways can you use a card catalog to research a subject?

4. What is a CD-ROM? What kinds of information does it contain?

5. Why would it be helpful for you to know how to use a variety of reference sources?

THE STRUGGLE FOR FREEDOM CONTINUES

READ ALOUD

Felix Haywood, a former slave from Texas, recalled how he felt when the war ended. "Everybody went wild. . . . We were free! Just like that, we were free. . . . Right off, folks started on the move. They seemed to want to get closer to freedom, so they'd know what it was—like it was a place or city."

THE BIG PICTURE

Less than a week after the Confederate forces surrendered, President Lincoln was watching a play at Ford's theater in Washington, D.C. Suddenly a gunshot rang out. John Wilkes Booth, a Confederate supporter, had shot the President. The next morning, April 15, 1865, Abraham Lincoln died. The nation had lost the leadership it so badly needed for the difficult days ahead.

The South was in ruins. Lincoln had spoken of Reconstruction, or rebuilding the South. He had hoped that all Americans would act "with malice toward none, with charity for all . . . to bind up the nation's wounds." These hopes did not become a reality. Neither did the freedom that African Americans had dreamed of.

REJOINING THE UNION

Vice President Andrew Johnson of Tennessee became President. He followed Lincoln's plan for Reconstruction. To form a new state government, one tenth of a Confederate state's voters had to swear loyalty to the Union. The new government then had to approve the Thirteenth Amendment to the Constitution. This amendment abolished slavery.

Johnson Clashes with Congress

By December of 1865, every Confederate state but Texas had followed the steps Johnson had outlined. He was ready to declare Reconstruction complete, but Congress would not admit the South's newly elected officials to Congress. Many Southern leaders had been Confederate leaders. Also, the new state governments had passed black codes. These laws kept black and white people separated. They prevented freed African Americans from living in certain areas or holding any job other than farmer or laborer. African Americans without jobs could be fined, arrested, or jailed.

A New Start for African Americans

Millions of newly free African Americans had no homes or jobs. One African American said "We had no land, no house, not so much as a place to lay our head . . . we were brothers on the battlefield, but in the peaceful pursuits [activities] of life it seems that we are strangers." In response, Congress created the Freedmen's Bureau in 1865 to provide food, clothing, shelter, medical care, jobs, and legal help.

The Bureau also started over 4,000 schools for newly freed people. Charlotte Forten, a free African American from Philadelphia, traveled to South Carolina to teach reading and writing. She reported that she "never before saw children so eager to learn. . . . They come here as other children go to play."

The Freedmen's Bureau founded schools like this one in Charleston, South Carolina.

OPPORTUNITY AND HARDSHIP

Planters came up with a system called sharecropping. Landowners divided their land and rented it to sharecroppers, people who would farm it. The landowner took part of the crop—as much as half—as rent.

Many poor whites and freed blacks became sharecroppers. It was a hard life. Sharecroppers often had to borrow money to buy seeds and supplies. Prices for crops were often low. Many sharecroppers slipped into debt. Even so, Thomas Johns of Arkansas felt that "there is something about being free that makes up for all the hardships."

New Amendments

The Thirteenth Amendment had freed the slaves, but gave them no rights. In 1868 the Fourteenth Amendment became law. It made African Americans citizens of the United States. Many whites, however, were still divided about whether these African American citizens should be allowed to vote. Finally, in 1870, Congress passed the Fifteenth Amendment. The amendment said simply:

> The right of citizens of the United States to vote shall not be denied or abridged [limited] by the United States or any state on account of race, color, or previous condition of servitude [slavery].

The President on Trial

Congress passed other Reconstruction laws regarding African Americans in the South. The Civil Rights Act of 1866 told the military to protect their rights. The First Reconstruction Act stated that the Union army would rule the South until the southern states gave voting rights to African Americans. As a result of these laws, more than 500 African American officials held state office during Reconstruction. Blanche Bruce and Hiram Revels, were two of the 16 African Americans who sat in Congress.

President Johnson refused to enforce these laws and the Fourteenth Amendment. He also refused to obey laws Congress had passed to limit his power. In 1868 the House of Representatives voted to impeach Johnson. To impeach means to charge a government official with wrongdoing.

At his trial, however, Johnson remained in office—by only one vote.

African Americans participated in debates (below) in state legislatures during Reconstruction. Hiram Revels (left) from Mississippi was the first African American to serve in the United States Senate.

RECONSTRUCTION ENDS

Many white Southerners did not like having the Union army in the South. They could not accept former slaves holding government positions. Many disliked paying the high taxes that state governments demanded to rebuild the roads and railroads, and to provide public education for both black and white children.

Violence

Riots followed the passage of the Civil Rights Act and the First Reconstruction Act. Some Southerners started secret societies such as the Ku Klux Klan. "The Ku Klux Klan [is] riding nightly over the country . . . robbing, whipping, . . . and killing our people," said a Kentucky petition to Congress in 1871. Violence was used to stop blacks from voting. Sometimes whites kept voting places secret from blacks, or closed the polls before blacks had the chance to vote.

Jim Crow Laws

In 1877 the last Union soldiers left the South, and Reconstruction was over. Southern states passed Jim Crow laws. Under Jim Crow laws, blacks and whites could not use the same schools, hotels, or parks. The laws made segregation, the separation of white and black people, legal.

WHY IT MATTERS

Reconstruction gave African Americans citizenship. Yet sharecropping and segregation had bound African Americans into lives of poverty and unequal rights. Not until the Civil Rights movement of the 1950s and 1960s would African Americans begin to gain the rights guaranteed to all citizens by the Thirteenth, Fourteenth, and Fifteenth amendments to the Constitution.

✓✓ Reviewing Facts and Ideas

MAIN IDEAS

● After Lincoln was killed, President Andrew Johnson followed Lincoln's plan of Reconstruction. The Freedmen's Bureau assisted African Americans.

● Congress passed the Thirteenth, Fourteenth, and Fifteenth amendments.

● After Reconstruction ended, Southern states passed segregation laws.

THINK ABOUT IT

1. Why did Congress disagree with Johnson about Reconstruction?

2. How did the Freedmen's Bureau help freed African Americans?

3. **FOCUS** What changes did Reconstruction bring to African Americans in the South?

4. **THINKING SKILL** What _effect_ did the black codes have on the lives of freed African Americans in the South?

5. **WRITE** Write a paragraph explaining why you think the Civil Rights Act and the First Reconstruction Act were necessary.

CHAPTER 18 REVIEW

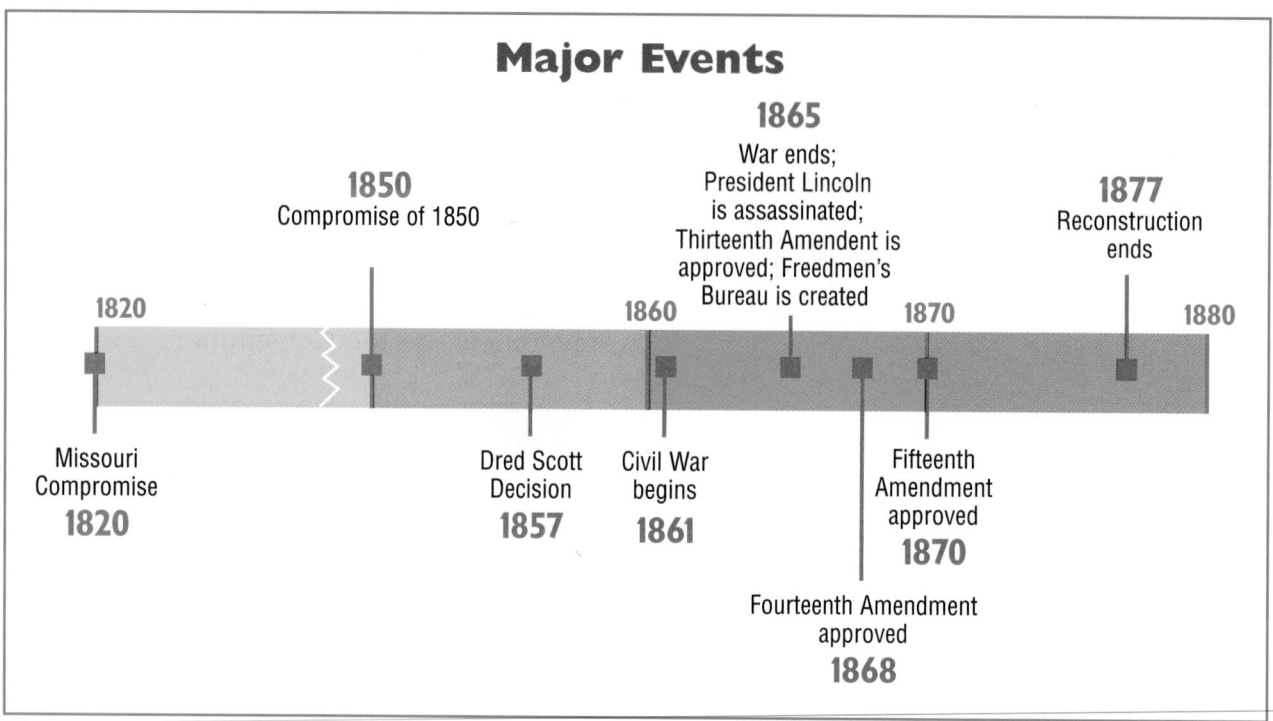

Major Events

1865
War ends; President Lincoln is assassinated; Thirteenth Amendent is approved; Freedmen's Bureau is created

1850
Compromise of 1850

1877
Reconstruction ends

1820

Missouri Compromise **1820**

1860

Dred Scott Decision **1857**

Civil War begins **1861**

1870

Fifteenth Amendment approved **1870**

1880

Fourteenth Amendment approved **1868**

THINKING ABOUT VOCABULARY

Number a sheet of paper from 1 to 10. Beside each number write the word or term from the list below that matches the description.

abolitionists	Freedmen's Bureau
Dred Scott Decision	Jim Crow laws
	Missouri Compromise
Emancipation Proclamation	Reconstruction
	segregation
free state	states' rights

1. a government agency that provided food and other help to African Americans

2. a law that created an imaginary line; slavery would be allowed south of the line, and not allowed north of the line

3. the period of rebuilding the South after the Civil War

4. the belief that states should make their own decisions about important issues

5. laws passed in the South that made the separation of whites and blacks legal

6. a state that did not allow slavery

7. Lincoln's announcement that freed some enslaved people in the Confederacy

8. separation on the basis of race

9. people who, like Frederick Douglass, wanted to end slavery

10. the Supreme Court judgment that said slaves were property

THINKING ABOUT FACTS

1. How did Frederick Douglass and William Lloyd Garrison fight against slavery?

2. Why did Congress pass the compromise laws?

3. What were some segregation laws passed during Reconstruction?

4. What gains did African Americans make during the early years of Reconstruction? Did they last? Why or why not?

5. Look at the time line above. What can you conclude about the years following the end of the Civil War?

THINK AND WRITE

WRITING A COMPARE/CONTRAST PARAGRAPH

Compare and contrast two women, Harriet Tubman and Harriet Beecher Stowe. Include information about how each person aided enslaved people.

WRITING A LETTER

Suppose that during the Civil War you are an African American who fights for the Union. Write a letter to a friend describing your experiences, the people you meet, and how you became involved in the war effort.

WRITING AN EDITORIAL

Suppose that you are the editor of a newspaper in 1860 in either the North or the South. Write an editorial in which you react to Abraham Lincoln's election as President.

APPLYING THINKING SKILLS

USING REFERENCE SOURCES

1. What is a reference source? List five reference sources.

2. When would you use an atlas? A CD-ROM?

3. If you wanted to write a report on Abraham Lincoln what resource would you use first? Why?

4. What is the purpose of a call number?

5. What sources would help you write a research report on the Missouri Compromise?

Summing Up the Chapter

Copy the main idea table on a separate sheet of paper. Review the chapter to find details to complete the table. When you have finished, use the information in the table to write a paragraph that answers the question, "How did Lincoln's actions help the cause of African Americans?"

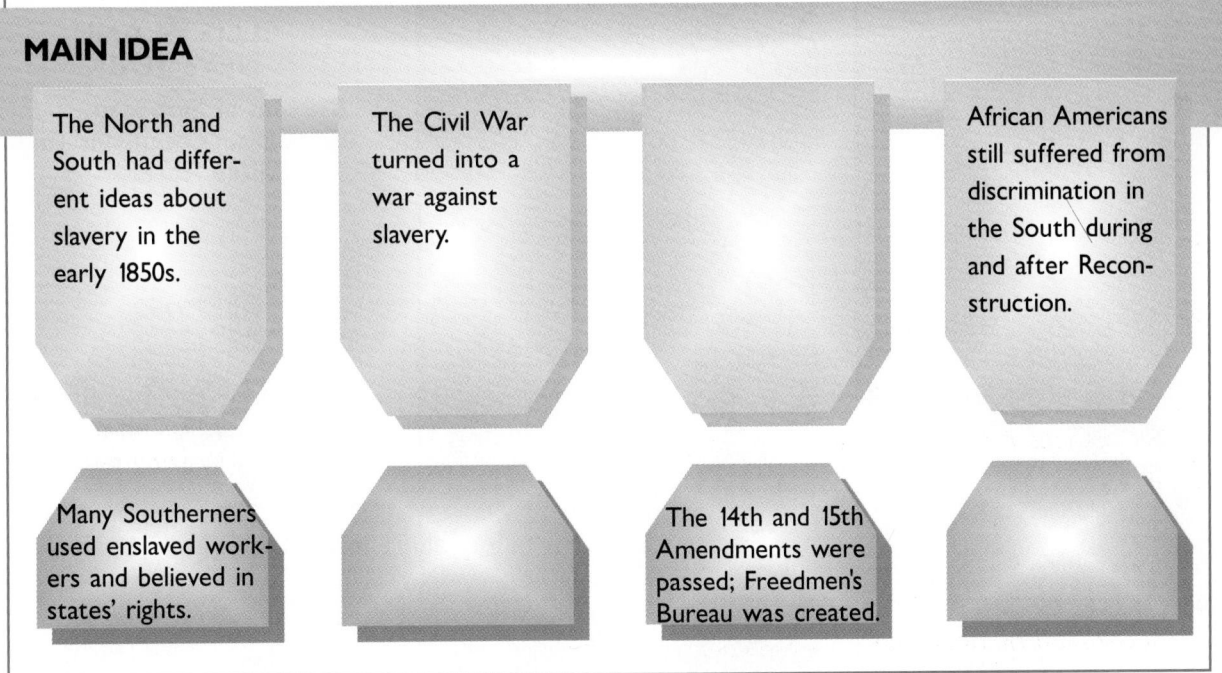

MAIN IDEA

The North and South had different ideas about slavery in the early 1850s.	The Civil War turned into a war against slavery.		African Americans still suffered from discrimination in the South during and after Reconstruction.
Many Southerners used enslaved workers and believed in states' rights.		The 14th and 15th Amendments were passed; Freedmen's Bureau was created.	

CHAPTER 19

Migrants and Immigrants

THINKING ABOUT
HISTORY AND GEOGRAPHY

This is a unique nation—most of its population came from other countries. As newcomers arrived, and as people moved from one region of the country to another, they all helped shape our history. You have read about the contributions made by Native Americans, African Americans, colonists, and the settlers of the West. After the Civil War, millions of new immigrants from Europe and Asia came to the United States. These immigrants added contributions of their own. Together with those who had arrived earlier, the newcomers formed a nation that reflects the many cultures of its population.

Los Angeles

PACIFIC OCEAN

1860s
SIERRA NEVADA MOUNTAINS

Chinese workers in California build the transcontinental railroad

1873
PITTSBURGH, PENNSYLVANIA

Andrew Carnegie helps build a new steel mill

1890s
ELLIS ISLAND, NEW YORK

Millions of European immigrants begin entering the United States

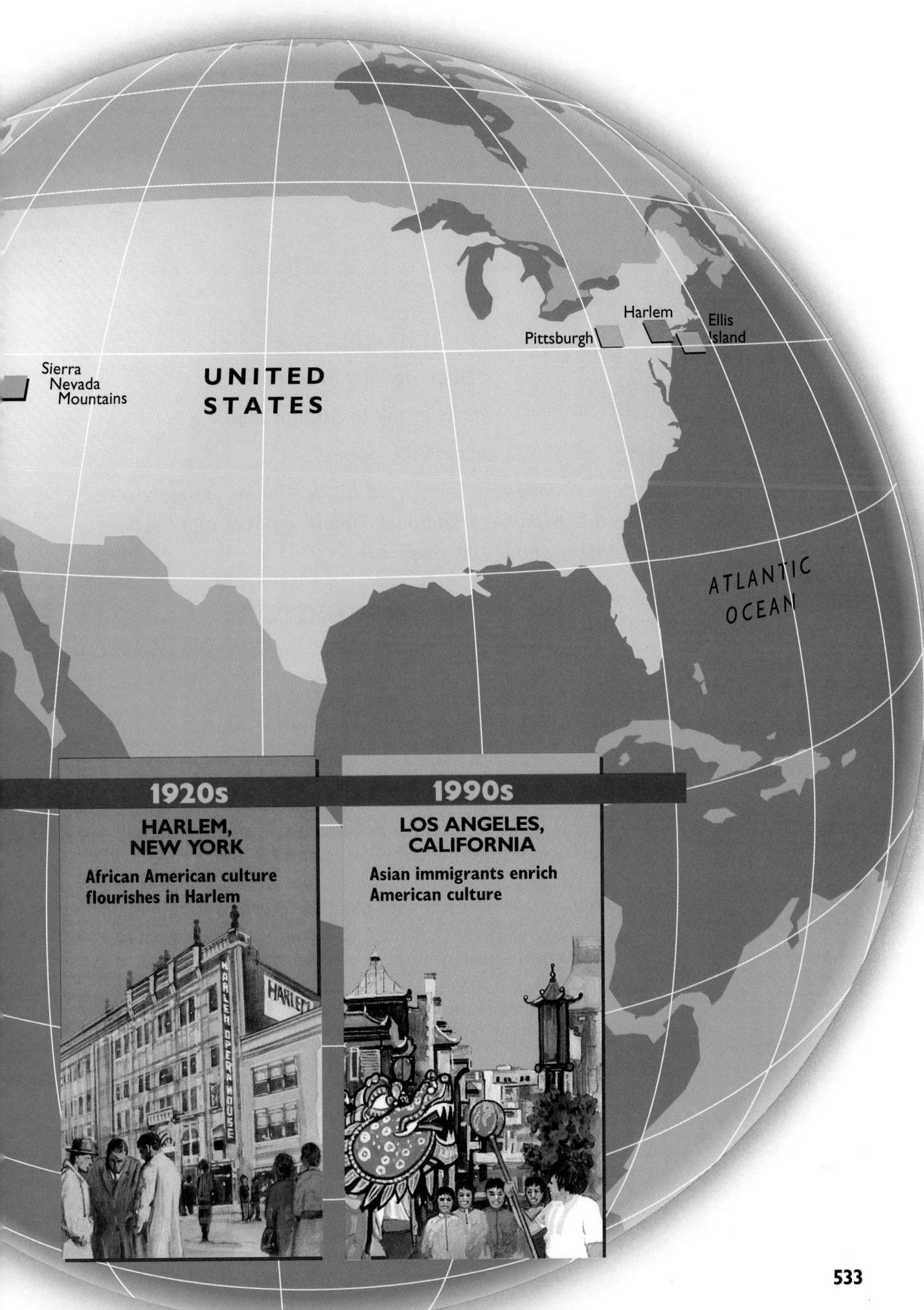

Sierra
Nevada
Mountains

**UNITED
STATES**

Pittsburgh

Harlem

Ellis
Island

ATLANTIC
OCEAN

1920s

**HARLEM,
NEW YORK**

African American culture
flourishes in Harlem

1990s

**LOS ANGELES,
CALIFORNIA**

Asian immigrants enrich
American culture

JOBS FOR ALL

READ ALOUD

"Huge dreams of fortune

go with me to foreign lands,

across the ocean."

A Japanese immigrant to the United States wrote this haiku—a traditional Japanese poem of 17 syllables—about 100 years ago.

Focus Activity

READ TO LEARN
How did immigrants change businesses and industries in the United States?

VOCABULARY
transcontinental railroad
exodusters
sweatshop
labor union
strike

PEOPLE
Andrew Carnegie
Mary Harris Jones
Samuel Gompers

THE BIG PICTURE

The years after the Civil War, in the late nineteenth century, brought great changes to our country. The North and South were united once again, and the country put most of its energies into business. Railroads were built, open plains were turned into farmland, and factories grew even larger and more numerous.

Much of this growth came from new immigrants. You read in Chapter 16 about a wave of immigrants who came to this country in the 1840s. Since the days of the English colonies, immigrants have made this country grow. In the late nineteenth century, beginning around 1880s, our country saw another great wave of immigrants from Europe, Latin America, and Asia.

Unlike earlier immigrants, most of the new arrivals went to large cities where industries offered jobs in factories and mills. They were joined in eastern and midwestern cities by African Americans migrating from the South and Mexican Americans migrating from the West and Southwest. All of these people in motion were looking for a better future. Some were trying to escape war, poverty, or discrimination.

A NATION ON THE MOVE

Our growing economy meant that more trade was taking place. Farmers shipped their crops to markets hundreds or even thousands of miles away. Factories sent shoes, light bulbs, and other products to stores across North America. How did these goods and people travel so far?

The New Railroads

In 1869, workers completed the nation's first transcontinental railroad, which crossed the entire continent. It linked California with the East.

Other railroads were also built. Laying so many miles of track gave jobs to thousands of laborers. Most of them were immigrants from Ireland and China and Mexican American migrants from the West and Southwest.

The new railroads opened up huge areas of land. Thousands of African Americans traveled by rail from the South. Some went to northern cities to work in industry, while others moved to the Middle West. In 1879, more than 20,000 African Americans started new farms in Kansas. The movement of thousands of people from a region is called an exodus—so the African Americans who moved to Kansas were known as exodusters.

Immigrants such as Taro Murata came to the United States later, around the turn of the century. What kind of work did he find?

MANY VOICES
PRIMARY SOURCE

Excerpt from an essay by Taro Murata, Collected in *American Mosaic* published in 1980.

When I came over, Japan was very, very poor. People traveled around to beg for something to eat. I had heard that the United States was a nice place to make money. The first job I got was on the railroad in the State of Washington. There were about two thousand Japanese working there at that time. Young boys, most of us . . . building the road or laying the tracks or spreading the stones . . . I worked nine hours a day—hard work—and I would earn about $1.25. After two years I got $90 a month from the railroad. We lived in a little car right on the railroad track and we cooked our own food—rice, vegetables, sometimes some meat.

It was mostly immigrants working for the railroad—Japanese, Italian, [and] Irish.

These exodusters (below) stopped to rest in Topeka, Kansas, in 1880.

All Colored People
THAT WANT TO
GO TO KANSAS,
On September 5th, 1877,
Can do so for $5.00

INDUSTRY CHANGES THE COUNTRY

Unlike Taro Murata, some immigrants came to this country to farm. Often they brought skills from their old homes to farms here. In Oregon, a man from China named Ah Bing bred the famous Bing cherry. In Florida, Lue Gim Gong bred a frost-resistant orange. That was the start of the state's famous citrus industry.

Railroads, new plows, and windmills allowed farming to begin on the Great Plains. Immigrants from Russia brought a kind of wheat that was perfect for the dry, windy plains.

In Texas and the West, raising cattle had also become a big business. Often the original rancheros and vaqueros were pushed out of business. Cowboys herded cattle to train lines that carried the animals to Chicago, which became the world's largest meatpacking center. From Chicago, meat was shipped all over the nation in refrigerated train cars.

New Inventions

Of the nearly 18 million people who immigrated to the United States between 1880 and 1910, the largest number became laborers in mines, factories, and mills. The hours there were long and the wages were low, but the jobs paid more than most immigrants could have earned in their homelands.

At this time many new inventions appeared that would change forever the way people lived and worked. Between 1891 and 1895, over 100,000 new inventions were created in our nation. The Infographic on page 537 shows some of these inventions. New inventions created great wealth for a few people. Andrew Carnegie came here as a poor Scottish immigrant in 1848. Using a new way of making steel, he started the American steel industry. The steel industry was located in Pennsylvania, where Carnegie built a new steel mill in 1873. By 1900 he was one of the world's richest people.

Women and Children Workers

Many immigrant women and children worked in factories for California's canning industry or New York's garment industry. Factories in the garment industry were known as sweatshops. They were dirty, hot, and crowded.

Children were paid less than women, and women were paid half as much as men. Pauline Newman, a young immigrant from Lithuania, earned $1.50 a week in a clothing factory. She described her work: "We were given little scissors to cut the threads off. It was not heavy work, but it was [boring], because you did the same thing from seven-thirty in the morning until nine at night."

Andrew Carnegie built steel mills like the one in this painting.

infographic

Inventors and Industry

In the late 1800s American inventors helped change everyday life in the United States. The immigrant Jan Matzeliger invented a machine that helped produce footwear quickly and cheaply—and the public could now afford new shoes. Thanks to Alexander Graham Bell, another immigrant, they could also make telephone calls. By 1900, millions of Bell's telephones were in use. In 1888 George Eastman produced the first simple, inexpensive camera. In fact, many of the products we use today were introduced during the late 1800s.

By the end of the 1800s, Isaac Singer's company sold more than a million sewing machines a year.

E. Remington and Son made the first version of the modern typewriter in 1874.

Thomas Edison produced more than 1,000 inventions; he made the first light bulb in 1879.

Light bulbs were improved by Lewis Latimer, who discovered how to make them last much longer.

LABOR FIGHTS BACK

Workers spent up to 80 hours a week in working conditions that were often dangerous. Mine workers might die in explosions. Factory workers might lose limbs in accidents. Workers began fighting to improve their working conditions.

Organize!

Workers formed organizations called labor unions. The members of a labor union were united in their fight for better wages and working conditions. Business owners often tried to fire people who joined unions, but a union with a lot of members had power.

Sometimes labor unions called a strike. In a strike, union members refuse to work until the business owners meet their demands. Business owners often hired "strikebreakers" to scare, hurt, or even kill strikers. They also hired nonunion workers—often people of a different ethnic background—to replace the strikers.

Pauline Newman became an organizer for the International Ladies' Garment Workers' Union (ILGWU). In 1911 a terrible fire broke out at the Triangle Shirtwaist Factory in New York City. The fire killed 145 workers, mostly young women. The doors that led outside were locked, and the workers could not escape from the buildings. Despite an ILGWU strike two years earlier, the company's owners had refused the workers' demands for fire escapes and unlocked doors.

One of the most famous leaders in labor's fight was the Irish immigrant Mary Harris Jones, known as "Mother Jones." When coal miners went on strike in Pennsylvania in 1900, Mother Jones organized a group of women to stop strikebreakers from taking their jobs. In 1903 she led a march of children who worked in mines to protest child labor. As a result of her efforts, Pennsylvania passed a law in 1905 that made it illegal to hire children who were under 14 years of age.

In the late 1800s, many immigrants worked long hours at large factories like this one in Michigan. Mother Jones (above) helped end child labor in the United States.

Until labor leaders like Mother Jones and Samuel Gompers organized protests against child labor, some young workers had full-time jobs. These children worked long hours in a coal mine.

AMERICAN FEDERATION OF LABOR

In 1886 a Dutch Jewish immigrant named Samuel Gompers founded the American Federation of Labor, or AFL. The AFL was made up of labor unions of skilled workers.

Gompers fought against laws forbidding strikes, which he described as "the protest of the workers against unjust conditions." He fought for better conditions for women and young workers, even though the AFL had few women or children members. The AFL worked for laws that shortened work hours, ended child labor, and made employers pay workers for injuries received at work. However, the federation was for skilled labor only, and Gompers himself would not fight for minorities. African Americans and Asian Americans were not welcome in the AFL.

Even though it did not fight for all workers, the AFL helped make the nation aware of workers and their rights. Many of the laws that govern the workplace today are the result of the battles that the AFL and other unions fought.

WHY IT MATTERS

Immigrants brought new cultures and ideas along with their hopes of finding better lives. The growth of new technologies helped industry to advance. Industry also changed in response to the struggles of the labor unions. Workers in most industries today work eight hours a day, five days a week. Many also receive paid vacations and other benefits.

✓ Reviewing Facts and Ideas

MAIN IDEAS

- In the 1870s railroads opened new regions in the United States to millions of immigrants and migrants.
- Industrial growth in the United States relied on immigrants for innovations and labor.
- Workers organized unions to fight for better working conditions.

THINK ABOUT IT

1. How did inventors contribute to the growth of industry?

2. Why might Andrew Carnegie have considered the United States a "land of opportunity"?

3. **FOCUS** How did the arrival of large numbers of immigrants in the late 1800s allow industry to grow?

4. **THINKING SKILL** _Compare_ the power of a labor union and that of an individual worker to change workers' rights.

5. **WRITE** Write a letter from Pauline Newman to her family in Lithuania, describing her feelings about her work.

GEOGRAPHY SKILLS

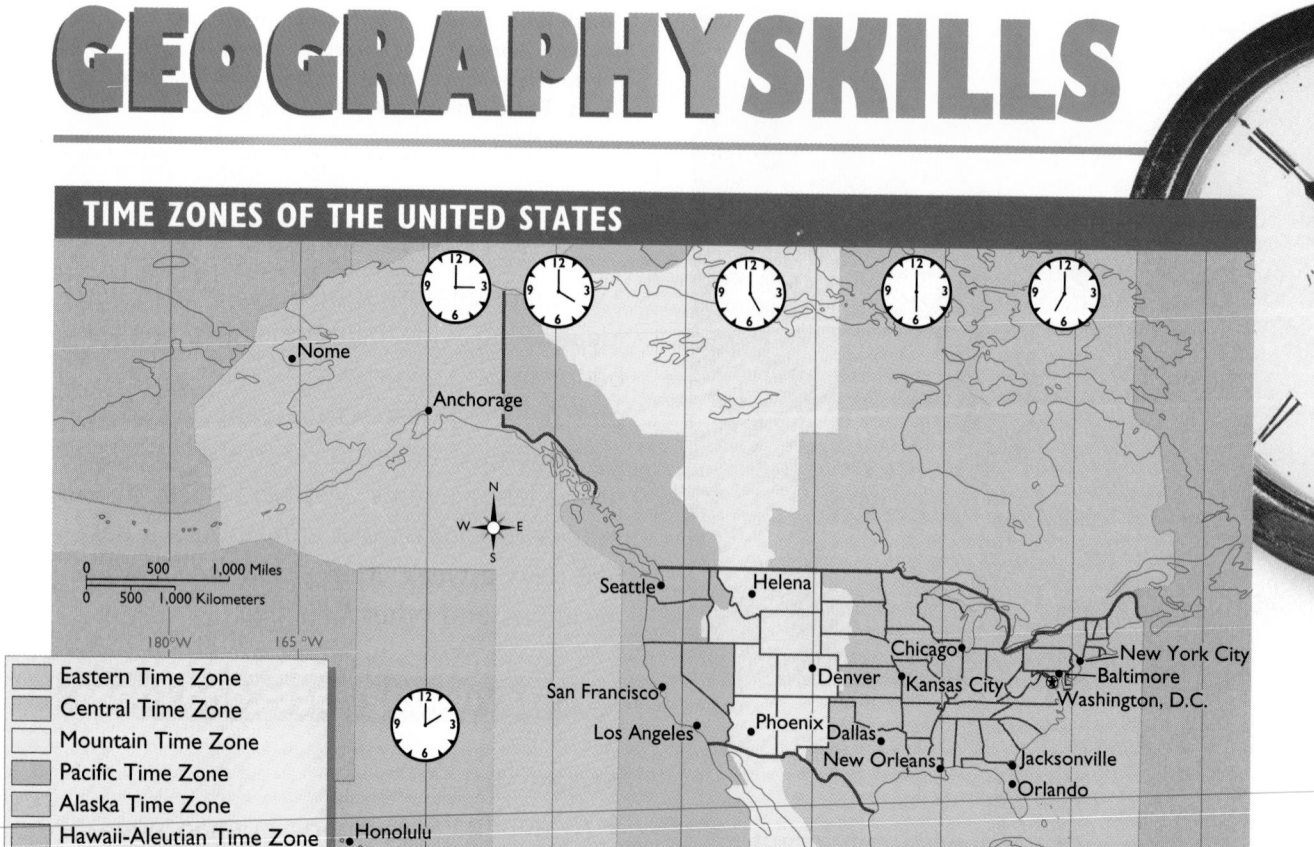

TIME ZONES OF THE UNITED STATES

Eastern Time Zone
Central Time Zone
Mountain Time Zone
Pacific Time Zone
Alaska Time Zone
Hawaii-Aleutian Time Zone

Reading Time Zone Maps

VOCABULARY

time zone

WHY THE SKILL MATTERS

By 1880 over 93,000 miles of railroads crisscrossed the United States. Many of the tracks were made of Carnegie steel and laid by immigrants. As business and industry grew, railroads became a common method of transport.

The increase in long-distance travel caused a problem. Every town and city across the country set its own time by the location of the sun in the sky. When the sun was directly overhead in Chicago, it was noon. When it was noon in Chicago, the sun had already passed this high point farther east in New York. A person traveling by train from New York to Chicago might be confused about what the time was in each town along the way.

USING THE SKILL

In the late 1800s the fact that every town had a different time troubled the people who set the train schedules. Travelers had to ask, "Is the train going to arrive at 6:00 P.M. our time or their time?" To solve this problem, time zones were set up in 1884. The world was divided into 24 different time zones—one for each hour in a day. Starting from the prime meridian at Greenwich, England, the time zones were laid out at every 15 degrees of longitude. Every town and city in a single time zone would use the same time.

As you can see from the map key on this page, the United States has six time zones. The map shows that the borders of the time zones no longer follow exactly the longitude lines. Today's time zone borders take into account national and state borders.

The time zone map can help you figure out what time it is in different parts of the United States. The time in any zone *east* of you is always *later* than it is in your zone.

The time in any zone *west* of you is always *earlier* than it is in your zone. As you move to the east, add one hour to your watch for each time zone that you cross. As you move west, subtract one hour for each time zone that you cross.

Suppose that you are a new immigrant living in Chicago. You have relatives in San Francisco, California, and New York, New York. If you take a train to either city, you want to set your watch for the correct time at your destination.

To figure out what time it is in New York, count the number of time zones east of Illinois through New York. Because Illinois and New York are one time zone apart, add one hour to 12:00 P.M. Thus, when it is noon in Chicago it is 1:00 P.M. in New York City.

To figure out what time it is in San Francisco, count the number of time zones west of Chicago through San Francisco. Chicago and San Francisco are two time zones apart. You must subtract two hours from 12:00 P.M. Thus, it will be 10:00 A.M. in San Francisco when it is noon in Chicago.

TRYING THE SKILL

Using the time zone map, find out which time zone Denver, Colorado, is in. Then, using the Helping Yourself box on this page, figure out the following time zone problems.

HELPING Yourself

- **A time zone is one of 24 divisions of Earth used to measure standard time.**

- **Find your starting point on the map.**

- **Add an hour for each time zone east of you. Subtract an hour for each time zone west of you.**

What time zone is to the west of Denver? What time zone is to the east? If the President planned to broadcast a live speech from Denver at 5:00 P.M., what time would the broadcast air in Seattle, Washington? How did you calculate the broadcast times?

Suppose that your family is planning a trip from Denver to Orlando, Florida. You plan to call the visitor center in Orlando to find out what kinds of fun things there are to do. The visitor center is open from 9:00 A.M. to 5:00 P.M. You get home from school at 4:00 P.M. Will you be able to call the office before it closes? Why or why not?

Suppose your mother wants to visit a family member in Los Angeles. She leaves Denver on a 6:00 P.M. flight that takes three hours. At what time will she arrive in Los Angeles? How did you calculate your answer?

REVIEWING THE SKILL

1. What is a time zone?

2. What time zone do you live in?

3. When people in Washington, D.C., are getting up at 7:00 A.M., what time is it in Kansas City? In Anchorage, Alaska? How do you know?

4. Between which two cities could you take a one-hour plane trip and arrive at the same time you left: New Orleans to Dallas or Kansas City to Denver?

5. Why might knowing how to read time zone maps be an important skill to have when planning a trip by airplane?

THE CHANGING CITY

READ ALOUD

Ernesto Galarza moved to California from Mexico in the early 1900s, and grew up in the barrio—the part of the city in which nearly all of the people are Hispanic. In his book Barrio Boy, *Galarza recorded memories of the barrio:*

"We came to know families from Chihuahua, Sonora, Jalisco, and Durango. Some had come to the United States even before the [Mexican] revolution, living in Texas before migrating to California. Like ourselves, our Mexican neighbors had come this far moving step by step, working and waiting."

THE BIG PICTURE

As you read in Lesson 1, a huge wave of immigrants came to this country from about 1880 to 1920. By 1920, in fact, a quarter of the population had been born in another country. Many of these immigrants moved to large cities, especially in the Northeast and Middle West, to find jobs. Immigrants and migrants helped our urban population to double between 1860 and 1900.

Many immigrants settled in communities with others of their ethnic groups. Neighborhoods such as the barrios of Los Angeles and Chicago, the Jewish Lower East Side and the Little Italy in New York, Boston's Irish End, and San Francisco's Chinatown changed the culture of our cities. Ethnic neighborhoods offered new immigrants a place where their languages and cultures would be familiar. But these places were often very poor, and life there could be very difficult.

Focus Activity

READ TO LEARN
What was city life like for immigrants of the late 1800s and early 1900s?

VOCABULARY
Great Migration
Harlem Renaissance
discrimination
Chinese Six Companies
settlement house
reform
suffrage
Nineteenth Amendment

PEOPLE
Jane Addams
Theodore Roosevelt
Lucretia Mott
Elizabeth Cady Stanton
Susan B. Anthony

PLACES
Angel Island
Seneca Falls

IMMIGRANTS IN THE CITIES

The Gold Rush of 1849 brought thousands of Chinese immigrants to the West Coast. Most worked in California's goldfields, or building the railroads. Others started their own laundry services, opened cigar factories, and helped expand California's fishing and agricultural industries. The Chinese started communities—Chinatowns—in many cities. The first, and largest, was in San Francisco.

Cities in California, Arizona, Texas, and New Mexico became homes to thousands of Mexican immigrants. Although many intended to return to Mexico, wars, revolutions, and poverty there kept them in the United States. By the 1930s, one-tenth of Mexico's population had immigrated into the United States. They were welcomed as cheap labor. Mexican women took jobs as servants or waitresses, or worked in canneries or garment factories.

In the East, about one-and-a-half million Irish immigrants arrived during the 1850s. The destruction of their potato crop by disease led to the death of thousands from starvation. Boston and New York were home to most of the Irish immigrants. In fact, by 1880 one-third of New York City's population was Irish. At first, they had to take the lowest-paying jobs. Irish women were often maids or worked in factories or sweatshops. They were "despised and kicked about" said one Irish laborer. However, as their numbers grew, the Irish became quite powerful.

By 1905 there were half a million Jews living in New York's Lower East Side. Jacob Riis, a Danish immigrant, described the neighborhood: "A five story house . . . contained apartments for 18 or 20 families, a population frequently amounting to 100 people, and sometimes increased by boarders and lodgers to 150 or more." Most of the Jewish immigrants were from Russia, where many had been segregated and treated unfairly because of their religion.

New York's Lower East Side (below) was an important immigrant community by 1900. San Francisco's Chinatown (left) was the first in the nation.

THE GREAT MIGRATION

After Reconstruction, many African Americans left the South to escape unfair laws, segregation, and poverty. They migrated to northern cities such as New York, Chicago, and Detroit. Others went west to California cities such as Oakland. Historians call this movement of African Americans from the rural South the Great Migration.

This migration increased after 1917, when the United States entered World War I. Americans of all ethnic groups fought. However, so many white men left to serve in the war that businesses began to hire African Americans and women to fill their jobs.

Some companies sent recruiters to the South to hire black workers. In Chicago alone the Great Migration caused the African American population to climb from 44,000 to 110,000 between 1910 and 1920. The following excerpt is from a letter an Alabama farmer sent to the African American newspaper *Chicago Defender* in 1917. It explains why he planned to migrate north:

We are not doing anything here we can get a living out of. . . . Some of [us] are farmers and some are cooks, barbers, and blacksmiths. We all want to leave this hard luck place.

The Harlem Renaissance

Another city to which many African Americans migrated was New York City. There they developed a lively community in the part of the city known as Harlem. By the 1920s it had become a center for black writers, artists, and musicians. Their new expression of the arts became known as the Harlem Renaissance. The word *renaissance* means "rebirth."

Artists in Harlem celebrated African American life and traditions in music and paintings. The poet Langston Hughes wrote poems using the rhythms of African American music. Writers such as Countee Cullen and Zora Neale Hurston described the people and energy of the Harlem Renaissance.

The artist Jacob Lawrence painted many scenes of the Great Migration.

FACING DISCRIMINATION

For centuries, Native Americans, African Americans, and Spanish-speaking Americans had been victims of discrimination—the act of treating people unfairly because of skin color, language, religion, or country of origin. In the late 1800s, immigrants such as the Irish and Japanese also faced discrimination.

Trouble, East and West

In San Francisco in the 1870s, anti-Chinese gangs kept Chinese people indoors after dark. The nation's laws also discriminated—Chinese people and all other nonwhites were not allowed to become citizens. An association known as the Chinese Six Companies was formed to speak for the Chinese community and fight laws that discriminated. Still, for the 60 years following 1882, the nation's borders were closed by Congress to nearly all Chinese immigrants.

After 1910, Asian immigrants who did enter the country came through Angel Island, an immigration station in San Francisco Bay. Some were held there for months or even years. Unlike

Asian immigrants wait in line at Angel Island.

Ellis Island in New York, Angel Island was for Asians only.

Mexican Americans in California, Texas, and elsewhere also faced discrimination. Many of them had owned land in the South and Southwest long before it was part of the United States. Often, their land was taken from them. One Mexican American, Policarpo Castro, described discrimination in the 1920s: "I know that if I want to amount to something in any work I will have to do it there in Mexico, because the Americans only despise us."

In New York in 1899 several Jewish societies in Brooklyn complained that "no Jew here can go on the street without exposing himself to the danger of being pitilessly beaten." Some people resented Jews who had become successful. Some colleges changed their rules to allow fewer Jewish students. As Jews became active in labor unions, business owners such as Henry Ford led fights against Jewish immigration. In 1924, Congress passed a law that limited immigration by country of origin.

THE AGE OF REFORM

Although the United States was a land of great promise, immigrants and migrants also faced hardships. Jane Addams, a young Chicago woman, decided to help. In 1889 she and a friend began holding readings and slide shows in a house once owned by Charles Hull. But they soon realized that their neighbors had more immediate needs. Hull House became the nation's first settlement house, a community center that provides services to a neighborhood. Hull House offered English and citizenship classes. It sponsored summer camps and playgrounds.

Addams also spoke out for reform, a change designed to make things better. Many citizens shared Addams's desire for reform. Writers known as "muckrakers" brought attention to unfair practices. Upton Sinclair wrote about dangerous and unclean conditions in the meat packing industry. His writings spurred Congress to pass laws calling for meat to be inspected before it was sold.

In 1903 a muckraking reporter named Ida Tarbell published articles about the Standard Oil Company. Standard Oil had a monopoly. That means it controlled almost the entire oil industry. Tarbell charged that because no other businesses could compete with Standard Oil, it was able to charge customers too much. "They had never played fair," she wrote.

President Theodore Roosevelt agreed. Roosevelt had been elected in 1904 saying that he would "see to it that every man has a square deal, no less and no more." By "square deal," he meant that government and business would deal with people fairly. Roosevelt forced Standard Oil and 24 other monopolies to divide into smaller companies.

The reform movement also gave a boost to an old cause. In 1848, two abolitionists, Lucretia Mott and Elizabeth Cady Stanton, had organized a convention in Seneca Falls, New York. The subject was women's suffrage, or right to vote. Susan B. Anthony and others continued the fight 24 years later by voting illegally as a protest. During the age of reform, citizens' participation in government seemed more important than ever. Women already had the right to vote in some states. In 1919 Congress passed the Nineteenth Amendment, which made women's suffrage the law for our country.

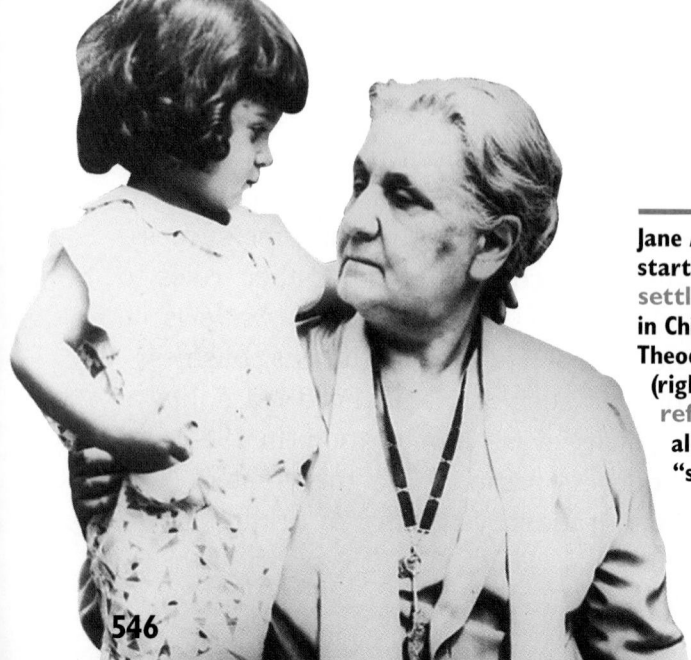

Jane Addams (left) started the first settlement house in Chicago. President Theodore Roosevelt (right) supported reforms to give all Americans a "square deal."

Immigration officials at Ellis Island interview a newcomer to the United States.

WHY IT MATTERS

Immigrants and migrants brought the cultures and experiences of their old homes to new lands. Yet the "open door" with which our country had welcomed most immigrants was about to close. Some Americans blamed problems our country faced on new immigrants. It was a bad thing, these people felt, that our culture was changing from their contributions. Congress began to pass laws restricting immigration. Between 1914 and 1950, fewer than 9 million people immigrated to the United States.

Reviewing Facts and Ideas

MAIN IDEAS

- A huge wave of immigrants came to the United States during the late 1800s and early 1900s.

- Many immigrants of the late 1800s settled in large cities where they created ethnic neighborhoods.

- During the Great Migration African Americans moved north for new jobs and to escape segregation.

- Reformers worked for laws to make life safer and fairer for all citizens.

THINK ABOUT IT

1. Give at least two reasons for the immigration of Mexicans to the United States in the early 1900s.

2. What were the causes of the Great Migration?

3. **FOCUS** How did the immigrants of the late 1800s and early 1900s change city life?

4. **THINKING SKILL** What were some *causes* and *effects* of discrimination against immigrants?

5. **WRITE** Write a newspaper editorial about the contributions of immigrants to businesses in the United States in the early 1900s.

TODAY'S IMMIGRANTS— A NEW MOSAIC

Focus Activity

READ TO LEARN
What events have caused immigrants to come to the United States since 1945?

VOCABULARY
refugee
World War II
diverse
Holocaust

READ ALOUD

Roberto Ortiz came to the United States from Cuba in 1962. Here's how he sees his new homeland: "This is still the land of opportunity. Over here, you can accomplish whatever you want to do. If you want to be a lawyer, you work hard and you are a lawyer. If you want to open a store, you open a store. You work hard, you make it go . . . it's a great country."

THE BIG PICTURE

Many immigrants have come to the United States as refugees, people who flee their country because of racial, religious, or political unrest. Since 1945 there have been two waves of immigration to the United States. The first was made up of refugees from Europe after World War II. In this war many nations joined together to stop Germany, Italy, and Japan from invading other nations. The war lasted from 1939 to 1945 and was fought in Europe, Africa, and Asia. It resulted in the deaths of about 50 million people.

The second wave of immigration started after the 1960s. Most of these later immigrants have been Asian and Latin American, and like Roberto Ortiz, many have come as refugees. Each immigrant group has helped make the United States the world's most diverse nation, or one made up of people from many different cultures.

THE NEW IMMIGRANTS

As you read, the United States has provided a home for many people who were in danger in their own countries.

European Immigrants

After World War II, thousands of European Jews immigrated to this country as refugees. German Nazis had murdered about 6 million Jews during the war in an attempt to destroy the Jewish people. This terrible crime is known as the Holocaust, a Greek word meaning "destruction by fire."

Another large immigration of Jews to the United States started in 1991. The Jews in the Soviet Union had long been victims of discrimination. When the Soviet Union broke up in 1991, many Jews left the former Soviet nations with only what they could carry. About 40,000 Jews immigrated to the United States each year for several years. When civil wars and unrest broke out in Eastern European countries such as Yugoslavia, thousands of refugees fled to the United States.

Asian Immigrants

Since 1975 more than half a million Southeast Asians have come to the United States, fleeing wars and poverty. Newcomers from Vietnam, Laos, Thailand, and Cambodia have established communities throughout the nation.

Other immigrants have come from Korea, Taiwan, and the Philippines.

Took Took Thongthiraj, the daughter of immigrants from Thailand, says that she follows the cultures of her old and new lands by being "100 percent American and 100 percent Asian."

Latin American Immigrants

During the 1970s and 1980s the United States also opened its doors to many refugees from civil wars in the Central American nations of El Salvador and Nicaragua. Many Mexicans also came here, mainly to escape poverty. More than one-fourth of recent immigrants were born in Mexico.

Too Many or Too Few?

Some Americans worry that these newcomers will take jobs from native-born Americans and change American culture.

Others believe that immigrants help the country. They argue that newcomers start businesses and bring new life to dying neighborhoods.

Today many immigrants come from such Asian countries as China and Korea.

Infographic

Great Contributions

Our culture and our economy benefit from the ideas and hard work of people from other countries. Many immigrants become leaders in their fields. Where would our country be without the immigrants on this page, and many others?

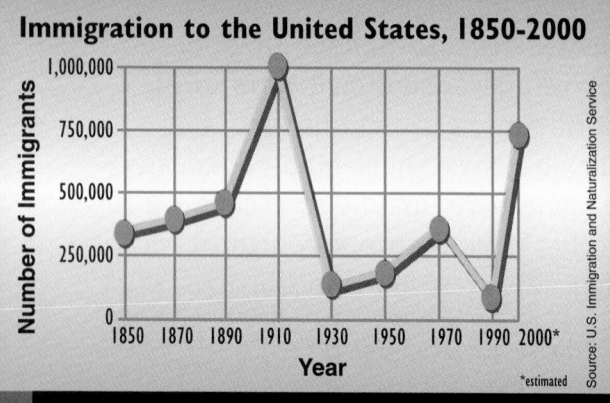

Immigration to the United States, 1850-2000

Source: U.S. Immigration and Naturalization Service

Number of Immigrants / Year

*estimated

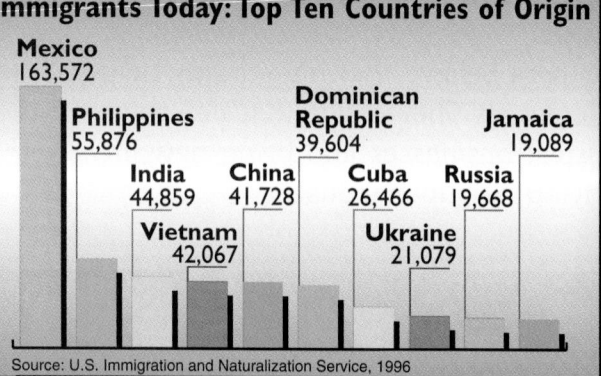

Immigrants Today: Top Ten Countries of Origin

Mexico 163,572
Philippines 55,876
Dominican Republic 39,604
Jamaica 19,089
India 44,859
China 41,728
Cuba 26,466
Russia 19,668
Vietnam 42,067
Ukraine 21,079

Source: U.S. Immigration and Naturalization Service, 1996

One of the best-selling books of the 1920s was *Home to Harlem* by **Claude McKay**. McKay came from Jamaica to New York City and became a leading figure of the Harlem Renaissance.

The violinist **Midori** came to this country from Japan to study at the famous Julliard School of Music. She is now recognized as one of the world's best violinists.

I. M. Pei, an immigrant from China, is one of the world's most famous architects. He has designed skyscrapers, housing projects, and museums, including the Rock-and-Roll Hall of Fame in Cleveland, Ohio.

One of this century's greatest ballet dancers, **Natalia Makarova** left the Soviet Union in 1970. She joined the American Ballet Theater in New York.

Writer **Isabel Allende** grew up in Chile and lived in many countries before settling in the United States. Among her many popular books are the novels *Eva Luna* and *The House of the Spirits.*

Albert Einstein was one of the greatest scientists of all time. He left Germany in the 1930s to escape being persecuted as a Jew, and taught at Princeton University in New Jersey.

WHY IT MATTERS

Immigrants—famous and unknown—are making our country a more diverse place. A typical elementary school in Los Angeles may have students from 35 different countries. "Now," says one school principal, "we've got the whole world in our classroom." In some ways, you might see the whole world in every aspect of the United States. The challenge facing all Americans is to find ways to enjoy our differences as well as the beliefs we have in common.

Reviewing Facts and Ideas

MAIN IDEAS

- After World War II, many people immigrated to the United States as refugees. Thousands of people have arrived from countries in Eastern Europe, Southeast Asia, and Central America.

- Immigrants have made the United States the world's most diverse nation.

THINK ABOUT IT

1. How have immigration patterns in the United States changed during this century?

2. Why did many people from El Salvador and Nicaragua immigrate to the United States?

3. **FOCUS** What events that took place in other countries after 1945 caused people to immigrate to the United States?

4. **THINKING SKILL** How might _bias_ affect people's views on immigration?

5. **WRITE** Write a paragraph explaining why immigration has been so important to the United States.

STORIES ON STAGE

Do you like telling stories? Telling stories on stage through music and drama has long been a tradition in many cultures around the world.

In the United States, many immigrants have used characters and stories from their home countries to create plays for the American stage. Sometimes these works have described what growing up in the United States was like for these newcomers.

Theater today—whether written in the United States or elsewhere—continues the legacy of inspiring, educating, and entertaining all Americans.

Above is a scene from the Chinese drama *Ching-Shih Mountain*, performed in New York City.

This 1915 poster (left) advertises a play called *The Green Millionaire,* performed in one of New York's Yiddish theaters.

The Asian American dancer (above) is performing in a traditional Cambodian play in the United States. The lights of Broadway (left) in New York City attract people to its many plays and musicals.

553

CHAPTER 19 REVIEW

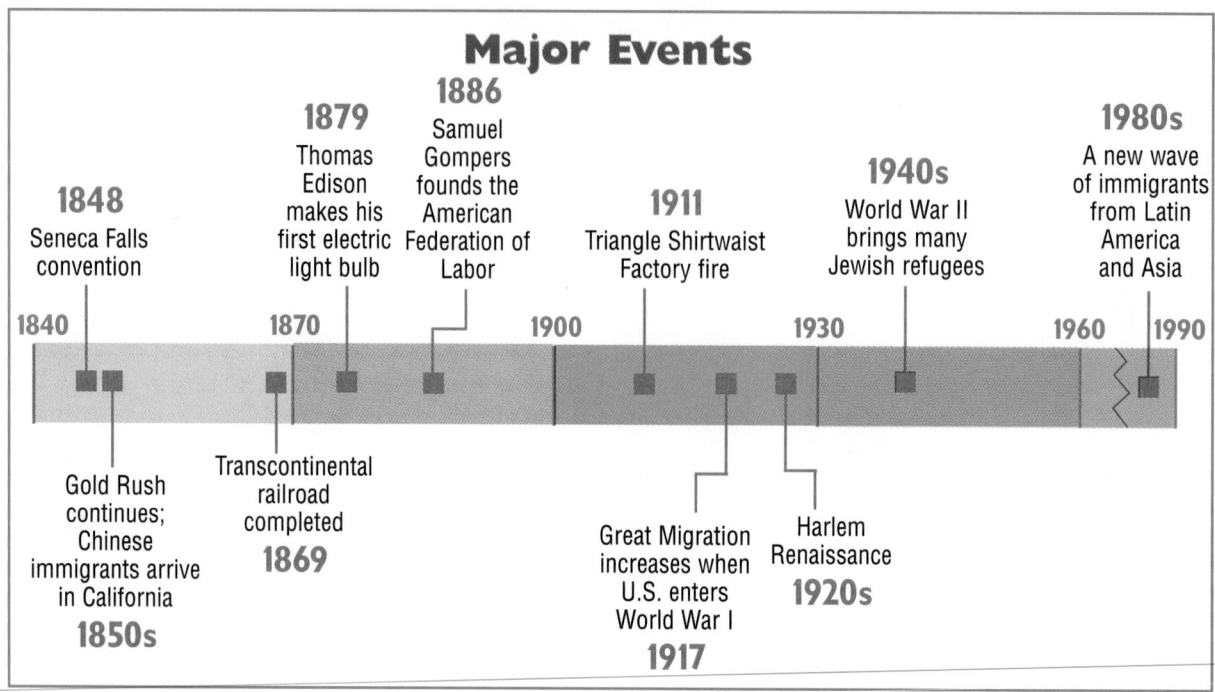

Major Events

1848
Seneca Falls convention

1879
Thomas Edison makes his first electric light bulb

1886
Samuel Gompers founds the American Federation of Labor

1911
Triangle Shirtwaist Factory fire

1940s
World War II brings many Jewish refugees

1980s
A new wave of immigrants from Latin America and Asia

1840   1870   1900   1930   1960   1990

Gold Rush continues; Chinese immigrants arrive in California
1850s

Transcontinental railroad completed
1869

Great Migration increases when U.S. enters World War I
1917

Harlem Renaissance
1920s

THINKING ABOUT VOCABULARY

Number a sheet of paper from 1 to 10. Beside each number, write the word or term from the list below that best completes each sentence.

discrimination
diverse
Great Migration
Harlem
  Renaissance
labor unions

refugees
strike
sweatshops
transcontinental
  railroad
World War II

1. During _____ the Germans tried to destroy the Jewish people.

2. Huge numbers of African Americans moved to the North during the _____.

3. African American literature, art, and music flourished during the _____.

4. _____ are small factories with dirty, crowded, often airless conditions.

5. A _____ society is one made up of people from many different cultures.

6. _____ are organizations of workers who have the same goals.

7. Many Jews left Europe as _____.

8. By 1869 a _____ linked the east and west coasts.

9. Many immigrants were victims of _____, or unfair treatment.

10. When workers _____, they refuse to work until owners meet their demands.

THINKING ABOUT FACTS

1. From which countries did many immigrants come to the United States beginning in the 1880s?

2. How did immigration in the early 1900s help the growth of industry?

3. List three countries that immigrants to the United States came from after the 1960s. What were some of the reasons they left their countries?

4. What are some ways that immigrants have contributed to the diversity of the United States?

5. Look at the time line above. What dates were important to the growth of industry in California?

THINK AND WRITE

WRITING AN EDITORIAL
Write an editorial that might have appeared in a newspaper in the late 1800s about changes in industry. You may support big businesses or the labor unions or both. Include facts to support your point of view.

WRITING A LETTER
Suppose that you are planning to move to Harlem, New York, during the Harlem Renaissance. Write a letter to a friend explaining why you have chosen to live in this community.

WRITING A REPORT
Conduct further research and write a report about the Chinese Six Companies. Give facts about what the organization did, who it helped, and why its help was needed.

APPLYING GEOGRAPHY SKILLS

Reading Time Zone Maps

1. What difficulties existed before the introduction of time zones?

2. How many time zones are there across the United States including Alaska and Hawaii?

3. Is the time in a zone *east* of you later or earlier than the time in your zone?

4. If you are in Los Angeles and need to telephone someone in Chicago at 6:00 P.M., at what time in your zone do you need to make the call?

5. Why is it useful to be able to read a time zone map?

Summing Up the Chapter

Copy the flow chart on a separate sheet of paper. Review the chapter to find information about immigrants and migrants during each time period. Then use the chart to answer the question, "How have immigrants and migrants contributed to American business and culture from the 1850s to the 1920s?"

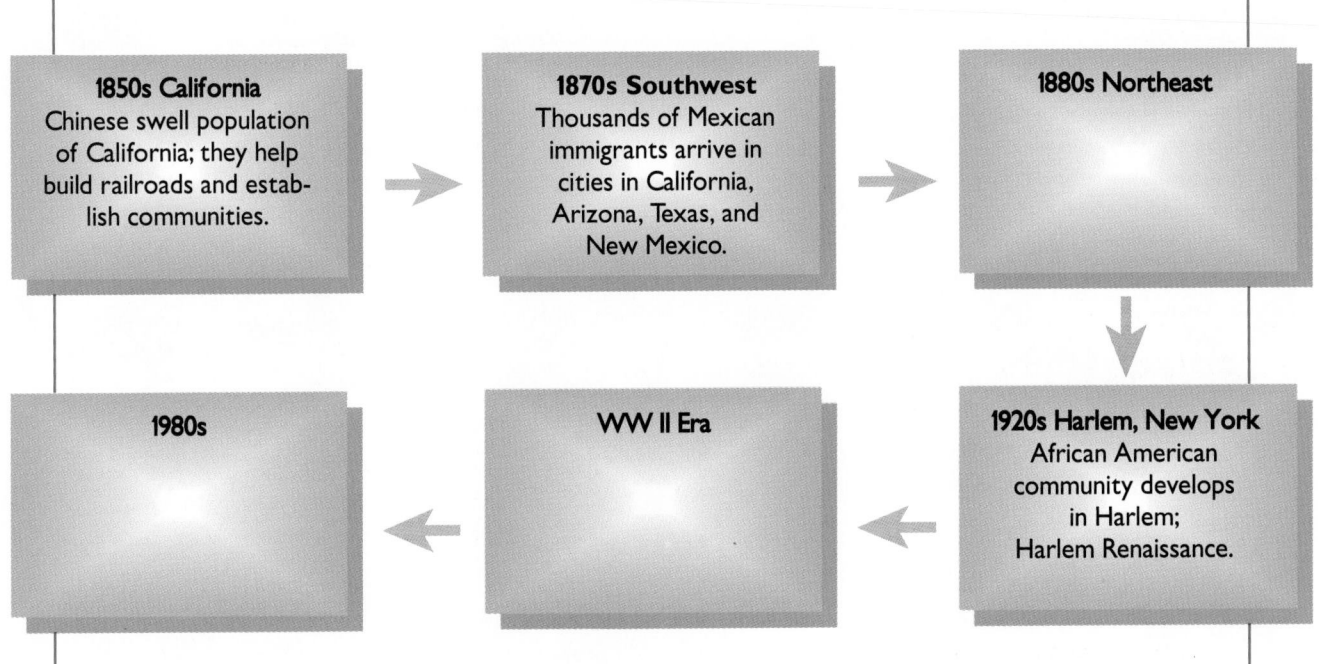

1850s California
Chinese swell population of California; they help build railroads and establish communities.

1870s Southwest
Thousands of Mexican immigrants arrive in cities in California, Arizona, Texas, and New Mexico.

1880s Northeast

1920s Harlem, New York
African American community develops in Harlem; Harlem Renaissance.

WW II Era

1980s

CHAPTER 20

Freedom and Justice for All

THINKING ABOUT HISTORY AND GEOGRAPHY

Chapter 20 brings the story of the struggle for equal rights up to the present day. It describes how many groups including women, African Americans, Native Americans, and Hispanics worked for civil rights and fair and equal treatment. As the century closes, all Americans continue to protect their rights by understanding their responsibilities as citizens.

Alcatraz Island

PACIFIC OCEAN

Southern California

1920
WASHINGTON, D.C.

Women finally win the right to vote when the Nineteenth Amendment is passed

1955
MONTGOMERY, ALABAMA

Martin Luther King, Jr., leads the boycott against segregation on city buses

1962
SOUTHERN CALIFORNIA

Cesar Chavez and Dolores Huerta start the NFWA

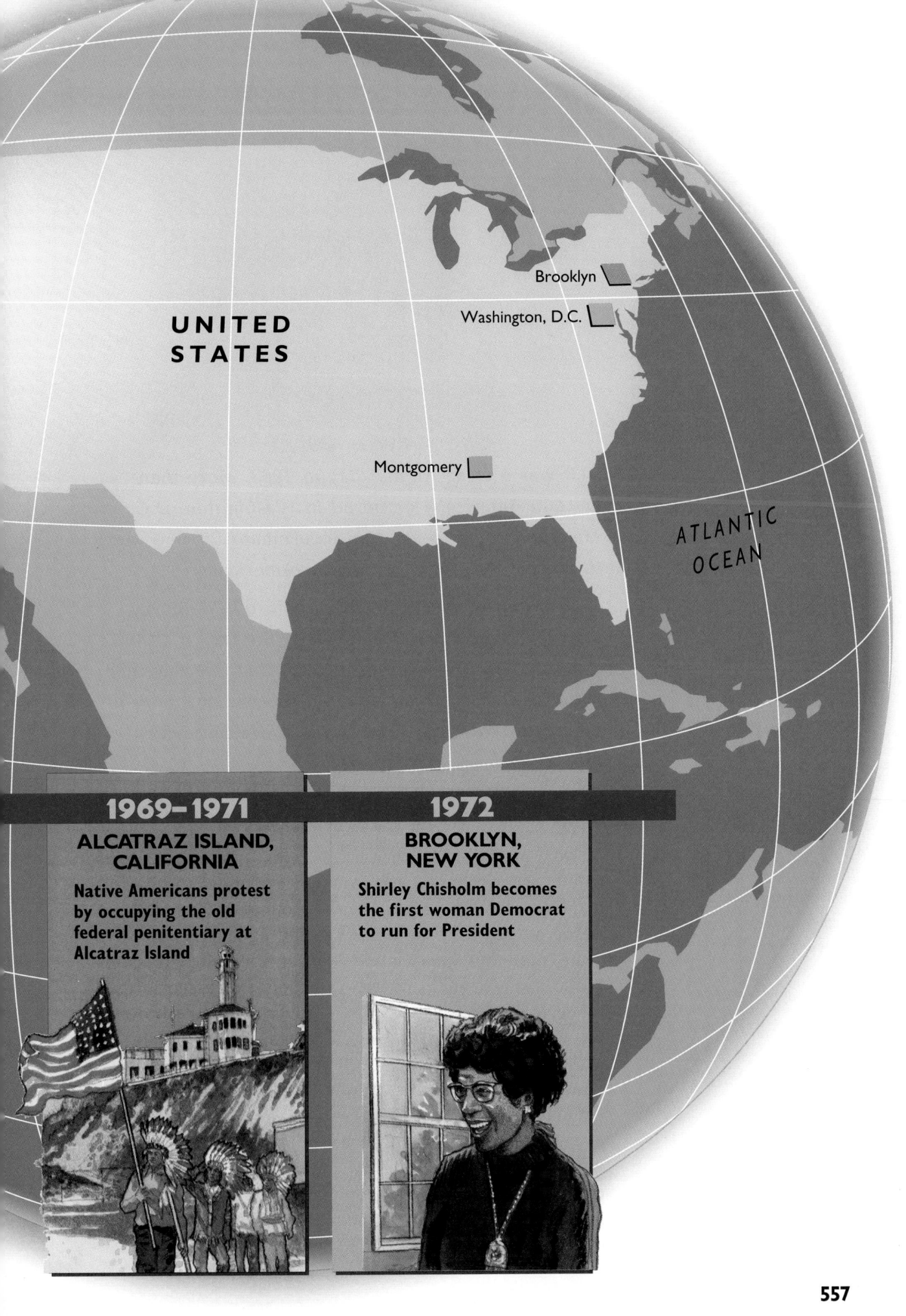

Brooklyn

Washington, D.C.

UNITED
STATES

Montgomery

ATLANTIC
OCEAN

1969–1971

ALCATRAZ ISLAND, CALIFORNIA

Native Americans protest by occupying the old federal penitentiary at Alcatraz Island

1972

BROOKLYN, NEW YORK

Shirley Chisholm becomes the first woman Democrat to run for President

THE STRUGGLE FOR EQUAL RIGHTS

Focus Activity

READ TO LEARN
How have African Americans and other groups struggled to gain equality?

VOCABULARY
NAACP
AIM
"La Causa"

PEOPLE
Martin Luther King, Jr.
Shirley Chisholm
Thurgood Marshall
Rosa Parks
Cesar Chavez
Dolores Huerta

PLACES
Montgomery, Alabama

READ ALOUD

It was a clear August day in 1963. More than 250,000 Americans gathered in Washington, D.C. They had come to ask the government for new laws to protect the rights of African Americans.

Standing on the steps of the Lincoln Memorial, Martin Luther King, Jr., spoke to the crowd. "I have a dream," King's voice rang out, "that one day this nation will rise up and live out the true meaning of its creed: 'We hold these truths to be self-evident, that all men are created equal . . .'"

THE BIG PICTURE

Dr. Martin Luther King, Jr., was quoting the Declaration of Independence because it expresses the basic beliefs on which this nation was founded. One of these beliefs is that all people are created equal. As you have read, after the American Revolution the colonists established a government based on beliefs expressed in the Declaration. The plan for their government is set out in the Constitution of the United States, the foundation of our government for over 200 years.

However, the fight for equality has continued in the United States as Americans' beliefs and interpretations of the Constitution have changed. When it was first written, many people in the United States thought that only white males should have rights. Women, African Americans, and other groups have led the struggle to change such long-held beliefs.

THE CONSTITUTION

Throughout our nation's history, people from around the world have come here seeking freedom and opportunity. As a result, the United States has become a land of many different beliefs and ethnic and national backgrounds. Our national motto, *e pluribus unum*, reflects our diversity. It is Latin for "from many, one." The diversity of our population is one of the greatest strengths of the United States.

A Strong Foundation

When lawmakers gathered in 1787 to write the Constitution and create a new government for the United States, they faced a huge challenge. They had to turn the principles of the Declaration of Independence into a workable system of government.

As you read in Chapter 14, the authors divided power between different parts of the government. In addition, they gave some citizens the power to vote for their leaders. The creators of the Constitution knew that the United States would change with time. The new government had to be able to change, too. In response, the authors wrote into the Constitution a process for making amendments to it.

A Bill of Rights

The first ten amendments, known as the Bill of Rights, describe the basic freedoms of every American citizen. Two of the rights protected in the Bill of Rights are freedom of religion and freedom of speech. Freedom of religion means that Congress cannot make laws that set up an official religion or prevent people from practicing their own religion. Freedom of speech means that Congress cannot stop people or the press from saying what they want to say if it does not harm others without cause.

During the 1700s only white men with property had the right to vote. Many Americans—such as women and African Americans—fought long political battles to win the right to vote. It was not until the 1800s and 1900s that amendments to the Constitution gave certain groups the right to vote. Find the amendments on pages R39–R49.

Native Americans drew attention to their battle for rights by claiming Alcatraz Island in 1964—just 40 years after they first won the right to vote.

THE STRUGGLE FOR EQUALITY

You read in Chapter 19 about the passage of the Nineteenth Amendment, which guaranteed women's suffrage, or right to vote. In some ways, however, women felt that their lives had not changed enough.

Women made little progress in the workplace. They had done "men's work" during wars, keeping the nation's factories running. They did not, however, get "men's pay."

The Women's Movement

In 1963 Congress passed the Equal Pay Act, stating that women should receive equal pay for equal work. However, women were often discouraged from seeking careers. Some people felt that the most important job a woman could have was in the home. Others wanted the same freedom as men to have jobs outside the home. One leader who felt this way was Betty Friedan. In 1966 she helped found the National Organization for Women, or NOW, to support women's rights.

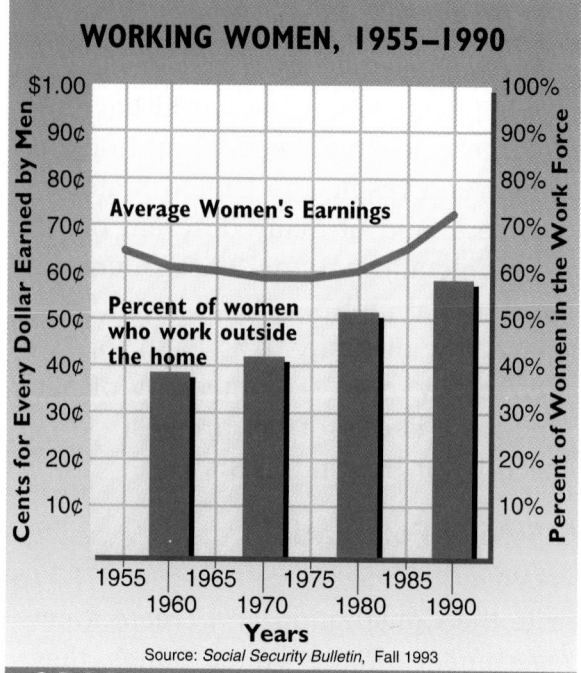

WORKING WOMEN, 1955–1990

Average Women's Earnings

Percent of women who work outside the home

Cents for Every Dollar Earned by Men: $1.00, 90¢, 80¢, 70¢, 60¢, 50¢, 40¢, 30¢, 20¢, 10¢

Percent of Women in the Work Force: 100%, 90%, 80%, 70%, 60%, 50%, 40%, 30%, 20%, 10%

Years: 1955, 1960, 1965, 1970, 1975, 1980, 1985, 1990

Source: *Social Security Bulletin,* Fall 1993

GRAPH WORK

Information for the line graph is found on the left side and for the bar graph, on the right side. In which years did both women's earnings and the number of women in the work force increase?

Today many women have jobs such as astronaut or firefighter that were once only held by men. Women also represent other Americans in government. In 1968 Shirley Chisholm became the first African American congresswoman, and in 1972, the first woman from a major party to run for President. Sandra Day O'Connor became Justice of the Supreme Court in 1981. Madeleine K. Albright became Secretary of State in 1996. California was the first state to have two women in the Senate, Dianne Feinstein and Barbara Boxer.

Shirley Chisholm (left) was the first African American congresswoman.

The Civil Rights Movement

In 1909 a group of blacks and whites had founded the National Association for the Advancement of Colored People, or **NAACP**, to fight discrimination.

During the 1950s, African Americans were still denied basic rights—even the right to vote in some states. Legal segregation was widespread, particularly in the South. Blacks could not live in the same neighborhoods, attend the same schools, or eat in the same restaurants as whites. During the 1940s and 1950s **Thurgood Marshall** led a team of NAACP lawyers. Marshall argued the case *Brown* versus *Board of Education of Topeka, Kansas* before the Supreme Court in 1954. The court ruled that segregation in public schools was unconstitutional.

In **Montgomery, Alabama**, in 1955 **Rosa Parks** said "no" when a bus driver told her to give her seat to a white person. Parks was arrested. In response, African Americans refused to ride city buses for over a year. Read the following description from a person who was part of this protest. How did Joseph Lacey feel about taking part?

MANY VOICES
PRIMARY SOURCE

Excerpt from a memoir by Joseph Lacey, published in *Freedom's Children* in 1993.

*When the boycott started, I just couldn't wait for morning to come because I wanted to see what was happening. I walked to school. As the buses passed me and my schoolmates, we said, "Nobody's on the bus! Nobody's on the bus!" It was a day to behold to see nobody on the bus. Everybody stuck together on the **boycott**. It lasted over a year, and we walked and we enjoyed walking. . . . Everybody had a part.*

boycott: a refusal to use a product or service

The Movement Grows

In 1956 the Supreme Court ordered Montgomery to end segregation on its buses. Martin Luther King, Jr, an organizer of the boycott, and other civil rights leaders led a march on Washington to persuade Congress to pass new civil rights laws. The next year the Civil Rights Act was passed, making segregation in public places illegal. A 1965 law protected African Americans' right to vote.

Even so, many African Americans still suffered discrimination. Their anger erupted in riots in many cities. In a section of Los Angeles called Watts, riots in 1965 lasted six days, and 34 people were killed.

Today discrimination still exists. Some housing is not available to African Americans, and only a small number of African Americans head major businesses.

As a leader in the bus boycott arising from the arrest of Rosa Parks (left), Martin Luther King, Jr., (far left) was also arrested.

561

THE FIGHT CONTINUES

African Americans are not the only group fighting for civil rights. Native Americans were not made citizens of the United States until 1924. In the 1960s, they continued to fight for land rights promised them by the United States government.

Native Americans

In 1968 Russell Means, a Sioux, and Dennis Banks, a Chippewa, joined others to form the American Indian Movement, or AIM. To focus attention on Native American problems, AIM took over the abandoned Alcatraz Island in San Francisco Bay from 1969 to 1971. Activists also briefly occupied Ellis Island and Mount Rushmore.

"La Causa"

In the 1960s migrant farm workers were among the poorest-paid laborers in the nation. As seasonal workers, they move from farm to farm picking different crops. Migrant workers often work long hours and live in very poor housing.

In 1962 two Mexican Americans in California decided to form a labor union for migrant workers. Cesar Chavez (SEH zahr CHAH vez) and Dolores Huerta (WAIR tah) founded the National Farm Workers Association (NFWA) to fight for better working conditions. From California to Florida, they led the NFWA in strikes, boycotts, and protest marches. Their fight was called *La Causa*—"the cause" or "the struggle"—and won better treatment for migrant farm workers.

WHY IT MATTERS

Although the Constitution promises every American the same rights, some groups continue to struggle to achieve equality. Discrimination still exists, but our country has come closer to the ideal of "liberty and justice for all."

✔️ **Reviewing Facts and Ideas**

MAIN IDEAS

- Americans are guaranteed certain basic rights in the Constitution.
- Women won the right to vote in 1920. They began to enter the workforce in record numbers in the 1960s.
- In the 1950s and 1960s African Americans began to achieve equality.
- Native Americans and migrant workers continue to fight for civil rights.

THINK ABOUT IT

1. What is suffrage?
2. List two gains African Americans made in the 1950s and 1960s.
3. **FOCUS** What are some ways that women and minority groups have worked for equality?
4. **THINKING SKILL** List one *cause* and one *effect* of the 1960s women's movement.
5. **WRITE** Write an outline of a new amendment to the Constitution.

Chavez and Huerta held many protests for migrant farm workers' rights.

CITIZENSHIP
MAKING A DIFFERENCE

Taking Another View

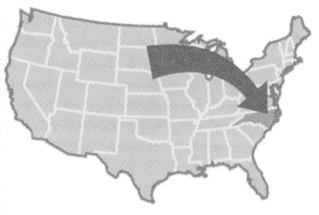

CHARLOTTE, NORTH CAROLINA. What is it like always to be seated in a world where everyone else can stand? Laura Stinson and Sharaye (shah RAY) LaMothe can answer that question. Both girls have depended on wheelchairs for many years.

When the two girls were in the sixth grade at Lebanon Elementary School, they decided to share their outlook on the world with other students. In April 1993 the two girls created "Chairs 'R Us," a show-and-tell program for younger students at their school. Laura and Sharaye begin their sessions by explaining how uncomfortable they feel when people stare at them. "We would prefer them to come to us and ask us questions if they like," Sharaye says.

"The only thing wrong with me," says Sharaye, "is I can't use my legs. I can think, talk, cook, draw, and even dance." The "Chairs 'R Us" team told the students about the challenges that people with disabilities face at amusement parks and shopping malls. "We can't really go on the rides because of the steps," Sharaye says. Laura points out, "I can't ride the Ferris wheel because they don't stop the ride long enough for me to get out of my wheelchair and into the seat."

After each session the girls give two students a chance to use a wheelchair. "At first they thought it was fun," said Laura, "but then they'd get tired. It showed them how hard it was for us to get around sometimes." Both girls agreed that "Chairs 'R Us" had made a difference. Laura said, "We helped some kids understand that people with disabilities have feelings. They want people to treat them normally. They want a fair chance and they don't want obstacles." Sharaye added, "I learned something too. I learned that when people stare, they're not trying to be mean. They are just wondering what it's like to be in a wheelchair."

" . . . come to us and ask us questions . . . "

Sharaye LaMothe

Laura Stinson

THINKINGSKILLS

WE DEMAND! AN END TO BIAS NOW!

FREEDOM MARCH ★

WE MARCH FOR EFFECTIVE CIVIL RIGHTS LAWS NOW!

Identifying Bias

VOCABULARY
bias

WHY THE SKILL MATTERS

Imagine that a public meeting was held in your town to hear people's views on requiring students to wear school uniforms. The next day a newspaper article described those who spoke in favor of uniforms as "thoughtful" and "well informed." Those against uniforms were described as "clueless" and "shallow."

Clearly the writer of the article was in favor of school uniforms and presented a bias. A bias is a slanted or strongly one-sided presentation of information. A person can have a bias *for* or *against* something.

Biased accounts are not completely accurate. Being able to identify bias will help you determine the accuracy of information you read or hear.

USING THE SKILL

Read the following comments about the women's movement. They were made by an American homemaker in 1969.

> *Men and women are different. Everyone knows that. Women can never achieve equality, so why even try? All the women I know who work are miserable, and any woman who would rather go to work than stay home and take care of her husband and children is crazy.*

Do this woman's comments show bias for or against the women's movement? The Helping Yourself box on the next page contains steps for identifying bias.

There are several clues in this passage that reveal the woman's bias. Her tone is angry, and she uses several "loaded" words. For example, "miserable" and "crazy" are words that create a negative feeling about the subject. She also exaggerates when she says "women can *never* achieve equality" and "*any* woman who would rather go to work." These are phrases that overstate or change what is probably true. Many women do enjoy careers outside the home. Use of loaded words and exaggerations are strong clues that the speaker is biased against the women's movement.

TRYING THE SKILL

Now read another passage. Use the Helping Yourself box to identify bias, if any exists.

This strike is absolutely appropriate. Anyone who stops to think about it for a moment will understand why. These courageous strikers couldn't go on working for peanuts while the boss got rich. And they couldn't go on working without being guaranteed that their jobs would last. So they are taking a stand—and each of us should thank them. People like these strikers can change our world. We should all support them.

HELPING Yourself

- **Bias is a one-sided or slanted presentation of information.**
- **Look for clues such as "loaded" words or exaggerated statements.**
- **Determine if only one side is presented.**
- **State the side or bias.**

Does the writer show bias for or against the strike? Are there any exaggerations or loaded words? Is more than one side presented?

REVIEWING THE SKILL

1. What is bias?
2. What clues can help you identify bias?
3. Did the speaker in the quote above reveal bias? If so, state the bias in your own words. Support your answer with evidence.
4. Why is it important to be alert to bias?

Garment workers in New York City went on strike in 1913.

SAFEGUARDING OUR FREEDOMS

Focus Activity

READ TO LEARN
How can citizens of the United States protect their rights?

VOCABULARY
Americans with Disabilities Act
naturalization

PEOPLE
Loretta Sanchez
Christopher Reeve

READ ALOUD

"This country . . . I am so proud of it! I am so proud of the law of this country. This is something you can fight for." Armande Roc, originally from Haiti, spoke these words as she watched her niece become a citizen of the United States. All around her on that cold day in January 1998 were immigrants from many other lands. They were gathered at Ellis Island, New York, to recite the oath of allegiance to the United States. Afterward the new American citizens hugged, shook hands, and cried with joy.

THE BIG PICTURE

Our country, of which Ms. Roc is so proud, is a land of physical wonders. It is a land of diverse peoples. It is also a land united in its belief in freedom for individuals.

Do you use your rights? If you have made a speech at a school meeting you have exercised your right to freedom of speech. If you have written a letter to the editor of a newspaper you have made use of the freedom of the press. If you have attended religious services, you have exercised your freedom of religion.

Our nation's rights are precious. So are our responsibilities as citizens. Each one of us shares in the responsibility of protecting our rights.

PEOPLE REACH OUT

You have read about many well-known Americans who have shaped our nation. It has also been shaped and defined—one day at a time—by ordinary people who participate in the American system.

Representing the People

One way ordinary people participate in the American system is by running for government office. After the 1996 elections, there were more women than ever before in Congress—51 congresswomen and 9 senators.

Loretta Sanchez represents a district in Orange County, California. She never planned to go into politics. But in recent years Sanchez and other Latinos and Latinas in her district began to feel their views were not being represented by their congressperson. Sanchez entered the race—and won. She takes her new position very seriously. "For these people who came out to vote for me," says Sanchez, "imagine what might happen if I don't deliver."

Landmark Law for Americans with Disabilities

Another way to participate in the American system is to organize large groups to take action. Although millions of Americans use wheelchairs, it used to be difficult or impossible to attend public school or visit a restaurant or museum in a wheelchair. Stairs and revolving doors often blocked the way.

Americans with disabilities have fought against such restrictions. In 1990

they won a battle when the Americans with Disabilities Act was passed. The table on this page describes some parts of the act. One United States senator called it "the emancipation proclamation for disabled Americans."

Christopher Reeve knows first-hand how important this law is. In 1995 he was badly injured in a horse-riding accident. He still cannot move from the neck down.

Disability has not stopped Reeve. Instead it has motivated him to work on behalf of all disabled people. The money that Reeve raises is used to assist those with disabilities and pays for research that may help Reeve and others with similar injuries.

Christopher Reeve (right) has worked as a film director as well as a spokesperson for Americans with disabilities. The majesty of the Rocky Mountains (left) is a source of pride for many Americans.

This Land Is Your Land

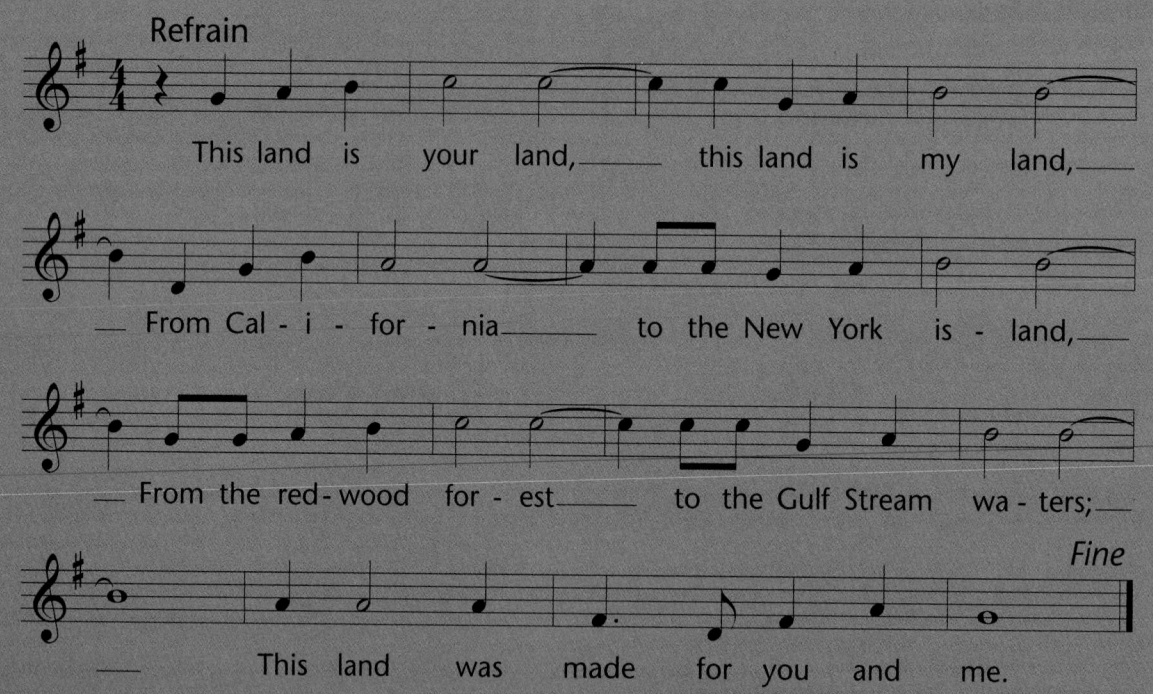

Refrain

This land is your land,____ this land is my land,____

____ From Cal - i - for - nia____ to the New York is - land,____

____ From the red - wood for - est____ to the Gulf Stream wa - ters;____

Fine

____ This land was made for you and me.

UNITED STATES CITIZENS

Most Americans became citizens of this country at birth. For those not born here, the process of becoming a citizen is called naturalization. Those who wish to become naturalized must live here for five years, and must read and write English. After passing a test on American history and government, they must swear an oath of allegiance to the United States.

Being a Responsible Citizen

Naturalized citizens have almost exactly the same rights—and responsibilities—as those born in the United States.

Some of these responsibilities are obeying laws, serving on juries, paying taxes, and taking an active part in government. One of the first ways most of us participate in government is by voting. In order to vote intelligently we must be well informed on important issues.

Being informed is important for another reason. We cannot protect our rights and those of others if we do not know what those rights are. We cannot contribute to our community if we do not know what is going on around us. Getting an education and keeping up with the news help us stay informed.

WHY IT MATTERS

Citizenship brings with it both freedom and responsibility. This country is the responsibility of everyone, as the song "This Land Is Your Land" on the opposite page reminds us. One of our responsibilities is to take an active part in safeguarding the freedoms that we as a nation have come to expect. By participating in the American system of voting, running for office, and organizing action groups, citizens continue to ensure the protection of their rights.

These new citizens swear an oath of allegiance to the United States at a ceremony in San Antonio, Texas.

✓/// Reviewing Facts and Ideas

MAIN IDEAS

- Citizens can protect their rights by taking part in government. Disabled-rights groups won a victory in 1990 with the passage of the Americans with Disabilities Act.

- A person becomes a U.S. citizen either by birth or by naturalization.

- All citizens have a responsibility to vote, to stay informed, to respect the rights of others, and to contribute to their communities.

THINK ABOUT IT

1. What are some ways of participating in the American system?

2. How did Loretta Sanchez exercise her rights under the Constitution?

3. **FOCUS** How can groups of Americans make sure their rights are protected?

4. **THINKING SKILL** Identify two forms of *bias* that might be demonstrated in newspaper editorials.

5. **WRITE** Write a paragraph about an injustice and how to correct it.

569

CHAPTER 20 REVIEW

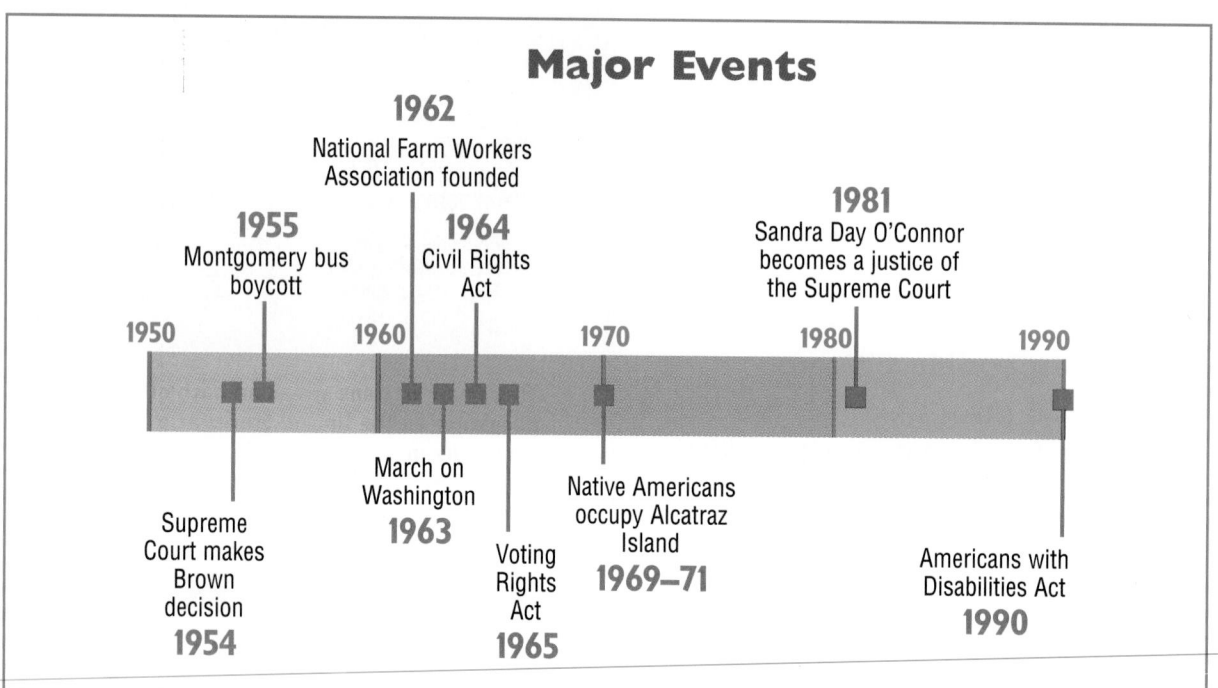

Major Events

1962
National Farm Workers Association founded

1955
Montgomery bus boycott

1964
Civil Rights Act

1981
Sandra Day O'Connor becomes a justice of the Supreme Court

1950   1960   1970   1980   1990

Supreme Court makes Brown decision
1954

March on Washington
1963

Voting Rights Act
1965

Native Americans occupy Alcatraz Island
1969–71

Americans with Disabilities Act
1990

THINKING ABOUT VOCABULARY

Number a sheet of paper from 1 to 5. Beside each number, write the word or term from the list below that completes the sentence.

AIM

Americans with Disabilities Act

La Causa

NAACP

naturalization

1. The process of becoming a citizen is called _____ .

2. Native American activists in _____ occupied several federal locations in the 1960s.

3. The _____ prohibits discrimination against people with disabilities.

4. The _____ was founded in 1909 to fight discrimination.

5. The farm workers' struggle was known by its Spanish name, _____ .

THINKING ABOUT FACTS

1. What did the Supreme Court decide in the Brown decision in 1954?

2. How did the Equal Pay Act of 1963 help women?

3. How have women's roles changed since the 1960s?

4. Who was Rosa Parks? What was the result of her actions?

5. Why did Martin Luther King, Jr., lead a march on Washington?

6. What caused the riots of 1965?

7. Who were Cesar Chavez and Dolores Huerta? What conditions were they trying to change?

8. What steps must a person take to become a naturalized citizen?

9. What are some of the responsibilities of being a citizen?

10. Name two things that were changed by the Americans with Disabilities Act.

THINK AND WRITE

WRITING A BIOGRAPHY
Conduct further research and write a biography of Shirley Chisholm, Sandra Day O'Connor, or another woman who has served in our government. Find facts about your subject's upbringing, work history, and how she contributed to our nation.

WRITING A SPEECH
Suppose that you are an African American who lives in Montgomery, Alabama, in 1955. Write a speech giving your reasons for either joining or not joining the bus boycott.

WRITING A LETTER
Suppose that you are a naturalized citizen who immigrated to this country from Mexico. Write a letter to a friend from home describing the process of naturalization, and what your new citizenship means to you.

APPLYING STUDY SKILLS

IDENTIFYING BIAS
1. What is a biased opinion?
2. How can you identify a bias?
3. Is a bias only against something or someone? Explain.
4. Why do arguments that support a particular point of view often show bias?
5. How can identifying bias help you when you are reading a newspaper?

Summing Up the Chapter

Copy the semantic map on a separate sheet of paper. Then review the chapter to complete the main ideas. After you have finished, answer the following question, "How have people worked to win equal rights?"

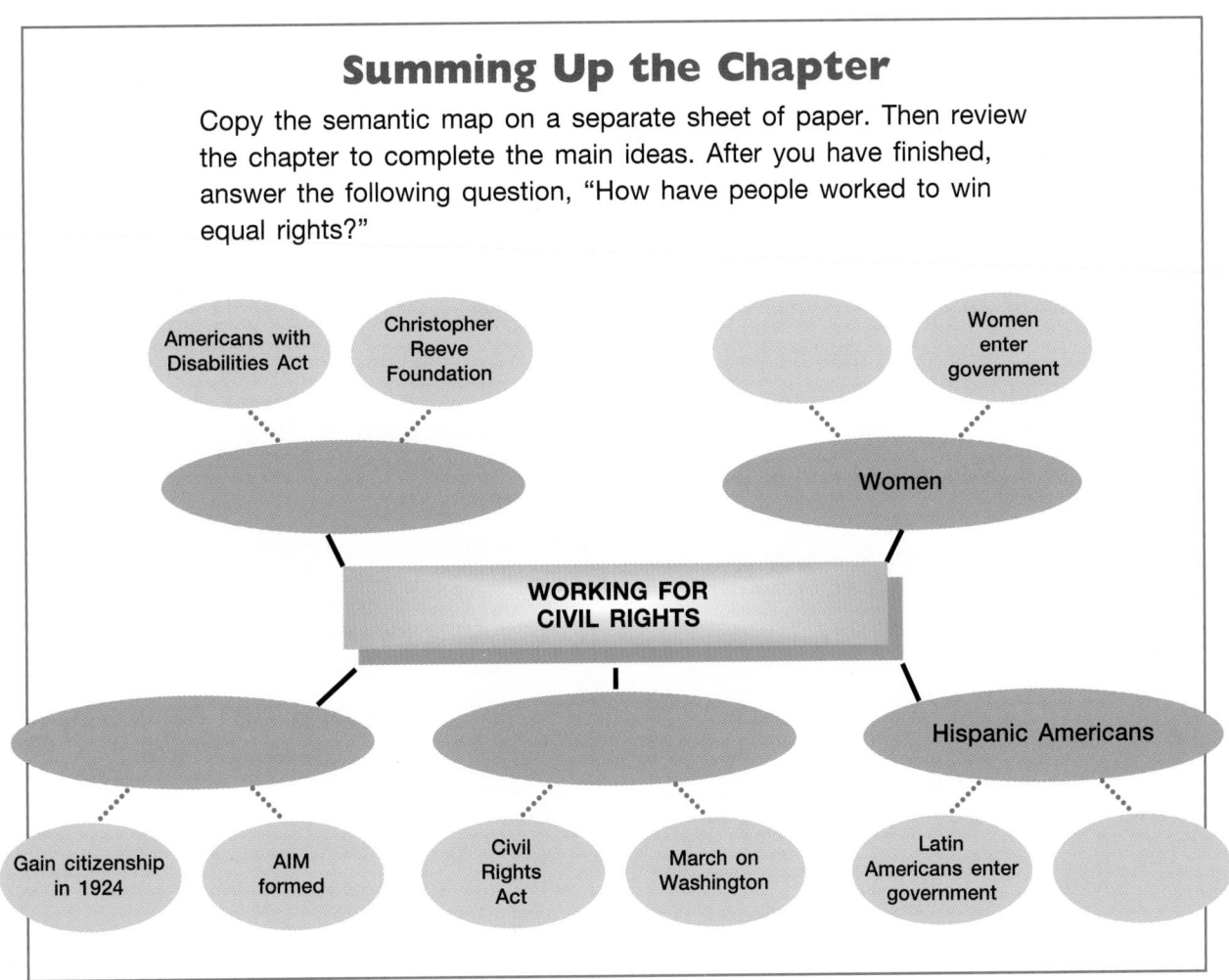

UNIT 8 REVIEW

THINKING ABOUT VOCABULARY

Number a paper from 1 to 10. Beside each number write the word or term from the list below that best matches the description.

Angel Island
Dred Scott Decision
Harlem Renaissance
Holocaust
impeach

refugee
seccession
strike
transcontinental railroad
Underground Railroad

1. one who leaves his or her homeland because of persecution or danger

2. immigration center for Asians arriving on the West Coast

3. the refusal of union members to work until their demands are met

4. the first railroad that crossed America from east to west

5. A network of secret routes to the North used by people escaping enslavement

6. the murder of six million European Jews during World War II

7. a Supreme Court ruling that slaves were property and could be taken into free territories

8. the act of breaking away from or leaving the Union

9. a period of great creative energy by African Americans in the 1920s

10. to charge a government official with wrongdoing

THINK AND WRITE

WRITING A REPORT

Conduct further research and write a report about a civil rights leader you have read about in this unit, such as Frederick Douglass, Dolores Huerta, or Martin Luther King, Jr. Include facts in your report about your subject's accomplishments.

WRITING A SPEECH

Suppose that "Mother Jones" has asked you to help her convince business owners to stop using child labor. As a young person, write a speech in which you present your views.

WRITING ABOUT PERSPECTIVES

Write several paragraphs in which you explain the different perspectives a naturalized citizen and a native-born citizen might have on the importance of democracy and equality and the responsibilites of being a citizen.

BUILDING SKILLS

1. **Reference sources** Why is it important to know how to use different kinds of reference sources?

2. **Reference sources** How are bibliographies at the end of encyclopedia articles useful?

3. **Time Zone Maps** How many time zones are there around the world?

4. **Time Zone Maps** If it is 7:00 P.M. in Los Angeles, what time is it in Boston?

5. **Identifying Bias** What clues can help you identify bias?

YESTERDAY, TODAY & *TOMORROW*

How did the immigrants you read about in this unit experience the United States differently from the way earlier immigrants had? In what ways were their experiences similar? What do you know about immigrants to the United States today? How do you think immigrants in the future might experience this country?

READING ON YOUR OWN

Here are some books you might find at the library to help you learn more.

ROSA PARKS: MY STORY
by Rosa Parks & Jim Haskins
This is the autobiography of the woman known as the "mother of the civil rights movement."

TEN MILE DAY: AND THE BUILDING OF THE TRANSCONTINENTAL RAILROAD
by Mary Ann Fraser
The author describes how workers on the transcontinental railroad laid ten miles of track in a day.

DIA'S STORY CLOTH
by Dia Cha
A Hmong worman tells the story of her own life and the history of her people. Her words accompany the pictures of a story cloth—a folk art form that uses needlework to create illustrations on cloth.

UNIT REVIEW PROJECT

Conduct a Get-Out-the Vote Campaign

1. Review the unit to see how women and African Americans won the right to vote.
2. With your group, write a list of reasons why it is important for people to vote. Include reasons from the unit as well as your own opinion.
3. Think of ways you can get your message across. You might want to start with a poster. Use a large piece of oak tag, write a slogan, and decorate it with colored paper, glitter and paints. Be sure to list reasons to vote.
4. You may also want to create pamphlets, a banner, or make stickers and buttons.
5. Have your group present your get-out-the vote poster and campaign to the class.

REFERENCE SECTION

The Reference Section has many parts,

each with a different type of information.

Use this section to look up people,

places, and events as you study.

Atlas

Maps of our country, our hemishpere, and the world

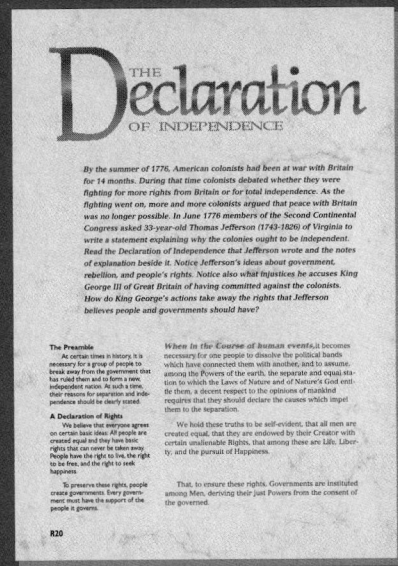

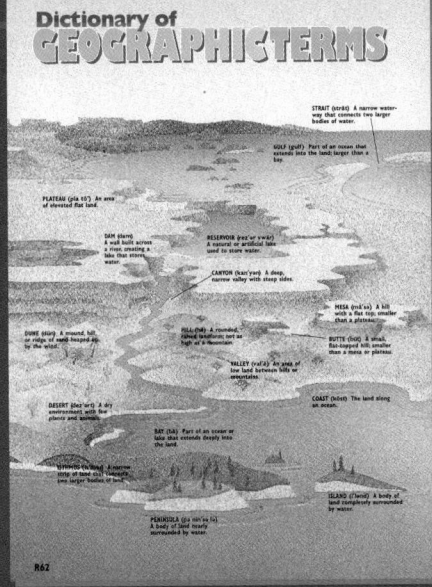

THE UNITED STATES: Political

RUSSIA

ARCTIC OCEAN

70°N

ALASKA

Arctic Circle

180°

60°N

Nome

Yukon

Fairbanks

CANADA

Anchorage

Juneau ★

PACIFIC OCEAN

170°W   160°W   150°W   140°W

0   250   500 Miles
0   250   500 Kilometers

CANADA

River

Seattle
Spokane

Olympia ★ **WASHINGTON**

Great Falls   Missouri River

Helena ★

MONTANA

Columbia

Portland

★ Salem

Eugene

OREGON

IDAHO

Boise ★

Billings

WYOMING

Snake River

Pocatello

Casper

40°N

Great Salt Lake

Ogden

Salt Lake City ★

Provo

Cheyenne ★

NEVADA

Reno
Carson City ★

San Francisco

★ Sacramento

Oakland
San Jose

COLORADO

UTAH

Denver ★

Colorado Springs

Pueblo

CALIFORNIA

Las Vegas

30°N

Los Angeles
Long Beach

San Diego

PACIFIC OCEAN

130°W

Colorado River

ARIZONA

★ Phoenix

Tucson

Santa Fe ★

Albuquerque

NEW MEXICO

El Paso

Rio Grande

N

W ★ E

S

160°W   PACIFIC OCEAN   155°W

Kauai

Niihau   Oahu

Honolulu ★   Molokai

Lanai   Maui

HAWAII   Kahoolawe

Hawaii   Hilo

20°N

0   100   200 Miles
0   100   200 Kilometers

20°N

MEXICO

R4

120°W   110°W

CANADA

MAINE
★ Augusta

Burlington • ★ Montpelier • Portland
VERMONT **NEW**
HAMPSHIRE ★ Concord

Lake Superior

NORTH
DAKOTA
Grand
Forks •
★ Bismarck • Fargo

Duluth •

MICHIGAN

Lake Huron

MINNESOTA

WISCONSIN

Lake Ontario

NEW
YORK
Albany ★
MASSACHUSETTS ★ Boston
• Providence

• Buffalo

SOUTH
DAKOTA
★ Pierre

Minneapolis • ★ St. Paul

Green
Bay •

Lake Michigan

Grand
Rapids •
Lansing ★

Hartford ★
CONNECTICUT

RHODE
ISLAND

Madison • Milwaukee •
★

Detroit •

Lake Erie

PENNSYLVANIA

Newark • • New York
Trenton ★
NEW JERSEY

Sioux
Falls •

Missouri River

Rockford •

Chicago •

• Gary

Toledo •

Cleveland •

Pittsburgh •
Harrisburg ★

Philadelphia •
Dover

NEBRASKA

IOWA

Cedar
Rapids •

Davenport •

Fort
Wayne •

OHIO

Wheeling •

Columbus •

Baltimore •

Annapolis ★
DELAWARE
MARYLAND

Lincoln ★

Omaha •
Des
Moines •

Peoria •

INDIANA

Springfield ★

★ Indianapolis

Cincinnati •

Washington,
D.C.

Platte River

MISSOURI

ILLINOIS

Ohio River

Evansville •

Louisville •

Frankfort ★

WEST
VIRGINIA
Charleston •

VIRGINIA

Richmond ★

Kansas
City •

KANSAS

Topeka ★

Kansas
City •

Jefferson
City ★

St.
Louis •

Mississippi River

KENTUCKY

• Norfolk

Wichita •

Arkansas River

Tulsa •

Oklahoma
★ City

OKLAHOMA

ARKANSAS

Fort
Smith •

Little
★ Rock

Memphis •

★ Nashville

TENNESSEE

Knoxville •

NORTH
CAROLINA
★ Raleigh

• Charlotte

ATLANTIC OCEAN

Tennessee River

SOUTH
★ Columbia
CAROLINA

• Charleston

Red River

Fort
Worth •
• Dallas

Shreveport •

MISSISSIPPI

Birmingham •

ALABAMA

Jackson ★

★ Atlanta

Columbus •

GEORGIA

• Savannah

TEXAS

LOUISIANA

Montgomery ★

• Mobile

★ Tallahassee

Jacksonville •

★ Austin

Baton Rouge ★

Biloxi •

New Orleans •

FLORIDA

Houston •

• San
Antonio

Gulf of Mexico

Tampa •

THE
BAHAMAS

Laredo •

Corpus
Christi •

Miami •

⊛ National capital ★ State capital • Other city

0   150   300 Miles

0   150   300 Kilometers

CUBA

R5

ARCTIC OCEAN

RUSSIA

BROOKS RANGE
ALASKA
CANADA

70°N

Yukon
River

Bering
Strait

ALASKA RANGE

▲ Mt. McKinley
20,320 ft.
(6,194 m)

60°N

170°W

Bering
Sea

160°W   150°W   140°W

0   250   500 Miles
0   250   500 Kilometers

CANADA

Missouri   River

Puget
Sound

Mt. Rainier
14,410 ft.
(4,391 m)

▲ Mt. St. Helens
8,366 ft.
(2,550 m)

Columbia   River

▲ Mt. Hood
11,235 ft.
(3,424 m)

Yellowstone River

COAST RANGES

CASCADE   RANGE

COLUMBIA PLATEAU

Snake   River

ROCKY MOUNTAINS

TETON RANGE

Granite Peak
12,799 ft.
(3,900 m) ▲

BLACK
HILLS

40°N

30°W

Cape Mendocino

▲ Mt. Shasta
14,162 ft.
(4,316 m)

Sacramento River

COAST

SIERRA NEVADA

CENTRAL VALLEY

GREAT

BASIN

Great
Salt
Lake

GREAT
SALT LAKE
DESERT

RANGE

WASATCH

Kings Peak
13,528 ft.
(4,123 m) ▲

GREAT

PLAINS

San Francisco Bay

Lake
Tahoe

San Joaquin   River

PACIFIC OCEAN

RANGES

▲ Mt. Whitney
14,491 ft.
(4,418 m)

Lake
Mead

Colorado   River

Mt. Elbert
14,433 ft.
(4,398 m) ▲

Pikes Peak
14,107 ft.
(4,301 m) ▲

COLORADO
PLATEAU

DEATH
VALLEY

Colorado

MOJAVE
DESERT

▲ Humphreys Peak
12,633 ft.
(3,850 m)

Wheeler Peak
13,065 ft.
(3,982 m) ▲

30°N

Salton
Sea

SONORA
DESERT

Gila   River

Pecos   River

Guadalupe Peak
8,751 ft.
(2,667 m) ▲

EDWARDS
PLATEAU

Rio Grande

Gulf of California

160°W   PACIFIC
OCEAN   155°W

N
W   E
S

Kauai

Oahu

Maui

HAWAII

20°N

Hawaii   ▲ Mauna Kea
13,796 ft.
(4,205 m)

0   100   200 Miles
0   100   200 Kilometers

MEXICO

120°W

110°W

CANADA

Lake of
the Woods

Lake Superior

GREAT

LAKES

St. Lawrence River

WHITE MTS.

Mt. Washington
6,288 ft.
(1,917 m)

MESABI RANGE

Lake Michigan

Lake Huron

Gulf of St. Lawrence

GREEN MTS.

Mississippi

ADIRONDACK
MTS.

Lake Ontario

Cape Cod

Hudson River

CENTRAL PLAINS

River

Lake Erie

ALLEGHENY
PLATEAU

Susquehanna
River

Long Island

APPALACHIAN MOUNTAINS

Platte River

River

Wabash

Ohio

River

ALLEGHENY MOUNTAINS

Potomac River

Delaware Bay

Missouri

River

River

Chesapeake Bay

Arkansas

INTERIOR PLAINS

OZARK
PLATEAU

River

Mt. Mitchell
6,684 ft.
(2,037 m)

PIEDMONT

ATLANTIC COASTAL PLAIN

Cape Hatteras

River

Tennessee

River

River

ATLANTIC OCEAN

OUACHITA
MOUNTAINS

Mississippi

River

Savannah River

Red

River

Alabama

Chattahoochee

Brazos

River

GULF COASTAL PLAIN

River

Colorado

River

Mobile Bay

Galveston Bay

Mississippi Delta

Lake
Okeechobee

Bahama Islands

Gulf of Mexico

Florida Keys

Straits of Florida

0   150   300 Miles

0   150   300 Kilometers

N
W   E
S

CUBA

R7

50° N

40° N

70° W

30° N

80° W

90° W

RUSSIA

ARCTIC OCEAN

160°E

180°

160°W

60°E

60°N

Bering Sea

Arctic Circle

AK

80°

40°N

Gulf of Alaska

PACIFIC   OCEAN

WA

OR

CA   NV

⊛ National capital

0		500		1,000 Miles

0   500   1,000 Kilometers

Tropic of Cancer

20°N

HI

60°W

N

W   E

S

140°W

120°W

CANADA

Greenland
(DENMARK)

Hudson Bay

Great Lakes

MT

ND

MN

MI

ID

SD

WI

MI

ME

VT

NY

NH

WY

NE

IA

MA

CT

RI

UT

CO

IL

IN

OH

PA

NJ

Washington, D.C.

MD

DE

WV

AZ

NM

KS

MO

KY

VA

ATLANTIC OCEAN

OK

AR

TN

NC

TX

LA

MS

AL

GA

SC

FL

Gulf of Mexico

MEXICO

CUBA

R9

ARCTIC OCEAN

GREENLAND)
(DENMARK)

ALASKA (U.S.)

Arctic Circle

CANADA

NORTH
AMERICA

UNITED STATES

BERMUDA
(U.K.)

ATLANTIC
OCEAN

MIDWAY ISLANDS
(U.S.)

MEXICO

See inset below

Tropic of Cancer

HAWAII (U.S.)

Caribbean Sea

VENEZUELA

GUYANA
SURINAME

PACIFIC OCEAN

COLOMBIA

FRENCH GUIANA
(FRANCE)

GALÁPAGOS ISLANDS
(ECUADOR)

ECUADOR

SOUTH
AMERICA

Equator

PERU

BRAZIL

SAMOA

AMERICAN SAMOA
(U.S.)

FRENCH POLYNESIA
(FRANCE)

BOLIVIA

TONGA

PARAGUAY

URUGUAY

CHILE

ARGENTINA

FALKLAND ISLANDS
(U.K.)

SOUTH
GEORGIA
(U.K.)

Antarctic Circle

ANTARCTICA

Central America and West Indies

Gulf of Mexico

FLORIDA
(U.S.)

THE
BAHAMAS

Tropic of Cancer

TURKS AND
CAICOS IS. (U.K.)

ATLANTIC OCEAN

CUBA

VIRGIN ISLANDS
(U.K.)

ST. KITTS
AND NEVIS

CAYMAN ISLANDS
(U.K.)

JAMAICA

HAITI

DOMINICAN
REPUBLIC

ANTIGUA AND
BARBUDA

MEXICO

BELIZE

PUERTO RICO
(U.S.)

VIRGIN ISLANDS
(U.S.)

GUADELOUPE
(FRANCE)

DOMINICA

GUATEMALA

MARTINIQUE
(FRANCE)

ST. LUCIA

HONDURAS

Caribbean Sea

EL SALVADOR

ST. VINCENT AND
THE GRENADINES

NICARAGUA

ARUBA
(NETHERLANDS)

NETHERLANDS
ANTILLES
(NETHERLANDS)

BARBADOS

GRENADA

PACIFIC
OCEAN

TRINIDAD AND
TOBAGO

COSTA
RICA

PANAMA

VENEZUELA

250   500 Miles

250   500 Kilometers

COLOMBIA

GUYANA

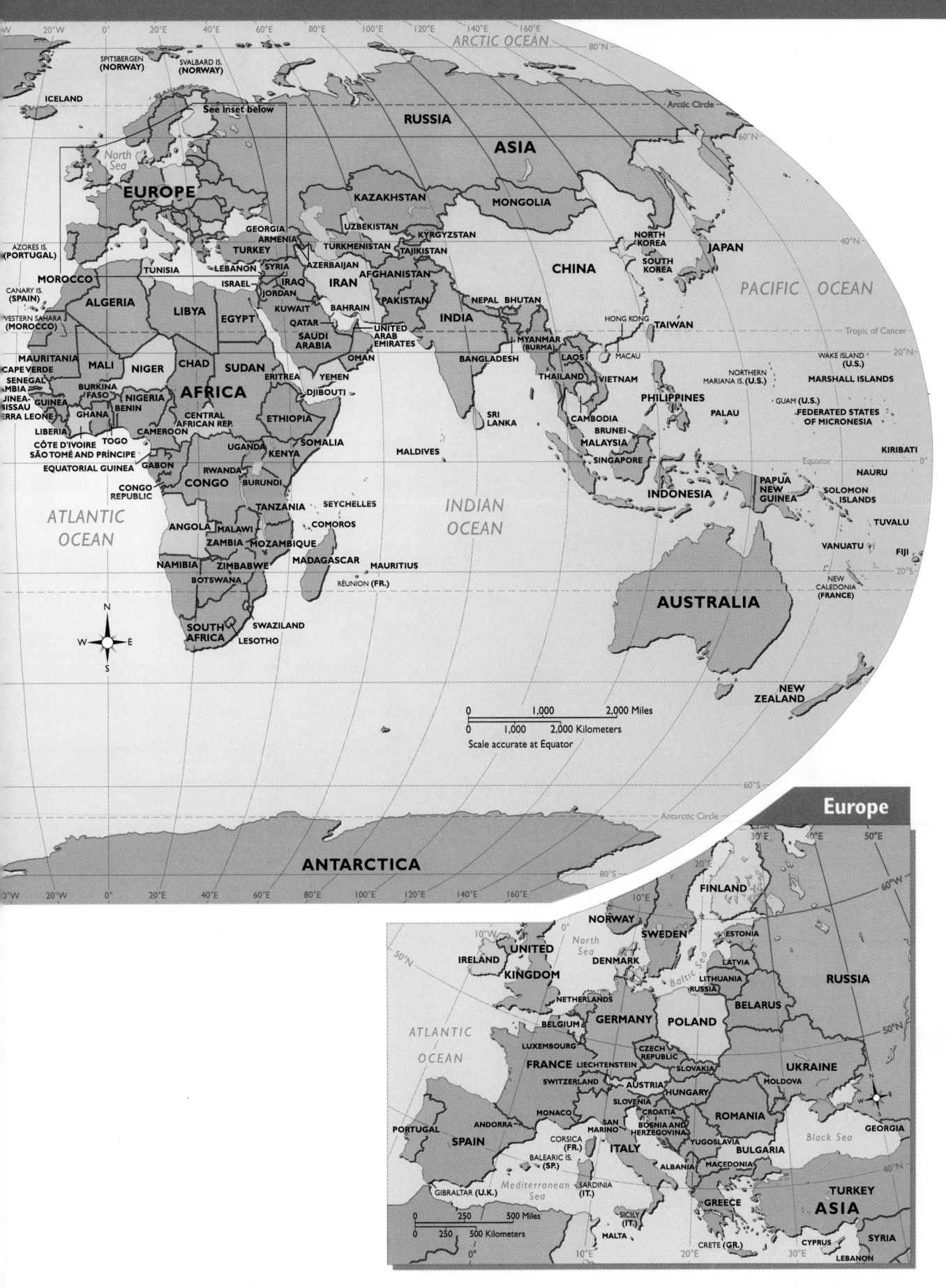

ARCTIC OCEAN

RUSSIA

ASIA

80°N

Arctic Circle

SPITSBERGEN
(NORWAY)

SVALBARD IS.
(NORWAY)

60°N

ICELAND

See Inset below

North
Sea

EUROPE

KAZAKHSTAN

MONGOLIA

40°N

AZORES IS.
(PORTUGAL)

GEORGIA
ARMENIA
TURKEY

UZBEKISTAN
TURKMENISTAN
KYRGYZSTAN
TAJIKISTAN

NORTH
KOREA
SOUTH
KOREA

JAPAN

PACIFIC OCEAN

MOROCCO

TUNISIA

LEBANON SYRIA
ISRAEL
JORDAN

AZERBAIJAN

AFGHANISTAN

CHINA

CANARY IS.
(SPAIN)

ALGERIA

LIBYA

EGYPT

IRAQ

IRAN

PAKISTAN

NEPAL BHUTAN

HONG KONG

TAIWAN

WESTERN SAHARA
(MOROCCO)

KUWAIT
QATAR
SAUDI
ARABIA

BAHRAIN

INDIA

Tropic of Cancer

20°N

MAURITANIA
CAPE VERDE
SENEGAL
GAMBIA
GUINEA-
BISSAU
SIERRA LEONE

MALI

NIGER

CHAD

SUDAN

OMAN

UNITED
ARAB
EMIRATES

MYANMAR
(BURMA)

LAOS

BANGLADESH

MACAU

WAKE ISLAND
(U.S.)

BURKINA
FASO

NIGERIA
BENIN

AFRICA

ERITREA

YEMEN

THAILAND

VIETNAM

NORTHERN
MARIANA IS. (U.S.)

MARSHALL ISLANDS

GUINEA
GHANA

DJIBOUTI

PHILIPPINES

GUAM (U.S.)

LIBERIA

CÔTE D'IVOIRE
TOGO
SÃO TOMÉ AND PRÍNCIPE

CENTRAL
AFRICAN REP.

CAMEROON

ETHIOPIA

SOMALIA

SRI
LANKA

CAMBODIA
BRUNEI
MALAYSIA

PALAU

FEDERATED STATES
OF MICRONESIA

EQUATORIAL GUINEA

GABON

UGANDA

KENYA

SINGAPORE

KIRIBATI

Equator

0°

CONGO
REPUBLIC

CONGO

RWANDA
BURUNDI

MALDIVES

INDONESIA

PAPUA
NEW
GUINEA

SOLOMON
ISLANDS

NAURU

ATLANTIC
OCEAN

TANZANIA

SEYCHELLES

INDIAN
OCEAN

TUVALU

ANGOLA

MALAWI

ZAMBIA

COMOROS

MOZAMBIQUE

VANUATU

FIJI

20°S

NAMIBIA

ZIMBABWE

BOTSWANA

MADAGASCAR

MAURITIUS

RÉUNION (FR.)

NEW
CALEDONIA
(FRANCE)

N
W   E
S

SOUTH
AFRICA

SWAZILAND

LESOTHO

AUSTRALIA

0   1,000   2,000 Miles

0   1,000   2,000 Kilometers

Scale accurate at Equator

NEW
ZEALAND

60°S

Antarctic Circle

80°S

ANTARCTICA

20°W   0°   20°E   40°E   60°E   80°E   100°E   120°E   140°E   160°E

Europe

FINLAND

NORWAY

SWEDEN

ESTONIA

10°W

0°

North
Sea

Baltic Sea

LATVIA

RUSSIA

IRELAND

UNITED
KINGDOM

DENMARK

LITHUANIA

RUSSIA

50°N

NETHERLANDS

BELARUS

ATLANTIC
OCEAN

BELGIUM

GERMANY

POLAND

LUXEMBOURG

CZECH
REPUBLIC

UKRAINE

FRANCE

LIECHTENSTEIN

SLOVAKIA

MOLDOVA

SWITZERLAND

AUSTRIA

HUNGARY

SLOVENIA

ROMANIA

MONACO

SAN
MARINO

CROATIA

BOSNIA AND
HERZEGOVINA

YUGOSLAVIA

BULGARIA

GEORGIA

PORTUGAL

ANDORRA

Black Sea

SPAIN

ITALY

MACEDONIA

CORSICA
(FR.)

ALBANIA

40°N

BALEARIC IS.
(SP.)

SARDINIA
(IT.)

GIBRALTAR (U.K.)

Mediterranean
Sea

SICILY
(IT.)

GREECE

TURKEY

ASIA

MALTA

CRETE (GR.)

CYPRUS

SYRIA

LEBANON

0   250   500 Miles

0   250   500 Kilometers

WESTERN HEMISPHERE: Political

ARCTIC OCEAN

Beaufort Sea

Baffin Bay

GREENLAND (DENMARK)

ALASKA (U.S.)

Yukon River
Fairbanks
Anchorage

Arctic Circle

Mackenzie River

Yellowknife

Hudson Bay

Iqaluit

Nuuk

Davis Strait

Arctic Circle

Labrador Sea

60°N

NORTH AMERICA

CANADA

Edmonton

Vancouver
Winnipeg
Seattle
Portland

Missouri River

Great Lakes

Quebec
Ottawa

Gulf of St. Lawrence

Minneapolis
UNITED
Salt Lake
City
Great Salt Lake
San Francisco
Denver
STATES
Phoenix
Los Angeles

Detroit
Chicago
St. Louis

Toronto
Boston
New York City
Washington, D.C.

ATLANTIC OCEAN

30°N

Colorado River

Rio Grande

Houston
New Orleans

Atlanta

BERMUDA (U.K.)

Tropic of Cancer

HAWAII (U.S.)

MEXICO
Monterrey

Gulf of Mexico

Miami

THE BAHAMAS
Nassau

PACIFIC OCEAN

Guadalajara
Mexico City

Havana
CUBA
HAITI
Port-au-Prince
BELIZE
Belmopan
JAMAICA
Guatemala City
Kingston
HONDURAS
GUATEMALA
Tegúcigalpa
San Salvador
NICARAGUA
EL SALVADOR
Managua
San José
Panama
COSTA RICA
City
PANAMA

DOMINICAN REPUBLIC
Santo Domingo
San Juan
PUERTO
RICO
(U.S.)

ST. KITTS AND NEVIS
ANTIGUA AND BARBUDA
DOMINICA
ST. LUCIA
BARBADOS
GRENADA
ST. VINCENT AND THE GRENADINES
TRINIDAD AND TOBAGO

Maracaibo
Caracas
VENEZUELA
SURINAME
Bogotá
Georgetown
Paramaribo
Cayenne
COLOMBIA
GUYANA
FRENCH GUIANA
(FRANCE)

Caribbean Sea

Quito

GALAPAGOS ISLANDS (ECUADOR)

ECUADOR
Guayaquil

Manaus
Amazon River

Belém

0° Equator

SOUTH AMERICA

Recife

PERU
Callao
Lima

BRAZIL

BOLIVIA
La Paz
Santa Cruz
Sucre

Brasília

Bahia

Antofagasta

PARAGUAY

Tropic of Capricorn

N
W   E
S

Tucumán

Asunción

São Paulo

Rio de Janeiro

Porto Alegre

30°S

CHILE

Valparaíso
Concepción
Santiago

Rosario
Buneos
Aires
La Plata

URUGUAY
Montevideo

Mar del Plata

ARGENTINA

Comodoro
Rivadavia

⊛ National capital   • Other city

0   1,000   2,000 Miles
0   1,000   2,000 Kilometers

Punta Arenas

Strait of Magellan

FALKLAND ISLANDS (U.K.)

SOUTH GEORGIA (U.K.)

R12

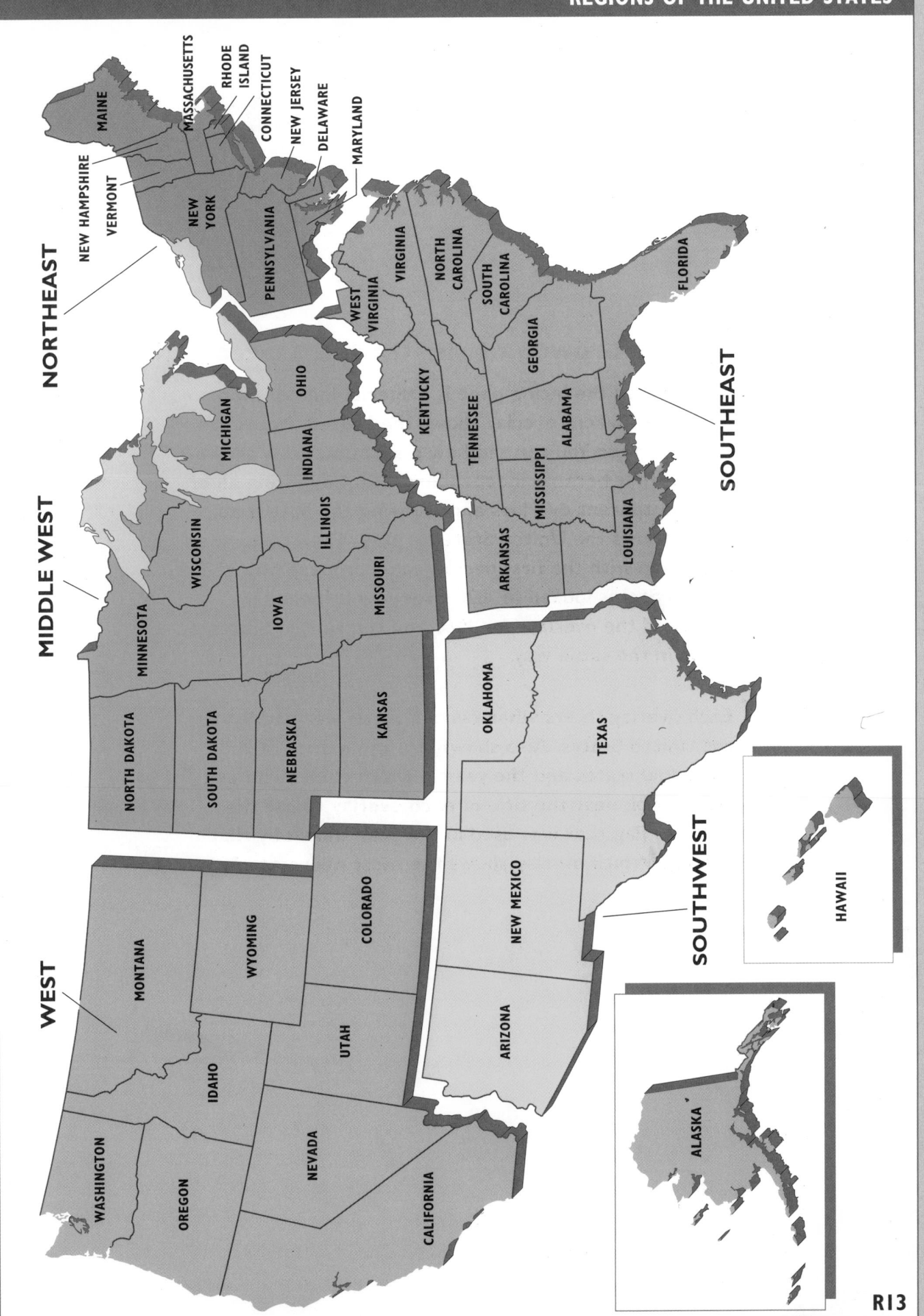

NORTHEAST

MIDDLE WEST

WEST

SOUTHEAST

SOUTHWEST

MAINE

MASSACHUSETTS
RHODE ISLAND
CONNECTICUT
NEW JERSEY
DELAWARE
MARYLAND

NEW HAMPSHIRE
VERMONT

NEW YORK

PENNSYLVANIA

WEST VIRGINIA

VIRGINIA

NORTH CAROLINA

SOUTH CAROLINA

GEORGIA

FLORIDA

OHIO

INDIANA

MICHIGAN

KENTUCKY

TENNESSEE

ALABAMA

MISSISSIPPI

WISCONSIN

ILLINOIS

MINNESOTA

IOWA

MISSOURI

ARKANSAS

LOUISIANA

NORTH DAKOTA

SOUTH DAKOTA

NEBRASKA

KANSAS

OKLAHOMA

TEXAS

MONTANA

WYOMING

COLORADO

NEW MEXICO

UTAH

ARIZONA

IDAHO

NEVADA

CALIFORNIA

WASHINGTON

OREGON

HAWAII

ALASKA

R13

Map Builder

Map Builder

The Growth of the United States

The map on the facing page is a special kind of map. Each transparent overlay shows the United States in a different year. You can see how our country has grown since it first became independent. Start by lifting all of the transparent overlays and studying the base map, which shows the United States in 1790. Then cover the base map with the first overlay and compare how the United States looked in 1820 with how it looked in 1790. Add the overlays for 1860 and the United States today in the same way.

Each overlay shows when certain areas were added to the United States. Also shown are the names of the individual states and the year in which each became a state. Look near the title of each overlay to see the national flag that was used in the year shown by that overlay. Which overlay shows the most new states?

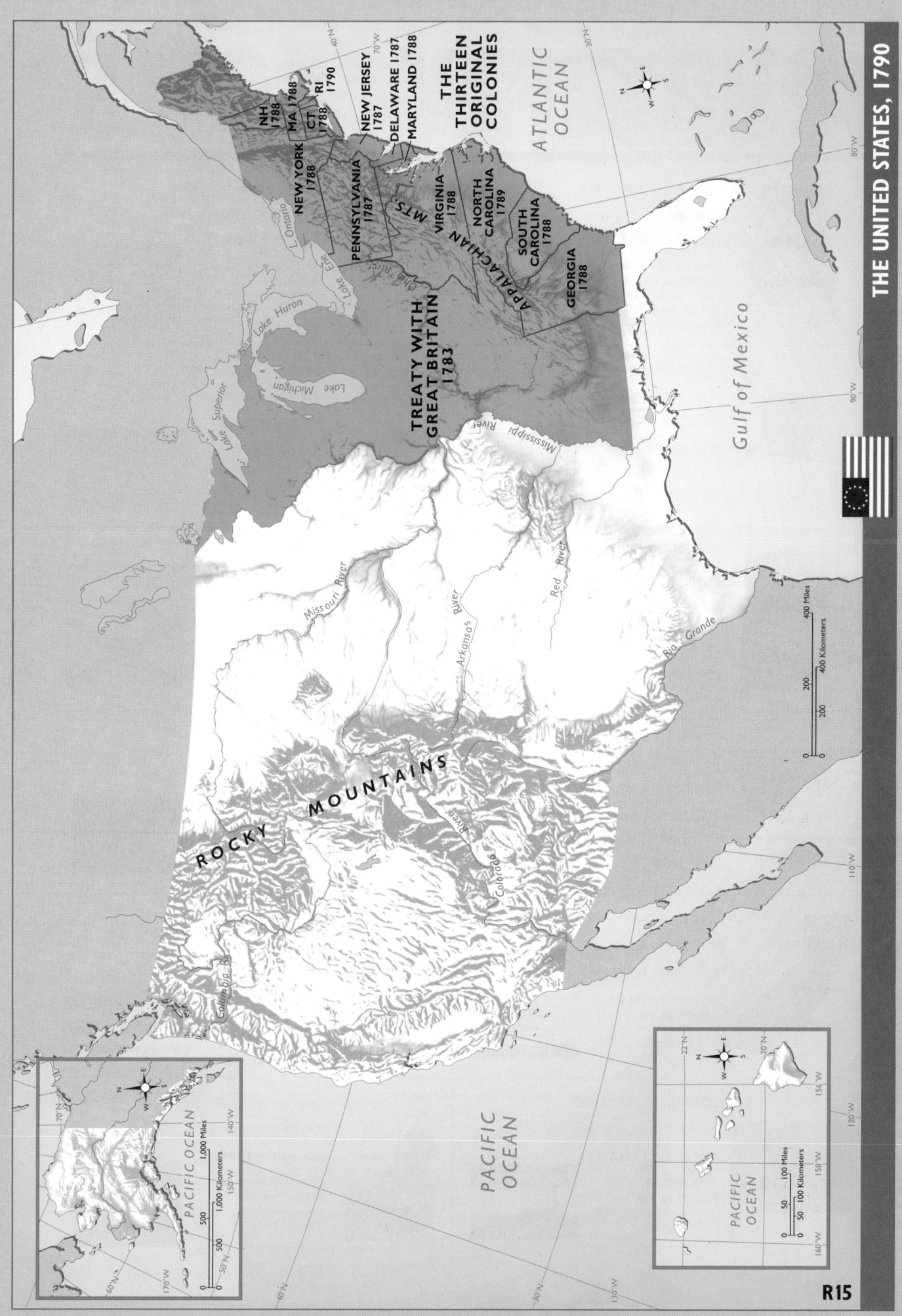

THE
THIRTEEN
ORIGINAL
COLONIES

NH
1788

MA 1788

CT
1788

RI
1790

NEW JERSEY
1787

DELAWARE 1787

MARYLAND 1788

NEW YORK
1788

PENNSYLVANIA
1787

VIRGINIA
1788

NORTH
CAROLINA
1789

SOUTH
CAROLINA
1788

GEORGIA
1788

ATLANTIC
OCEAN

APPALACHIAN MTS.

Ohio River

TREATY WITH
GREAT BRITAIN
1783

Mississippi River

L. Ontario

Lake Erie

Lake Huron

Lake Michigan

Lake Superior

Gulf of Mexico

Missouri River

Arkansas River

Red River

Rio Grande

ROCKY MOUNTAINS

Colorado
River

Columbia R.

PACIFIC
OCEAN

400 Miles

400 Kilometers

200

200

0

0

PACIFIC OCEAN

1,000 Miles

1,000 Kilometers

500

500

0

0

PACIFIC
OCEAN

100 Miles

100 Kilometers

50

50

0

0

OUR FIFTY STATES

ALABAMA
★ Montgomery

DATE OF STATEHOOD 1819

NICKNAME Heart of Dixie

POPULATION 4,273,084

AREA 52,423 sq mi;
135,776 sq km

REGION Southeast

CONNECTICUT
★ Hartford

DATE OF STATEHOOD 1788

NICKNAME Constitution State

POPULATION 3,274,238

AREA 5,544 sq mi;
14,359 sq km

REGION Northeast

ALASKA
Juneau ★

DATE OF STATEHOOD 1959

NICKNAME The Last Frontier

POPULATION 607,007

AREA 656,424 sq mi;
1,700,138 sq km

REGION West

DELAWARE
★ Dover

DATE OF STATEHOOD 1787

NICKNAME First State

POPULATION 724,842

AREA 2,489 sq mi;
6,447 sq km

REGION Northeast

DECEMBER 7, 1787

ARIZONA
★ Phoenix

DATE OF STATEHOOD 1912

NICKNAME Grand Canyon State

POPULATION 4,428,068

AREA 114,006 sq mi;
295,276 sq km

REGION Southwest

FLORIDA
★ Tallahassee

DATE OF STATEHOOD 1845

NICKNAME Sunshine State

POPULATION 14,399,985

AREA 65,758 sq mi;
170,313 sq km

REGION Southeast

ARKANSAS
★ Little Rock

DATE OF STATEHOOD 1836

NICKNAME Land of Opportunity

POPULATION 2,509,793

AREA 53,182 sq mi;
137,741 sq km

REGION Southeast

ARKANSAS

GEORGIA
★ Atlanta

DATE OF STATEHOOD 1788

NICKNAME Peach State

POPULATION 7,353,225

AREA 59,441 sq mi;
153,952 sq km

REGION Southeast

CALIFORNIA
★ Sacramento

DATE OF STATEHOOD 1850

NICKNAME Golden State

POPULATION 31,878,234

AREA 163,707 sq mi;
424,001 sq km

REGION West

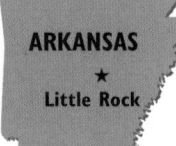
CALIFORNIA REPUBLIC

HAWAII
★ Honolulu

DATE OF STATEHOOD 1959

NICKNAME The Aloha State

POPULATION 1,183,723

AREA 10,932 sq mi;
28,314 sq km

REGION West

COLORADO
Denver ★

DATE OF STATEHOOD 1876

NICKNAME Centennial State

POPULATION 3,822,676

AREA 104,100 sq mi;
269,619 sq km

REGION West

IDAHO
★ Boise

DATE OF STATEHOOD 1890

NICKNAME Gem State

POPULATION 1,189,251

AREA 83,574 sq mi;
216,457 sq km

REGION West

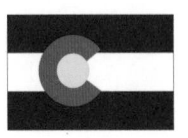
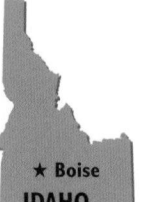

ILLINOIS
★
Springfield

DATE OF STATEHOOD 1818

NICKNAME The Prairie State

POPULATION 11,846,544

AREA 57,918 sq mi; 150,008 sq km

REGION Middle West

MAINE
Augusta
★

DATE OF STATEHOOD 1820

NICKNAME Pine Tree State

POPULATION 1,243,316

AREA 35,387 sq mi; 91,652 sq km

REGION Northeast

INDIANA
★
Indianapolis

DATE OF STATEHOOD 1816

NICKNAME Hoosier State

POPULATION 5,840,528

AREA 36,420 sq mi; 94,328 sq km

REGION Middle West

MARYLAND
Annapolis ★

DATE OF STATEHOOD 1788

NICKNAME Free State

POPULATION 5,071,604

AREA 12,407 sq mi; 32,134 sq km

REGION Northeast

IOWA
★
Des Moines

DATE OF STATEHOOD 1846

NICKNAME Hawkeye State

POPULATION 2,851,792

AREA 56,276 sq mi; 145,755 sq km

REGION Middle West

Boston ★

MASSACHUSETTS

DATE OF STATEHOOD 1788

NICKNAME Bay State

POPULATION 6,092,352

AREA 10,555 sq mi; 27,337 sq km

REGION Northeast

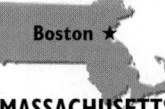

Topeka ★

KANSAS

DATE OF STATEHOOD 1861

NICKNAME Sunflower State

POPULATION 2,572,150

AREA 82,282 sq mi; 213,110 sq km

REGION Middle West

MICHIGAN
★
Lansing

DATE OF STATEHOOD 1837

NICKNAME Wolverine State

POPULATION 9,594,350

AREA 96,810 sq mi; 250,738 sq km

REGION Middle West

KENTUCKY
★
Frankfort

DATE OF STATEHOOD 1792

NICKNAME Bluegrass State

POPULATION 3,883,723

AREA 40,411 sq mi; 104,664 sq km

REGION Southeast

MINNESOTA

St. Paul ★

DATE OF STATEHOOD 1858

NICKNAME North Star State

POPULATION 4,657,758

AREA 86,943 sq mi; 225,182 sq km

REGION Middle West

LOUISIANA

Baton Rouge ★

DATE OF STATEHOOD 1812

NICKNAME Pelican State

POPULATION 4,350,579

AREA 51,843 sq mi; 134,273 sq km

REGION Southeast

MISSISSIPPI
★
Jackson

DATE OF STATEHOOD 1817

NICKNAME Magnolia State

POPULATION 2,716,115

AREA 48,434 sq mi; 125,444 sq km

REGION Southeast

OUR FIFTY STATES

MISSOURI
★ Jefferson City

DATE OF STATEHOOD 1821

NICKNAME Show Me State

POPULATION 5,358,692

AREA 69,709 sq mi; 180,546 sq km

REGION Middle West

MONTANA
★ Helena

DATE OF STATEHOOD 1889

NICKNAME Treasure State

POPULATION 879,372

AREA 147,046 sq mi; 380,849 sq km

REGION West

NEBRASKA
Lincoln ★

DATE OF STATEHOOD 1867

NICKNAME Cornhusker State

POPULATION 1,652,093

AREA 77,358 sq mi; 200,357 sq km

REGION Middle West

NEVADA
★ Carson City

DATE OF STATEHOOD 1864

NICKNAME Silver State

POPULATION 1,603,163

AREA 110,567 sq mi; 286,369 sq km

REGION West

NEW HAMPSHIRE
Concord ★

DATE OF STATEHOOD 1788

NICKNAME Granite State

POPULATION 1,162,481

AREA 9,351 sq mi; 24,219 sq km

REGION Northeast

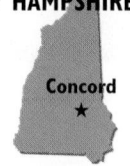

NEW JERSEY
★ Trenton

DATE OF STATEHOOD 1787

NICKNAME Garden State

POPULATION 7,987,933

AREA 8,722 sq mi; 22,590 sq km

REGION Northeast

NEW MEXICO
★ Santa Fe

DATE OF STATEHOOD 1912

NICKNAME Land of Enchantment

POPULATION 1,713,407

AREA 121,598 sq mi; 314,939 sq km

REGION Southwest

NEW YORK
Albany ★

DATE OF STATEHOOD 1788

NICKNAME Empire State

POPULATION 18,184,774

AREA 54,475 sq mi; 141,090 sq km

REGION Northeast

NORTH CAROLINA
Raleigh ★

DATE OF STATEHOOD 1789

NICKNAME Tar Heel State

POPULATION 7,322,870

AREA 53,821 sq mi; 139,396 sq km

REGION Southeast

NORTH DAKOTA
Bismarck ★

DATE OF STATEHOOD 1889

NICKNAME Peace Garden State

POPULATION 643,539

AREA 70,704 sq mi; 183,123 sq km

REGION Middle West

OHIO
★ Columbus

DATE OF STATEHOOD 1803

NICKNAME Buckeye State

POPULATION 11,172,782

AREA 44,828 sq mi; 116,105 sq km

REGION Middle West

OKLAHOMA
★ Oklahoma City

DATE OF STATEHOOD 1907

NICKNAME Sooner State

POPULATION 3,300,902

AREA 69,903 sq mi; 181,049 sq km

REGION Southwest

OREGON
★ Salem

DATE OF STATEHOOD 1859

NICKNAME Beaver State

POPULATION 3,203,735

AREA 98,386 sq mi; 254,820 sq km

REGION West

PENNSYLVANIA
Harrisburg ★

DATE OF STATEHOOD 1787

NICKNAME Keystone State

POPULATION 12,056,112

AREA 46,058 sq mi; 119,290 sq km

REGION Northeast

RHODE ISLAND
Providence ★

DATE OF STATEHOOD 1790

NICKNAME Ocean State

POPULATION 990,226

AREA 1,545 sq mi; 4,002 sq km

REGION Northeast

SOUTH CAROLINA
★
Columbia

DATE OF STATEHOOD 1788

NICKNAME Palmetto State

POPULATION 3,698,746

AREA 32,007 sq mi; 82,898 sq km

REGION Southeast

SOUTH DAKOTA
Pierre ★

DATE OF STATEHOOD 1889

NICKNAME Mount Rushmore State

POPULATION 732,405

AREA 77,121 sq mi; 199,743 sq km

REGION Middle West

TENNESSEE
★Nashville

DATE OF STATEHOOD 1796

NICKNAME Volunteer State

POPULATION 5,319,654

AREA 42,146 sq mi; 109,158 sq km

REGION Southeast

TEXAS
Austin ★

DATE OF STATEHOOD 1845

NICKNAME Lone Star State

POPULATION 19,128,261

AREA 268,601 sq mi; 695,677 sq km

REGION Southwest

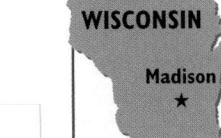

UTAH
★
Salt Lake City

DATE OF STATEHOOD 1896

NICKNAME Beehive State

POPULATION 2,000,494

AREA 84,904 sq mi; 219,901 sq km

REGION West

VERMONT
★
Montpelier

DATE OF STATEHOOD 1791

NICKNAME Green Mountain State

POPULATION 588,654

AREA 9,615 sq mi; 24,903 sq km

REGION Northeast

VIRGINIA
Richmond ★

DATE OF STATEHOOD 1788

NICKNAME Old Dominion

POPULATION 6,675,451

AREA 42,769 sq mi; 110,772 sq km

REGION Southeast

WASHINGTON
★ Olympia

DATE OF STATEHOOD 1889

NICKNAME Evergreen State

POPULATION 5,532,939

AREA 71,303 sq mi; 184,675 sq km

REGION West

WEST VIRGINIA
★ Charleston

DATE OF STATEHOOD 1863

NICKNAME Mountain State

POPULATION 1,825,754

AREA 24,231 sq mi; 62,758 sq km

REGION Southeast

WISCONSIN
Madison ★

DATE OF STATEHOOD 1848

NICKNAME Badger State

POPULATION 5,159,795

AREA 65,503 sq mi; 169,653 sq km

REGION Middle West

WYOMING
Cheyenne ★

DATE OF STATEHOOD 1890

NICKNAME Equality State

POPULATION 481,400

AREA 97,818 sq mi; 253,349 sq km

REGION West

Sources: population—U.S. Bureau of Census; area—U.S. Bureau of Census, 1991; capital—*World Almanac*, 1995.

THE Declaration OF INDEPENDENCE

By the summer of 1776, American colonists had been at war with Britain for 14 months. During that time colonists debated whether they were fighting for more rights from Britain or for total independence. As the fighting went on, more and more colonists argued that peace with Britain was no longer possible. In June 1776 members of the Second Continental Congress asked 33-year-old Thomas Jefferson (1743-1826) of Virginia to write a statement explaining why the colonies ought to be independent. Read the Declaration of Independence that Jefferson wrote and the notes of explanation beside it. Notice Jefferson's ideas about government, rebellion, and people's rights. Notice also what injustices he accuses King George III of Great Britain of having committed against the colonists. How do King George's actions take away the rights that Jefferson believes people and governments should have?

The Preamble

At certain times in history, it is necessary for a group of people to break away from the government that has ruled them and to form a new, independent nation. At such a time, their reasons for separation and independence should be clearly stated.

A Declaration of Rights

We believe that everyone agrees on certain basic ideas: All people are created equal and they have basic rights that can never be taken away. People have the right to live, the right to be free, and the right to seek happiness.

To preserve these rights, people create governments. Every government must have the support of the people it governs.

When in the Course of human events, it becomes necessary for one people to dissolve the political bands which have connected them with another, and to assume, among the Powers of the earth, the separate and equal station to which the Laws of Nature and of Nature's God entitle them, a decent respect to the opinions of mankind requires that they should declare the causes which impel them to the separation.

We hold these truths to be self-evident, that all men are created equal, that they are endowed by their Creator with certain unalienable Rights, that among these are Life, Liberty, and the pursuit of Happiness.

That, to ensure these rights, Governments are instituted among Men, deriving their just Powers from the consent of the governed.

That, whenever any Form of Government becomes destructive of these ends, it is the Right of the People to alter or to abolish it, and to institute new Government, laying its foundation on such Principles, and organizing its powers in such form, as to them shall seem most likely to effect their Safety and Happiness.

Prudence, indeed, will dictate that Governments long established should not be changed for light and transient causes; and, accordingly all experience hath shown, that mankind are more disposed to suffer, while evils are sufferable, than to right themselves by abolishing the forms to which they are accustomed. But, when a long train of abuses and usurpations, pursuing invariably the same Object, evinces a design to reduce them under absolute Despotism, it is their right, it is their duty, to throw off such Government, and to provide new Guards for their future security.

Such has been the patient sufferance of these Colonies; and such is now the necessity which constrains them to alter their former Systems of Government. The history of the present King of Great Britain is a history of repeated injuries and usurpations, all having in direct object the establishment of an absolute Tyranny over these States.

To prove this, let Facts be submitted to a candid world.

He has refused his Assent to Laws the most wholesome and necessary for the public good.

He has forbidden his Governors to pass Laws of immediate and pressing importance, unless suspended in their operation till his Assent should be obtained; and when so suspended, he has utterly neglected to attend to them.

He has refused to pass other Laws for the accommodation of large districts of People, unless those People would relinquish the right of Representation in the Legislature, a right inestimable to them and formidable to tyrants only.

He has called together legislative bodies at places unusual, uncomfortable, and distant from the depository of their Public Records, for the sole purpose of fatiguing them into compliance with his measures.

If a government loses this support or tries to take away basic freedoms, people have the right to change their government or to get rid of it and form a new government that will protect their rights.

However, people should not change governments that have long been in power for minor or temporary problems. We have learned from history that people are usually more willing to put up with a bad government than to get rid of it. But when people see their government misusing its power and mistreating its people time after time, it is the right and duty of the people to get rid of their government and to form a new one.

A List of Abuses

The colonies have suffered patiently long enough, and it is now time to change our government. King George III of Great Britain has ruled badly for many years. His main goal has been to establish total control over the colonies.

These statements are proven by the following facts:

King George III has rejected much-needed laws passed by the colonists.

He has not permitted important laws to be passed by his governors in America.

He has refused to redraw the borders of large voting districts unless the people living there agreed to give up their right to be represented in the legislature.

He has ordered lawmakers in the colonies to meet far from their homes and offices in places that are unusual and difficult to get to. His only reason for doing this has been to tire out the lawmakers so that they will accept his rule.

When lawmakers have criticized the king for attacking their rights, he has broken up the legislature's meetings.

After breaking up their meetings, the king has refused to allow new elections. As a result, colonists have been living in danger, unable to protect themselves or pass new laws.

He has tried to stop colonists from moving west and settling in new lands. He has also tried to prevent people from foreign countries from settling in America by making it hard for newcomers to become citizens.

In some places, he has not let colonists set up a system of courts.

He has forced colonial judges to obey him by deciding how long they can serve and how much they are paid.

He has sent officials from Britain to fill new government offices in the colonies. These officials have mistreated people and demanded unfair taxes.

In times of peace, he has kept soldiers in the colonies even though Americans did not want them.

He has tried to give soldiers power over colonial legislatures.

He and other leaders in Great Britain have passed laws for the colonies that Americans did not want. In these laws the British government has:

forced colonists to house and feed British soldiers;

protected these soldiers by giving them phony trials and not punishing them for murdering colonists;

cut off trade between Americans and people in other parts of the world;

demanded taxes that colonists never agreed to;

prevented colonists accused of crimes from having their trials decided fairly by a jury;

He has dissolved Representative Houses repeatedly, for opposing, with manly firmness, his invasions on the rights of the people.

He has refused for a long time, after such dissolutions, to cause others to be elected; whereby the Legislative Powers, incapable of Annihilation, have returned to the People at large for their exercise; the State remaining in the mean time exposed to all the dangers of invasion from without, and convulsions within.

He has endeavoured to prevent the Population of these States; for that purpose obstructing the Laws of Naturalization of Foreigners; refusing to pass others to encourage their migration hither, and raising the conditions of new Appropriations of Lands.

He has obstructed the Administration of Justice by refusing his Assent to Laws for establishing judiciary Powers.

He has made judges dependent on his Will alone, for the tenure of their offices, and the amount and payment of their salaries.

He has erected a multitude of New Offices, and sent hither swarms of Officers to harass our People, and eat out their substance.

He has kept among us, in times of Peace, Standing Armies, without the Consent of our legislature.

He has affected to render the Military independent of and superior to the Civil Power.

He has combined with others to subject us to a jurisdiction foreign to our constitution, and unacknowledged by our laws; giving his Assent to their Acts of pretended Legislation:

For quartering large bodies of armed troops among us:

For protecting them, by a mock Trial, from Punishment for any Murders which they should commit on the Inhabitants of these States:

For cutting off our Trade with all parts of the world:

For imposing Taxes on us without our Consent:

For depriving us, in many cases, of the benefits of Trial by jury:

For transporting us beyond Seas to be tried for pretended offences:

For abolishing the free System of English Laws in a neighbouring Province, establishing therein an Arbitrary government, and enlarging its Boundaries, so as to render it at once an example and fit instrument for introducing the same absolute rule into these Colonies:

For taking away our Charters, abolishing our most valuable Laws, and altering fundamentally the Forms of our Governments:

For suspending our own Legislatures, and declaring themselves invested with Power to legislate for us in all cases whatsoever.

He has abdicated Government here, by declaring us out of his Protection and waging War against us.

He has plundered our seas, ravaged our Coasts, burnt our towns, and destroyed the Lives of our People.

He is at this time transporting large Armies of foreign Mercenaries to compleat the works of death, desolation and tyranny, already begun with circumstances of Cruelty & perfidy scarcely paralleled in the most barbarous ages, and totally unworthy the Head of a civilized nation.

He has constrained our fellow Citizens taken Captive on the high Seas to bear Arms against their Country, to become the executioners of their friends and Brethren, or to fall themselves by their Hands.

He has excited domestic insurrections amongst us, and has endeavoured to bring on the inhabitants of our frontiers, the merciless Indian Savages, whose known rule of warfare, is an undistinguished destruction of all ages, sexes and conditions.

In every stage of these Oppressions We have Petitioned for Redress in the most humble terms: Our repeated Petitions have been answered only by repeated injury. A Prince, whose character is thus marked by every act which may define a Tyrant, is unfit to be the ruler of a free People.

brought colonists falsely accused of crimes to Great Britain to be put on trial;

extended the borders of the neighboring province of Quebec to include lands stretching to the Ohio River, thus forcing colonists in this region to obey harsh French laws rather than English laws. The goal of the British government is to force all colonists to obey these harsh laws;

taken away our charters, or documents that make governments legal, canceled important laws, and completely changed our forms of government;

broken up our legislatures and claimed that Great Britain has the right to pass all laws for the colonies.

King George III has ended government in the colonies by waging war against us and not protecting us.

He has robbed American ships at sea, burned down our towns, and ruined people's lives.

He is right now bringing foreign soldiers to the colonies to commit horrible and brutal deeds. These actions by the king are some of the cruelest ever committed in the history of the world.

He has forced colonists captured at sea to join the British navy and to fight and kill Americans.

He has urged enslaved people in the colonies to rebel, and he has tried to get Native Americans to fight against colonists.

Statement of Independence
For years we have asked King George III to correct these probems and safe-guard our rights. Unfortunately, the king has refused to listen to our complaints and he continues to treat us badly. The king is such an unfair ruler that he is not fit to rule the free people of America.

We have also asked the British people for help. We have told them many times of our problems and pointed out the unfair laws passed by their government. We hoped they would listen to us because they believed in reason and justice. We hoped they would listen to us because we are related to each other and have much in common. But we were wrong: The British people have not listened to us at all. They have ignored our pleas for justice. We must, therefore, break away from Great Britain and become a separate nation.

Nor have We been wanting in attention to our British brethren. We have warned them from time to time of attempts by their legislature to extend an unwarrantable jurisdiction over us. We have reminded them of the circumstances of our emigration and settlement here. We have appealed to their native justice and magnanimity, and we have conjured them by the ties of our common kindred to disavow these usurpations, which, would inevitably interrupt our connections and correspondence. They too have been deaf to the voice of justice and of consanguinity. We must, therefore, acquiesce in the necessity, which denounces our Separation, and hold them, as we hold the rest of mankind, Enemies in War, in Peace Friends.

Signers

Button Gwinnett (Ga.)
Lyman Hall (Ga.)
George Walton (Ga.)

William Hooper (N.C.)
Joseph Hewes (N.C.)
John Penn (N.C.)
Edward Rutledge (S.C.)
Thomas Heyward, Jr. (S.C.)
Thomas Lynch, Jr. (S.C.)
Arthur Middleton (S.C.)

John Hancock (Mass.)
Samuel Chase (Md.)
William Paca (Md.)
Thomas Stone (Md.)
Charles Carroll of Carrollton (Md.)
George Wythe (Va.)
Richard Henry Lee (Va.)
Thomas Jefferson (Va.)
Benjamin Harrison (Va.)
Thomas Nelson, Jr. (Va.)
Francis Lightfoot Lee (Va.)
Carter Braxton (Va.)

We, therefore, the Representatives of the United States of America, in General Congress Assembled, appealing to the Supreme judge of the world for the rectitude of our intentions, do, in the Name, and by Authority of the good People of these Colonies, solemnly publish and declare, That these United Colonies are, and of Right ought to be Free and Independent States; that they are Absolved from all Allegiance to the British Crown, and that all political connection between them and the State of Great Britain, is and ought to be totally dissolved; and that as Free and Independent States, they have full Power to levy War, conclude Peace, contract Alliances, establish Commerce, and to do all other Acts and Things which Independent States may of right do. And for the support of this Declaration, with a firm reliance on the protection of divine Providence, we mutually pledge to each other our Lives, our Fortunes and our sacred Honour.

In the name of the American people, we members of the Continental Congress declare that the United States of America is no longer a colony of Great Britain but is, instead, a free and independent nation. The United States now cuts all its relations with Great Britain. As a free nation, the United States has the right and power to make war and peace, make agreements with other nations. conduct trade, and do all the things that independent nations have the right to do. To support this Declaration of Independence, we promise to each other our lives, our fortunes, and our personal honor.

Robert Morris (Pa.)
Benjamin Rush (Pa.)
Benjamin Franklin (Pa.)
John Morton (Pa.)
George Clymer (Pa.)
James Smith (Pa.)
George Taylor (Pa.)
James Wilson (Pa.)
George Ross (Pa.)
Cæsar Rodney (Del.)
George Read (Del.)
Thomas McKean (Del.)

William Floyd (N.Y.)
Philip Livingston (N.Y.)
Francis Lewis (N.Y.)
Lewis Morris (N.Y.)
Richard Stockton (N.J.)
John Witherspoon (N.J.)
Francis Hopkinson (R.I.)
John Hart (N.J.)
Abraham Clark (N.J.)

Josiah Bartlett (N.H.)
William Whipple (N.H.)
Samuel Adams (Mass.)
John Adams (Mass.)
Robert Treat Paine (Mass.)
Elbridge Gerry (Mass.)
Stephen Hopkins (R.I.)
William Ellery (R.I.)
Roger Sherman (Conn.)
Samuel Huntington (Conn.)
William Williams (Conn.)
Oliver Wolcott (Conn.)
Matthew Thornton (N.H.)

THE Constitution
OF THE UNITED STATES

PREAMBLE

We the People of the United States, in Order to form a more perfect Union, establish Justice, insure domestic Tranquility, provide for the common defense, promote the general Welfare, and secure the Blessings of Liberty to ourselves and our Posterity, do ordain and establish this Constitution for the United States of America.

Explanation and Summary

The following text explains the meaning of the Constitution and its Amendments. Crossed out sentences are no longer in effect.

The people of the United States make this Constitution for several reasons: to form a stronger and more united nation; to ensure peace, justice, and liberty; to defend its citizens; and to improve the lives of its people.

Article 1. THE LEGISLATIVE BRANCH

Section 1. The Congress

All legislative powers herein granted shall be vested in a Congress of the United States, which shall consist of a Senate and House of Representatives.

Congress has the power to make laws. Congress is made up of two houses: the Senate and the House of Representatives.

Section 2. The House of Representatives

1. The House of Representatives shall be composed of members chosen every second year by the people of the several states, and the electors in each state shall have the qualifications requisite for electors of the most numerous branch of the state legislature.

1. Members of the House of Representatives are elected every two years by qualified voters in each state.

2. No person shall be a Representative who shall not have attained to the age of twenty-five years, and been seven years a citizen of the United States, and who shall not, when elected, be an inhabitant of that state in which he shall be chosen.

2. To be a member of the House of Representatives, a person must be at least 25 years old, a United States citizen for at least seven years, and live in the state he or she represents.

3. Representatives ~~and direct taxes~~ shall be apportioned among the several states which may be included within this Union, according to their respective numbers, ~~which shall be determined by adding to the whole number of free persons, including those bound to service for a term of years, and excluding Indians not taxed, three fifths of all other persons.~~ The actual enumeration shall be made within three years after the first meeting of the Congress of the United

3. The number of Representatives for each state is based on the population, or number of people, who live in that state. Every ten years a census, or count, must be taken to determine the population of each state. At first, this census of the population included indentured servants but not most Native Americans. Each enslaved

States, and within every subsequent term of ten years, in such manner as they shall by law direct. The number of Representatives shall not exceed one for every 30,000, but each state shall have at least one Representative; ~~and until such enumeration shall be made, the state of New Hampshire shall be entitled to choose three, Massachusetts, eight, Rhode Island and Providence Plantations, one, Connecticut, five, New York, six, New Jersey, four, Pennsylvania, eight, Delaware, one, Maryland, six, Virginia, ten, North Carolina, five, South Carolina, five, and Georgia, three.~~

person was counted as three-fifths of a free person. Today all people are counted equally. (The crossed-out sections of the Constitution are no longer in effect.)

4. When vacancies happen in the representation from any state, the executive authority thereof shall issue writs of election to fill such vacancies.

4. Special elections called by the state's governor must be held to fill any empty seat in the House of Representatives.

5. The House of Representatives shall choose their Speaker and other officers; and shall have the sole power of impeachment.

5. Members of the House of Representatives choose their own leaders. House members alone have the power to impeach, or accuse, government officials of crimes in office.

Section 3. The Senate

1. The Senate of the United States shall be composed of two Senators from each state, ~~chosen by the legislature thereof,~~ for six years; and each Senator shall have one vote.

1. Each state has two Senators. Each Senator serves a term of six years and has one vote in the Senate. At first, state legislatures elected Senators, but the 17th Amendment changed the way Senators are chosen. Senators are now elected directly by the people.

2. ~~Immediately after they shall be assembled in consequence of the first election, they shall be divided as equally as may be into three classes. The seats of the Senators of the first class shall be vacated at the expiration of the second year, of the second class at the expiration of the fourth year, and of the third class at the expiration of the sixth year, so that one-third may be chosen every second year; and if vacancies happen by resignation, or otherwise, during the recess of the legislature of any state, the executive thereof may make temporary appointments until the next meeting of the legislature, which shall then fill such vacancies.~~

2. One-third of the Senate seats are up for election every two years. The 17th Amendment changed the way empty seats are filled.

3. No person shall be a Senator who shall not have attained to the age of thirty years, and been nine years a citizen of the United States, and who shall not, when elected, be an inhabitant of that state for which he shall be chosen.

3. To be a Senator, a person must be at least 30 years old, a citizens of the United States for at least nine years, and live in the state he or she represents.

4. The Vice President of the United States shall be president of the Senate, but shall have no vote, unless they be equally divided.

4. The Vice President of the United States is the officer in charge of the Senate but votes only to break a tie.

5. The Senate shall choose their other officers, and also a president pro tempore, in the absence of the Vice President,

5. Senators choose their own leaders. When the Vice President is absent, the Senate leader is called the

President *pro tempore* (prō tem′pə rē), or temporary President.

6. The Senate holds all impeachment trials. When the President of the United States is impeached, the Chief Justice of the Supreme Court is the judge for the trial. Conviction, or judgment of guilt, is decided by a two-thirds vote.

or when he shall exercise the office of the President of the United States.

6. The Senate shall have the sole power to try all impeachments. When sitting for that purpose, they shall be on oath or affirmation. When the President of the United States is tried, the Chief Justice shall preside; and no person shall be convicted without the concurrence of two-thirds of the members present.

7. Impeached officials convicted by the Senate can be removed from office and barred from serving again in government. Regular courts of law can decide other punishments.

7. Judgment in cases of impeachment shall not extend further than to removal from office, and disqualification to hold and enjoy any office of honor, trust or profit under the United States; but the party convicted shall nevertheless be liable and subject to indictment, trial, judgment and punishment, according to law.

Section 4. Elections and Meetings of Congress

1. State lawmakers set rules for Congressional elections. Congress can change some of these rules.

1. The times, places and manner of holding elections for Senators and Representatives shall be prescribed in each state by the legislature thereof; but the Congress may at any time by law make or alter such regulations, ~~except as to the places of choosing Senators~~.

2. Congress meets at least once a year, beginning in December. The 20th Amendment changed this date to January 3.

2. The Congress shall assemble at least once in every year ~~and such meeting shall be on the first Monday in December, unless they shall by law appoint a different day~~.

Section 5. Rules of Procedure for Congress

1. The Senate and House of Representatives decide if their members were elected fairly and are qualified to take their seats. At least half the members of each house of Congress must be present for Congress to do most business. Absent members can be required to attend sessions of Congress.

1. Each house shall be the judge of the elections, returns and qualifications of its own members, and a majority of each shall constitute a quorum to do business; but a smaller number may adjourn from day to day, and may be authorized to compel the attendance of absent members, in such manner, and under such penalties as each house may provide.

2. Each house of Congress may set its own rules and punish members for breaking them. A two-thirds vote is needed to expel, or force out, a member.

2. Each house may determine the rules of its proceedings, punish its members for disorderly behavior, and with the concurrence of two-thirds, expel a member.

3. Each house of Congress keeps and publishes a record of its activities. Secret matters may be left out of the published record. If one-fifth of the members demand it, a vote on any matter will be published.

3. Each house shall keep a journal of its proceedings, and from time to time publish the same, excepting such parts as may in their judgment require secrecy; and the yeas and nays of the members of either house on any question shall, at the desire of one-fifth of those present, be entered on the journal.

4. Neither house, during the session of Congress, shall, without the consent of the other, adjourn for more than three days, nor to any other place than that in which the two houses shall be sitting.

4. During a session of Congress, neither house can stop meeting for more than three days or decide to meet somewhere else unless the other house agrees.

Section 6. Privileges and Restrictions of Members of Congress

1. The Senators and Representatives shall receive a compensation for their services, to be ascertained by law, and paid out of the Treasury of the United States. They shall in all cases, except treason, felony and breach of the peace, be privileged from arrest during their attendance at the session of their respective houses, and in going to and returning from the same; and for any speech or debate in either house, they shall not be questioned in any other place.

1. Each member of Congress receives a salary from the United States government. Except for very serious crimes, no member can be arrested in the place where Congress is meeting while in session. Members cannot be arrested for anything they say in Congress.

2. No Senator or Representative shall, during the time for which he was elected, be appointed to any civil office under the authority of the United States, which shall have been created, or the emoluments whereof shall have been increased during such time; and no person holding any office under the United States, shall be a member of either house during his continuance in office.

2. Senators and Representatives may not hold any other job in the federal government while they serve in Congress.

Section 7. How Laws Are Made

1. All bills for raising revenue shall originate in the House of Representatives; but the Senate may propose or concur with amendments as on other bills.

1. All money and tax bills must begin in the House of Representatives. The Senate can later pass or change these bills.

2. Every bill which shall have passed the House of Representatives and the Senate, shall, before it become a law, be presented to the President of the United States. If he approve he shall sign it, but if not he shall return it, with his objections to that house in which it shall have originated, who shall enter the objections at large on their journal, and proceed to reconsider it. If after such reconsideration two-thirds of that house shall agree to pass the bill, it shall be sent, together with the objections, to the other house, by which it shall likewise be reconsidered, and if approved by two-thirds of that house, it shall become a law. But in all such cases the votes of both houses shall be determined by yeas and nays, and the names of the persons voting for and against the bill shall be entered on the journal of each house respectively. If any bill shall not be returned by the President within ten days (Sundays excepted) after it shall have been presented to him, the same shall be a law, in like manner as if he had signed it, unless the Congress by their adjournment prevent its return, in which case it shall not be a law.

2. After a bill, or suggested law, passes both the House of Representatives and the Senate, it goes to the President. If the President signs the bill, it becomes a law. If the President vetoes, or rejects, the bill, it goes back to Congress. A President's veto can be overridden, or upset, if Congress votes again and two-thirds of the members of each house vote in favor of the bill. The bill then becomes a law. If the President neither signs nor vetoes a bill within 10 days (not counting Sundays) of first receiving it, the bill becomes a law. If Congress stops meeting *before* 10 days have passed, however, the bill does *not* become a law. This last type of action is called a "pocket veto."

3. Every act passed by Congress must be presented to the President either to be signed or vetoed. The only exception is when Congress votes to adjourn, or stop meeting.

Congress has the power to:

1. raise and collect taxes to both pay debts and to protect and serve the nation, but taxes must be the same everywhere in the United States;

2. borrow money;

3. control trade with foreign nations, between states, and with Native Americans;

4. decide how people from foreign countries can become citizens of the United States and to make laws dealing with people and businesses unable to pay their debts;

5. print money, set its value, and set the standards of weights and measures used throughout the nation;

6. punish people who make counterfeit, or fake, money and bonds;

7. set up post offices and roads for mail delivery;

8. protect the rights and creations of scientists, artists, authors, and inventors;

9. create federal, or national, courts lower than the Supreme Court;

10. punish crimes committed at sea;

11. declare war;

12. establish and support an army, but no amount of money set aside for this purpose can be for a term longer than two years;

13. establish and support a navy;

3. Every order, resolution, or vote to which the concurrence of the Senate and House of Representatives may be necessary (except on a question of adjournment) shall be presented to the President of the United States; and before the same shall take effect, shall be approved by him, or being disapproved by him, shall be repassed by two-thirds of the Senate and House of Representatives, according to the rules and limitations prescribed in the case of a bill.

Section 8. Powers Granted to Congress

1. The Congress shall have power to lay and collect taxes, duties, imposts and excises, to pay the debts and provide for the common defense and general welfare of the United States; but all duties, imposts and excises shall be uniform throughout the United States;

2. To borrow money on the credit of the United States;

3. To regulate commerce with foreign nations, and among the several states, and with the Indian tribes;

4. To establish a uniform rule of naturalization, and uniform laws on the subject of bankruptcies throughout the United States;

5. To coin money, regulate the value thereof, and of foreign coin, and fix the standard of weights and measures;

6. To provide for the punishment of counterfeiting the securities and current coin of the United States;

7. To establish post offices and post roads;

8. To promote the progress of science and useful arts, by securing for limited times to authors and inventors the exclusive right to their respective writings and discoveries;

9. To constitute tribunals inferior to the Supreme Court;

10. To define and punish piracies and felonies committed on the high seas and offenses against the law of nations;

11. To declare war, ~~grant letters of marque and reprisal~~, and make rules concerning captures on land and water;

12. To raise and support armies, but no appropriation of money to that use shall be for a longer term than two years;

13. To provide and maintain a navy;

14. To make rules for the government and regulation of the land and naval forces;

15. To provide for calling forth the militia to execute the laws of the Union, suppress insurrections and repel invasions;

16. To provide for organizing, arming, and disciplining, the militia, and for governing such part of them as may be employed in the service of the United States, reserving to the states respectively, the appointment of the officers, and the authority of training the militia according to the discipline prescribed by Congress;

17. To exercise exclusive legislation in all cases whatsoever, over such district (not exceeding ten miles square) as may, by cession of particular states, and the acceptance of Congress, become the seat of the government of the United States, and to exercise like authority over all places purchased by the consent of the legislature of the state in which the same shall be, for the erection of forts, magazines, arsenals, dockyards, and other needful buildings;—and

18. To make all laws which shall be necessary and proper for carrying into execution the foregoing powers, and all other powers vested by this Constitution in the government of the United States, or in any department or officer thereof.

Section 9. Powers Denied to Congress

1. ~~The migration or importation of such persons as any of the states now existing shall think proper to admit, shall not be prohibited by the Congress prior to the year one thousand eight hundred and eight, but a tax or duty may be imposed on such importation, not exceeding ten dollars for each person.~~

2. The privilege of the writ of habeas corpus shall not be suspended, unless when in cases of rebellion or invasion the public safety may require it.

3. No bill of attainder or ex post facto law shall be passed.

4. No capitation, or other direct, tax shall be laid, unless in proportion to the census or enumeration herein before directed to be taken.

5. No tax or duty shall be laid on articles exported from any state.

14. make rules for the armed forces;

15. call the militia (today called the National Guard) to enforce federal laws, put down rebellions, and fight invasions;

16. organize, train, and discipline the National Guard. States have the power to name officers and train soldiers in the National Guard under rules set by Congress;

17. govern the capital and military sites of the United States; and

18. make all laws necessary to carry out the powers of Congress. This is called the "elastic clause" because it stretches the powers of Congress.

Congress does *not* have the power to:

1. stop enslaved people from being brought into the United States before 1808. In 1808, the first year allowed, Congress passed a law banning the slave trade;

2. arrest and jail people without charging them with a crime. The only exception is during a rebellion or emergency;

3. punish a person without a trial in a court of law; nor punish a person for doing something wrong that was not against the law when the person did it;

4. pass a direct tax (such as an income tax) unless it is in proportion to the population. The 16th Amendment allowed an income tax;

5. tax goods sent out of a state;

6. give ports of one state an advantage over ports of another state; nor can one state tax the ships of another state that enter its borders;

7. spend money without both passing a law and keeping a record of all its accounts;

8. grant any title of nobility (such as king or queen); nor may any worker in the federal government accept any gift or title from a foreign government.

State governments do *not* have the power to:

1. make treaties, print money, or do anything forbidden to the federal government outlined in Section 9 of the Constitution, above;

2. tax goods sent into and out of a state unless Congress agrees;

3. keep armed forces, go to war, or make agreements with others states or foreign countries unless Congress agrees.

1. The President has the power to execute, or carry out, the laws of the United States. The President and Vice President together serve a term of four years.

2. The President is chosen by electors from each state. Today these electors are chosen by the voters and called the *Electoral College*. The number of

6. No preference shall be given any regulation of commerce or revenue to the ports of one state over those of another; nor shall vessels bound to, or from, one state, be obliged to enter, clear, or pay duties in another.

7. No money shall be drawn from the Treasury, but in consequence of appropriations made by law; and a regular statement and account of the receipts and expenditures of all public money shall be published from time to time.

8. No title of nobility shall be granted by the United States; and no person holding any office of profit or trust under them, shall, without the consent of the Congress, accept of any present, emolument, office, or title, of any kind whatever, from any king, prince, or foreign state.

Section 10. Powers Denied to the States

1. No state shall enter into any treaty, alliance, or confederation; grant letters of marque and reprisal; coin money; emit bills of credit; make anything but gold and silver coin a tender in payment of debts; pass any bill of attainder, ex post facto law, or law impairing the obligation of contracts, or grant any title of nobility.

2. No state shall, without the consent of the Congress, lay any imposts or duties on imports or exports, except what may be absolutely necessary for executing its inspection laws; and the net produce of all duties and imposts, laid by any state on imports or exports, shall be for the use of the Treasury of the United States; and all such laws shall be subject to the revision and control of the Congress.

3. No state shall, without the consent of Congress, lay any duty of tonnage, keep troops, or ships of war in time of peace, enter into any agreement or compact with another state, or with a foreign power, or engage in war, unless actually invaded, or in such imminent danger as will not admit of delay.

Article 2. THE EXECUTIVE BRANCH

Section 1. Office of President and Vice President

1. The executive power shall be vested in a President of the United States of America. He shall hold his office during the term of four years, and, together with the Vice President, chosen for the same term, be elected, as follows:

2. Each state shall appoint, in such manner as the legislature thereof may direct, a number of electors, equal to the whole number of Senators and Representatives to which the

state may be entitled in the Congress; but no Senator or Representative, or person holding an office or trust or profit under the United States, shall be appointed an elector.

electoral votes for each state is determined by adding up the number of the state's Senators and Representatives.

3. ~~The electors shall meet in their respective states, and vote by ballot for two persons, of whom one at least shall not be an inhabitant of the same state with themselves. And they shall make a list of all the persons voted for, and of the number of votes for each; which list they shall sign and certify, and transmit sealed to the seat of the government of the United States, directed to the president of the Senate. The president of the Senate shall, in the presence of the Senate and House of Representatives, open all the certificates, and the votes shall then be counted. The person having the greatest number of votes shall be the President, if such number be a majority of the whole number of electors appointed; and if there be more than one who have such majority, and have an equal number of votes, then the House of Representatives shall immediately choose by ballot one of them for President; and if no person have a majority, then from the five highest on the list the said House shall in like manner choose the President. But in choosing the President, the votes shall be taken by states, the representation from each state having one vote; a quorum for this purpose shall consist of a member or members from two-thirds of the states, and a majority of all the states shall be necessary to a choice. In every case, after the choice of the President, the person having the greatest number of votes of the electors shall be the Vice President. But if there should remain two or more who have equal votes, the Senate shall choose from them by ballot the Vice President.~~

3. This part of the Constitution describes an early method of electing the President and Vice President. The 12th Amendment changed this method. Originally, the person who received the most electoral votes became President and the person who received the next highest number became Vice President.

4. The Congress may determine the time of choosing the electors, and the day on which they shall give their votes; which day shall be the same throughout the United States.

4. Congress decides when Presidential electors are chosen and when they vote. The electors vote on the same day throughout the United States. Today people vote for the electors on the Tuesday after the first Monday of November. Presidential elections take place every four years.

5. No person except a natural born citizen, ~~or a citizen of the United States, at the time of the adoption of this Constitution~~, shall be eligible to the office of the President; neither shall any person be eligible to that office who shall not have attained to the age of thirty-five years, and been fourteen years a resident within the United States.

5. To be President, a person must be a citizen born in the United States, at least 35 years old, and have lived in the United States for at least 14 years.

6. In case of the removal of the President from office, or of his death, resignation, or inability to discharge the powers and duties of the said office, the same shall devolve on the Vice President, and the Congress may by law provide for

6. If the President leaves office for any reason or can no longer serve as President, the Vice President becomes President. If there is no Vice

President, Congress may decide who becomes President. The 25th Amendment changed the method of filling these vacancies, or empty offices.

7. The President receives a set salary that can neither be raised nor lowered during the President's term of office. The President can receive no other gift or salary from the United States or any of the states while in office.

8. Before taking office, the person elected President takes an oath. In this oath, the person promises to carry out the laws of the United States and defend the Constitution.

1. The President is in charge of the armed forces and state militias (today the National Guard) of the United States. The President can demand advice and opinions, in writing, of the people in charge of each executive department. These advisers are called the President's Cabinet. The President also has the power to pardon, or free, people convicted of federal crimes, except in cases of impeachment.

2. The President has the power to make treaties, but they must be approved by two-thirds of the Senate. The President also has the power to name ambassadors, important government officials, and judges of the Supreme Court and other federal courts, with the approval of the Senate.

3. The President has the power to fill empty offices for a short time when the Senate is not meeting.

The President must inform Congress from time to time on the condition of

the case of removal, death, resignation, or inability, both of the President and Vice President, declaring what officer shall then act as President, and such officer shall act accordingly, until the disability be removed, or a President shall be elected.

7. The President shall, at stated times receive for his services, a compensation, which shall neither be increased nor diminished during the period for which he shall have been elected, and he shall not receive within that period any other emolument from the United States, or any of them.

8. Before he enter on the execution of his office, he shall take the following oath or affirmation:—"I do solemnly swear (or affirm) that I will faithfully execute the office of President of the United States, and will to the best of my ability, preserve, protect and defend the Constitution of the United States."

Section 2. Powers Granted to the President

1. The President shall be Commander in Chief of the Army and Navy of the United States, and of the militia of the several states, when called into the actual service of the United States; he may require the opinion, in writing, of the principal officer in each of the executive departments, upon any subject relating to the duties of their respective offices, and he shall have power to grant reprieves and pardons for offenses against the United States, except in cases of impeachment.

2. He shall have power, by and with the advice and consent of the Senate, to make treaties, provided two-thirds of the Senators present concur; and he shall nominate, and by and with the advice and consent of the Senate, shall appoint ambassadors, other public ministers and consuls, judges of the Supreme Court, and all other officers of the United States, whose appointments are not herein otherwise provided for, and which shall be established by law; but the Congress may by law vest the appointment of such inferior officers, as they think proper, in the President alone, in the courts of law, or in the heads of departments.

3. The President shall have power to fill up all vacancies that may happen during the recess of the Senate, by granting commissions which shall expire at the end of their next session.

Section 3. Duties of the President

He shall from time to time give to the Congress information of the state of the Union, and recommend to their consideration such measures as he shall judge necessary and expedient; he may, on extraordinary occasions, convene both houses, or either of them, and in case of disagreement between them, with respect to the time of adjournment, he may adjourn them to such time as he shall think proper; he shall receive ambassadors and other public ministers; he shall take care that the laws be faithfully executed, and shall commission all the officers of the United States.

the nation. Today, this speech is called the State of the Union address and is given once a year, usually in late January. In this message, the President recommends laws to improve the nation. The President can also, in time of emergency, call Congress to meet. If, in other situations, Congress cannot decide whether or not to adjourn, the President can make this decision. The President receives foreign officials, makes sure the nation's laws are carried out, and signs orders naming officers in the armed forces.

Section 4. Removal from Office

The President, Vice President and all civil officers of the United States, shall be removed from office on impeachment for, and conviction of, treason, bribery, or other high crimes and misdemeanors.

The President, Vice President, and other non-military officers of the United States may be impeached, or accused of committing crimes, and removed from office if found guilty.

Article 3. THE JUDICIAL BRANCH

Section 1. Federal Courts

The judicial power of the United States shall be vested in one Supreme Court, and in such inferior courts as the Congress may from time to time ordain and establish. The judges, both of the Supreme and inferior courts, shall hold their offices during good behavior, and shall, at stated times, receive for their services, a compensation, which shall not be diminished during their continuance in office.

The judicial power, or the power to make decisions in courts of law, is held by the Supreme Court and other lower federal, or national, courts that Congress may set up. Supreme Court and other federal judges hold office for life if they act properly. Judges receive a set salary that cannot be lowered.

Section 2. Powers of Federal Courts

1. The judicial power shall extend to all cases, in law and equity, arising under this Constitution, the laws of the United States, and treaties made, or which shall be made, under their authority; to all cases affecting ambassadors, other public ministers and consuls; to all cases of admiralty and maritime jurisdiction; to controversies to which the United States shall be a party; to controversies between two or more states; between a state and citizens of another state; between citizens of different states, between citizens of the same state claiming lands under grants of different states, and between a state, or the citizens thereof, and foreign states, citizens or subjects.

1. Federal courts have legal authority over:

a) all laws made under the Constitution;

b) treaties made with foreign governments;

c) cases involving matters occurring at sea;

d) cases involving the federal government;

e) cases involving different states or citizens of different states; and

f) cases involving foreign citizens or governments.

The 11th Amendment partly limits which cases federal courts can hear.

2. In all cases affecting ambassadors, other public ministers and consuls, and those in which a state shall be party, the

2. In cases involving either states or ambassadors and government officials, the Supreme Court is the first and only court that makes a judgment. All other cases begin in lower courts but may later be appealed to, or reviewed by, the Supreme Court.

3. All criminal cases, except those of impeachment, are judged by trial and jury in the state where the supposed crime took place. If a crime occurs outside of any state, Congress decides where the trial takes place.

1. Treason is the crime of making war against the United States or helping its enemies. To be found guilty of treason, a person must confess to the crime or two witnesses must swear to having seen the crime committed.

2. Congress decides the punishment for treason. Relatives of people convicted of treason cannot also be punished for the crime.

Each state must respect the laws, records, and court decisions of every other state in the United States. Congress may pass laws to help carry out these matters.

1. Citizens are guaranteed all their basic rights when visiting other states.

2. A person charged with a crime, who flees to another state, must be returned to the state where the crime took place if the governor of the state demands.

3. A person enslaved in one state, who escapes to another state, is still considered enslaved and must be returned to the person's owner. The 13th Amendment, which outlawed slavery, nullified, or overturned, this section of the Constitution.

Supreme Court shall have original jurisdiction. In all the other cases before mentioned, the Supreme Court shall have appellate jurisdiction, both as to law and fact, with such exceptions, and under such regulations as the Congress shall make.

3. The trial of all crimes, except in cases of impeachment, shall be by jury; and such trial shall be held in the state where the said crimes shall have been committed; but when not committed within any state, the trial shall be at such place or places as the Congress may by law have directed.

Section 3. The Crime of Treason

1. Treason against the United States shall consist only in levying war against them, or in adhering to their enemies, giving them aid and comfort. No person shall be convicted of treason unless on the testimony of two witnesses to the same overt act, or on confession in open court.

2. The Congress shall have power to declare the punishment of treason, but no attainder of treason shall work corruption of blood, or forfeiture except during the life of the person attainted.

Article 4. RELATIONS AMONG THE STATES

Section 1. Recognition by Each State of Acts of Other States

Full faith and credit shall be given in each state to the public acts, records, and judicial proceedings of every other state. And the Congress may by general laws prescribe the manner in which such acts, records and proceedings shall be proved, and the effect thereof.

Section 2. Rights of Citizens in Other States

1. The citizens of each state shall be entitled to all privileges and immunities of citizens in the several states.

2. A person charged in any state with treason, felony, or other crime, who shall flee from justice, and be found in another state, shall on demand of the executive authority of the state from which he fled, be delivered up, to be removed to the state having jurisdiction of the crime.

3. No person held to service or labor in one state, under the laws thereof, escaping into another, shall, in consequence of any law or regulation therein, be discharged from such service or labor, but shall be delivered up on claim of the party to whom such service or labor may be due.

Section 3. Treatment of New States and Territories

1. New states may be admitted by the Congress into this Union; but no new state shall be formed or erected within the jurisdiction of any other state; nor any state be formed by the junction of two or more states, or parts of states, without the consent of the legislatures of the states concerned as well as of the Congress.

1. Congress may let new states become part of the United States. No new state can be formed from another state or by joining parts of other states, unless Congress and the legislatures of the states involved approve.

2. The Congress shall have power to dispose of and make all needful rules and regulations respecting the territory or other property belonging to the United States; and nothing in this Constitution shall be so construed as to prejudice any claims of the United States, or of any particular state.

2. Congress has the power to make all laws and rules over territories and government properties of the United States.

Section 4. Guarantees to the States

The United States shall guarantee to every state in this Union a republican form of government, and shall protect each of them against invasion; and on application of the legislature, or of the executive (when the legislature cannot be convened) against domestic violence.

The federal government guarantees that the people of each state have the right to elect their leaders. The federal government also promises to protect each state from invasion, rebellion, and violent disorders.

Article 5. AMENDING THE CONSTITUTION

The Congress, whenever two-thirds of both houses shall deem it necessary, shall propose amendments to this Constitution, or, on the application of the legislatures of two-thirds of the several states, shall call a convention for proposing amendments, which, in either case, shall be valid to all intents and purposes, as part of this Constitution, when ratified by the legislatures of three-fourths of the several states, or by conventions in three-fourths thereof, as the one or the other mode of ratification may be proposed by the Congress; provided that ~~no amendment which may be made prior to the year one thousand eight hundred and eight shall in any manner affect the first and fourth clauses in the Ninth Section of the First Article; and that~~ no state, without its consent, shall be deprived of its equal suffrage in the Senate.

There are two ways to make amendments, or changes, to the Constitution: two-thirds of each branch of Congress can suggest an amendment; or, two-thirds of the state legislatures can call a convention to suggest an amendment. Once the amendment has been suggested, three-fourths of the state legislatures or three-fourths of special state conventions must approve the amendment for it to become part of the Constitution. No state can be denied its equal vote in the Senate without its approval. No amendment could be made before 1808 that affected either the slave trade or certain direct taxes.

Article 6. DEBTS, FEDERAL SUPREMACY, OATHS OF OFFICE

Section 1. Prior Debts of the United States

All debts contracted and engagements entered into, before the adoption of this Constitution, shall be as valid against the United States under this Constitution, as under the Confederation.

The United States government promises to pay back all debts and honor all agreements made by the government under the Articles of Confederation.

The Constitution and all the laws and treaties made under it are the supreme, or highest, law in the United States. If state or local laws disagree with federal law, the federal law must be obeyed. All judges must follow this rule.

All officials of the federal and state governments must promise to support the Constitution. A person's religion may never be used to qualify or disqualify a person from holding federal office.

The Constitution will become law when special conventions in 9 (of the 13 original) states approve it.

This Constitution is completed by the agreement of everyone at this convention on September 17, 1787, in the 12th year of the independence of the United States of America.

The people present have signed their names below.

Section 2. The Supreme Law of the Land

This Constitution, and the laws of the United States which shall be made in pursuance thereof; and all treaties made, or which shall be made, under the authority of the United States, shall be the supreme law of the land; and the judges in every state shall be bound thereby, anything in the constitution or laws of any state to the contrary notwithstanding.

Section 3. Oaths of Office

The Senators and Representatives before mentioned, and the members of the several state legislatures, and all executive and judicial officers, both of the United States and of the several states, shall be bound by oath or affirmation, to support this Constitution; but no religious test shall ever be required as a qualification to any office or public trust under the United States.

Article 7. RATIFICATION OF THE CONSTITUTION

The ratification of the conventions of nine states, shall be sufficient for the establishment of this Constitution between the states so ratifying the same.

Done in convention by the unanimous consent of the States present the Seventeenth day of September in the year of our Lord one thousand seven hundred and eighty seven, and of the Independence of the United States of America the Twelfth.

In witness whereof we have hereunto subscribed our names.

George Washington, President and deputy from Virginia

DELAWARE
George Read
Gunning Bedford, Jr.
John Dickinson
Richard Bassett
Jacob Broom

MARYLAND
James McHenry
Daniel of St. Thomas
* Jenifer*
Daniel Carroll

VIRGINIA
John Blair
James Madison, Jr.

NORTH CAROLINA
William Blount
Richard Dobbs Spaight
Hugh Williamson

SOUTH CAROLINA
John Rutledge
Charles Cotesworth
* Pinckney*
Charles Pinckney
Pierce Butler

GEORGIA
William Few
Abraham Baldwin

NEW HAMPSHIRE
John Langdon
Nicholas Gilman

MASSACHUSETTS
Nathaniel Gorham
Rufus King

CONNECTICUT
William Samuel Johnson
Roger Sherman

NEW YORK
Alexander Hamilton

NEW JERSEY
William Livingston
David Brearley
William Paterson
Jonathan Dayton

PENNSYLVANIA
Benjamin Franklin
Thomas Mifflin
Robert Morris
George Clymer
Thomas FitzSimons
Jared Ingersoll
James Wilson
Gouverneur Morris

Attest: William Jackson,
* Secretary.*

AMENDMENTS TO THE CONSTITUTION

Amendment 1. *Freedom of Religion, Speech, Press, Assembly, and Petition (1791)*

Congress shall make no law respecting an establishment of religion, or prohibiting the free exercise thereof; or abridging the freedom of speech, or of the press; or the right of the people peaceably to assemble, and to petition the government for a redress of grievances.

Amendment 2. *Right to Keep Weapons (1791)*

A well-regulated militia, being necessary to the security of a free state, the right of the people to keep and bear arms shall not be infringed.

Amendment 3. *Protection Against Quartering Soldiers (1791)*

No soldier shall, in time of peace, be quartered in any house, without the consent of the owner, nor in time of war, but in a manner to be prescribed by law.

The first ten amendments to the Constitution ensure basic freedoms and are known as the Bill of Rights. Under the First Amendment, Congress cannot make laws:

1) setting up an official religion;

2) preventing people from practicing their religion;

3) stopping people or the press from saying what they want;

4) preventing people from gathering peacefully and asking the government to listen to their complaints and to correct problems.

People have the right to keep weapons and be part of the state militia (today the National Guard).

During peacetime, people cannot be forced to quarter, or house and feed, soldiers in their homes. During time of war, Congress may set other rules.

People are protected against unreasonable arrests and searches of their homes and property. To search a person's home or property, the government must get a search warrant, or special approval, describing exactly what place is to be searched and what items are expected to be found.

Amendment 4. *Freedom from Unreasonable Search and Seizure (1791)*

The right of the people to be secure in their persons, houses, papers, and effects, against unreasonable searches and seizures, shall not be violated, and no warrants shall issue, but upon probable cause, supported by oath or affirmation, and particularly describing the place to be searched, and the persons or things to be seized.

A person cannot be charged with a serious crime unless a grand jury, or a group of citizens appointed to study criminal evidence, decides that a good reason exists to put the person on trial. (The only exceptions are cases involving people in the armed forces.) A person judged innocent by a court of law cannot be put on trial again for the same crime. People on trial cannot be forced to testify, or speak in court, against themselves. A person cannot have life, liberty, or property taken away unless fairly decided by a court of law. If the government takes away property for public use, a fair price must be paid the owner.

Amendment 5. *Rights of Persons Accused of a Crime (1791)*

No person shall be held to answer for a capital, or otherwise infamous, crime, unless on a presentment or indictment of a grand jury, except in cases arising in the land or naval forces, or in the militia, when in actual service in time of war or public danger; nor shall any person be subject for the same offense to be twice put in jeopardy of life or limb; nor shall be compelled in any criminal case to be a witness against himself, nor be deprived of life, liberty, or property, without due process of law; nor shall private property be taken for public use, without just compensation.

In all criminal cases, a person accused of a crime has the right to a fast, public trial by a fair jury in the place where the crime took place. All persons accused of a crime have the right to:

1) know the charges against them;

2) hear the evidence and witnesses against them;

3) call witnesses in their defense;

4) have a lawyer.

Amendment 6. *Right to a Jury Trial in Criminal Cases (1791)*

In all criminal prosecutions, the accused shall enjoy the right to a speedy and public trial, by an impartial jury of the state and district wherein the crime shall have been committed, which district shall have been previously ascertained by law, and to be informed of the nature and cause of the accusation; to be confronted with the witnesses against him; to have compulsory process for obtaining witnesses in his favor, and to have the assistance of counsel for his defense.

A person has the right to a trial by jury in civil, or noncriminal, cases involving more than $20.

Amendment 7. *Right to a Jury Trial in Civil Cases (1791)*

In suits at common law, where the value in controversy shall exceed twenty dollars, the right of trial by jury shall be preserved, and no fact tried by a jury shall be otherwise re-examined in any court of the United States than according to the rules of the common law.

Amendment 8. *Protection from Unfair Fines and Punishment (1791)*

The government cannot require very high bail, or deposit of money, from a

Excessive bail shall not be required, nor excessive fines imposed, nor cruel and unusual punishments inflicted.

Amendment 9. *Other Rights of the People (1791)*

The enumeration in the Constitution, of certain rights, shall not be construed to deny or disparage others retained by the people.

The rights of the people are not limited to those stated in the Constitution.

Amendment 10. *Powers of the States and the People (1791)*

The powers not delegated to the United States by the Constitution, nor prohibited by it to the states, are reserved to the states respectively, or to the people.

Powers not granted to the United States government and not forbidden to the states are left to the states or to the people.

Amendment 11. *Limiting Law Cases Against States (1798)*

The judicial power of the United States shall not be construed to extend to any suit in law or equity, commenced or prosecuted against one of the United States, by citizens of another state, or by citizens or subjects of any foreign state.

A state government cannot be sued in a federal court by people of another state or by people from a foreign country.

Amendment 12. *Election of President and Vice President (1804)*

The electors shall meet in their respective states, and vote by ballot for President and Vice President, one of whom, at least, shall not be an inhabitant of the same state with themselves; they shall name in their ballots the person voted for as President, and in distinct ballots the person voted for as Vice President, and they shall make distinct lists of all persons voted for as President, and of all persons voted for as Vice President, and of the number of votes for each, which lists they shall sign and certify, and transmit, sealed, to the seat of government of the United States, directed to the President of the Senate; the President of the Senate shall, in the presence of the Senate and House of Representatives, open all the certificates and the votes shall then be counted; the person having the greatest number of votes for President shall be the President, if such number be a majority of the whole number of electors appointed; and if no person have such majority, then from the persons having the highest numbers not exceeding three on the list of those voted for as President, the House of Representatives shall choose immediately, by ballot, the President. But in choosing the President, the votes shall be taken by states, the representation from each state having one vote; a quorum for this purpose shall consist of a member or members from two-thirds of the states, and a majority of all the states shall be neces-

person accused of a crime. People convicted of crimes cannot be fined an unfairly high amount. Nor can they be punished in a cruel or unusual way.

This amendment changed the method of choosing a President and Vice President. This method is called the Electoral College. The main change caused by this amendment is that candidates for President and Vice President now run for office together, and each elector casts only one vote. Before, candidates for President and Vice President ran for office separately, and each elector cast two votes. Under the Electoral College, people called electors meet in their home states and vote for President and Vice President. Electors choose one person for President and a different person for Vice President. (One of the people voted for must be from a different state than the elector.) These electoral votes are then sent to the United States Senate where all the electoral votes for President are counted. The person who receives more than half the electoral votes for President is elected President. The person who receives more than half the electoral votes for Vice President is elected Vice President. If no person receives more than half the electoral votes for President, the House of Representatives chooses the President. A list of the top three vote-getters is sent to the House of Representatives. From this list, the Representatives vote for President with each state entitled to one vote. The person who receives more than half the votes of the states in the House of Representatives is elected President. If no person receives more than half the vote, the Representatives vote again. If the Representatives fail to elect a President by March 4 (later changed to January 20), the Vice President serves as President. If no person receives at least half the electoral votes for Vice President, no one becomes Vice President and a list of the top two vote-getters is sent to the Senate. From this list, the Senators then vote for Vice President, with each Senator entitled to one vote. The person who receives more than half the votes in the Senate becomes Vice President. Qualifications for the office of Vice President are the same as those of President.

Slavery is outlawed in the United States.

sary to a choice. ~~And if the House of Representatives shall not choose a President whenever the right of choice shall devolve upon them, before the fourth day of March next following, then the Vice President shall act as President, as in the case of the death or other constitutional disability of the President~~. The person having the greatest number of votes as Vice President, shall be the Vice President, if such number be a majority of the whole number of electors appointed, and if no person have a majority, then from the two highest numbers on the list, the Senate shall choose the Vice President; a quorum for the purpose shall consist of two-thirds of the whole number of Senators, and a majority of the whole number shall be necessary to a choice. But no person constitutionally ineligible to the office of President shall be eligible to that of Vice President of the United States.

Amendment 13. *Slavery Outlawed (1865)*

Section 1. *Abolition of Slavery*

Neither slavery nor involuntary servitude, except as a punishment for crime whereof the party shall have been duly convicted, shall exist within the United States, or any place subject to their jurisdiction.

Congress can pass any laws necessary to carry out this amendment.

Section 2. *Enforcement*

Congress shall have power to enforce this article by appropriate legislation.

Amendment 14. *Rights of Citizens (1868)*

Section 1. *Citizenship*

All people born in or made citizens by the United States are citizens of both the United States and the state in which they live. No state can deny any citizen the basic rights outlined in the 5th Amendment. All states must treat people equally under the law. This amendment made formerly enslaved people citizens of both the United States and the states in which they lived.

All persons born or naturalized in the United States and subject to the jurisdiction thereof, are citizens of the United States and of the state wherein they reside. No state shall make or enforce any law which shall abridge the privileges or immunities of citizens of the United States; nor shall any state deprive any person of life, liberty, or property, without due process of law; nor deny to any person within its jurisdiction the equal protection of the laws.

The number of a state's Representatives in Congress can be lowered if the state prevents qualified citizens

Section 2. *Representation in Congress*

Representatives shall be apportioned among the several states according to their respective numbers, counting the whole number of persons in each state, ~~excluding Indians not taxed~~. But when the right to vote at any election for the choice of electors for President and Vice President of the United States, Representatives in Congress, the executive and judicial officers of a state, or the members of the legislature thereof, is denied to any of the ~~male~~ inhabitants of such state, being ~~twenty-one years of age and~~ citizens of the United States, or in any way abridged, except for participation in rebellion, or other crime, the basis of representation therein shall be reduced in the proportion which the number of such ~~male~~ citizens shall bear to the whole number of ~~male~~ citizens ~~twenty-one years of age~~ in such state.

from voting. This section aimed to force states in the South to allow African Americans to vote.

Section 3. Penalties for Confederate Leaders

No person shall be a Senator or Representative in Congress, or elector of President and Vice President, or hold any office, civil or military, under the United States, or under any state, who, having previously taken an oath, as a member of Congress, or as an officer of the United States, or as a member of any state legislature, or as an executive or judicial officer of any state, to support the Constitution of the United States, shall have engaged in insurrection or rebellion against the same, or given aid or comfort to the enemies thereof. But Congress may, by vote of two-thirds of each house, remove such disability.

Any official of the federal or state governments who took part in the Civil War against the United States cannot again hold any federal or state office. But Congress can remove this restriction by a two-thirds vote.

Section 4. Responsibility for Public Debt

The validity of the public debt of the United States, authorized by law, including debts incurred for payment of pensions and bounties for services in suppressing insurrection or rebellion, shall not be questioned. But neither the United States nor any state shall assume or pay any debt or obligation incurred in aid of insurrection or rebellion against the United States ~~or any claim for the loss or emancipation of any slave~~; but all such debts, obligations, and claims shall be held illegal and void.

All money borrowed by the United States government to fight the Civil War is to be paid back. No debts owed to the Confederate states or to the Confederate government to pay for the Civil War are to be paid back by the federal or state governments. No money would be paid to anyone for the loss of people they once held in slavery.

Section 5. Enforcement

The Congress shall have power to enforce, by appropriate legislation, the provisions of this article.

Congress can pass any laws necessary to carry out this amendment.

Amendment 15. *Voting Rights (1870)*

Section 1. Black Suffrage

The right of citizens of the United States to vote shall not be denied or abridged by the United States or any state on account of race, color, or previous condition of servitude.

No federal or state government can prevent people from voting because of their race, color, or because they were once enslaved. This amendment aimed to give black men the right to vote.

Congress can pass any laws necessary to carry out this amendment.

Section 2. Enforcement

The Congress shall have power to enforce this article by appropriate legislation.

Amendment 16. *Income Tax (1913)*

Congress has the power to collect an income tax regardless of the population of any state.

The Congress shall have the power to lay and collect taxes on incomes, from whatever source derived, without apportionment among the several states, and without regard to any census or enumeration.

Amendment 17. *Direct Election of Senators (1913)*

Section 1. *Method of Election*

Senators are to be elected by the voters of each state. This amendment changed the method by which state legislatures elected Senators as outlined in Article 1, Section 3, Clause 1 of the Constitution.

The Senate of the United States shall be composed of two Senators from each state, elected by the people thereof, for six years; and each Senator shall have one vote. The electors in each state shall have the qualifications requisite for electors of the most numerous branch of the state legislatures.

Section 2. *Vacancies*

Special elections can be held to fill empty seats in the Senate. State legislatures may permit the governor to name a person to fill an empty seat for a short time until the next election.

When vacancies happen in the representation of any state in the Senate, the executive authority of such state shall issue writs of election to fill such vacancies: *provided* that the legislature of any state may empower the executive thereof to make temporary appointments until the people fill the vacancies by election as the legislature may direct.

Section 3. *Those Elected under Previous Rules*

This amendment does not affect the election or term of office of any Senator in office before the amendment becomes part of the Constitution.

This amendment shall not be so construed as to affect the election or term of any Senator chosen before it becomes valid as part of the Constitution.

Amendment 18. *Prohibition of Alcoholic Drinks (1919)*

Section 1. *Prohibition*

Making, selling, or transporting alcoholic, or intoxicating, drinks in the United States is illegal. This amendment was called the Prohibition Amendment because it prohibited, or banned, the use of alcohol.

After one year from the ratification of this article the manufacture, sale, or transportation of intoxicating liquors within, the importation thereof into, or the exportation thereof from, the United States and all territory subject to the jurisdiction thereof for beverage purposes is hereby prohibited.

Section 2. *Enforcement*

Both Congress and the states can pass any laws necessary to carry out this amendment.

The Congress and the several states shall have concurrent power to enforce this article by appropriate legislation.

Section 3. Time Limit on Ratification

~~The article shall be inoperative unless it shall have been ratified as an amendment to the Constitution by the legislatures of the several states, as provided in the Constitution, within seven years from the date of the submission hereof to the states by the Congress.~~

This amendment is to become part of the Constitution only if it is approved within seven years. It was repealed, or canceled, by the 21st Amendment.

Amendment 19. *Women's Right to Vote (1920)*

Section 1. Women Made Voters

The right of citizens of the United States to vote shall not be denied or abridged by the United States or by any state on account of sex.

No federal or state government can prevent people from voting because of their sex. This amendment grants women the right to vote.

Section 2. Enforcement

Congress shall have power to enforce this article by appropriate legislation.

Congress can pass any laws necessary to carry out this amendment.

Amendment 20. *Terms of Office (1933)*

Section 1. Start of Terms of Office

The terms of the President and Vice President shall end at noon on the 20th day of January, and the terms of Senators and Representatives at noon on the 3rd day of January, of the years in which such terms would have ended if this article had not been ratified; and the terms of their successors shall then begin.

The terms of office for the President and Vice President begin on January 20. This date is called Inauguration Day. The terms of office for members of Congress begin on January 3. Originally their terms began on March 4.

Section 2. Meeting Time of Congress

The Congress shall assemble at least once in every year, and such meeting shall begin at noon on the 3rd day of January, unless they shall by law appoint a different day.

Congress must meet at least once a year beginning at noon on January 3. However, Congress may pick a different day to first meet.

Section 3. Providing for a Successor of the President-Elect

If at the time fixed for the beginning of the term of the President, the President-elect shall have died, the Vice President-elect shall become President. If a President shall not have been chosen before the time fixed for the beginning of his term, or if the President-elect shall have failed to qualify, then the Vice President-elect shall act as President until a President shall have qualified; and the Congress may by law provide for the case wherein neither a President-elect nor a Vice President-elect shall have qualified, declaring who shall then act as President, or the manner in which one who is to act shall be selected, and such person shall act accordingly until a President or Vice President shall have qualified.

If the person elected President dies before taking office, the Vice President becomes President. If no person is elected President before the term of office begins, or if the person elected President is not qualified to serve, then the Vice President acts as President until a qualified President is chosen. If both the person elected President and the person elected Vice President are disqualified from holding office, Congress selects the President.

If, during the time Congress is selecting the President and Vice President, one of these two people dies, Congress may pass a law determining how to choose the President and Vice President.

Section 4. Elections Decided by Congress

The Congress may by law provide for the case of the death of any of the persons from whom the House of Representatives may choose a President whenever the right of choice shall have devolved upon them, and for the case of the death of any of the persons from whom the Senate may choose a Vice President whenever the right of choice shall have devolved upon them.

Section 5. Effective Date

Sections 1 and 2 shall take effect on the 15th day of October following the ratification of this article.

Sections 1 and 2 of this amendment take effect on the 15th day of October after this amendment becomes part of the Constitution.

This amendment is to become part of the Constitution only if it is approved by three-fourths of the state legislatures within seven years.

Section 6. Time Limit on Ratification

This article shall be inoperative unless it shall have been ratified as an amendment to the Constitution by the legislatures of three-fourths of the several states within seven years from the date of its submission.

Amendment 21. Repeal of Prohibition (1933)

Section 1. Prohibition Ends

The 18th Amendment is repealed, or no longer in effect.

The Eighteenth article of amendment to the Constitution of the United States is hereby repealed.

Section 2. Protection of State and Local Prohibition Laws

Any state or territory of the United States may pass prohibition laws.

The transportation or importation into any state, territory, or possession of the United States for delivery or use therein of intoxicating liquors, in violation of the laws thereof, is hereby prohibited.

Section 3. Time Limit on Ratification

This amendment is to become part of the Constitution only if state conventions approve it within seven years.

This article shall be inoperative unless it shall have been ratified as an amendment to the Constitution by conventions in the several states, as provided in the Constitution, within seven years from the date of the submission hereof to the states by the Congress.

Amendment 22. President Limited to Two Terms (1951)

Section 1. Limit on Number of Terms

No person can be elected more than two times to the office of President. No person can be elected more than once to the office of President who has served more than two years of another President's term. This amend-

No person shall be elected to the office of the President more than twice, and no person who has held the office of President, or acted as President, for more than two years of a term to which some other person was elected President shall be elected to the office of the President more than once. ~~But this Article shall not apply to any person holding the office of President when this Article was proposed by the Congress, and shall not prevent any person who may be holding the office of President, or acting as President, during the term within which this Article becomes operative from holding the office of President or acting as President during the remainder of such term.~~

ment does not affect any President who is in office when this amendment becomes part of the Constitution.

Section 2. Time Limit on Ratification

~~This Article shall be inoperative unless it shall have been ratified as an amendment to the Constitution by the legislatures of three-fourths of the several states within seven years from the date of its submission to the states by the Congress.~~

This amendment is to become part of the Constitution only if three-fourths of the state legislatures approve it within seven years.

Amendment 23. *Presidential Elections for the District of Columbia (1961)*

Section 1. Presidential Electors in the District of Columbia

The District constituting the seat of Government of the United States shall appoint in such manner as the Congress may direct: A number of electors of President and Vice President equal to the whole number of Senators and Representatives in Congress to which the District would be entitled if it were a State, but in no event more than the least populous State; they shall be in addition to those appointed by the States, but they shall be considered, for the purposes of the election of President and Vice President, to be electors appointed by a State; and they shall meet in the District and perform such duties as provided by the twelfth article of amendment.

People living in Washington, D.C. (the District of Columbia), have the right to vote in Presidential elections. The number of electoral votes of Washington, D.C., can never be more than the number of electoral votes of the state with the fewest number of people.

Section 2. Enforcement

The Congress shall have power to enforce this article by appropriate legislation.

Congress can pass any laws necessary to carry out this amendment.

Amendment 24. *Poll Tax Ended (1964)*

Section 1. Poll Taxes Not Allowed in Federal Elections

The right of citizens of the United States to vote in any primary or other election for President or Vice President, for electors for President or Vice President, or for Senator or Representative in Congress, shall not be denied or abridged by the United States or any state by reason of failure to pay any poll tax or other tax.

No person can be prevented from voting in a federal election for failing to pay a poll tax or any other kind of tax.

Congress can pass any laws necessary to carry out this amendment.

Section 2. Enforcement

The Congress shall have the power to enforce this article by appropriate legislation.

Amendment 25. *Presidential Succession (1967)*

Section 1. *Filling the Vacant Office of President*

In case of the removal of the President from office or of his death or resignation, the Vice President shall become President.

If the President dies, resigns, or is removed from office, the Vice President becomes President.

Section 2. *Filling the Vacant Office of Vice President*

Whenever there is a vacancy in the office of the Vice President, the President shall nominate a Vice President who shall take the office upon confirmation by a majority vote of both houses of Congress.

If the office of Vice President becomes empty, the President names a new Vice President, with the approval of both houses of Congress.

Section 3. *Disability of the President*

Whenever the President transmits to the President pro tempore of the Senate and the Speaker of the House of Representatives his written declaration that he is unable to discharge the powers and duties of his office, and until he transmits to them a written declaration to the contrary, such powers and duties shall be discharged by the Vice President as Acting President.

If the President is unable to carry out the powers and duties of office, the President may inform the leaders of Congress. The Vice President then serves as Acting President. The President may return to office only when he or she informs the leaders of Congress that he or she can again carry out the powers and duties of office.

Section 4. *When Congress Designates an Acting President*

Whenever the Vice President and a majority of either the principal officers of the executive departments or of such other body as Congress may by law provide, transmit to the President pro tempore of the Senate and the Speaker of the House of Representatives their written declaration that the President is unable to discharge the powers and duties of his office, the Vice President shall immediately assume the powers and duties of the office as Acting President. Thereafter, when the President transmits to the President pro tempore of the Senate and the Speaker of the House of Representatives his written declaration that no inability exists, he shall resume the powers and duties of his office unless the Vice President and a majority of either the principal officers of the executive departments or of such other body as Congress may by law provide, transmit within four days to the President pro tempore of the Senate and the Speaker of the House of Representatives their written declaration that the President is unable to discharge the powers and duties of his office. Thereupon Congress shall decide the issue, assembling within 48 hours for that purpose if not in ses-

If the Vice President and at least half the Cabinet, or President's top advisers (or a special committee), inform the leaders of Congress that the President cannot carry out the powers and duties of office, the Vice President immediately becomes Acting President. If the President informs the leaders of Congress that he or she is able to serve as President, he or she again becomes President. But if, within four days, the Vice President and at least half the Cabinet (or a special committee) inform the leaders of Congress that the President still cannot carry out the powers and duties of office, the President does not return to office. Instead, Congress must meet within 48 hours. In the next 21 days, Congress must decide if the President is able to carry out the powers and duties of office. If two-thirds of both houses of Congress vote that the President is unable to serve, the Presision. If the Congress, within 21 days after receipt of the latter written declaration, or, if Congress is not in session, within 21 days after Congress is required to assemble, determines by two-thirds vote of both houses that the President is unable to discharge the powers and duties of his office, the Vice President shall continue to discharge the same as Acting President; otherwise, the President shall assume the powers and duties of his office.

dent is removed from office and the Vice President becomes Acting President. If two-thirds do not vote this way, the President stays in office.

Amendment 26. *Vote for Eighteen-Year-Olds (1971)*

Section 1. Voting Age

The right of citizens of the United States, who are 18 years of age or older, to vote shall not be denied or abridged by the United States or any state on account of age.

No federal or state government can prevent people 18 years of age or older from voting because of their age. This amendment grants people who are at least 18 years old the right to vote.

Section 2. Enforcement

The Congress shall have the power to enforce this article by appropriate legislation.

Congress can pass any laws necessary to carry out this amendment.

Amendment 27. *Limits on Salary Changes (1992)*

No law, varying the compensation for the services of the Senators and Representatives, shall take effect, until an election of Representatives shall have intervened.

No law changing the salaries of members of Congress can take effect until after the next election of the House of Representatives.

Time Line of Our PRESIDENTS

George Washington
(1732-1799)

Years in Office 1789-1797
Vice President John Adams
Home State Virginia
Occupation Planter, military leader
First Lady Martha Dandridge Washington
Religion Episcopalian

New States
Vermont 1791; Kentucky 1792; Tennessee 1796

Major Events
- 1789 Roman Catholics found Georgetown University
- 1790 First spinning mill in U.S. opened
- 1790 First U.S. census
- 1791 First recorded Cabinet meeting
- 1791 Bill of Rights added to Constitution
- 1791 (First) Bank of the U.S. established
- 1792 New York Stock Exchange founded
- 1796 Washington's Farewell Address

John Adams
(1735-1826)

Years in Office 1797-1801
Vice President Thomas Jefferson
Home State Massachusetts

Occupation Lawyer
First Lady Abigail Smith Adams
Religion Unitarian

Major Events
- 1798 Navy Department established
- 1798-1800 Undeclared war with France
- 1801 John Marshall appointed Chief Justice

Thomas Jefferson
(1743-1826)

Years in Office 1801-1809
Vice Presidents Aaron Burr 1801-1805; George Clinton 1805-1809
Home State Virginia
Occupation Lawyer
First Lady (none)
Religion No specific denomination

New States
Ohio 1803

Major Events
- 1802 West Point military academy opens
- 1803 Louisiana Purchase
- 1804-1806 Lewis and Clark expedition
- 1807 Trial run of steamboat *Clermont*
- 1808 Importing slaves into U.S. ends

James Madison
(1751-1836)

Years in Office 1809-1817
Vice Presidents George Clinton 1809-1812, died; Elbridge Gerry 1813-1814, died
Home State Virginia
Occupation Lawyer
First Lady Dolley Payne Madison
Religion Episcopalian

New States
Louisiana 1812; Indiana 1816

Major Events
- 1811 Construction of National Road begins
- 1812-1814 War of 1812
- 1814 "Star-Spangled Banner" written
- 1814 Building of new White House begins
- 1815 Battle of New Orleans
- 1816 (Second) Bank of the U.S. established

James Monroe
(1758-1831)

Years in Office 1817-1825
Vice President Daniel D. Tompkins
Home State Virginia
Occupation Lawyer, soldier
First Lady Elizabeth Kortright Monroe
Religion Episcopalian

New States
Mississippi 1817; Illinois 1818; Alabama 1819; Maine 1820; Missouri 1821

Major Events
- 1817 American Colonization Society founded
- 1817-1818 First Seminole War
- 1819 Washington Irving's "Rip Van Winkle" and "The Legend of Sleepy Hollow"
- 1819 Adams-Onís Treaty with Spain gives Florida to U.S.
- 1820 Missouri Compromise
- 1823 Monroe Doctrine

John Quincy Adams
(1767-1848)

Years in Office 1825-1829
Vice President John C. Calhoun
Home State Massachusetts
Occupation Lawyer
First Lady Louisa Johnson Adams
Religion Unitarian

Major Events
- 1825 Erie Canal completed
- 1826 First railway steam locomotive
- 1827 *Freedom's Journal,* first African American newspaper published
- 1828 Congress passes the "tariff of abominations"
- 1828 Noah Webster publishes dictionary

Andrew Jackson
(1767-1845)

Years in Office 1829-1837
Vice Presidents John C. Calhoun 1829-1832, resigned; Martin Van Buren 1833-1837
Home State Tennessee
Occupation Lawyer

First Lady (none)
Religion Presbyterian

New States
Arkansas 1836; Michigan 1837

Major Events
- 1829 First commercial railroad, the Baltimore & Ohio
- 1832 Black Hawk War
- 1832-1833 Nullification crisis
- 1835-1842 Second Seminole War
- 1836 Texas Revolution against Mexico
- 1836 Jackson issues *Species Circular*
- 1837 Panic of 1837

Martin Van Buren
(1782-1862)

Years in Office 1837-1841
Vice President Richard M. Johnson
Home State New York
Occupation Lawyer
First Lady (none)
Religion Dutch Reformed

Major Events
- 1837 Methodists found Oberlin College, first U.S. coed college
- 1837 Horace Mann establishes U.S. Board of Education
- 1837 Samuel F.B. Morse files for telegraph patent
- 1838-1839 Trail of Tears
- 1839 Aroostock War
- 1839 Abner Doubleday lays out first baseball diamond

William Henry Harrison
(1773-1841)

Years in Office 1841-1841(one month; died in office)
Vice President John Tyler
Home State Ohio
Occupation Military leader
First Lady Anna Symmes Harrison
Religion Episcopalian

Major Events
- 1841 10-hour work day established for federal workers
- 1841 Horace Greeley founds the New York *Tribune*
- 1841 Harrison becomes first President to die in office

John Tyler
(1790-1862)

Years in Office 1841-1845
Vice President (none)
Home State Virginia
Occupation Lawyer
First Ladies Letitia Christian Tyler, died 1842; Julia Gardiner Tyler
Religion Episcopalian

New States
Florida 1845

Major Events
- 1842 Webster-Ashburton Treaty
- 1844 Charles Goodyear, Sr., patents rubber-hardening process

James K. Polk
(1795-1849)

Years in Office 1845-1849
Vice President George M. Dallas
Home State Tennessee
Occupation Lawyer
First Lady Sarah Childress Polk
Religion Presbyterian

New States
Texas 1845; Iowa 1846; Wisconsin 1848

Major Events
- 1846 Ether used as anesthetic
- 1846 Smithsonian Institution founded
- 1846-1847 War with Mexico
- 1848 Treaty of Guadalupe Hidalgo
- 1848 Stephen Foster writes "Oh, Susanna"
- 1848 Gold discovered in California
- 1848 First women's rights convention held in Seneca Falls, NY

Zachary Taylor
(1784-1850)

Years in Office 1849-1850 (died in office)
Vice President Millard Fillmore
Home State Kentucky
Occupation Planter, military leader
First Lady Margaret Smith Taylor
Religion Episcopalian

Major Events
- 1849 California Gold Rush
- 1849 Interior Department established
- 1850 Compromise of 1850 proposed by Henry Clay

Millard Fillmore
(1800-1874)

Years in Office 1850-1853
Vice President (none)
Home State New York
Occupation Lawyer
First Lady Abigail Powers Fillmore
Religion Unitarian

New States
California 1850

Major Events
- 1850 Compromise of 1850, included the Fugitive Slave Law
- 1851 First U.S. chapter of the YMCA opens
- 1852 *Uncle Tom's Cabin* published
- 1852 Commodore Perry sent to open trade with Japan

Franklin Pierce
(1804-1869)

Years in Office 1853-1857
Vice President William R. King, died 1853
Home State New Hampshire
Occupation Lawyer
First Lady Jane Appleton Pierce
Religion Episcopalian

Major Events
- 1853 Gadsden Purchase
- 1854 Kansas-Nebraska Act
- 1854 Henry David Thoreau's *Walden*
- 1855 Walt Whitman's *Leaves of Grass*

James Buchanan
(1791-1868)

Years in Office 1857-1861
Vice President John C. Breckinridge
Home State Pennsylvania
Occupation Lawyer
First Lady (none)
Religion Presbyterian

New States
Minnesota 1858; Oregon 1859; Kansas 1861

Major Events
- 1857 First amateur baseball clubs formed
- 1857 Dred Scott Decision
- 1859 John Brown's raid at Harpers Ferry, Virginia
- 1860 South Carolina secedes
- 1861 Confederate States of America formed

Abraham Lincoln
(1809-1865)

Years in Office 1861-1865 (assassinated)
Vice Presidents Hannibal Hamlin 1861-1865; Andrew Johnson 1865
Home State Illinois
Occupation Lawyer
First Lady Mary Todd Lincoln
Religion No specific denomination

New States
West Virginia 1863; Nevada 1864

Major Events
- 1861 Civil War begins
- 1862 Homestead, Pacific Railroad, and Land-Grant acts passed

- 1862 Julia Ward Howe's "The Battle Hymn of the Republic" published
- 1863 Henry Wadsworth Longfellow publishes "Paul Revere's Ride"
- 1863 Emancipation Proclamation
- 1865 Civil War ends

Andrew Johnson
(1808-1875)

Years in Office 1865-1869
Vice President (none)
Home State Tennessee
Occupation Lawyer
First Lady Eliza McCardle Johnson
Religion No specific denomination

New States
Nebraska 1867

Major Events
- 1867 University of Illinois, one of first land-grant colleges, founded
- 1867 U.S. buys Alaska from Russia
- 1868 Johnson impeached; found not guilty
- 1869 John Wesley Powell explores Grand Canyon

Ulysses S. Grant
(1822-1885)

Years in Office 1869-1877
Vice Presidents Schuyler Colfax 1869-1873; Henry Wilson 1873-1875, died
Home State Illinois
Occupation Farmer, military leader
First Lady Julia Dent Grant
Religion Methodist

New States
Colorado 1876

Major Events
- 1869 Transcontinental railroad is completed
- 1871 Great Chicago Fire
- 1872 Yellowstone is made first national park
- 1876 Bell invents telephone
- 1876 Battle of the Little Bighorn

Rutherford B. Hayes
(1822-1893)

Years in Office 1877-1881
Vice President William A. Wheeler
Home State Ohio
Occupation Lawyer, soldier
First Lady Lucy Webb Hayes
Religion Methodist

Major Events
- 1877 Reconstruction ends
- 1877 Chief Joseph surrenders after Nez Percé War
- 1879 Edison invents light bulb
- 1879 First inter-city telephone communications
- 1880 U. S. branch of Salvation Army formed

James A. Garfield
(1831-1881)

Years in Office 1881-1881 (assassinated)
Vice President Chester A. Arthur
Home State Ohio
Occupation Teacher, soldier
First Lady Lucretia Rudolph Garfield
Religion Disciples of Christ

Major Events
- 1881 Barton founds the American Red Cross
- 1881 Shootout at the OK Corral in Tombstone, AZ

Chester A. Arthur
(1829-1886)

Years in Office 1881-1885
Vice President (none)
Home State New York
Occupation Lawyer, teacher
First Lady (none)
Religion Episcopalian

Major Events
- 1881 Tuskegee Institute established by Booker T. Washington
- 1883 Brooklyn Bridge opens
- 1884 Statue of Liberty cornerstone laid
- 1884 First skycraper built, in Chicago

Grover Cleveland
(1837-1908)

Years in Office 1885-1889, 1893-1897
Vice Presidents Thomas A. Hendricks, died 1885; Adlai E. Stevenson 1893-1897
Home State New York
Occupation Lawyer
First Lady Frances Folsom Cleveland
Religion Presbyterian

New States
Utah 1896

Major Events
- 1887 Interstate Commerce Act
- 1888 First *National Geographic* magazine published
- 1891 Sears & Roebuck Company founded
- 1894 Labor Day holiday established

Time Line of Our PRESIDENTS

Benjamin Harrison
(1833-1901)

Years in Office 1889-1893
Vice President Levi P. Morton
Home State Indiana
Occupation Lawyer
First Lady Caroline Scott Harrison
Religion Presbyterian

New States
Washington, Montana, North Dakota, South Dakota 1889; Wyoming, Idaho 1890

Major Events
- 1889 Jane Addams starts Hull House
- 1889 Johnstown, PA Flood
- 1890 Sherman Anti-Trust Act limits monopolies
- 1891 James Naismith invents basketball
- 1892 Ellis Island begins accepting immigrants
- 1893 First gasoline-powered automobile

William McKinley
(1843-1901)

Years in Office 1897-1901 (assassinated)
Vice Presidents Garret A. Hobart 1897-1899, died; Theodore Roosevelt 1901
Home State Ohio
Occupation Lawyer, teacher

First Lady Ida Saxton McKinley
Religion Methodist

Major Events
- 1898 Spanish-American War
- 1898 U.S. gains Puerto Rico, Guam, and the Philippines
- 1900 U.S. troops enter China to fight in the Boxer Rebellion

Theodore Roosevelt
(1858-1919)

Years in Office 1901-1909
Vice President Charles W. Fairbanks (1905-1909)
Home State New York
Occupation Law enforcement, military leader
First Lady Edith Carow Roosevelt
Religion Dutch Reformed

New States
Oklahoma 1907

Major Events
- 1903 First national wildlife refuge established, in Florida
- 1903 Wright brothers make first successful plane flight
- 1903 U.S. acquires Panama Canal Zone
- 1905 National Audubon Society formed
- 1906 Sinclair's *The Jungle* published
- 1906 San Francisco earthquake

William Howard Taft
(1857-1930)

Years in Office 1909-1913
Vice President James S. Sherman 1909-1912, died
Home State Ohio
Occupation Lawyer
First Lady Helen Herron Taft
Religion Unitarian

New States
New Mexico, Arizona 1912

Major Events
- 1909 Ford produces Model T
- 1909 NAACP founded
- 1909 Robert Edwin Peary's expedition reaches North Pole
- 1910 Boy Scouts founded
- 1911 First transcontinental airplane flight
- 1912 First state minimum wage law
- 1912 Girl Scouts founded
- 1912 *Titanic* sinks

Woodrow Wilson
(1856-1924)

Years in Office 1913-1921
Vice President Thomas R. Marshall
Home State New Jersey
Occupation University professor and president
First Ladies Ellen Louise Axson Wilson, died 1914; Edith Bolling Galt Wilson
Religion Presbyterian

Major Events
- 1913 Congress passes income tax law

- 1913 Federal Reserve Bank established
- 1914 Panama Canal opens
- 1915 New York and San Francisco linked by telephone
- 1915 Sinking of the *Lusitania*
- 1917-1918 U.S. in World War I
- 1919-1933 Prohibition
- 1920 Nineteenth Amendment ratified, giving women the right to vote

---

Warren G. Harding
(1865-1923)

Years in Office 1921-1923 (died in office)
Vice President Calvin Coolidge
Home State Ohio
Occupation Journalist, publisher
First Lady Florence King DeWolfe Harding
Religion Baptist

Major Events
- 1921 Washington Conference limits weapons
- 1921 Einstein visits New York to discuss Theory of Relativity
- 1922 Teapot Dome Scandal begins
- 1922 Lincoln Memorial dedicated

Calvin Coolidge
(1872-1933)

Years in Office 1923-1929
Vice President Charles G. Dawes (1925-1929)
Home State Massachusetts
Occupation Lawyer
First Lady Grace Goodhue Coolidge
Religion Congregationalist

Major Events
- 1924 All Native Americans made citizens

- 1924 Immigration from Europe limited
- 1926 First artifacts of prehistoric life in New Mexico found
- 1927 First talking movie shown in theaters
- 1927 Lindbergh flies solo across the Atlantic Ocean

Herbert Hoover
(1874-1964)

Years in Office 1929-1933
Vice President Charles Curtis
Home State California
Occupation Engineer, businessman
First Lady Lou Henry Hoover
Religion Quaker

Major Events
- 1929 Stock market crashes; Great Depression begins
- 1930 U.S. astronomers discover Pluto
- 1931 "Star-Spangled Banner" made national anthem
- 1932 Reconstruction Finance Corporation established
- 1932 Earhart becomes first woman pilot to cross Atlantic

Franklin D. Roosevelt
(1882-1945)

Years in Office 1933-1945 (died in office)
Vice Presidents John Nance Garner 1933-1941; Henry Wallace 1941-1945; Harry S. Truman 1945
Home State New York
Occupation Lawyer
First Lady Anna Eleanor Roosevelt
Religion Episcopalian

Major Events
- 1933 New Deal begins

- 1934 Drought creates Dust Bowl
- 1937 Golden Gate Bridge opens
- 1939 Marian Anderson sings at Lincoln Memorial
- 1939 John Steinbeck's *The Grapes of Wrath* published
- 1939 The film *Gone With the Wind* opens
- 1941 "Four Freedoms" speech
- 1941 Japanese Attack Pearl Harbor
- 1941-1945 U.S. in World War II

Harry S. Truman
(1884-1972)

Years in Office 1945-1953
Vice President Alben W. Barkley (1949-1953)
Home State Missouri
Occupation Farmer, businessman, judge
First Lady Elizabeth (Bess) Wallace Truman
Religion Baptist

Major Events
- 1945 United Nations formed
- 1945 Commercial television broadcasting begins
- 1947 Jackie Robinson begins playing for Brooklyn Dodgers
- 1950 U.S. enters Korean War
- 1952 U.S. tests hydrogen bomb
- 1952 Puerto Rico becomes U.S. commonwealth

Dwight D. Eisenhower
(1890-1969)

Years in Office 1953-1961
Vice President Richard M. Nixon
Home State New York
Occupation Military leader
First Lady Marie (Mamie) Doud Eisenhower
Religion Presbyterian

New States
Alaska, Hawaii 1959

Major Events
- 1954 Supreme Court rules against school segregation
- 1954 Jonas Salk develops polio vaccine
- 1955-1956 Montgomery bus boycott
- 1956 Building of interstate highway system begins
- 1957 First nuclear power plant opens, in Shippingport, PA

John F. Kennedy
(1917-1963)

Years in Office 1961-1963 (assassinated)
Vice President Lyndon B. Johnson
Home State Massachusetts
Occupation Legislator
First Lady Jacqueline Bouvier Kennedy
Religion Roman Catholic

Major Events
- 1961 Peace Corps established
- 1961 Alan B. Shepherd, Jr., becomes the first American in outer space
- 1962 Cuban Missile Crisis

- 1962 National Farm Workers Association founded
- 1962 Rachel Carson publishes *Silent Spring*
- 1963 March on Washington for civil rights

Lyndon Baines Johnson
(1908-1973)

Years in Office 1963-1969
Vice President Hubert H. Humphrey
Home State Texas
Occupation Teacher, legislator
First Lady Claudia (Lady Bird) Taylor Johnson
Religion Disciples of Christ

Major Events
- 1964 Johnson's War on Poverty begins
- 1964 Civil Rights Act
- 1965 Voting Rights Act
- 1968 Tet Offensive signals turning point in Vietnam War
- 1968 César Chávez protests for migrant workers' rights with his first hunger strike

Richard M. Nixon
(1913-1994)

Years in Office 1969-1974 (resigned)
Vice Presidents Spiro T. Agnew 1969-1973, resigned; Gerald R. Ford 1973-1974
Home State New York
Occupation Lawyer
First Lady Thelma (Pat) Ryan Nixon
Religion Quaker

Major Events
- 1969 U.S. lands first astronauts on the moon
- 1972 Nixon visits communist China
- 1972-1974 Watergate Scandal
- 1973 U.S. troops leave Vietnam

Gerald R. Ford
(1913-   )

Years in Office 1974-1977
Vice President Nelson A. Rockefeller
Home State Michigan
Occupation Lawyer
First Lady Elizabeth (Betty) Bloomer Ford
Religion Episcopalian

Major Events
- 1974 Ford pardons Nixon for Watergate acts
- 1975 *Apollo-Soyuz* joint U.S.-USSR space mission
- 1975 *Viking* sends first close-up photographs of Mars
- 1976 U.S. celebrates Bicentennial

James Earl Carter
(1924-   )

Years in Office 1977-1981
Vice President Walter F. Mondale
Home State Georgia
Occupation Farmer, businessman, navy officer
First Lady Rosalynn Smith Carter
Religion Baptist

Major Events
- 1977 U.S. signs treaty to give Panama Canal Zone to Panama in 2000

- 1979 Carter negotiates peace treaty between Egypt and Israel
- 1979-1981 American hostages held in Iran

Ronald W. Reagan
(1911-   )

Years in Office 1981-1989
Vice President George Bush
Home State California
Occupation Radio announcer, actor, labor union official
First Lady Nancy Davis Reagan
Religion Presbyterian

Major Events
- 1981 Reagan survives assassination attempt
- 1981 Sandra Day O'Connor becomes first woman Supreme Court justice
- 1981 Henry Cisneros becomes first Latino mayor of a major city, San Antonio, TX
- 1982 Vietnam War Memorial, designed by Maya Lin, unveiled
- 1983 U.S. troops invade Grenada
- 1986 Space Shuttle *Challenger* explodes
- 1986-1988 Iran-Contra affair
- 1988-1989 U.S. and USSR sign treaty to reduce nuclear weapons

George Bush
(1924-   )

Years in Office 1989-1993
Vice President J. Danforth (Dan) Quayle
Home State Texas
Occupation Businessman
First Lady Barbara Pierce Bush
Religion Episcopalian

Major Events
- 1989 U.S. troops invade Panama
- 1989 L. Douglas Wilder becomes first African American governor
- 1991 Persian Gulf War
- 1989-1992 Cold War ends
- 1992 NAFTA treaty
- 1992-1994 U.S. troops lead U.N. sponsored peace-keeping force in Somalia

William Jefferson Clinton
(1946-   )

Years in Office 1993-
Vice President Albert Gore, Jr.
Home State Arkansas
Occupation Law professor, attorney
First Lady Hillary Rodham Clinton
Religion Baptist

Major Events
- 1994 U.S. troops restore democratically elected government in Haiti
- 1995 U.S. troops take part in peacekeeping mission in Bosnia
- 1995 A bomb explodes in a federal building in Oklahoma City, Oklahoma, killing 162 people
- 1996 Astronaut Shannon Lucid ends a 188-day stay in space— longer than any other woman
- 1997 *Sojourner* spacecraft lands on Mars
- 1998 John Glenn, at age 77, returns to space aboard the space shuttle *Discovery*
- 1998 Clinton becomes the first elected U.S. President to be impeached by the House of Representatives

Sources: *New Columbia Encyclopedia*, 1975; *The Complete Book of U.S. Presidents*, 1993; *World Almanac*, 1995.

PEOPLES OF THE AMERICAS

NATIVE AMERICANS

| 1500 | 1550 | 1600 |

1500
The Aztec civilization is at its peak in what is now Mexico; the Inca empire stretches along the west coast of South America.

1570
The Peace Maker and Hiawatha develop the Great Laws of the Iroquois Confederacy of the Eastern Woodlands.

1609
The Lenape welcome Henry Hudson as he and his crew sail up the Hudson River. Hudson is amazed at their huge stores of crops.

SPANISH

| 1500 | 1550 | 1600 |

← **1492**
Spanish ships led by the Italian Christopher Columbus carry the first Europeans to reach the Americas in 500 years.

1542
Juan Rodríguez Cabrillo sets out to explore California.

1565
Spain founds its first permanent settlement north of Mexico at St. Augustine, Florida.

1598–1605
Don Juan de Oñate explores much of the land between the present-day states of California and Kansas.

FRENCH/DUTCH

| 1500 | 1550 | 1600 |

1534
Jacques Cartier claims land for the French along the St. Lawrence River. He names the land *Canada*, after the Huron word for "village."

1626
Peter Minuit buys Manhattan Island and founds the city of New Amsterdam for the Dutch.

ENGLISH

| 1500 | 1550 | 1600 |

1585
English colonists establish their first settlement at Roanoke Island.

1607
Captain John Smith founds the Jamestown colony in Virginia.

1620
The Pilgrims sign the Mayflower Compact before they set ashore at Cape Cod.

TIME LINE

1500 TO 1750

1650 — **1700** — **1750**

1680
Popé leads the Pueblo Revolt against the Spanish in New Mexico.

1740
The Tlingit of Alaska trade furs with Russian, French, Spanish, and English traders.

1650 — **1700** — **1750**

1769
Father Junípero Serra founds San Diego, the first Spanish mission in California.

1650 — **1700** — **1750**

1673
French explorers Marquette and Jolliet reach the Mississippi River.

1763
After the French and Indian War, France gives up almost all of its North American claims to Britain.

1725
French trappers in New France trade with the Huron, Chippewa, and Ottawa.

1650 — **1700** — **1750**

1682
William Penn makes a land treaty with the Lenape, and founds the colony of Pennsylvania.

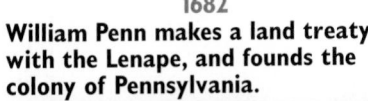

1732
James Oglethorpe founds Georgia, the last of the 13 English Colonies.

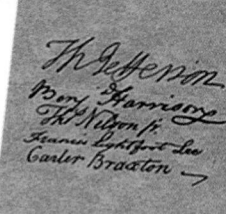

1776
Thomas Jefferson writes the Declaration of Independence.

A YOUNG NATION

NORTHEAST

1800 — 1810 — 1820

1790
All 13 states ratify the
United States
Constitution.

1812
The USS *Constitution* sinks a
British warship in one of the
first battles of the War of 1812.

1825
New York governor
DeWitt Clinton com-
pletes the Erie Canal,
connecting Lake Erie
to the Hudson River.

SOUTHEAST

1800 — 1810 — 1820

1810
Plantations in the South become
increasingly wealthy producing cotton
with the newly invented cotton gin.

MIDDLE WEST

1800 — 1810 — 1820

1803
President Thomas Jefferson purchases
Louisiana from France for $15 million,
doubling the size of the United States.

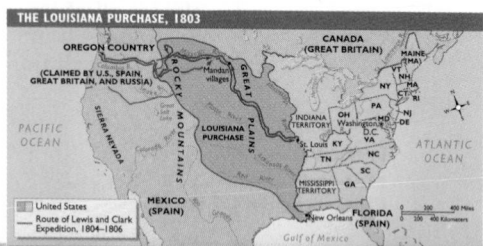

THE LOUISIANA PURCHASE, 1803

1811–1813
The Shawnee chief Tecumseh
travels thousands of miles
trying to form a Native
American confederacy.

1820
The Missouri
Compromise is
passed, keeping
the balance of
free and slave
states in
Congress.

WEST & SOUTHWEST

1800 — 1810 — 1820

1805
With some help from
Sacajawea and the
Shoshone, Lewis and
Clark reach the
Pacific Ocean.

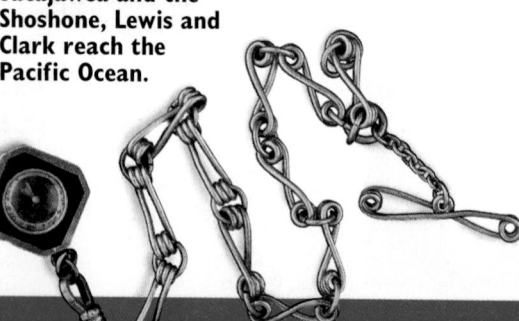

1821
Inspired by Miguel
Hidalgo, Mexicans
gain independence
from Spain—Texas
and California
become part of
Mexico.

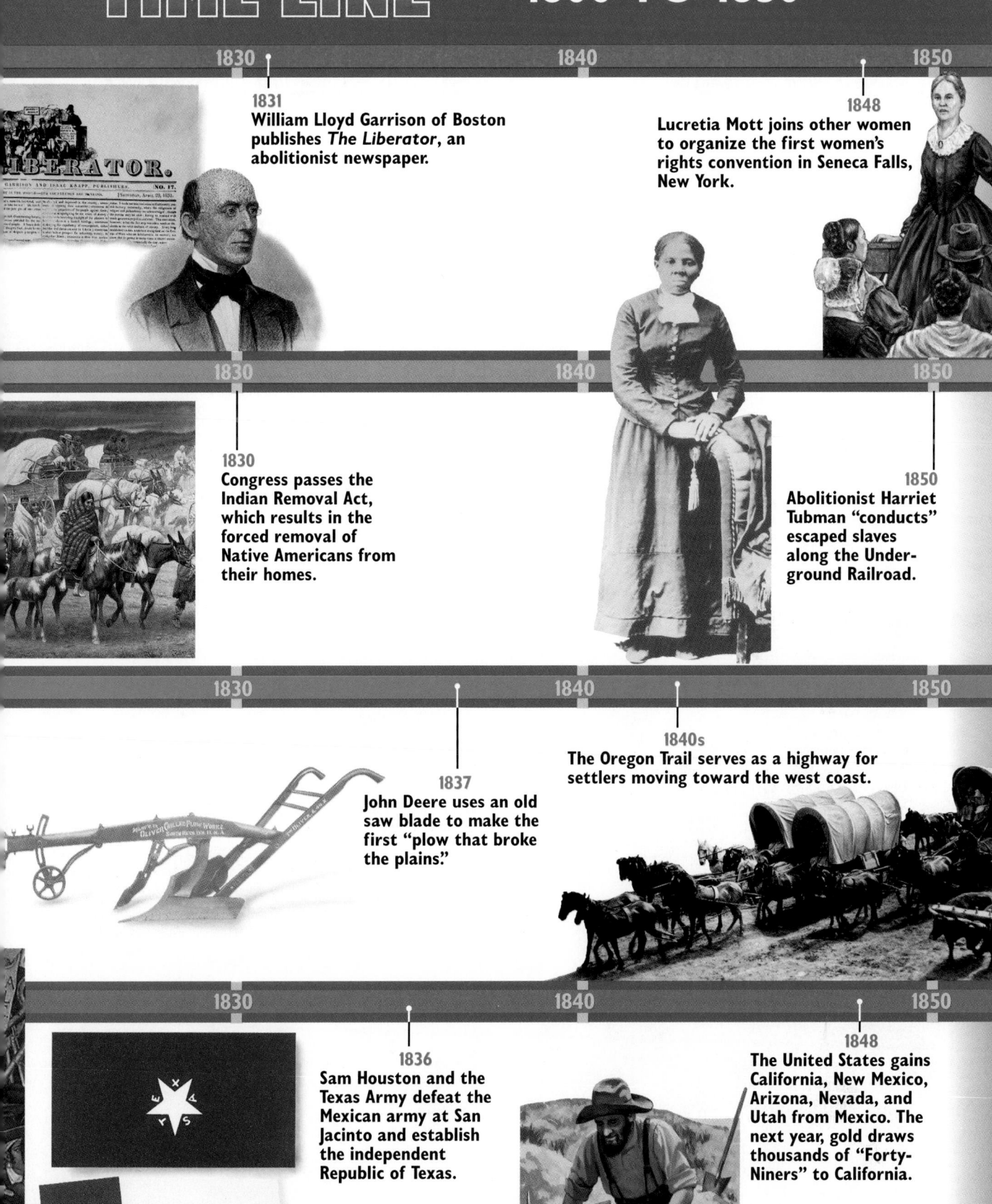

1830   **1840**   **1850**

1831
William Lloyd Garrison of Boston publishes *The Liberator*, an abolitionist newspaper.

1848
Lucretia Mott joins other women to organize the first women's rights convention in Seneca Falls, New York.

1830
Congress passes the Indian Removal Act, which results in the forced removal of Native Americans from their homes.

1850
Abolitionist Harriet Tubman "conducts" escaped slaves along the Underground Railroad.

1837
John Deere uses an old saw blade to make the first "plow that broke the plains."

1840s
The Oregon Trail serves as a highway for settlers moving toward the west coast.

1836
Sam Houston and the Texas Army defeat the Mexican army at San Jacinto and establish the independent Republic of Texas.

1848
The United States gains California, New Mexico, Arizona, Nevada, and Utah from Mexico. The next year, gold draws thousands of "Forty-Niners" to California.

Dictionary of GEOGRAPHIC TERMS

STRAIT (strāt) A narrow water-way that connects two larger bodies of water.

GULF (gulf) Part of an ocean that extends into the land; larger than a bay.

PLATEAU (pla tō′) An area of elevated flat land.

DAM (dam) A wall built across a river, creating a lake that stores water.

RESERVOIR (rez′ər vwär) A natural or artificial lake used to store water.

CANYON (kan′yən) A deep, narrow valley with steep sides.

MESA (mā′sə) A hill with a flat top; smaller than a plateau.

DUNE (dün) A mound, hill, or ridge of sand heaped up by the wind.

HILL (hil) A rounded, raised landform; not as high as a mountain.

BUTTE (būt) A small, flat-topped hill; smaller than a mesa or plateau.

VALLEY (val′ē) An area of low land between hills or mountains.

DESERT (dez′ərt) A dry environment with few plants and animals.

COAST (kōst) The land along an ocean.

BAY (bā) Part of an ocean or lake that extends deeply into the land.

ISTHMUS (is′məs) A narrow strip of land that connects two larger bodies of land.

ISLAND (ī′lənd) A body of land completely surrounded by water.

PENINSULA (pə nin′sə lə) A body of land nearly surrounded by water.

VOLCANO (vol kā'nō) An opening in Earth's surface through which hot rock and ash are forced out.

MOUNTAIN (moun'tən) A high landform with steep sides; higher than a hill.

PEAK (pēk) The top of a mountain.

HARBOR (här'bər) A sheltered place along a coast where boats dock safely.

GLACIER (glā'shər) A huge sheet of ice that moves slowly across the land.

CANAL (kə nal') A channel built to carry water for irrigation or navigation.

LAKE (lāk) A body of water completely surrounded by land.

PORT (pôrt) A place where ships load and unload their goods.

TRIBUTARY (trib'yə ter ē) A smaller river that flows into a larger river.

SOURCE (sôrs) The starting point of a river.

TIMBERLINE (tim'bər lin) A line beyond which trees do not grow.

RIVER BASIN (riv'ər bā'sin) All the land that is drained by a river and its tributaries.

WATERFALL (wô'tər fôl) A flow of water falling vertically.

MOUNTAIN RANGE (moun'tən rānj) A row or chain of mountains.

PLAIN (plān) A large area of nearly flat land.

RIVER (riv'ər) A stream of water that flows across the land and empties into another body of water.

BASIN (bā'sin) A bowl-shaped landform surrounded by higher land.

DELTA (del'tə) Land made of silt left behind as a river drains into a larger body of water.

MOUTH (mouth) The place where a river empties into a larger body of water.

MOUNTAIN PASS (moun'tən pas) A narrow gap through a mountain range.

OCEAN (ō'shən) A large body of salt water; oceans cover much of Earth's surface.

R63

Gazetteer

This Gazetteer is a geographical dictionary that will help you to pronounce and locate the places discussed in this book. Latitude and longitude are given for cities and some other places. The page numbers tell you where each place appears on a map or in the text.

A

Africa (af′ri kə) One of Earth's seven continents. (m. G5, 111, t. 110–113)

Alamo, The (al′ə mō) A mission in San Antonio, Texas, where Mexican troops defeated Texan defenders in 1836; 30°N, 98°W. (t. 476)

Angel Island (ān′jəl i′lənd) An island in San Francisco Bay, California, which served as the West Coast entry point for immigrants from the 1880s to the early 1920s; 38°N, 122°W. (t. 545)

Antarctica (ant ärk′ti kə) One of Earth's seven continents. (m. G5, 149, t. G4)

Antarctic Circle (ant ärk′tik sûr′kəl) A line of latitude at 66°33'S. (m. 149)

Appalachian Mountains (ap ə lā′chē ən moun′tənz) Chain of mountains stretching from Canada to Alabama. (m. 33, 231, t. 230)

Appomattox Court House (ap ə mat′əks kôrt hous) A town in central Virginia, where Confederate General Lee surrendered to Union General Grant in 1865, ending the Civil War; 37°N, 79°W. (t. 523)

Arctic Circle (ärk′tik sûr′kəl) A line of latitude at 66° 30'N. (m. 149, t. 162)

Arctic Ocean (ärk′tik ō′shən) The smallest of Earth's four oceans. (m. G5, t. G4)

Asia (ā′zhə) The largest of Earth's seven continents. (m. G5, 106, t. G4, 104–107)

Atlantic Ocean (at lan′tik ō′shən) One of Earth's four oceans. (m. G4, t. G4)

B

Bahama Islands (bə hä′mə i′ləndz) A chain of islands in the West Indies, east of Florida. (m. 133, t. 135)

Baltimore (bôl′tə môr) The largest city in Maryland and a port on Chesapeake Bay; 39°N, 77°W. (m. 249, t. 426)

Bering Strait (ber′ing strāt) A narrow waterway connecting the Bering Sea and the Arctic Ocean. (m. R6, t. 61)

Beringia (bə rin′jē ə) A sunken land bridge that once connected North America and Asia. It is now the Bering Strait; 62°N, 167°W. (t. 61)

Black Hills (blak hilz) A mountain range in southwestern South Dakota and northeastern Wyoming. (m. 32, t. 88)

Boonesborough (bünz′bər ə) A town in east-central Kentucky, now Boonesboro; site of fort founded in 1775 by Daniel Boone; 38°N, 84°W. (m. 412, t. 414)

Boston (bôs′tən) Capital and largest city of Massachusetts; 42°N, 71°W. (m. 193, t. 193)

Boswash (bôs′wôsh) Unofficial name given to the megalopolis of cities running south from Boston, Massachusetts, to Washington, D.C. (m. 34, t. 34)

Brazil (brə zil′) The largest country in South America, in the eastern part of the continent. (m. R12, t. 142)

C

Cahokia (kə hō′kē ə) A city founded around 1,300 years ago by mound-building peoples near the Mississippi River, in present-day Illinois; 38°N, 90°W. (m. 61, t. 60)

California Trail (kal ə fôr′nyə trāl) A trail to the California gold fields used by "Forty-Niners" in 1849. (m. 485, t. 494)

Canada (kan′ə də) A country in northern North America, bordering the United States. It is made up of ten provinces and two territories. (m. 308, t. 306)

Cape Cod (kāp kod) A peninsula in southeastern Massachusetts, enclosing Cape Cod Bay. (m. 177, t. 175)

Cape of Good Hope (kāp əv gùd hōp) The southernmost tip of Africa; 34°S, 18°E. (m. 120, t. 121)

Caribbean Sea (kar ə bē′ən sē) A part of the Atlantic Ocean, due east of Central America. (m. 133, 136, t. 137)

pronunciation key

a	at	i	ice	u	up	th	thin
ā	ape	îr	pierce	ū	use	th	this
ä	far	o	hot	ü	rule	zh	measure
âr	care	ō	old	ù	pull	ə	about, taken,
e	end	ô	fork	ûr	turn		pencil, lemon,
ē	me	oi	oil	hw	white		circus
i	it	ou	out	ng	song		

Cascade Range (kas kād′ rānj) A mountain range extending from northern California through Oregon and Washington. (m. G10)

Central America (sen′trəl ə mer′i kə) A region occupying the southern part of the North American continent south of Mexico. (m. 136, t. 60)

Charleston (chärlz′tən) A coastal city in southeastern South Carolina, originally Charles Town; 33°N, 80°W. (m. 33, t. 521)

Charlestown (chärlz′taun) A town in Massachusetts across the Charles River from Boston; the Battle of Bunker Hill was fought near there in 1775; 42°N, 71°W. (m. 337, 368, t. 340)

Chesapeake Bay (ches′ə pēk bā) A long arm of the Atlantic Ocean surrounded by Maryland and Virginia. (m. 33, t. 166)

Chicago (shi kä′gō) A city in northeastern Illinois, the largest city in the state, a transportation and manufacturing center; 42°N, 88°W. (m. R5, t. 309)

China (chī′nə) A country in eastern Asia, the most populous in the world. (m. 106, t. 104–107)

Coast Ranges (kōst rānj′əz) The mountain ranges along the Pacific Coast of North America. (m. G10)

Columbia River (kə lum′bē ə riv′ər) A river in northwestern North America which flows between Oregon and Washington into the Pacific Ocean. (m. G10, t. 421)

Concord (kong′kərd) A town in eastern Massachusetts, site of one of the first battles of the American Revolution; 42°N, 71°W. (m. 337, 368, t. 337)

Conestoga Valley (kän ə stō gə) A valley in southeastern Pennsylvania where the Conestoga Wagon was invented. (t. 235)

Continental Divide (kon′tə nen′təl di vīd′) An elevation of land that runs along the tops of the Rocky Mountains. Rivers to the west drain into the Pacific Ocean and rivers to the east drain into the Atlantic Ocean or Gulf of Mexico. (m. 30, t. 30)

Corn Belt (kôrn belt) An area of the Middle West well-suited to growing corn. (m. 32, t. 32)

Cuba (kū′bə) An island country in the Caribbean Sea, the largest and westernmost of the West Indies. (m. 133, 144, t. 144)

Cumberland Gap (kum′bər lənd gap) A natural pass through the Cumberland Mountains, of Kentucky. 37°N, 84°W. (m. 412, t. 413)

D

Death Valley (deth val′ē) The lowest point in the Western Hemisphere, part of the Mojave Desert in California; 37°N, 117°W. (m. 30, t. 37)

Detroit (di troit′) An important manufacturing center in southeastern Michigan; 42°N, 83°W. (m. 308, t. 309)

District of Columbia (dis′trikt uv kə lum′bē ə) An area encompassing the capital of the United States; 39°N, 77°W. (m. 419, t. 416)

E

Eastern Hemisphere (ēs′tərn hem′is fêr) The half of Earth that lies east of the Prime Meridian (0° longitude) and west of 180° longitude. (m. G5, t. G4)

El Camino Real (el cä mē′nō rā äl) A number of routes that connected Spain's colonies in the American Southwest to Mexico from the late 1500s to the middle 1800s. (m. 302, t. 299)

England (ing′glənd) A part of the United Kingdom. England occupies the southern part of the island of Great Britain. (m. R11, t. 166)

equator (i kwā′tər) An imaginary line encircling Earth halfway between the North Pole and the South Pole, designated as 0° latitude. (m. G4, t. G4)

Erie Canal (ir′ē kə nal′) A human-made waterway across New York State, connecting the Hudson River with Lake Erie. (m. 449, t. 451)

Europe (yùr′əp) One of seven continents, between Asia and the Atlantic Ocean. (m. G5, 120, t. 114–121)

F

Florida Keys (flōr′i də kēz) A chain of small islands off the southern coast of Florida. (m. 33)

Fort Duquesne (fôrt dù kān′) A fort built by the French in 1754 where Pittsburgh stands today. (t. 315)

Fort Laramie (fôrt lar′ ə mē) In present-day Wyoming, the sight of the treaty of Fort Laramie between the United States government and Native American chiefs from the region. (m. 485, t. 490)

Fort Necessity (fôrt nə ses′i tē) A temporary fort built 60 miles south of Fort Duquesne in 1754 by troops under George Washington's command; 40°N, 80°W. (t. 315)

Fort Orange (fôrt or′ inj) A fort built by the Dutch on the Hudson River that later became Albany. 42°N, 73°W (m. 219, t. 219)

Fort Sumter (fôrt səm′tər) A fort guarding the entrance to Charleston Harbor, South Carolina; site of the first battle of the Civil War; 33°N, 80°W. (t. 521)

Fort Ticonderoga (fôrt tī kon də rō′gə) A fort on Lake Champlain, New York; site of important battles in the American Revolution; 44°N, 74°W. (m. 368, t. 340)

Fort Vincennes (fôrt vin senz′) A fort on the site of present-day Vincennes, Indiana; 39°N, 88°W. (m. 368, t. 365)

Gazetteer

Four Corners (fôr kôr′nərz) The place at which the states of Arizona, New Mexico, Utah, and Colorado meet; 37°N, 109°W. (m. 61, t. 64)

France (frans) A country in western Europe. (m. R11, t. 306)

Frankfort (frangk′fərt) Capital of Kentucky; 38°N, 85°W. (m. 33)

G

Gao (gou) In the 1400s, the capital of the African kingdom of Songhai; 16°N, 0°W. (m. 111, t. 112)

Grand Canyon (grand kan′yən) A vast and richly colored canyon on the Colorado River in northwestern Arizona. (m. 31, t. 31)

Great Lakes (grāt lāks) A group of five large lakes in North America between Canada and the United States. The Great Lakes are Lake Superior, Lake Michigan, Lake Huron, Lake Erie, and Lake Ontario. (m. G9, 308, t. 92)

Great Salt Lake (grāt sôlt lāk) A lake in northwestern Utah, the largest salt lake in North America; 41°N, 113°W. (m. 30, t. 486)

Great Wall (grāt wôl) A fortified barrier of stone and earth that winds continuously over 1,500 miles in northern China. (m. 106, t. 105)

Gulf of Mexico (gulf əv mek′si kō) An arm of the Atlantic Ocean, between the United States and Mexico. (m. 136)

H

Harlem (här′ləm) A district of New York City, on Manhattan Island. (t. 544)

Hispaniola (his pən yō′la) An island in the Greater Antilles, in the Caribbean. (m. 133)

Hodenosaunee Trail (hō den ō sä′nē trāl) A 250-mile path connecting the homelands of five Iroquois peoples in the 1500s. (m. 94, t. 94)

Hudson Bay (hud′sən bā) A large inland sea in northeastern Canada. (m. R9, 316)

Hudson River (hud′sən riv′ər) A river in New York that empties into the Atlantic Ocean. (m. 219, t. 163)

Hudson River valley (hud′ sən riv′ər val′ ē) A valley on either side of the Hudson River in New York. (m. 219, t. 219)

I

India (in′dē ə) A large peninsular country in southern Asia. (m. 106, t. 106)

Indian Ocean (in′dē ən ō′shən) One of Earth's four oceans. (m. G5, t. G4)

Indian Territory (in′dē ən ter′i tôr ē) Land set aside by the Indian Removal Act of 1830 as a place for Native Americans forced from their homelands. (m. 468, t. 466)

Italy (it′ə lē) A country in southern Europe. (R11, t. 114)

J

Jamestown (jāmz′toun) A town in southeastern Virginia; first permanent English settlement in North America, founded in 1607; 37°N, 77°W. (m. 249, t. 168–171)

Jenne (je nā′) A city located on the Niger River in present-day Mali, in Africa; 14°N, 5°W. (m. 111, t. 111)

Jerusalem (jə rü′ sə ləm) A city in present-day Israel considered holy by Jews, Muslims, and Christians; 31°N, 35°E. (t. 115)

Juneau (jü′nō) Capital of Alaska; 58°N, 135°W. (m. 30)

K

Klamath River (klam′ əth ri′ vər) A river that runs from southern Oregon through northern California and empties into the Pacific Ocean. (t. 74)

L

Lake Erie (lāk îr′ē) The southernmost of the Great Lakes, bordering Canada and the United States. (m. G9, t. 450)

Lake Huron (lāk hyùr′ən) Second-largest of the Great Lakes, bordering Canada and the United States. (m. G9)

Lake Michigan (lāk mish′i gən) Third-largest of the Great Lakes, between Michigan and Wisconsin. (m. G9)

Lake Ontario (lāk on târ′ē ō) The smallest of the Great Lakes, bordering Canada and the United States. (m. G9)

Lake Superior (lāk sə pîr′ē ər) The largest of the Great Lakes, bordering Canada and the United States. (m. G9)

Lancaster County (lan′ kə stər koun′ tē) A county in southeastern Pennsylvania and birthplace of the Kentucky Rifle. (t. 235)

Latin America (lat′in ə mer′i kə) The part of the Western Hemisphere south of the United States—including Mexico, Central America, South America, and the West Indies. (m. R10, t. 549–550)

Lexington (lek′sing tən) A town in eastern Massachusetts, site of one of the first battles of the American Revolution; 42°N, 71°W. (m. 337, 368, t. 337)

Los Angeles (läs an′jə ləs) A city in southwestern California, the largest city in the state, the second largest city in the United States; 34°N, 118°W. (m. R4, t. 303)

Lowell (lō′əl) A city in northeastern Massachusetts; 42°N, 71°W. (t. 444)

M

Manhattan Island (man hat′ ən ī′ lənd) An island in southeastern New York and borough of New York City. 41°N, 74°W (m. 219, t. 219)

Mesa Verde (mā′sə vərd′ē) The name given an Anasazi village built around A.D. 900 in present-day Colorado; 57°N, 108°W. (m. 61, t. 64)

Mexico (mek′si kō) A North American country on the southern border of the United States. (m. 152, t. 150)

Mexico City (mek′si kō sit′ē) Capital and largest city in Mexico, the second largest city in the world; 19°N, 99°W. (m. 152, t. 150)

Middle Colonies (mid′əl kol′ə nēz) The name given to the English colonies of Delaware, New Jersey, New York, and Pennsylvania. (m. 222, t. 216–239)

Mississippi River (mis ə sip′ē riv′ər) A river in the central United States, flowing from Minnesota to the Gulf of Mexico; the longest river in the United States. (m. G9, t. 33)

Missouri River (mi zùr′ē riv′ər) A large tributary of the Mississippi, flowing from Montana to the Mississippi River north of St. Louis. (m. 419, t. 420)

Mojave Desert (mō hä′vē dez′ərt) A desert in southeastern California; 35°N, 117°W. (m. R6, t. 37)

Monticello (mänt ə sel′ō) The home designed by Thomas Jefferson, southeast of Charlottesville, Virginia; 38°N, 78°W. (t. 350)

Mormon Trail (môr′mən trāl) A route west named for the 20,000 Mormons who migrated from Nauvoo, Illinois, between 1837 and 1847. (m. 485, t. 486)

Mother Lode Country (muth′ ər lōd kun′ trē) The western face of the Sierra Nevada where the richest deposits of gold were found in the 1850s. (t. 494)

Mount McKinley (mount mə kin′lē) The highest mountain in North America, elevation 20,320 feet (6,194 m), located in south-central Alaska; also known as Denali, or "Great One"; 64°N, 153°W. (m. R6)

Mount Vernon (mount vûr′nən) The Virginia home and burial place of George Washington, on the Potomac River; 39°N, 77°W. (t. 358)

Mount Whitney (mount hwit′nē) The highest mountain in the contiguous United States, elevation 14,494 (4,418 m), located in California; 37°N, 118°W. (m. R6)

N

National Road (nash′ə nəl rōd) A road built in the first half of the 1800s. It ran from Maryland to the Mississippi River. (m. 449, t. 448)

New Amsterdam (nü am′stər dam) An early Dutch settlement in New Netherland, on the site of present-day New York City; 41°N, 74°W. (m. 219, t. 219)

New England (nü ing′glənd) Northeastern region of the United States, containing the states of Maine, Vermont, New Hampshire, Massachusetts, Connecticut, and Rhode Island. (m. 193, t. 190–215)

New France (nü frans) French possessions in North America during colonial times. It included large parts of what are now Canada and the United States. (m. 308, t. 306–313)

New Netherland (nü neth′ər lənd) A Dutch colony in North America from 1609 to 1664 that included parts of present-day New York, New Jersey, and Connecticut. (m. 219, t. 218–223)

New Orleans (nü ôr′lē ənz) A city in southern Louisiana, largest in the state and a major port; 30°N, 90°W. (m. R5, t. 316)

New Spain (nü spān) Colonial lands held by Spain, mainly in North America. New Spain included parts of what are now the United States, Mexico, Central America, and islands in the West Indies. (m. 152, t. 150–155)

New Sweden (nü swē′dən) A Swedish colony along the Delaware River from 1638 to 1664 in what are now New Jersey, Pennsylvania, and Delaware. (m. 219, t. 220)

New York City (nü yôrk sit′ē) The largest city in the United States, located in southeastern New York State; 41°N, 74°W. (m. 222, t. 223)

North America (nôrth ə mer′i kə) The third-largest of Earth's seven continents. It includes Canada, Central America, Mexico, the West Indies and the United States. (m. G4, G5, t. G4)

Northern Hemisphere (nôr′thərn hem′i sfîr) The half of Earth north of the equator. (m. G5, t. G4)

North Pole (nôrth pōl) The northernmost point on Earth; the northern end of Earth's axis; 90°N. (m. G4, G5, t. G4)

Northwest Territory (nôrth west′ ter′i tôr ē) The land organized as a territory in 1787, including what became the states of Indiana, Wisconsin, Ohio, Michigan, and Illinois. (m. 386, t. 386)

pronunciation key

a **at**; ā **ape**; ä **far**; âr **care**; e **end**; ē **me**; i **it**; ī **ice**; îr **pierce**; o **hot**; ō **old**; ô **fork**; oi **oil**; ou **out**; u **up**; ū **use**; ü **rule**, ù **pull**; ûr **turn**; hw **white**; ng **song**; th **thin**; th **this**; zh **measure**; ə **about, taken, pencil, lemon, circus**

Gazetteer

O

Ohio River (ō hī′ō riv′ər) A river in the east-central United States, flowing from Pennsylvania, southwest into the Mississippi River. (m. 32, 316, t. 315)

Ohio River valley (ō hī′ō riv′ər val′ē) The region along the banks of the Ohio River. (m. 316, t. 315)

Old Oraibi (ōld ō rä ē′bē) A pueblo in Arizona inhabited by the Hopi for about 800 years, one of the oldest continuously populated settlements in the United States; 36°N, 111°W. (t. 81)

Oregon Territory (or′i gən ter′i tōr ē) The area of the Western region of the United States during the middle 1800s. It comprised all or parts of what are now the states of Oregon, Washington, Idaho, Wyoming, and Montana. (m. 485, t. 480–483)

Oregon Trail (ôr′i gən trāl) A route west used by pioneers in the 1840s that stretched from Independence, Missouri, to northwestern Oregon. (m. 485, t. 482)

P

Pacific Ocean (pə sif′ik ō′shən) The largest of Earth's four oceans. (m. G4, G5, t. G4)

Persia (pûr′zhə) An ancient empire in southwest Asia centered in what is now the country of Iran. (m. 106, t. 105)

Philadelphia (fil ə del′fē ə) A city in southeastern Pennsylvania; the largest city in the state. From 1790 to 1800 it was the capital of the United States; 40°N, 75°W. (m. R5, t. 227)

Piedmont (pēd′ mänt) A plateau stretching through the Middle and Southern Colonies. (t. 249)

Pikes Peak (piks pēk) A mountain in the Rocky Mountains, in east-central Colorado, elevation 14,110 (4,301 m); 39°N, 105°W. (m. R6)

Plymouth (plim′əth) A town in southeastern Massachusetts, founded by the Pilgrims in 1620; 42°N, 71°W. (m. 177, t. 177)

Portsmouth (pôrts′məth) A town in southeastern Rhode Island founded in 1637 by Anne Hutchinson; 43°N, 71°W. (m. 193, t. 203)

Portugal (pôr′chə gəl) A country in southwestern Europe. (m. 120, t. 120)

Prime Meridian (prīm mə rid′ē ən) The meridian, or line of longitude, that passes through Greenwich, England, and from which longitudes east and west are measured; 0° longitude. (m. G5, t. 40)

Providence (prov′i dəns) Capital and largest city of Rhode Island; 42°N, 71°W. (m. 34, t. 202)

Pueblo Bonito (pweb′lō bə nē′tō) An Anasazi village that flourished from about A.D. 950 to 1300, located in what is now northwestern New Mexico; 36°N, 108°W. (m. 59, t. 56–57)

Puget Sound (pū′jit sound) An arm of the Pacific Ocean, extending into the northwestern part of Washington state. (m. G10)

Q

Quebec (kwi bek′) The largest province of Canada in the eastern part of the country; also the capital city of this province; 47°N, 71°W. (m. 308, t. 307)

R

Richmond (rich′mənd) Capital of Virginia; Confederate capital from 1861 to 1865; 38°N, 78°W. (m. 33)

Rio Grande (rē′ō grand′) A river in southwestern North America, flowing from Colorado into the Gulf of Mexico. It forms part of the border between the United States and Mexico. (m. R6, 478, t. 478)

Roanoke Island (rō′ə nōk ī′lənd) An island off the coast of North Carolina, the site of the "Lost Colony" founded by Sir Walter Raleigh in 1587; 36°N, 76°W. (m. 167, t. 167)

Rocky Mountains (rok′ē moun′tənz) A high, rugged mountain chain in western North America stretching from Alaska into Mexico. (m. 30, t. 30)

S

Sacramento (sak rə men′tō) Capital of California; 39°N, 122°W. (m. G6)

Sahara (sə har′ə) The largest desert in the world, stretching across most of North Africa. (m. 111, t. 110)

St. Augustine (sānt ô′gə stēn) A port city in northeast Florida; the oldest city in the United States, founded by the Spanish in 1565; 30°N, 81°W. (m. 164, t. 299)

St. Lawrence River (sānt lôr′əns riv′ər) A river in eastern North America between the United States and Canada, flowing from Lake Ontario into the Atlantic Ocean. (m. 308, t. 306)

St. Louis (sānt lü′is) A city in Missouri located near the joining of the Missouri and the Mississippi rivers; 39°N, 90°W. (m. 308, t. 309)

Salem (sā′ləm) A city in Massachusetts settled in 1626 and the scene of the Salem witch trials in 1692. 42°N, 71°W (m. 193, t. 205)

Salt Lake City (sôlt lāk sit′ē) Capital and largest city of Utah; 41°N, 112°W. (m. 485, t. 486)

San Diego (san dē ā′gō) A port city in southern California; 33°N, 117°W. (m. G6, t. 302)

San Francisco (san frən sis′kō) A city in west-central California; 38°N, 122°W. (m. G6, 302, t. 303)

San Jacinto River (san jə sint′ō riv′ər) A river in southeastern Texas that flows into Galveston Bay. (t. 476)

San Salvador (san sal′və dôr) Capital and largest city of El Salvador; 14°N, 89°W (m. 661, t. 650) Also one of the Bahama Islands, also known as Watling Island. It is believed to be the site of Columbus's first landing in North America, in 1492; 24°N, 75°W. (m. 136, t. 135)

Santa Fe (san′tə fā′) Capital of New Mexico; 35°N, 106°W. (m. 302, t. 299)

Saratoga (sar ə tō′gə) Site in northeastern New York of an important Patriot victory in the Revolutionary War; 43°N, 75°W. (m. 368, t. 360)

Savannah (sə van′ə) A port city in southeastern Georgia, site of important battles in the American Revolution; 32°N, 81°W. (m. 249, 368, t. 246)

Schuylkill River (skül′ kil ri′ vər) A 130-mile long river in southeastern Pennsylvania that runs into the Delaware at Philadelphia. (t. 227)

Seneca Falls (sen′i kə fôlz) A village in west-central New York, site of the first women's rights convention in the United States, in 1848; 43°N, 77°W. (t. 546)

Sierra Nevada (sē er′ə nə vad′ə) A mountain range in eastern California. (m. 532, t. 27)

Silk Road (silk rōd) An ancient network of overland trade routes that stretched from China to what is now Iran. (m. 106, t. 105)

Sitka (sit′kə) A city on Baranof Island, Alaska, in the Alexander chain of islands; 57°N, 135°W. (m. 59, t. 72)

Snake River (snāk riv′ər) A river in the northwestern United States that flows into the Columbia River. (m. 419, t. 421)

Songhai (sông′hī) A powerful and wealthy kingdom that ruled a large part of West Africa in the 1400s. (m. 111, t. 110–113)

South America (south ə mer′i kə) One of Earth's seven continents. (m. G4, G5, t. 151)

Southern Colonies (suth′ərn kol′ə nēz) The name given to the English colonies of Georgia, Maryland, North Carolina, South Carolina, and Virginia. (m. 249, t. 242)

Southern Hemisphere (suth′ərn hem′i sfîr) The half of Earth that lies south of the equator. (m. G5, t. G4)

South Pole (south pōl) The southernmost point on Earth; the southern end of Earth's axis; 90°S. (m. G4, G5, t. G4)

Spain (spān) A country in southwestern Europe. (m. 120, t. 134)

Strait of Magellan (strāt əv mə jel′ən) The narrow waterway between the southern tip of South America and Tierra del Fuego that links the Atlantic Ocean to the Pacific Ocean. (m. 149, t. 149)

Sutter's Mill (su′tərz mil) The sawmill on the American River where gold was discovered in California in 1848, starting the California gold rush; 39°N, 121°W. (m. 473, t. 492)

T

Tenochtitlán (te nōch tē tlän′) The capital of the ancient Aztec empire, on the site of present-day Mexico City; 19°N, 99°W. (m. 61, t. 65)

Tidewater (tīd′ wät ər) A 75-mile wide strip along the Virginia coast that was fertile ground for tobacco farming in the 1600s. (t. 249)

Tikal (ti käl′) An ancient Maya city in northern Guatemala; 17°N, 90°W. (m. 61, t. 62)

Timbuktu (tim buk tü′) A West African city in the present-day country of Mali; 17°N, 03°W. (m. 111, t. 112)

Trenton (tren′tən) Site of an important battle in the American Revolution; 40°N, 75°W. (m. 34, 368, t. 359)

V

Valley Forge (val′ē fōrj) A village in southeastern Pennsylvania where George Washington and his army camped during the harsh winter of 1777–1778; 40°N, 75°W. (m. 368, t. 360)

Vicksburg (viks′ bûrg) A city in west-central Mississippi on the Mississippi River, site of a major Civil War battle; 32°N, 91°W. (t. 522)

W

Washington, D.C. (wô′shing tən) Capital of the United States; 39°N, 77°W. (m. R5, 409, t. 12, 408)

West Indies (west in′dēz) The islands stretching from Florida in North America to Venezuela in South America. (m. 277, t. 275)

Wilderness Road (wil′dər nis rōd) An early road across the Appalachians, between western Virginia and eastern Kentucky. (m. 412, t. 414)

Williamsburg (wil′yəmz bûrg) Colonial capital of Virginia from 1699 to 1779, where the House of Burgesses met; 37°N, 77°W. (m. 249, t. 243)

Y

Yorktown (yôrk′toun) A town in southeastern Virginia, site of the last major battle of the American Revolution; 37°N, 77°W. (m. 368, 373, t. 365, 370)

---

pronunciation key

a **at**; ā **ape**; ä **far**; âr **care**; e **end**; ē **me**; i **it**; ī **ice**; îr **pierce**; o **hot**; ō **old**; ô **fork**; oi **oil**; ou **out**; u **up**; ū **use**; ü **rule**; u **pull**; ûr **turn**; hw **white**; ng **song**; th **thin**; th **this**; zh **measure**; ə **about, taken, pencil, lemon, circus**

Biographical Dictionary

Biographical Dictionary

This Biographical Dictionary tells you about the people you have learned about in this book. The Pronunciation Key tells you how to say their names. The page numbers tell you where each person first appears in the text.

A

Adams, Abigail (ad'əmz), 1744–1818 First Lady to President John Adams. She wrote many letters about the role of women in the new country. (p. 331)

Adams, John (ad'əmz), 1735–1826 Second President of the United States, 1797 to 1801. Member of Continental Congress, Constitutional Convention. (p. 325)

Adams, Samuel (ad'əmz), 1722–1803 Patriot and leader in the American Revolution. He was a member of the Sons of Liberty and a cousin of John Adams. (p. 329)

Addams, Jane (ad'əmz), 1860–1935 Reformer who founded Hull House in Chicago in 1889, the first settlement house in the United States.

Africanus, Leo (lē'ō af ri kā'nəs), 1485–1554 Arab historian from Spain who wrote one of the earliest descriptions of the Songhai kingdom. (p. 112)

Allen, Ethan (al'ən), 1738–1789 Leader of the "Green Mountain Boys," the Vermont militiamen who captured Fort Ticonderoga in the American Revolution. (p. 340)

Allen, Richard (al'ən), 1760–1831 Abolitionist, founded Free African Society, 1787. Helped found first African Methodist Episcopal Church with Absalom Jones. (p. 384)

Anthony, Susan B. (an'thə nē), 1820–1906 A leader in the movement for women's suffrage. (p. 546)

Applegate, Jesse (a' pəl gāt), 1811–1888 Pioneer who led 900 people to Oregon in 1841. (p. 482)

Armistead, James (är'mə sted), 1760–1832 Patriot spy who helped defeat the British general Charles Cornwallis at Yorktown in 1781. (p. 370)

Arnold, Benedict (är'nəld), 1741–1801 General in Continental Army, later traitor to the American Revolution. (p. 361)

Attucks, Crispus (at'əks), 1723?–1770 Patriot, former slave, first person killed in Boston Massacre, 1770. (p. 330)

Austin, Stephen F. (ôs'tən), 1793–1836 Pioneer who led about 300 American families to Texas in 1822. (p. 475)

B

Balboa, Vasco Núñez de (bal bō'ə, väs'kō nu'ñez dā), 1475–1519 Explorer, led first European expedition across Panama to Pacific Ocean, 1513. (p. 146)

Baltimore, Lord (bol tim' ôr), see **Calvert, George**.

Banneker, Benjamin (ban'i kər), 1731–1806 Scientist, writer, planner of District of Columbia; probably first African American hired by federal government. (p. 416)

Beckwourth, James (bek'wûrth), 1798–1866 Runaway slave turned mountain man who found a route through the Sierra Nevada to California in 1850. (p. 481)

Berkeley, Lord John (bərk' lē), 1600s With Sir George Carteret, given the land between the Delaware and Hudson rivers by James, Duke of York in 1665. (p. 223)

Bonaparte, Napoleon (bō'nə pärt, nə pō'lē ən), 1769–1821 Emperor of France who sold the Louisiana Purchase to the United States in 1803. (p. 417)

Boone, Daniel (bün), 1734–1820 Virginia pioneer, trailblazer, nicknamed "the Pathfinder." Guided settlers through Cumberland Gap into Kentucky. (p. 412)

Braddock, Edward (brad'ək), 1695–1755 British general of French and Indian War, died at Battle of Fort Duquesne. (p. 315)

Bradford, William (brad'fərd), 1590–1657 Governor of the Plymouth Colony beginning in 1621. (p. 176)

Bradstreet, Ann (brad'strēt), 1612–1672 First poet in English colonies. (p. 210)

Brant, Joseph (brant), 1742–1807 Mohawk leader, sided with the British in the American Revolution. (p. 371)

Brent, Margaret (brent), 1600?–1671 First woman to own land in Maryland. As a landowner she unsuccessfully sought suffrage in the colony's assembly. (p. 244)

Brown, John (broun), 1800–1859 Abolitionist who led a raid on Harper's Ferry, Virginia, in 1859. (p. 517)

Bruce, Blanche K. (brüs), 1841–1898 The first African American to serve a full term in the United States Senate from 1875 to 1881. (p. 528)

Burgoyne, John (bər goin'), 1722–1792 British general whose defeat at the Battle of Saratoga in 1777 marked a turning point in the American Revolution. (p. 360)

C

Cabeza de Vaca, Álvar Núñez (kä bā'sä dā vä'kä, äl'vär nün' yāz), 1490?–1560? Spanish explorer who was the first to reach Texas. (p. 146)

Cabot, John (kab'ət), 1450?–1498? Italian sea captain in the service of England. First European to explore North America seeking Northwest Passage. (p. 164)

Cabral, Pedro Álvares (kä' bräl), 1467 or 1468–1520 Portuguese explorer who discovered present-day Brazil and claimed it for the Portuguese crown in 1500. (p. 148)

pronunciation key

a	at	ī	ice	u	up	th	thin
ā	ape	îr	pierce	ū	use	th	this
ä	far	o	hot	ü	rule	zh	measure
âr	care	ō	old	ù	pull	ə	about, taken,
e	end	ô	fork	ûr	turn		pencil, lemon,
ē	me	oi	oil	hw	white		circus
i	it	ou	out	ng	song		

Cabrillo, Juan Rodríguez (kä brē′ yō), ?–1543 Portuguese explorer working for Spain, sailed north from west coast of Mexico, landed in San Diego Bay, 1542; continued north up California coast. (p. 152)

Calvert, George (kal vûrt), 1580?–1632 English noble with the title of Lord Baltimore whose son founded Maryland in 1634 as a haven for Catholics. (p. 244)

Carnegie, Andrew (kär′ni gē), 1835–1919 Business leader who developed the steel industry and philanthropist who established many charities. (p. 536)

Carter, Robert "King" (kär′ tûr), 1728–1804 Wealthy owner of 300,000-acre Nomini Hall plantation in Virginia; had 17 children, 1,000 enslaved workers. (p. 258)

Carteret, Sir George (kart′ ə ret), 1610–1690 British naval officer, with Lord John Berkeley, given the land between Hudson and the Delaware by James, Duke of York, 1664. (p. 223)

Carteret, Phillip (kart′ ə ret), 1639–1682 English colonist appointed first governor of New Jersey by his cousin, Sir George, in 1665. (p. 223)

Cartier, Jacques (kär tyä′, zhäk), 1491–1557 French explorer, first European on St. Lawrence River, 1534. (p. 164)

Carver, John (kär′ vûr), 1576–1621 Elected first governor of Plymouth aboard the Mayflower in 1620. (p. 176)

Champlain, Samuel de (sham plān′), 1567–1635 Explorer and founder of Quebec, the first permanent French settlement in North America, in 1608. (p. 307)

Charles I (chärlz), 1600–1649 King of England, gave Puritans a charter for Massachusetts Bay Colony, 1629. (p. 192)

Chavez, Cesar (chä′vez, sā′zär), 1927–1993 A founder of the National Farm Workers Association. (p. 562)

Chisholm, Shirley (chiz′əm), 1924– United States Representative from New York, 1969–1983. First African American woman elected to Congress. (p. 560)

Clark, George Rogers (klärk), 1752–1818 Revolutionary War general and frontier leader who defeated the British at Fort Vincennes in 1779. (p. 365)

Clark, William (klärk), 1770–1838 Explorer of the Louisiana Purchase with Meriwether Lewis. He was the brother of George Rogers Clark. (p. 419)

Clay, Henry (klā), 1777–1852 United States Senator who helped work out the Missouri Compromise in 1820 and the Compromise of 1850. (p. 424)

Clinton, DeWitt (klin′tən), 1769–1828 New York governor, supported building the Erie Canal. (p. 450)

Columbus, Christopher (kə lum′bəs), 1451?–1506 Italian sea captain, explorer. Sailing for Spain, he reached the Americas in 1492 seeking a sea route to Asia. (p. 134)

Cooper, Peter (kü′pər), 1791–1883 New York merchant, invented steam-driven train, the *Tom Thumb*. (p. 452)

Cornwallis, Charles (kôrn wol′is), 1738–1805 British general who surrendered at Yorktown, the last major battle of the American Revolution, in 1781. (p. 367)

Coronado, Francisco de (kôr ə nä′dō), 1510–1554 Spanish explorer of American Southwest, 1540–1542. (p. 152)

Cortés, Hernán (kôr tez′, er nän′), 1485–1547 Spaniard who defeated the Aztec in 1521. (p. 144)

Cotton, John (kot′ ən), 1585–1652 Conservative Puritan minister; "The Patriarch of New England." (p. 207)

Cuauhtémoc (kwä tä′mok), 1495?–1525 Aztec ruler after Moctezuma II's death; led Aztec in battle for Tenochtitlán. (p. 145)

D

Da Gama, Vasco (də gäm′ə, väs′kō), 1460–1524 Portuguese navigator who was the first European to sail from Europe to Asia in 1498. (p. 121)

Davis, Jefferson (dā′vis), 1808–1889 United States Senator who was President of the Confederate States of America from 1861 to 1865. (p. 520)

Dawes, William (dôz′), 1745–1799 Patriot who rode with Paul Revere on April 18, 1775, to warn colonists that British troops were coming. (p. 337)

Deere, John (dîr), 1804–1886 Illinois blacksmith who invented the steel plow in 1837. (p. 446)

De Soto, Hernando (dā sō′tō, er nän′dō), 1500?–1542 Spanish explorer of the Southeast from 1539 to 1542. First European to see the Mississippi River. (p. 147)

Dias, Bartholomeu (dē′əsh, bâr tù lù mā′ù), 1450?–1500 Portuguese ship captain, reached Cape of Good Hope in 1487, opening a Europe–Asia sea route. (p. 121)

Douglass, Frederick (dug′ləs), 1817–1895 Abolitionist writer, attacked slavery by describing his enslavement. (p. 515)

Duke of York, James (dūk əv yôrk) 1633–1701 English leader who took over New Netherland in 1665; king of Great Britain, 1685–1688. (p. 221)

Du Sable, Jean Baptiste Point (dü sä′blə, zhän′ bap tēst′ pwän′), 1745–1818 Haitian fur trader, started a trading post that later became Chicago. (p. 309)

E

Elizabeth I (i liz′ə bəth), 1533–1603 Queen of England during Roanoke colony, defeat of Spanish Armada. (p. 167)

Equiano, Olaudah (i kwē ä′nō, ōl′ə dä), 1750–1797 African who wrote of being kidnapped, enslaved, and transported to North America. (p. 269)

Ericson, Leif (er′ik sən, lēf), 980?–1025? Viking leader who was probably the first European to explore North America, around A.D. 1000. (p. 132)

Estevanico (es tā vä nē′kō), 1500s African scout whose story of "Seven Cities of Gold" convinced Coronado to explore American Southwest, 1540. (p. 152)

F

Ferdinand (fûr′də nand), 1452–1516 King of Spain who, with his wife Queen Isabella, paid for Columbus's voyages to the Americas. (p. 134)

Findley, John (find′lē), 1722–1772? Frontier trader, blazed trails with Daniel Boone over Cumberland Gap. (p. 412)

Forten, Charlotte (fôr′tən), 1837–1914 African American writer who taught freed African Americans in South Carolina during the Civil War. (p. 527)

Franklin, Benjamin (frang′klən), 1706–1790 Writer, scientist, delegate to the Continental Congress, signer of the Declaration of Independence, and delegate to the Constitutional Convention. (p. 282)

Biographical Dictionary

Fray Marcos de Niza (frā mär'kōs dā nē zä), 1500s Roman Catholic priest from Spain, with Coronado on his search for "Seven Cities of Gold." (p. 152)

Frémont, John Charles (frā' môn), 1813–1890 Western explorer who mapped routes for the United States government. (p. 493)

Fulton, Robert (fŭl'tən), 1765–1815 Builder of the first successful steamboat, the *Clermont*, in 1807. (p. 450)

G

Gálvez, Bernardo de (gäl'vāth), 1746–1786 Spanish Governor of Louisiana, Patriot ally in American Revolution. (p. 367)

Garrison, William Lloyd (gar'ə sən), 1805–1879 Abolitionist, founder of newspaper *The Liberator*, 1831. (p. 516)

George III (jôrj), 1738–1820 King of England during the American Revolution. (p. 317)

Gompers, Samuel (gom'pərz), 1850–1924 Union leader, founded American Federation of Labor, 1886. (p. 539)

Grant, Ulysses S. (grant), 1822–1885 The 18th President of the United States from 1869 to 1877. He was Commander of the Union Army from 1864 to 1865. (p. 522)

Greene, Nathanael (grēn), 1742–1786 Patriot general during the American Revolution who forced the British out of Georgia and the Carolinas. (p. 367)

Grimké, Angelina Emily (grim'kē), 1805–1879 Southern abolitionist who, with her sister Sarah, spoke out against slavery. (p. 516)

Grimké, Sarah Moore (grim'kē), 1792–1873, Southern abolitionist who, with her sister Angelina, spoke out against slavery. (p. 516)

Gutenberg, Johannes (gü'tən bûrg, yō hän'əs), 1400?–1468 German printer whose invention of the printing press in 1436 helped spread learning. (p. 116)

H

Hale, Nathan (hāl), 1755–1776 Patriot hanged by the British as a spy in the American Revolution. (p. 356)

Hamilton, Alexander (ham'əl tən), 1757–1804 Delegate to the Constitutional Convention, and first Secretary of the Treasury from 1789 to 1795. (p. 388)

Hammon, Britton (ham' ən), 1700s African American, won his freedom from slavery by becoming a sailor. (p. 279)

Hancock, John (han'kok), 1737–1793 Patriot, president of Continental Congress, 1775–1777. (p. 337)

Harrison, William Henry (har ris' ən), 1773–1841 Ninth President of the United States. (p. 426)

Hays, Mary Ludwig (hāz), 1752–1832 American Patriot; known as "Molly Pitcher." (p. 366)

Henry, Patrick (hen'rē), 1736–1799 Virginia Burgess who encouraged the colonists to fight for their independence from Great Britain. (p. 329)

Henry, Prince (hen'rē), 1394–1460 Prince of Portugal, founded school for sailors; "the Navigator." (p. 120)

Hiawatha (hī ə wä'thə), 1500s A founder of the Iroquois Confederacy in 1570. (p. 96)

Hooker, Thomas (hùk'ər), 1586–1647 Puritan who founded the colony of Connecticut in 1639. (p. 201)

Hoskens, Jane (häs'kənz), 1694–? Indentured servant, autobiography tells of colonial Pennsylvania. (p. 270)

Houston, Sam (hūs'tən), 1793–1863 Leader of Texas army during Texas Revolution and first president of the Republic of Texas, 1836. (p. 476)

Howe, William (hou), 1729–1867 Commander of British forces in American colonies, 1775 to 1778. (p. 347)

Hudson, Henry (hud'sən), ?–1611 English explorer, sought Northwest Passage in North America from 1609 on. (p. 162)

Huerta, Dolores (wer'tä), 1929– A founder of the National Farm Workers Association. (p. 562)

Hutchinson, Anne (huch'ən sən), 1591–1643 Puritan founder of Portsmouth, Rhode Island, 1636. (p. 201)

I

Isabella (iz ə bel'ə), 1451–1504 Queen of Spain who, with her husband King Ferdinand, paid for Columbus's voyages to the Americas. (p. 134)

J

Jackson, Andrew (jak'sən), 1767–1845 Seventh President of the United States from 1829 to 1837. He defeated the British at the Battle of New Orleans during the War of 1812. (p. 426)

James I (jāmz), 1566–1625 King of England who granted the Jamestown Charter. (p. 168)

Jefferson, Thomas (jef'ər sən), 1743–1826 Third President of the United States, 1801–1809; also author of the Declaration of Independence. (p. 349)

Johnson, Andrew (jon'sən), 1808–1875 The 17th President of the United States, 1865–1869. (p. 527)

Jolliet, Louis (jō'lē et), 1645–1700 French explorer who sailed with Jacques Marquette through the Great Lakes and down the Mississippi. (p. 308)

Jones, Absalom (jōnz), 1746–1818 Abolitionist, helped found first African Methodist Episcopal Church, 1816. (p. 457)

Jones, John Paul (jōnz), 1747–1792 American sea captain of *Bonhomme Richard*, defeated British ship *Serapis*, 1779. (p. 365)

Jones, Mary Harris (jōnz), 1830–1930 American labor union leader, fought against child labor, called "Mother Jones." (p. 538)

K

Key, Francis Scott (kē), 1779–1843 Writer of "The Star-Spangled Banner" during the War of 1812. This poem later became the national anthem. (p. 426)

King, Martin Luther, Jr. (king), 1929–1968 Baptist minister, major civil rights leader in 1950s and 1960s. (p. 558)

Knox, Henry (noks), 1750–1806 Revolutionary War officer, helped drive British from Boston, 1776. (p. 347)

Kosciuszko, Thaddeus (kos ē us'kō), 1746–1817 Patriot from Poland, served in Continental Army, 1776–1784. (p. 360)

L

Lafayette, Marquis de (laf ē et', mär kē' də), 1757–1834 French general who joined the Continental Army during the American Revolution. (p. 360)

La Salle, Robert (lə sal'), 1643–1687 French explorer who reached mouth of the Mississippi River in 1682, claimed the Mississippi River valley for France. (p. 309)

Las Casas, Bartolomé de (läs käs´äs, bär tō lō mä´ dä), 1474–1566 Roman Catholic missionary from Spain, opposed the mistreatment of Indians in New Spain. (p. 153)

Lee, Richard Henry (lē), 1732–1794 Virginia planter, patriot, signer of Declaration of Independence. (p. 324)

L'Enfant, Pierre (län fän´, pē yâr´), 1754–1825 French engineer, architect of the District of Columbia. (p. 416)

Lewis, Meriwether (lü´is), 1774–1809 United States Army officer and scout who explored the Louisiana Purchase with William Clark from 1803 to 1806. (p. 419)

Lincoln, Abraham (ling´kən), 1809–1865 The 16th President of the United States, 1861–1865, led the country during the Civil War, wrote the Gettysburg Address, was called the "Great Emancipator." (p. 415)

Locke, John (lok), 1632–1704 English philosopher whose thinking influenced Thomas Jefferson in the writing of the Declaration of Independence. (p. 350)

Lowell, Francis Cabot (lō´əl), 1775–1817 Cloth factory owner, built first power loom in the United States, 1813. (p. 444)

M

Madison, Dolley (mad´ə sən), 1768–1849 First Lady to President James Madison, who saved George Washington's portrait from British forces invading Washington, D. C., during the War of 1812. (p. 426)

Madison, James (mad´ə sən), 1751–1836 Fourth President of the United States from 1809 to 1817 and author of *The Federalist Papers*. He was known as the "Father of the Constitution" because of his influence at the Constitutional Convention. (p. 388)

Magellan, Ferdinand (mə jel´ən, fûr´də nand), 1480?–1521 Portuguese explorer sailing for Spain who led the first-known voyage around the world. (p. 147)

Marina, Doña (mä rē´nä, dōn´yə), 1501?–1550 Aztec princess also called Malinche (mä lēn´ chä), aided Hernán Cortés's conquest of Tenochtitlán, 1521. (p. 144)

Marion, Francis (mâr´ē ən), 1732–1795 Revolutionary War commander, fought British army throughout the Carolinas; known as the "Swamp Fox." (p. 367)

Marquette, Jacques (mär ket´, zhäk), 1637–1675 Roman Catholic priest from France, sailed with Louis Jolliet through the Great Lakes, down the Mississippi to the mouth of the Arkansas River, 1673. (p. 308)

Marshall, James Wilson (mär´shəl), 1810–1885 First found gold in California, January, 1848. (p. 494)

Marshall, Thurgood (mär´shəl), 1907–1993 The first African American Supreme Court justice from 1967 to 1991. He was a civil rights lawyer who helped end segregation in public schools in 1954. (p. 561)

Mason, George (mā´sən), 1725–1792 Constitutional Convention delegate, called for a bill of rights. (p. 389)

Massasoit (mas´ə soit), 1580?–1661 Grand Wampanoag sachem, who made a peace agreement with the Pilgrims at Plymouth. (p. 178)

Mather, Cotton (math´ ər), 1663–1728 Puritan minister, set up a school for African Americans, formed the Negro Society to improve lives of enslaved people. (p. 197)

McCormick, Cyrus (mə kôr´mək), 1809–1884 Inventor of the reaper in 1832. (p. 446)

Meijeterma (me´ he ter mä), 1600s One of Lenape sachems, sold Manhattan island to the Dutch, 1626. (p. 220)

Metacomet (met ə käm´ət), 1639?–1676 Wampanoag sachem, also known as King Philip; led one of last Native American battles against colonists in New England, 1676. (p. 204)

Minuit, Peter (min ə wit), 1580–1638 First Dutch governor of New Amsterdam who bought the island of Manhattan from the Lenape in 1626. (p. 220)

Moctezuma II (mäk tə zü´mə), 1480?–1520 Aztec emperor, defeated by conquistador Hernán Cortés, 1520. (p. 143)

Monroe, James (mən rō´), 1758–1831 Fifth President of the United States, 1817–1825; proclaimed Monroe Doctrine, opposing European interference in Western Hemisphere. (p. 428)

Mott, Lucretia (mot), 1793–1880 Abolitionist, women's rights leader; with Elizabeth Cady Stanton, organized Seneca Falls Convention, 1848. (p. 546)

N

Nampeyo (näm pā´ō), 1859?–1942 Hopi potter who renewed interest in traditional Hopi pottery. (p. 83)

O

Oglethorpe, James (ō´gəl thôrp), 1696–1785 British military officer, founded colony of Georgia, 1732. (p. 246)

Openchancanough (ō pən chän´kən awf), 1545?–1644 Powhatan chief, led one of the last major Native American battles against English in Virginia, 1622. (p. 171)

Osceola (ä sē ō´lə), 1800–1838 Seminole chief who resisted his people's removal from Florida. (p. 468)

P

Paine, Thomas (pān), 1737–1809 American Patriot who wrote *Common Sense* in 1776. (p. 347)

Parker, John (pär´kər), 1729–1775 Patriot captain at the Battle of Lexington on April 19, 1775, where the first shots in the American Revolution were fired. (p. 338)

Parks, Rosa (pärks), 1913– Civil rights leader, fought segregation on city buses in Montgomery, Alabama, 1955; "Mother of the Civil Rights Movement." (p. 561)

The Peace Maker (<u>th</u>ə pēs māk´ ər), 1500s Iroquois leader, along with Hiawatha helped develop Iroquois Confederacy and the Great Laws, 1570. (p. 96)

Penn, William (pen), 1644–1718 Quaker leader who founded the colony of Pennsylvania in 1681. (p. 224)

---

pronunciation key

a **at**; ā **ape**; ä **far**; âr **care**; e **end**; ē **me**; i **it**; ī **ice**; îr **pierce**; o **hot**; ō **old**; ô **fork**; oi **oil**; ou **out**; u **up**; ū **use**; ü **rule**, ù **pull**; ûr **turn**; hw **white**; ng **song**; th **thin**; <u>th</u> **this**; zh **measure**; ə **about, taken, pencil, lemon, circus**

Biographical Dictionary

Perry, Oliver Hazard (per'ē), 1785–1819 United States Navy captain who defeated the British in the Battle of Lake Erie during the War of 1812. (p. 425)

Pinckney, Elizabeth Lucas (pink'nē), 1722?–1793 South Carolina planter who made indigo a major cash crop for the Southern Colonies. (p. 249)

Pizarro, Francisco (pi zär'ō), 1471?–1541 Spanish conquistador who defeated the Inca in 1533. (p. 146)

Pocahontas (pō kə hon'təs), 1595?–1617 Daughter of Chief Powhatan whose marriage to John Rolfe led to the "Peace of Pocahontas" from 1614 to 1617. (p. 169)

Polo, Marco (pō'lō), 1254?–1324? Italian merchant whose book about his travels through China from 1274 to 1292 stirred European interest in Asia. (p. 114)

Ponce de León, Juan (pons də lā ōn'), 1460?–1521 Spanish explorer who reached Florida in 1513. (p. 147)

Pontiac (pon'tē ak), 1720–1769 Ottawa chief, led attacks against British after losing French and Indian War, 1763. (p. 317)

Popé (pō pā'), ?–1688 Pueblo leader, drove Spanish out of New Mexico for 12 years, from 1680. (p. 301)

Powhatan, Chief (pou ə tan'), 1550?–1618 Chief of the Powhatan who helped the English settlement at Jamestown. (p. 168)

Punch, John (punch), 1600s In 1640, after running away from being an indentured servant, he became the first enslaved person in the colonies. (p. 250)

Putnam, Israel (pət'nəm), 1718–1790 Patriot general at the Battle of Bunker Hill. (p. 341)

R

Raleigh, Sir Walter (rô'lē), 1552?–1618 English explorer, historian, and soldier who started two unsuccessful colonies at Roanoke Island, in 1584 and 1587. (p. 167)

Reeve, Christopher (rēv), 1952– Film director/actor as well as spokesperson for disabled people. (p. 567)

Revels, Hiram (rev'əlz), 1822–1901 First African American Senator, who finished the term of Jefferson Davis from 1870 to 1871. (p. 528)

Revere, Paul (rə vîr'), 1735–1818 Boston Patriot silversmith; on night of April 18, 1775, rode warning Lexington that British troops were coming. (p. 337)

Rolfe, John (rälf), 1585–1622 Jamestown leader; his tobacco-curing method made it a successful cash crop. (p. 170)

Roosevelt, Theodore (rō'zə velt), 1858–1919 The 26th President of the United States from 1901 to 1909. (p. 546)

Ross, John (rôs), 1790–1866 Cherokee chief, 1828–1866; his people forced to march to Indian Territory, 1838. (p. 464)

S

Sacajawea (sak ə jə wē'ə), 1787?–1812 Shoshone guide, translator, Lewis and Clark expedition, 1805–1806. (p. 420)

Salem, Peter (sā'ləm), 1750?–1816 Patriot and former slave whose shot killed British Colonel Pitcairn at the Battle of Bunker Hill. (p. 341)

Salomon, Haym (sal'ə mən), 1740–1785 Business leader who raised money for the Continental Army during the American Revolution. (p. 366)

Samoset (sam'ə set), 1590?–1655 Wampanoag sachem, among first to meet Pilgrims at Plymouth, 1620. (p. 177)

Sampson, Deborah (samp' sən), 1760–1827 Fought in the American Revolution disguised as a man. (p. 366)

Sanchez, Loretta (sän' chez), 1960– Congresswoman elected in 1996 who represents Orange County, California, in the House of Representatives. (p. 567)

Santa Anna, Antonio López de (san'tə an'ə), 1795–1876 Mexican general who defeated the Texans defending The Alamo in 1836. (p. 476)

Seguín, Juan (sā gēn'), 1806–1889 Tejano leader who organized volunteers to fight the Mexican army in the Texas Revolution. (p. 476)

Sequoyah (si kwoi'ə), 1766?–1843 Cherokee leader who invented an alphabet for his people's language. (p. 465)

Serra, Junípero (ser'ə, hū nē'pe rō), 1713–1784 Roman Catholic missionary, built missions in California, 1700s. (p. 302)

Sewall, Samuel (sü' wəl), 1642–1730 Judge in the Salem witch trials who sentenced people to death and then later regretted it. (p. 205)

Seyseys (sā sās'), 1600s His full name was Seyseychkimus. One of Lenape sachems who sold parts of what is now New York City to the Dutch, 1626. (p. 220)

Shays, Daniel (shāz), 1747?–1825 American Revolutionary officer, led rebellion of Massachusetts farmers against state courts, 1786. (p. 385)

Sherman, Roger (shûr'mən), 1721–1793 Patriot who proposed the Great Compromise at the Constitutional Convention in 1787. (p. 392)

Slater, Samuel (slā'tər), 1768–1835 English engineer; built first water-powered spinning mill in United States, 1789. (p. 443)

Smith, Jedediah (smith), 1799–1831 Explorer who found routes to California through the Mojave desert and the Sierra Nevada Mountains. (p. 493)

Smith, John (smith), 1579?–1631 English army captain; his strict discipline helped Jamestown settlement survive. (p. 169)

Smith, Martha Turnstall (smith) Whaling merchant in New York in the 1700s. (p. 222)

Squanto (skwon'tō), 1585?–1622 Pawtuxet Native American, helped Pilgrims at Plymouth survive. (p. 178)

Standish, Miles (stan'dish), 1584?–1656 English army captain at Plymouth, defended Pilgrim colony. (p. 175)

Stanton, Elizabeth Cady (stant'ən), 1815–1902 Abolitionist and women's rights leader who helped write the "Declaration of Rights and Sentiments" at the Seneca Falls Convention in 1848. (p. 546)

Steuben, Frederich von (stü'bən), 1730–1794 Patriot officer from Germany, trained the Continental Army at Valley Forge during American Revolution. (p. 360)

Stowe, Harriet Beecher (stō), 1811–1896 Abolitionist and writer of *Uncle Tom's Cabin* in 1851. (p. 516)

Stuyvesant, Peter (stī' və sänt), 1610–1672 Sent from the Netherlands in 1647 to govern New Netherland; captured New Sweden, 1654; and in 1664 he surrendered New Netherland to the English. (p. 220)

Sunni Ali (sü'nē ä'lē), ?–1492 King of Songhai in West Africa in the late 1400s. (p. 111)

Sutter, John (sut′ ər), 1803–1880 Explorer of the West and owner of the land in California where gold was first found in 1848. (p. 494)

T

Taylor, Zachary (tā′lər), 1784–1850 The 12th President of the United States, from 1849 to 1850. He led United States forces during the War with Mexico. (p. 477)

Tecumseh (tə kum′sə), 1768–1813 Shawnee chief who attempted to unite Native American peoples against new settlers in the Northwest Territory. (p. 426)

Tenskwatawa (tens kwō tō′ wō), 1768–1834? Tecumseh's brother and popular Native American religious leader known as the "Prophet." (p. 426)

Tituba (ti chü′ bə), 1700s An enslaved woman from Barbados; first woman accused as a witch in Salem witch trials; later accused many other women of witchcraft. (p. 205)

Tomochichi (tō mä chē′chē), 1650?–1739 Chief of the Yamacraw who gave James Oglethorpe land for the Savannah settlement. (p. 246)

Truth, Sojourner (trüth), 1797–1883 Abolitionist who escaped from slavery in 1827 and spoke out for women's rights. (p. 516)

Tubman, Harriet (tub′mən), 1820?–1913 Abolitionist, Underground Railroad conductor, and spy for the Union Army during the Civil War. She helped hundreds of enslaved African Americans escape to freedom. (p. 516)

V

Verrazano, Giovanni da (vâr ə zä′nō, jō vän′ nē də), 1485?–1528? Italian sea captain in the service of France who searched for a Northwest Passage in 1524. (p. 164)

Vizcaíno, Sebastian (vith kä′ ē nō), 1550?–1616 Spanish merchant who in 1602, extended Cabrillo's route north along the California coast. (p. 152)

W

Warren, Mercy Otis (wôr′ən), 1728–1814 Patriot, poet, and playwright, urged women to give up tea and other British taxable goods in the 1760s. (p. 330)

Washington, George (wô′shing tən), 1732–1799 First President of the United States, 1789–1797. He fought in the French and Indian War, led the Continental Army during the American Revolution. (p. 314)

Washington, Martha (wô′shing tən), 1731–1802 First Lady to President George Washington, assisted the Continental Army during American Revolution. (p. 358)

Wheatley, Phillis (hwēt′lē), 1753?–1784 Enslaved American poet whose poems called for fair treatment for all people. (p. 327)

White, John (hwīt), 1500s Leader of the English colony of Roanoke in 1587. (p. 167)

White Cloud (wīt kloud), 1800s Lakota chief, 1840s. (p. 489)

Whitney, Eli (hwit′nē), 1765–1825 Inventor of the cotton gin in 1793. (p. 443)

Williams, Roger (wil′yəmz), 1603–1684 Puritan minister, founded the colony of Rhode Island, 1636. (p. 201)

Winthrop, John (win′thrəp), 1588–1649 First governor of the Massachusetts Bay Colony in 1630. (p. 193)

Y

Yanga (yang′gə), 1500s–1600s Leader of a slave revolt in New Spain in 1609. (p. 154)

York (yôrk), 1770–1832? William Clark's slave, member of Lewis and Clark expedition, 1804 to 1806. (p. 420)

Young, Brigham (yung), 1801–1877 Mormon leader who brought the Mormons from Illinois to Utah, where they founded Salt Lake City. (p. 486)

Z

Zavala, Lorenzo de (zä vä′lä), 1788–1836 The first vice president of the Texas Republic in 1836. (p. 476)

Zenger, John Peter (zeng′ər), 1697–1746 Newspaper printer whose trial in 1734 helped to establish the idea of freedom of the press. (p. 326)

Zheng He (jäng hə), 1371?–1433? Chinese sea captain; his voyages opened Chinese exploration, trade, early 1400s. (p. 106)

Zhu Di (zhü dē), 1360–1424 Emperor of China, encouraged exploration, trade, early 1400s. (p. 105)

---

pronunciation key

a **at**; ā **ape**; ä **far**; âr **care**; e **end**; ē **me**; i **it**; ī **ice**; îr **pierce**; o **hot**; ō **old**; ô **fork**; oi **oil**; ou **out**; u **up**; ū **use**; ü **rule**, u̇ **pull**; ûr **turn**; hw **white**; ng **song**; th **thin**; th **this**; zh **measure**; ə **about, taken, pencil, lemon, circus**

Glossary

This Glossary will help you to pronounce and understand the meaning of the vocabulary in this book. The page number at the end of the definition tells you where the word first appears.

A

abolitionist (ab ə lish′ə nist) A person who wanted to end slavery in the United States. (p. 515)

acid rain (asid rān) Precipitation containing harmful chemical pollution that can destroy trees and wildlife and poison water. *See* **precipitation**. (p. 45)

Act Concerning Religion (akt kən sûrn′ ing ri lij′ ən) Written in 1649 by Lord Baltimore to bring peace to Protestants and Catholics in Maryland by granting religious freedom to all Christians. (p. 244)

A.D. (ā dē) "Anno Domini," Latin for "in the year of the Lord." Used before a numeral to indicate a year occurring since the birth of Jesus Christ. (p. 68)

adobe (ə dō′bē) A type of clay traditionally used as a building material by Native Americans and later by Spanish colonists in the Southwest. (p. 82)

almanac (ôl′mə nak) A reference book containing facts and figures. (p. 283)

amendment (ə mend′mənt) An addition to the Constitution. *See* **Constitution**. (p. 396)

American Revolution (ə mer′ i kən rev ə lü′shən) The war between Great Britain and its thirteen American colonies from 1775 to 1783 that led to the founding of the United States of America. (p. 336)

Americans with Disabilities Act (ə mer′ i kənz with dis′ ə bil i tēz) Passed in 1990, the act gives disabled people greater access to jobs, public places, and public services. (p. 567)

ancestor (an′ses tər) A relative who lived before you. (p. 9)

Antifederalist (an′tē fed′ər ə list) An opponent of a strong central government in the late 1700s. *See* **Federalist**. (p. 401)

apprentice (ə pren′ tis) A person learning a craft or trade from a master. (p. 209)

archaeologist (är kē ol′ə jist) A scientist who looks for and studies artifacts. (p. 61)

arid (ar′id) Dry. (p. 37)

Articles of Confederation (är′ti kəlz uv kən fed ə rā′shən) The first plan of government of the United States. It gave more power to the states than the central government. *See* **Constitution**. (p. 385)

assembly (ə sem′blē) A lawmaking body. (p. 322)

astrolabe (as′trə lāb) An instrument that helped sailors and desert travelers find their way by the stars. (p. 135)

atlas (at′ləs) A book of maps. *See* **reference source**. (p. 525)

autobiography (ô tə bī og′rə fē) The story of a person's own life written by himself or herself. (p. 269)

B

backcountry (bak′kən trē) In colonial times, the name given to the eastern foothills of the Appalachian Mountains. (p. 249)

barn raising (bärn rāz′ ing) A custom where entire communities gathered to build a barn for a person or family. A barn could be raised in a day. (p. 233)

Battle of Bunker Hill (ba′təl uv bung′kər hil) Costly British "victory" in 1775 over Colonial forces at a site near Charlestown, Massachusetts. (p. 341)

Battle of New Orleans (bat′əl uv nü ôr′lē ənz) A United States victory over British forces in the last battle of the War of 1812. *See* **War of 1812** (p. 428)

B.C. (bē sē) "Before Christ." Used after a numeral to indicate a year occurring before the birth of Jesus Christ. (p. 68)

bias (bī′ əs) Prejudice, preference, or opinion. (p. 564)

Bill of Rights (bil uv rīts) The first ten amendments to the Constitution, ratified in 1791. *See* **amendment** *and* **Constitution**. (p. 402)

pronunciation key

a	at	ī	ice	u	up	th	thin
ā	ape	îr	pierce	ū	use	<u>th</u>	this
ä	far	o	hot	ü	rule	zh	measure
âr	care	ō	old	ù	pull	ə	about, taken,
e	end	ô	fork	ûr	turn		pencil, lemon,
ē	me	oi	oil	hw	white		circus
i	it	ou	out	ng	song		

black codes (blak kōdz) Laws passed by the Southern states after the Civil War that severely limited the rights of the newly freed African Americans. (p. 527)

Boston Tea Party (bôs′tən tē pär′tē) A 1773 protest against British taxes in which colonists disguised as Mohawks dumped tea into Boston Harbor. (p. 332)

boycott (boi′kot) To refuse to do business or have contact with a person, group, company, country, or product. (p. 330)

C

Cabinet (kab′ə nit) The officials appointed by the President to be advisers and to head each department in the executive branch. See **executive branch** and **secretary**. (p. 403)

call number (kôl num′bər) A series of letters and numbers giving the exact location of a book on a library shelf. See **card catalog**. (p. 525)

canal (kə nal′) A human-built waterway. See **lock**. (p. 450)

caravan (kar′ə van) A group of people traveling together for safety, especially through desert areas. (p. 110)

caravel (kar′ə vel) A fast sailing ship that could be steered easily and hold large amounts of cargo. (p. 117)

card catalog (kärd kat′ə lôg) A listing by call number of all the books a library contains. The catalog is arranged alphabetically by author, title, and subject. See **call number**. (p. 525)

cardinal direction (kär′də nəl di rek′shən) One of the four main points of the compass; north, south, east, and west. See **compass rose**. (p. G6)

cash crop (kash krop) A crop that is grown to be sold for profit. See **profit**. (p. 170)

cause (kôz) Something that makes something else happen. See **effect**. (p. 98)

CD-ROM (sē dē räm′) A type of reference source similar to a compact disc that is "read" by a computer. It combines text, sound, and even short films. See **reference source**. (p. 525)

census (sen′səs) An official count of all the people living in a country or region. (p. 10)

century (sen′chə rē) A period of 100 years. (p. 68)

charter (chär′tər) An official document giving a person permission to do something, such as settle in an area. (p. 167)

checks and balances (cheks and bal′ən səz) The system that balances power among the branches of government. (p. 398)

Chinese Six Companies (chi′ nēz′ siks cum′ pən ēz) The group of various organizations in San Francisco in the 1870s that helped Chinese immigrants in labor and immigration disputes. (p. 545)

circle graph (sûr′kəl graf) A kind of graph that shows how something can be divided into parts. (p. 109)

citizen (sit′ə zən) A person born in a country or who legally becomes a member of that country. (p. 13)

civil rights (siv′əl rīts) The individual rights of all citizens to be treated equally under the law. (p. 14)

Civil War (siv′əl wôr) In the United States, the war between the Union and the Confederacy from 1861 to 1865. (p. 521)

civilization (siv ə lə zā′shən) A culture that has developed complex systems of government, education, and religion. Civilizations usually have large populations with many people living in cities. (p. 60)

clan (klan) A group of families who share the same ancestor. (p. 95)

clarify (klar′i fī) To make clear. (p. 16)

climate (klī′mit) The weather of an area over a number of years. (p. 36)

colony (kol′ə nē) A settlement far away from the country that rules it. (p. 137)

Columbian exchange (kə lum′bē ən eks chānj′) The movement of people, plants, animals, and germs in either direction across the Atlantic Ocean following the voyages of Columbus. (p. 136)

Committees of Correspondence (kə mit′ēz uv kōr ə spon′dəns) Groups organized in the 1770s to keep colonists informed of important events. (p. 331)

common (kom′ ən) The village green or center of Puritan villages characterized by the presence of a Puritan church or meeting house. (p. 194)

compass rose (kum′pəs rōz) A drawing that indicates directions on a map, especially cardinal and intermediate directions. See **cardinal direction** and **intermediate direction**. (p. G6)

compromise (kom′prə mīz) The settling of a dispute by each side agreeing to give up part of its demands. (p. 97)

Compromise of 1850 (kom′prə mīz uv āt′tēn′ fif′tē) A law passed by Congress admitting California to the Union, allowing people in the territories to decide on the issue of slavery for themselves, and obtaining the North's agreement to obey the Fugitive Slave Law. (p. 496)

conclusion (kən klü′zhən) A statement reached by pulling together all the information about something. (p. 312)

Conestoga (kon ə stō′gə) A sturdy wagon used by colonists and pioneers to carry people and goods. (p. 235)

Confederate States of America (kən fed′ər it stāts uv ə mer′i kə) The name adopted by the Southern states that seceded from the Union during the Civil War. (p. 520)

Glossary

congregation (kong′gri gā′ shən) A gathering of people. In Puritan times the congregation was made up of all male villagers who followed the Puritan religion. Only members of the congregation could vote. (p. 196)

conquistador (kon kēs′tə dôr) A name for the Spanish conquerors who first came to the Americas in the 1500s. (p. 142)

conservation (kon sər vā′shən) The protection and careful use of natural resources. (p. 46)

Constitution (kon sti tü′shən) A plan of government. In the United States it is the supreme law and plan of the national government, adopted in 1789. (p. 12)

Constitutional Convention (kon sti tü′shə nəl kən ven′shən) The meeting of twelve states' delegates in Philadelphia, Pennsylvania, that replaced the Articles of Confederation with a new Constitution. *See* **Articles of Confederation** *and* **Constitution**. (p. 388)

continent (kon′tə nənt) One of Earth's seven large bodies of land, including Africa, Antarctica, Asia, Australia, Europe, North America, and South America. (p. G4)

Continental Army (kon′tə nen′təl är′mē) The army created by the Second Continental Congress in May 1775, with George Washington as commander-in-chief. *See* **Second Continental Congress**. (p. 348)

cotton gin (kot′ən jin) A machine that separates cotton from its seeds, invented by Eli Whitney in 1793. (p. 443)

coup stick (kü stik) A special weapon used by a Lakota Sioux soldier to show his bravery by touching, but not killing, his enemy. (p. 88)

coureur de bois (kü rər′ də bwä′) In New France, a person who trapped furs without permission from the French government. (p. 310)

credibility (cred ə bil′i tē) Accuracy or believability. (p. 254)

Crusades (krü′ sädz) A series of wars fought for about 200 years by European Christians to gain parts of western Asia where Christianity began. (p. 115)

culture (kul′chər) The entire way of life of a people, including their customs, beliefs, and language. (p. 8)

D

dame school (dām skül) A school for Puritan children up to the age of seven, usually taught in a woman's home. (p. 208)

dateline (dāt′līn) A line at the beginning of a newspaper article that tells when and where the story was written. (p. 455)

debtor (det′ər) A person who owes money. (p. 246)

decade (dek′ād) A period of ten years. (p. 68)

Declaration of Independence (dek lə rā′shən əv in di pen′dəns) The official document issued on July 4, 1776, announcing that the American colonies were breaking away from Great Britain. (p. 349)

define (di fīn′) To name (a problem) or give meaning to a word. (p. 16)

degree (di grē′) A unit of measurement. It can be used for calculating latitude and longitude. (p. 40)

delegate (del′i git) A member of an elected assembly. *See* **assembly**. (p. 325)

democracy (di mok′rə sē) A form of government in which the people make the laws and run the government. (p. 12)

discrimination (di skrim′ə nā shən) An unfair difference in the treatment of people. (p. 545)

diverse (di′ vûrs) Different, varied. (p. 548)

Dred Scott Decision (dred skät di sizh′ən) An 1857 Supreme Court decision that said slaves were private property. (p. 517)

E

economy (i kon′ə mē) The way a country's people use natural resources, money, and knowledge to produce goods and services. (p. 44)

editor (ed′i tər) A person who helps to run a publication, such as a newspaper or a magazine. (p. 455)

editorial (ed′i tôr′ē əl) A newspaper article in which the editors give their opinions. (p. 455)

effect (i fekt′) Something that happens as a result of a cause. *See* **cause**. (p. 98)

elevation (el′ə vā′shən) The height of an area above sea level. *See* **elevation map**. (p. 230)

elevation map (el′ə vā′shən map) A physical map that uses colors to show the elevation, or height, of land above sea level. *See* **physical map**. (p. G10)

Emancipation Proclamation (ē man si pā′shən prok lə mā′shən) An official announcement issued by President Abraham Lincoln in 1862 that led to the end of slavery in the United States. (p. 522)

emigration (em′ i grā′ shən) The movement of people to a new place. (p. 492)

empire (em′pīr) An area in which different groups of people are controlled by one ruler or government. (p. 65)

encomienda (en kō mē en′də) A very large piece of land in New Spain given by the Spanish government to certain Spanish colonists during the 1500s. (p. 150)

encyclopedia (en sī klə pē′dē ə) A book or set of books that gives information about people, places, things, and past events. (p. 524)

environment (en vĩ'rən mənt) All the surroundings in which people, plants, and animals live. (p. 44)

equator (i kwā'tər) An imaginary line encircling Earth halfway between the North Pole and the South Pole, designated as 0° latitude. See **latitude**. (p. G4)

Era of Good Feelings (îr'ə uv gŭd fē'lingz) The name given to the period of peace and prosperity that followed the War of 1812. (p. 428)

established church (e stab' lisht chûrch) The official church of a state or country. (p. 244)

ethnic group (eth'nik grüp) People who share the same customs and language, and often a common history. (p. 9)

evaluate (i val' ū āt) To judge the accuracy or quality of something. (p. 16)

executive branch (eg zek'yə tiv branch) The part of government, headed by the President, that carries out the laws. (p. 391)

exoduster (ek'sō dus tər) The term describing one of the many African Americans from the South who went to Kansas in the 1860s. (p. 535)

expedition (ek spi dish'ən) A journey made for a special purpose. (p. 134)

export (ek'spôrt) To send goods to other countries for sale or use. See **import**. (p. 274)

F

fact (fakt) A statement that can be checked and proved true. See **opinion**. (p. 172)

feature article (fē'chər är'ti kəl) A detailed newspaper report on a person, an issue, or an event. (p. 455)

federal (fed'ər əl) The word describing the central, or national, government. (p. 12)

Federalist (fed'ər ə list) A supporter of a strong federal system of government in the late 1700s. See **Antifederalist**. (p. 401)

federal system (fed'ər əl sis'təm) A system of government in which power is shared between the central government and the state governments. The United States has a federal system of government. See **states' rights**. (p. 397)

Fifteenth Amendment (fif'tēnth' ə mend'mənt) An amendment to the Constitution, ratified in 1870, that made it illegal to withhold voting rights "on account of race or color." See **amendment** and **ratify**. (p. 528)

First Continental Congress (fûrst kon'tə nen'təl kong'gris) The assembly of colonial delegates from every colony except Georgia that met in 1774 in Philadelphia to oppose the Intolerable Acts. See **Intolerable Acts** and **Second Continental Congress**. (p. 336)

Forty-Niners (fôr'tē ni'nərz) People who came to California in 1849 in search of gold. (p. 494)

fossil fuel (fos'əl fū'əl) A fuel, such as oil, natural gas, or coal, that is formed from the remains of plants and animals that lived millions of years ago. (p. 43)

Fourteenth Amendment (fôr'tēnth' ə mend'mənt) An amendment to the Constitution, ratified in 1868, that officially established blacks as citizens with the same legal rights as whites. See **amendment** and **ratify**. (p. 528)

free enterprise (frē en'tər prīz) An economic system in which people can own property and businesses and are free to decide what to make, how much to produce, and what price to charge. (p. 275)

free state (frē stāt) A state that did not permit slavery before the Civil War. (p. 496)

Freedmen's Bureau (frēd'mənz byūr'ō) A government agency created in 1865 that provided food, schools, and medical care for freed slaves and others in the South. (p. 527)

French and Indian War (french ənd in'dē ən wôr) A conflict between Great Britain and France in North America from 1756 to 1763. (p. 314)

G

geography (jē og'rə fē) The study of Earth and the way people live on it and use it. (p. 28)

gold rush (gōld rush) The sudden rush of people to an area where gold has been discovered. (p. 492)

grammar school (gram' ər skül) A secondary school first set up by the Puritans in 1647, in villages that had 100 or more families. (p. 194)

graph (graf) A diagram that presents information in a way that makes it easy to detect patterns, trends, or changes over time. (p. 108)

Great Awakening (grāt ə wā' kə ning) A religious movement in the middle 1700s which aimed to strengthen people's religious beliefs and feelings. (p. 285)

Glossary

Great Compromise (grāt kom′ prə mīz) The plan drawn up by Roger Sherman at the Constitutional Convention in 1787. It proposed the establishment of two houses of Congress. (p. 392)

Great Migration (grāt mī grā′shən) The journey of hundreds of thousands of African Americans from the South to northern cities in the early 1900s. (p. 544)

grid (grid) A set of squares formed by crisscrossing lines that can help you to determine locations, such as on a map or globe. (p. 41)

H

Harlem Renaissance (här ləm ren′ ə säns) Movement in the Harlem section of New York City in the 1920s, where many African American artists, writers, poets, and musicians developed distinctly African American art forms. (p. 544)

headline (hed′līn) A sentence or phrase printed in large type across the top of a news article to get the reader's attention. (p. 454)

hemisphere (hem′i sfîr) One half a sphere or globe. Earth can be divided into four hemispheres. The equator divides Earth into the Northern and Southern hemispheres. The prime meridian divides it into the Eastern and Western hemispheres. See **equator** and **prime meridian**. (p. G4)

historian (hi stōr′ē ən) A person who studies the past. (p. 19)

historical atlas (hi stôr′i kəl at′ləs) A book that includes maps of important events from the past. See **reference source**. (p. 525)

history (his′tə rē) The study or record of what happened in the past. (p. 18)

Holocaust (hol′ə kôst) The murder of 6 million Jews by Nazi Germany during World War II. (p. 549)

Holy Experiment (hō′ lē ek sper′ ə mənt) The name William Penn gave to his planned Quaker colony that would later become Pennsylvania. (p. 226)

hornbook (hôrn bük) The alphabet, numbers, and a prayer printed on a piece of paper attached to clear horn. It was used to teach Puritan children. (p. 208)

House of Burgesses (hous uv bûr′jis əz) The law-making body of colonial Virginia, established in Jamestown in 1619. (p. 243)

House of Representatives (hous uv rep ri zen′tə tivz) The house of Congress in which each state's number of representatives is determined by its population. See **legislative branch** and **Senate**. (p. 392)

humid (hū′mid) Wet; moist. (p. 37)

I

immigrant (im′i grənt) A person who leaves one country to live in another. (p. 9)

impeach (im pēch′) To charge a government official with wrongdoing. (p. 528)

import (im′pōrt′) To bring goods from another country for sale or use. See **export**. (p. 274)

indentured servant (in den′chərd sûr′vənt) A person who worked for someone in colonial America for a set time in exchange for the ocean voyage. (p. 170)

Indian Removal Act (in′dē ən ri mü′vəl akt) A law passed by Congress in 1830 forcing Native Americans to move to what is now Oklahoma. (p. 466)

indigo (in′di gō) A plant that is used to produce a blue dye. See **cash crop**. (p. 249)

Industrial Revolution (in dus′trē əl rev ə lü′shən) The dramatic change from making goods by hand at home to making them by machine in factories. (p. 442)

interchangeable parts (in tər chān′jə bəl pärts) Parts of a product built to a standard size so that they can be easily replaced. (p. 446)

interdependent (in′tər di pen′dənt) Depending on each other to meet needs and wants. (p. 35)

intermediate direction (in′tər mē′dē it di rek′shən) A direction halfway between two cardinal directions; northeast, northwest, southwest, southeast. (p. G6)

Intolerable Acts (in tä′lər ə bəl akts) The laws passed by the British Parliament in 1774 that closed Boston Harbor, dissolved the Massachusetts assembly, and forced colonists to house British soldiers. (p. 333)

investor (in vest′ər) A person who uses money to buy or make something in order to produce a profit. See **profit**. (p. 451)

Iroquois Confederacy (ir′i kwä kən fed′ər ə sē) The union of the five major Iroquois peoples beginning about 1570. (p. 96)

irrigation (ir i gā′shən) A method of supplying dry land with water through a series of ditches or pipes. (p. 64)

J

jerky (jûr′kē) Thin strips of sun-dried meat. (p. 89)

Jim Crow laws (jim krō lôz) Laws passed by Southern states after Reconstruction that established segregation, or separation of the races. (p. 529)

journeyman (jûr′ nē mən) A person practicing a trade or craft who is not yet called a master but who has completed an apprenticeship. (p. 209)

judicial branch (jü dish′əl branch) The part of government that decides the meaning of the laws. See **Supreme Court**. (p. 391)

K

kachina (kə chē′nə) In Pueblo religion, the living spirit of an ancestor who helps bring rains and makes crops grow. (p. 82)

Kansas-Nebraska Act (kan′zəs nə bras′kə akt) An 1854 law passed by Congress that allowed the Kansas and Nebraska territories to decide whether to become free states or slave states. (p. 514)

Kentucky rifle (kən tu kē′ rif′ əl) The name given to a light, easily reloadable rifle. (p. 235)

L

labor union (lā′bər ūn′yən) A group of workers united to gain better wages and working conditions. (p. 538)

La Causa (lä kou′ sə) Spanish name given to the struggle of farm workers for better conditions and wages, meaning "the cause." (p. 562)

landform (land′fôrm) A shape on Earth's surface, such as a mountain or hill. (p. 30)

large-scale map (lärj skāl map) A map that shows a smaller area in greater detail. See **small-scale map**. (p. 372)

latitude (lat′i tüd) An imaginary line, or parallel, measuring distance north or south of the equator. See **equator** and **parallel**. (p. 40)

legacy (leg′ə sē) A part of our past that we value in our lives today. (p. 22)

legislative branch (lej′is lā tiv branch) The law-making part of government, with the power to raise the money needed to run the government. See **House of Representatives** and **Senate**. (p. 391)

liberty (lib′ər tē) Freedom. (p. 328)

line graph (līn graf) A kind of graph that shows changes over time. See **graph**. (p. 108)

locator (lō kā′tər) A small map inset in a larger map that helps you see where the subject area of the larger map is located. (p. G8)

lock (lok) A water elevator that moves boats within a canal to higher or lower levels. See **canal**. (p. 451)

lodge (loj) A type of home made of logs, grasses, sticks, and soil which the Native Americans of the Plains used when living in their villages. See **teepee**. (p. 86)

longhouse (lông′hous) A home shared by several related Iroquois families. (p. 94)

longitude (lon′ji tüd) An imaginary line, or meridian, measuring distance east or west of the prime meridian. See **meridian** and **prime meridian**. (p. 40)

Louisiana Purchase (lü ē zē an′ə pûr′chəs) The territory purchased by the United States from France in 1803, reaching from the Mississippi River to the Rocky Mountains and from the Gulf of Mexico to Canada. (p. 419)

Loyalist (loi′ə list) A colonist who supported Great Britain in the American Revolution. (p. 357)

M

magnetic compass (mag net′ik kum′pəs) An instrument invented by the Chinese about A.D. 100 to help sailors find north and south. (p. 106)

malaria (mə lâr′ē ə) A disease caused by the bite of a certain mosquito. (p. 113)

Manifest Destiny (man′ ə fest des′ tə nē) Belief in the early 1800s that the United States was to stretch west to the Pacific Ocean and south to the Rio Grande. (p. 474)

map key (map kē) A guide telling you what each symbol on a map stands for. See **symbol**. (p. G8)

map scale (map skāl) A line like a measuring stick drawn on a map which uses a unit of measurement, such as an inch, to represent a real distance on Earth. (p. 372)

Mayflower Compact (mā′flou ər kom′pakt) An agreement the Pilgrims made before landing in New England to make and obey "just and equal laws." (p. 176)

megalopolis (meg ə lop′ə lis) A group of cities that have grown so close together that they seem to form one city. (p. 34)

mercenary (mûr′sə ner ē) A soldier paid to fight for another country. (p. 356)

merchant (mûr′ chənt) A person who buys, sells, and trades goods for a profit. (p. 114)

meridian (mə rid′ē ən) Any line of longitude east or west of Earth's prime meridian. See **longitude** and **prime meridian**. (p. 40)

Mexican War (mek′si kən wôr) A war between the United States and Mexico from 1846 to 1848. See **Treaty of Guadalupe Hidalgo**. (p. 477)

Middle Passage (mid′əl pas′ij) The middle leg of the colonial trade route in which captive Africans were shipped to the West Indies. See **triangular trade**. (p. 276)

---

pronunciation key

a **at**; ā **ape**; ä **far**; âr **care**; e **end**; ē **me**; i **it**; ī **ice**; îr **pierce**; o **hot**; ō **old**; ô **fork**; oi **oil**; ou **out**; u **up**; ū **use**; ü **rule**; ù **pull**; ûr **turn**; hw **white**; ng **song**; th **thin**; th **this**; zh **measure**; ə **about, taken, pencil, lemon, circus**

militia (mi lish'ə) A group of volunteers who fought in times of emergency during the colonial period and the American Revolution. *See* **minutemen**. (p. 325)

mineral (min'ər əl) A substance found in the earth that is neither plant nor animal. (p. 43)

minutemen (min'it men) Well-trained volunteer soldiers who defended the American colonies against the British at a minute's notice. (p. 336)

mission (mish'ən) A settlement where missionaries lived and worked. (p. 298)

missionary (mish'ə ner ē) A person who teaches his or her religion to others who have different beliefs. (p. 153)

Missouri Compromise (mi zùr'ē kom'prə mīz) A law passed by Congress in 1820 that divided the Louisiana Territory into areas allowing slavery and areas outlawing slavery. (p. 514)

Monroe Doctrine (mən rō dok'trin) A declaration of United States foreign policy made by President James Monroe in 1823 that opposed European colonization or interference in the Western Hemisphere. (p. 429)

N

national anthem (nash'ə nəl an'thəm) A country's official song, such as "The Star-Spangled Banner." (p. 426)

nationalism (nash' ə nə liz əm) Strong loyalty to one's country and culture. (p. 428)

natural resource (nach'ər əl rē'sôrs) A material found in nature that people use to meet their needs and wants. (p. 42)

navigation (nav i gā'shən) The science of determining a ship's location and direction. (p. 117)

neutral (nü'trəl) Not taking sides. (p. 424)

The New England Primer (thə nü ing' lənd pri' mər) A book used from 1690 to 1830 to teach Puritan children spelling, vocabulary, and Puritan religious beliefs, using simple rhymes. (p. 208)

New Jersey Plan (nü jûr'zē plan) The plan offered by the small states at the Constitutional Convention of 1787 to give all states an equal number of representatives in Congress. *See* **Virginia Plan**. (p. 391)

news article (nüz är'ti kəl) A newspaper story that factually describes an important recent event. (p. 454)

Nineteenth Amendment (nīn'tēnth' ə mend'mənt) An amendment to the Constitution, ratified in 1920, that gave women the right to vote. *See* **amendment** and **ratify**. (p. 546)

nonrenewable resource (non ri nü'ə bəl rē'sôrs) A material found in nature that cannot be replaced, such as coal, oil, or natural gas. (p. 42)

Northwest Ordinance (nôrth'west' ôr'də nəns) A law passed in 1787 organizing the Northwest Territory for settlement and eventual statehood. (p. 386)

Northwest Passage (nôrth'west' pas'ij) A water route believed to flow through North America to Asia that European explorers searched for from the 1500s to the 1700s. (p. 162)

O

ocean (ō'shən) One of Earth's four large bodies of water. The Arctic, Atlantic, Indian, and Pacific. (p. G4)

opinion (ə pin' yən) A personal view or belief. (p. 172)

oral history (ôr'əl his'tə rē) Spoken records, including stories that have been passed from one generation to the next. (p. 19)

outline (out'līn) A plan for organizing written information about a subject. (p. 272)

overseer (ō'vər sē ər) A person hired to be the boss of a plantation. (p. 252)

P

parallel (par'ə lel) A line of latitude. *See* **latitude**. (p. 40)

Patriot (pā'trē ət) An American colonist who supported the fight for independence. (p. 357)

patroon (pə trün') The name given to wealthy Dutch landowners who were given land to farm along the Hudson river by the Dutch West India Company in the 1600s. (p. 219)

perspective (pər spek'tiv) Point of view. *See* **point of view**. (p. 19)

petition (pə tish'ən) A written request signed by many people. (p. 336)

physical map (fiz'i kəl map) A map that highlights Earth's natural features. (p. G10)

pilgrim (pil' grəm) A person who travels to a sacred place for religious reasons. (p. 174)

pioneer (pī ə nîr') A person who settles a new part of the country. (p. 410)

plantation (plan tā'shən) A large farm that often grows one crop. (p. 250)

point of view (point uv vū) The position from which a person looks at an issue or situation. (p. 394)

political cartoon (pə lit'i kəl kär tün') A drawing that shows a cartoonist's opinion about a political person, event, or issue. (p. 334)

political map (pə lit'i kəl map) A map that shows the boundaries of states and countries. (p. G9)

Glossary

political party • republic

political party (pə lit′i kəl pär′tē) A group of people who share similar ideas about government. (p. 404)

pollution (pə lü′shən) Anything that dirties the air, soil, or water. (p. 45)

population (pop yə lā′shən) The total number of people living in a particular area or place. (p. 10)

portage (pôr′tij) A land route from one body of water to another. (p. 309)

potlatch (pot′lach) A special feast given by Native Americans of the Northwest Coast, in which the guests receive gifts. (p. 73)

prairie (prâr′ē) Flat or gently rolling land covered mostly with grasses and wildflowers. (p. 87)

Preamble (prē′am bəl) The introduction to the Constitution. (p. 397)

precipitation (pri sip i tā′shən) The moisture that falls to Earth as rain or snow. (p. 36)

prejudice (prej′ə dis) A negative opinion formed without proof. (p. 11)

presidio (pri sid′ē ō) A type of fort the Spanish built to house Spanish soldiers protecting the missions. (p. 299)

primary source (prī′ mer ē sôrs) A firsthand account of an event or an artifact created during the period of history that is being studied. *See* **secondary source**. (p. 198)

prime meridian (prīm mə rid′ē ən) The line of longitude labeled 0° longitude. Any place east of the prime meridian is labeled E, any place west of it is labeled W. *See* **longitude**. (p. 40)

problem (prob′ləm) A question or issue that needs to be answered or solved. (p. 16)

Proclamation of 1763 (prok lə mā′shən) An official announcement by King George III of Great Britain outlawing colonial settlement west of the Appalachian Mountains. (p. 317)

profit (prof′it) The money remaining after the costs of a business have been paid. (p. 115)

proprietor (prə prī′i tər) A person who owns a property or a business. (p. 245)

public school (pub lik′ skül) A school open to all children, funded by taxes. (p. 194)

pueblo (pweb′ lō) A Spanish word meaning "village" used to refer to the apartment-style homes of the Native Americans of the Southwest. (p. 81)

Quaker (kwā′ kər) A member of the Society of Friends, a Christian sect founded in the seventeenth century. (p. 224)

ratify (rat′ə fī) To give official approval—for example, to the Constitution or amendments to it. (p. 400)

reaper (rē′pər) A machine that uses sharp blades to harvest grain. (p. 446)

rebel (ri bel′) To oppose those in charge, even to the point of fighting them with weapons, because of different ideas about what is right. (p. 328)

Reconstruction (rē kən struk′shən) The period following the Civil War in which Congress passed laws designed to rebuild the country and bring the Southern states back into the Union. (p. 526)

recycle (rē sī′kəl) To save discarded items, like cans or bottles, so that they can be used again. (p. 48)

reference source (ref′ər ens sôrs) A book or other source that contains facts about many different subjects. (p. 524)

reform (ri fôrm′) A change to make government or business work better. (p. 546)

refugee (ref yù jē′) A person who flees his or her country because of racial, religious, or political persecution. (p. 548)

region (rē′jən) A large area with common features that set it apart from other areas. (p. 29)

relief (ri lēf′) The difference in height between land areas. *See* **relief map**. (p. 231)

relief map (ri lēf′ map) A physical map that uses shading to show the difference in height between areas of land. *See* **relief** and **physical map**. (p. 231)

Renaissance (ren′ ə säns) A period of cultural and artistic growth in Europe that began in Italy in the 1300s. (p. 116)

renewable resource (ri nü′ə bəl rē′sôrs) A material found in nature that can be replaced, such as forests. (p. 42)

repeal (ri pēl′) To withdraw or cancel. (p. 329)

republic (ri pub′lik) A form of government in which the people elect representatives to run the country. (p. 12)

pronunciation key**

a at; ā ape; ä far; âr care; e end; ē me; i it; ī ice; îr pierce; o hot; ō old; ô fork; oi oil; ou out; u up; ū use; ü rule; ù pull; ûr turn; hw white; ng song; th thin; <u>th</u> this; zh measure; ə about, taken, pencil, lemon, circus

R83

S

sachem (sā'chəm) The leader or chief of any group of Native Americans in the Eastern Woodlands and Great Lakes regions. (p. 178)

scale (skāl) A guide that explains the relationship between real distances on Earth and distances on a map. (p. G7)

secession (si sesh' ən) The act of breaking away from a group, such as the Southern states from the Union in 1861. (p. 520)

secondary source (sek'ən der ē sôrs) An account of the past based on information from primary sources and written by someone who was not an eyewitness to those events. See **primary source**. (p. 198)

Second Continental Congress (sek'ənd kon'tə nen'təl kong'gris) A meeting in Philadelphia in 1775 of delegates from all 13 colonies which established a colonial army and declared American independence. See **Continental Army** and **Declaration of Independence**. (p. 348)

secretary (sek'rə ter ē) The head of each department in the executive branch of government. As a group the secretaries are called the President's Cabinet. See **Cabinet**. (p. 403)

segregation (seg ri gā'shən) The separation of people, usually based on race or religion. (p. 529)

Senate (sen'it) The house of Congress in which each state has an equal number of representatives, or Senators, regardless of population. See **legislative branch** and **House of Representatives**. (p. 392)

separatists (sep' ər ə tists) Protestants who believed in separating from the Church of England in the early 1600s. (p. 174)

settlement house (set'əl mənt hous) A community center providing services such as child care and education to immigrants and others in need. (p. 546)

sharecropping (shâr'krop ing) A system common in the South in the late 1800s and early 1900s in which farmers rented land from a landowner by promising to pay the owner with a share of their crop. (p. 528)

Shays's Rebellion (shāz ri bel'yən) A revolt in 1786 of Massachusetts farmers, led by Daniel Shays, who opposed tax decisions of the state courts. (p. 385)

slave codes (slāv cōdz) Rules made by colonial planters that controlled the lives of enslaved Africans. (p. 252)

slavery (slā'və rē) The practice of people owning other people and forcing them to work. (p. 67)

slave state (slāv stāt) A state that allowed slavery before the Civil War. (p. 496)

small-scale map (smôl skāl map) A map that shows a large area but not much detail. See **large-scale map**. (p. 372)

Sons of Liberty (sunz uv lib'ər tē) Groups of colonists who organized themselves to protest against the British government. (p. 329)

specialize (spesh'ə līz) To spend most of one's time doing one kind of job. (p. 62)

stagecoach (stāj'kōch) A large, horse-drawn carriage in the 1800s that transported passengers, baggage, and mail on a regular schedule. (p. 448)

Stamp Act (stamp akt) A law passed by the British Parliament in 1765 requiring colonists to pay a tax on newspapers, pamphlets, legal documents, and even playing cards. (p. 329)

statehood (stāt'hùd) Becoming a state in the United States. (p. 386)

states' rights (stāts rīts) The belief that each state should be allowed to make its own decisions about issues affecting it. (p. 521)

steamboat (stēm' bōt) Boat powered by steam that made traveling upstream easier. The first steamboat was built by Robert Fulton in 1807. (p. 450)

steam engine (stēm en'jin) An engine powered by the energy produced from steam. (p. 448)

steerage (stîr' ij) The part of a ship where people paying the lowest fare travel. (p. 269)

strike (strīk) A refusal of all the workers in a business to work until the owners meet their demands. (p. 538)

suffrage (suf'rij) The right to vote. (p. 546)

Supreme Court (sü prēm' kôrt) The head of the judicial branch of the federal government. It is the highest court in the country. See **judicial branch**. (p. 391)

surplus (sûr'plus) An amount greater than what is needed. (p. 61)

sweatshop (swet'shop) A small, crowded factory where people work, usually in unsafe conditions. (p. 536)

symbol (sim'bəl) Something that stands for something else. See **political cartoon**. (p. 334)

T

technology (tek nol'ə jē) The design and use of tools, ideas, and methods to solve problems. (p. 72)

teepee (tē'pē) A cone-shaped tent made of animal skins used by Native Americans of the Plains. (p. 87)

temperature (tem'pər ə chər) The measurement of heat and cold. (p. 36)

territory (ter'i tôr ē) An area of land that belongs to a government. (p. 386)

Thirteenth Amendment (thûr′tēnth′ ə mend′mənt) An 1865 amendment to the Constitution that abolished slavery. *See* **amendment** *and* **ratify**. (p. 527)

time line (tīm′ līn) A diagram showing the order in which events took place. (p. 68)

time zone (tīm zōn) One of the 24 areas into which Earth is divided for measuring time. (p. 540)

tolerate (tol′ə rāt) Allowing people to have different beliefs from your own. (p. 201)

totem pole (tō′təm pōl) A tall carved log used by Native Americans of the Northwest Coast to honor an important person or to mark a special event. (p. 72)

town meeting (toun mē′ting) Gathering of a town's citizens to discuss and solve local problems. (p. 196)

Townshend Acts (taún′zend akts) Taxes passed by Parliament in 1767 for goods brought into the colonies. (p. 330)

Trail of Tears (trāl uv tîrz) The name given to the 800-mile forced march of 15,000 Cherokee in 1838 from their homes in Georgia to the Indian Territory. (p. 467)

traitor (trā′tər) Someone who turns against his or her country. *See* **treason**. (p. 349)

transcontinental railroad (trans′ kon ti nen′təl rāl′rōd) A railroad that crosses an entire continent. (p. 535)

travois (trə voi′) A sled-like device constructed by Native Americans of the Plains. (p. 87)

treason (trē′zən) The betrayal of one's country by giving help to an enemy. *See* **traitor**. (p. 329)

Treaty of Guadalupe Hidalgo (trē′tē uv gwäd′əl üp ā ē däl′gō) The treaty signed in 1848 that ended the Mexican War. *See* **Mexican War**. (p. 478)

Treaty of Paris of 1763 (trē′tē uv par′is) An agreement signed by Great Britain and France that brought an end to the French and Indian War. (p. 317)

Treaty of Paris of 1783 (trē′tē uv par′is) The peace treaty in which Great Britain recognized the United States as an independent country. (p. 370)

triangular trade (trī ang′gyə lər trād) The three-sided trade route between Africa, the West Indies, and colonial New England which involved the slave trade as well as the trading of goods. *See* **Middle Passage**. (p. 276)

tribute (trib′ūt) Forced payment, usually made in the form of valuable goods. (p. 67)

U

Underground Railroad (un′dər ground rāl′rōd) A system of secret routes used by escaping slaves to reach freedom in the North or in Canada. (p. 516)

unity (ū′ni tē) Being as one or in agreement. (p. 8)

V

values (val′ūz) The beliefs or ideals that guide the way people live. (p. 9)

veto (vē′tō) To refuse to approve. (p. 398)

Virginia Plan (vər jin′yə plan) The plan, drawn up by James Madison and adopted by the Constitutional Convention in 1787, that established three branches of the federal government. *See* **New Jersey Plan**. (p. 390)

voyageur (vwä yā zhûr′) A trader who transported furs by canoe in New France. (p. 310)

W

wagon train (wag′ ən trān) A group of covered wagons that follow one another closely like a railroad train. (p. 481)

Walking Purchase (wôk′ ing pûr′ chəs) The agreement made by William Penn with the Lenape in Pennsylvania in which he traded for the land a man could walk in a day and a half. (p. 225)

wampum (wom′pəm) Polished beads used in gift-giving and trading by the Iroquois and other Native Americans. (p. 94)

War Hawks (wôr hôks) Members of Congress from the South and the West in the early 1800s who wanted the United States to go to war against Great Britain. *See* **War of 1812**. (p. 424)

War of 1812 (wôr uv ā′tēn′twelv) War between Great Britain and the United States from 1812 to 1815. *See* **Battle of New Orleans** *and* **War Hawks**. (p. 425)

World War II (wûrld wôr tü) War between the Axis and the Allies that involved most of the countries of the world. It was fought from 1939 to 1945. The United States joined the Allies on Dec. 8, 1941. (p. 548)

---

pronunciation key

a **at**; ā **ape**; ä **far**; âr **care**; e **end**; ē **me**; i **it**; ī **ice**; îr **pierce**; o **hot**; ō **old**; ô **fork**; oi **oil**; ou **out**; u **up**; ū **use**; ü **rule**; u̇ **pull**; ûr **turn**; hw **white**; ng **song**; th **thin**; <u>th</u> **this**; zh measure; ə **about, taken, pencil, lemon, circus**

index

CREDITS

Cover: McGraw-Hill School Division

Maps: Geosystems

Charts and Graphs: Eliot Bergman: pp. 242, 243; Dale Glasgow & Associates: pp. 38, 44–45; Hima Pamoedjo: pp. 144, 287, 348, 405, 445, 473, 497, 595, 621, 632; Shelley Rena: pp. 458, 550

Chapter Opener Globes: Greg Wakabayashi

Illustrations: Hal Brooks: pp. 134, 139, 140, 145, 433, 465, 543, 611, 633; Margaret Cusack: pp. 389, 427; Don Dyden: pp. 161, 556, 557; John Edens: pp. 190, 191, 344–345, 440, 441; Peter Fiore: pp. 76–77; Joseph Forte: pp. 266–267; George Gaadt: pp. 130–131, 296–297; Stephen Gardner, 130, 409, 532, 533; Michael Hampshire: pp. 195, 207; Adam Hook: pp. 66, 510; David McCall Johnston: pp. 166–167, 538–539; Dave Joly: pp. 13, 39, 113, 171, 191, 219, 233, 247, 261, 269, 291, 311, 327, 335, 345, 371, 387, 391, 429, 477; Rosanne Kakos-Main: pp. 47; Dennis Lyall: pp. 430–431, 484–485; Ron Mahoney: pp. 408–409; Angus McBride: pp. 102–103, 320–321; Jim McMahon: pp. 232, 278; Ed Parker: pp. 332–333, 368–369; Hima Pamoedjo: pp. 90, 108, 109, 138, 323, 327, 347, 363, 389, 390, 443, 521; Rudica Prado: pp. 117, 176–177; Jame Seward: pp. 216, 217, 240, 241, 472, 473; Neil Shigley: pp. 463; Remy Simard: pp. 487; Victor Stabin: pp. 258, 300; Dan Tesser: pp. 209, 237, 409, 482, 557; Robert Van Nutt: pp. 202–203, 239, 251, 340–341, 382–383, 412, 451, 470–471, 480, 510, 511, 616–617; Gregory Wakabayshi: pp. 191, 216, 241, 473; Nina Wallace: pp. 495, 513; Steve Wells: pp. 510; Eli Woods: pp. 568

Photography Credits: All photographs are by the McGraw-Hill School Division (MSD) except as noted below.

iii: b. The Image Bank. iv: b.l. National Museum, Mexico City; m. Bridgeman Art Library. v: m.l. The Metropolitan Museum of Art; b.l. The Granger Collection. v: t. Adam Woolfit/Robert Harding Picture Library; b. The Granger Collection. vi: t.r. National Portrait Gallery, London/Superstock; m.l. Guilford Courthouse National Millitary Park, Greensboro, NC; b.l. The Granger Collection; b.m. The Granger Collection. vii: t.l. Nawrocki Stock Photo, Inc.; r. Colonial Williamsburg Foundation. viii: t.l. The Granger Collection; m.l. Michael Bryant/Woodfin Camp & Associates; b. Steve Elmore/The Stock Market. ix: t.l. UPI/Corbis-Bettmann; b.l. UPI/Corbis-Bettmann. **Chapter 1** 2: b.r. David Woodfall/Tony Stone Images. 2-3: m. The Image Bank. 4: t. Phil Schermeister/National Geographic Society; b. Galen Rowell/National Geographic Society. 4-5: Harold Sund/National Geographic Society. 7: Jimmy Rudnick/The Stock Market. 8: Joe Sohm/The Stock Market. 9: David Young-Wolff/PhotoEdit. 10-11: b. Comstock. 10: t. Dianne Arandt/Superstock. 11: Davi Conklin/Index Stock Photography/The Picture Cube. 12: The Stock Market. 13: Judy Griesdick/Black Star; r. UPI/Corbis-Bettmann. 14: i. Dennis Brack/Black Star. 14-15: Marc Muench/Tony Stone Images. 16: Elliott Smith/International Stock. 18: Miro Vintoniv/Stock Boston. 19: t. National Museum of American Art, Smithsonian Institution/Art Resource, Inc.; b. Jerry Jacka Photography. 20: l. UPI/Corbis-Bettmann; m. courtesy of Yoshihiko Ito. 20-21: Brown Brothers. 21: r. Photo Researchers, Inc. 22-23: Corbis-Bettmann. 23: t. Addison Thompson; b.l. White House Collection; b.r. James Blank/Photophile. **Chapter 2** 27: t. Donald C. Johnson/The Stock Market; t.m. Bill Ross/Tony Stone Images; m. Mark A. Leman/Tony Stone Images; b.m. Nigel Atherton/Tony Stone Images; b. Terry Qing/FPG International. 28: t.l. Paul Steel/The Stock Market. 29: t. Grant Heilman/ProFiles West; b. Henryk T. Kaiser/Index Stock Photography/The Picture Cube. 30: t. Jeff Gnass/West Stock, Inc.; b. Anne Griffiths/Woodfin Camp & Associates. 31: t. Larry Ulrich/Tony Stone Images; b. Jim Richardson/Corbis-Westlight. 32: t. Peter Beck/The Stock Market; b. David Noble/FPG International. 34-35: National Snow & Ice Data Center/Photo Researchers. 34: David Forbert/Superstock. 36: t. Reuters/Corbis-Bettmann. 38: t. Daryl Benson/Masterfile. 42: t. Jack Stein Grove/ProFiles West. 45: t.r. John Elk III/Stock Boston; t.l. Andre Jenny/Unicorn Stock Photos. 46: b.l. Paul S. Howell/Gamma Liaison; b.r. Steve Chenn/Corbis-Westlight. 47: Francis Clark Westfield. 48: b.l. Bob Daemmrich/The Image Works. 53: b. Monica Stevenson/MSD. 54: t.l. National Geographic Society; b. Lawrence Migdale/Photo Researchers, Inc. 54-55: Lawrence Migdale/Photo Researchers, Inc. 55: t.l. The Bridgeman Art Library; t.r. Scala/Art Resource, Inc.; b.r. The Bridgeman Art Library. 56: t. Richard Alexander Cooke III/National Geographic Society. 56-57: Michael A. Hampshire/National Geographic Society. 57: t. David Brill/National Geographic Society; b. Richard Alexander Cooke III/National Geographic Society. **Chapter 3** 60: D. Donne Bryant. 61: l. Craig Aurness/Woodfin Camp & Associates. 62: t. The Granger Collection; b. D. Donne Bryant. 63: Superstock. 64: l. Jerry Jacka Photography/courtesy Arizona State Museum; r. Tom Bean/The Stock Market. 65: t. Michael Fogden/DRK Photo; b. National Museum of Anthropology & History, Mexico City. 67: b. David Hiser/Photographers Aspen. 70: Jeff Greenberg/PhotoEdit. 71: Natalie B. Fobes. 72: l. Alan Hicks/Tony Stone Images; r. Mark Newman/Tom Stack & Associates. 73: t. Reader's Digest Association; b. Art Wolfe/Tony Stone Images. 74: t. National Museum of the American Indian. 75: l. New York State Historical Association; r. Smithsonian Institution. 78: l. The Brooklyn Museum; r. Lawrence Migdale for MSD. 79: l. Lawrence Migdale for MSD; t.r. Grace Hudson Museum; b.r. Lawrence Migdale for MSD. 80: National Geographic Society. 81: l. Adam Woolfitt/Woodfin Camp & Associates; r. Stephen Trimble. 82: l. The Heard Museum/Jerry Jacka Photography; t.r. National Museum of the American Indian. 83: l. Southwest Museum, Adam Clark Vroman; r. Stephen Trimble. 84: The Heard Museum/Jerry Jacka Photography. 85: Michael McDermott. 86: Robert Frerck/Odyssey Productions. 87: i. Buffalo Bill Historical Center, Cody, WY, gift of Mr. & Mrs. Irving H. "Larry" Larom; b. R. P. Kingston/Index Stock Photography/The Picture Cube. 88: Superstock. 90: National Museum of the American Indian. 92: Rochester Museum. 93: Rochester Museum. 94: The Granger Collection. 96: Mike Greencar/The Image Works. 97: Kevin King. 98: Rochester Museum. **Chapter 4** 104: Jeff Foott/Bruce Coleman, Inc. 105: i. Georg Gerster/Comstock; b. Lawrence Migdale/Photo Researchers, Inc. 106: Science & Society Picture Library. 107: Art Resource, Inc. 110-111: b. Superstock. 112: t.l. Superstock; t.r. Superstock; b.r. Betty Press/Woodfin Camp & Associates, Inc. 113: Michael Holford. 114: Bodleian Library, Oxford/Robert Harding Picture Library. 115: l. Bridgeman Art Library; r. El Escorial/Arxiu Mas. 116: l. Giraudon/Alinari; r. The Pierpont Morgan Library. 118: t. Boltin Picture Library; b. Science Museum, London/Science and Society Picture Library. 119: t.l. North Wind Picture Archives; t.r. Stock Montage, Inc.; m. Science Museum, London/Science and Society Picture Library; b. The Granger Collection. 120: Boltin Picture Library. 121: t.r. National Geographic Society; b.l. Odyssey Productions. 126: t. British Museum; m.l. British Museum/Superstock; m.r. Lotos Film; b.l. Smithsonian Institution; b.r. Ashmolean Museum, Oxford. 127: b.r. Adam Woolfit/Robert Harding Picture Library. 128-29: Bob Sacha. 128: b. Bob Sacha. 129: t. Naval Museum, Madrid. **Chapter 5** 132: North Wind Picture Archive. 133: i. The Granger Collection. 134: Museo Navale, Genua-Pegli/Superstock. 135: t. The Granger Collection; b. Florida Museum of Natural History, 1994. 136: The Granger Collection. 137: t.l. The Granger Collection; t.r. Dag Sundberg/The Image Bank; b. John E. Swedberg/Bruce Coleman, Inc. 140: Architect of the Capital. 141: t. The Granger Collection; b. Patrimonio Nacional, Madrid/Arxiu Mas; m. The Granger Collection. 142: t.l. Felipe Davalos/National Geographic Society. 143: l. Adam Woolfitt/Woodfin Camp & Associates; t.r. Jonathan Blair/Woodfin Camp & Associates; b.r. Lotos Film. 144: l. Eric Lessing/Art Resource, Inc.; r. Galleria degli Uffizi/Art Resource, Inc. 145: Biblioteca Nacional, Madrid/Arxiu Mas. 148: North Wind Picture Archives. 150-151: l. Haroldo Castro/FPG International. 150: Museo de America, Madrid/Carousel. 153: Biblioteca Colombina, Sevilla/Arxiu Mas. 154: t. The Granger Collection; b. The Detroit Institute of Art. 155: t. Robert Frerck/Odyssey Productions. 156: Dion Ogust/The Image Works. 157: t. Porterfield/Chickering/Photo Researchers, Inc.; m. Superstock; b. Jerome R. Sangler/Uniphoto. **Chapter 6** 162: t.l. The Granger Collection. 163: t. New York Historical Association; b. Superstock. 166: t. Superstock; b. Larry Ulrich/Tony Stone Images. 167: t. The Granger Collection. 168: Ashmolean Museum, Oxford. 169: l. The Granger Collection; m. North Wind Picture Archives; r. The Granger Collection. 170: Greig Cranna/Stock Boston. 171: r. The Granger Collection. 172: l. Boltin Picture Library. 172-173: The Granger Collection. 173: r. Boltin Picture Library. 174: Bonnie McGrath/Index Stock Photography/The Picture Cube. 176: Pilgrim Hall Museum. 177: Superstock. 175: t. Wayne McLoughlin/National Geographic Society. 178: t. Corbis-Bettmann; b.r. Walter Edwards/National Geographic Society. 180: The Norman Rockwell Museum, Stockbridge. 181: t.l. Bob Daemmrich/The Image Works; m.r. Painting by Sidney King/courtesy of the Berkeley Plantation and Bicast Publishing Co., Williamsburg, VA; b.l. Gene Peach/Index Stock Photography/The Picture Cube. 186: t. Boltin Picture Library; m. Colonial Williamsburg Foundation. b. The Granger Collection. 187: t.l. The Granger Collection; t.r. National Portrait Gallery, London/Superstock; b.r. The Metropolitan Museum of Art. 188-189: David Alan Harvey. 188: b. Colonial Williamsburg Foundation. 189: t. Colonial Williamsburg Foundation; b. Colonial Williamsburg Foundation. **Chapter 7** 192: t. Superstock. 193: The Metropolitan Museum of Art. 194: The Massachusetts Historical Society. 196: t.l. Margo & Taussig/New England Stock Photo; t.r. Paula Lerner/Index Stock Photography/The Picture Cube. 197: Nantucket Historical Association. 198: New York Historical Society. 199: Stratford Historical Society. 200: Architect of the Capitol, Washington, DC. 200-201: Vanessa Vick/Photo Researchers, Inc. 201: t. The Granger Collection; b. Kindra Clineff/Index Stock Photography/The Picture Cube. 203: t.l. Runk Schoenberger/Grant Heilman Photography; t.r. North Wind Picture Archive; b. Linda Detrick/Photo Researchers, Inc. 204: t. The Shelburne Museum, Shelburne, VT; b. Superstock. 205: r. Stock Montage. 206: t.l. The Winterthur Museum. 206-207: Kim Nielsen/The Smithsonian Institution. 207: b.l. The Winterthur Museum. 207: b.r. The Worcester Art Museum. 208: t. The Granger Collection. 209: t. The Winterthur Museum; b. The Pilgrim Society, Plymouth, MA. 210: t. St. Botolph's Church, Boston, England; b. Wadsworth Atheneum. 211: Boston Parks & Recreation Commission/Museum of Fine Arts, Boston. 212: Massachesetts Historical Society. 213: t. American Antiquarian Society; b. Museum of Fine Arts, Boston. **Chapter 8** 218: t. Westmoreland Museum of American Art, Greensburg, PA. 220: b. Tom McHugh/Photo Researchers, Inc. 220-221: Museum of The City of New York. 221: t.r. Stock Montage. 222: The Granger Collection. 223: Victoria & Albert Museum/The Bridgeman Art Library. 224: The Granger Collection. 225: t.l. Historical Society of Pennsylvania; t.r. Superstock. 226: t.r. Colonial Williamsburg. 227: H. Mark Weidman. 228: Museum of Fine Art, Boston. 229: Francis Clark Westfield. 232: Colonial Williamsburg Foundation. 233: b.l. Eric Crossan; t.r. Lee Snider/The Image Works. 234-235: The Winterthur Museum. 236: l. The Winterthur Museum; r. New York Historical Society. **Chapter 9** 242: New York Public Library/Art Resource, Inc. 243: b. Steve Solum/West Stock. 244: l. Pratt Free Library, Baltimore, MD; r. The Maryland Historical Society. 245: Colonial Williamsburg Foundation. 246: t. The Granger Collection; b. The Winterthur Museum. 248: The Granger Collection. 249: l. John Henley/Uniphoto; r. Superstock. 250: Christie's Images. 252: b.l. Superstock; b.r. Smithsonian Institution. 253: Colonial Williamsburg Foundation. 254: North Carolina Division of Archives & History. 255: The Granger Collection. 256-257: Tony Stone Images. 258: Metropolitan Museum of Art. 259: David Forb/Superstock. 260: b. Colonial Williamsburg Foundation. 260-261: Metropolitan Museum of Art. 262: l. Library of Congress; r. Corbis-Bettmann. 263: t. Archive Photos; m. UPI/Corbis-Bettmann; b. Corbis-Bettmann. **Chapter 10** 268: The Granger Collection. 269: National Maritime Museum, London/Bridgeman Art Library. 270: The Granger Collection. 272: Phelps Collection/New York Public Library/Art Resource, Inc. 273: Fine Art Photographic Library/Art Resource, Inc. 274: t.l. Superstock. 274-275: b. New York State Historical Association. 275: t.r. Charleston Library Society. 276: l. Superstock; m. Jeff Greenberg/Archive Photos; r. Gene Peach/Index Stock Photography/The Picture Cube, Inc. 277: Corbis-Bettmann. 279: The Winterthur Museum. 280: t. Museum of Fine Arts, Boston, gift of Joseph W., William B., and Edward H.R. Revere; b. National Geographic Society. 281: t. Colonial Williamsburg Foundation; m.l. The Minneapolis Institute of Arts; m.r. Museum of The City of New York. 282: Cigna Museum & Art Collection. 283: t. The Granger Collection; b. The Granger Collection. 284-285: The Library Company of Philadelphia. 284: b.l. The Library Company of Philadelphia. 285: b.r. American Philosophical Society. 287: Massachusetts Historical Society. 292: t.l. Charles Martin/National Geographic Society; b.l. The Granger Collection; t.r. Guilford Courthouse National Military Park, Greensboro, NC. 293: t. The Museum of Fine Arts, Boston & The National Portrait Gallery; b.r. Colonial Williamsburg Foundation. **Chapter 11** 298: t. Michael J. Howell/ProFiles West. 299: l. John Lewis Stage/The Image Bank; r. Richard Elliot/Tony Stone Images. 301: i. The Granger Collection; r. Brownie Harris/The Stock Market. 302: t. The Granger Collection. 302-303: Branson Reynolds/ProFiles West. 304: t.l. The Granger Collection. 304-305: Superstock. 305: t.l. David Stoecklein/The Stock Market; t.r. John Eastcott & Yva Momatiuk/The Image Works; b. David Carriere/Tony Stone Images. 306: Stock Montage, Inc. 307: t. National Archives of Canada; b. National Museum of the American Indian. 309: t.l. The Granger Collection; b.l. National Postal Museum; b.r. David Noble/FPG International. 310: t. Buffalo Bill Historical Center, Cody, WY, gift of Mrs. Karl Frank; b. The Granger Collection. 312: The Granger Collection. 313: Corbis-Bettmann. 314: H. Mark Weidman. 315: Archive Photos. 317: Superstock. **Chapter 12** 322: Corbis-Bettmann. 323: City of Norfolk, VA/The Chrysler Museum. 324: t. Colonial Williamsburg Foundation; b. Corbis-Bettmann. 325: t. Corbis-Bettmann; b. Archive Photos. 326: b.l. The Metropolitan Museum of Art; b.r. Corbis-Bettmann. 327: Corbis-Bettmann. 328: North Wind Picture Archives. 329: t. The Granger Collection; b. The Granger Collection. 330: The Museum of Fine Arts, Boston. 331: b.l. The Granger Collection; t.r. Massachusetts Historical Society; b.r. Corbis-Bettmann. 332: b.l. The Granger Collection; t.r. The Granger Collection. 332-333: The Winterthur Museum. 334: The Granger Collection. 335: Kirk Anderson. 336: John Coletti/Stock Boston. 338: Corbis-Bettmann. 339: The Granger Collection. 340: t. H. Mark Weidman; b. Yale University Art Gallery. 341: The Granger Collection. **Chapter 13** 346: Kenneth Garrett/Woodfin Camp & Associates. 347: l. National Geographic

Society; r. Ticonderoga Museum. 348: t. Andre Jenny/Stock South; b. H. Mark Weidman. 349: t. Stock Boston; b. The Museum of Fine Arts, Boston. 350: l. Andre Jenny/Stock South; r. National Geographic Society Image Collection. 351: l. The Granger Collection; r. Superstock. 352: Yale University Art Gallery. 354: George Chan/Photo Researchers, Inc. 355: t. Superstock; m. Superstock; b. Catherine Karnow/Woodfin Camp and Associates. 356: H. Mark Weidman. 357: t. Rhode Island Historical Society; b. Nawrocki Stock Photo, Inc. 358: Superstock. 359: Henley & Savage/Tony Stone Images. 360: Stock Montage. 361: Superstock. 362: Superstock 363: t. Frick Library; m. Pennsylvania Historical Society. 364: Superstock. 365: Nawrocki Stock Photo, Inc. 366: l. The Granger Collection; t.r. Nawrocki Stock Photo, Inc.; b.r. The Granger Collection. 367: Valentine Museum, Richmond, VA. 369: t. Nawrocki Stock Photo, Inc. 369: b.l. Murray Alcosser/The Image Bank; b.r. Ted Spiegel. 370: Yale University Art Gallery. 372: Nawrocki Stock Photo, Inc. 378: t.l. Colonial Williamsburg Foundation; t.m. Culver Pictures; t.r. Missouri Historical Society; b.l. Glenn Kulbako/Index Stock Photography/The Picture Cube; b.r. North Wind Picture Archives. 379: t.r. Nawrocki Stock Photo, Inc.; b.r. Michael Bryant/Woodfin Camp & Associates. **Chapter 14** 384: North Wind Picture Archives. 385: l. Corbis/Bettmann; r. Nawrocki. 386: Corbis/Bettmann. 388: The Granger Collection. 389: Superstock. 391: The Library of Congress. 392: The Granger Collection. 393: t. The Pennsylvania Academy of The Fine Arts; b. Michael Bryant/Woodfin Camp & Assoc. 394: l. The Granger Collection; r. The Granger Collection. 395: North Wind Picture Library. 396: Independence National Historical Park. 399: FPG International. 400: Superstock. 401: t. Corbis-Bettmann; m. The Granger Collection; b. Shelburne Museum. 403: l. Glenn Kulbako/The Picture Cube; r. Superstock. 404: Colonial Williamsburg Foundation. **Chapter 15** 410: Kenneth Murray/Photo Researchers, Inc. 410-411: Leonard Lee Rue III/Tony Stone Images. 411: Diane Padys/FPG International. 412: Fort Boonesborough State Park. 413: The Granger Collection. 414: Fort Boonesborough State Park. 415: University of Michigan Museum of Art, bequest of Henry C. Lewis. 416: UPI/Corbis-Bettmann. 417: b.l. The Granger Collection; t.r. Superstock; b.r. Culver Pictures. 418: t. Chuck Fishman/Woodfin Camp & Associates, Inc.; b. Chicago Historical Society. 419: Missouri Historical Society. 420: Montana Historical Society. 421: Larry Ulrich/Tony Stone Images. 422-423: The New York Historical Society. 423: t.l. The Smithsonian Institution; t.r. North Wind Picture Archives; b. Renee Lynn/Davis Lynn Photography. 424: The Granger Collection. 425: l. The Granger Collection; r. Corbis-Bettmann. 426: l. The Granger Collection; r. The New York Historical Society. 428: t. National Portrait Gallery/Art Resource; b. The Historical New Orleans Collection. 431: Archive Photos. 436: t.r. The Granger Collection; m. Steve Elmore/The Stock Market; b. Don Mason/The Stock Market. 437: t. Nawrocki Stock Photo, Inc.; b. Brown Brothers. 438-439: Phil Schermeister/National Geographic Society. 438: t. Karen Keeney/National Geographic Society; b. Phil Schermeister/National Geographic Society. 439: Haynes Foundation Collection, Montana Historical Society. **Chapter 16** 442: Corbis-Bettmann. 443: t. Grant Heilman Photography; b. Corbis-Bettmann. 444: North Wind Picture Archive. 445: National Geographic Society. 447: t. Brown Brothers; b. Lester Sloan/Woodfin Camp & Associates 448: Superstock. 449: Archive Photos. 450: b.Corbis-Bettmann; i. Nawrocki Stock Photo, Inc. 451: i. North Wind Picture Archive. 452: Corbis-Bettmann. 456: Nawrocki Stock Photo, Inc. 457: t. The National Portrait Gallery/Smithsonian Institution/Art Resource, Inc.; b. American Museum of Bath/Bridgeman Art Library/Superstock. 458: Bridgeman Art Library. 459: Corbis-Bettmann. 460: t.l. Corbis-Bettmann; b.r. Nawrocki Stock Photo, Inc. 462: Brown Brothers. 463: b. Chuck Pefley/Tony Stone Images. 464: The Granger Collection. 465: l. Corbis-Bettmann; r: New Echota State Historic Site. 466: Pablo Prints/Superstock. 467: The Granger Collection. 468: Pablo Prints/Superstock. 469: t. National Anthropological Archives, Smithsonian Institution; b. New York State Historical Association. **Chapter 17** 474: Willard Clay/Tony Stone Images. 475: t. Institute of Texan Cultures; b. Michael Salas/The Image Bank. 476: t.r. Superstock; m. Texas State Library, Archives Division; b.r. New York Public Library/Art Resource, Inc.. 477: Library of Congress. 479: University of Southern California. 480: Joe Bensen/Stock Boston. 481: l. North Wind Picture Archive; r. Museum of The City of New York. 482: Geoffrey Clifford/Woodfin Camp & Associates. 483: t. The Granger Collection; b. Culver Pictures. 484: t. National Archives, U.S. Army Signal Corps Collection; b. Nebraska Game and Parks Commission. 485: Nawrocki Stock Photo, Inc. 486: t. Corbis-Bettmann; b. Superstock. 487: Culver Pictures. 488: t. Superstock. 488-489: Richard A. Cooke III/Tony Stone Images. 490: Billy E. Barnes/Stock Boston; i. Superstock. 491: Jarvis Photo/Uniphoto. 492: Superstock. 493: t. The Granger Collection; b. The Society of California Poineers. 494: Brown Brothers. 495: California Historical Society. 496: California Historical Society; i. California Historical Society. 497: Oakland Museum History Department. 498: L. Kolvoord/The Image Works. 499: Mark Burnett/Stock Boston. 500: Stock Montage. 501: t. North Wind Picture Archive; m. Brown Brothers; b. North Wind Picture Archive. 506: t.l. Brown Brothers; t.r. Karen Yamauchi for Chermayeff & Geismer, Inc./Metaform, Inc.; b. UPI/Corbis-Bettmann. 507: t.l. Larry Sherer/Time Life Books, Inc.; t.r. Evan Agostini/Gamma Liaison; b. Bob Adelman/Magnum Photos, Inc. b. UPI/Corbis-Bettmann. **Chapter 18** 512: USDA Photo/Library of Congress. 512-513: Lance Nelson/The Stock Market. 514: The Granger Collection. 515: Superstock. 516: t.l. Corbis-Bettmann; t.r. The Granger Collection; b.r. The Granger Collection. 517: The Granger Collection. 518: t. Lyle LeDuc/Gamma Liaison; b. St. John Fisher College. 519: t.l. Library Company of Philadelphia; m.l. National Postal Museum, Smithsonian Institution. 520: The Granger Collection. 521: Brown Brothers. 522: t. North Wind Picture Archive; b. Superstock. 523: The Granger Collection. 524: l. Ken Cavanaugh/MSD; r. Henley & Savage/The Stock Market. 526: t. Superstock; b. Stock Montage. 527: The Granger Collection. 528: The Granger Collection. **Chapter 19** 534: Brown Brothers 535: b. Kansas Collection, University of Kansas Libraries. 536: l. Superstock. 537: t.l. The Granger Collection. 537: t.r. The Granger Collection. 537: b.l. The Granger Collection. 537: b.m. Smithsonian Institution. 537: b.r. Queens Borough Library/Latimer Family Collection. 538: t. Corbis-Bettman. 538: b. Corbis-Bettmann. 540541: Corbis-Bettmann. 542: UPI/Corbis-Bettmann. 543: l. Andrew Rokczy/Bruce Coleman, Inc. 543: r. Brown Brothers. 544: b. The Philipps Collection, Washington, DC. 545: Tom Myers. 546: James Blank/West Stock, Inc. 547: Brown Brothers. 548: John W. Warren/Superstock. 549: Deborah Davis. 550: Evan Agostini/Gamma Liaison. 551: l. A. Helitzer/T. Lechner/Still Productions; r. A. Helitzer/T. Lechner/Still Productions. 552: Jack Vartoogian. 552553: Paul Simcock/The Image Bank. 553: t.l. Chermayeff and Geismar, Inc; r. Jack Vartoogian. **Chapter 20** 558: AP/Wide World Photos. 559: UPI/Corbis-Bettmann. 560: UPI/Corbis-Bettman 561: l. AP/Wide World; r. Charles Moore/Black Star. 562: UPI/Corbis-Bettmann. 563: r. Courtesy of Sharaye LaMothe. 565: Brown Brothers. 566: t. Stock Market. 566567: Kathleen Campbell/Gamma Liaison. 567: b.l. Reuters/Gary Hershorn/Archive Photos. 568: Uniphoto. 569: Bob Daemmrich/The Image Works. R50: t.l. National Geographic Society/White House Historical Assoc. R50: b.l. National Geographic Society/White House Historical Association; m. National Geographic Society/White House Historical Association; t.r. National Geographic Society/White House Historical Association; b.r. National Geographic Society/White House Historical Association. R51: t.l. National Geographic Society/White House Historical Association; b.l. National Geographic Society/White House Historical Association; m. National Geographic Society/White House Historical Association; t.r. National Geographic Society/White House Historical Association; b.r. National Geographic Society/White House Historical Association. R52: t.l. National Geographic Society/White House Historical Association; b.l. National Geographic Society/White House Historical Association; t.m. National Geographic Society/White House Historical Association; b.m. National Geographic Society/White House Historical Association; t.r. National Geographic Society/White House Historical Association; b.r. National Geographic Society/White House Historical Association. R53: t.l. National Geographic Society/White House Historical Association; b.l. National Geographic Society/White House Historical Association; t.m. National Geographic Society/White House Historical Association; b.m. National Geographic Society/White House Historical Association; t.r. National Geographic Society/White House Historical Association; b.r. National Geographic Society/White House Historical Association. R54: t.l. National Geographic Society/White House Historical Association; b.l. National Geographic Society/White House Historical Association; m. National Geographic Society/White House Historical Association; t.r. National Geographic Society/White House Historical Association; b.r. National Geographic Society/White House Historical Association. R55: t.l. National Geographic Society/White Hosue Historical Association; b.l. National Geographic Society/White House Historical Association; t.m. National Geographic Society/White House Historical Association; b.m. National Geographic Society/White House Historical Association; r. National Geographic Society/White House Historical Association. R56: t.l. National Geographic Society/White House Historical Association; b.l. National Geographic Society/White House Historical Associaition; t.m. National Geographic Society/White House Historical Association; b.m. National Geographic Society/White House Historical Association; t.r. National Geographic Society/White House Historical Association; t.r. National Geographic Society/White House Historical Association. R57: t.l. National Geographic Society/White House Historical Association; b.l. Robert Sherbow/Uniphoto. R58: row 1, l. Boltin Picture Library; row 2, l. National Museum, Mexico City; row 2, r. Adam Woolfit/Robert Harding Picture Library; row 4, l. The Granger Collection. R59: row 1, r. Jeff Greenberg/PhotoEdit; row 2, l. The Granger Collection; row 2, r. James Blank/Photophile; row 3, l. National Archives at Canada; row 3, r. Stock Montage, Inc.; row 4, l. Bonnie McGrath/Index Stock Photography/The Picture Cube; row 4, m. Historical Society of Pennsylvania; row 4, r. The Granger Collection. R60: row 1, r. The Granger Collection; row 3 Archive Photos; row 2, l. The Granger Collection; row 4, l. Missouri Historical Society; row 4, r. Robert Ferck/Odyssey Productions. R61: row 1, l. Corbis-Bettmann; row 1, m. The Granger Collection; row 1, r. The Granger Collection; row 2, l. The Granger Collection; row 2, r. The Granger Collection; row 3, l. Floyd County Historical Society; row 3, r. Superstock.

(continued from page ii)
Acknowledgments
"The Strangers Did Not Sleep" by Felipe Waman Puma, translated by Ronald Wright, from **Stolen Continents: The Indian Story.** Copyright 1992 by John Murray.
From **Bartolome de Las Casas: A Selection of His Writings** edited and translated by George Sanderlin. Copyright 1971 by Alfred A. Knopf, Inc./Random House.
From **The American Heritage History of the Thirteen Colonies** edited by Richard M. Ketchum and Alvin M. Josephy, Jr. Copyright 1967 by American Heritage Publishing Company.
From **Narratives of Early Virginia, 1606-1625** edited by Lyon Gardiner Tyler, L.L.D. Copyright 1946 by Barnes & Noble. Reprinted in 1966.
From **Of Plymouth Plantation** by William Bradford. Copyright 1952 by Samuel Eliot Morison. Reprinted by Alfred A. Knopf, 1963.
From **Saga of the Pilgrims: From Europe to the New World** by John Harris. Copyright 1990 by the Globe Pequot Press.
From **The Pilgrim Reader** by George F. Willison. Published by Doubleday & Company, Inc. Copyright 1953 by George F. Willison.
From **The Pilgrims and Plymouth Colonies** by the editors of American Heritage. Copyright 1961 by American Heritage Publishing Co., Inc.
"In Freedom's Footsteps" from **The African Background to the Civil War** by Charles H. Wesley. Copyright 1978 by The Association of Afro-American Life and History.
From **Narratives of Early Pennsylvania, West New Jersey, and Delaware, 1630-1707** edited by Albert Cook Myers. Copyright 1912 by Charles Scribner & Sons. Copyright renewed 1940 by Barnes & Noble, Inc.
From **The Colonial Experience** by David Hawke. Copyright 1966 by the Bobbs-Merrill Company, Inc.
From **Home Life in Colonial Days** by Alice Morse Earle. Copyright 1975 by Jonathan David Publishers, New York.
From **Narratives of New Netherland, 1609-1664** edited by J. Franklin Jameson, Ph.D., L.L.D Copyright renewed 1937 by Barnes & Noble, Inc., reprinted 1959.
From **A Historical Album of New York** by Monique Avakian & Carter Smith 111. Copyright 1993 by the Millbrook Press, Inc.
From **Colonial American Home Life** by John F. Warner. Published by Franklin Watts. Copyright 1993 by John F. Warner.
From **A Sweet and Alien Land: The Story of Dutch New York.** Published by Viking Press. Copyright 1978 by Henri & Barbara van der Zee.
From **Life and Times in Colonial Philadelphia** by Joseph J. Kelley, Jr. Published by Stackpole Books. Copyright 1973 by the Stackpole Company.
From Pennsylvania, **The Colonial Years, 1681-1776** by Joseph J. Kelley, Jr. Published by Doubleday & Company, Inc., New York. Copyright 1980 by Joseph J. Kelley.
From **The Puritan Family** by Edmund S. Morgan. Copyright 1966 by Harper & Row Publishers, New York.
From **The Negro in Colonial New England** by Lorenzo Johnston Greene. Copyright 1974 by Atheneum.
From **Old Plantation Hymns** by William E. Barton. Published by AMS Press, NY, 1972.
From **Black Americans of Achievement Book Series: Frederick Douglass and Harriet Tubman.** Published by Chelsea House Publishers. Copyright 1988 by Chelsea House Publishers.
From **Frederick Douglass And the Fight From Freedom.** Copyright 1988 by Douglas T. Miller. Used by permission of Facts on File, Inc.
From **The Colonial Experience** by David Hawke. Published by the Bobbs-Merrill Company, Inc. Copyright 1966 by the Bobbs-Merrill Company, Inc.
From **Cities in the Wilderness** by Carl Bridenbaugh. Published by Alfred A. Knopf, Inc. Copyright 1938 by Carl Bridenbaugh.
From **Black Jacks: African American Seamen in the Age of Sail** by Jeffrey W. Bolster. Copyright 1997 by Harvard University Press.
From **"When I Came Over..."** from **American Mosaic** by Joan Morrison and Charlotte Fox Zabusky. Published by University of Pittsburgh Press. Copyright 1980 by Joan Morrison and Charlotte Fox Zabusky.
From **Freedom's Children** by Ellen Levine. Published by G.P. Putnam's Sons. Copyright 1993 by Ellen Levine.
From **Luzena Stanley Wilson, Forty-Niner: Memories Recalled for Her Daughter.** Published by Eucalyptus Press. Copyright 1937

The Princeton Review
— Handbook of —
Test-Taking Strategies

DEDUCTION AND OUTSIDE KNOWLEDGE

Many questions on standardized multiple-choice tests ask you to look at a map, a chart, a graph, or a drawing. Then you must choose the correct answer based on what you see. On these questions, the information you need to answer the question will be on the map, chart, graph, or drawing. The process of looking, finding the answer to the question, and choosing the correct answer from among the answer choices is called DEDUCTION. You've been doing this ever since you learned how to read a map or a chart, or any other visual information.

Sometimes, however, multiple-choice tests will ask you to remember a fact that you learned in social studies class. You won't be able to find the correct answer on a map, chart, graph, or drawing; the correct answer will be in your memory. We call these OUTSIDE KNOWLEDGE questions.

Use the map below to answer question 1. Question 2 asks you to use outside knowledge.

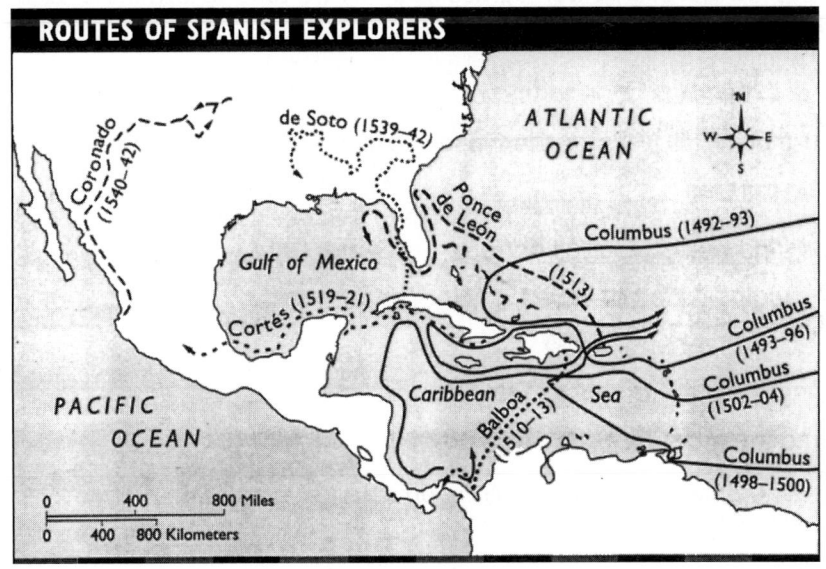

ROUTES OF SPANISH EXPLORERS

1 Which Spanish explorer traveled farthest west in the Americas?

  A   Hernando Cortés
  B   Francisco Vásquez de Coronado
  C   Ponce de León
  D   Christopher Columbus

2 What was the main goal of the Spanish explorers in the Americas?

  F   To find gold and other riches and bring them back to Spain
  G   To make friends with Native Americans
  H   To settle in a land where they could practice their religion in freedom
  J   To preserve the rain forests

PROCESS OF ELIMINATION

When you take a multiple-choice test, you have an advantage that you don't have on other tests. On most tests, you must come up with the answers to the questions all on your own. For example, a test might ask "Who was the first President of the United States?" You would then have to write the name "George Washington" on your answer sheet.

On a multiple-choice test, however, the correct answer is already written down for you; it is among the answer choices! All you have to do is figure out which of the answer choices is the correct one.

This is good news for you! It means that you can still answer a question correctly *even if you can't come up with the correct answer on your own*. That's because you can ELIMINATE choices that you know are *incorrect*. Eliminating answers this way will be especially helpful on OUTSIDE KNOWLEDGE questions. Sometimes you will be able to eliminate all of the choices except one. When that happens, it means that you have found the best answer by the PROCESS OF ELIMINATION.

Try using the process of elimination to answer this question:

1 In 1899, the President of the United States was

A Richard Nixon

B William McKinley

C Thomas Jefferson

D George Bush

Were you able to eliminate any *incorrect* answers? How many?

Now try using the process of elimination to answer this question:

2 In the early 1800s, which of these inventions enabled the South to increase agricultural production?

F Telephone

G Airplane

H Cotton Gin

J Gas Lighting

Remember: Do not write in your textbook.

TABLES

On many multiple-choice tests, you are provided with the information you need to answer the question. The information will come in many different forms. It might appear in a time line, a flow chart, a map, or a graph. Sometimes, the information will be included in a table.

The table below compares the climate in two United States cities. Study the table. Then answer questions 1 and 2.

Climate in Two Cities					Rainfall		Snowfall Average Annual (in.)
Average Monthly Temperature (°F)					Average (in.)	Annual (days)	
City	Jan.	Apr.	July	Oct.			
Albany, NY	21	47	71	51	36	134	66
El Paso, TX	44	64	83	64	8	47	5

Source: *Information Please Almanac, 1995*

1 On an average July day in Albany, NY, what is the temperature?

   A 21°F

   B 51°F

   C 64°F

   D 71°F

2 Based on the information in the table, which of these statements is most likely true?

   F It snows more in the northern United States than in the southern United States.

   G It rains more in the southern United States than in the northern United States.

   H It is colder in the southern United States than in the northern United States.

   J The southern United States has more days of precipitation than the northern United States has.

Remember: Do not write in your textbook.

FLOW CHARTS

A flow chart shows the sequence of steps used to complete an activity. It shows the steps in the order they happen. A flow chart usually uses arrows to show which step happens next.

The first thing to do when you look at a flow chart is to see if it has a title. The title will tell you what the flow chart is about. The next thing you should do is find the arrows. The arrows tell you the order in which you should read the chart.

Read flow charts carefully. Don't just look at the illustrations; make sure to read any text beneath the illustrations. Careless errors are the most common mistakes made when answering flow chart questions. If you take a little extra time, you can eliminate these errors.

Use the flow chart below to answer questions 1 and 2.

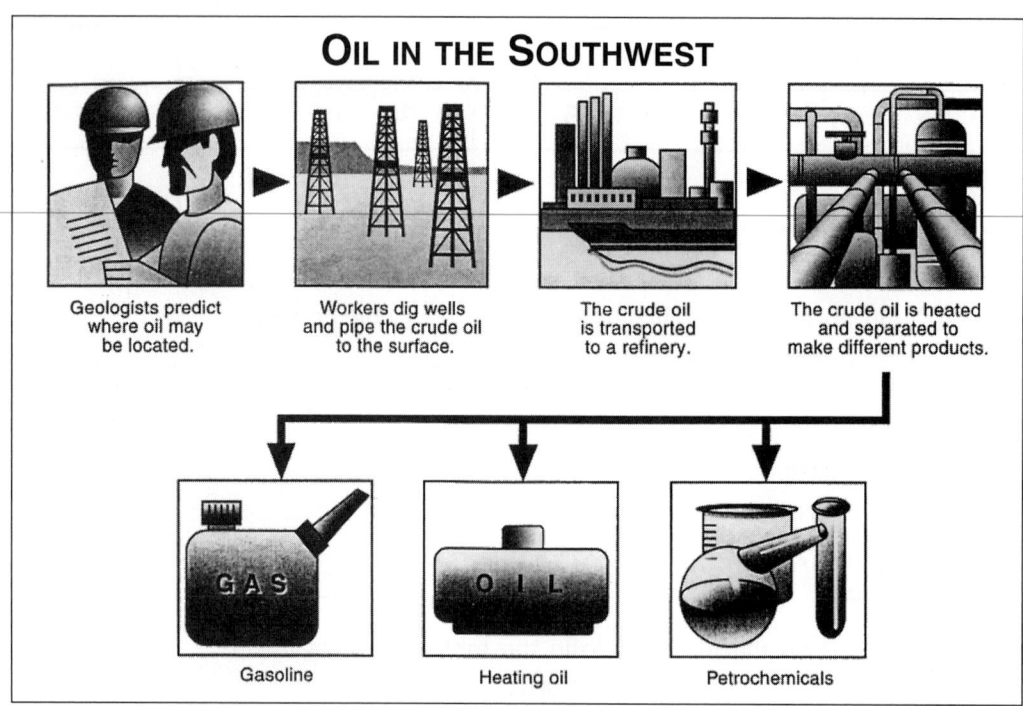

OIL IN THE SOUTHWEST

Geologists predict where oil may be located.

Workers dig wells and pipe the crude oil to the surface.

The crude oil is transported to a refinery.

The crude oil is heated and separated to make different products.

Gasoline

Heating oil

Petrochemicals

1 Who is responsible for predicting where oil is located?

    A   Geologists

    B   Workers

    C   Refiners

    D   Heating Oil Salespersons

2 What does the flow chart show about the oil industry?

    F   Which states produce the most crude oil

    G   How much money it costs to refine oil

    H   How crude oil is turned into useful products

    J   How petrochemicals are turned into plastic

Remember: Do not write in your textbook.

DIFFERENT TYPES OF GRAPHS

Different types of graphs are used to present numerical information. A **line graph** shows how something changes over time. A line graph might be used to show how the population of the United States has grown over the years. A **bar graph** compares amounts. A bar graph might show the populations of different United States cities. A **circle graph** shows how a whole is divided into smaller parts. For example, a circle graph might show how the government divides its funds to pay for roads, defense, education, and other services.

Sometimes you will see a set of questions accompanied by more than one graph. Each question will contain clues to tell you which graph you should read to find the answer. Take the extra time to make sure you are looking at the correct graph.

Use the graphs below to answer questions 1 and 2.

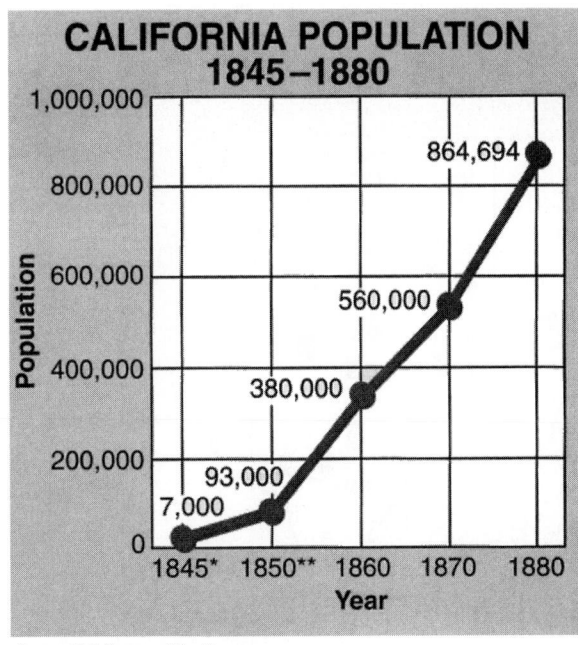

Source: U.S. Bureau of the Census

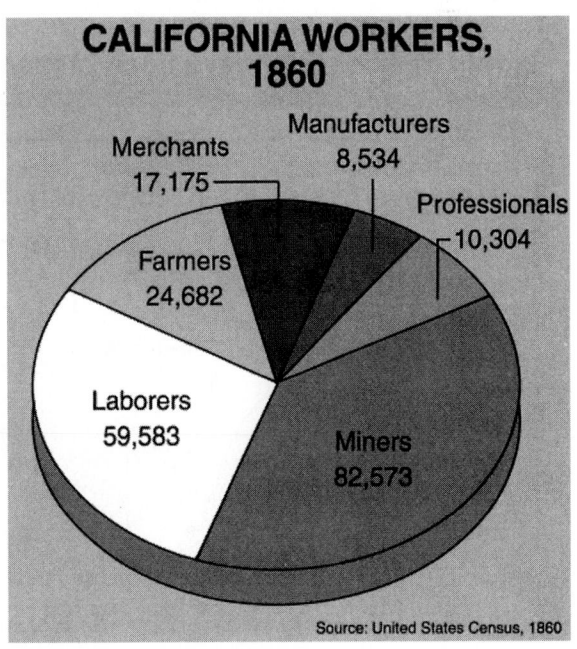

1   What was the population of California in 1870?

   A   59,583
   B   82,573
   C   380,000
   D   560,000

2   In 1860, the greatest number of workers in California were

   F   professionals
   G   miners
   H   merchants
   J   farmers

Remember: Do not write in your textbook.

MAPS

The ability to read and understand maps is an important skill in social studies. Many of the multiple-choice tests you take will require you to read a map.

Look carefully at all the parts of a map. Maps contain a lot of information. Whenever you see a map, you should ask yourself questions like these:

- What does the title of the map tell you?
- Where is the map key?
- What symbols are on the map key? What do they stand for?
- Where is the compass rose?
- What does the compass rose tell you?
- Is there a map scale?

Look at the map of the Southwest. Use the map to answer questions 1 and 2.

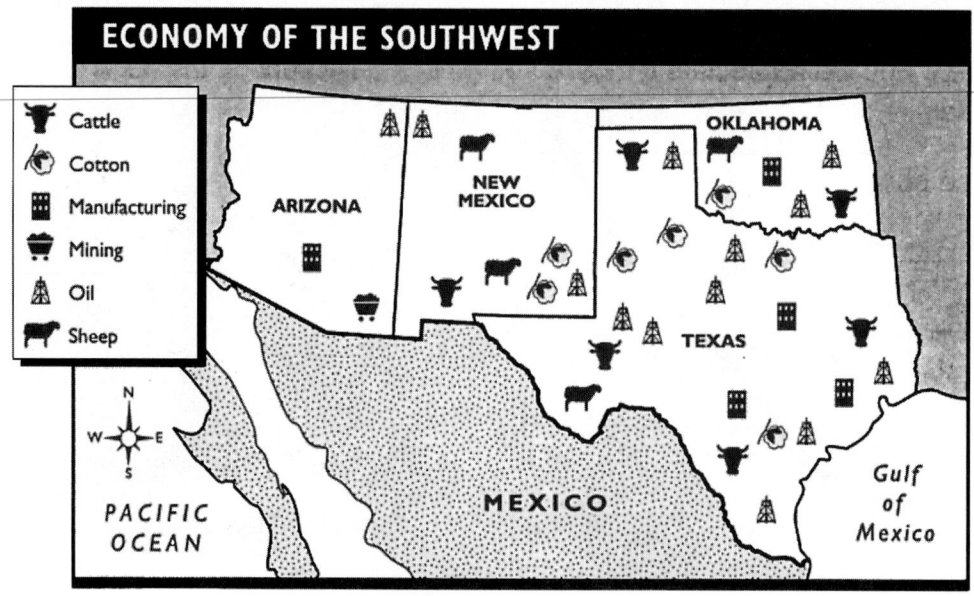

1 Mining is a part of the economy of which state?

   A   Arizona

   B   New Mexico

   C   Oklahoma

   D   Texas

2 According to the map, what is a major industry in the southernmost part of Texas?

   F   Manufacturing

   G   Radio

   H   Oil

   J   Mining

Remember: Do not write in your textbook.

POLITICAL CARTOONS

Some tests will ask you to look at and interpret a political cartoon. A political cartoon is an illustration or drawing that expresses a political point of view.

When you look at a political cartoon, ask yourself the following questions:

- What do the images in the cartoon represent? Are they **symbols** for something else? Uncle Sam is an example of a symbol. When he appears in a cartoon, he is being used as a **symbol** of the United States.
- What is the cartoonist's point of view? Is the cartoonist for, or against, the political issue that is the subject of the drawing? Look carefully at the details of the drawing. Do they provide hints about the artist's point of view?

Now look at the cartoon below. It was drawn during the American Revolution. Use the cartoon to answer questions 1 and 2.

The Horse America, Throwing His Master

1 What does the rider of the horse symbolize?

- **A** France
- **B** The American colonies
- **C** England
- **D** George Washington

2 What detail shows that the master has been very cruel to the horse?

- **F** The type of saddle the master is using
- **G** The type of riding crop the master is holding
- **H** The type of uniform the master is wearing
- **J** The look of surprise on the master's face

Remember: Do not write in your textbook.

TIME LINES

Historical information is sometimes presented in the form of a time line. A time line shows events in the order in which they occurred. It is usually read from left to right, like a sentence. If the time line is drawn vertically, it is usually read from top to bottom.

Some questions may ask you to find information on a time line. They may also ask you to remember outside knowledge about the subject of the time line.

Study the time line below. Then do questions 1 and 2.

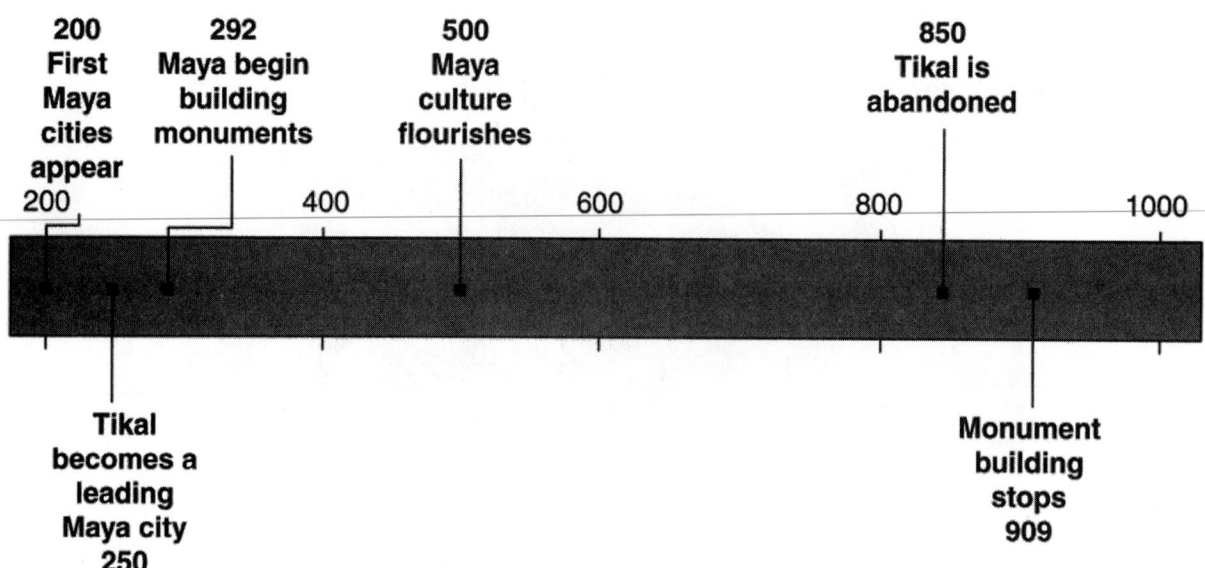

Maya History, A.D. 200–A.D. 1000

200 First Maya cities appear

292 Maya begin building monuments

500 Maya culture flourishes

850 Tikal is abandoned

200 — 400 — 600 — 800 — 1000

Tikal becomes a leading Maya city **250**

Monument building stops **909**

---

1 In what year did the Maya abandon the city of Tikal?

A 250
B 292
C 850
D 909

2 The area in which the ancient Maya lived includes present-day

F Central America
G Africa
H Canada
J Asia

Remember: Do not write in your textbook.